Green Intrusion Detection Systems for IoT

Intelligent Data-Centric Systems

Green Intrusion Detection Systems for IoT

Saeid Jamshidi
Software Engineering Department
SWAT Lab
Polytechnique Montréal
Montréal, QC, Canada

Kawser Wazed Nafi
Software Engineering Department
SWAT Lab
Polytechnique Montréal
Montréal, QC, Canada

Foutse Khomh
Software Engineering Department
SWAT Lab
Polytechnique Montréal
Montréal, QC, Canada

Amin Nikanjam
Software Engineering Department
SWAT Lab
Polytechnique Montréal
Montréal, QC, Canada

ELSEVIER
ACADEMIC PRESS
An imprint of Elsevier

Academic Press is an imprint of Elsevier
125 London Wall, London EC2Y 5AS, United Kingdom
50 Hampshire Street, 5th Floor, Cambridge, MA 02139, United States

ISBN: 978-0-443-44249-0

For information on all Academic Press publications
visit our website at https://www.elsevier.com/books-and-journals

Publisher: Mara Conner
Editorial Project Manager: Asmi Bharati
Production Project Manager: Omer Mukthar
Cover Designer: Raman Kumar

Typeset by VTeX

This book is dedicated to my parents, whose endless love, sacrifices, and encouragement have made everything possible. Their belief in me has been my greatest strength. To my sister, for always being there with support, patience, and motivation during every step of this journey.

– Saeid Jamshidi

This book is dedicated to my beloved parents, whose love has been my greatest strength and whose sacrifices have paved the way for my dreams. No words can adequately express my gratitude for all they have done for me.

– Kawser Wazed Nafi

Contents

Preface

The rapid expansion of the Internet of Things (IoT) has transformed modern digital infrastructures, enabling intelligent, interconnected systems across domains such as smart cities, healthcare, and industrial environments. However, this transformation has also introduced significant security challenges, particularly in the context of resource-constrained and large-scale IoT networks. Traditional intrusion detection systems have primarily focused on detection performance, often overlooking the critical constraints of energy consumption, scalability, and environmental impact inherent to IoT ecosystems. This limitation highlights the need for a new generation of security solutions that not only ensure robust protection but also operate efficiently within sustainable computing paradigms. This book addresses this gap by introducing the concept of **Green Intrusion Detection Systems**, which integrate cybersecurity, AI, and sustainability principles into a unified framework. It explores lightweight, energy-efficient, and intelligent IDS models tailored for IoT networks, leveraging ML, FL, and distributed detection mechanisms. Through a combination of theoretical foundations, practical methodologies, and real-world case studies, this work aims to provide a comprehensive perspective on the design of secure and sustainable IoT systems. The presented approaches emphasize the balance between detection accuracy, computational efficiency, and environmental responsibility. This book is intended for researchers, practitioners, and students seeking to advance the development of next-generation IoT security solutions aligned with global sustainability goals and emerging technological demands.

Acknowledgements

The completion of this work would not have been possible without the support and contributions of many individuals. I would like to express my sincere gratitude to my supervisor and academic advisor, Professor Foutse Khomh, for his invaluable guidance, insightful feedback, and continuous support throughout this project. His expertise and mentorship have significantly strengthened the quality and direction of this work. I am also deeply thankful to my collaborators, particularly Amin Nikanjam and Kawser Wazed Nafi, who authored chapters 6 through 10, for their valuable contributions, technical insights, and constructive discussions that enhanced the depth and rigor of this book. I would like to acknowledge the support of the SWAT Laboratory at Polytechnique Montréal, which provided an excellent research environment and resources that enabled this work.

CHAPTER

1 Introduction to IoT security and sustainability

1.1 Background and motivation

The Internet of Things (IoT) has emerged as one of the most transformative technological paradigms of the twenty-first century, enabling pervasive interconnection between physical and cyber systems. IoT comprises a large-scale ecosystem of heterogeneous devices endowed with sensing, communication, and computational capabilities. These devices range from low-power environmental sensors and RFID tags to advanced embedded controllers, wearable platforms, autonomous vehicles, industrial machinery, and critical infrastructure components. Through continuous data acquisition, processing, and actuation, IoT systems facilitate intelligent services and real-time decision-making capabilities that extend well beyond the scope of traditional computing environments.

The rapid proliferation of IoT technologies has had a substantial impact on social, economic, and industrial sectors. In consumer contexts, smart home systems integrate intelligent thermostats, surveillance solutions, and energy management platforms that dynamically adapt to user behavior and environmental conditions. In industrial domains, Industrial IoT (IIoT) enables automation, predictive maintenance, and real-time operational intelligence, resulting in improved efficiency, reduced downtime, and lower operational costs. At the urban scale, smart city infrastructures employ IoT solutions to enhance traffic management, environmental monitoring, waste management, and public safety services. Similarly, healthcare systems utilize wearable devices, implantable sensors, and remote monitoring platforms to facilitate early diagnosis, continuous patient monitoring, and reduced clinical workload. Collectively, these developments position IoT as a foundational enabler of emerging paradigms such as *Industry 4.0*, *ubiquitous computing*, and Cyber-Physical Systems (CPS).

Despite its transformative potential, the inherent characteristics of IoT systems introduce significant technical and security challenges. The large-scale, distributed, and heterogeneous nature of IoT deployments complicates system integration, interoperability, and resource management. The coexistence of diverse hardware platforms, communication protocols, data formats, and network topologies creates an expanded attack surface that adversaries can readily exploit. Moreover, many IoT devices are designed under strict cost and energy constraints, resulting in limited processing power, memory, and storage. These limitations often preclude the

Green Intrusion Detection Systems for IoT. https://doi.org/10.1016/B978-0-44-344249-0.00008-9

deployment of conventional security mechanisms, leading to weak authentication, insufficient encryption, outdated firmware, and the absence of patching mechanisms.

Security risks are further amplified by the deployment environments and operational characteristics of IoT systems. Devices are frequently installed in physically accessible and uncontrolled locations, such as homes, public spaces, industrial facilities, and remote agricultural fields, making them vulnerable to physical tampering. In addition, reliance on wireless communication exposes IoT networks to eavesdropping, replay attacks, spoofing, and jamming. The integration of IoT devices with cloud platforms, edge computing infrastructures, and mobile systems further expands the threat landscape, enabling multi-layer, cross-domain cyberattacks.

Beyond security, the unprecedented scale of IoT deployments raises critical concerns regarding energy consumption and environmental sustainability. Billions of IoT devices operate continuously, many of which rely on batteries and energy-harvesting mechanisms. The cumulative energy demand of these systems contributes significantly to global energy consumption and associated carbon emissions. Frequent battery replacement, particularly in large-scale or remote deployments, increases maintenance overhead, operational costs, and electronic waste (e-waste) generation. Even marginal inefficiencies at the device level can translate into substantial environmental impact when aggregated across large IoT networks.

Importantly, security and sustainability in IoT systems are deeply interconnected. Compromised devices participating in malware propagation, botnets, and Denial-of-Service (DoS) attacks may exhibit excessive computation, leading to abnormal energy consumption and accelerated hardware degradation. Repeated system failures, firmware corruption, and forced resets can further shorten device lifespan and increase replacement frequency. Conversely, poorly designed security mechanisms may impose excessive computational and communication overhead, undermining energy efficiency and limiting system longevity. These interactions highlight that security and sustainability should be treated as interdependent dimensions rather than isolated design objectives. Addressing these dual challenges requires developing a Green IDS tailored to IoT networks. In contrast to conventional IDS, which assumes abundant computational resources and a stable power supply, Green IDS must operate under strict resource constraints. Such systems are required to minimize CPU usage, memory footprint, and communication overhead while maintaining effective threat detection capabilities. Green IDS solutions emphasize energy-aware algorithms, lightweight data processing models, distributed and collaborative detection strategies, and adaptive mechanisms that dynamically respond to device state and network conditions. The concept of "green" in this context extends beyond reduced power consumption to encompass a holistic sustainability-oriented design philosophy, including:

- **Energy efficiency**: Minimizing energy consumption during sensing, communication, and analysis phases.
- **Resource awareness**: Adapting detection algorithms to constrained computational and memory resources.

- **Environmental responsibility**: Extending device lifespan and reducing electronic waste generation.
- **Long-term sustainability**: Supporting durable, scalable, and environmentally conscious IoT security deployments.

Developing effective Green IDS raises several open research questions, including the identification of energy-efficient features for IDS, adaptation and compression of learning models for low-power devices, reduction of communication overhead through distributed detection, integration of energy-harvesting mechanisms, and the definition of evaluation metrics that capture trade-offs between detection accuracy, latency, and energy consumption. This book is motivated by the lack of resources that address IoT security from a sustainability-centered perspective. While extensive research exists on traditional IDS and energy-efficient IoT design independently, their intersection, namely, the systematic design of *sustainable, energy-aware, and secure IDS for IoT*, remains insufficiently explored. By synthesizing principles, methodologies, and practical implementation strategies for Green IDS, this book aims to bridge this gap and provide a unified framework for next-generation IoT security solutions.

1.2 The IoT paradigm

The IoT represents a fundamental shift in how digital systems interact with the physical environment. Rather than relying solely on conventional computing platforms such as desktops, servers, and mobile devices, IoT introduces a large-scale network of heterogeneous, interconnected objects capable of autonomous sensing, communication, and decision-making. This paradigm extends computational intelligence into everyday artifacts, infrastructures, and operational environments, thereby reshaping both technological ecosystems and human activities. Although the concept of device interconnection for information exchange has existed for several decades, recent advances in embedded systems, wireless communication technologies, edge computing, and Artificial Intelligence (AI) have enabled IoT deployments to scale to billions of connected devices. Advances in hardware miniaturization, energy-efficient processing units, low-power communication modules, and cloud-based analytics have collectively expanded IoT well beyond earlier machine-to-machine communication models. Contemporary IoT ecosystems exhibit a multi-layered architecture in which physical entities seamlessly integrate with cyber infrastructure to support continuous, context-aware functionality. This section provides a conceptual and an architectural foundation for IoT, establishing the basis for understanding its distinctive security requirements and the motivation for developing Green IDS.

1.2.1 Definition and core concepts

The term IoT broadly refers to the interconnection of physical entities equipped with sensors, actuators, processors, and communication interfaces that enable autonomous

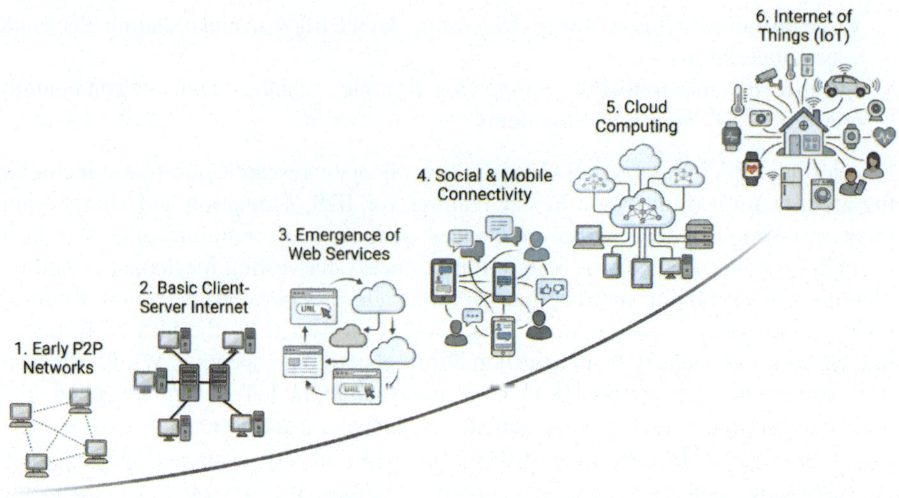

FIGURE 1.1

Evolution of the Internet from early peer-to-peer networks and World Wide Web architectures toward social platforms and the contemporary IoT, illustrating the transition toward universal connectivity across location, objects, time, and users.

sensing, data collection, processing, and exchange. As illustrated in Fig. 1.1, the Internet has evolved from early peer-to-peer networks and Web-based architectures toward social platforms and contemporary IoT systems, enabling connectivity across locations, objects, time, and users. Definitions proposed by standards bodies, research communities, and industrial consortia differ in scope and emphasis, yet they consistently share a set of foundational characteristics that define IoT systems.

- **Ubiquitous connectivity**. IoT devices communicate through both wired and wireless channels, forming large-scale, distributed networks. Connectivity may follow device-to-device, device-to-gateway, and hierarchical edge-to-cloud interaction models. Such pervasive communication supports continuous data exchange across geographical and infrastructural boundaries.
- **Sensing and actuation**. IoT devices monitor a wide range of physical and environmental phenomena, including temperature, humidity, biochemical indicators, vibration, motion, and structural conditions. Actuation capabilities enable direct control of physical processes through real-time feedback mechanisms.
- **Data-driven intelligence**. Raw sensory streams are transformed into actionable knowledge through edge computing, fog-based processing, and cloud analytics. These mechanisms support predictive maintenance, anomaly identification, behavioral modeling, forecasting, and autonomous system operation.
- **Interoperability**. IoT ecosystems incorporate devices developed under heterogeneous standards, operating systems, and communication technologies. Mid-

dleware platforms, semantic frameworks, and interoperability standards enable coordinated interaction among diverse system components.

- **Context-awareness**. IoT platforms leverage contextual attributes, including spatial information, user preferences, temporal dynamics, and environmental states, to deliver adaptive, personalized, and optimized services.
- **Autonomy and distributed operation**. Numerous IoT applications require fully autonomous behavior under dynamic and uncertain conditions, often with minimal human supervision. Distributed decision-making mechanisms have become essential due to scalability limitations inherent in centralized control architectures.

From a technological perspective, IoT embodies the convergence of previously independent domains, including wireless sensor networks, embedded computing, machine-to-machine communication, CPSs, cloud services, mobile platforms, and AI. The defining contribution of IoT resides not only in connecting everyday objects but in enabling intelligence, autonomy, and deep integration across interconnected physical and digital systems.

1.2.2 Typical layered architecture

Due to the inherent complexity of IoT ecosystems, layered architectural models are commonly adopted to abstract functional components and support systematic analysis. As illustrated in Fig. 1.2, an extended IoT architecture can be organized into perception, network, support, and application layers, each associated with representative security considerations. Such models facilitate structured evaluation of system performance, security characteristics, and energy efficiency across different functional levels, thereby enabling rigorous design and optimization of large-scale IoT deployments.

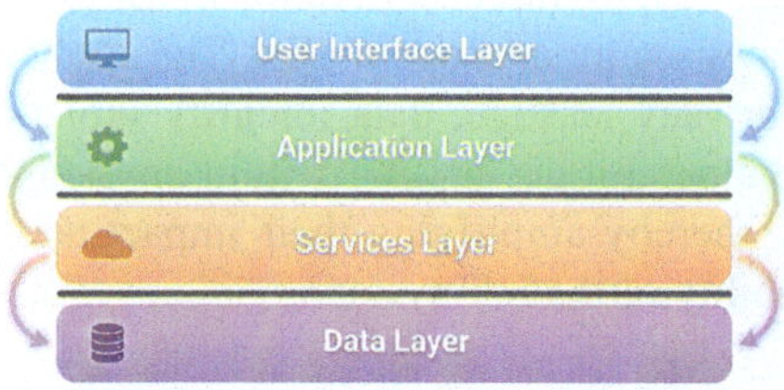

FIGURE 1.2

Illustration of an extended IoT layered architecture comprising perception, network, support, and application layers, with representative security considerations associated with each layer.

1. **Perception (Device) Layer**. This layer encompasses physical sensing and actuation components, including RFID tags, temperature sensors, inertial measurement units, smart meters, and biosensors. Owing to stringent constraints on cost, memory capacity, processing power, and energy availability, devices at this layer

typically operate with limited computational capability and minimal embedded security mechanisms.

2. **Network (Transport) Layer**. The network layer supports data transmission between IoT devices, gateways, and backend infrastructures through various communication technologies, including Wi-Fi, Bluetooth Low Energy, Zigbee, 6LoWPAN, LoRaWAN, NB-IoT, and fifth-generation cellular networks. It manages addressing, routing, and packet forwarding functions, while remaining particularly vulnerable to threats such as jamming, spoofing, and man-in-the-middle attacks.
3. **Application Layer**. This layer delivers end-user services and domain-specific functionalities across application domains, including smart residential environments, industrial automation, healthcare monitoring, and mobility analytics. It interfaces with cloud-based infrastructures, interprets processed data, and facilitates interaction between human users and intelligent systems.

More advanced architectural frameworks extend the conventional three-layer model through the inclusion of additional functional layers:

- **Middleware layer**, which enables semantic data processing, service coordination, and device abstraction through virtualization mechanisms.
- **Business layer**, which supports system-wide management functions, analytics, monetization strategies, regulatory compliance, and high-level policy enforcement.
- **Edge computing layer**, which has gained increasing importance due to its ability to reduce latency, limit bandwidth consumption, and improve energy efficiency by relocating computation closer to data sources.

Each architectural layer introduces distinct challenges related to performance, security, and system dependability. Resource limitations at the perception layer constrain the feasibility of robust cryptographic operations, while protocol diversity at the network layer complicates secure interoperability. The application layer faces heightened risks, including privacy leakage, data integrity violations, and authentication failures. Importantly, vulnerabilities arising within any single layer may propagate across adjacent layers, thereby amplifying their impact and threatening the overall resilience and sustainability of the IoT system.

1.2.3 IoT application domains

The IoT paradigm encompasses a diverse range of application domains, each characterized by distinct operational constraints, performance requirements, communication patterns, and security challenges. A clear understanding of these domains is essential for designing effective, energy-aware, and sustainable IDS mechanisms tailored to heterogeneous IoT networks.

Smart homes and buildings

IoT deployments in residential and commercial buildings include smart thermostats, lighting controllers, heating and cooling systems, surveillance cameras, access control devices, household appliances, and energy meters. These technologies support the automation of daily activities, improve energy efficiency, enhance occupant comfort, and strengthen physical security. However, their integration with external networks and cloud-based platforms introduces significant privacy exposure and attack surfaces. Compromised devices may lead to leakage of sensitive personal information, unauthorized physical access, and lateral movement within local networks.

IIoT and Industry 4.0

Within industrial environments, IoT technologies monitor equipment condition, detect structural abnormalities, manage production workflows, and coordinate robotic and autonomous systems to enhance operational efficiency and productivity. These capabilities enable predictive maintenance, reduced downtime, and increased productivity. At the same time, IIoT infrastructures frequently support mission-critical processes. A compromised sensing and actuation component may disrupt industrial operations, damage physical assets, and introduce serious safety risks. Consequently, strong real-time security mechanisms remain indispensable in such settings.

Healthcare and medical IoT

Medical IoT systems encompass wearable health monitors, implantable sensing devices, remote patient monitoring platforms, intelligent hospital infrastructure, and connected medical imaging systems. These technologies collect highly sensitive physiological data and, in certain cases, directly influence therapeutic interventions. Security failures within this domain may result in privacy violations, compromised patient safety, and manipulation of clinical outcomes. Additionally, strict energy-efficiency requirements apply to implanted and wearable devices, where reliability and battery longevity directly impact patient well-being.

Smart cities and urban infrastructure

Urban-scale IoT ecosystems support intelligent transportation management, adaptive street lighting, waste-collection optimization, environmental sensing, emergency response coordination, and public safety services. Such deployments commonly involve large numbers of distributed nodes across extensive geographic areas, requiring high availability, resilient security mechanisms, and long-term operational sustainability. Cyberattacks targeting smart city infrastructure may trigger widespread disruptions, degrade traffic management, and impair emergency response capabilities.

Agriculture, environmental monitoring, and natural resource management

IoT technologies deployed in agricultural and environmental contexts monitor soil conditions, crop health, livestock behavior, air and water quality, weather patterns, and ecological indicators. These systems frequently operate in remote and harsh environments characterized by limited accessibility and severe energy constraints. Sustainability and energy efficiency, therefore, represent core design requirements. System failures and malicious compromises may lead to reduced agricultural yields, delayed hazard detection, and ineffective environmental management.

Transportation and mobility systems

Connected vehicles, autonomous driving platforms, intelligent fleet management solutions, and smart logistics systems depend extensively on IoT technologies. These applications impose stringent demands on real-time data processing, communication reliability, and system security, given their safety-critical nature. Cyber attacks targeting transportation-related IoT components may disrupt navigation functions, manipulate vehicle-to-infrastructure communication, and undermine autonomous control decisions.

Energy and utility management

IoT-enabled energy infrastructure encompasses smart grids, advanced metering systems, distribution automation platforms, and renewable energy control units that support efficient power delivery, demand-side management, fault localization, and predictive maintenance. Security breaches within these systems may cause large-scale service disruptions, unauthorized manipulation of consumption data, and destabilization of grid operations. Collectively, these application domains demonstrate the pronounced heterogeneity of IoT ecosystems. A single, uniform security solution cannot adequately address the diverse requirements present across all scenarios. Instead, IDS mechanisms, particularly Green IDS, must carefully balance general applicability with domain-specific adaptation, accounting for differences in device capabilities, deployment environments, communication characteristics, latency sensitivity, and energy constraints.

1.3 Security challenges in IoT systems

Despite the transformative capabilities of the IoT, its rapid expansion has introduced security challenges fundamentally different from those encountered in conventional computing environments. IoT ecosystems combine heterogeneous devices, distributed architectures, constrained hardware resources, and diverse communication technologies. These characteristics collectively expand the attack surface, complicate threat mitigation, and demand security mechanisms specifically designed for the operational constraints of IoT. This section presents a systematic examination of the primary security challenges inherent in IoT systems. Fig. 1.3 illustrates representative smart-home IoT security threats. It analyzes the enlarged attack surface created by large-scale deployments, identifies common vulnerabilities and systemic weaknesses, characterizes the evolving IoT threat landscape, and explains why conventional security solutions cannot be directly transferred to IoT networks. Moreover, these insights motivate the need for lightweight, energy-aware, and sustainable IDS mechanisms.

1.3.1 Expanded attack surface

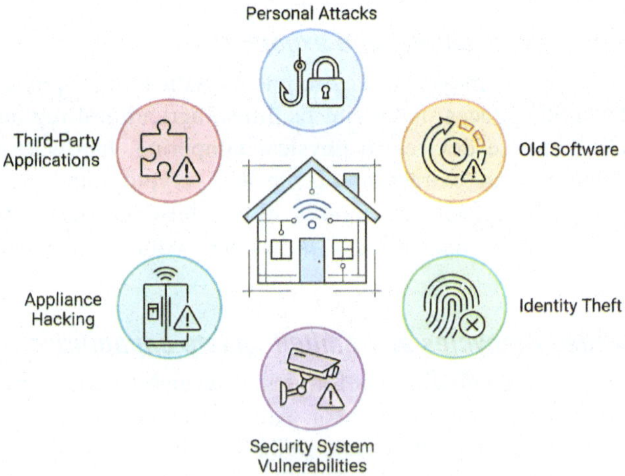

FIGURE 1.3

Illustration of prevalent smart-home IoT security threats, including personal data exposure, outdated software components, device compromise, insecure protection mechanisms, appliance exploitation, and vulnerabilities introduced by third-party applications.

IoT deployments substantially expand the attack surface compared to traditional information technology infrastructures. This expansion arises from several intrinsic characteristics of IoT networks, each of which contributes to heightened exposure to cyber threats.

1.3.1.1 Massive scale and device proliferation

The population of IoT devices continues to grow at an unprecedented rate, with projections indicating tens of billions of interconnected nodes within the coming years. Each deployed device, irrespective of its functional complexity, constitutes a potential entry point for adversaries. The distributed nature of IoT infrastructures enables a single compromised sensor node to facilitate lateral movement, compromise adjacent devices, and inject malicious traffic into wider network segments. Consequently, large-scale IoT deployments create conditions that enable adversaries to conduct systematic reconnaissance and exploitation.

1.3.1.2 Device heterogeneity and complex ecosystems

IoT ecosystems exhibit pronounced heterogeneity across processing capabilities, operating systems, firmware versions, communication protocols, and security configurations. This diversity complicates centralized security administration and undermines the feasibility of uniform defensive strategies. Adversaries frequently exploit inconsistencies among firmware implementations, protocol stacks, and vendor-specific configurations, targeting the weakest component to gain a foothold within the broader ecosystem.

1.3.1.3 Physical accessibility and exposure

Many IoT devices are deployed in environments with limited physical protection. Installations in public spaces, industrial facilities, agricultural regions, and remote outdoor locations expose devices to physical tampering, hardware probing, side-channel exploitation, and extraction of sensitive cryptographic material. Direct physical access enables firmware modification, abuse of debug interfaces, and component manipulation that remain infeasible within controlled data center environments.

1.3.1.4 Extended lifecycles and limited update capabilities

In contrast to personal computing platforms that receive frequent software updates, IoT devices often remain operational for extended deployment lifetimes spanning many years. A significant portion lacks reliable over-the-air update mechanisms, and vendor support may cease shortly after the product's release. As a result, vulnerable firmware versions persist within operational environments, exposing known weaknesses over prolonged periods. These long-term maintenance limitations increase the attractiveness of IoT devices as targets for persistent adversaries.

1.3.1.5 Interdependence of devices and services

IoT systems operate through tightly coupled dependencies among devices, gateways, cloud platforms, mobile applications, and external service interfaces. A compromise at any point in this interconnected chain may propagate across multiple components. For instance, exploitation of a vulnerability within a centralized cloud service can simultaneously impact large populations of dependent devices deployed across diverse locations.

1.3.2 Common vulnerabilities and weaknesses

Extensive empirical studies, vulnerability repositories, and incident investigations consistently identify recurring categories of weaknesses in IoT devices. These vulnerabilities typically stem from constrained hardware resources, aggressive cost optimization, limited vendor security expertise, and the absence of mature, standardized security practices across the IoT ecosystem.

1.3.2.1 Default, weak, and hard-coded credentials

One of the most widespread security weaknesses involves devices shipped with default credentials, trivially guessable passwords, and embedded hard-coded authentication data. Such credentials are rarely modified by end users, allowing adversaries to gain unauthorized access with minimal effort. Large-scale botnets, most notably Mirai, have successfully exploited this weakness to compromise vast populations of IoT devices.

1.3.2.2 Absence of secure communication and encryption

A significant proportion of IoT devices transmit sensitive information using plaintext channels and legacy cryptographic schemes. Resource limitations frequently discourage manufacturers from deploying robust encryption algorithms, secure key management mechanisms, and mutual authentication protocols. Adversaries exploit these weaknesses through traffic interception, replay techniques, and man-in-the-middle exploitation, enabling data manipulation and malicious injection.

1.3.2.3 Insecure web interfaces and application programming interfaces

Web-based management interfaces and vendor-provided application programming interfaces are common components of IoT systems. These interfaces are frequently vulnerable to cross-site scripting, command injection, insecure session management, and insufficient authentication enforcement. Deficient interface design exposes administrative functionality and sensitive device data to unauthorized entities.

1.3.2.4 Firmware weaknesses and lack of integrity verification

Firmware deployed on IoT devices often lacks robust integrity verification mechanisms. Unsigned firmware images and inadequately validated update processes allow adversaries to install malicious firmware, perform downgrade attacks that reintroduce known vulnerabilities, and deactivate embedded security controls. Constraints on storage capacity and processing capability further limit the adoption of advanced protection mechanisms, such as secure boot processes and runtime attestation frameworks.

1.3.2.5 Weak authentication and insufficient access control

To reduce computational overhead and simplify deployment, many IoT devices implement minimal authentication mechanisms alongside coarse-grained access control policies. Deficiencies such as poor user-role separation, lack of multi-factor authentication, and unrestricted debugging interfaces substantially increase the exposure to attacks.

1.3.2.6 Inadequate process isolation and software sandboxing

Due to hardware limitations, many IoT platforms lack effective process isolation mechanisms and hardware-supported sandboxing. Consequently, compromise of a single software component, such as a management interface, may provide full system-level access, enabling unauthorized interaction with additional subsystems. This architectural weakness significantly expands the impact radius of successful attacks and facilitates privilege escalation across device layers. Collectively, these vulnerabilities reflect systemic design challenges in IoT development practices, including prioritizing usability and cost efficiency over security robustness, limited engineering resources, and fragmented standardization efforts.

1.3.3 Threat landscape and attack vectors

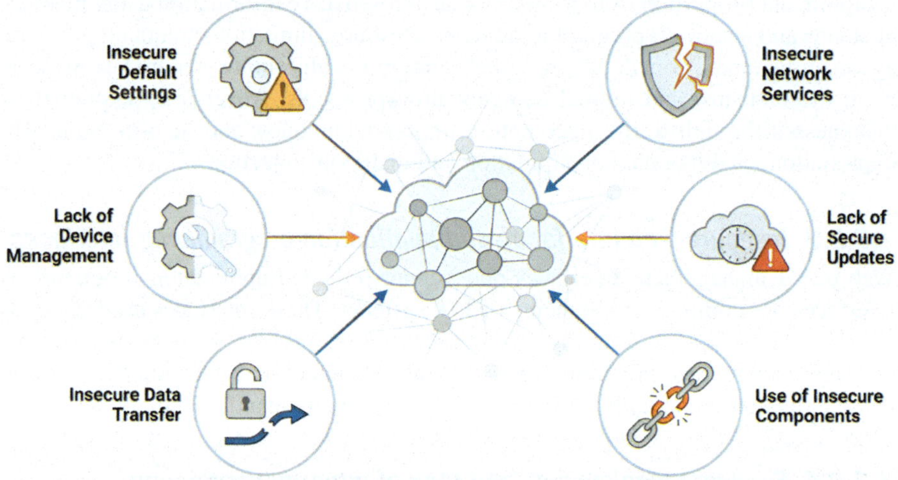

FIGURE 1.4

Representative IoT attack vectors across multiple deployment domains, including residential automation, automotive platforms, healthcare systems, and consumer electronics, illustrating potential compromise of physical processes, sensitive data, and service availability.

The IoT threat landscape is highly diverse and continues to evolve rapidly. Fig. 1.4 illustrates representative IoT attack vectors across multiple deployment domains. Adversaries exploit both technical weaknesses and socio-technical behaviors to compromise devices, exfiltrate sensitive information, and disrupt system functionality.

1.3.3.1 Botnet formation and distributed attacks

Compromised IoT devices are frequently incorporated into large-scale botnets that conduct Distributed Denial-of-Service (DDoS) attacks. These attacks exploit the massive number of network-connected IoT nodes and their persistent online presence. Botnets such as Mirai, Hajime, and Reaper have demonstrated the destructive capacity of coordinated IoT-based attack campaigns. Such botnets generate traffic volumes capable of overwhelming major online platforms and critical infrastructure services.

1.3.3.2 Data exfiltration and privacy violations

IoT deployments routinely collect sensitive personal, industrial, and medical data. Adversaries exploit insecure communication links, weak cryptographic protections, misconfigured cloud infrastructures, and compromised companion applications to extract confidential information. Resulting breaches expose behavioral patterns, location traces, health indicators, and proprietary industrial knowledge, underscoring the fragility of privacy safeguards in IoT ecosystems.

1.3.3.3 Service disruption and availability attacks

System availability is a critical requirement for IoT deployments across healthcare services, transportation systems, industrial automation platforms, and smart energy infrastructure. Adversaries target availability through DoS campaigns, radio-frequency interference, selective packet forwarding, and battery depletion strategies. Even localized disruption may escalate into severe operational failures, financial loss, and safety hazards.

1.3.3.4 Manipulation of physical processes

IoT systems maintain direct interaction with physical environments. Adversaries that gain control over sensing and actuation components may alter environmental measurements, disrupt automated control logic, and manipulate physical processes. Documented attack scenarios include malicious adjustments to thermostats, unauthorized control of robotic arms, falsified industrial sensor readings, and interference with life-sustaining medical device parameters.

1.3.3.5 Supply chain and third-party risks

IoT products incorporate hardware components, firmware modules, and software libraries sourced from extensive supply chains involving multiple vendors and subcontractors. A compromised component introduced at any stage of this chain may propagate malicious functionality across large device populations. Adversaries increasingly exploit third-party dependencies, cloud service interfaces, containerized components, and insecure update infrastructures to distribute malicious payloads. The distributed and interconnected nature of IoT networks enables rapid propagation of such attacks across devices, networks, and cloud platforms, necessitating coordinated and multi-layered defense strategies.

1.3.4 Constraints on traditional security mechanisms

Security techniques originally designed for resource-rich enterprise computing environments cannot be directly applied to IoT deployments. The distinctive constraints of IoT systems require fundamental rethinking of security architectures and detection mechanisms.

1.3.4.1 Limited processing capacity

Many IoT platforms rely on low-power microcontrollers characterized by restricted clock frequencies, simplified instruction sets, and minimal parallel processing capability. Computationally intensive cryptographic operations, complex anomaly detection pipelines, and large rule-based engines rapidly exhaust available resources. Consequently, security algorithms require careful redesign to meet minimal computational footprints.

1.3.4.2 Memory and storage limitations

Constraints on volatile memory and persistent storage further restrict the deployment of sophisticated security libraries, Deep Learning (DL) models, and extensive signature repositories. Even relatively lightweight IDS mechanisms may exceed device memory budgets. Efficient memory utilization and compact model design, therefore, remain essential.

1.3.4.3 Severe energy constraints

A substantial proportion of IoT devices operate on battery power, making energy conservation a primary design objective. Security mechanisms that demand continuous monitoring, frequent communication, and sustained processor utilization significantly reduce device lifetime. These constraints motivate the development of energy-aware and power-efficient security solutions.

1.3.4.4 Bandwidth limitations and intermittent connectivity

Low-power communication technologies, such as LoRaWAN, Zigbee, and NB-IoT, offer limited data throughput and intermittent connectivity. Continuous transmission of security telemetry and centralized log aggregation remain infeasible under these conditions. Conventional centralized monitoring approaches, therefore, fail to scale within IoT networks.

1.3.4.5 Real-time and safety-critical constraints

IoT applications supporting healthcare delivery, industrial control systems, and autonomous transportation impose stringent real-time performance requirements. Security mechanisms must operate with minimal latency and high reliability, since delays and excessive false alarms may compromise system safety. These demands drive ongoing research into fast, adaptive, and lightweight IDS techniques. Collectively, these constraints explain the growing research focus on *Green IDS*, which seeks to provide effective security monitoring while minimizing computational overhead, energy consumption, and environmental impact.

1.4 Sustainability in IoT: energy and environment

FIGURE 1.5

Representative environmentally oriented IoT applications, including smart energy management, extreme weather monitoring, vehicle tracking, intelligent waste handling, air and water quality assessment, biodiversity protection, commercial agriculture, and pollution mitigation.

The rapid expansion of the IoT has intensified global concern regarding sustainability, energy efficiency, and environmental responsibility. With billions of interconnected devices continuously sensing, processing, and transmitting data, IoT ecosystems now account for a major share of worldwide digital energy consumption. As shown in Fig. 1.5, IoT deployments support environmentally oriented applications across smart energy management, extreme weather monitoring, vehicle tracking, intelligent waste handling, air and water quality assessment, biodiversity protection, commercial agriculture, and pollution mitigation. As IoT deployments extend across critical domains including healthcare, transportation, energy systems, agriculture, and urban infrastructure, careful examination of their environmental footprint becomes imperative. Sustainability within IoT encompasses energy-efficient system design, environmentally responsible manufacturing, effective lifecycle management, and security mechanisms that limit ecological impact.

1.4.1 Energy consumption in IoT ecosystems

Energy availability is the dominant constraint in IoT systems, particularly in large-scale, remote deployments that rely on battery power and energy-harvesting technologies. Energy consumption directly influences device lifetime, operational reliability, maintenance overhead, environmental impact, and system resilience. Device-level energy expenditure may be approximated as:

$$E_{\text{total}} = E_{\text{compute}} + E_{\text{communication}} + E_{\text{sensing}} + E_{\text{idle}}, \tag{1.1}$$

where E_{compute} corresponds to processing activities such as feature extraction, learning inference, and cryptographic operations, $E_{\text{communication}}$ denotes transmission and reception costs, E_{sensing} captures interaction with physical environments, and E_{idle} reflects baseline consumption during standby and low-power states.

1.4.1.1 Communication as the primary energy driver

In wireless IoT platforms, communication accounts for the majority of overall energy expenditure. Long-range transmissions consume substantially more energy than local computation, while multi-hop routing and mesh networking further amplify overhead. Security-related exchanges, including authentication procedures, key establishment, and encrypted payload transmission, account for a significant share of communication energy costs.

1.4.1.2 Security-induced energy overhead

Security mechanisms introduce unavoidable energy overhead. Cryptographic primitives increase computational demand, continuous intrusion monitoring elevates processing and communication requirements, and secure communication protocols expand the packet size and increase the retransmission frequency. Without careful optimization, such mechanisms may reduce device lifetime by more than half.

1.4.2 Environmental impact and electronic waste

Beyond operational energy use, IoT systems impose environmental costs throughout their lifecycles. Projections exceeding seventy-five billion deployed devices by 2035 position IoT among the fastest-growing contributors to electronic waste.

1.4.2.1 Carbon footprint

Semiconductor fabrication, battery production, and antenna manufacturing involve energy-intensive industrial processes. Operational energy consumption further scales with deployment size, making efficiency essential for carbon mitigation. Sustainable IoT design emphasizes reduced material impact, power-aware algorithms, integration of renewable energy, and device-level carbon optimization.

1.4.2.2 Electronic waste accumulation

Many IoT devices have limited service lifetimes due to poor repairability, tightly integrated hardware designs, and firmware obsolescence resulting from vendor support termination. These characteristics accelerate disposal cycles and intensify waste accumulation.

1.4.2.3 Resource depletion

IoT hardware relies on critical raw materials, including rare-earth elements and strategic metals such as lithium, cobalt, copper, and gold. Extraction and refinement processes generate ecological degradation, toxic by-products, and significant greenhouse gas emissions. Rising demand amplifies supply chain fragility and long-term resource scarcity.

1.4.3 IoT sustainability and the United Nations sustainable development goals

Aligning IoT development with the United Nations Sustainable Development Goals remains essential for global sustainability. IoT contributes directly to goals related to clean energy, resilient infrastructure, sustainable cities, responsible consumption, climate action, and ecosystem protection through intelligent monitoring, optimization, and data-driven decision support. Achieving alignment requires sustainable hardware engineering, lifecycle-aware system design, carbon-conscious computation, energy-aware algorithm deployment, efficient security enforcement, and responsible end-of-life management.

1.4.4 Sustainability and security as a unified objective

Security and sustainability form mutually reinforcing objectives within IoT ecosystems. Secure devices avoid malware-induced energy drain, resist premature replacement, and sustain predictable operational behavior over extended lifetimes. Simultaneously, energy-efficient systems experience reduced hardware stress, maintain reliable update processes, and support consistent, secure communication without disabling protective mechanisms. Sustainability, therefore, functions as a foundational enabler of resilient IoT security architectures.

1.4.4.1 Motivation for Green IDS

Green IDS aims to deliver effective threat monitoring while adhering to stringent resource constraints. Their objectives include minimizing energy consumption, reducing communication overhead through localized inference and edge aggregation, adapting computational complexity to device conditions, and maintaining strong security guarantees with minimal environmental impact.

1.5 IDS in IoT

IDSs constitute a core security mechanism within IoT ecosystems. In contrast to conventional computing environments, IoT deployments exhibit high heterogeneity, distributed operation, constrained resources, and extensive reliance on wireless communication. These characteristics substantially increase exposure to cyber threats while limiting the feasibility of traditional security controls. Consequently, IDS in IoT must operate with minimal resource overhead while maintaining reliable detection capabilities under dynamic, large-scale conditions.

1.5.1 Role of IDS in IoT

IoT networks frequently lack perimeter defenses, hardware firewalls, continuous human oversight, and device isolation. As a result, IDS serves as the primary mechanism for system-wide visibility and threat identification across devices, networks, and services. Its function extends beyond passive monitoring to the early detection of unauthorized access, abnormal behavior, protocol misuse, and coordinated cyberattacks before they propagate across interconnected nodes.

1.5.1.1 Network-level observation

Network monitoring remains a fundamental capability of IoT-oriented IDS. Low-power wireless networks are particularly vulnerable to routing manipulation, spoofing, replay attacks, selective forwarding, jamming, and DDoS flooding. IDS evaluates traffic characteristics to identify deviations from expected communication behavior. IDS analyzes:

- **Traffic flows**, using statistical metrics, entropy analysis, and flow aggregation to detect abnormal transmission volumes, burst patterns, and silent node behavior indicative of DoS activity and isolation attacks.
- **Routing behavior**, examining rank fluctuations, inconsistent advertisements, and unstable routing tables within protocols such as RPL, ZigBee, AODV, and 6LoWPAN.
- **Protocol compliance**, validating header formats, message sequencing, timing consistency, and protocol state transitions in lightweight protocols including MQTT, CoAP, and BLE.
- **Connection patterns**, identifying unauthorized associations, abnormal peer discovery, and communication with previously unseen identities.

Network-level visibility provides crucial protection across deployments spanning public infrastructure, industrial environments, and large-scale sensing systems.

1.5.1.2 Device behavior analysis

Many IoT attacks do not immediately manifest through network anomalies. Host-level behavioral inspection enables detection of compromised firmware, logic manipulation, and stealthy malware execution. IDS examines:

- **CPU and memory usage**, where deviations from predictable consumption profiles indicate unauthorized execution or malicious workload injection.
- **System call and library patterns**, revealing firmware modification, privilege escalation attempts, and unauthorized module loading.
- **Energy signatures**, detecting abnormal radio activity, disabled sleep states, and malware-induced power drain unique to IoT platforms.
- **Operational timing**, identifying implausible sensor activation rates, unsafe actuation sequences, and manipulated environmental readings.

Due to deterministic duty cycles and constrained functionality, even minor behavioral deviations frequently indicate compromise in IoT devices.

1.5.1.3 Multi-device event correlation

IoT attacks commonly exploit the distributed nature of propagation and the coordinated behavior of multiple devices. IDS therefore performs correlation across nodes, gateways, and aggregation layers to identify collective attack patterns. Correlation mechanisms support:

- detection of synchronized anomalies across device groups,

- identification of multi-stage attack progression,
- recognition of lateral movement across network paths,
- temporal alignment of coordinated malicious actions.

Cross-layer correlation enhances detection confidence while minimizing false alarms in large-scale deployments, such as smart cities and industrial IoT.

1.5.1.4 Runtime resilience and response

IDS in IoT networks must support timely mitigation to preserve operational continuity and safety. Runtime response capabilities include isolating compromised devices, updating rules and models adaptively, generating attack fingerprints, and redirecting traffic through trusted communication paths. Such resilience is essential in healthcare systems, autonomous platforms, and industrial control environments where delayed response may result in physical harm or economic loss.

1.5.2 Classification of IDS

IDS classification within IoT extends beyond detection logic to incorporate data sources, architectural structure, and operational behavior. Modern research organizes IDS along four complementary dimensions: detection methodology, data origin, architectural deployment, and response behavior. Fig. 1.6 summarizes this taxonomy.

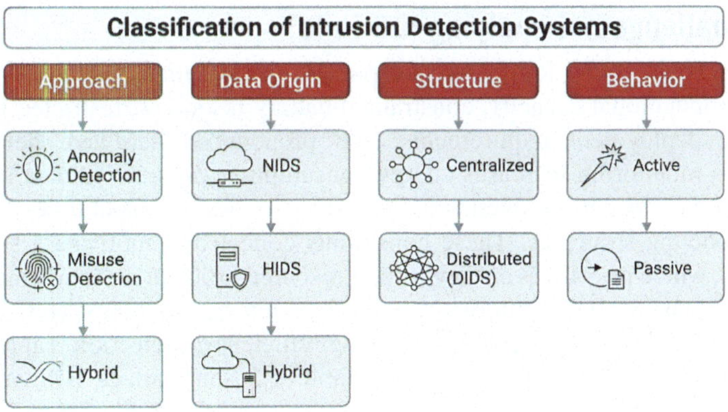

FIGURE 1.6

Taxonomy of IDS across detection methodology, data origin, architectural structure, and operational behavior.

Detection methodology

Anomaly-based IDS models normal operational behavior and flags deviations indicative of unknown attack activity, making it well-suited for evolving IoT threat patterns. Signature-based detection identifies known attack fingerprints with low computational overhead, but it is limited in its adaptability. Hybrid approaches integrate lightweight local signature checks with higher-level anomaly analysis at gateways, fog nodes, and cloud layers, achieving scalability and robustness.

Data origin

Network-based IDS inspects inter-device communication and routing behavior, enabling detection of flooding, spoofing, and coordinated botnet activity. Host-based IDS analyzes the internal behavior of devices, including resource usage and firmware integrity. Combined host-network systems correlate both perspectives, significantly strengthening the evidence of intrusion.

Architectural deployment

Centralized IDS provides powerful analytics but introduces latency, communication overhead, and single points of failure. Distributed IDS shifts partial detection to edge devices and gateways, improving scalability, energy efficiency, and resilience.

Response behavior

Passive IDS focuses on monitoring and generating alerts, making it suitable for safety-critical deployments. Active IDS enables automated containment actions such as device isolation and privilege revocation, improving responsiveness while requiring careful control to avoid unintended disruption.

1.5.3 Challenges of applying IDS in IoT

Deploying IDS within IoT networks presents substantial challenges, including limited computational capacity, constrained battery resources, restricted bandwidth, large-scale deployment requirements, and pronounced hardware heterogeneity. Continuous monitoring increases energy consumption, centralized data aggregation amplifies communication overhead, and diverse device capabilities complicate unified modeling strategies. These constraints collectively motivate a shift toward Green IDS, which prioritizes energy-aware, resource-efficient detection mechanisms. Table 1.1 contrasts IDS solutions across detection methodology and data source dimensions, highlighting trade-offs among efficiency, detection capability, and operational cost under IoT constraints. Table 1.2 summarizes IDS architectural and operational distinctions relevant to IoT deployments. Table 1.3 compares IDS categories with respect to energy demand, detection effectiveness, and computational burden.

1.6 Green IDS

Green IDS integrates cybersecurity with sustainability by minimizing resource consumption while preserving detection performance. These systems rely on lightweight learning models, adaptive sampling, hierarchical computation distribution, and

Table 1.1 Comparison of IDS based on detection methodology and data source.

Category	Type	Characteristics
Detection Method	Signature-Based IDS	Lightweight pattern matching with low energy demand; limited effectiveness against novel threats.
	Anomaly-Based IDS	Behavioral modeling enabling discovery of unknown attacks; increased energy use and training complexity.
	Hybrid IDS	Combined local signature checks with higher-layer anomaly analysis; balanced accuracy and efficiency.
Data Source	Network-Based IDS	Inspection of traffic and routing behavior; limited visibility into internal device state.
	Host-Based IDS	Monitoring of CPU usage, memory activity, and firmware behavior; constrained by device resources.
	Combined Host–Network IDS	Correlated visibility across layers; highest detection accuracy with elevated overhead.

Table 1.2 Comparison of IDS architectural structure and operational behavior.

Category	Type	Characteristics
Architecture	Centralized IDS	Deep correlation capabilities with high communication overhead and reduced resilience.
	Distributed IDS	Localized detection across devices and gateways; improved scalability and energy efficiency.
Operation	Passive IDS	Monitoring and alert generation without intervention; suitable for safety-critical deployments.
	Active IDS	Automated mitigation actions; increased responsiveness with careful false-action control.

context-aware inference strategies. Table 1.4 summarizes IDS categories by IoT suitability, sustainability contribution, and SDG alignment.

1.6.1 Concept and design principles

Green IDS dynamically adjusts monitoring intensity, computational placement, and model complexity based on device state and environmental conditions. Computation migrates toward gateways under constrained energy conditions, while lightweight inference remains local. This approach extends device lifetime, reduces communication overhead, and aligns security with sustainability objectives.

Table 1.3 Energy demand, detection effectiveness, and computational burden of IDS categories.

IDS Category	Energy Demand	Detection Capability	Computational Load
Signature-Based IDS	Minimal energy consumption	Reliable detection of known threats	Very low processing overhead
Anomaly-Based IDS	Moderate to high energy consumption	Strong detection of unknown threats	High computational complexity
Hybrid IDS	Balanced energy profile	Highest overall detection robustness	Moderate processing overhead
Network-Based IDS	Low to moderate energy consumption	Effective for traffic-level threats	Moderate packet inspection cost
Host-Based IDS	Moderate energy consumption	Accurate detection of device compromise	Moderate local processing cost

Table 1.4 IoT suitability, sustainability contribution, and SDG alignment of IDS categories.

IDS Type	IoT Suitability	Sustainability Contribution	Aligned SDGs
Signature-Based IDS	Highly suitable for constrained devices	Extends battery life and reduces replacement	SDG 9, SDG 12
Anomaly-Based IDS	Suitable for data-rich environments	Increased energy demand with optimized scheduling	SDG 11, SDG 13
Hybrid IDS	Applicable across IoT layers	Balanced energy consumption and strong protection	SDG 9, SDG 11, SDG 12, SDG 13
Centralized IDS	Limited suitability	High communication and processing footprint	SDG 7, SDG 13
Distributed IDS	Highly scalable for massive deployments	Reduced transmission overhead and emissions	SDG 7, SDG 9, SDG 12
Active IDS	Suitable for autonomous systems	Prevents cascading failures	SDG 11, SDG 13
Passive IDS	Appropriate for safety-critical systems	Energy-efficient monitoring	SDG 3, SDG 12

1.6.2 Key characteristics

Green IDS employs compact learning models optimized for microcontrollers, distributes inference across device–edge–cloud hierarchies, and implements energy-aware scheduling to suppress redundant processing and contextual detection to limit unnecessary communication.

1.7 Scope and objectives of this book

This book systematically integrates cybersecurity and sustainability by embedding energy efficiency, lifecycle awareness, and environmental responsibility into the design and evaluation of IDS for IoT networks. It positions Green IDS. as a unifying paradigm that reconciles robust security guarantees with long-term ecological viability in resource-constrained and large-scale IoT deployments. The primary objectives of this book are fourfold. First, it establishes the foundational principles of IoT architectures, threat models, and security constraints under energy- and resource-limited conditions. Second, it critically analyzes the limitations of conventional IDS when applied to heterogeneous, low-power IoT ecosystems. Third, it develops theoretical, algorithmic, and architectural models for Green IDS, with a particular emphasis on lightweight cryptography, Machine Learning (ML), driven detection, distributed and federated IDS frameworks, and energy-aware optimization strategies. Finally, the book introduces comprehensive evaluation methodologies that jointly consider security effectiveness, computational overhead, energy consumption, and environmental impact. By explicitly aligning IoT security innovation with global sustainability initiatives, particularly the United Nations Sustainable Development Goals (SDG 9: Industry, Innovation, and Infrastructure; SDG 11: Sustainable Cities and Communities; and SDG 13: Climate Action), this book provides a coherent framework for designing IDS mechanisms that are not only secure but also environmentally responsible and future-proof.

1.8 Organization of the book

The book consists of ten chapters that progress from foundational concepts to advanced sustainable security architectures and future research directions.

Chapter 1

introduces the evolution of IoT systems, emerging sustainability challenges, and the motivation for Green IDS.

Chapter 2

examines IoT architectures, communication stacks, and layered security constraints inherent to resource-constrained environments.

Chapter 3

presents IDS theories, models, and algorithms, including anomaly-based, signature-based, and hybrid approaches.

Chapter 4

discusses lightweight cryptography, secure communication protocols, and trust mechanisms tailored for low-power IoT devices.

Chapter 5

focuses on energy-efficient IoT networking, optimization techniques, and power-aware system design.

Chapter 6

analyzes IoT threat models, attack surfaces, and attack taxonomies across perception, network, and application layers.

Chapter 7

explores ML, DL, Federated Learning (FL), and TinyML techniques for IDS in constrained IoT Networks.

Chapter 8

details Green IDS architectures, design frameworks, and distributed detection strategies that balance security performance with energy efficiency.

Chapter 9

defines evaluation methodologies and performance metrics that explicitly incorporate energy consumption, computational efficiency, and environmental sustainability alongside traditional security metrics.

Chapter 10

discusses future research directions, including circular IoT, edge intelligence, post-quantum security, and the long-term sustainability of cybersecurity infrastructures.

CHAPTER

Foundations of intrusion detection system for IoT

2

2.1 Introduction

Intrusion Detection Systems (IDS) play a central role in maintaining the security and reliability of modern digital ecosystems. While IDS technologies have matured significantly within traditional Information Technology (IT) infrastructures, their direct application to the IoT remains challenging due to the heterogeneous, distributed, and resource-constrained nature of IoT networks. As billions of low-power, often remotely deployed devices proliferate across smart cities, industrial automation, healthcare, transportation, and energy systems, the attack surface grows proportionally, making IDS one of the most critical defense components. IoT networks differ fundamentally from classical computing platforms. Devices are typically characterized by limited CPU capacity, constrained memory, low-power wireless communication, and a reliance on batteries and energy-harvesting mechanisms. Consequently, IDS mechanisms designed for conventional systems often impose unacceptable overhead when deployed on IoT devices, leading to excessive energy consumption, increased latency, and reduced operational lifetime. These limitations necessitate the development of lightweight, energy-efficient, and context-aware IDS architectures. An additional and increasingly important dimension in modern IDS design is the *sustainability* of cybersecurity systems. AI-driven cybersecurity solutions are recognized not only for their defensive capabilities but also for their environmental and energy implications. The application of Machine Learning (ML), Deep Learning (DL), and Deep Reinforcement Learning (DRL) methods in IDS imposes significant computational and energy demands, directly affecting carbon emissions, operational costs, and long-term device reliability. As IoT continues to expand globally, IDS systems must align with energy-efficiency requirements and the Sustainable Development Goals (SDGs), particularly SDG 7 (Clean Energy), SDG 9 (Industry, Innovation, and Infrastructure), and SDG 11 (Sustainable Cities). Furthermore, IoT networks face a diverse range of cyber threats, including Distributed Denial-of-Service (DDoS) attacks, botnet infections such as Mirai and Gafgyt, port scanning, spoofing, and protocol manipulation. Attackers frequently exploit weak authentication mechanisms, unencrypted communication channels, default configurations, and vulnerable firmware to compromise devices at scale. These threats highlight the urgency of developing adaptive IDS strategies capable of operating efficiently at the network edge with minimal computational overhead. This chapter establishes the foundational concepts necessary

Green Intrusion Detection Systems for IoT. https://doi.org/10.1016/B978-0-44-344249-0.00009-0

for understanding IDS in IoT networks. It covers architectural principles of IoT networks, attack taxonomies, IDS classification models, ML foundations, sustainability metrics, and emerging trends such as green security and energy-aware IDS.

2.2 IoT architecture and threat landscape

IoT networks represent one of the most rapidly expanding and heterogeneous technological domains. Industry projections estimate that deployments will exceed 30 billion devices by 2030, spanning smart homes, industrial automation, healthcare systems, transportation networks, and critical infrastructure. This large-scale proliferation expands the global attack surface and exposes IoT networks to a range of cyber threats. In contrast to traditional IT infrastructures, IoT devices operate under strict constraints in processing power, memory, energy, and communication bandwidth. These limitations restrict the deployment of heavyweight security mechanisms and increase susceptibility to large-scale exploitation, including malware propagation, DDoS campaigns, spoofing, routing manipulation, and resource exhaustion. Botnets such as Mirai and Gafgyt have demonstrated how systemic weaknesses in constrained deployments can be weaponized at scale.

2.2.1 IoT architectural models

IoT networks are commonly represented through layered architectural abstractions that describe the end-to-end lifecycle of data, from physical sensing to cloud-based service delivery. These models clarify device interaction, communication flows, and data-processing pipelines. From a security standpoint, layered architectures enable systematic identification of attack surfaces across the device–cloud continuum and support structured threat modeling.

2.2.1.1 Three-layer IoT architecture

The three-layer architecture (Fig. 2.1) serves as the foundational abstraction for IoT networks. Despite its simplicity, it captures the essential separation between sensing, communication, and service provisioning.

Perception layer

The perception layer forms the interface between the physical and digital environments. It includes sensors, RFID tags, cameras, GPS modules, embedded microcontrollers, and actuators responsible for environmental data acquisition and actuation control. Devices at this layer are typically resource-constrained and battery-powered, often lacking secure boot mechanisms, hardware trust anchors, and strong cryptographic support. These limitations increase the risk of firmware injection, sensor spoofing, side-channel exploitation, physical tampering, and authentication bypass. Compromise at this layer may propagate corrupted data throughout the IoT pipeline.

Network layer

The network layer ensures reliable data transmission between devices, gateways, and cloud infrastructures. It integrates heterogeneous communication technologies, including Wi-Fi, Zigbee, Bluetooth Low Energy (BLE), 6LoWPAN, LTE-M, NB-IoT, and LoRaWAN. As the communication backbone, this layer is a frequent target for adversarial manipulation, including packet injection, replay attacks, routing manipulation, jamming, MITM attacks, and DDoS flooding. Protocol diversity and legacy integration further enlarge the attack surface and complicate unified security enforcement.

Application layer

The application layer delivers domain-specific services, including remote monitoring, smart home automation, predictive maintenance, industrial analytics, and healthcare management. Operating across edge and cloud environments, it exposes APIs, dashboards, and analytics engines to users and administrators. Common vulnerabilities include insecure APIs, weak authentication, misconfigured access controls, inadequate encryption, and improper cloud configurations, which can lead to large-scale data leakage and privacy compromises. While the three-layer model provides conceptual clarity, it abstracts intermediate orchestration layers such as edge/fog computing and middleware services. Nevertheless, it remains a useful foundation for analyzing threat propagation paths and structuring IoT security architectures.

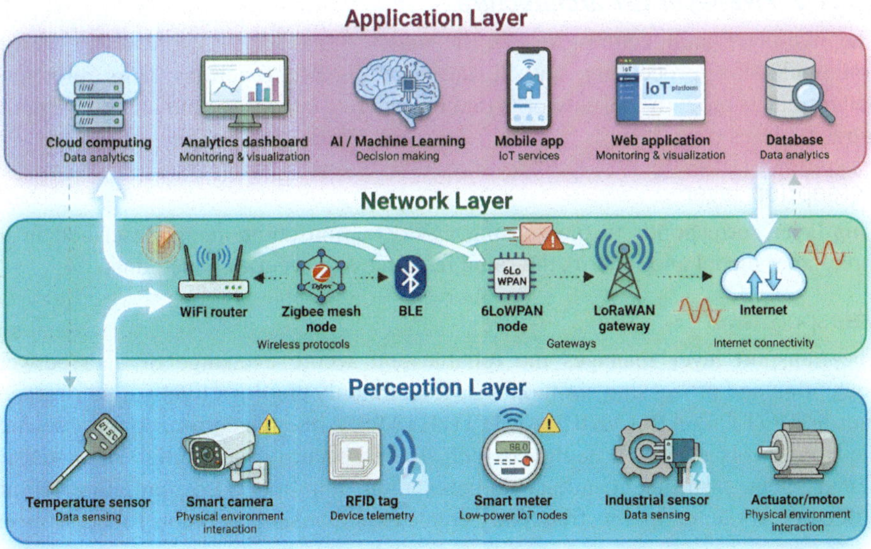

FIGURE 2.1

Three-layer IoT architecture illustrating perception, network, and application components.

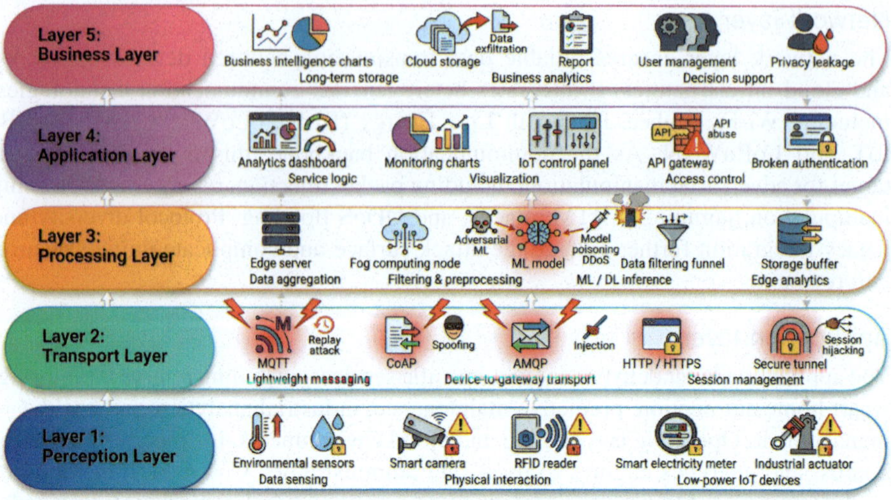

FIGURE 2.2

Five-layer IoT architecture with transport and processing layers. Red-highlighted areas denote typical injection points for attacks.

2.2.1.2 Five-layer IoT architecture

The five-layer architecture extends the classical model by explicitly separating communication, processing, and business intelligence functions. This refinement better reflects modern IoT networks that incorporate edge, fog, and cloud computing infrastructures (Fig. 2.2).

Perception layer

This layer corresponds to the sensing and actuation components described in the three-layer model and inherits the same resource and security constraints.

Transport layer

The transport layer manages the reliable and secure exchange of data between perception and processing components. It commonly employs lightweight protocols such as MQTT, CoAP, AMQP, and HTTP/HTTPS. Although optimized for efficiency, these protocols are often deployed with limited security hardening. Weak session management, insufficient mutual authentication, improper TLS configuration, and unsecured broker endpoints frequently create exploitable entry points for adversaries.

Processing layer

The processing layer performs aggregation, filtering, storage, analytics, and ML inference. It includes edge servers, fog nodes, and cloud analytics engines. Due to its computational role, this layer is exposed to adversarial ML manipulation, resource exhaustion, inference tampering, and service-disruption attacks. Compromise at this layer may corrupt decision-making pipelines and degrade system availability.

Application layer

The application layer provides user-facing services such as dashboards, automation interfaces, and predictive analytics tools. Typical weaknesses include insecure APIs, improper authorization controls, and data leakage risks.

Business layer

The business layer supports strategic oversight, reporting, billing, and long-term analytics. Because it aggregates high-value operational and user data, it is a prime target for large-scale data exfiltration and privacy compromise. Compared to the three-layer abstraction, the five-layer model enables more granular threat modeling and clearer mapping between attack surfaces and defensive controls, making it better suited to contemporary IoT security architecture design.

2.2.2 IoT communication protocols

Communication protocols form the connective fabric of IoT networks. In contrast to traditional Internet applications, IoT deployments operate under strict constraints on bandwidth, latency, and memory footprint, and energy availability. As a result, many IoT protocols prioritize lightweight operation and reduced overhead over strong security defaults. While this optimization enables the large-scale deployment of constrained devices, it also introduces protocol-specific attack surfaces. Understanding these trade-offs is essential to designing a secure IoT architecture. Table 2.1 summarizes these protocol-level strengths and vulnerabilities across commonly used IoT communication protocols.

2.2.3 IoT threat landscape

The IoT threat landscape is significantly broader and more heterogeneous than that of traditional IT systems. This expansion stems from the large-scale distribution of devices, heterogeneous communication technologies, limited hardware resources, and the frequent absence of uniform security policies. In contrast to conventional networks, where endpoints are relatively standardized, IoT networks include constrained sensors, embedded controllers, edge gateways, cloud services, and mobile interfaces, each with distinct attack surfaces. The compromise of a single low-power device may laterally propagate across the network, enabling large-scale disruption, such as botnet formation and DDoS attacks. Fig. 2.3 categorizes the most prevalent IoT threat classes, adapted from prior analyses. These threats span multiple architectural layers and may simultaneously target availability, integrity, confidentiality, and control logic.

2.2.3.1 Malware and botnet attacks

Malware-driven botnet formation represents one of the most disruptive threat categories in IoT networks. In contrast to traditional malware that targets high-

Table 2.1 Security-oriented comparison of commonly used IoT communication protocols.

Protocol	Transport	Operational Strengths	Common Security Vulnerabilities
MQTT	TCP	Publish/Subscribe model, low header overhead, scalable broker architecture	Broker-targeted DDoS, session hijacking, weak ACL configuration, unauthorized topic subscription
CoAP	UDP	REST-like lightweight design, minimal packet size	Replay attacks, spoofing, amplification abuse, lack of built-in encryption without DTLS
Zigbee	RF Mesh	Energy-efficient mesh networking, self-healing topology	Weak key management, default keys, eavesdropping, unauthorized device joining
BLE	RF	Very low power consumption, short-range connectivity	Man-in-the-Middle (MITM), insecure pairing modes, address tracking
6LoWPAN	IPv6/UDP	IPv6 compatibility for constrained networks, mesh routing	Routing manipulation, neighbor spoofing, fragmentation-based attacks
LoRaWAN	LPWAN	Long-range communication, low power wide-area coverage	Key extraction from devices, gateway impersonation, replay vulnerabilities

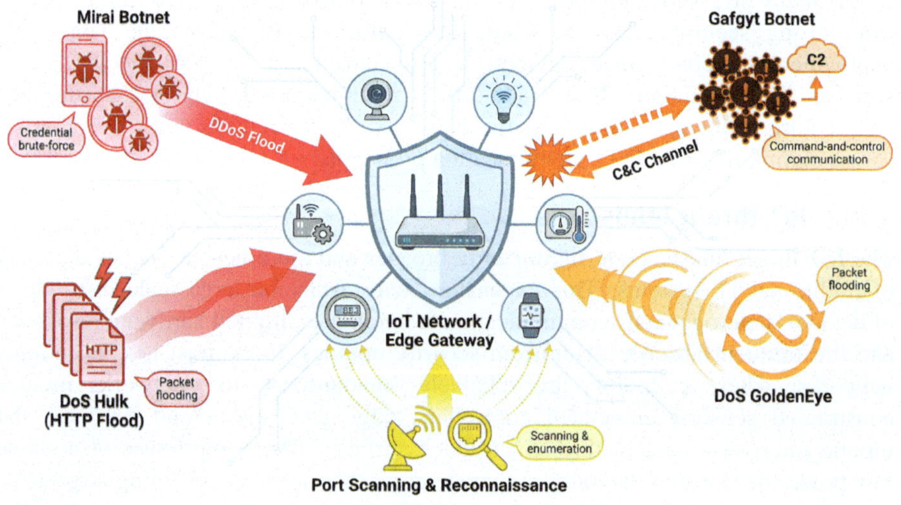

FIGURE 2.3

Representative IoT attack model including DoS Hulk, DoS attacks (GoldenEye, Mirai, Gafgyt) and port-scanning.

performance computing systems, IoT botnets exploit large populations of resource-constrained devices to achieve scale rather than computational sophistication.

Prominent malware families such as Mirai, Gafgyt, Tsunami, Hajime, and Bashlite have demonstrated how insecure IoT deployments can be rapidly weaponized. In particular, Mirai and Gafgyt extensively analyzed ways to exploit systemic weaknesses commonly observed in IoT networks, including factory-default credentials, exposed Telnet and SSH services, outdated firmware, weak password policies, and unencrypted communication channels. The botnet lifecycle typically follows a structured propagation sequence. First, infected nodes perform large-scale scanning of public IP ranges to identify vulnerable devices. Second, brute-force authentication attempts are launched against exposed management interfaces. Upon successful access, a malicious payload is downloaded and executed. Moreover, the compromised device registers with a command-and-control server, enabling coordinated large-scale attacks such as DDoS, cryptomining, and lateral propagation. The architectural implications are substantial. Because IoT devices often operate continuously and lack real-time monitoring mechanisms, compromised nodes may remain undetected for extended periods. Moreover, large-scale homogeneous deployments amplify systemic risk, allowing malware to propagate across thousands of devices within minutes. Fig. 2.4 summarizes this malware infection cycle, showing how Mirai- and Gafgyt-like botnets progress from vulnerable-device discovery to payload execution and command-and-control registration.

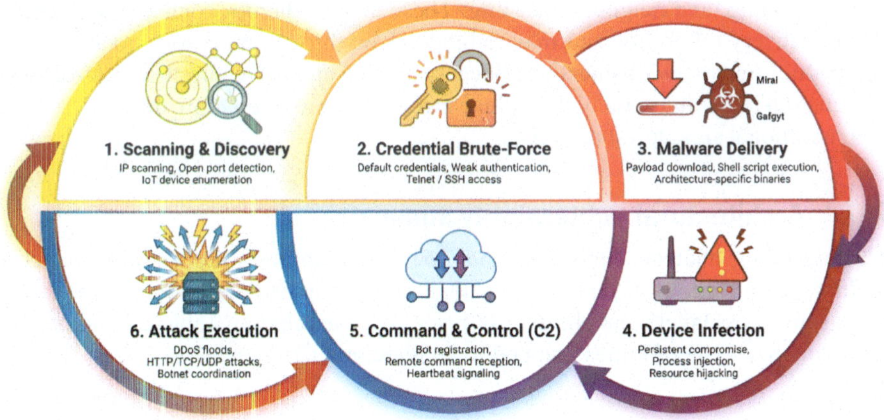

FIGURE 2.4

Typical malware infection cycle for Mirai and Gafgyt botnets.

2.2.3.2 DDoS attacks

DDoS attacks aim to exhaust network bandwidth, computational resources, or application-layer capacity by generating massive volumes of malicious traffic. In IoT networks, DDoS attacks are particularly disruptive due to the limited processing power and constrained energy budgets of gateways and edge nodes. Common IoT-related DDoS variants include HTTP-based floods such as DoS Hulk and DoS

GoldenEye, TCP SYN floods, UDP floods, and high-rate application-layer request bursts. In contrast to volumetric attacks targeting traditional cloud servers, IoT-focused DDoS campaigns often target edge gateways, where even moderate traffic surges can degrade service.[1]

2.2.3.3 Port scanning and reconnaissance

Port scanning and reconnaissance activities represent the initial stage of most IoT intrusion campaigns. Attackers systematically probe IP ranges to identify open ports, active devices, exposed services, firmware versions, and configuration weaknesses. Although reconnaissance traffic may appear benign due to its low volume, it serves as an intelligence-gathering mechanism that enables subsequent exploitation phases. Adaptive defense mechanisms are therefore essential. DRL-based security pattern frameworks introduce dynamic behavioral adaptation capabilities to detect and mitigate evolving reconnaissance patterns before large-scale exploitation occurs.[2]

2.2.3.4 Routing attacks

IoT routing protocols such as RPL and 6LoWPAN introduce additional attack surfaces at the network layer. Due to multi-hop mesh communication and decentralized topology control, routing logic becomes a strategic target for adversaries. Representative routing attacks include sinkhole, wormhole, selective forwarding, routing table poisoning, and neighbor spoofing. These attacks disrupt connectivity, degrade packet delivery reliability, and may redirect traffic through malicious nodes for data interception and malware injection. Because routing attacks manipulate control-plane information rather than solely data-plane traffic, they are often more difficult to detect with traditional signature-based IDS.

2.2.4 Architectural vulnerability summary

The preceding analysis highlights that IoT vulnerabilities are distributed across multiple architectural layers. Rather than remaining isolated, weaknesses often propagate across layers, enabling cross-layer attack escalation. Table 2.2 summarizes representative vulnerabilities mapped to architectural components.

2.3 Fundamentals of IDS

IDS constitutes a central pillar of modern cybersecurity architectures. Rather than merely identifying malicious traffic, contemporary IDS frameworks form an

[1] S. Jamshidi, A. Amirnia, A. Nikanjam, K.W. Nafi, F. Khomh, and S. Keivanpour, "Self-adaptive cyber defense for sustainable IoT: A DRL-based IDS optimizing security and energy efficiency," *Journal of Network and Computer Applications*, 2025. https://doi.org/10.1016/j.jnca.2025.104176.

[2] S. Jamshidi, A. Nikanjam, K.W. Nafi, and F. Khomh, "A Dynamic Security Pattern Selection Framework Using Deep Reinforcement Learning," IEEE, Institute of Electrical and Electronics Engineers.

Table 2.2 Layer-wise mapping of representative vulnerabilities and attack vectors across the IoT architecture.

Layer	Representative Vulnerabilities and Attack Vectors
Perception	Weak authentication, insecure firmware updates, sensor spoofing, physical tampering, hardware backdoors
Network	Packet injection, traffic spoofing, routing manipulation, DDoS (Hulk, GoldenEye, SYN, UDP), RF jamming
Transport	Replay attacks, session hijacking, amplification abuse (CoAP), insecure TLS/DTLS configuration
Processing	ML model poisoning, adversarial inference attacks, CPU-exhaustion DDoS, storage compromise
Application	API abuse, identity spoofing, insecure cloud endpoints, access control misconfiguration
Business	Data exfiltration, privacy breaches, long-term analytics manipulation, configuration tampering

integrated ecosystem of monitoring, representation learning, probabilistic reasoning, and adaptive response. Their objective extends beyond detection toward preserving confidentiality, integrity, availability, and increasingly, operational efficiency. In IoT networks, IDS design becomes significantly more complex. Systems must operate under severe constraints, including limited CPU resources, reduced memory capacity, intermittent connectivity, heterogeneous protocols, and noisy telemetry streams. Consequently, IoT-oriented IDS architectures require optimization not only for accuracy, but also for latency, scalability, and energy sustainability.

2.3.1 Theoretical foundations of IDS

From a security-theoretic perspective, IDS differ from preventive mechanisms such as firewalls and access control systems. While preventive systems attempt to block unauthorized access a priori, IDS operates in a detective and reactive paradigm. Their core objectives include continuous monitoring, behavioral modeling, probabilistic threat estimation, multi-stage decision-making under uncertainty, and automated response orchestration. Formally, an IDS can be represented as a mapping function:

$$D : X \rightarrow Y$$

where X denotes the feature space derived from observed network and host behavior, and $Y = \{0, 1, 2, \ldots, K\}$ represents the decision space, corresponding to benign activity and one of K attack classes. In classical systems, D may be implemented through rule engines and statistical thresholds. In modern architectures, however, this mapping is learned using ML, DL, and DRL. In DRL-based IDS frameworks, the function D is extended to a policy-learning formulation that jointly optimizes detection accuracy and operational cost, including energy-aware adaptation of security patterns.

2.3.2 Advanced IDS operational pipeline

Although traditional IDS models are often described as linear pipelines, IoT-oriented IDS implementations adopt a hierarchical, multi-layered processing architecture.

1. Signal acquisition layer

This layer captures raw telemetry and communication signals, including packet headers and payload features, device-level telemetry (CPU load, temperature, battery status), communication metrics (RSSI, jitter, modulation rate), system logs, and time-series behavioral traces. In contrast to enterprise IT systems, where traffic is relatively stable, IoT networks generate sparse, bursty, and heterogeneous signals, making this stage critically important.

2. Transformation layer

The transformation layer performs packet parsing, flow reconstruction, protocol dissection, temporal windowing, and noise filtering. Statistical distortions introduced by attacks such as IoT-targeted DDoS frequently manifest at this stage as anomalous flow timing distributions and irregular packet inter-arrival patterns.

3. Representation learning layer

Raw input signals are converted into structured feature representations. Classical ML-based IDS relies on handcrafted statistical descriptors, whereas DL-based systems employ neural encoders:

$$\mathbf{z} = f_\theta(\mathbf{x}),$$

where f_θ denotes a parameterized neural transformation (e.g., Convolutional Neural Network (CNN), Convolutional Neural Network (RNN), Gated Recurrent Unit (GRU), and Autoencoder (AE) that maps raw input $\mathbf{x}$ into a latent embedding vector $\mathbf{z}$.

4. Detection engine layer

The detection engine constitutes the analytical core of the IDS. Depending on architectural design, it may implement signature-based matching, statistical anomaly detection, supervised classification, deep neural inference, and DRL-based policy evaluation. In advanced IoT networks, ensemble and hybrid detectors are frequently employed to reduce false positives while maintaining adaptability.

5. Decision and policy layer

Outputs from detection modules are aggregated to produce a final decision:

$$y = \arg\max_{c \in C} P(c \mid \mathbf{z}),$$

where $P(c \mid \mathbf{z})$ denotes the posterior probability of class c given the learned representation. In adaptive systems, this stage may also incorporate cost-sensitive thresholds and risk-aware decision logic.

6. Action layer

The final stage executes defensive actions such as alert generation, traffic blocking, connection throttling, device isolation, dynamic security policy adjustment, and reconfiguration of IoT gateway parameters. In DRL-enhanced systems, this layer may further optimize long-term reward functions, balancing detection performance and resource consumption.

2.3.3 Mathematical view of IDS detection

Consider an incoming network flow stream $\{x_1, x_2, x_3, \ldots\}$, where each observation $x_t \in \mathbb{R}^d$ represents a multivariate feature vector extracted from packet headers, flow statistics, and device telemetry at time t. An IDS computes a decision statistic:

$$S_t = g(x_t),$$

where $g(\cdot)$ denotes a scoring and classification function and S_t represents either an anomaly score and a predicted attack class.

Anomaly-based detection

Let normal traffic follow a baseline distribution N characterized by mean μ_N and covariance Σ_N. Deviation-based detection evaluates:

$$A_t = \|x_t - \mu_N\|_{\Sigma_N^{-1}},$$

where the distance captures multivariate deviation by measuring how far an observation is from the mean of a reference distribution, while accounting for the data's covariance structure. An alert is triggered when the computed distance exceeds a predefined statistical threshold.[3]

$$A_t \geq \theta,$$

with θ representing an adaptive threshold derived from statistical learning. In IoT networks, θ must account for bursty traffic, device heterogeneity, and temporal variability to avoid excessive false positives.

Supervised ML-based detection

In supervised settings, a classifier f_θ performs:

$$\hat{y}_t = f_\theta(x_t),$$

where $\hat{y}_t \in \{0, 1, \ldots, K\}$ denotes the predicted class. Model complexity must be constrained in IoT deployments to balance accuracy, latency, and energy consumption.

[3] R. De Maesschalck, D. Jouan-Rimbaud, and D.L. Massart, "The Mahalanobis distance," *Chemometrics and Intelligent Laboratory Systems*, vol. 50, no. 1, pp. 1–18, 2000.

DRL-based adaptive detection

In DRL-enhanced IDS frameworks, intrusion detection is modeled as a sequential decision-making problem defined by a Markov Decision Process (MDP).[4] A policy network learns:

$$\pi(a_t \mid s_t),$$

where s_t represents the current network state and a_t corresponds to an adaptive security action such as pattern switching, throttling, blacklist updates, and gateway reconfiguration. The objective is to maximize long-term reward:

$$\max_{\pi} \mathbb{E}\left[\sum_{t=0}^{T} \gamma^t r_t\right],$$

balancing detection performance, response latency, and energy efficiency.

2.3.4 Deep technical comparison of IDS categories

Table 2.3 presents a detailed technical comparison of the principal IDS detection paradigms in IoT networks, highlighting their underlying detection logic and operational trade-offs under resource-constrained conditions. As shown in Table 2.3, signature-based systems rely on deterministic pattern matching and therefore provide low-latency detection with minimal computational overhead, making them suitable for constrained edge devices; however, they lack adaptability against zero-day and polymorphic attacks. In contrast, anomaly-based approaches leverage statistical modeling and ML techniques to detect previously unseen threats, offering broader detection coverage at the cost of higher computational complexity and increased false-positive sensitivity in noisy IoT telemetry. Specification-based IDS operates through formally defined behavioral constraints derived from device-level specifications, which makes them effective for predictable sensor-driven systems but less scalable in heterogeneous deployments. Furthermore, hybrid IDS architectures integrate multiple detection engines to enhance robustness and coverage, though this integration typically increases resource consumption unless coordinated via adaptive optimization mechanisms, such as DRL-driven policy control.

[4] F. Garcia and E. Rachelson, "Markov decision processes," in: *Markov Decision Processes in Artificial Intelligence*, 2013, pp. 1–38. A Markov Decision Process is a mathematical framework for modeling sequential decision-making under uncertainty, formally defined by the tuple (S, A, P, R, γ), where S denotes the state space, A the action space, P the state-transition probability function, R the reward function, and γ the discount factor.

Table 2.3 Technical comparison of IDS detection paradigms in IoT networks.

Category	Detection Principle	Technical Strengths and Limitations in IoT
Signature-Based	Deterministic rule and pattern matching	Low computational cost and minimal latency; effective for known threats; ineffective against zero-day attacks and polymorphic IoT malware; requires continuous rule updates.
Anomaly-Based	Statistical deviation modeling and ML-based scoring	Capable of detecting unknown threats; sensitive to noisy IoT telemetry; higher false positive rates; computationally heavier than signature-based systems.
Specification-Based	Formal behavioral rules derived from device specifications	Suitable for predictable IoT devices (e.g., periodic sensors); limited adaptability; high maintenance complexity in heterogeneous networks.
Hybrid IDS	Multi-engine fusion of signature, anomaly, and specification models	Improved robustness and detection coverage; increased resource consumption unless optimized through adaptive and DRL-based control.

2.4 IDS taxonomies

IDS have evolved from static pattern-matching engines into adaptive, learning-driven cybersecurity frameworks capable of analyzing multi-layered network and device behavior. This evolution mirrors the transformation of digital infrastructure, particularly with the rapid expansion of IoT networks. IoT networks introduce extreme heterogeneity in device capability, protocol diversity, traffic patterns, and operational constraints. Devices often operate under limitations in energy, memory, computational power, and connectivity stability. Consequently, IDS design for IoT networks requires architectural, algorithmic, and operational adaptations beyond those used in traditional enterprise networks. A structured taxonomy of IDS is therefore essential. Taxonomies clarify operational philosophies, detection assumptions, scalability properties, computational costs, and suitability for resource-constrained networks. This section presents a multi-dimensional IDS taxonomy covering detection methodology, deployment topology, processing location, temporal analysis strategy, behavioral modeling paradigm, and sustainability considerations. Insights from AI-driven and DRL-based IDS frameworks such as, as well as energy-aware security principles discussed in, are integrated to ground the taxonomy in modern IoT security research.

2.4.1 Detection method taxonomy

Detection methodology defines how an IDS interprets observed data and transforms it into security decisions. Four primary categories dominate the literature: signature-based, anomaly-based, specification-based, and hybrid systems.

2.4.1.1 Signature-based IDS

Signature-based IDS relies on predefined patterns representing known malicious behaviors. These signatures may include byte sequences, protocol anomalies, rule-based logic, malware fingerprints, and regular expressions. Formally, detection can be modeled as:

$$D(x) = \begin{cases} 1 & \text{if } x \in \mathcal{S} \\ 0 & \text{otherwise} \end{cases}$$

where $\mathcal{S}$ denotes the set of known attack signatures. Signature-Based IDS are computationally efficient and deterministic, making them attractive for lightweight IoT networks. However, they cannot detect zero-day attacks and polymorphic malware variants such as evolving Mirai and Gafgyt strains. As signature databases grow, lookup latency and memory requirements increase, potentially exceeding the capacity of constrained devices. Encrypted traffic further reduces payload visibility, thereby limiting the effectiveness of signatures.

2.4.1.2 Anomaly-based IDS

Anomaly-based IDS assumes that malicious activity deviates statistically and behaviorally from normal system operation. Rather than matching known patterns, these systems learn a model of legitimate behavior and flag deviations exceeding a threshold. Let N represent the normal behavior distribution. An anomaly score is computed as:

$$A(x) = \text{dist}(x, N),$$

and an alert is triggered if $A(x) \geq \theta$. Anomaly-based detection is particularly valuable in IoT networks due to the rapid evolution of botnets and the prevalence of zero-day exploits. It remains effective even under encrypted traffic by leveraging metadata features such as timing, flow statistics, and interaction patterns. However, IoT noise and device heterogeneity can inflate false positive rates. Additionally, training and maintaining accurate behavioral models consume computational and energy resources. DRL-enhanced approaches mitigate these issues by dynamically adjusting detection sensitivity and selecting resource-aware policies.

2.4.1.3 Specification-based IDS

Specification-based IDS enforces predefined behavioral rules derived from protocol semantics and expected device functionality. Any deviation from these formally defined constraints triggers an alert. This approach is highly effective for deterministic IoT devices, such as periodic environmental sensors and fixed-function actuators. When specifications are precise, false positives remain low. However, constructing and maintaining accurate specifications in heterogeneous IoT deployments is labor-intensive and requires deep domain knowledge. Specification-Based IDS are therefore best suited for controlled networks with well-defined operational logic.

2.4.1.4 Hybrid IDS

A hybrid IDS combines multiple detection paradigms to improve robustness and coverage. A typical hybrid system may employ signature-based detection for known threats, anomaly-based detection for emerging attacks, and specification validation for critical device behaviors. Modern AI-driven IDS often employs fusion architectures that aggregate outputs from multiple detectors via an ensemble. In DRL-based systems, behavioral scores, rule-based alerts, and specification checks are treated as state inputs to a policy network that selects optimal security actions. Such architectures enhance adaptability while balancing computational overhead and energy constraints. Hybrid IDS represents the most comprehensive detection paradigm for IoT networks, particularly when deployed within edge-centric architectures that offload computationally intensive tasks from constrained devices.

2.4.2 Deployment mode taxonomy

The deployment mode taxonomy examines where within the network an IDS is positioned and how its physical, logical placement impacts visibility, latency, scalability, and resource utilization. Deployment strategies vary significantly between host-level, network-level, edge-level, cloud-based, and distributed architectures. The suitability of each mode depends heavily on the specific characteristics of the IoT ecosystem.

2.4.2.1 Host-based IDS

Host-based IDS is deployed directly on individual IoT devices and analyzes system calls, log entries, firmware activity, memory usage, and CPU load fluctuations. Because IoT devices often run minimal operating systems such as RTOSes and stripped-down Linux distributions, Host-Based IDS must be designed for extreme efficiency, minimal memory consumption, and limited processing overhead. The computational complexity of the detection algorithm must remain safely below the device's maximum allowable cycle budget to avoid depleting battery life and interfering with the device's primary functionality. Despite these limitations, Host-Based IDS provides unmatched visibility into host-level indicators of compromise.

2.4.2.2 Network-based IDS

Network-based IDS operates at routers, gateways, and other aggregation points where it can monitor packet streams, flow records, protocol interactions, and temporal patterns across multiple devices. This deployment mode provides broad visibility and is particularly effective for identifying DDoS attacks, scanning activity, and large-scale botnet activity. Although Network-Based IDS provides powerful detection capabilities, its effectiveness may be reduced by encrypted payloads.

2.4.2.3 Edge/fog-based IDS

Edge-based IDS is deployed on fog nodes, gateway controllers, and intermediate computing infrastructure situated between IoT devices and the cloud. They balance computational power and latency by providing more resources than individual IoT nodes while achieving significantly lower latency than cloud-based systems. Edge IDS can support DL inference and DRL-based policy selection.

2.4.2.4 Cloud-based IDS

Cloud-based IDS relies on remote servers with abundant processing power and storage capacity. They are capable of training large-scale ML models and aggregating global threat intelligence. Although cloud IDS offers unmatched computational capabilities, its applicability in IoT settings is limited by communication delays and bandwidth consumption.

2.4.2.5 Distributed IDS

Distributed IDS coordinates multiple detection agents across nodes, enabling collaborative threat analysis and cross-device information sharing. These systems improve scalability and resilience but introduce communication overhead that may consume significant energy in constrained IoT deployments.

2.4.3 Processing taxonomy

The processing taxonomy describes where IDS computations occur and how processing location affects resource consumption, latency, and detection quality. On-device processing offers privacy and minimal latency but is constrained by limited resources. Edge processing balances computational capacity and responsiveness, while cloud processing supports computationally intensive offline tasks.

2.4.4 Timing taxonomy

Timing taxonomy refers to whether analysis occurs in real time, near real time, and offline. Real-time IDS must meet strict inference deadlines to prevent the propagation of attacks, such as botnet spread and DDoS bursts.

2.4.5 Data granularity taxonomy

IDS systems differ in the granularity of the data they analyze. Packet-level systems inspect fine-grained traffic properties, flow-level systems aggregate packets into connection flows, and behavioral-level systems analyze the device activity over longer time windows.

2.4.6 Sustainability-oriented taxonomy

Sustainability-oriented IDS adopts energy-efficient and carbon-aware strategies to minimize resource consumption. Energy-aware systems optimize CPU cycles and inference time to preserve device battery life. Adaptive IDS mechanisms adjust detection thresholds and processing modes to balance security and energy consumption. Table 2.4 compares major IDS detection methods in terms of strengths, limitations, and IoT suitability. Table 2.5 summarizes common IDS deployment modes and their practical trade-offs across IoT networks.

Table 2.4 Comparison of IDS Detection Methods in IoT networks.

IDS Type	Strengths	Limitations	IoT Suitability
Signature-Based	High precision for known attacks; low computational cost; mature technology	Fails against zero-day attacks; poor performance under encryption; requires constant signature updates	Moderate for constrained devices, poor for evolving threats
Anomaly-Based	Detects unknown attacks; works with encrypted traffic; adaptable to new threats	High false positives; requires training; computationally heavier	High suitability with optimized ML and edge computing
Specification-Based	Low false positives; ideal for deterministic IoT devices; no training required	Difficult to scale; costly specification creation; not adaptable	High suitability for sensors and fixed-function IoT
Hybrid IDS	Combines strengths of multiple methods; best detection accuracy; adaptable with DRL	Complex architecture; higher resource demand; requires coordination	Excellent for edge and distributed IoT deployments

Table 2.5 Comparison of IDS Deployment Modes for IoT networks.

Deployment Mode	Advantages	Challenges	Best Use Cases
Host-Based IDS	Direct insight into device behavior; detects firmware and process-level attacks	Resource constraints; limited logging; battery drain risks	Critical devices requiring fine-grained monitoring
Network-Based IDS	Broad visibility; captures large-scale attacks; efficient at gateways	Encrypted traffic limits analysis; cannot detect host-level compromise	Smart home hubs, industrial edge routers
Edge/Fog IDS	Low latency; suitable for DRL models; balanced resources	Gateway overload risk; requires reliable fog infrastructure	Real-time IoT security, industrial IoT
Cloud IDS	High computational capacity; supports large-scale ML models	High latency; privacy risks; expensive bandwidth overhead	Historical analysis, global threat intelligence
Distributed IDS	High scalability; collaborative detection; resilient to single-node failures	Communication overhead; energy burden on IoT devices	Large-scale sensor networks, smart cities

2.5 Behavioral modeling taxonomy

Behavioral modeling constitutes a foundational pillar of modern IDS, particularly within IoT networks characterized by heterogeneous devices, intermittent connectivity, environmental variability, and constrained resources. In contrast to enterprise IT systems, where user and system behavior often follow relatively stable patterns, IoT networks exhibit diverse operational profiles including periodic sensing, event-driven actuation, and adaptive transmission schedules, and context-dependent interactions impactd by environmental and hardware conditions. Effective behavioral modeling in IoT IDS, therefore, requires dynamic, multi-dimensional analysis encompassing temporal evolution, protocol semantics, spatial interaction patterns, and resource utilization. Rather than relying on static baselines, IoT behavioral models must capture device-specific operational signatures while remaining adaptive to legitimate environmental drift. Fig. 2.5 presents a visual taxonomy of the principal behavioral modeling strategies adopted in IoT IDS.

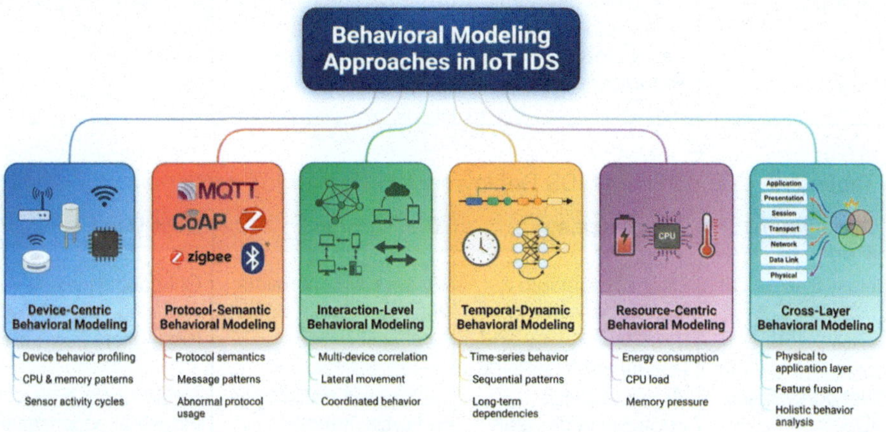

FIGURE 2.5

Taxonomy of behavioral modeling approaches in IoT IDS, including device-centric, protocol-semantic, interaction-level, temporal-dynamic, resource-centric, and cross-layer behavioral modeling strategies.

2.5.1 Primary behavioral modeling dimensions

Behavioral modeling in IoT IDS can be categorized along several complementary dimensions, each emphasizing a distinct interpretative strategy.

1. Device-centric behavioral modeling

Device-centric modeling constructs individualized behavioral profiles for each IoT device. These profiles typically encode transmission frequency, protocol usage, payload size distribution, CPU load patterns, energy consumption cycles, and operational state transitions. Such models are particularly effective for detecting device-level compromise. For example, a thermostat exhibiting sudden high-frequency outbound connections and repeated TCP SYN emissions may indicate botnet enrollment. However, maintaining per-device models in large-scale heterogeneous deployments introduce scalability challenges and increase monitoring overhead.

2. Protocol-semantic modeling

Protocol-semantic modeling interprets behavioral deviations at the level of communication semantics rather than raw packet statistics. IoT protocols such as MQTT, CoAP, Zigbee, BLE, and LoRaWAN exhibit characteristic message patterns and session structures. An IDS employing semantic modeling analyzes control-flow structures, message sequencing, topic usage, and session lifecycles. This approach remains partially effective even under encryption, leveraging metadata and structural features. However, protocol diversity and semantic ambiguity increase computational complexity in constrained networks.

3. Interaction-level behavioral modeling

Interaction-level modeling evaluates relationships among multiple devices within an IoT ecosystem. Rather than treating devices independently, it analyzes cross-correlated events, causal sequences, and multi-hop communication patterns. This approach is well-suited for detecting coordinated attacks and lateral movement. However, constructing and maintaining dynamic dependency graphs introduces computational and communication overhead, particularly in real-time deployments.

4. Temporal-dynamic modeling

Temporal modeling focuses on sequential behavior over time. IoT attacks often manifest through distinctive temporal signatures such as scanning bursts, periodic command-and-control beaconing, and delayed payload activation. Sequential models, including LSTMs, GRUs, Temporal Convolutional Networks (TCNs), Hidden Markov Models (HMMs), and other recurrent architectures, capture long-range dependencies:

$$\mathbf{h}_t = f(\mathbf{x}_t, \mathbf{h}_{t-1})$$

While powerful, these models require extended observation windows and increased computational resources, often necessitating edge-level acceleration.

5. Resource-centric behavioral modeling

Resource-centric modeling monitors device-level metrics, including CPU usage, memory allocation, radio frequency transmission power, battery drain rate, and thermal stability. Malware activity frequently produces measurable resource anomalies, including persistent CPU spikes, abnormal energy consumption. This modeling dimension aligns closely with sustainability-aware IDS design, but distinguishing malicious resource usage from legitimate environmental variation remains challenging.

Table 2.6 Comparative analysis of behavioral modeling paradigms in IoT IDS.

Modeling Category	Behavioral Focus	Technical Strengths	IoT Limitations
Device-Centric	Device-level operational cycles and telemetry patterns	High granularity; strong detection of device compromise	Requires per-device modeling; scalability challenges
Protocol-Semantic	Message structure and protocol behavior	Works under encryption; captures malformed protocol flows	Parsing overhead; protocol diversity complexity
Interaction-Level	Multi-device correlations and ecosystem relationships	Detects coordinated attacks and lateral movement	Graph construction overhead; real-time complexity
Temporal-Dynamic	Sequential behavioral evolution	Captures slow-and-low and multi-phase attacks	Training cost; drift sensitivity
Resource-Centric	Energy, CPU, memory, and RF patterns	Detects hidden processes and cryptojacking; sustainability alignment	Environmental fluctuation sensitivity
Cross-Layer	Multi-layer aggregated behavioral vectors	Robust multi-layer anomaly detection	High-dimensional processing cost

6. Cross-layer behavioral aggregation

Cross-layer modeling integrates behavioral signals across physical, MAC, network, transport, and application layers into high-dimensional feature vectors. Because IoT malware often modifies behavior at multiple layers simultaneously, cross-layer aggregation enhances detection robustness. However, high-dimensional feature extraction increases computational load and is generally unsuitable for purely on-device execution without edge offloading.

2.5.2 Comparative analysis of behavioral modeling approaches

Table 2.6 presents a comparative analysis of behavioral modeling paradigms in IoT IDS, highlighting the distinct observational layers at which anomalous behavior can be captured. As shown in Table 2.6, each modeling category focuses on a different abstraction level of system behavior, ranging from fine-grained device telemetry to cross-layer aggregated representations. Device-centric approaches provide high-resolution insight into individual node compromise but suffer from scalability constraints in large-scale deployments. Protocol-semantic models shift the focus toward message structure and communication semantics, enabling detection even under encrypted traffic conditions, albeit at the cost of parsing overhead and protocol heterogeneity. Interaction-level modeling extends visibility to ecosystem-wide correlations, making it suitable for identifying coordinated or lateral attacks, though real-time graph construction introduces computational complexity. Temporal-dynamic approaches capture sequential behavioral evolution and are particularly effective against multi-stage, yet they remain sensitive to concept drift and training cost. Resource-centric modeling aligns closely with sustainability-aware IDS design by monitoring energy and computational anomalies, but it must carefully distinguish malicious deviations from legitimate environmental variation. In addition, cross-layer paradigms integrate multiple behavioral dimensions to enhance robustness, though this aggregation increases the demands on high-dimensional processing. Collectively, the table illustrates that no single modeling paradigm is universally optimal; instead, effective IoT IDS design often requires adaptive.

2.6 IDS evaluation metrics and benchmark frameworks

Evaluating the efficacy, reliability, robustness, and sustainability of IDS in IoT networks requires a holistic set of metrics coupled with repeatable benchmarking procedures. In contrast to enterprise IDS, IoT IDS operates under constraints on CPU, memory, connectivity stability, and energy availability, while facing rapidly evolving threats such as botnets (e.g., Mirai and Gafgyt), protocol abuse, scanning, and device-level manipulation. Consequently, IoT IDS evaluation must extend beyond classical classification metrics to include latency, throughput, resource cost, sustainability impact, and resilience under drift and adversarial pressure. IoT evaluation is further complicated by heterogeneity. Performance must be interpreted relative to device class and deployment conditions: a model optimized for gateway-level inference may be infeasible on battery-powered sensors. In addition, IoT workloads exhibit strong temporal variability (diurnal cycles, seasonal behavior, event-driven bursts), meaning that evaluation must include multi-scenario testing rather than a single static dataset split.

2.6.1 Classical classification metrics

The confusion matrix remains the foundational construct for IDS evaluation, as it explicitly captures the four possible outcomes of a binary detection decision and forms the basis of nearly all classical performance metrics:

	Predicted Normal	Predicted Attack
Actual Normal	TN	FP
Actual Attack	FN	TP

From this matrix, standard metrics are defined as:

Accuracy

$$\text{Accuracy} = \frac{TP + TN}{TP + TN + FP + FN}$$

Accuracy quantifies the overall proportion of correct decisions. While intuitive, it can be highly misleading in IoT IDS scenarios where benign traffic significantly outweighs malicious traffic. In highly imbalanced datasets, a model may achieve high accuracy while failing to detect rare but critical attacks.

Precision

$$\text{Precision} = \frac{TP}{TP + FP}$$

Precision measures the reliability of positive alerts. High precision indicates that when the IDS signals an attack, it is likely correct. In operational IoT deployments, low precision results in excessive false alarms, which may overload edge monitoring systems and reduce operator trust in automated defenses.

Recall (true positive rate)

$$\text{Recall} = \frac{TP}{TP + FN}$$

Recall evaluates the detection coverage of actual attacks. In safety-critical IoT networks, such as healthcare monitoring and industrial control networks, high recall is often prioritized because missed detections (false negatives) may enable botnet propagation, firmware compromise, and unsafe actuator manipulation.

False positive rate (FPR)

$$\text{FPR} = \frac{FP}{FP + TN}$$

The False Positive Rate quantifies the proportion of benign traffic incorrectly classified as malicious. In resource-constrained IoT networks, high FPR can trigger unnecessary mitigation responses, increase computational overhead, and waste battery power through redundant security actions.

F1-score

$$F1 = 2 \times \frac{\text{Precision} \cdot \text{Recall}}{\text{Precision} + \text{Recall}}$$

The F1-score provides a harmonic balance between precision and recall, making it particularly useful when class imbalance exists. In contrast to accuracy, F1 emphasizes the trade-off between detection coverage and alert reliability, offering a more informative metric for anomaly-based and adaptive IDS models. In IoT IDS contexts, accuracy alone is insufficient for robust evaluation due to traffic imbalance and heterogeneous attack distributions. Metrics such as recall, F1-score, and FPR provide deeper insight into operational reliability, especially when IDS decisions directly impact automated mitigation policies and DRL-based adaptive defense mechanisms. In many IoT scenarios, minimizing false negatives is critical because undetected compromises may cascade across interconnected devices, amplifying systemic risk.

2.6.2 Advanced statistical metrics

Advanced statistical metrics provide a more nuanced assessment of IDS performance, particularly in class-imbalanced settings, probabilistic decision-making, and threshold-sensitive detection scenarios commonly observed in IoT networks.

Matthews correlation coefficient (MCC)

MCC provides a balanced assessment in imbalanced datasets:

$$MCC = \frac{TP \cdot TN - FP \cdot FN}{\sqrt{(TP + FP)(TP + FN)(TN + FP)(TN + FN)}}$$

In contrast to accuracy, MCC incorporates all four components of the confusion matrix and remains informative even when class distributions are skewed. In IoT IDS, where benign traffic typically dominates, MCC provides a stable, correlation-based measure of classifier quality, preventing inflated performance estimates under extreme imbalance.

AUC-ROC and AUC-PR

AUC-ROC measures the TPR–FPR trade-off across thresholds and is useful for score-based IDS operating with adjustable sensitivity levels. However, in highly imbalanced IoT datasets, AUC-PR is often more informative because it focuses on precision-recall behavior under rare-event detection. Since IoT attacks may represent only a small fraction of traffic; PR-based evaluation better reflects the reliability of operational alerts, particularly for anomaly-based and adaptive models.

2.6.3 Resource, energy, and sustainability metrics

Resource-aware evaluation is fundamental in IoT deployments, particularly for on-device and edge IDS designs, where hardware constraints, limited battery capacity, and thermal constraints directly limit the feasible model complexity. In contrast to cloud-centric security systems, IoT IDS must operate within strict computational and energy envelopes while maintaining reliable detection performance.

CPU utilization

$$U_{\text{CPU}} = \frac{\text{Active CPU Time}}{\text{Total Time}} \times 100\%$$

Sustained high CPU utilization may reduce device lifetime, increase thermal stress, and interfere with primary application tasks, e.g., sensing and actuation. In multi-tenant embedded platforms, excessive CPU occupation can introduce scheduling delays and degrade Quality of Service (QoS).

Memory consumption

$$M_{\text{use}} = M_{\text{peak}} - M_{\text{idle}}$$

Memory overhead is critical in constrained IoT devices with limited RAM and flash storage. Elevated memory usage increases the risk of buffer exhaustion, firmware instability, and unexpected reboots. Lightweight models must therefore balance representational capacity with bounded memory footprints.

Energy consumption

$$E = \int_0^T P(t)\,dt$$

This integral formulation captures time-varying power behavior rather than static approximations, enabling accurate profiling under bursty traffic, adaptive inference, and dynamic workload shifts. Fine-grained power sampling is especially important for battery-operated devices.

Energy per detection

$$E_{\text{det}} = \frac{E}{\text{Total Alerts}}$$

Energy per detection reflects the marginal cost of security enforcement and enables direct comparison between lightweight statistical IDS and DL-based architectures. This metric is particularly useful when evaluating adaptive DRL-based systems that dynamically adjust model complexity.

Carbon-weighted energy score

A carbon-aware proxy can be defined as:

$$CIS = \alpha \cdot E,$$

where α denotes the local electricity carbon intensity. This metric extends energy evaluation toward environmental impact assessment and aligns IDS benchmarking with sustainability objectives. Energy-aware IDS, including DRL-based pattern-selection approaches can reduce sustained consumption by dynamically switching between lightweight and intensive detection modes based on contextual risk estimation and attack likelihood.

2.6.4 Timing and latency metrics

IoT IDS must support real-time and near-real-time response, especially under scanning, flooding, and rapid compromise attempts, where delayed mitigation can amplify cascading failures across interconnected devices.

Detection latency

$$t_{\text{det}} = t_{\text{alert}} - t_{\text{event}}$$

Detection latency quantifies the reaction delay between the onset of malicious activity and alert generation. In edge-centric deployments, low t_{det} is critical to prevent lateral propagation, botnet synchronization, or coordinated command-and-control activation.

Inference time per sample

$$t_{\text{infer}} = \frac{1}{N}\sum_{i=1}^{N} t_i$$

Inference time reflects the computational overhead per processed instance and directly impacts scalability on constrained IoT hardware. Excessive inference delay may lead to queue buildup and packet drops under high traffic conditions.

Throughput

$$\text{Throughput} = \frac{\text{Packets Processed}}{\text{Second}}$$

Throughput measures sustainable processing capacity under load and determines whether the IDS can maintain stable performance during traffic bursts and distributed flooding attacks. Latency evaluation should incorporate stress conditions, e.g., bandwidth saturation, device churn, topology changes, intermittent connectivity, and partial disconnection. Static laboratory benchmarks often underestimate timing constraints observed in dynamic field deployments.

2.6.5 Robustness, resilience, and adversarial metrics

Beyond accuracy, efficiency, and timing, IoT IDS must maintain operational integrity under adversarial pressure, environmental variability, and long-term behavioral evolution.

Adversarial robustness

$$R_{\text{adv}} = 1 - \frac{\text{Successful Attacks}}{\text{Total Attempts}}$$

This metric evaluates resistance to evasion strategies, adversarial perturbations, adaptive malware, and model exploitation techniques. For learning-based IDS, robustness testing should include white-box and black-box adversarial scenarios.

Drift magnitude

$$D_{\text{drift}} = \| P_t(x) - P_{t+\Delta t}(x) \|$$

Drift magnitude quantifies distributional shifts over time, capturing firmware updates, environmental fluctuations, device aging, and evolving usage patterns. Drift-aware IDS must incorporate adaptive retraining and online learning mechanisms.

Resilience

$$\mathcal{R} = \frac{\text{Recovered Performance}}{\text{Baseline Performance}}$$

Resilience measures the system's ability to restore its detection capability after degradation caused by attacks, poisoning attempts, and concept drift. High resilience implies stable recovery dynamics and minimal long-term performance collapse. Robustness benchmarking should include stealthy low-rate attacks, adversarial perturbations, poisoning scenarios (for learning-based IDS), and long-horizon drift tests reflecting firmware updates and device aging. In IoT networks, sustained reliability often outweighs peak benchmark accuracy, making resilience-centric evaluation essential for secure long-term deployment.

2.7 IoT IDS datasets and evaluation frameworks

The rapid evolution of IoT security threats has intensified the demand for high-quality datasets and rigorous evaluation frameworks that reflect the complexity, diversity, and multimodality of IoT behavior. While traditional IDS research relied on enterprise-oriented benchmarks, e.g., KDD99, NSL-KDD, and UNSW-NB15; these datasets do not adequately represent IoT networks characterized by lightweight protocols, periodic telemetry, constrained payload structures, device heterogeneity, and cyber-physical coupling. Modern IoT deployments span a wide spectrum of devices, operating systems, and communication stacks. Consequently, IoT IDS datasets must capture not only network traffic, but also device telemetry, control-plane interactions, application-layer semantics, and in some settings, physical process signals. This requirement has motivated the development of IoT-centric datasets targeting botnets (e.g., Mirai, Gafgyt, Mozi), protocol abuse (MQTT/CoAP manipulation), reflection-based flooding, and IIoT controller attacks. Despite progress, IoT datasets remain fragmented across modalities and collection methodologies. Some emphasize flow-level records, others provide host telemetry and logs, while botnet-focused corpora capture only a narrow threat class. As a result, IDS evaluation is often biased by dataset assumptions, synthetic traffic artifacts, and unrealistic deployment conditions.

This section reviews major IoT IDS datasets and summarizes evaluation frameworks, highlighting design trade-offs, attack coverage, feature implications, and suitability for ML- and DRL-based IDS.

2.7.1 Characteristics of IoT IDS datasets

IoT IDS datasets differ from enterprise datasets in structure and intent. Key distinguishing characteristics include periodicity, burstiness, protocol heterogeneity, and device-specific behavioral signatures. A realistic IoT dataset should ideally support multi-layer observation across:

1. **Device layer:** sensor readings, firmware logs, CPU cycles, memory utilization, and duty-cycle behavior.
2. **Network layer:** packet traces, flow summaries, and protocol interactions (Wi-Fi, Zigbee, BLE, LoRaWAN, Ethernet).
3. **Application layer:** MQTT topics, CoAP messages, REST calls, payload semantics, and command patterns.
4. **Cloud/service layer:** authentication events, session management, shadow-state updates, and telemetry ingestion.
5. **Physical process layer:** signals reflecting cyber-physical interaction (e.g., control loops, actuator dynamics).

Few datasets capture all five layers simultaneously. This limitation motivates multi-dataset evaluation and cross-domain testing, since models trained on one modality (e.g., packet-level traces) may not generalize to semantic or cloud-driven anomalies.

2.7.2 Major IoT IDS datasets

This subsection summarizes the most widely adopted IoT and IIoT IDS datasets used in academic benchmarking. These datasets differ substantially in realism, telemetry modality, attack coverage, temporal dynamics, feature dimensionality, and deployment assumptions. No single dataset comprehensively captures all IoT threat dimensions across device, network, application, and cyber-physical layers; therefore, cross-dataset validation is strongly recommended to avoid overfitting to the dataset-specific artifacts and narrow threat classes.

N-BaIoT contains traffic collected from nine commercial IoT devices infected with Mirai and Gafgyt botnets.[5] It reflects realistic scanning, probing, and flooding behaviors derived from real infected hardware deployments. However, it focuses primarily on botnet-related activity and exhibits significant class imbalance, limiting its representativeness for broader attack categories. Bot-IoT is a large-scale synthetic IoT dataset generated using realistic network topologies combined with scripted

[5] Y. Meidan et al., "N-BaIoT: Network-Based Detection of IoT Botnet Attacks Using Deep Autoencoders," *IEEE Pervasive Computing*, 2018. https://arxiv.org/abs/1805.03409.

multi-stage attack scenarios.[6] It includes DDoS, DoS, reconnaissance, and data exfiltration attacks, offering high attack diversity, although the realism of benign traffic is comparatively limited due to synthetic generation mechanisms. IoT-23 consists of real malware traffic captured from honeypots deployed in operational environments.[7] It provides full PCAP traces with strong temporal realism and multi-stage campaign traces, yet device diversity remains constrained.

TON_IoT integrates network flows, operating system logs, and IoT sensor telemetry, enabling cross-layer correlation between host-level and network-level signals.[8] While it supports multimodal IDS evaluation, certain scenarios exhibit constrained heterogeneity in device behavior. Edge-IIoTset targets industrial IoT networks incorporating PLC-like and SCADA-like components.[9] It includes reconnaissance, spoofing, MITM, and cyber–physical manipulation scenarios. Its high feature dimensionality enables rich modeling but may increase computational overhead for lightweight IDS deployment. MedBIoT provides medium-scale IoT botnet traces collected from controlled testbeds.[10] It supports malware family classification tasks but covers fewer attack categories compared to broader synthetic corpora.

The CIC IoT dataset series (2022, 2023, IoMT, and IoV variants) emphasizes protocol abuse, encrypted traffic analysis, and large-scale IoT topology simulation.[11] These datasets extend evaluation toward application-layer and encrypted communication scenarios, although deployment assumptions remain controlled. MQTTset focuses specifically on MQTT protocol abuse, including malformed publish/subscribe messages, flooding, and broker manipulation attacks.[12] It is particularly useful for protocol-semantic IDS evaluation but is limited in scale and attack diversity. WUSTL-IIoT-2021 captures industrial IIoT traffic traces to support anomaly-detection research in industrial control environments.[13] While industrial realism is emphasized, attack diversity is narrower relative to multi-category datasets. CICIoMT2024 focuses on Internet of Medical Things (IoMT) security scenarios and supports healthcare intrusion detection experiments.[14] However, it is confined to controlled laboratory conditions. CICIoV2024 targets Internet-of-Vehicles ecosystems and ECU-level anomalies.[15] It enables automotive IDS benchmarking but does not generalize directly to consumer IoT domains. Finally, UNSW-NB15 and CICIDS2017, although not IoT-native, remain widely used baseline intrusion detection

[6] N. Koroniotis et al., "Towards the Development of Realistic Botnet Dataset in the Internet of Things," *Future Generation Computer Systems*, 2019. https://doi.org/10.1016/j.future.2018.05.041.

[7] Stratosphere IPS, IoT-23 Dataset. https://www.stratosphereips.org/datasets-iot23.

[8] A. Moustafa, "TON_IoT Telemetry Dataset," *IEEE Access*, 2020.

[9] A. Ferrag et al., "Edge-IIoTset," *IEEE Access*, 2022.

[10] MedBIoT Dataset, TalTech. https://cs.taltech.ee/research/data/medbiot/.

[11] Canadian Institute for Cybersecurity (CIC). https://www.unb.ca/cic/datasets/.

[12] MQTTset Dataset. https://pmc.ncbi.nlm.nih.gov/articles/PMC7698741/.

[13] WUSTL-IIoT Dataset. https://www.cse.wustl.edu/~jain/iiot2/.

[14] CICIoMT2024 Dataset. https://www.unb.ca/cic/datasets/iomt-dataset-2024.html.

[15] CICIoV2024 Dataset. https://www.unb.ca/cic/datasets/iov-dataset-2024.html.

Table 2.7 Comparison of representative IoT IDS datasets.

Dataset	Attack Coverage	Modalities	Strengths / Limitations
N-BaIoT	Botnets (Mirai/Gafgyt)	Packet/Flow + Features	Real infected devices; strong botnet realism; limited beyond botnets; heavy class imbalance.
Bot-IoT	DDoS/DoS, Recon, Theft	Flow-centric	Large-scale multi-attack corpus; synthetic benign behavior.
IoT-23	Malware Campaigns	Full PCAP	Real honeypot captures; strong temporal realism; limited device heterogeneity.
TON_IoT	Multi-category	Network + Logs + Sensors	Cross-layer modeling; supports host-network fusion; uneven distribution.
Edge-IIoTset	IIoT + Cyber-Physical	Network + Process Signals	Industrial realism; high dimensionality; computationally intensive.
MedBIoT	IoT Botnets	Network Flows	Medium-scale dataset; focused attack families.
CIC IoT Series	Protocol/Topology Abuse	Application + Encrypted Traffic	Modern IoT exploits; protocol semantics; moderate scale.
MQTTset	MQTT Attacks	Application-layer	Strong protocol focus; smaller scale.
WUSTL-IIoT	Industrial Anomalies	IIoT Traffic	Industrial relevance; narrower scope.
CICIoMT2024	Medical IoT Attacks	Network + Medical Signals	Healthcare realism; limited deployment diversity.
CICIoV2024	Vehicular Attacks	ECU / CAN Traffic	Automotive-specific; domain-constrained.
UNSW/CICIDS	Generic IDS	Flow/PCAP	Baseline reference; not IoT-specific.

datasets.[16] They provide comprehensive general attack coverage but lack IoT-specific telemetry patterns, lightweight protocol characteristics, and device-level behavioral signatures.

Table 2.7 compares representative datasets across attack coverage, modality, realism, and research suitability, highlighting the necessity of multi-dataset evaluation strategies for robust IoT IDS benchmarking.

[16] UNSW-NB15: https://ieeexplore.ieee.org/document/7348942; CICIDS2017: https://www.unb.ca/cic/datasets/ids-2017.html.

2.7.3 Synthetic data generation and DRL-based simulation networks

Because collecting real IoT security data is costly, privacy-sensitive, and operationally constrained, synthetic data generation and simulation-based networks are widely adopted for controlled experimentation. In large-scale IoT networks, real attack campaigns are difficult to reproduce deterministically; therefore, simulation environments enable systematic variation of the device behavior, communication patterns, noise characteristics, protocol stacks, and adversarial strategies. This controlled flexibility is particularly important for DRL-based IDS frameworks, where agents require repeated, stateful interactions with the environment to converge on stable policies. A DRL simulation environment can be formally modeled as a MDP:

$$\langle S, A, P, R, \gamma \rangle,$$

where S denotes IoT system states (e.g., traffic statistics, device telemetry, energy levels, anomaly scores), A represents IDS actions (e.g., security pattern selection, mitigation strategy activation, traffic throttling, isolation), $P(s'|s, a)$ captures probabilistic state transitions under both benign dynamics and adversarial manipulation, $R(s, a)$ encodes reward as a trade-off between detection performance and operational cost, and $\gamma \in (0, 1]$ is the discount factor controlling long-term optimization. In a practical IoT IDS design, the reward function can be formulated as:

$$R = \alpha \cdot \text{TPR} - \beta \cdot \text{FPR} - \lambda \cdot E - \mu \cdot L,$$

where E denotes energy consumption, L represents detection latency, and $\alpha, \beta, \lambda, \mu$ are tunable weights reflecting deployment priorities. This multi-objective formulation allows DRL agents to balance security effectiveness with sustainability and real-time constraints. Simulation networks further support multi-stage attack modeling, including reconnaissance, initial compromise, lateral propagation, privilege escalation, resource exhaustion, and coordinated botnet activation. By explicitly modeling adversarial policies, the environment can incorporate adaptive attackers that modify scanning frequency, payload signatures, and traffic timing to evade static detection thresholds. Such adversarially adaptive environments are essential for evaluating robust and self-healing IDS architectures.

2.7.4 Evaluation frameworks for IoT IDS

A complete IoT IDS evaluation pipeline requires more than dataset availability. It must support reproducible traffic replay, scalable device emulation, adversarial stress testing, and cyber-physical validation under resource constraints. Evaluation should reflect realistic deployment conditions, including encrypted traffic, network instability, device churn, and heterogeneous firmware stacks.

Traffic replay and injection frameworks

Replay-based evaluation injects packet traces and flow records into controlled networks for real-time observation. Tools such as `tcpreplay`, programmable traffic generators, and SDN-controlled injection frameworks allow controlled replay of scanning bursts, volumetric flooding waves, slow-and-low stealth attacks, and topology churn. Replay fidelity is critical: timestamp preservation, inter-arrival timing accuracy, and packet ordering must be maintained to avoid artificially inflating IDS performance.

Device emulation and firmware sandboxes

Device emulation frameworks (e.g., QEMU-based hardware emulation and containerized firmware sandboxes) enable controlled execution of IoT operating systems and protocol stacks without requiring large physical hardware fleets. Emulation supports host-based telemetry collection (CPU, memory, RF usage), firmware instrumentation, and exploit reproducibility. Such frameworks are particularly useful for evaluating host-based IDS components and resource-centric anomaly detection.

Cyber-physical simulation and digital twins

Cyber-physical simulation frameworks (e.g., MiniCPS industrial networks and DRL-enabled digital twins) model physical processes such as temperature dynamics, pressure regulation, valve movement, and motor control. These environments allow the injection of sensor spoofing, actuator manipulation, and control-loop corruption scenarios. In contrast to purely network-level evaluation, cyber-physical validation requires temporal consistency checks, multi-sensor correlation, and process-invariant monitoring. Digital twins further enable predictive anomaly detection by comparing real-time telemetry against physics-based expected trajectories. Collectively, synthetic simulation, replay infrastructure, emulation platforms, and digital twin systems provide complementary evaluation layers. When combined, they enable reproducible, adversarially adaptive, and resource-aware benchmarking of IoT IDS across device, network, and physical domains.

2.8 Computational and energy constraints in IoT IDS

The design and deployment of IDS in IoT networks must explicitly account for the severe computational and energy constraints intrinsic to embedded devices. In contrast to enterprise-grade endpoints, many IoT nodes use low-power microcontrollers with limited clock frequencies, shallow instruction pipelines, small memory footprints, and battery-powered and energy-harvesting subsystems. These architectural limitations impose strict bounds on the IDS model size, feature extraction complexity, inference latency, communication overhead, and sustained operational lifetime. The core challenge lies in the fundamental trade-off between 1) deploying sufficiently expressive detection models capable of identifying stealthy, adaptive, and distributed adversaries, and 2) maintaining feasibility within constrained hardware without degrading primary device functionality. Modern IoT threat actors employ polymorphic malware, low-rate stealth scanning, coordinated botnet propagation (e.g., Mirai, Gafgyt, and Mozi-like behaviors), and resource-exhaustion strategies, all of which require robust, adaptive detection mechanisms. Consequently, IoT IDS design becomes a multi-objective optimization problem, balancing detection accuracy, robustness, latency, energy consumption, memory footprint, and communication cost. This tension motivates the adoption of multi-tier architectures, lightweight feature engineering, energy-aware anomaly detection, model compression techniques, and RL-based security pattern optimization that dynamically adapts IDS behavior to the current resource availability.

2.8.1 Computational constraints of IoT devices

Many IoT nodes are built on microcontrollers optimized for low-power embedded computation rather than high-throughput numerical processing. Typical devices operate at clock frequencies in the tens of MHz range, with RAM budgets often limited to tens and hundreds of kilobytes and constrained flash storage. These architectural limitations restrict both model capacity and the intermediate activation memory required during inference. In practice, even modest neural network models can exceed available RAM once feature buffers, stack allocations, intermediate tensors, and DMA-related overhead are taken into account. Two primary constraints dominate: computational throughput and memory availability. Let a deployed IDS model require C_{ops} multiply-accumulate (MAC) operations per inference. If the effective device throughput is T_{cpu} operations per second, the minimum per-sample inference time is:

$$t_{\text{inf}} = \frac{C_{\text{ops}}}{T_{\text{cpu}}}.$$

For real-time monitoring, t_{inf} must satisfy:

$$t_{\text{inf}} \leq T_{\text{ctrl}},$$

where T_{ctrl} denotes the control-loop period and telemetry reporting interval. When this condition is violated, IDS execution competes with primary device tasks, potentially degrading sensing accuracy, actuator responsiveness, and safety-critical timing guarantees. Memory constraints impose an additional feasibility bound. If M_{model} represents model parameters and M_{act} denotes peak activation memory during inference, deployment requires:

$$M_{\text{model}} + M_{\text{act}} \leq M_{\text{RAM}},$$

where M_{RAM} is available device memory. This constraint is frequently more restrictive than computational throughput, particularly for deep models with large intermediate representations. These limitations motivate architectural strategies such as model pruning, quantization, feature dimensionality reduction, and approximate inference. Alternatively, computation may be offloaded to edge gateways and cloud back-ends. However, offloading introduces additional latency L_{net} and communication energy cost E_{tx}, transforming IDS design into a joint optimization problem over compute, delay, and energy:

$$\min f(\text{detection accuracy}, t_{\text{inf}}, E_{\text{tx}}, L_{\text{net}}).$$

Consequently, IoT IDS deployment must balance local inference feasibility against distributed processing overhead, often leading to hierarchical or adaptive execution policies.

2.8.2 Energy constraints and power models

Energy is often the dominant constraint for battery-powered IoT devices and energy-harvesting nodes. Continuous IDS execution can significantly reduce operational lifetime, degrade sensing availability, and increase maintenance overhead in large-scale deployments. In contrast to enterprise endpoints connected to stable power supplies, IoT devices must carefully allocate limited energy budgets across sensing, communication, computation, and standby states. Energy consumption over a time horizon T can be modeled as:

$$E = \int_0^T P(t)\, dt,$$

where instantaneous power draw decomposes into computational, memory, and radio components:

$$P(t) = P_{\text{cpu}}(t) + P_{\text{mem}}(t) + P_{\text{tx}}(t) + P_{\text{rx}}(t) + P_{\text{idle}}(t).$$

In microcontroller-based systems, CPU power typically consists of dynamic and leakage components. A common approximation for dynamic power consumption is:

$$P_{\text{cpu}}^{\text{dyn}} = C_L V^2 f,$$

where C_L is effective load capacitance, V is supply voltage, and f is clock frequency. Increased IDS workload increases the active cycle count and often requires a higher operating frequency, leading to quadratic growth with voltage scaling. Static leakage power may further contribute to long-lived deployments. Communication energy is frequently more expensive than computation in low-power wireless IoT networks. If E_{tx} and E_{rx} denote per-bit transmission and reception energy, then radio-related energy over B transmitted bits can be approximated as:

$$E_{\text{radio}} \approx B \cdot (E_{\text{tx}} + E_{\text{rx}}),$$

making frequent telemetry export, cloud offloading, and raw packet streaming unsustainable for constrained nodes. Energy-aware IDS therefore, employs adaptive sampling, duty cycling, local feature summarization, model quantization, compression, and RL-based policies that dynamically adjust detection granularity based on residual energy. This can be formulated as a constrained optimization problem: given an energy budget E_{lim}, learn a policy π that maximizes long-term security utility U^{π} while satisfying:

$$\mathbb{E}\left[E^{\pi}\right] \leq E_{\text{lim}}.$$

More generally, the problem can be formulated as a constrained Markov decision process (CMDP), where energy serves as a cumulative cost signal. Such formulations enable adaptive IDS strategies that trade off detection fidelity for sustainability under dynamic workloads and adversarial pressure.

2.8.3 Memory constraints and feature extraction costs

Memory limitations constrain both the deployed model footprint and the feature extraction pipeline required for intrusion detection. Packet- and flow-based IDS commonly compute statistics, e.g., inter-arrival times, windowed byte counts, TCP flag distributions, burst descriptors, entropy measures, and temporal correlations. These statistics typically require buffering recent observations over sliding windows, which directly increases RAM consumption. Maintaining a sliding window of n items of size s requires:

$$M_{\text{req}} = n \cdot s + M_{\text{meta}},$$

where M_{meta} accounts for indexing structures, buffer alignment, stack usage, and bookkeeping overhead. On resource-constrained microcontrollers with M_{RAM} in the tens of kilobytes, the feasibility condition becomes:

$$M_{\text{req}} + M_{\text{model}} \leq M_{\text{RAM}}.$$

Even modest window sizes can violate this bound once concurrent tasks and interrupt-driven buffers are considered. To mitigate this limitation, IoT IDS often relies on compact streaming representations such as incremental statistics, exponential moving averages, Bloom filters, probabilistic counting sketches, and compressed summaries. A common memory-efficient approach is sketch-based flow summarization, e.g., the count-min sketch:

$$\hat{f}(x) = \min_{i} C_i\left[h_i(x)\right],$$

where C_i are sketch arrays of width w and depth d, and $h_i(\cdot)$ are pairwise-independent hash functions. The memory requirement is approximately $O(w \cdot d)$ counters, typically fitting within a few kilobytes. Although sketches introduce bounded approximation error, they provide sub-linear memory scaling while preserving heavy-hitter detection and frequency estimation. Such approximate representations trade precision for scalability; therefore, IDS design must explicitly account for the impact of approximation errors on detection thresholds and false-positive rates.

2.8.4 Communication constraints and bandwidth limitations

Communication frequently accounts for the majority of energy consumption in wireless IoT networks. Even when IDS computation is partially offloaded, limited bandwidth and low-rate links (e.g., LPWAN technologies such as LoRaWAN and NB-IoT) constrain the frequency and granularity of transmitted telemetry. Let a device transmit d bytes per second over a link with capacity B; link utilization is:

$$U = \frac{d}{B}.$$

To maintain stable operation, U must satisfy:

$$U < U_{\max},$$

where $U_{\max}$ denotes the congestion threshold beyond which queuing delay and packet loss increase sharply. If packet arrivals follow rate λ and service rate is $\mu = B/\bar{s}$ (with $\bar{s}$ average packet size), queuing delay grows as $\lambda \to \mu$, increasing detection latency and potentially obscuring time-sensitive threats such as scanning bursts, lateral propagation, and coordinated botnet activation. Consequently, effective IoT IDS architectures minimize transmission volume through local feature summarization, event-triggered reporting, adaptive sampling, hierarchical aggregation at edge gateways, and compressed anomaly descriptors. The resulting design becomes a trade-off between detection visibility and communication sustainability under strict bandwidth and energy constraints.

2.8.5 Multi-tier IDS architectures mitigating constraints

To address device-level computational, memory, energy, and communication constraints, modern IoT IDS architectures increasingly adopt multi-tier designs that distribute responsibilities across device, edge/fog, and cloud layers. Rather than executing full-scale detection locally, these architectures decompose the IDS pipeline into hierarchical components aligned with resource availability. Lightweight on-device modules typically perform minimal detection tasks, such as feature extraction, threshold-based anomaly screening, or sketch-based summarization. Let F_d denote device-level features and $g_d(\cdot)$ a lightweight detector; local inference produces a coarse anomaly score:

$$a_d = g_d(F_d),$$

which may trigger selective reporting to higher tiers. Edge gateways perform higher-cost inference, cross-device correlation, temporal modeling, and adaptive policy selection. By aggregating signals from multiple devices $\{a_{d_i}\}$, edge nodes construct contextualized risk estimates:

$$R_{\text{edge}} = h\left(a_{d_1}, a_{d_2}, \ldots, a_{d_k}\right),$$

enabling coordinated attack detection, such as lateral propagation and distributed scanning. Cloud services support large-scale model training, long-horizon analytics, fleet-wide threat intelligence aggregation, and periodic model updates. This tiered separation reduces device burden while preserving low-latency decision-making near the data source. It also enables hybrid defense mechanisms in which device-level signals inform edge-level correlation and cloud-level retraining, forming a closed feedback loop across tiers.

2.8.6 Model compression techniques for IoT IDS

Model compression enables learning-based IDS deployment on constrained hardware without requiring full architectural redesign. Common techniques include quantization, pruning, weight sharing, low-rank approximation, and knowledge distillation. Quantization reduces numerical precision (e.g., FP32 to INT8), lowering memory footprint and arithmetic complexity. Let C_{fp} and C_{int} denote the per-operation cost of floating-point and integer arithmetic, respectively. A rough computational speedup proxy is:

$$S_{\text{quant}} \approx \frac{C_{\text{fp}}}{C_{\text{int}}},$$

while memory reduction scales proportionally with bit-width compression. Pruning eliminates redundant weights and filters, reducing the number of multiply-accumulate (MAC) operations. If a model initially requires C_{ops} operations and pruning removes fraction ρ, the post-pruning complexity becomes:

$$C'_{\text{ops}} = (1 - \rho)C_{\text{ops}}.$$

Knowledge distillation transfers representational knowledge from a large teacher model f_T to a compact student model f_S, minimizing divergence between output distributions:

$$\mathcal{L}_{\text{KD}} = D_{\text{KL}}(f_T(x) \parallel f_S(x)).$$

Additionally, these techniques reduce model footprint, inference latency, and energy consumption while preserving detection accuracy within acceptable degradation margins.

2.8.7 Energy-aware RL for IDS decision-making

RL provides a principled mechanism for optimizing IDS behavior under dynamic resource constraints. Rather than statically fixing detection parameters, an energy-aware RL-based IDS can adaptively select actions such as activating advanced feature extraction, adjusting sampling rates, offloading computation, and switching between lightweight and heavyweight detection models. Let s_t represent the system state at time t, including traffic statistics, anomaly scores, residual energy, CPU load, and link utilization. The agent selects action a_t from action set $\mathcal{A}$ to maximize cumulative expected reward. A typical reward function trades detection gain against resource cost:

$$R_t = \alpha \cdot \text{DetectionGain}_t - \beta \cdot E_t - \gamma \cdot L_t,$$

where E_t denotes energy consumption, L_t latency cost, and α, β, γ control the security–efficiency trade-off. More formally, the problem can be expressed as a constrained Markov decision process (CMDP):

$$\max_{\pi} \mathbb{E}\left[\sum_{t=0}^{\infty} \gamma^t R_t\right] \quad \text{s.t.} \quad \mathbb{E}\left[\sum_{t=0}^{\infty} E_t\right] \leq E_{\text{lim}},$$

where E_{lim} denotes the cumulative energy budget. Such adaptive policies enable sustainable IDS operation by allocating computational resources according to contextual risk, workload intensity, and remaining device capacity. Under low-risk conditions, the system may operate in lightweight monitoring mode; during elevated threat levels, it can escalate detection depth while respecting global resource constraints.

2.9 Unified conceptual model and chapter summary

This chapter established complementary foundations for IoT IDS, encompassing IDS taxonomies, threat landscapes, behavioral modeling strategies, evaluation metrics, dataset considerations, and resource constraints. While each perspective provides valuable insight, effective IoT security design requires a unified conceptual model that synthesizes these dimensions into a coherent blueprint. Such a model clarifies how IDS components interact across device, network, edge/fog, cloud, and cyber-physical layers within heterogeneous IoT networks. The unified model serves two primary purposes: 1) to formalize the end-to-end flow of telemetry, detection signals, and control decisions across the IoT security stack, and 2) to connect architectural design choices, including detection methodology, deployment tier, behavioral abstraction level, and sustainability strategy, to measurable evaluation objectives.

2.9.1 Unified conceptual model for IoT IDS

The unified IoT IDS model can be conceptualized as an end-to-end, multi-layer pipeline spanning five interdependent layers, as shown in Fig. 2.6:

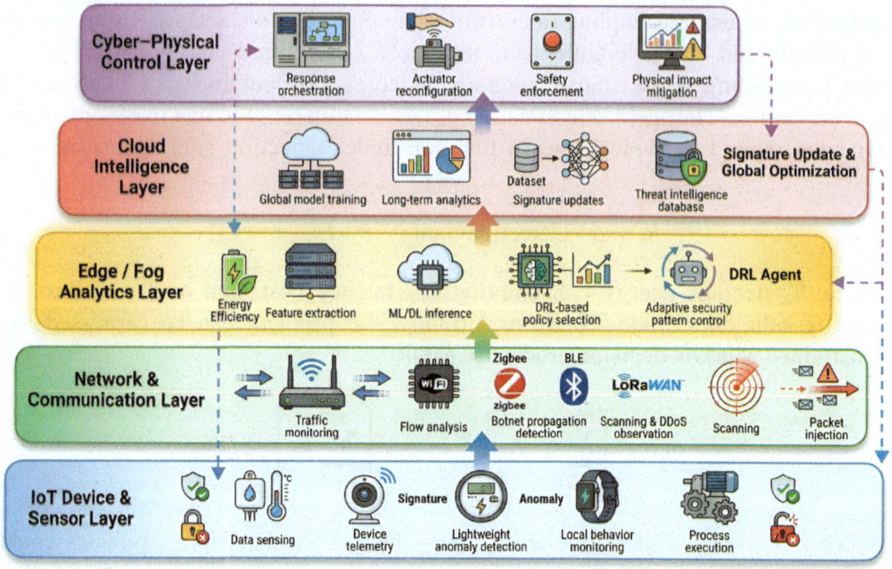

FIGURE 2.6

Unified cross-layer conceptual model for IoT IDS, illustrating the bidirectional flow of telemetry (bottom-up) and security intelligence/policies (top-down) across device, network, edge/fog, cloud, and cyber-physical control layers.

1. **Device and Sensor Layer:** Constrained local sensing, lightweight monitoring, feature summarization, and minimal anomaly screening under strict energy and memory budgets.
2. **Network and Communication Layer:** Traffic observation, protocol-aware anomaly detection, flow analytics, and monitoring of propagation patterns across interconnected devices.
3. **Edge/Fog Analytics Layer:** Low-latency inference, cross-device correlation, multi-stage attack detection, adaptive policy selection, and localized response orchestration.
4. **Cloud Intelligence Layer:** Large-scale model training, long-horizon behavioral analytics, global threat intelligence fusion, and coordinated fleet-wide model updates.
5. **Cyber–Physical Control Layer:** Safety-aware actuation decisions, device isolation, mitigation enforcement, and physical-process resilience management.

Each layer offers distinct observability, computational capacity, and control authority. Device-level IDS prioritizes feasibility under computational and energy constraints. Network- and edge-level components emphasize correlation, temporal modeling, and responsiveness. Cloud-level intelligence enables global learning and coordinated adaptation. Cyber-physical integration ensures that detection outputs translate into safe and reliable control actions when IoT networks interact with physical processes.

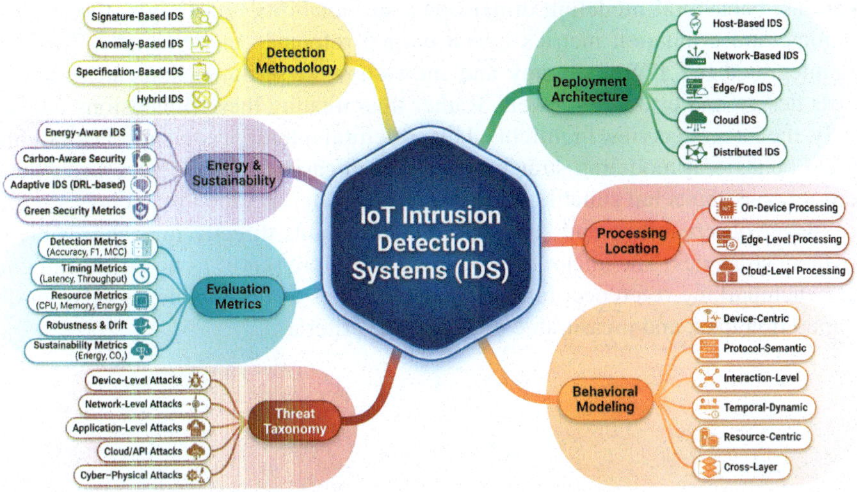

FIGURE 2.7

Integrated IoT IDS taxonomy linking detection paradigms, deployment architectures, behavioral modeling dimensions, and sustainability constraints, threat classes, and evaluation metrics as a unified meta-framework for design and benchmarking.

Collectively, these layers form a hierarchical yet interdependent architecture in which detection depth, decision latency, and resource allocation are jointly optimized.

2.9.2 Unified cross-layer interaction model

In the unified cross-layer interaction model, telemetry and security-relevant signals propagate upward from devices through the network and edge components toward cloud analytics, while refined threat intelligence, detection parameters, and policy updates propagate downward. Detection functions operate concurrently across layers, exchanging contextual information when necessary. Modern IoT IDS effectiveness emerges from the collaboration between 1) device-level behavioral deviations capturing localized anomalies, and 2) edge-level correlation mechanisms identifying coordinated, distributed, and multi-stage attacks. This bidirectional interaction enables dynamic adjustment of detection sensitivity, feature granularity, and computational intensity according to contextual risk and available resources. Cross-layer coordination is particularly critical in detecting stealthy adversaries whose behavior may appear benign at a single layer but becomes anomalous when aggregated across spatial and temporal dimensions.

2.9.3 Unified IDS taxonomy integration

To consolidate the taxonomies developed throughout this chapter, the integrated taxonomy diagram merges detection paradigms, deployment architectures, processing locations, behavioral modeling dimensions, sustainability constraints, threat classifications, and evaluation metrics into a unified reference model. Fig. 2.7 presents this integrated IoT IDS taxonomy and shows how these dimensions are connected across design and evaluation levels. Rather than treating these dimensions independently, the integrated view highlights their structural interdependencies. For example, certain behavioral modeling strategies may be infeasible at the device layer due to memory constraints but suitable at the edge. Similarly, specific threat classes require cross-layer observability, and sustainability constraints directly impact feasible deployment strategies. The integrated taxonomy therefore serves as both a design guide and benchmarking reference, linking attack surfaces to observable signals, feasible computation tiers, and measurable performance criteria.

CHAPTER

Foundations of lightweight security in IoT

3

3.1 Introduction

Lightweight security in the IoT arises from a fundamental tension between security requirements and physical constraints. Modern digital infrastructures demand confidentiality, integrity, authentication, and resilience against increasingly sophisticated adversaries. Yet the devices tasked with enforcing these guarantees often operate under extreme resource limitations. Typical IoT nodes operate within energy budgets measured in microjoules per duty cycle, with memory footprints limited to kilobytes, and use low-power microcontrollers (e.g., ARM Cortex-M and RISC-V RV32E) architectures that lack advanced processing capabilities. These realities render many assumptions of traditional security engineering, abundant computation, persistent connectivity, and generous buffering, practical in embedded environments. In resource-constrained systems, security cannot simply be downsized; it must be reengineered. Lightweight cryptographic primitives, compact authentication protocols, and minimal-footprint IDS mechanisms form the foundation of this redesign. The objective is not merely to reduce computational cost, but to construct mechanisms whose security guarantees remain robust under strict energy, timing, and memory constraints. Designing secure IoT systems, therefore, extends beyond algorithm selection. It requires careful protocol engineering, adaptive authentication strategies, and cross-layer coordination that balance protection with resource availability. As IoT systems expand across smart infrastructure, industrial automation, healthcare monitoring, and critical systems, lightweight security becomes not a niche optimization problem but a core architectural principle of embedded computing.

3.1.1 Motivation for lightweight security models

The motivation for lightweight security arises from the structural realities of IoT systems. In contrast to traditional computing infrastructures, where systems are relatively homogeneous, centrally managed, and physically protected, IoT systems consist of billions of heterogeneous devices operating across uncontrolled, distributed, and often hostile environments. Industrial automation controllers, implantable medical devices, environmental sensors, smart agriculture nodes, vehicular control units, and RF-powered passive tags coexist within a globally interconnected and continuously evolving attack surface. This unprecedented scale

Green Intrusion Detection Systems for IoT. https://doi.org/10.1016/B978-0-44-344249-0.00010-7

and diversity introduce systemic complexity that fundamentally reshapes classical security assumptions. Security can no longer be treated as a perimeter-based defense; instead, it must be embedded in every constrained device on the network. Many IoT devices operate unattended for extended periods, lack secure boot mechanisms, fail to verify firmware integrity, and remain physically exposed to tampering and environmental interference. They frequently maintain intermittent and persistent internet connectivity while relying on limited update mechanisms that may not support rapid patch deployment. These characteristics substantially increase systemic risk: compromise of even a low-capability node may enable lateral movement across the network, data exfiltration, botnet formation, and coordinated infrastructure disruption. In distributed IoT systems, vulnerabilities propagate non-linearly, meaning the system's overall security posture is often determined by its weakest embedded node rather than its strongest defense. Consequently, security must be engineered under the assumption that adversaries will target the most resource-constrained components. The challenge is further intensified by severe hardware limitations. A typical battery-powered IoT node operates within a tightly constrained resource envelope:

$$\text{RAM} \approx 16\text{-}64 \text{ kB}, \qquad \text{Flash} \approx 64\text{-}512 \text{ kB}, \qquad \text{Clock} \approx 16\text{-}48 \text{ MHz},$$
$$\text{Energy Budget} \approx 0.2\text{-}3 \text{ mJ per duty cycle.}$$

These limits fundamentally reshape what security implementation means in embedded systems. Mechanisms that are routine in server-class environments, such as full TLS handshakes, RSA-based key exchange, large-hash computations, and deep neural inference, can exceed the total computational and energy budget of an IoT node by orders of magnitude. Even a single asymmetric cryptographic operation may consume more energy than an entire sensing cycle, directly affecting device lifetime and operational reliability. Lightweight security is therefore not an optional optimization but a necessity dictated by physics, hardware architecture, and energy availability. Security mechanisms in such environments must be energy-proportional, consuming power in relation to the level of protection delivered; computationally bounded, executing within deterministic cycle limits compatible with duty cycling; and memory-minimal, fitting within strict RAM and flash constraints while preserving operational stability. The objective is to enforce strong security guarantees without compromising device longevity, destabilizing duty cycles, and degrading primary sensing functionality. In this sense, lightweight security becomes a systems-engineering discipline that integrates algorithmic design, architectural awareness, and energy modeling rather than a simple reduction of existing cryptographic schemes.

3.1.2 Constraints governing IoT security design

Lightweight security is governed by strict, quantitatively measurable constraints that shape both algorithmic design and architectural decisions. These constraints stem from the physical limitations of embedded hardware and the operational characteristics of IoT systems. From a computational standpoint, most IoT microcontrollers lack floating-point units, instruction-level parallelism, branch prediction, and vector acceleration. As a result, lightweight algorithms must rely primarily on integer arithmetic, minimize branching to preserve execution predictability, employ compact substitution–permutation and ARX-based structures, and maintain small internal state representations. Execution time must remain deterministic and bounded to ensure compatibility with real-time sensing and communication schedules. Let T_{crypto} denote the total number of CPU cycles required to execute a cryptographic primitive. If the processor operates at frequency f_{clk} and the device is active for a time window Δt_{slot} within each duty cycle, then the available computational budget is defined as:

$$T_{\text{budget}} = f_{\text{clk}} \cdot \Delta t_{\text{slot}}.$$

Secure execution must satisfy

$$T_{\text{crypto}} \leq T_{\text{budget}},$$

and in practice, a strict inequality $T_{\text{crypto}} \ll T_{\text{budget}}$ is desirable to preserve timing margins and avoid interference with sensing and radio operations. Modern lightweight cryptographic designs achieve substantial cycle reductions compared to traditional public-key schemes, enabling symmetric security primitives to operate within millisecond-scale windows on constrained microcontrollers. Memory constraints impose an equally stringent boundary. The memory footprint of security mechanisms must satisfy:

$$M_{\text{security}} = M_{\text{code}} + M_{\text{state}} + M_{\text{buffers}} \leq M_{\text{avail}},$$

where M_{code} denotes flash storage for implementation, M_{state} represents runtime internal state, and M_{buffers} accounts for temporary storage. Typical deployment limits restrict M_{code} to approximately 15–25 kB and M_{state} to 512–2048 bytes. These restrictions motivate the adoption of compact cryptographic primitives with small S-boxes, reduced round structures, and minimal lookup tables. Authenticated encryption modes are particularly attractive in this context because they unify confidentiality and integrity within a single construction, thereby reducing redundant code and state overhead. Energy remains the dominant limiting factor in battery-powered and energy-harvesting IoT systems. The total energy consumed per security cycle can be expressed as:

$$E_{\text{sec}} = E_{\text{CPU}} + E_{\text{radio}} + E_{\text{mem}},$$

where E_{CPU} corresponds to computational energy, E_{radio} to transmission and reception energy, and E_{mem} to memory access costs. Empirical observations indicate that radio transmission frequently dominates overall consumption:

$$E_{\text{radio}} \approx 20\text{-}45\ \mu\text{J per packet}.$$

This asymmetry implies that reducing communication overhead often yields greater energy savings than optimizing computation alone. Consequently, lightweight security architectures prioritize compressed authentication headers, minimized handshake exchanges, session resumption techniques, and local anomaly detection to reduce continuous cloud offloading. Communication constraints further limit the feasibility of protocol design. Low-Power Wide-Area Networks (LPWAN) such as LoRaWAN, Sigfox, and NB-IoT restrict payload sizes to:

$$\text{Max Payload} \in [8, 51] \text{ bytes.}$$

Within such constrained frames, encrypted data, authentication tags, nonces, and protocol headers must coexist without exceeding strict size limits. Classical TLS handshakes become impractical without structural adaptation. Lightweight security models, therefore, reduce handshake size, eliminate certificate chains where feasible, and employ pre-shared keys and compact authenticated encryption mechanisms tailored for narrow-band communication. Temporal constraints associated with longevity and duty cycling introduce an additional design dimension. IoT devices frequently remain in sleep mode for 95–99% of operational time to conserve energy. Active computation windows are typically limited to:

$$t_{\text{active}} \approx 2\text{–}20 \text{ ms.}$$

Security computations must therefore complete within tight real-time bounds and support checkpointing for intermittent execution in energy-harvesting systems. Algorithms that assume continuous power availability risk state inconsistency during brownouts and aggressive sleep scheduling.

3.1.3 Fundamental lightweight security trade-offs

Lightweight security design can be formalized as a constrained multi-objective optimization problem:

$$\min\{C, M, E, L\} \quad \text{subject to} \quad S \geq S_{\text{req}},$$

where C denotes computational cycles, M the memory footprint, E the energy consumption, L the communication latency, and S the achieved security strength. The solution space is inherently non-linear and multi-dimensional. Increasing cryptographic strength generally increases computational and energy costs; reducing the memory footprint may require additional transformation rounds and limit key size; minimizing communication latency may shift the processing burden to local computation; and simplifying IDS mechanisms may reduce statistical robustness. Lightweight security engineering, therefore, requires balancing competing objectives under deterministic physical constraints rather than optimizing a single metric in isolation. It is the art of achieving maximal security effectiveness within the immutable boundaries imposed by embedded hardware.

Table 3.1 Resource constraints and corresponding feasible security capabilities across IoT device classes.

IoT Device Class	Typical RAM	Energy per Cycle	Feasible Security Capability
Passive RFID Tag	< 512 bytes	< 10 μJ	Bitwise ultra-lightweight primitives
Batteryless Sensor	1-4 kB	50-300 μJ	Stateless micro-crypto
Wearable Node	8-32 kB	0.2-1 mJ	Lightweight block ciphers + tiny IDS
Industrial Controller	32-256 kB	2-10 mJ	Full LWC + compact ML-based IDS
Smart Gateway	256 kB-1 MB	> 10 mJ	Hybrid crypto + full IDS stack

3.1.4 Comparative constraints across IoT classes

The progression from passive RFID tags to smart gateways demonstrates that lightweight security is not a single fixed design, but rather a spectrum of implementations tailored to device-class constraints. At the lowest extreme, passive RFID tags operate with less than 512 bytes of RAM and microjoule-level energy availability. Such devices cannot support conventional block ciphers, public-key cryptography, and even moderately sized state machines. Their feasible security capability is therefore restricted to ultra-lightweight bitwise primitives, minimal challenge–response mechanisms, and physically assisted security techniques. In these environments, even storing a 128-bit key may consume an insignificant fraction of available memory, forcing designers to rethink key management, randomness sources, and authentication protocols at the most fundamental level. Batteryless sensors, typically equipped with 1–4 kB of RAM and powered through energy harvesting, allow slightly more expressive security constructions. However, intermittent power availability introduces additional constraints, as cryptographic state must survive brownouts and support stateless reinitialization. Stateless micro-cryptographic constructions, compact authenticated encryption schemes, and carefully bounded hashing mechanisms become feasible, provided that execution can complete within tight energy windows. Wearable nodes represent a mid-category class with 8–32 kB of RAM and millijoule-scale energy budgets per cycle. At this level, lightweight block ciphers and compact authenticated encryption schemes can be deployed reliably, and minimal IDS logic becomes practical. However, continuous high-dimensional machine learning remains infeasible, necessitating quantized models and statistical detectors with extremely small feature vectors.

Industrial controllers, typically equipped with tens to hundreds of kilobytes of RAM and multi-millijoule energy budgets, can support full lightweight cryptographic stacks and compact ML-based IDS. Here, authenticated key exchange, key rotation, and anomaly scoring mechanisms can coexist without destabilizing primary control functionality. Nevertheless, even in this class, energy efficiency remains critical for long-term operational sustainability and real-time guarantees.

At the highest category, smart gateways possess comparatively abundant memory and energy resources, often in the range of hundreds of kilobytes to megabytes of RAM and energy budgets exceeding 10 mJ per cycle. These devices can support hybrid cryptographic stacks, deep inspection logic, and full IDS orchestration layers. Importantly, gateways serve as security amplifiers within the IoT hierarchy: they compensate for the limitations of lower-category nodes by aggregating telemetry, performing higher-order inference, and coordinating policy updates. Table 3.1 underscores a central architectural principle: security mechanisms must be stratified across device classes. Uniform deployment of identical security stacks across all nodes is neither feasible nor efficient. Instead, lightweight security must be context-aware, scaling in sophistication and resource consumption according to the hardware envelope of each device class.

3.1.5 Lightweight security pipeline: structural model

Lightweight IoT security can be conceptualized as a layered interaction model in which cryptography, authentication, key management, IDS, and edge-level policy enforcement operates as a tightly coupled component within a constrained computational pipeline. In contrast to traditional network security architectures, where individual mechanisms may be implemented independently on powerful hardware, embedded IoT security must be architected as a coordinated system in which each layer respects strict energy, memory, timing, and communication constraints while collectively preserving end-to-end security guarantees. Fig. 3.1 illustrates this structural model as a multi-stage security pipeline extending from the physical communication layer to edge-level verification and adaptive policy control. At the lowest level, physical-layer communication establishes the channel through which data and control signals propagate. This layer defines bandwidth limits, modulation constraints, duty-cycle patterns, and link reliability, all of which directly impact the feasibility of security operations. Because radio transmission often accounts for most energy consumption, security mechanisms must be designed to minimize packet expansion and redundant signaling.

The second stage of the pipeline consists of lightweight cryptographic primitives responsible for confidentiality and integrity protection. These primitives operate within deterministic computational bounds and small internal state spaces, ensuring compatibility with the device's duty-cycle schedule. Cryptographic execution must complete within the computation window available per cycle, as defined previously by $T_{\text{budget}} = f_{\text{clk}} \cdot \Delta t_{\text{slot}}$. The design of this stage emphasizes compact state machines, minimized memory usage, and bounded execution time to prevent interference with sensing and communication tasks.

Authentication and key management form the next structural layer. In constrained IoT systems, key establishment mechanisms must minimize asymmetric operations, reduce handshake size, and support session resumption and pre-shared key models. Key rotation strategies must account for limited flash endurance and restricted RAM buffers. Importantly, this layer acts as a control boundary: it governs trust relationships, identity verification, and secure session establishment while operating within strict resource envelopes. On-device anomaly detection constitutes the fourth stage of the pipeline. Lightweight statistical models, quantized ML classifiers, and threshold-based detectors analyze traffic patterns and behavioral signals locally, thereby reducing the need to continuously transmit raw data to gateways and cloud infrastructure. By performing early anomaly filtering on-device, the system reduces communication overhead and conserves energy. However, these models must remain computationally bounded and memory-aware, ensuring that IDS does not destabilize core sensing operations. Following local detection and cryptographic protection, compact secure transmission ensures that only necessary, authenticated, and compressed information is transmitted to upstream nodes. This stage reflects the principle that communication cost dominates embedded energy consumption. Secure payload construction, therefore, integrates encryption, authentication, tagging, and header minimization in a unified process to preserve bandwidth and energy. At the top of the pipeline, edge-level verification and policy enforcement provide global oversight. Gateways and edge nodes aggregate telemetry from multiple constrained devices, perform higher-order analysis, coordinate anomaly thresholds, and enforce adaptive response policies. Feedback channels from the edge to devices enable dynamic adjustment of detection thresholds, key lifetimes, and communication rates based on observed risk levels.

3.1.6 Security implications of constrained environments

Severe computational and energy limitations do not merely restrict performance; they fundamentally reshape the threat landscape of embedded systems. In conventional computing environments, surplus computational headroom allows designers to incorporate layered defenses, randomized execution patterns, complex cryptographic constructions, and redundancy mechanisms. In constrained IoT nodes, however, the absence of computational margin introduces structurally embedded vulnerabilities that arise directly from resource scarcity. One of the most critical implications concerns entropy generation. Hardware random number generators implemented on ultra-low-cost microcontrollers frequently rely on limited noise sources such as oscillator jitter, thermal noise, and metastability in digital circuits. When sampling resolution, environmental variability, and buffering capacity are restricted, the resulting entropy rate may be significantly reduced. Low-entropy pools increase susceptibility to prediction, state-reconstruction, and bias-exploitation attacks in key generation and nonce construction. In systems where entropy extraction must operate within tight cycle and memory bounds, insufficient randomness can silently degrade cryptographic strength without obvious functional failure.

Timing predictability represents a second structural vulnerability. Lightweight implementations often simplify control flow to minimize branching and reduce cycle count. While this improves performance and energy efficiency, it may also produce highly deterministic timing patterns. In the absence of countermeasures such as masking, blinding, and randomized scheduling, deterministic execution enables

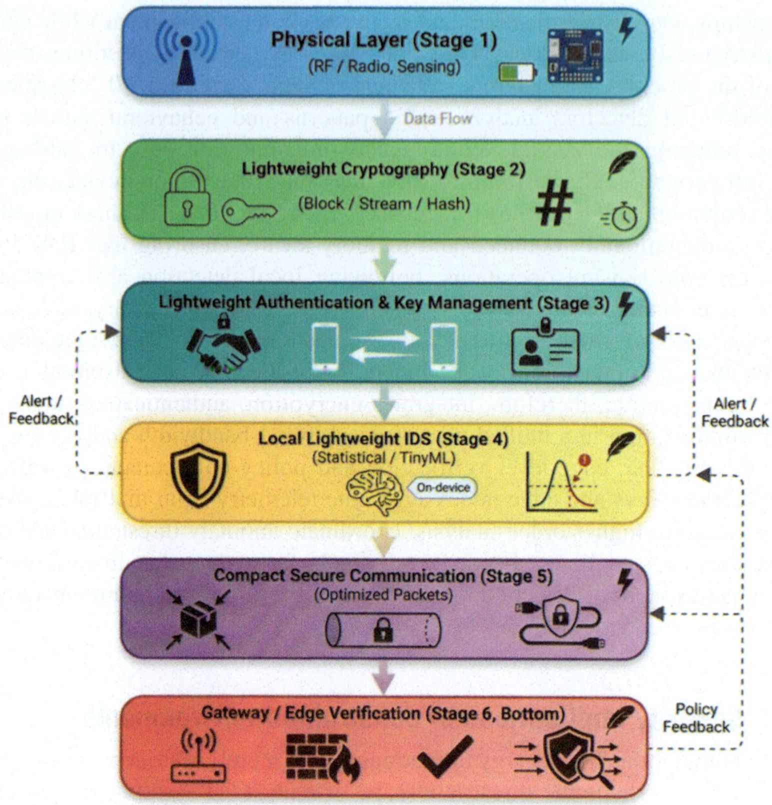

FIGURE 3.1

Multi-stage lightweight security architecture for resource-constrained IoT systems. The framework integrates physical-layer communication, lightweight cryptography, authentication and key management, on-device anomaly detection, compact secure transmission, and edge-level verification with adaptive feedback channels.

timing analysis and power-side-channel attacks. Because adding side-channel protections typically increases code size and energy consumption, designers must balance leakage resilience against strict resource ceilings. Aggressive footprint minimization can also affect the internal algebraic structure of cryptographic primitives. Simplified S-boxes, reduced round counts, and constrained permutation layers may lower hardware gate count and memory usage, but can inadvertently increase exposure to differential, linear, and algebraic cryptanalysis if not rigorously designed. The challenge is therefore to preserve provable and empirically validated cryptographic strength while operating within extremely small state spaces. Resource constraints similarly limit the expressive capacity of IDS. Lightweight IDS implementations frequently rely on small feature vectors, integer arithmetic, and shallow statistical and quantized models. While such designs conserve memory and energy, they may reduce anomaly separability in high-dimensional traffic environments. Complex, multi-stage attack patterns may remain indistinguishable when only a restricted subset of behavioral indicators can be processed locally. This creates a detection–efficiency trade-off that must be managed through architectural stratification, where higher-order analysis is delegated to edge and gateway nodes.

Intermittent execution further complicates the provision of security guarantees in energy-harvesting and aggressively duty-cycled systems. Unstable power supplies may interrupt cryptographic state machines mid-execution, potentially leading to desynchronized key schedules, partial state exposure, and nonce reuse if state persistence mechanisms are not carefully engineered. Brownout conditions can also corrupt memory buffers and disrupt secure session state, creating subtle reliability and security hazards. These factors collectively demonstrate that lightweight security cannot be designed as a scaled-down replica of conventional architectures. Instead, it must adopt a co-design philosophy that integrates cryptographic primitives, protocol state management, secure randomness generation, side-channel awareness, and system-level IDS into a unified and resource-aware framework. In constrained environments, security weaknesses are often not additive but emergent, arising from interactions between limited entropy, deterministic timing, and constrained memory structures.

3.1.7 Energy modeling for lightweight security

Energy-aware design requires explicit modeling of security-related consumption rather than treating energy as an abstract constraint. In battery-powered and energy-harvesting IoT systems, every cryptographic operation, memory access, and radio transmission must be evaluated in terms of its energetic footprint. The total energy cost per security operation can be expressed as

$$E_{\text{sec}} = \sum_{i=1}^{k} (C_i \cdot E_{\text{cycle}}) + E_{\text{radio}} + E_{\text{mem}},$$

where C_i represents the cycle count of each computational component, E_{cycle} denotes the energy consumed per clock cycle, E_{radio} captures transmission and reception costs, and E_{mem} accounts for memory access and buffer management overhead. Microcontroller datasheets for ARM Cortex-M0 and Cortex-M3 class devices typically report

$$E_{\text{cycle}} \approx 35\text{-}70 \text{ pJ per cycle.}$$

Under this model, a lightweight block cipher requiring approximately 2000 cycles consumes

$$E \approx 0.07\text{-}0.14\ \mu\text{J},$$

which remains several orders of magnitude smaller than the energy required for radio transmission in low-power wide-area networks. Radio transmission frequently exceeds

$$20\text{-}45\ \mu J \text{ per packet,}$$

indicating that communication accounts for the majority of energy expenditure in typical IoT workloads.

This asymmetry carries profound architectural implications. Although optimizing cryptographic cycle count remains important, minimizing communication overhead yields disproportionately greater energy savings. Consequently, security architectures should prioritize local anomaly detection, compressed authentication tags, reduced handshake exchanges, and aggregated reporting. Instead of continuously offloading raw telemetry to cloud-based analysis engines, constrained devices should perform preliminary filtering and transmit only essential, authenticated summaries. Energy modeling, therefore, transforms security design into an optimization problem spanning both computational and communication domains. Effective lightweight security systems shift complexity away from energy-expensive radio transmissions toward carefully bounded local computation, thereby achieving maximal protection per microjoule consumed. This perspective establishes the quantitative foundation for green security architectures and energy-aware multi-agent coordination models developed in later chapters.

3.2 Lightweight cryptography: theory, design principles, and algorithms

Lightweight cryptography constitutes the mathematical and algorithmic foundation of secure Internet of Things systems. In contrast to classical computing platforms, IoT nodes operate within sub-milliwatt power envelopes, kilobyte-scale memory footprints, and intermittently available energy supplies. Under such constraints, conventional cryptographic primitives, including full AES implementations, SHA-256 hashing, RSA-2048 modular exponentiation, and high-degree elliptic curve constructions often impose computational and energy demands that exceed the practical capabilities of microcontroller-class hardware. The modern lightweight cryptographic paradigm, therefore, redefines efficiency as a primary design objective alongside security strength. Rather than adapting legacy algorithms to constrained platforms, lightweight cryptography develops primitives whose internal structure is inherently resource-aware. This paradigm emphasizes minimal hardware gate count, compact software code size, predictable constant-time execution to mitigate timing leakage, low RAM and stack consumption, and resilience against both classical cryptanalysis and side-channel analysis. The NIST Lightweight Cryptography standardization effort, culminating in the selection of Ascon as the primary standardized authenticated encryption algorithm represents a major milestone in formalizing secure and energy-efficient primitives for constrained devices. Beyond symmetric constructions, ongoing research explores compact public-key mechanisms and post-quantum candidates tailored to microcontroller-level hardware.

3.2.1 Foundations of lightweight cryptographic design

A lightweight cryptographic primitive must reconcile two competing objectives: maximizing security strength and minimizing implementation cost. This design tension can be formalized through a constrained multi-objective optimization framework:

$$\min_{\theta \in \Theta} (w_C C(\theta) + w_M M(\theta) + w_E E(\theta) + w_L L(\theta)) \quad \text{subject to} \quad S(\theta) \geq S_{\min},$$

where $C(\theta)$ denotes computational complexity measured in cycles per block, $M(\theta)$ represents memory footprint, $E(\theta)$ captures energy consumption, $L(\theta)$ models latency and communication overhead, and $S(\theta)$ defines achieved security strength relative to a minimum acceptable threshold $S_{\min}$. The weighting coefficients reflect deployment priorities across device classes. In contrast to conventional cryptography, in which efficiency impacts implementation details while the algorithmic structure remains largely fixed, lightweight cryptography integrates resource constraints directly into the construction of its primitives. State size, round function complexity, algebraic structure, and key scheduling mechanisms are deliberately engineered to operate within deterministic bounds defined by hardware limitations.

3.2.2 Architectural considerations for lightweight symmetric design

Symmetric cryptography dominates the lightweight landscape due to its computational efficiency and predictable performance. Two principal structural paradigms define most lightweight block ciphers: substitution–permutation networks (SPN) and ARX constructions. In SPN-based designs, confusion and diffusion are achieved through the repeated application of a nonlinear substitution followed by a structured permutation. The transformation can be expressed as

$$x \mapsto P(S(x) \oplus k),$$

where S denotes a compact S-box and P a bit-level permutation layer. Lightweight SPNs use small S-boxes, typically 4 and 8 bits, to minimize hardware area and memory footprint. Permutation layers are carefully engineered to reduce routing complexity in ASIC implementations while preserving diffusion properties. ARX-based constructions rely exclusively on modular addition, bit rotation, and XOR operations:

$$x \mapsto ((x \oplus k) + (x \lll r)) \bmod 2^n.$$

These operations map efficiently to microcontroller instruction sets without requiring lookup tables, thereby reducing memory overhead and improving software efficiency.

The absence of S-boxes simplifies side-channel countermeasures and enables compact implementations.

3.2.3 Lightweight block ciphers

Block ciphers remain central to confidentiality in constrained systems due to their structural regularity and predictable resource requirements. PRESENT, a 64-bit block cipher with 31 rounds and key sizes of 80 and 128 bits, exemplifies minimalistic SPN design. It's a round transformation

$$x \mapsto P(S(x \oplus k))$$

employs a 4-bit S-box and a fixed-bit-permutation layer. With an approximate hardware footprint of 1570 gate equivalents (GE), PRESENT achieves strong diffusion within a compact architecture. If each round consumes C_r cycles, the total computational cost is

$$C_{\text{PRESENT}} = 31 \cdot C_r.$$

Measured energy consumption is approximately 0.85 μJ per 64-bit block. GIFT refines this philosophy by optimizing permutation structure and reducing wiring complexity, achieving an area of approximately 1300 GE while improving diffusion efficiency. Its design illustrates how careful structural reorganization can simultaneously enhance security margin and reduce hardware footprint. SIMON and SPECK represent ARX-based alternatives. SPECK's round function

$$(x, y) \mapsto ((x \lll \alpha + y) \oplus k,\ y \ggg \beta \oplus x)$$

maps efficiently to microcontroller instructions, yielding measured energy consumption near 0.65 μJ per block. Table comparisons demonstrate that ARX constructions often provide superior software performance, whereas SPN designs may offer advantages in hardware synthesis.

3.2.4 Lightweight stream ciphers

In applications that generate continuous data, stream ciphers provide low-latency encryption with minimal buffering. Designs such as Grain and Trivium rely on compact shift registers and nonlinear feedback functions. The Trivium state update equation

$$s_{t+288} = s_{t+65} \oplus (s_{t+90} \cdot s_{t+91}) \oplus s_{t+92} \oplus 1$$

illustrates reliance solely on AND and XOR operations, making the design well-suited for constrained hardware with minimal combinational logic.

3.2.5 Lightweight hash functions

Integrity verification, device authentication, firmware validation, and key derivation demand compact hash constructions. SPONGENT employs an SPN-based permutation within a sponge construction:

$$H(M) = \text{Sponge}[f, r](M).$$

The hardware area typically ranges from 1400 to 2500 GE, depending on digest size. PHOTON adopts an AES-inspired permutation with simplified diffusion layers and reduced S-box complexity, supporting digest sizes from 80 to 256 bits while maintaining a compact round structure.

3.2.6 Authenticated encryption for IoT

Authenticated encryption with associated data (AEAD) combines confidentiality and integrity into a single primitive, eliminating redundant hashing steps and reducing overhead. The NIST LWC competition identified several candidates optimized for constrained platforms, including Ascon, GIFT-COFB, TinyJAMBU, Romulus, and Grain-128AEAD. Ascon's permutation-based AEAD construction can be expressed abstractly as

$$C = M \oplus f(K, N, A),$$

where a 320-bit internal state partitioned into five 64-bit lanes enables efficient operation on 32-bit microcontrollers. Its design balances the side-channel resilience, software efficiency, and hardware compactness.

3.2.7 Lightweight public-key cryptography

Despite their computational expense, public-key primitives remain essential for authentication and secure bootstrapping. Elliptic curve scalar multiplication

$$Q = kP$$

typically requires 10^5 to 10^6 cycles, depending on the curve selection and implementation strategy. Curves such as Curve25519 and FourQ reduce multiplication latency through optimized field arithmetic. Emerging post-quantum schemes, including Kyber512, NewHope-Simple, and FrodoKEM-640, leverage structured polynomial arithmetic that can be optimized for constrained microcontrollers. Although memory demands remain significant, ongoing research continues to reduce the footprint through parameter tuning and algorithmic refinement.

Fig. 3.2 presents the layered architecture of lightweight cryptographic primitives for IoT systems, illustrating how symmetric encryption and hashing form the foundational layer, authenticated encryption provides integrated protection, and public-key mechanisms enable secure key establishment. Across all layers, memory footprint, energy consumption, latency,, and packet size impose continuous design pressure. Lightweight cryptography thus represents a vertically integrated discipline in which mathematical construction, hardware synthesis, and system-level constraints are inseparable.

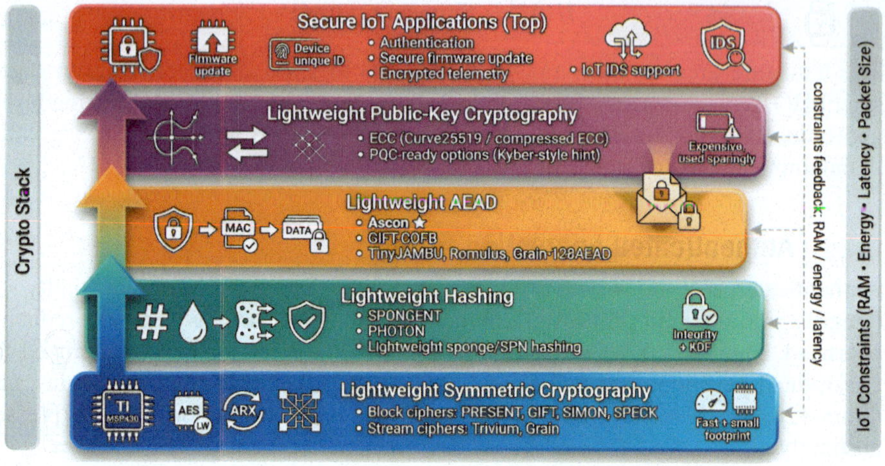

FIGURE 3.2

Layered architecture of lightweight cryptographic primitives for IoT systems. The stack progresses from lightweight symmetric cryptography and hashing at the lower layers, through authenticated encryption with AEAD and lightweight public-key cryptography, to secure IoT systems at the top. Design constraints, such as memory footprint, energy consumption, latency, and packet size, affect algorithm selection across all layers.

3.3 Lightweight authentication and key management

Lightweight authentication and key management in IoT systems are among the most mathematically demanding yet resource-constrained areas of security engineering. Classical distributed infrastructures rely on certificate hierarchies, multi-round TLS negotiations, and computationally intensive elliptic-curve operations. In contrast, IoT microcontrollers operate with tens of kilobytes of RAM and milliwatt-scale power budgets. Many cannot execute even a single RSA signature within acceptable energy limits. Authentication mechanisms must therefore be redesigned so that computational complexity, transmission volume, and memory usage remain tightly bounded while preserving mutual authentication, forward secrecy, replay protection, and session integrity.

3.3.1 Lightweight authenticated key exchange

A lightweight authenticated key exchange protocol must minimize both the transmitted data volume and the number of elliptic-curve scalar multiplications. The total transmitted message size is

$$|M_{\text{total}}| = \sum_{i=1}^{R} |M_i|,$$

while computational cost is dominated by scalar multiplications

$$C_{\text{ECC}} = m \cdot C_{\text{mul}}.$$

Handshake latency can be modeled as

$$L_{\text{handshake}} = L_{\text{prop}} + L_{\text{ecc}} + L_{\text{txrx}}, \quad L_{\text{ecc}} \approx \frac{C_{\text{ECC}}}{f_{\text{cpu}}}.$$

In constrained environments, protocol design compresses authentication into two andthree rounds in order to limit both radio usage and asymmetric computation.

Fig. 3.3 depicts the temporal structure of a lightweight authenticated key exchange between a constrained IoT initiator and a gateway responder. The initiator performs a compressed elliptic-curve key exchange using reduced coordinate representation to minimize transmission size. Certificate chains are deliberately omitted, and authentication is derived from pre-established trust anchors and lightweight credential bindings. The diagram illustrates that the responder completes its scalar multiplication while the initiator remains in low-power standby, reducing overlap between radio transmission and computation. An optional third message enables explicit key confirmation, strengthening integrity guarantees without imposing excessive additional overhead. Session-caching mechanisms are implemented to avoid redundant elliptic-curve computations during repeated interactions, thereby significantly reducing cumulative energy consumption over device lifetimes. The figure therefore visualizes how computation, transmission, and timing are co-optimized within a strict energy envelope.

3.3.2 Compressed ECC and micro-curve arithmetic

Elliptic-curve cryptography is computationally intensive because scalar multiplication requires repeated point doublings and additions. Lightweight implementations restructure this arithmetic using fixed-base precomputation, flash-resident window tables, bit-sliced register optimization, and uniform Montgomery-ladder execution to ensure constant control flow. Public key compression further reduces transmission overhead. A compressed key is represented as

$$pk = (x, b_y), \quad b_y = y \mod 2.$$

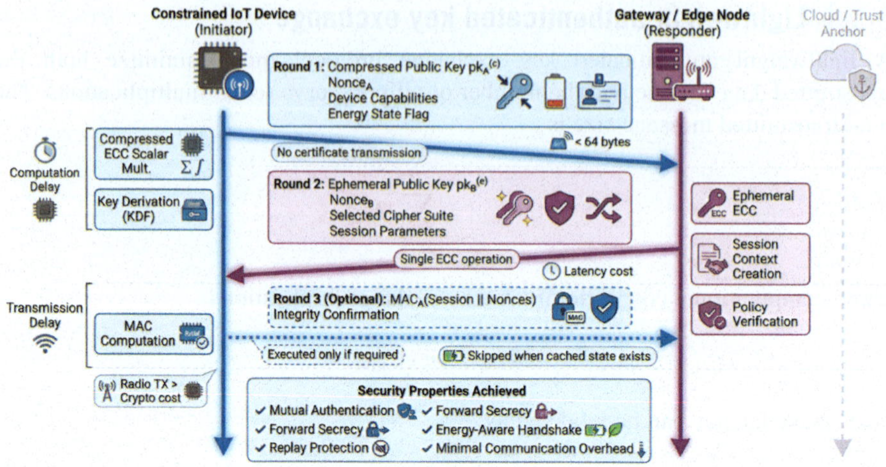

FIGURE 3.3

Timing structure of a lightweight authenticated key exchange protocol for constrained IoT devices.

The missing coordinate is reconstructed through

$$y = \sqrt{x^3 + ax + b} \mod p.$$

In practice, constrained nodes avoid computing modular square roots locally by delegating reconstruction to gateways andselecting curve forms that simplify arithmetic. Table 3.2 quantifies trade-offs between naïve implementations and optimized micro-architectural variants, demonstrating that bit-sliced arithmetic reduces cycle count and leakage current, while flash-table acceleration lowers multiplication latency at the cost of increased code size. These trade-offs illustrate that ECC efficiency is determined not only by mathematical structure but also by memory layout and instruction-level optimization.

Table 3.2 Micro-architectural trade-offs in lightweight ECC implementations.

ECC Variant	Code Size (KB)	Cycles per Mul	Gate Leakage (nA)
Naïve C implementation	28 KB	2.8M	39
Optimized bit-sliced impl.	18 KB	1.9M	27
Montgomery-ladder impl.	22 KB	1.5M	29
Flash-table accelerated impl.	35 KB	0.9M	45

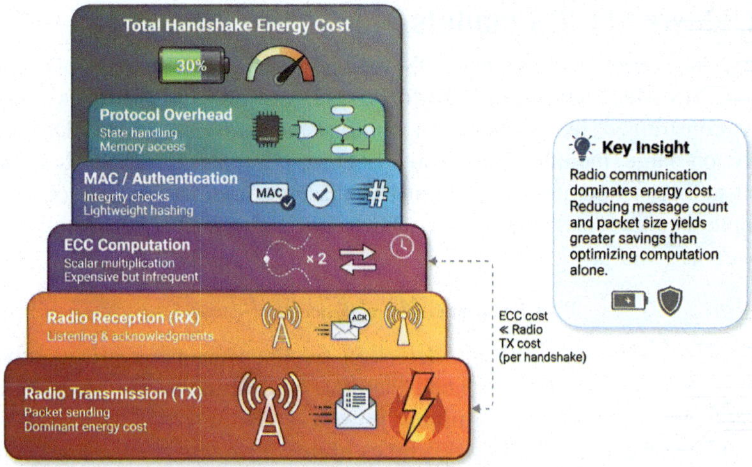

FIGURE 3.4

Energy contribution distribution during a lightweight IoT authentication handshake.

3.3.3 Energy-aware handshake models

Energy modeling reveals the dominant contributors to authentication cost. Typical IoT radios consume

$$E_{\text{tx}} = 25\text{–}60\,\mu\text{J per packet},$$

while elliptic-curve scalar multiplication may require

$$E_{\text{ecc}} = 9\text{–}20\,\text{mJ}.$$

Total handshake energy is therefore

$$E_{\text{handshake}} = n_{\text{tx}} E_{\text{tx}} + n_{\text{rx}} E_{\text{rx}} + n_{\text{ecc}} E_{\text{ecc}} + E_{\text{MAC}}.$$

Fig. 3.4 illustrates the qualitative distribution of these energy components. The visual comparison shows that radio transmission and reception account for the bulk of cumulative expenditure, while symmetric message authentication incurs minimal additional cost. The figure reinforces a central architectural principle: reducing message count and packet size produces greater energy savings than optimizing computational primitives alone. Efficient authentication, therefore, requires simultaneous minimization of elliptic-curve operations, transmission rounds, and payload expansion. This integrated energy-aware perspective transforms handshake design into a constrained optimization problem spanning computation, communication, and session management.

3.4 Lightweight IDS models

This section extends lightweight IDS architectures to include deeply optimized statistical, TinyML, hybrid, and reinforcement-learning-ready models tailored for severely constrained IoT devices. In contrast to enterprise-grade IDS platforms that rely on large memory pools and floating-point acceleration, IoT detection mechanisms must operate within tight bounds on computation, memory footprint, per-sample energy cost, and latency. The overarching design objective can be formalized as

$$\min(C_{\text{compute}}, M_{\text{ram}}, E_{\text{sample}}, L_{\text{latency}})$$

subject to maintaining sufficient detection accuracy under realistic adversarial conditions. IoT IDS modules typically operate with kilobyte RAM, lack floating-point hardware, experience intermittent power availability, rely on bursty wireless links, and must meet strict timing deadlines imposed by sensing and communication schedules. These constraints fundamentally reshape detection model design, favoring compact, integer-based, low-latency mechanisms.

3.4.1 Statistical IDS models

Statistical anomaly detection remains dominant in ultra-low-power IoT devices due to its minimal memory requirements and deterministic execution profile. A generalized anomaly score may be defined as

$$A(x) = \sum_{i=1}^{d} w_i |x_i - \mu_i|,$$

where μ_i represents baseline statistics and w_i denotes importance weights assigned to each feature dimension. Temporal smoothing can be incorporated through exponential moving averages,

$$S_t = \lambda S_{t-1} + (1 - \lambda)|x_t - \mu|,$$

with normalized deviation computed as

$$Z_t = \frac{S_t - \sigma}{\sigma}.$$

An alert condition is triggered when

$$Z_t > \tau.$$

The memory footprint of this approach remains tightly bounded,

$$M_{\text{stat}} \leq 8d \text{ bytes},$$

making it feasible for always-on monitoring even on microcontrollers with limited RAM. Statistical IDS models provide predictable latency and extremely low energy per sample, though their detection power may diminish in high-dimensional attack spaces.

3.4.2 TinyML IDS models

TinyML-based IDS extends statistical detection by introducing learned representations while remaining executable on microcontrollers without floating-point support. Model compression and integer quantization transform floating-point weights w into fixed-width integer representations,

$$w_q = \text{round}\left(\frac{w}{s}\right), \qquad s = \frac{\max|w|}{2^{q-1}-1}.$$

Inference then reduces to integer accumulation,

$$y = \sum_i w_{q,i} x_{q,i}.$$

A representative TinyML architecture may consist of an 8-dimensional input vector followed by two compact dense layers, forming a pipeline

$$\text{In} \rightarrow \text{Dense}(16) \rightarrow \text{Dense}(4) \rightarrow \text{Out}.$$

In such configurations, weight storage occupies approximately 256 bytes, activation buffers require roughly 32 bytes, and stack usage remains near 64 bytes, resulting in total RAM consumption below 400 bytes. The resource footprint comparison in Table 3.3 demonstrates how different compressed architectures trade parameter count against latency and memory usage. Quantized perceptrons achieve minimal latency, micro-CNNs increase representational capacity at moderate cost, quantized GRUs introduce temporal modeling with higher memory consumption, and shallow hybrid multilayer perceptrons provide a balanced middle ground.

Table 3.3 Resource characteristics of compact TinyML-based IDS architectures.

Model	Params	RAM (Bytes)	Latency (μs)
Quantized Perceptron	64	160	22
1D Micro-CNN (1 filter)	320	900	140
Quantized GRU (4 units)	1024	2200	380
Shallow Hybrid MLP	256	680	90

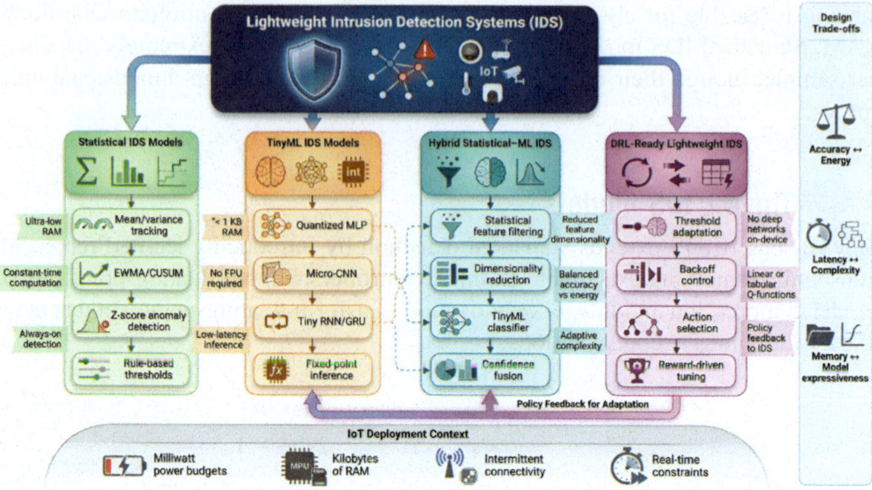

FIGURE 3.5

Taxonomy of lightweight IDS models for constrained IoT systems.

3.4.3 Hybrid statistical-ML models

Hybrid IDS architectures combine low-cost statistical pre-filtering with lightweight learned inference. The statistical stage performs coarse anomaly filtering,

$$x_t^{(\text{stat})} = \text{Filter}(x_t),$$

after which, reduced features are forwarded to a TinyML classifier,

$$\hat{y}_t = f_{\text{tinyML}}(x_t^{(\text{stat})}).$$

This layered design reduces feature dimensionality by 50–90 percent, thereby lowering computational and memory requirements while preserving improved detection accuracy relative to purely statistical approaches. Fig. 3.5 presents the structural taxonomy of lightweight IDS strategies. The figure organizes IDS approaches into statistical detection, TinyML inference, hybrid pipelines, and reinforcement-learning-ready mechanisms. It visually captures the trade-offs among detection performance, memory footprint, latency, and energy consumption. Statistical models occupy the lowest resource category; TinyML approaches introduce compact learned representations; hybrid systems balance filtering and inference; and DRL-ready modules enable adaptive policy control without deploying deep networks directly on constrained nodes.

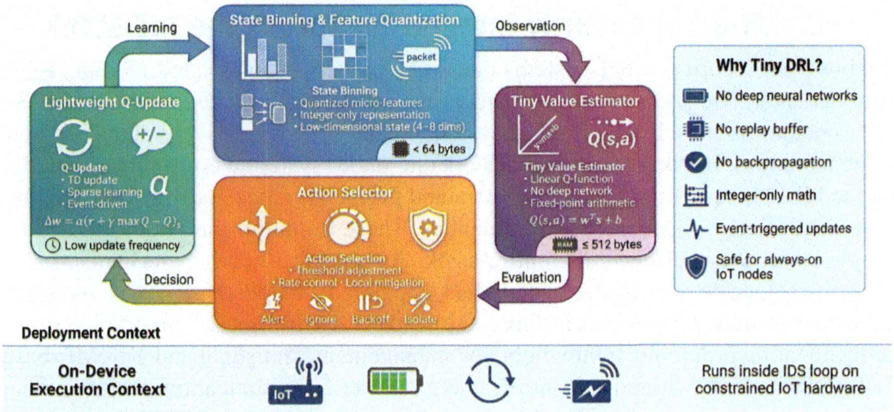

FIGURE 3.6

Compact DRL-ready IDS agent for ultra-constrained IoT devices.

3.4.4 DRL-ready lightweight agents

Full DRL is infeasible on severely constrained IoT hardware due to limited memory and computational resources. Instead, DRL-ready lightweight agents employ compressed value-function approximators defined as

$$\hat{Q}(s,a) = w_a^{\top} s + b_a,$$

where s represents a quantized feature vector of 4–8 dimensions, w_a is a compact integer weight vector occupying 8–16 bytes, and b_a is an integer bias. Parameter updates follow a simplified temporal-difference rule,

$$\Delta w_a = \alpha(r + \gamma \max_{a'} \hat{Q}(s',a') - \hat{Q}(s,a))s.$$

Memory consumption remains tightly bound,

$$M_{\text{DRL}} < 512 \text{ bytes}.$$

Fig. 3.6 illustrates the architecture of such a Tiny DRL-style IDS agent. The model relies exclusively on integer arithmetic, feature binning, and event-driven updates, eliminating the need for replay buffers and backpropagation. Action selection dynamically adjusts IDS thresholds, transmission backoff intervals, and channel access control parameters, enabling adaptive response while preserving strict energy and latency constraints. It demonstrates how RL can be safely embedded in resource-limited IoT hardware by reducing the model to its essential linear components.

3.5 Lightweight security integration across the IoT stack

Lightweight security in IoT systems cannot be treated as an isolated module. In traditional enterprise architectures, cryptography, authentication, key management, and IDS operate as loosely coupled subsystems layered over relatively abundant hardware resources. In contrast, IoT nodes operate under systemic constraints, including limited RAM, strict duty cycling, constrained flash endurance, narrow CPU architectures, and energy-expensive radio semantics. These limitations are not localized to a single layer; they permeate the entire stack. As a result, security mechanisms must be co-designed across layers rather than appended independently. The integrated security discipline developed in this section spans lightweight cryptography, micro-authentication protocols, lightweight key management, statistical and TinyML-based IDS, DRL-assisted adaptive control, energy-aware communication primitives, and stack-level co-optimization. The IoT protocol stack can be abstracted as

$$\mathcal{S} = \{L_{\text{phys}}, L_{\text{mac}}, L_{\text{net}}, L_{\text{trans}}, L_{\text{app}}, L_{\text{sec}}\},$$

where each layer contributes to global energy consumption and security strength:

$$E_{\text{total}} = \sum_{i=1}^{6} E(L_i), \qquad S_{\text{total}} = \bigcap_{i=1}^{6} S(L_i).$$

A viable lightweight design minimizes E_{total} while maintaining S_{total} above required thresholds, subject to device capability limits.

3.5.1 Cross-layer security coupling

IoT systems operate under tight vertical coupling, meaning that physical-layer modulation patterns, MAC duty-cycle schedules, packet timing structures, and application semantics collectively expose observable behavior. Security must therefore extend beyond encryption and authentication into timing control, packet shaping, and behavior modeling. Consider a constrained device deploying a lightweight block cipher such as PRESENT, compressed elliptic-curve authentication, periodic LAKE key refresh, a statistical IDS pre-filter, a TinyML anomaly classifier, and a DRL-based threshold tuner. If these components operate independently without coordination, redundant computation may occur, radio scheduling may conflict with IDS sampling intervals, and encryption overhead may distort packet timing assumptions used by anomaly detection. A cryptographic mode that expands packet size by a factor of four can directly alter MAC-layer scheduling and invalidate statistical baselines. Stack-level cooperation, therefore, becomes mandatory rather than optional.

3.5.2 Unified lightweight security pipeline

A deeply integrated pipeline across the IoT stack is illustrated in Fig. 3.7. The figure depicts security functions embedded from the physical and MAC layers upward

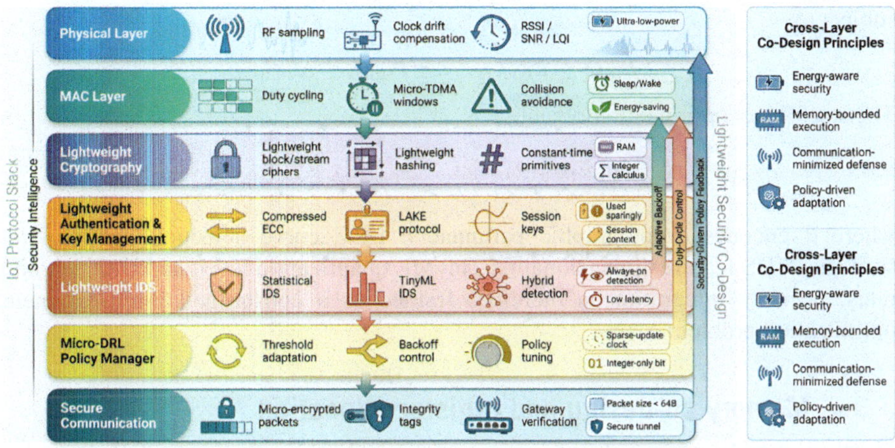

FIGURE 3.7

Integrated lightweight security pipeline across the IoT protocol stack.

through lightweight cryptography, authenticated key exchange, key management, IDS, and adaptive policy control. Lower layers provide channel state, duty-cycle timing, and transmission metadata. Cryptographic layers enforce confidentiality and integrity using compact primitives. Authentication and key management layers regulate trust relationships through compressed ECC and LAKE-style handshakes. IDS modules process statistical features and TinyML representations to detect anomalous behavior. A micro-DRL policy engine adjusts detection thresholds, backoff timing, and communication frequency based on observed patterns. Cross-layer feedback loops coordinate behavior, ensuring that computation, memory allocation, and radio scheduling remain aligned with energy constraints. The figure, therefore, depicts a vertically integrated system in which security intelligence propagates bidirectionally rather than linearly.

3.5.3 Mathematical model of multi-layer co-design

Each lightweight security component consumes computational, memory, and communication energy:

$$E = E_{\text{comp}} + E_{\text{mem}} + E_{\text{txrx}}.$$

At the stack level, the aggregate cost becomes

$$E_{\text{total}} = \sum_{i=1}^{N} \left(E_{\text{crypto}}^{(i)} + E_{\text{auth}}^{(i)} + E_{\text{ids}}^{(i)} + E_{\text{policy}}^{(i)} + E_{\text{comm}}^{(i)} \right),$$

subject to

$$E_{\text{total}} \leq E_{\text{budget}}, \qquad M_{\text{total}} \leq M_{\text{ram}}.$$

The stack-level optimization objective is

$$\min_{\theta \in \Theta} E_{\text{total}}(\theta) \quad \text{s.t.} \quad S_{\text{total}}(\theta) \geq S_{\text{req}},$$

where θ encodes cryptographic parameters, ECC curve selection, compression strategies, IDS feature dimensionality, TinyML quantization level, and DRL learning rates. Security integration is therefore framed as a constrained multi-parameter optimization problem.

3.5.4 Memory co-design and register allocation

Memory sharing represents one of the most critical cross-layer challenges. IoT microcontrollers typically provide 8–64 KB of RAM, which must simultaneously support sensing buffers, communication stacks, cryptographic keys, IDS features, TinyML weights, DRL state variables, and system execution stacks. Total memory usage can be modeled as

$$M_{\text{total}} = M_{\text{stack}} + M_{\text{crypto}} + M_{\text{ids}} + M_{\text{drl}} + M_{\text{comm}}.$$

A safe design requires

$$M_{\text{total}} < M_{\text{ram}} - M_{\text{reserve}}.$$

Table 3.4 illustrates a representative memory allocation layout for an integrated lightweight node. The diagram shows how radio buffers occupy the largest contiguous region, followed by compressed ECC tables, cryptographic keys, IDS feature vectors, TinyML weight storage, DRL Q-values, and residual stack memory. The visual structure emphasizes that no component can expand independently without affecting the entire system footprint.

Table 3.4 Representative Memory Co-Design Layout for an Integrated Lightweight IoT Node.

Component	Memory Allocation	Role in System
Radio Buffers	2–4 KB	Packet TX/RX buffering (largest contiguous block)
Compressed ECC Tables	1–2 KB	Lightweight cryptographic operations
Cryptographic Keys	256–512 B	Secure authentication and key storage
IDS Feature Vectors	64–160 B	Real-time IDS inputs
TinyML Weights	200–800 B	Embedded inference parameters
DRL Q-Table	200–512 B	Adaptive policy learning storage
System Stack + Free RAM	Remaining Memory	Runtime execution and overflow margin

3.5.5 Integrated energy budget analysis

Energy availability determines operational viability. Total available energy is modeled as

$$E_{\text{budget}} = E_{\text{harvested}} + E_{\text{battery}},$$

with typical hourly availability

$$E_{\text{available}} \in [100, 500]\ \mu\text{J}.$$

A complete lightweight IDS-integrated cycle consumes

$$E_{\text{cycle}} = E_{\text{feat}} + E_{\text{model}} + E_{\text{crypto}} + E_{\text{comm}} + E_{\text{policy}}.$$

Operational feasibility requires

$$E_{\text{cycle}} \times N_{\text{cycles}} \leq E_{\text{available}}.$$

The integration resource Table 3.5 summarizes representative RAM and energy costs across stack components, demonstrating that radio transmission and compressed ECC dominate cost, whereas statistical IDS and DRL tuning remain comparatively lightweight.

Table 3.5 Resource requirements of integrated lightweight security components.

Component	RAM (Bytes)	Energy (μJ)	Notes
Lightweight Block Cipher	200–800	0.5–1.5	PRESENT, GIFT
Compressed ECC	1024–2048	6000–12000	Handshake only
LAKE Protocol State	128–256	1–3	Session tokens + MAC
Statistical IDS	64–200	0.03–0.08	Always-on
TinyML IDS	300–900	0.1–0.4	Quantized inference
DRL Agent	200–500	0.05–0.2	Periodic updates
Secure Radio TX	0	20–50 per packet	Dominant energy cost

3.5.6 Case study: fully integrated lightweight node

Consider a constrained IoT node deploying GIFT-64 encryption, compressed ECC for initial authentication, LAKE for key updates, a micro-feature statistical IDS, a quantized TinyML classifier, a DRL-based adaptive threshold controller, and TDMA-based duty cycling. Total runtime memory is approximately

$$M_{\text{total}} \approx 8.6\,\text{KB},$$

with per-cycle energy consumption

$$E_{\text{cycle}} \approx 17.4\ \mu\text{J}.$$

Given the hourly energy availability of

$$E_{\text{available}} \approx 200\text{–}400\ \mu\text{J},$$

The system remains fully self-sustainable while maintaining integrated security functions.

3.6 Multi-agent lightweight IDS deployment models

The deployment of IDS across massive, heterogeneous, and resource-constrained IoT systems introduce challenges that cannot be effectively addressed by isolated detection mechanisms operating independently on each device. Robust IoT security, however, requires a carefully engineered multi-agent ecosystem in which lightweight IDS nodes, gateway-level orchestrators, and cloud-side RL coordinators operate cooperatively. Prior sections have examined the internal mechanics of lightweight detection models and established the physical, energy, and architectural constraints that govern feasible IoT security systems. Building on these foundations, this section develops an integrated structural, mathematical, and procedural framework for multi-agent IDS deployment, emphasizing how distributed lightweight IDS agents can be configured, synchronized, and optimized to provide real-time protection under severe resource constraints. At a conceptual level, multi-agent lightweight IDS infrastructures must reconcile three conflicting operational realities. First, individual IoT nodes often lack the computational capacity to run full anomaly-detection pipelines continuously, forcing always-on intelligence to be minimalist, bounded, and predictable. Second, gateways, fog-layer controllers, and mesh aggregators provide larger computational budgets, yet remain bounded by latency constraints, communication noise, device mobility, and topology changes that can rapidly invalidate static policies. Third, cloud-level and edge-cloud nodes have sufficient scale for DRL, meta-learning, graph-based policy synthesis, and multi-agent coordination, yet they incur communication delays that prevent immediate reactive defense. A practical multi-agent IDS must therefore form a category pipeline in which each layer executes only the intelligence that can be supported locally, while coordinating with the remaining categories to preserve high detection fidelity and low false-positive rates without exhausting energy budgets. The remainder of this section formalizes that pipeline through role decomposition, distributed inference models, resource-aware partitioning, synchronization logic, and reinforcement-learning-driven coordination.

3.6.1 Architectural foundations of multi-agent lightweight IDS

A multi-agent IDS for IoT can be organized into three core agent classes that differ in computational budget, memory footprint, network position, and operational lifetime. Class-L agents operate directly on ultra-constrained IoT devices and implement

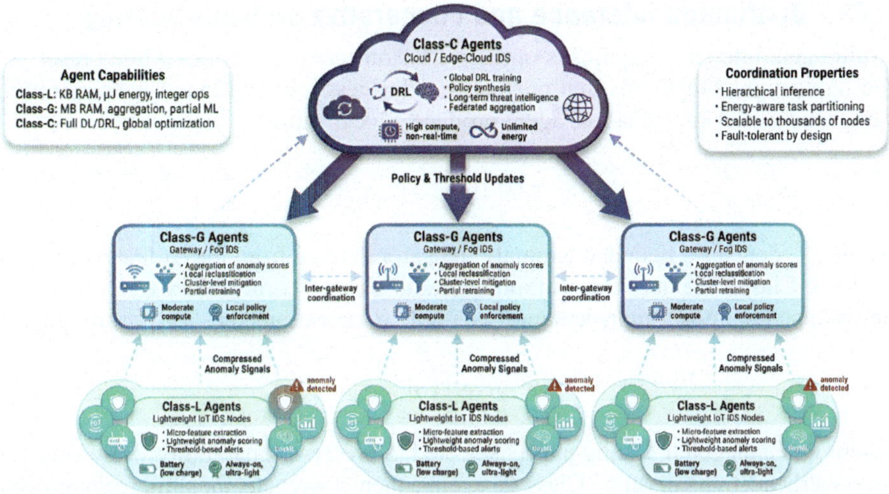

FIGURE 3.8

Hierarchical multi-agent lightweight IDS deployment across IoT, gateway/fog, and cloud categories.

always-on detection using micro-feature extraction and bounded anomaly scoring under strict duty-cycle constraints. Class-G agents reside at gateways and fog nodes, where they aggregate signals, execute hierarchical decision-making, perform partial reclassification, and enforce near-real-time mitigation under moderate compute and memory budgets. Class-C agents operate in cloud and edge-cloud infrastructure and provide global intelligence through long-horizon correlation, distributed or federated DRL training, and policy synthesis that coordinates the overall system. This hierarchy is depicted in Fig. 3.8, which illustrates the upward flow of compressed anomaly evidence from IoT nodes to gateways and onward to cloud intelligence, along with the downward flow of policy updates, threshold calibration, and coordinated response strategies that enable energy-aware, fault-tolerant operation at scale. The figure emphasizes that the multi-agent architecture is not merely a communications relay; it is a control system in which local sensing, mid-category fusion, and global policy learning jointly determine system-level security. Functionally, Class-L agents detect low-cost anomalies, such as abrupt shifts in packet interval, deviations in header structure, and symbolic-state transitions, using small feature sets. Class-G agents consolidate multi-source signals, perform hierarchical clustering of anomaly reports, execute local retraining when feasible, and enforce cluster-level mitigation actions. Class-C agents synthesize global policies through DRL training, update decision thresholds, coordinate distributed defense strategies, and dispatch compact control updates to lower categories in a manner consistent with bandwidth and latency constraints.

3.6.2 Distributed inference and cooperative anomaly scoring

Multi-agent inference requires cooperative fusion across categories while preserving the lightweight constraints that prevent IoT devices from continuously transmitting raw features. Let each Class-L agent produce a local anomaly score vector

$$s_i = (s_{i,1}, s_{i,2}, \ldots, s_{i,K}),$$

where $s_{i,k}$ denotes a bounded anomaly indicator derived from micro-feature vectors. Because Class-L devices must minimize radio usage, score vectors are compressed and mapped to integer representations suitable for constrained registers through

$$\tilde{s}_i = \lfloor \Gamma s_i \rfloor,$$

where Γ is a diagonal scaling matrix selected to preserve separability while enabling low-overhead transmission. Class-G agents then aggregate incoming compressed signals using cooperative weighted fusion,

$$S_G = \frac{1}{N} \sum_{i=1}^{N} w_i \tilde{s}_i,$$

where w_i reflects device reliability, historical detection quality, residual energy state, sensing role, and network criticality. This fusion step produces a gateway-level summary statistic that supports higher-level decisions without requiring the gateway to reconstruct raw features. At the top category, Class-C agents apply policy-driven DRL optimization to calibrate thresholds and mitigation strategies. Given aggregated gateway evidence S_G and a global environment representation e_t, the cloud policy selects an action

$$a_t = \pi_\theta(S_G, e_t),$$

where π_θ is a parameterized policy network whose parameters θ evolve during training. The resulting coordination can be interpreted as a multi-agent Markov decision process (MA-MDP) in which Class-L agents generate local observations, Class-G agents provide aggregated intermediate states, and Class-C agents supply policy guidance that is executed in a decentralized manner.

3.6.3 Resource-aware role assignment and task partitioning

Sustainable multi-agent IDS operation requires that tasks be partitioned according to device capabilities, network conditions, and instantaneous energy availability. Let each Class-L device be characterized by a resource vector

$$r_i = (c_i, m_i, e_i),$$

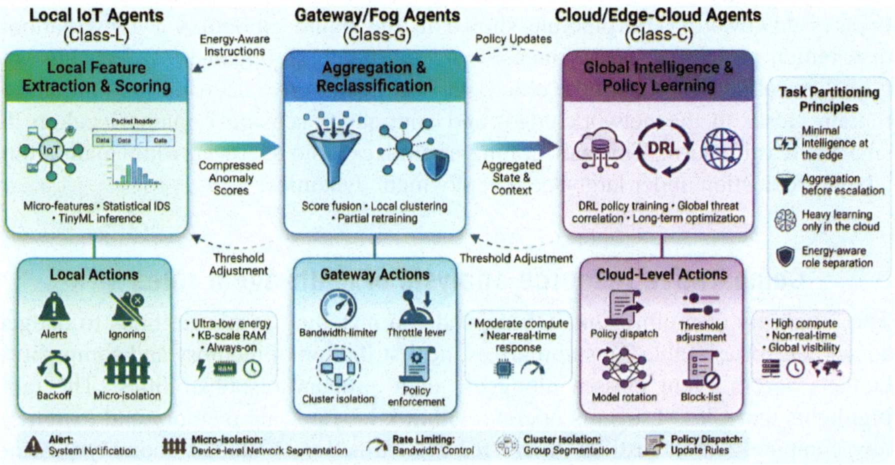

FIGURE 3.9

Task-flow pipeline among Class-L, Class-G, and Class-C IDS agents.

representing computational capacity, available memory, and current energy level. Task assignment can then be expressed as a constrained optimization problem

$$\min_{T} \sum_{i=1}^{N} \alpha_c C_i(T) + \alpha_m M_i(T) + \alpha_e E_i(T)$$

subject to

$$\text{security}(T) \geq \sigma_{\min},$$

where T is an assignment matrix mapping detection subtasks to devices, $C_i(T)$, $M_i(T)$, and $E_i(T)$ denote the induced compute, memory, and energy costs, and α_c, α_m, α_e control prioritization under constrained operation. In practice, Class-G agents approximate solutions to this problem using local heuristics driven by metadata and reliability history, thereby preserving responsiveness by avoiding reliance on the cloud for time-critical paths.

3.6.4 Multi-agent task flow pipeline

The category task-flow pipeline is illustrated in Fig. 3.9. The figure depicts the upward movement of Class-L agents' always-on micro-feature extraction, lightweight anomaly scoring, and TinyML inference, followed by aggregation, reclassification, score fusion, clustering, and near-real-time mitigation actions executed by Class-G agents. At the highest category, Class-C agents provide long-horizon correlation and policy learning, including DRL-based optimization and cross-domain threat intelligence synthesis, and then dispatch policy and threshold updates downward. The pipeline shown in the figure embodies a computational distribution principle: energy-intensive operations, high-dimensional learning, and global correlation remain in the cloud, while time-sensitive decisions and mitigation remain closer to the network edge, and continuous sensing remains local in the smallest feasible form. This partitioning minimizes radio overhead while maintaining adaptive detection under large-scale deployment dynamics.

3.6.5 Comparative resource analysis of multi-agent roles

The feasibility of multi-agent IDS depends on matching responsibilities to budgets across categories. Table 3.6 summarizes the distribution of memory and computation budgets across agent classes alongside their primary responsibilities. The table highlights that Class-L agents operate within kilobyte-scale memory and extremely low compute, which justifies micro-feature extraction, bounded anomaly scoring, and threshold-based alerting rather than complex inference. Class-G agents occupy a middle regime in which aggregation, local clustering, and partial reclassification become feasible while still respecting latency and throughput constraints. Class-C agents operate with high compute availability, enabling global DRL policy training, multi-agent coordination, and long-term correlation that would be infeasible on gateways and impossible on constrained devices. This category mapping between budgets and roles is the core reason multi-agent IDS becomes structurally necessary in IoT systems: it ensures that intelligence is placed where it can be supported energetically while maintaining system-level coherence.

Table 3.6 Resource and responsibility distribution across multi-agent IDS layers.

Agent Class	Memory Budget	Computation Budget	Primary Responsibilities
Class-L (Local)	2-32 kB	Very Low	Micro-feature extraction, anomaly scoring, thresholding
Class-G (Gateway)	256 kB-8 MB	Moderate	Aggregation, local reclassification, clustering, response coordination
Class-C (Cloud)	Unlimited	High	Global DRL policy training, multi-agent coordination, long-term analysis

3.6.6 Synchronization and temporal consistency

Multi-agent IDS must remain robust under asynchronous IoT conditions, including clock drift, intermittent connectivity, and bursty communication schedules that prevent strict temporal alignment. To maintain operational consistency without requiring synchronized clocks, gateways, and cloud categories rely on timestamp-independent ordering heuristics

$$\phi(\tilde{s}_i) = \text{local arrival order},$$

along with sliding aggregation windows

$$W = [t - \Delta, t],$$

In which anomaly evidence is fused despite irregular reporting. Gateways maintain windowed consistency by computing

$$S_G(t) = \frac{\sum_{i \in W} \tilde{s}_i}{|W|},$$

which supports reclassification and mitigation even when devices report sporadically due to duty cycling and channel contention. This temporal strategy ensures that the system remains stable under realistic network conditions while preserving low overhead.

3.6.7 Multi-agent RL for coordinated intrusion response

Class-C agents train coordinated DRL policies that align actions across categories while preserving decentralized execution. Each Class-L device operates with a reduced action set

$$A_L = \{\text{alert, ignore, local-backoff, local-isolation}\},$$

gateways operate with a richer set

$$A_G = \{\text{rate-limit, device-throttle, cluster-isolation, local-model-update}\},$$

and cloud controllers issue macro-scale actions

$$A_C = \{\text{policy-dispatch, threshold-update, model-rotation, global-block}\}.$$

Coordination is learned by maximizing a global reward function

$$R = w_d \cdot \text{detection score} - w_f \cdot \text{false positives} - w_e \cdot \text{energy cost} - w_l \cdot \text{latency},$$

where the weights encode trade-offs between detection fidelity, operational stability, and energy sustainability. Training typically follows centralized training and decentralized execution principles, enabling cloud-scale optimization while ensuring that devices execute only lightweight action logic consistent with local constraints.

3.6.8 Scalability and device churn management

Large-scale IoT systems exhibit continuous device churn due to mobility, battery exhaustion, intermittent connectivity, and environmental interference. Multi-agent

IDS must therefore adapt through lightweight membership management rather than heavy consistency protocols. Devices enter the system using compact join logic

$$\text{Join request} = \text{device ID} \parallel H(\text{baseline}),$$

and leave events are represented through timeout-based soft-state expiration

$$\text{Leave event} = \text{timeout}(T).$$

Gateways maintain membership tables with expiration-based removal, enabling scalable churn handling without imposing high communication overhead. This approach preserves system responsiveness while maintaining stable aggregation and policy execution under continuous topology evolution.

3.7 Energy-aware multi-agent coordination and load balancing

The sustainability of IDS in large-scale IoT systems hinges not merely on detection accuracy but also on the system's capacity to maintain operational longevity under tight energy budgets. While previous sections established lightweight detection models and multi-agent structures, this section introduces an integrated energy-aware coordination layer that orchestrates lightweight IDS behavior across the multi-agent hierarchy. In contrast to conventional architectures, where nodes operate independently under static policies, energy-aware multi-agent IDS frameworks continuously adapt sensing rates, inference frequencies, communication schedules, and cooperation modes to minimize power usage while preserving detection robustness. This capability is essential in deployments powered by small lithium cells, supercapacitors, RF harvesting, solar microcells, and other intermittent sources, where energy availability fluctuates over time and across nodes. Energy awareness in multi-agent IDS is not a superficial optimization layer; it is a system-level principle that determines where tasks execute, and how often devices participate in cooperative inference, and when costly actions such as anomaly reporting and synchronization should be deferred, compressed, aggregated, and suppressed. The remainder of this section provides a rigorous mathematical, algorithmic, and diagrammatic treatment of energy-aware coordination mechanisms, emphasizing how these mechanisms preserve security continuity while preventing premature node depletion.

3.7.1 Energy modeling for distributed IDS agents

Each IDS agent maintains a local energy state variable

$$E_i(t) \in [0, E_{\max,i}]$$

representing available energy for device i at time t. For battery-powered nodes, $E_i(t)$ corresponds to the remaining charge, expressed in an energy-equivalent unit.

For energy-harvesting nodes, $E_i(t)$ captures the dynamically fluctuating energy accumulated from environmental sources, making the state time-varying even in the absence of communication. The instantaneous energy expenditure for one operational cycle can be expressed as

$$C_i(t) = C_{\text{feat}} + C_{\text{infer}} + C_{\text{comm}}(t),$$

where C_{feat} denotes the cost of micro-feature extraction, C_{infer} denotes the cost of local anomaly detection, and $C_{\text{comm}}(t)$ denotes the time-dependent cost of transmission and reception for anomaly reporting and coordination. Empirically and structurally, communication dominates the energy hierarchy,

$$C_{\text{comm}}(t) \gg C_{\text{infer}} \gg C_{\text{feat}},$$

which implies that energy-aware coordination must prioritize radio minimization as the primary lever for sustainability, while still controlling inference and feature extraction in low-energy operating regimes. The energy state evolves according to

$$E_i(t+1) = E_i(t) - C_i(t) + H_i(t),$$

where $H_i(t)$ represents harvested energy, which can be modeled as a stochastic process that depends on environmental conditions and harvesting hardware. This evolution equation provides a tractable foundation for coordination policies that reason explicitly about future viability rather than making myopic decisions based solely on instantaneous energy.

3.7.2 Energy-aware inference scheduling

Each agent computes a binary inference schedule

$$f_i(t) \in \{0, 1\},$$

where $f_i(t) = 1$ indicates that the device performs anomaly detection at time t, while $f_i(t) = 0$ indicates that the device skips inference and may remain in a sensing-only, buffering, andsleep state. Scheduling is energy-coupled and risk-coupled through

$$f_i(t) = \mathbb{I}\left[E_i(t) \geq \theta_i(t)\right],$$

where $\theta_i(t)$ is a dynamic threshold rather than a fixed constant. A practical threshold must incorporate both local costs and global security context, yielding

$$\theta_i(t) = \beta_1 C_{\text{infer}} + \beta_2 \cdot \text{risk}(t) + \beta_3 \cdot \text{network\_state}(t).$$

The term risk(t) provides a global threat-intensity estimate supplied by the cloud-level coordination agent, which can be computed from aggregated gateway evidence and global environment state via

$$\text{risk}(t) = \pi_R(S_G(t), e_t),$$

where π_R denotes a learned risk estimation function. Under elevated risk, $\theta_i(t)$ effectively lowers the inference barrier, increasing sampling and detection frequency; under low risk, $\theta_i(t)$ increases, allowing devices to conserve energy without sacrificing system-level robustness. The network_state component captures macroscopic conditions such as contention level, mobility, packet loss, and gateway load, ensuring that inference schedules remain consistent with the feasibility of communication and coordination.

3.7.3 Gateway-level load balancing under energy constraints

Gateways must distribute IDS participation across local IoT nodes to prevent premature exhaustion of energy-critical devices while maintaining sufficient sensing coverage. Let the task assignment vector be

$$T = (T_1, T_2, \ldots, T_N),$$

where $T_i \in [0, 1]$ represents the fractional allocation of IDS workload assigned to device i within a cluster, such as the responsibility for higher-rate inference, richer micro-feature extraction, andmore frequent anomaly reporting. A gateway-level energy-aware objective that penalizes the overuse of low-energy nodes can be expressed as

$$\min_{T} \sum_{i=1}^{N} \frac{T_i}{E_i(t) + \epsilon}$$

subject to

$$\sum_{i=1}^{N} T_i = 1,$$

where ϵ is a small stabilizer that prevents division singularities. This formulation preferentially assigns a higher workload to nodes with larger current energy reserves and protects depleted nodes by reducing their participation. Gateways recompute T when cluster-wide anomaly thresholds are exceeded when a node's energy drops below a survival threshold, and when membership changes occur due to joins and departures, since each of these events change either the security demand and the feasible resource pool.

3.7.4 Energy-aware coordination loop

Energy-aware coordination emerges from continuous feedback among Class-L, Class-G, and Class-C agents, which is summarized in Fig. 3.10. It describes a closed-loop control process in which Class-L agents track local energy states while adjusting inference frequency and local responses such as throttling, sleeping, and selective suppression under low-energy conditions; Class-G gateway agents act as coordination kernels that fuse compressed anomaly evidence with energy telemetry, compute

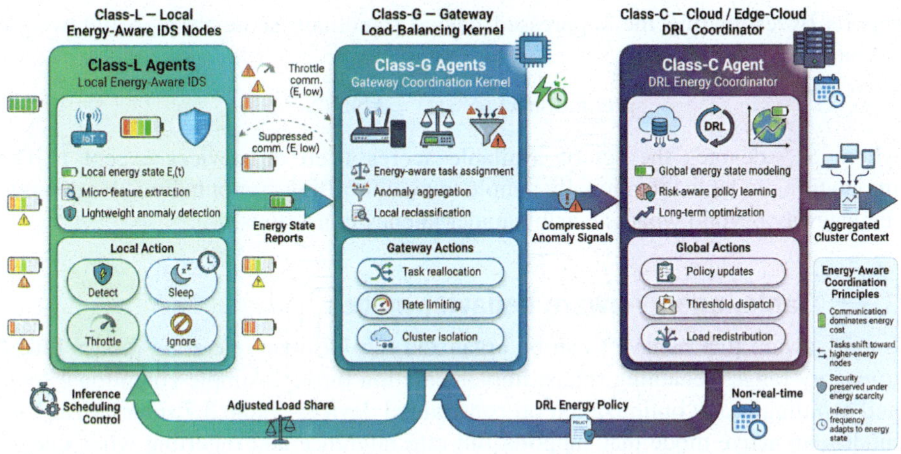

FIGURE 3.10

Energy-aware multi-agent coordination loop across hierarchical IDS categories.

energy-aware task assignment, and enforce cluster-level balancing decisions; Class-C cloud and edge-cloud agents train DRL-based coordination policies that model long-term energy dynamics and risk, then propagate a compact threshold and policy updates downward. The critical implication highlighted by Fig. 3.10 is that energy-aware IDS cannot be reduced to local power saving; it requires coordinated multi-category control, because local conservation decisions alter global observability, and global threat states must be considered when energy expenditure becomes justified for security.

3.7.5 Energy-triggered communication throttling

Because communication dominates energy cost, a central mechanism in energy-aware IDS is communication throttling, in which devices reduce reporting frequency under low energy while preserving the ability to signal severe events. A node may enter throttled mode when

$$E_i(t) < \lambda C_{\text{comm}},$$

where λ is a safety factor that reserves energy for baseline sensing and survival. In throttled mode, the device suppresses low-severity notifications and transmits only high-confidence alerts according to

$$\text{send}(s_i(t)) = \begin{cases} 1 & s_i(t) \geq \theta_{\text{severe}}, \\ 0 & s_i(t) < \theta_{\text{severe}}. \end{cases}$$

Suppressing non-severe messages reduces radio usage while preserving the ability to trigger a cluster response when attacks are likely. Gateways compensate for missing reports by estimating the suppressed device's anomaly score through lightweight imputation,

$$\text{prediction}(i) = \hat{s}_i(t) = \text{kNN}(S^{-i}),$$

where S^{-i} denotes the set of available scores from all devices except i. The imputation model is intentionally simple to avoid shifting computational burden into the gateway beyond what is feasible under latency constraints.

3.7.6 Table: energy-aware behavior modes

Energy-aware IDS behavior can be organized into discrete operating modes linked to energy ranges, enabling robust implementation through simple conditional logic and avoiding heavy optimization on constrained devices. Table 3.7 summarizes four modes: an active mode that supports full-rate inference and reporting when energy is abundant; an adaptive mode that reduces inference frequency and compresses scoring; a throttled mode that reports only severe anomalies while the gateway provides assisted detection; and a survival mode that disables IDS inference and reporting while maintaining minimal sensing functionality to preserve device availability. The table provides an implementable mapping between residual energy and behavior policy, enabling both predictable operation and coordination across clusters.

Table 3.7 Energy-aware operating modes of Class-L IoT nodes.

Energy Range	Mode	Behavior Description
$E_i(t) > 70\%$	Active IDS Mode	Full feature extraction, full-rate inference, full-rate reporting
$40\% < E_i(t) \leq 70\%$	Adaptive Mode	Reduced inference frequency, compressed anomaly scoring
$10\% < E_i(t) \leq 40\%$	Throttled Mode	Sparse inference, only severe anomalies reported, gateway-assisted detection
$E_i(t) \leq 10\%$	Survival Mode	No inference, no reporting; node maintains minimal sensing-only operation

3.7.7 Multi-agent RL for energy optimization

At the coordination category, the cloud-level agent trains a DRL policy for energy-aware orchestration using a global state representation

$$z(t) = (\{E_i(t)\},\ S_G(t),\ \text{topology}(t),\ \text{risk}(t)),$$

which captures energy distribution across devices, aggregated anomaly evidence, structural network dynamics, and threat intensity. The coordinated action space includes operations that alter how the system spends energy, such as threshold updates, reporting-interval adjustment, shifting tasks toward gateways, selective offloading, cluster isolation, and policy broadcast.

$$\begin{aligned} A_C = \{ & \text{update detection thresholds,} \\ & \text{adjust reporting intervals,} \\ & \text{shift selected tasks to gateway nodes,} \\ & \text{offload computation from constrained devices,} \\ & \text{isolate compromised andhigh-risk clusters,} \\ & \text{broadcast global security policies} \}. \end{aligned}$$

The reward must jointly encode security and sustainability through

$$\begin{aligned} R(t) = {} & \alpha \cdot \text{detection}(t) - \beta \cdot \text{energy\_usage}(t) - \gamma \cdot \text{false\_positives}(t) \\ & + \delta \cdot \text{network\_stability}(t), \end{aligned}$$

where $(\alpha, \beta, \gamma, \delta)$ tune the balance among detection fidelity, energy preservation, operational stability, and false-alarm suppression. This formulation supports deployment-specific prioritization, since industrial control contexts frequently tolerate higher energy expenditure for lower false negatives, while long-lived environmental sensing emphasizes survival and stability.

3.7.8 Load balancing under partial network failure

Energy-aware coordination must remain robust under partial network failure, including gateway outages caused by mobility, interference, network partitioning, or sustained attack. Let the set of active gateways be

$$\mathcal{G}(t) = \{g_1, g_2, \ldots, g_K\},$$

and let $\mathcal{D}(g_k)$ denote the device set served by gateway g_k. When gateway g_k fails at time t_f, the cluster workload can be reassigned through

$$\mathcal{D}(g_k) \rightarrow \arg\min_{g_j \neq g_k} \left(\text{load}(g_j) + \eta \cdot \text{latency}(g_j)\right),$$

where η controls the trade-off between computational load and proximity. Fig. 3.11 summarizes the recovery mechanism by showing how the Class-C coordination category detects failure through latency and reachability indicators, recomputes reallocation weights, and redirects orphaned nodes to active gateways without inserting cloud dependencies into the data path. The figure emphasizes continuous feedback of updated load and latency metrics, enabling rapid recovery while maintaining IDS continuity across large-scale deployments.

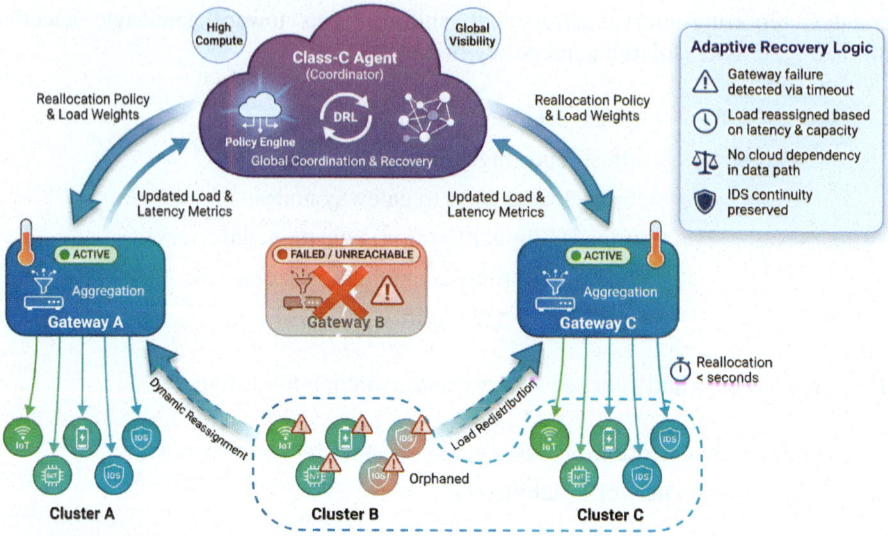

FIGURE 3.11

Adaptive gateway-failure recovery and load reallocation in hierarchical multi-agent IDS deployments.

3.7.9 Energy-neutral operation model

For energy-harvesting nodes, the objective is not minimal consumption but energy-neutral operation, defined by the long-run condition

$$\mathbb{E}[H_i(t)] \geq \mathbb{E}[C_i(t)].$$

Achieving energy neutrality requires adaptive control over inference duty cycling, micro-feature complexity, communication bursts, aggregation windows, and interaction frequency with gateways. Node survival over a horizon T can be expressed as

$$P_{\text{alive}} = \prod_{t=1}^{T} \mathbb{I}[E_i(t) > 0],$$

which captures the requirement that energy must remain positive at all times. DRL-based coordination aims to maximize fleet-wide survival while maintaining adequate security by optimizing

$$\max_{\pi} \sum_{i} P_{\text{alive}}^{(i)}(T),$$

thereby prioritizing policies that preserve long-term operation across the population rather than sacrificing low-energy nodes for short-term detection gains. This energy-neutral perspective closes the loop between sustainability and security, ensuring that multi-agent IDS remains viable in real deployments where energy availability is a first-class constraint rather than an afterthought.

3.8 Cross-layer lightweight security harmonization

Lightweight security is not the sum of isolated mechanisms but a tightly woven fabric spanning sensing hardware, embedded firmware, wireless protocols, network topologies, and cloud intelligence. In large-scale IoT systems, security failures often emerge at the boundaries between layers—where application semantics collide with network abstractions, where device-level constraints conflict with gateway-level enforcement, and where timing or packet-structure assumptions made at one layer silently invalidate defenses at another. This section presents a comprehensive cross-layer harmonization framework that unites lightweight cryptography, micro-authentication, statistical and ML-based IDS, energy-aware multi-agent coordination, and adaptive networking into a single coherent architecture. The core principle is cross-layer coupling, in which security actions at one layer dynamically modify, constrain, or enrich behavior at adjacent layers, enabling anomaly scoring to trigger MAC backoff reshaping, routing reconfiguration, sampling throttling, and micro-cryptographic refresh cycles without violating resource envelopes. The objective is to prevent attack propagation and policy inconsistency by ensuring that security signals are interpreted consistently across the protocol stack and translated into bounded, energy-aware control actions that remain implementable on constrained nodes.

3.8.1 Cross-layer interaction model

We define the IoT security stack as consisting of the following layers:

$$\mathcal{L} = \{\text{PHY}, \text{MAC}, \text{NET}, \text{TRANS}, \text{APP}, \text{SEC}\},$$

where SEC represents the ensemble of lightweight cryptography, lightweight IDS, authentication, and policy logic. Each layer exposes a set of control parameters

$$\theta_\ell = \{\theta_{\ell,1}, \theta_{\ell,2}, \ldots\}$$

that directly impact performance, energy, and security:

$$\begin{aligned}
\theta_{\text{PHY}} &= \text{TX power, modulation, coding} \\
\theta_{\text{MAC}} &= \text{duty cycle, backoff, contention window} \\
\theta_{\text{NET}} &= \text{routing paths, hop limit, neighbor trust} \\
\theta_{\text{TRANS}} &= \text{session parameters, retransmissions} \\
\theta_{\text{APP}} &= \text{sampling rate, data granularity} \\
\theta_{\text{SEC}} &= \text{crypto strength, IDS frequency, policies}
\end{aligned}$$

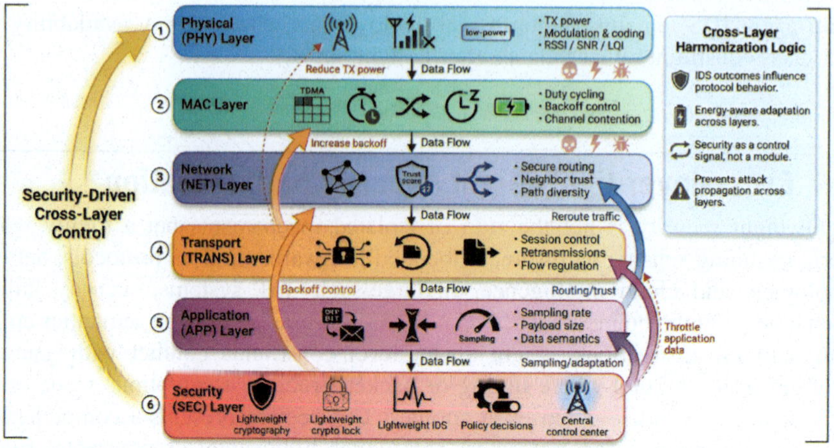

FIGURE 3.12

Cross-layer lightweight security harmonization loop across the IoT protocol stack.

Cross-layer harmonization is the process of adjusting the joint parameter set

$$\Theta(t) = \{\theta_{\mathrm{PHY}}, \theta_{\mathrm{MAC}}, \ldots, \theta_{\mathrm{SEC}}\}$$

based on a fused operational context

$$\mathcal{S}(t) = \{\mathrm{risk}(t),\ \mathrm{energy}(t),\ \mathrm{topology}(t),\ \mathrm{congestion}(t),\ \mathrm{attack\_surface}(t)\},$$

so that the harmonization engine selects

$$\Theta(t+1) = \pi_{\mathrm{harm}}(\mathcal{S}(t)),$$

where π_{harm} is a multi-agent, cross-layer decision policy that outputs bounded updates to layer parameters. Fig. 3.12 summarizes this closed-loop structure by showing how security-layer intelligence propagates as control signals to the application, transport, network, MAC, and physical layers, enabling coordinated adaptation such as dynamic sampling control, secure routing adjustments, contention shaping, and transmit-power modulation. The key implication emphasized by Fig. 3.12 is that security becomes an active driver of protocol behavior rather than a passive add-on, enabling attack containment and energy conservation through synchronized, stack-wide parameter updates rather than isolated reactions.

3.8.2 Cross-layer policy mapping

A harmonized stack requires a deterministic translation layer that converts security outcomes into network-layer control actions without ambiguity. We define a mapping function

$$\Phi : \mathcal{O}_{\text{SEC}} \rightarrow \bigcup_{\ell} \theta_{\ell},$$

where $\mathcal{O}_{\text{SEC}}$ denotes security-layer outcomes such as anomaly scores, authentication states, key-health indicators, and cryptographic state alerts, and the codomain is the union of actionable parameters across layers. For example, an elevated anomaly score can be mapped to contention and routing control through

$$\Phi(\text{high anomaly score}) = \{\theta_{\text{MAC}} \leftarrow \text{increase backoff}, \ \theta_{\text{NET}} \leftarrow \text{reroute}\},$$

while evidence of key compromise can be mapped to traffic shaping and session control through

$$\Phi(\text{key compromise}) = \{\theta_{\text{APP}} \leftarrow \text{reduce data rate}, \ \theta_{\text{TRANS}} \leftarrow \text{terminate session}\}.$$

This mapping serves as a reflex-like coupling between detection and protocol behavior, ensuring that responses to security evidence are implementable, energy-aware, and consistent across devices in the same operational context.

3.8.3 State fusion across layers

Cross-layer decisions require a unified state representation that captures the minimal sufficient statistics from each layer while remaining compressible into micro-state vectors. Each layer produces a local descriptor

$$s_{\ell}(t) \in \mathbb{R}^{k_{\ell}},$$

for example,

$$s_{\text{PHY}} = \{\text{RSSI, SNR, LQI}\}, \qquad s_{\text{MAC}} = \{\text{collision\_rate, backoff\_counter}\},$$
$$s_{\text{NET}} = \{\text{TTL, hop\_trust, path\_diversity}\}, \qquad s_{\text{APP}} = \{\text{sampling\_freq, payload\_size}\},$$
$$s_{\text{SEC}} = \{\text{anomaly, auth\_status, crypto\_state}\}.$$

The fused state is formed by concatenation,

$$s_{\text{fusion}}(t) = \bigoplus_{\ell} s_{\ell}(t),$$

then compressed into an integer-encoded representation suitable for constrained registers through

$$s'_{\text{fusion}} = Q_{\text{fxd}}\left(s_{\text{fusion}}\right),$$

where $Q_{\text{fxd}}(\cdot)$ denotes fixed-point quantization. This design preserves interpretability and supports fast updates, since each layer can update only its portion of the state while the fusion mechanism maintains a consistent global representation used by π_{harm}.

3.8.4 Table: cross-layer vulnerability mapping

Cross-layer harmonization is motivated by the fact that vulnerabilities manifest differently across layers, while mitigation often requires actions outside the layer where the vulnerability is observed. Table 3.8 summarizes common vulnerabilities per layer and highlights countermeasures that deliberately cross boundaries, such as using MAC duty-cycle reshaping to reduce exposure to PHY-layer jamming, using NET rerouting and trust-aware forwarding to reduce the impact of MAC spoofing, using security anomaly flags to trigger routing path pruning, and using transport-layer session control to contain replay and hijack attempts. The table formalizes the operational intent of harmonization: detection signals and resource constraints must be translated into coordinated controls that reduce attack effectiveness while preserving energy and stability.

Table 3.8 Cross-layer relationships between vulnerabilities and mitigation actions.

Layer	Common Vulnerabilities	Cross-Layer Countermeasures
PHY	Jamming, interference	MAC duty-cycle reshaping, security-layer throttling
MAC	Collision attacks, spoofed contention	NET-level rerouting, SEC-level authentication boost
NET	Sinkhole, blackhole, wormhole	PHY link diversity, SEC anomaly flags, MAC rate limiting
TRANS	Session hijack, replay	Crypto refresh, APP throttling, NET route switching
APP	Injection, crafted payloads	SEC lightweight ML, TRANS re-authentication
SEC	Key leaks, false positives	Cross-layer support for rekeying, MAC isolation

3.8.5 Mathematical model for cross-layer decision making

Let

$$a_\ell(t) \in A_\ell$$

denote a layer-specific action chosen from the feasible action set A_ℓ, such as TX power modulation at PHY, contention-window adjustment at MAC, route switching at NET, retransmission control at TRANS, sampling adaptation at APP, and cryptographic and IDS-policy updates at SEC. Cross-layer policy selects the joint action vector

$$A(t) = \{a_{\text{PHY}}, a_{\text{MAC}}, a_{\text{NET}}, a_{\text{TRANS}}, a_{\text{APP}}, a_{\text{SEC}}\}$$

to optimize a multi-objective utility that balances security against resource costs,

$$\max_{A(t)} \alpha \cdot \text{security}(A(t)) - \beta \cdot \text{energy}(A(t)) - \gamma \cdot \text{latency}(A(t)) + \delta \cdot \text{stability}(A(t)).$$

The weights are application-specific, since mission-critical control loops demand higher α, energy-harvesting deployments demand higher β, latency-sensitive sensing demands higher γ, and long-lived mesh networks demand higher δ. The policy computes the constrained optimum

$$A^*(t) = \arg\max_{A \in \mathcal{A}} U(A(t)),$$

where $\mathcal{A}$ is the set of jointly feasible actions that respect duty cycles, packet-size limits, memory bounds, and allowable protocol parameter ranges.

3.8.6 Lightweight cross-layer synchronization protocol

Cross-layer coupling requires lightweight coordination messages that allow nodes and gateways to share compact state and control updates without introducing heavy synchronization overhead. Each IoT device exchanges micro-state vectors, compressed anomaly flags, routing trust updates, MAC-layer congestion hints, and PHY-layer noise metrics within a constrained synchronization packet

$$P_{\text{sync}} = \left[\text{ID} \parallel s'_{\text{fusion}} \parallel \Delta\theta_\ell \parallel t \right],$$

where $\Delta\theta_\ell$ represents bounded updates to layer parameters and t denotes a local time marker and epoch counter used for windowing rather than strict global time. To remain feasible for IEEE 802.15.4 and LoRaWAN-style payload constraints, the packet size is capped by

$$|P_{\text{sync}}| \leq 32 \text{ bytes}.$$

Fig. 3.13 depicts this synchronization mechanism by showing how each node maintains a local cross-layer state, performs state fusion and quantization to produce compact messages, and exchanges these messages are opportunistically without requiring a global clock. The figure emphasizes a loss-tolerant, energy-aware sliding-window consistency model, which is critical in IoT systems with drift, intermittent links, and bursty schedules, as strict synchronization would impose energy and latency costs beyond feasible budgets.

3.8.7 Adaptive cross-layer backoff algorithm

When anomaly levels increase, nodes adapt MAC-layer parameters to reduce contention, preserve bandwidth for secure retransmissions, and prioritize gateway alerts. Let

$$A_i(t) = \text{anomaly score of node } i,$$

and define a MAC backoff multiplier

$$B_i(t) = B_0 \cdot (1 + kA_i(t)),$$

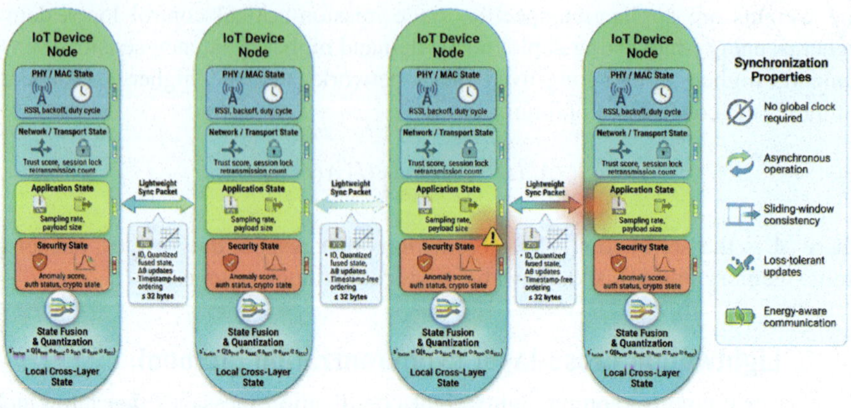

FIGURE 3.13

Cross-layer state synchronization between IoT devices using lightweight, asynchronous coordination.

clamped to a maximum permissible value to prevent starvation,

$$B_i(t) = \min(B_i(t), B_{\max}).$$

This rule provides a lightweight, implementable coupling between IDS evidence and MAC behavior, requiring only integer arithmetic and bounded memory while producing a monotonic response that suppresses medium contention under elevated suspicion.

3.8.8 Cross-layer attack containment mechanism

Attack containment is triggered when anomaly scores exceed a critical threshold.

$$A_i(t) \geq \theta_{\text{critical}}.$$

Containment requires coordinated layer actions that reduce propagation while preserving network stability: the PHY layer reduces TX power to shrink the effective attack radius; the MAC layer suppresses duty cycle participation to isolate the node, the NET layer removes the node from the routing tables and prunes paths that rely on it; the TRANS layer terminates active sessions to prevent hijack continuation, the APP layer suspends non-essential tasks to reduce exposure and conserve energy, and the SEC layer initiates re-authentication of neighbors and key refresh to limit lateral movement. The containment mechanism is cross-layer by construction, since a single-layer response typically leaves alternative propagation paths unaddressed, particularly in mesh topologies, where routing and contention patterns can amplify compromise.

3.8.9 Table: cross-layer reaction sequences

Cross-layer coupling becomes operationally meaningful when triggers map to ordered reaction cascades that are consistent, bounded, and implementable. Table 3.9 provides examples of such cascades, illustrating how a high anomaly trigger can activate a SEC→MAC response sequence, how key compromise can activate a SEC→TRANS→NET cascade that terminates sessions and reroutes traffic while rekeying, how congestion can propagate MAC→PHY→NET adjustments that reshape contention and modulation behavior, and how routing attacks can trigger NET→SEC actions that intensify IDS and prune paths. These sequences serve as practical templates for policy encoding inside π_{harm} and reduce ambiguity by specifying both the initiating layer and the downstream control targets.

Table 3.9 Examples of cross-layer cascade responses.

Trigger	Layer Activated	Reaction Sequence
High anomaly	SEC → MAC	Rate limiting, retransmission suppression
Key compromise	SEC → TRANS → NET	Session termination, rerouting, rekeying
Severe congestion	MAC → PHY → NET	TX power modulation, backoff reshaping
Routing attack	NET → SEC	Path pruning, trust-weighted IDS intensification

3.8.10 Cross-layer RL policy

A cross-layer DRL agent can be used to learn adaptive harmonization policies under non-stationary attack dynamics and time-varying energy states. The agent observes the fused quantized state

$$z(t) = s'_{\text{fusion}}(t)$$

and outputs a cross-layer action vector

$$a(t) = \pi_{\text{CL}}(z(t)),$$

where the action components correspond to bounded parameter updates across layers,

$$a(t) = \{\Delta\theta_{\text{PHY}}, \Delta\theta_{\text{MAC}}, \Delta\theta_{\text{NET}}, \Delta\theta_{\text{TRANS}}, \Delta\theta_{\text{APP}}, \Delta\theta_{\text{SEC}}\}.$$

The reward function must balance mitigation effectiveness with the costs of energy and network performance.

$$R(t) = \alpha \cdot \text{attack\_mitigation}(t) - \beta \cdot \text{energy}(t) - \gamma \cdot \text{collisions}(t) + \lambda \cdot \text{QoS}(t),$$

so that the learned policy prefers actions that contain attacks while preserving longevity, medium access efficiency, and service quality. In constrained deployments, the learned policy can be distilled into rule tables and low-dimensional function approximators suitable for gateway execution, while devices consume only compact

$\Delta\theta$ updates, ensuring the harmonization framework remains feasible across heterogeneous IoT classes.

3.9 Unified integration model, cross-layer synthesis, and final chapter conclusions

The preceding discussion, ranging from lightweight cryptographic foundations and authentication and key-management mechanisms to TinyML-based intrusion detection models, stack-level integration, multi-agent deployment architectures, energy-aware coordination, and cross-layer harmonization have collectively established a comprehensive and multi-layered framework for AI-driven, lightweight, and reinforcement-learning-based intrusion detection in IoT systems. Building on these components, this work synthesizes the individual elements into a unified conceptual, architectural, and mathematical representation that captures the complete lifecycle of intelligent IoT security, while also providing a forward-looking foundation for energy-centric and sustainability-oriented security frameworks. Modern IoT systems operate at the intersection of severe hardware constraints, heterogeneous communication standards, ultra-low-power execution, and continuously evolving attack surfaces. As demonstrated throughout this work, classical intrusion detection approaches based on static rules, signature matching, and manually engineered anomaly thresholds are fundamentally inadequate under such conditions. Effective IoT security instead requires the coordinated integration of lightweight cryptographic primitives, compact authentication and key-management protocols, micro-feature extraction pipelines, distributed lightweight intrusion detection models, deep learning inference at edge layers, and reinforcement-learning agents capable of self-adaptation under uncertainty and strict energy budgets. dgets.

3.9.1 Unified computational graph for IoT IDS

Building upon the lightweight detection models introduced in Section 3.4 and the multi-agent coordination mechanisms developed in Sections 3.6 and 3.7, the overall security system can be formalized as a stochastic computational graph

$$\mathcal{G} = (\mathcal{V}, \mathcal{E}, \Theta),$$

where each node $v \in \mathcal{V}$ corresponds to a functional block such as micro-feature extraction, lightweight cryptographic processing, anomaly scoring, policy evaluation, and mitigation selection, edges $e \in \mathcal{E}$ represent data-flow transitions across the IoT–edge–cloud hierarchy, and parameters Θ include model weights, decision thresholds, DRL policy parameters and energy-budget constraints.

Each IoT device i generates a data stream

$$X_i(t) = \{x_{i,1}, x_{i,2}, \ldots, x_{i,T}\},$$

which is processed locally using the lightweight mechanisms described in Sections 3.2, 3.3, and 3.4. This local processing produces an anomaly score

$$A_i(t) = f_\theta(X_i(t)),$$

where f_θ may represent a statistical detector, a TinyML classifier, a hybrid model, and a DRL-adjusted threshold selector as developed in Sections 3.4 and 3.5. These scores propagate upward through the multi-agent hierarchy defined in Section 3.6, enabling gateway and cloud components to reason over aggregated security states. At the orchestration level, introduced in Sections 3.7 and 3.8, the objective is to minimize a long-term expected risk functional

$$J(\pi) = \mathbb{E}\left[\sum_{t=0}^{\infty} \gamma^t \left(\lambda_1 C_{\text{inf}}(t) + \lambda_2 E_{\text{use}}(t) + \lambda_3 R_{\text{miss}}(t) - \lambda_4 D_{\text{det}}(t)\right)\right],$$

where $C_{\text{inf}}(t)$ represents computational cost arising from inference execution and model switching, $E_{\text{use}}(t)$ captures communication and computation energy expenditure as quantified in Section 3.7, $R_{\text{miss}}(t)$ models the cost of missed detections, and $D_{\text{det}}(t)$ denotes detection utility. This formulation unifies the goals of security fidelity, energy efficiency, and adaptive response that motivated the design choices throughout Chapter 3.

3.9.2 Cross-layer integrated IoT security architecture

Extending the cross-layer harmonization framework introduced in Section 3.8, the unified IDS architecture spans device, network, edge, and cloud layers and is formally represented as

$$\mathcal{L} = \{\mathcal{L}_{\text{dev}}, \mathcal{L}_{\text{net}}, \mathcal{L}_{\text{edge}}, \mathcal{L}_{\text{cloud}}\}.$$

This layered decomposition reflects a deliberate escalation of computational intelligence aligned with available resources, while preserving continuous security coverage across the entire IoT stack. As illustrated in Fig. 3.14, the architecture implements a vertically integrated security pipeline in which detection, aggregation, and control responsibilities are distributed across layers based on hardware capabilities, latency tolerance, and energy availability. At the device layer $\mathcal{L}_{\text{dev}}$, ultra-constrained IoT nodes always perform always-on micro-feature extraction, lightweight cryptographic protection, statistical anomaly detection, and TinyML inference using integer-only operations, consistent with the lightweight cryptographic and IDS constraints detailed in Sections 3.2 and 3.4. These nodes generate compressed anomaly indicators and protocol-level metadata rather than raw traffic, minimizing memory usage and radio transmission cost.

The network and MAC layer $\mathcal{L}_{\text{net}}$ acts as an intermediate security-aware substrate that enforces micro-protocol protection, secure routing, MAC backoff adaptation, and anomaly hint propagation, as developed in Section 3.5. This layer transforms low-level communication behavior into security-relevant context, enabling early detection

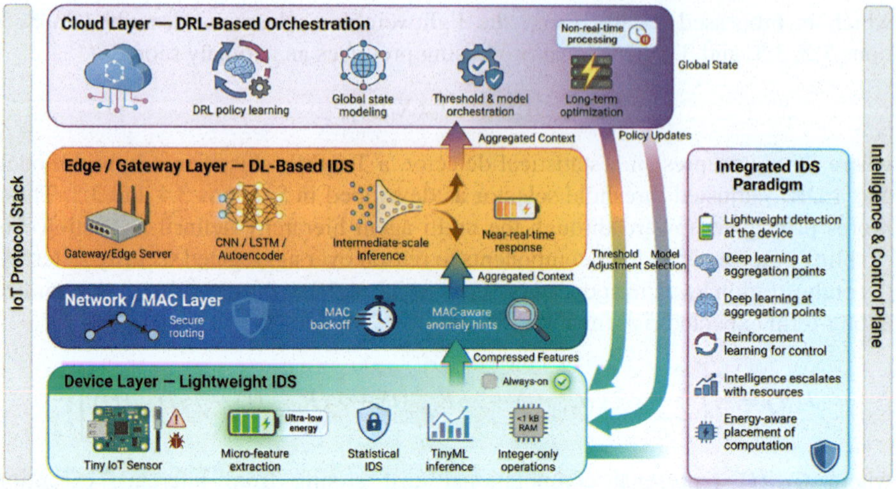

FIGURE 3.14

Unified cross-layer IDS architecture for IoT systems.

of volumetric, timing, and routing-based attacks without introducing heavyweight processing. At the edge and gateway layer $\mathcal{L}_{\text{edge}}$, aggregated contextual information from multiple devices is processed using more expressive deep learning models, including CNN-, LSTM-, and autoencoder-based IDS components. These models enable intermediate-scale inference and near-real-time response under moderate computational budgets, while coordinating multiple lightweight agents as formalized in Section 3.6. In addition, this layer hosts energy-aware decision logic that adapts inference frequency, reporting behavior, and mitigation actions based on cluster-level energy states, in accordance with the coordination mechanisms described in Section 3.7. Additionally, the cloud layer $\mathcal{L}_{\text{cloud}}$ provides global intelligence and long-term optimization. As shown in Fig. 3.14, this layer executes DRL–based orchestration, global state modeling, federated training, and policy synthesis across the entire IoT system. Rather than participating in time-critical detection loops, the cloud layer generates adaptive thresholds, model updates, and coordination policies that propagate downward to edge, network, and device layers, enabling continuous adaptation without violating latency andenergy constraints. Together, the bidirectional flow depicted in Fig. 3.14, where contextual information is aggregated upward while control and policy decisions propagate downward, constitutes the architectural embodiment of the unified IDS model developed throughout Chapter 3. This cross-layer integration ensures that detection complexity scales with available resources, energy consumption remains bounded, and security intelligence remains coherent across heterogeneous IoT systems.

3.9.3 Integrated lightweight–DL–DRL detection pipeline

Synthesizing the detection pipeline components introduced throughout Sections 3.4 through 3.7, the end-to-end IDS can be expressed as

$$\mathcal{P} = \mathcal{P}_{\text{feat}} \circ \mathcal{P}_{\text{light}} \circ \mathcal{P}_{\text{DL}} \circ \mathcal{P}_{\text{DRL}},$$

where $\mathcal{P}_{\text{feat}}$ denotes micro-feature extraction, $\mathcal{P}_{\text{light}}$ corresponds to lightweight statistical filtering, $\mathcal{P}_{\text{DL}}$ represents deeper latent analysis performed at gateways andedges, and $\mathcal{P}_{\text{DRL}}$ encapsulates policy-based mitigation and adaptation mechanisms.

CHAPTER

Energy-efficient IoT networks

4

4.1 Introduction

Energy efficiency is a foundational requirement for the design, deployment, and sustainable operation of IoT networks. In contrast to conventional computing infrastructures powered by stable electrical grids, IoT networks operate under severe, heterogeneous energy constraints. Devices frequently rely on coin-cell batteries, micro-energy harvesters, intermittent RF power delivery systems, together with extremely small rechargeable storage elements. In many deployment scenarios, such as environmental sensing, structural health monitoring, industrial telemetry, agricultural monitoring, and remote infrastructure supervision, battery replacement becomes logistically complex and economically costly. Under these constraints, every computational instruction, radio transmission, cryptographic primitive, IDS inference cycle, routing decision, and adaptive mitigation action consumes measurable energy. Even minor inefficiencies accumulate over time and translate into significant reductions in operational lifetime.

Previous chapters established lightweight security primitives, micro-IDS pipelines, together with adaptive DRL-driven detection strategies. The present section frames the constrained energy environment in which those mechanisms must operate. Energy-aware security in IoT is not merely an optimization layered on a fixed protocol stack; rather, it is a structural design principle. Communication, computation, storage, and detection must be co-designed under explicit energy constraints. This section formalizes foundational models, architectural principles, protocol behaviors, and cross-layer mechanisms that govern energy consumption across IoT communication stacks. The objective is to establish a unified analytical framework that later DRL-guided optimizers can exploit to balance sustainability and security performance.

4.1.1 Fundamental energy model for IoT devices

For an IoT device executing sensing, communication, and IDS-related tasks, the total energy consumption across an observation window T is expressed as

$$E_{\text{tot}}(T) = \int_0^T \Big(P_{\text{cpu}}(t) + P_{\text{radio}}(t) + P_{\text{mem}}(t) + P_{\text{sec}}(t)\Big)dt.$$

Green Intrusion Detection Systems for IoT. https://doi.org/10.1016/B978-0-44-344249-0.00011-9

This decomposition separates the dominant contributors to device-level energy expenditure. The computational term $P_{cpu}(t)$ captures energy consumed during sampling, feature extraction, IDS inference, DRL reasoning, routing computation, and protocol stack processing. The radio component $P_{radio}(t)$ reflects transmission, reception, idle listening, channel sensing, and contention backoff. The memory term $P_{mem}(t)$ accounts for volatile memory access, non-volatile writes, checkpoint updates, buffering operations, and state preservation. The security term $P_{sec}(t)$ includes cryptographic primitives, hashing, authentication exchanges, key derivation, secure channel establishment, and periodic rekeying.

Empirical measurements on low-power wireless platforms consistently show that radio operations account for the majority of total consumption in typical IoT networks. Transmission energy scales with distance and retransmissions, reception energy scales with network activity, and idle listening accumulates during poorly synchronized communication cycles. Consequently, energy-aware protocol design prioritizes minimizing

$$E_{radio} = E_{tx} + E_{rx} + E_{listen},$$

since idle listening frequently exceeds active transmission energy in dense networks. Effective energy control, therefore, requires precise radio scheduling rather than purely computational optimization.

4.1.2 Communication-centric energy optimization

Because communication dominates energy cost in wireless IoT networks, optimization must begin at the MAC and routing layers. Reducing algorithmic complexity alone yields limited lifetime extension if radio scheduling remains inefficient. Duty-cycling reduces radio activity by periodically disabling transceivers and activating them only during scheduled communication windows. The active ratio is defined as

$$\text{Active Ratio} = \frac{T_{awake}}{T_{cycle}},$$

with Active Ratio $\ll 1$ in optimized deployments. Lower active ratios directly reduce idle listening energy and contention overhead. However, aggressive duty cycling introduces trade-offs in latency, synchronization overhead, packet delivery reliability, and IDS visibility since fewer samples are collected during reduced awake intervals. Mechanisms such as low-power listening, TDMA scheduling, wake-up receivers, and adaptive beacon alignment synchronize communication windows with predicted traffic patterns, thereby transforming idle listening from a continuous drain into a structured activity. Routing decisions must simultaneously balance hop count, residual energy distribution, and link stability. Selecting the shortest paths without accounting for energy heterogeneity can lead to premature depletion of central nodes, e.g., cluster heads and gateways. A generalized routing cost metric is expressed as

$$C_{ij} = \alpha d_{ij} + \beta \frac{1}{E_j^{\mathrm{res}}} + \gamma \rho_{ij},$$

where d_{ij} represents path loss together with required transmission power between nodes i and j, E_j^{res} denotes residual energy at node j, and ρ_{ij} captures link quality together with congestion state. This formulation discourages the overuse of energy-depleted nodes and redistributes traffic toward nodes with healthier reserves and stable connectivity, thereby extending the overall network lifetime and preventing localized energy collapse.

4.1.3 Energy harvesting and sustainability-oriented operation

Energy harvesting transforms IoT nodes from static battery-limited devices into stochastic energy systems whose operational capacity fluctuates over time. Harvested energy is modeled as

$$E_{\mathrm{harvest}}(t) = \eta \cdot I_{\mathrm{source}}(t),$$

where η denotes conversion efficiency and $I_{\mathrm{source}}(t)$ represents environmental energy input, such as solar intensity, thermal gradient, kinetic vibration, together with ambient RF power density. The storage buffer evolves according to

$$B(t+1) = \min\Big(B_{\max}, B(t) - E_{\mathrm{use}}(t) + E_{\mathrm{harvest}}(t)\Big),$$

where $E_{\mathrm{use}}(t)$ aggregates computation, communication, sensing, and IDS costs. Sustainable operation requires that buffer dynamics remain bounded under stochastic harvesting conditions. A persistent deficit results in energy collapse, whereas a persistent surplus is constrained by storage capacity and leakage effects. Energy neutrality is achieved when

$$\mathbb{E}[E_{\mathrm{harvest}}] \geq \mathbb{E}[E_{\mathrm{use}}],$$

which guarantees an operationally unbounded lifetime. IDS mechanisms and DRL-based control policies must therefore operate within this constraint, dynamically adapting complexity and communication frequency according to instantaneous harvesting conditions and expected inflow.

4.1.4 Trade-off between security and energy

Security mechanisms introduce measurable computational and communication overhead. Cryptographic primitives increase $P_{\mathrm{cpu}}(t)$ together with memory access, while authentication exchanges increase $P_{\mathrm{radio}}(t)$ through additional message transmission. IDS inference adds costs for feature extraction, model execution, and alert communication. The feasibility constraint becomes

$$E_{\text{sec}} + E_{\text{comm}} + E_{\text{ids}} \leq E_{\text{budget}},$$

where E_{budget} denotes allowable energy expenditure within a scheduling interval. Violation of this constraint accelerates depletion and reduces device lifetime. This inequality forms the analytical foundation for adaptive DRL-driven balancing between security aggressiveness and energy sustainability.

4.1.5 Cross-layer energy modeling

Energy efficiency emerges from coordinated optimization across protocol layers rather than isolated parameter tuning. The global objective can be expressed as

$$\min_{\Pi} \left(E_{\text{phy}} + E_{\text{mac}} + E_{\text{net}} + E_{\text{sec}} + E_{\text{ids}}\right),$$

where Π represents the joint policy space spanning transmission power selection, modulation configuration, duty cycle adaptation, routing weight assignment, cryptographic scaling, and IDS threshold configuration. Cross-layer integration ensures that improvements at one layer do not inadvertently increase cost at another. For example, reducing transmission power lowers instantaneous energy consumption but may increase retransmissions, thereby increasing cumulative cost. Similarly, lowering IDS thresholds increases detection sensitivity but amplifies alert traffic, increasing radio expenditure, only coordinated control yields globally optimal behavior.

4.1.6 Energy-constrained IDS operation

In many IoT networks,

$$E_{\text{IDS}}^{\max} \ll E_{\text{comm}},$$

which implies that local inference is energetically preferable to frequent telemetry transmission. Communication is triggered only when anomaly confidence exceeds the threshold τ:

$$\text{Transmit alert} \iff A(x) > \tau.$$

The anomaly threshold τ becomes a tunable parameter within the cross-layer DRL optimization. Increasing τ reduces communication frequency and conserves energy at the potential cost of delayed detection. Decreasing τ improves sensitivity but increases radio overhead. The optimal threshold balances detection accuracy, false positive rate, and long-term sustainability within the available energy budget.

The conceptual architecture that operationalizes the previously introduced energy models and cross-layer optimization principles is illustrated in Fig. 4.1. The architecture is hierarchical, separating computation, aggregation, learning, and orchestration across four categories to align energy availability with computational intensity. At the IoT device layer, constrained nodes execute lightweight statistical

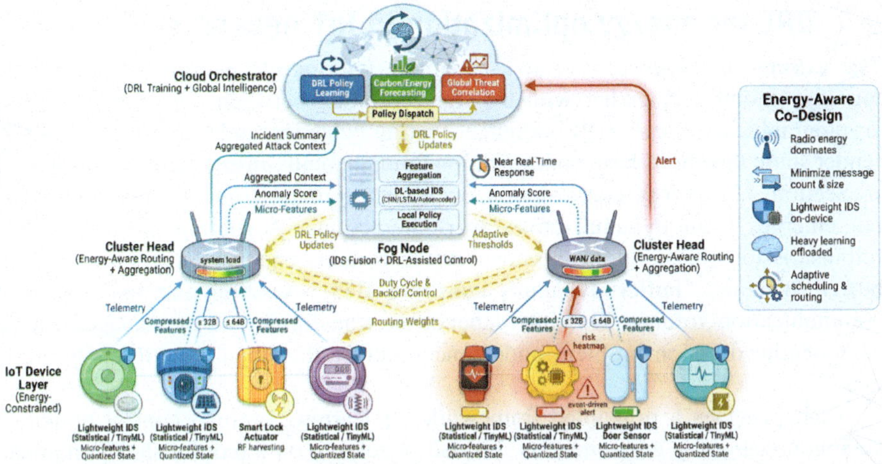

FIGURE 4.1

Multi-category energy-aware IoT security architecture with hierarchical IDS and DRL-assisted cross-layer control.

and TinyML-based IDS. Instead of transmitting raw traffic and high-dimensional features, devices generate quantized micro-features and anomaly scores. These compressed representations significantly reduce radio-on time and limit uplink energy consumption, which is critical since radio operations dominate device-level energy expenditure. Cluster heads act as intermediate aggregation points. They collect telemetry and anomaly indicators from multiple devices, perform local context fusion, and enforce energy-aware routing decisions. By compressing and summarizing information before forwarding it upward, cluster heads prevent unnecessary multi-hop traffic and reduce the probability of energy hotspots forming around frequently used relays. Fog nodes implement IDS fusion together with DRL-assisted cross-layer control. In this category, anomaly scores are correlated, adaptive thresholds are computed, and duty-cycle, backoff, and routing weights are dynamically updated. Because fog nodes have greater computational capacity than leaf devices; they can run deeper models while remaining closer to the edge than cloud backends, enabling near-real-time responses. The cloud orchestrator performs long-term DRL policy learning, carbon and energy forecasting, and global threat correlation across clusters. It periodically dispatches optimized policies downward, ensuring that device-level decisions remain aligned with global sustainability and security objectives. This hierarchical separation of micro-inference at devices, aggregation at cluster heads, adaptive control at fog nodes, and strategic learning at the cloud ensures that energy efficiency and security are co-designed rather than independently optimized.

4.2 DRL for energy optimization in IoT networks

The extreme heterogeneity of IoT networks, intermittent energy availability, and topology mobility, together with the tight coupling between communication cost, cryptographic overhead, IDS inference, routing behavior, and harvesting variability, render static threshold-based optimization fundamentally insufficient. As established in Section 4.1, energy consumption does not originate from isolated subsystems but emerges from dynamic cross-layer interactions. A routing change modifies retransmission rates; retransmissions increase radio energy; radio energy affects buffer dynamics; buffer dynamics constrain IDS activation and its impacts on communication volume. This interdependence transforms energy management into a sequential decision problem under uncertainty rather than a static configuration task.

DRL provides a principled framework for learning optimal control policies in such non-stationary environments. Instead of relying on fixed thresholds, manually tuned parameters and heuristic control loops, a DRL agent continuously observes network state variables, interacts with the environment, evaluates reward signals that encode sustainability and security objectives, and iteratively refines its policy through gradient-based updates. Energy optimization, therefore, becomes a closed-loop learning process capable of adapting to fluctuations in harvesting rate, traffic intensity, wireless channel quality, congestion state, and adversarial activity. In this context, the IoT network is treated as a dynamic environment in which actions have both immediate energy consequences and delayed sustainability implications. This section formalizes DRL-driven energy optimization using the MDP formulation and integrates routing control, duty-cycle scheduling, and offloading decisions, and IDS adaptation into a unified learning architecture.

4.2.1 Formulating energy optimization as the MDP

The IoT network is modeled as the MDP defined by the tuple

$$\mathcal{M} = (\mathcal{S}, \mathcal{A}, \mathcal{P}, R, \gamma),$$

where $\mathcal{S}$ denotes the state space, $\mathcal{A}$ the action space, $\mathcal{P}$ the stochastic transition kernel, R the reward function, and $\gamma \in (0, 1)$ the temporal discount factor. In contrast to deterministic control problems, the transition dynamics $\mathcal{P}$ are impacted by stochastic harvesting processes, wireless fading, traffic bursts, interference patterns, and adversarial disturbances. Exact modeling of $\mathcal{P}$ becomes impractical at scale; therefore, model-free DRL methods are adopted to learn policies directly from interactions. For device i at time t, the state representation is defined as

$$s_i(t) = [E_i(t), H_i(t), \lambda_i(t), L_i(t), A_i(t), \theta_i(t), \omega_i(t)],$$

where $E_i(t)$ denotes residual energy, $H_i(t)$ represents harvested energy together with forecast information, $\lambda_i(t)$ captures traffic load, $L_i(t)$ measures link quality metrics such as RSSI and packet error rate, $A_i(t)$ denotes IDS anomaly score, $\theta_i(t)$ represents duty-cycle configuration, and $\omega_i(t)$ describes routing role such as parent selection together with the cluster-head state. This compact state representation embeds energy status, communication conditions, and security context into a unified vector, enabling cross-layer optimization within a single learning framework. The action space includes energy-sensitive cross-layer controls expressed as

$$a_i(t) \in \{\text{TX power, sleep/wake, parent selection, channel selection,}\\ \text{IDS threshold, offload/local compute}\}.$$

Each action impacts immediate energy expenditure through transmission power and active time, while simultaneously shaping long-term stability through routing balance, congestion distribution, and detection fidelity. Consequently, the learning agent must evaluate both short-term cost and future sustainability when selecting actions.

4.2.2 Reward function design

The reward function encodes energy neutrality, latency guarantees, harvesting alignment, and detection quality into a unified objective. A composite reward is defined as

$$R(t) = \alpha R_{\text{energy}}(t) + \beta R_{\text{latency}}(t) + \chi R_{\text{security}}(t) + \delta R_{\text{harvest}}(t) + \zeta R_{\text{load}}(t),$$

where weighting coefficients regulate the trade-off between competing objectives. The energy component penalizes consumption relative to maximum capacity:

$$R_{\text{energy}}(t) = -\frac{E_{\text{use}}(t)}{E_{\max}},$$

encouraging minimal expenditure and discouraging unnecessary communication bursts. Latency deviation is captured through

$$R_{\text{latency}}(t) = -\big(D(t) - D_{\text{target}}\big)^{+},$$

ensuring quality-of-service constraints remain satisfied. Security performance is incorporated via

$$R_{\text{security}}(t) = \begin{cases} +\kappa, & A(t) \le \tau \text{ and benign,} \\ -\kappa, & A(t) > \tau \text{ and benign,} \\ +\kappa', & A(t) > \tau \text{ and attack.} \end{cases}$$

This formulation rewards correct anomaly discrimination while penalizing false alarms that unnecessarily trigger radio communication. Harvesting-aware incentives are introduced through

$$R_{\text{harvest}}(t) = \eta \frac{E_{\text{harvest}}(t)}{E_{\max}},$$

which aligns policy decisions with renewable availability, encouraging energy-intensive actions during favorable harvesting intervals. The combined structure of the reward enforces sustainability while maintaining security vigilance and performance guarantees.

4.2.3 Distributed and multi-agent DRL

Energy optimization in IoT networks is inherently multi-agent since each node maintains local constraints and impacts neighboring nodes through routing load and interference. The global network can be expressed as $\mathcal{M}_{\text{global}} = \bigcup_{i=1}^{N} \mathcal{M}_i$, where each device contributes to collective energy dynamics. A scalable implementation uses a decentralized actor alongside a centralized critic. In this architecture, fog nodes estimate a joint value function $Q_{\text{global}}(\mathbf{s}, \mathbf{a})$, while devices execute local policies $a_i(t) = \pi_i(s_i(t); \theta_i)$. This structure preserves scalability in large deployments while enabling coordination through shared value estimation.

4.2.4 Cross-layer DRL control mechanisms

Within this framework, duty-cycle adaptation is learned as

$$\theta_i(t+1) = f_\pi(s_i(t)),$$

reducing idle listening while preserving connectivity. Energy-aware routing is implemented via learned next-hop selection $a_i(t) = \text{select\_next\_hop}(s_i(t))$, balancing residual energy distribution and congestion mitigation. Computation offloading decisions compare long-term value estimates Q_{local} and Q_{fog} to determine whether inference should be executed locally and migrated to the fog infrastructure, taking into account radio costs and computational energy.

The unified DRL-based cross-layer control architecture defines a closed-loop learning pipeline in which IoT networks continuously generate state variables including residual energy, harvesting rate, link quality, traffic load, and IDS metrics. These variables feed into the DRL agent, which outputs cross-layer control actions affecting transmission power, MAC duty cycle, routing configuration, IDS threshold, and offloading policy. The environment then returns a composite reward that encodes energy consumption, latency deviation, harvesting balance, and detection accuracy. Through repeated interactions, policy parameters are updated until convergence toward an energy-neutral, security-aware operating point. This architecture visually emphasizes the feedback loop between the environment, the agent, and the reward signal, highlighting the iterative adaptation process that distinguishes DRL from static control schemes. Fig. 4.2 presents this unified DRL-based cross-layer control architecture.

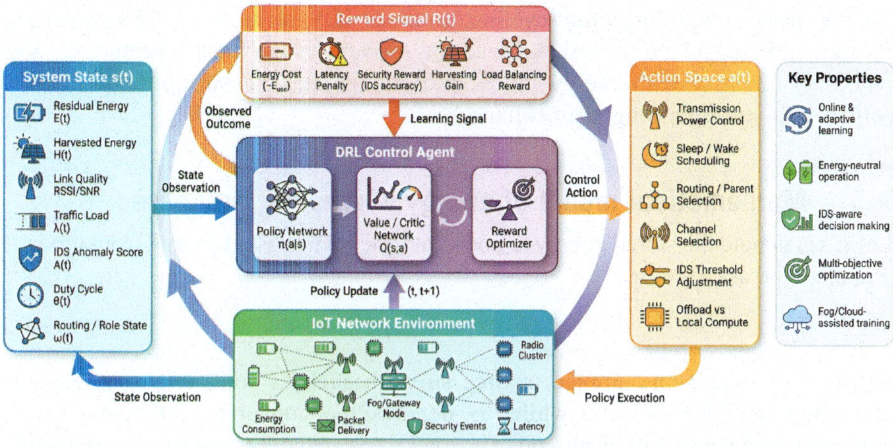

FIGURE 4.2

Unified DRL-based cross-layer energy optimization framework integrating energy state, harvesting forecasts, routing control, and IDS adaptation within a closed-loop learning architecture.

4.2.5 Integration with lightweight IDS

Integration with lightweight IDS mechanisms ensures that detection behavior remains energy-aligned. The DRL agent dynamically adjusts the DS threshold via

$$\tau(t+1) = \tau(t) + \Delta_\pi(s_i(t)),$$

and selects the operational mode based on the energy state. During scarcity, statistical detection with minimal feature extraction is preferred. During abundance, more expressive inference, together with optional retraining, can be activated. This adaptive mechanism ensures long-term sustainability while preserving responsiveness to anomalous activity.

4.3 Energy harvesting models and sustainable utilization strategies

Energy harvesting (EH) enables IoT devices to replenish operational energy from ambient sources, including solar radiation, radio-frequency (RF) waves, thermal gradients, vibration, fluid motion, inductive coupling, and biochemical reactions. In contrast to battery-powered systems that operate on finite stored reserves, harvesting-enabled IoT nodes exhibit dynamic, intermittent energy profiles that are often difficult to predict with high confidence. The feasibility of continuous operation, therefore, depends less on a static capacity assumption and more on the arrival rate, temporal variance, burstiness, and predictability of harvested energy. This shift fundamentally changes how scheduling, duty-cycling, routing, IDS activation, and computation prioritization must be designed. A harvesting-driven system must continuously align workload intensity with energy inflow and storage state, ensuring that short-term actions do not trigger long-term collapse.

4.3.1 Mathematical model of energy harvesting processes

Let $E_i(t)$ denote the stored energy at node i at time t. Harvested energy from modality j is modeled as

$$H_{i,j}(t) = \eta_j S_j(t),$$

where $S_j(t)$ represents ambient source strength such as solar intensity, vibration amplitude, and RF density, while η_j denotes the conversion efficiency of the corresponding harvesting front-end. The total harvested energy across N_h modalities is

$$H_i(t) = \sum_{j=1}^{N_h} H_{i,j}(t).$$

Energy storage dynamics are described by

$$E_i(t+1) = \min\Big(E_{\max},\ E_i(t) - E_{\text{use}}(t) + H_i(t)\Big),$$

where $E_{\max}$ is the storage capacity and $E_{\text{use}}(t)$ represents the total energy consumed by device operation during the interval. In harvesting-enabled IoT, $E_{\text{use}}(t)$ is naturally decomposed into radio, computation, IDS, and sleep components as

$$E_{\text{use}}(t) = E_{\text{TX}} + E_{\text{RX}} + E_{\text{listen}} + E_{\text{IDS}} + E_{\text{comp}} + E_{\text{sleep}}.$$

This model highlights a key systems coupling: harvesting variability affects the feasible duty cycle; the duty cycle affects radio-on time; radio-on time affects both communication overhead and IDS observability; and IDS observability impacts alerting behavior, which further increases radio expenditure. The resulting feedback loops motivate harvesting-aware control policies that jointly regulate communication and detection behavior. Long-term sustainable operation requires that the average harvested energy is not dominated by the average expenditure. A necessary energy-neutral condition is

$$\mathbb{E}[H_i(t)] \geq \mathbb{E}[E_{\text{use}}(t)],$$

which ensures that storage does not drift toward depletion over a long time horizons. In practical deployments, this condition must be enforced while meeting minimum sensing, connectivity, and security monitoring requirements, which motivates adaptive workload shaping rather than a static, always-on approach.

4.3.2 Stochastic harvesting models

Harvested energy is inherently stochastic and frequently non-stationary due to environmental dynamics. A general abstraction models harvesting as

$$H_i(t) \sim \mathcal{D}(t; \Theta),$$

where $\mathcal{D}$ denotes a time-varying distribution parameterized by Θ that captures modality-specific dynamics, diurnal patterns, and context-driven burstiness. Different harvesting modalities exhibit distinct statistical structures that directly shape feasible networking behavior. Solar harvesting follows diurnal periodicity and is commonly approximated as

$$H_i(t) = H_{\max} \max\left(0, \sin(\omega t + \phi) + \epsilon_t\right),$$

where ϵ_t captures atmospheric variability and shading effects. RF harvesting depends on ambient transmission density and can be expressed as

$$H_i(t) = \alpha P_{\text{ambient}}(t) + \epsilon_t,$$

which produces bursty fluctuations driven by nearby transmitters, mobility, and traffic cycles. Vibration-based harvesting frequently reflects event-driven energy opportunities in industrial systems and transportation environments, making the Poisson-like structure a useful approximation:

$$H_i(t) \sim \text{Pois}(\lambda_h).$$

These stochastic models are not merely descriptive; they define the uncertainty that a harvesting-aware controller must learn to manage. High-variance harvesting encourages conservative baseline operation with opportunistic bursts, while predictable periodic harvesting supports scheduled, heavier workloads during known energy-rich windows.

4.3.3 Energy storage constraints and leakage effects

Practical storage components exhibit leakage, self-discharge, and inefficiencies in charge–discharge cycles. Let λ denote the leakage rate. Leakage loss during the interval can be represented as

$$E_{\text{leak}}(t) = \lambda E_i(t),$$

which yields the modified storage evolution

$$E_i(t+1) = \min\Big(E_{\max},\ E_i(t)(1-\lambda) + H_i(t) - E_{\text{use}}(t)\Big).$$

Leakage introduces a structural penalty for energy over-accumulation and motivates timely utilization when energy inflow is high. In harvesting-enabled IoT, it becomes suboptimal to keep devices in overly conservative low-duty-cycle operation during energy-improvement intervals, as stored energy may be lost through leakage. This observation supports workload-shaping strategies that opportunistically allocate heavier computation and enhance IDS models when harvesting peaks are detected and forecast.

4.3.4 Energy-adaptive duty cycling

Duty cycle $\theta_i(t) = \frac{T_{\text{awake}}}{T_{\text{total}}}$ must adapt to instantaneous harvesting conditions and storage state. A sustainability constraint can be expressed as

$$\theta_i(t) \leq \frac{H_i(t)}{E_{\text{awake}}},$$

which defines a harvesting-driven upper bound on activity, with E_{awake} denoting the energy expenditure during a fully active interval. When harvested energy falls below the consumption required for a given duty cycle, storage will drift downward and risk energy collapse. An adaptive update rule is expressed as

$$\theta_i(t+1) = \theta_i(t) + \alpha_h \left(\frac{H_i(t)}{E_{\text{use}}(t)} - 1 \right),$$

which expands activity during energy surplus and contracts activity during deficit periods. This update rule can be interpreted as a feedback controller that regulates the activity ratio around an energy-neutral operating point. When harvesting is persistently low, the controller gradually reduces awake time, which reduces idle listening and compute overhead. As harvesting increases, the controller relaxes constraints and enables greater observability, improved connectivity, and higher-fidelity detection.

4.3.5 Energy-aware IDS activation

IDS inference incurs an energy cost associated with feature extraction and model execution. A compact representation is

$$E_{\text{IDS}} = C_{\text{model}} + C_{\text{feature}}.$$

In energy-harvesting systems, IDS cannot be assumed to be always-on; instead, it must be treated as an energy-scheduled workload. A basic activation policy is governed by

$$\text{IDS}(t) = \begin{cases} \text{ON}, & E_i(t) > E_{\text{thr}}, \\ \text{OFF}, & E_i(t) \leq E_{\text{thr}}. \end{cases}$$

To avoid abrupt security collapse, multi-level IDS modes enable graceful degradation across energy states. A representative hierarchy includes Level 0 disabling detection,

Level 1 activating lightweight statistical monitoring, Level 2 enables compact ML inference, and Level 3 performs full anomaly analysis with fog offloading when feasible. Mode selection is captured by

$$\text{mode}(t) = \arg\max_{m} \big(R_m(t) - E_m(t)\big),$$

which balances security reward against energy expenditure. This formulation explicitly states that higher-fidelity detection must be justified by energy feasibility and expected security benefits, which naturally supports adaptive detection strategies aligned with available harvested energy.

4.3.6 DRL for harvest forecasting and control

Harvest forecasting improves scheduling decisions by reducing uncertainty about near-future feasibility. A learning-based predictor estimates

$$\hat{H}_i(t+1) = f_\pi(s_i(t)),$$

where the forecasting state can be represented as

$$s_i(t) = [H_i(t), H_i(t-1), H_i(t-2), \text{time-of-day}, \text{weather-state}, \ldots].$$

Accurate prediction improves duty-cycle stability, routing persistence, IDS activation timing and transmission scheduling. Forecasting transforms purely reactive control into proactive sustainability management. When the controller anticipates a near-future energy deficit, it can preemptively lower the duty cycle and defer non-critical tasks. When the controller anticipates an energy-rich window, it can opportunistically enable more intensive IDS operation and perform energy-intensive maintenance tasks, such as calibration and local model refresh.

4.3.7 Sustainable routing under harvest variability

Nodes with higher harvesting capacity should assume greater routing responsibility since they can replenish energy more effectively than energy-scarce nodes. A harvesting ratio is defined as

$$\rho_i(t) = \frac{H_i(t)}{\max_j H_j(t)}.$$

A routing weight can then be defined as

$$w_i(t) = \beta_1 \rho_i(t) + \beta_2 L_i(t) + \beta_3 Q_i(t),$$

where $L_i(t)$ denotes link quality and $Q_i(t)$ denotes queue length. Parent selection becomes proportional to $w_i(t)$, thereby shifting the forwarding load toward energy-rich nodes while maintaining link reliability and queue stability. This strategy prevents premature depletion of low-harvest nodes and reduces network partition risk under intermittent energy inflow.

4.3.8 Harvesting modalities and networking implications

Different harvesting sources impose distinct constraints on networking behavior and IDS operation due to differences in predictability, variance, and available power budget. Table 4.1 summarizes how these modality characteristics shape feasible communication patterns and detection strategies. Solar harvesting provides predictable windows of higher energy, enabling richer IDS inference during peak intervals. RF ambient harvesting yields low and unpredictable power, motivating ultra-lightweight detection and sparse communication. Vibration harvesting is bursty and context-dependent, making it well-suited to industrial systems in which monitoring intensity can increase when machinery is active. Thermal harvesting is slower changing and comparatively stable, supporting continuous low-power sensing and steady IDS schedules. Piezoelectric harvesting is event-triggered, making it compatible with event-driven structural monitoring and burst-based anomaly checks.

Table 4.1 Comparison of energy harvesting modalities and their implications for networking behavior and harvesting-aware IDS scheduling in IoT networks.

Harvesting Source	Characteristics	Impact on IoT Networking and IDS Operation
Solar	Predictable periodicity, moderate-to-high power density	enables scheduled higher duty cycle and richer IDS inference during energy-rich intervals
RF Ambient	Low power density, highly variable, environment dependent	Requires ultra-lightweight micro-IDS and sparse communication to prevent energy collapse
Vibration	Event-driven bursts, context-dependent availability	Supports opportunistic routing load and intensified monitoring near active machinery cycles
Thermal	Slow dynamics, comparatively stable harvesting profile	enables continuous low-rate sensing and stable IDS sampling under energy-neutral constraints
Piezoelectric	Trigger-based energy opportunities, intermittent bursts	Aligns with event-driven structural monitoring and burst-mode anomaly detection checks

4.3.9 Unified energy harvesting control pipeline

The harvesting-to-utilization pipeline provides a conceptual summary of the energy flow from ambient sources to actionable networking decisions. Stochastic energy inputs are first rectified and conditioned, then stored in constrained buffers subject to capacity and leakage effects. An energy manager continuously monitors the

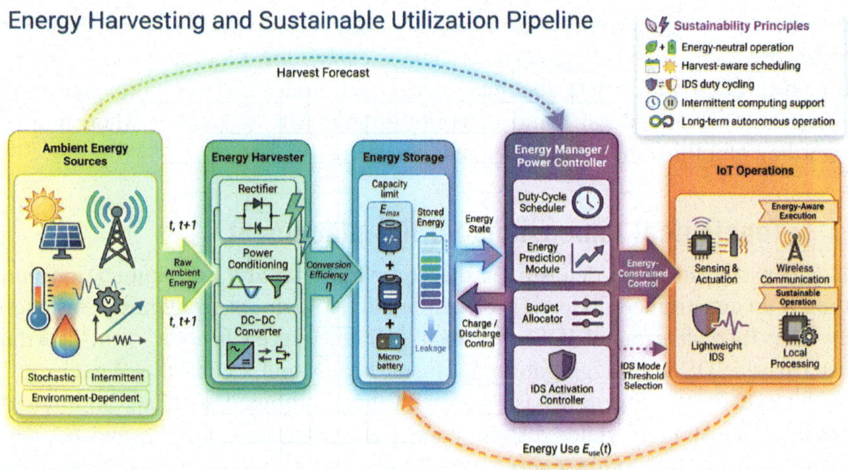

FIGURE 4.3

Harvesting-to-utilization pipeline for sustainable IoT operation, showing stochastic energy input, rectification, and storage dynamics, predictive energy management, and harvesting-aware allocation across communication, computation, and IDS workloads.

storage level, estimates near-term harvesting potential, and allocates energy budgets across sensing, communication, computation, and IDS subsystems. Harvesting-aware operation is fundamentally a closed-loop control process: harvested energy determines the feasible duty cycle, the duty cycle shapes radio activity, radio activity affects both connectivity and IDS observability, and IDS behavior feeds back into communication demand through alerting. By integrating harvesting forecasts into adaptive duty cycling and DRL-driven cross-layer policies, the pipeline supports energy-neutral, long-term autonomous operation despite intermittent supply, while preserving baseline security observability through graceful IDS mode selection. Fig. 4.3 illustrates this harvesting-to-utilization pipeline.

4.4 Wired and wireless IDS topologies in energy-constrained IoT networks

The design of IDS topologies in IoT networks is fundamentally shaped by the underlying communication medium. Wired and wireless infrastructures impose different constraints on physical-layer energy consumption, latency determinism, packet reliability, bandwidth stability, and achievable detection coverage. While traditional enterprise systems rely on predictable Ethernet backbones, IoT networks predominantly operate over wireless technologies such as LoRaWAN, BLE, Zigbee, 6LoWPAN, Wi-SUN, NB-IoT, and WiFi HaLow, each characterized by distinct transmission power profiles, modulation schemes, topology patterns, and link asymmetries. As a result, energy efficiency cannot be separated from topology; the path through which IDS features, alerts, and model updates propagate directly to determine device lifetime and detection granularity, especially when multi-hop forwarding amplifies the cumulative radio burden.

4.4.1 Topological dimensions for IDS placement

IDS processing location determines the computational and communication burden imposed on constrained nodes. Three canonical deployment strategies dominate IoT networks: fully distributed IDS with local inference at each node, semi-distributed cluster-based IDS with aggregation at cluster heads, and a centralized gateway IDS with feature forwarding to a base station. When combined with a communication modality, each strategy yields distinct energy characteristics. Let E_{tx} and E_{rx} denote transmission and reception energy per frame, and let E_{comp} denote computation cost for feature extraction and inference. In wired environments, $E_{\text{tx}} \ll E_{\text{comp}}$ because transmission does not activate high-power RF circuitry, while in wireless IoT networks, $E_{\text{tx}} \gg E_{\text{comp}}$, making radio operations the dominant contributor to total energy expenditure. This inequality dictates that wireless IDS designs must prioritize communication minimization, whereas wired systems can tolerate higher traffic volumes without destabilizing energy budgets.

4.4.2 Wired IDS topologies: properties and energy behavior

Although less common in battery-powered IoT, wired infrastructure remains prevalent in industrial automation, PLC networks, e.g., Modbus and PROFINET[1], smart manufacturing robotics, power-grid monitoring, automotive CAN, and Ethernet systems and building automation frameworks. Wired IDS deployments exhibit extremely high reliability with near-zero packet loss, negligible per-frame transmission energy compared to RF systems, and deterministic latency due to scheduled access mechanisms. Empirically, transmission energy in wired systems may be approximated as $E_{\text{tx}}^{wired} \approx 10^{-3} E_{\text{tx}}^{wireless}$, enabling frequent monitoring and large feature vector propagation without threatening device longevity. Consequently, wired IDS architectures can support high-frequency sampling, improved anomaly features, and inline enforcement without destabilizing node energy budgets.

Wired deployment models include inline IDS switches integrated at wire-speed routers, passive wire-tap IDS systems that mirror traffic to monitoring engines without latency impact, and dual-homed industrial endpoints performing local detection while forwarding summaries via wired backbones. These architectures provide deterministic control and stable bandwidth conditions, making them suitable

[1] PROFINET, or Process Field Network, is an industrial Ethernet protocol used for real-time communication between controllers, sensors, actuators, and field devices in automation systems.

for safety-critical industrial control systems, where predictability and coverage are primary requirements.

4.4.3 Wireless IDS topologies: energy dominance of radio operations

Wireless IoT networks dominate large-scale deployments due to flexibility and low installation cost; however, IDS placement in wireless environments is significantly more constrained. Link variability, asymmetric uplink and downlink power, multi-hop forwarding overhead, interference, and fading amplify energy consumption. Typical wireless transmission energy ranges between 30–80 μJ per frame, whereas lightweight IDS computation may require only 0.03–0.2 μJ, yielding $E_{\text{tx}}^{wireless} \gg E_{\text{comp}}$. Therefore, communication becomes the dominant design variable, and the feasibility of enhancing IDS operation is bounded by radio scheduling and the depth of the topology rather than local inference cost. Wireless IDS topologies include single-hop gateway aggregation, multi-hop mesh forwarding to cluster heads, cooperative distributed detection in which nodes exchange partial anomaly indicators, and hierarchical categoryed architectures combining leaf nodes, cluster heads, and gateways. In multi-hop systems, the total IDS communication energy follows

$$E_{\text{total}} = E_{\text{comp}} + H(E_{\text{tx}} + E_{\text{rx}}),$$

where H denotes hop count. Energy, therefore, scales proportionally with path length, directly linking the depth of the topology to battery depletion risk and making route selection, aggregation design, and reporting compression central to sustainability.

Fig. 4.4 illustrates the structural contrast between wired and wireless IDS deployment environments. The diagram emphasizes that wired infrastructures operate over stable, low-loss backbones with deterministic latency and insignificant incremental transmission energy relative to computation. As a result, wired IDS designs can support high-frequency sampling, full-flow monitoring, inline inspection, and passive mirroring without materially affecting device lifetime and network sustainability.

In contrast, wireless IoT networks are constrained by hop-dependent radio energy expenditure, variable link quality, contention, and retransmission overhead. In multi-hop topologies, each additional relay increases the cumulative transmission and reception costs, directly linking the IDS feature propagation to the risk of battery depletion. The figure highlights that sustainable wireless IDS operation, therefore, requires compressed micro-features reporting, adaptive sampling strategies, topology-aware aggregation at cluster heads, and risk-driven activation policies. The architectural implication is that communication efficiency becomes the primary determinant of IDS scalability in wireless networks, whereas computation cost dominates design trade-offs in wired infrastructures.

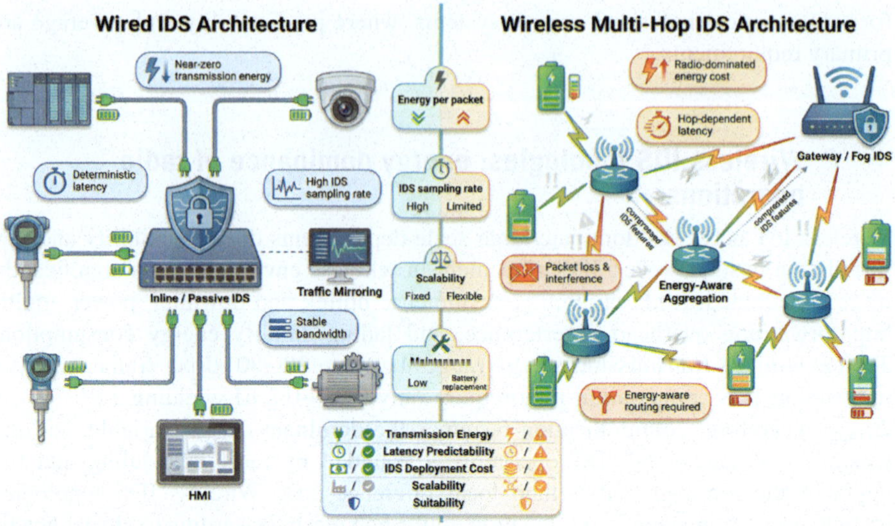

FIGURE 4.4

Structural comparison of wired and wireless IDS architectures. Wired backbones enable dense monitoring with minimal energy impact on transmission, whereas wireless multi-hop systems require communication-efficient aggregation and topology-aware reporting to sustain energy.

4.4.4 Energy comparison across communication modes

Transmission energy varies substantially across communication technologies. Wired Ethernet typically incurs less than 0.1 μJ per frame with very high reliability, supporting high-frequency IDS operation without meaningful energy penalty at endpoints. Zigbee and BLE frequently fall within 10–30 μJ per frame, supporting moderate IDS sampling rates under conservative duty cycling. LoRaWAN and NB-IoT exhibit substantially higher transmission energy requirements, along with duty-cycle constraints, limiting the feasible IDS reporting frequency and pushing designs toward event-driven summaries and micro-feature transmission. These disparities demonstrate that the selection of the communication medium directly constrains detection frequency, feature richness, and the feasible location of inference within the topology.

4.4.5 Hybrid IDS architectures

Hybrid deployments integrate wired reliability with wireless scalability. Industrial floors commonly use Ethernet-connected controllers with Zigbee sensors, smart buildings combine PoE cameras with wireless environmental sensors, and agricultural deployments link wired control centers with LoRaWAN field nodes. Hybrid IDS operation follows a categoryed propagation model in which lightweight detec-

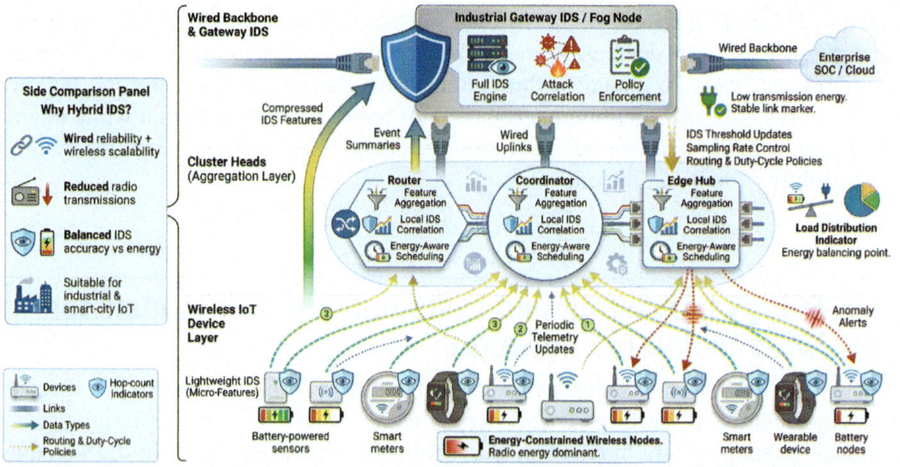

FIGURE 4.5

Hybrid wired-wireless IDS architecture in which energy-constrained wireless nodes perform lightweight detection and compressed reporting, while wired backbones support high-fidelity aggregation and correlation with minimal transmission energy impact.

tion occurs at wireless leaf nodes, cluster heads aggregate and compress anomaly indicators, and wired gateways run full IDS engines and forward correlated alerts to fog layers, along with cloud analytics services.

Fig. 4.5 illustrates a hybrid IDS architecture that strategically separates energy-constrained wireless segments from energy-abundant wired backbones. The diagram shows that lightweight detection and micro-feature extraction occurs at wireless leaf nodes, where radio energy dominates and device lifetime is highly sensitive to communication overhead. These nodes transmit compressed anomaly indicators rather than raw traffic, limiting multi-hop forwarding cost.

Cluster heads perform intermediate aggregation and contextual filtering, reducing redundancy before forwarding selected summaries toward the wired backbone. Once traffic reaches wired gateways, high-fidelity correlation, model fusion and global alert synthesis can be executed with negligible incremental transmission energy cost. This architectural partitioning preserves wireless device lifetime while maintaining system-wide detection visibility and enabling computationally intensive analysis at infrastructure-rich categories.

4.4.6 Topology-aware IDS sampling and energy-latency trade-off

IDS sampling frequency must adapt to the topology. Empirically, f_{IDS}^{wired} may be 5–20 times higher than $f_{\text{IDS}}^{wireless}$ without meaningful energy penalties. Wireless deployments favor event-driven activation, compressed micro-features, and sleep-aware anomaly detection. Let $E(f)$ denote energy cost and $L(f)$ denote detection latency at sampling rate f. In wireless systems, $E(f)$ increases approximately linearly while $L(f)$ decreases nonlinearly, yielding a pronounced energy-latency trade-off that must be managed through adaptive thresholds and reporting policies. In wired systems, the endpoint energy remains approximately constant while latency decreases rapidly with increased sampling, enabling aggressive detection without sustainability impact at the edge.

4.5 Energy harvesting and sustainable power models for IDS-enabled IoT networks

Energy harvesting is a central pillar of sustainable IoT network design, especially in large-scale and hard-to-access deployments where battery replacement and manual recharging are infeasible and economically prohibitive. In IDS-enabled IoT settings, the importance of harvesting is amplified because IDS introduces non-trivial computational and communication overheads that can rapidly shorten operational lifetime when powered solely by finite batteries. This section develops a comprehensive framework for integrating energy harvesting with IoT IDS operation, including the harvesting source modeling, storage dynamics, intermittency-aware execution, harvesting-constrained duty-cycle regulation, and scheduling architectures that explicitly couple IDS behavior to energy availability and threat risk.

4.5.1 The role of energy harvesting in sustainable IoT security

Conventional battery-powered IoT nodes are fundamentally limited by a fixed, finite energy reserve:

$$E_{\text{battery}} = \text{fixed finite energy reserve.}$$

Once depleted, devices become inoperable, making large-scale deployments dependent on costly maintenance cycles. When IDS logic is activated, energy drain accelerates due to feature extraction, model inference, and alert communication:

$$E_{\text{IDS}} = E_{\text{feat}} + E_{\text{model}} + E_{\text{tx}}.$$

Because radio transmission typically accounts for the majority of energy costs in wireless IoT networks, sustainable IDS operation requires minimizing communication while maintaining detection fidelity. Energy harvesting transforms the static battery model into a dynamic power model:

$$E_{\text{available}}(t) = E_{\text{stored}}(t) + E_{\text{harvested}}(t),$$

where $E_{\text{harvested}}(t)$ replenishes storage according to a time-varying, environmentally impacted process. The practical implication is that IDS decisions can no longer be designed under the assumption of stationarity power; instead, detection must be energy-adaptive, intermittency-aware, and opportunistic, allocating richer detection behaviors only when energy inflow and storage conditions permit, while preserving a minimum monitoring floor under scarcity.

4.5.2 Classification of energy harvesting sources

IoT nodes can harvest from multiple ambient sources, each characterized by distinct power density, temporal availability, predictability, and hardware overhead. These properties directly shape the feasible IDS sampling rate, the maximum allowable model complexity, and whether periodic retraining, together with offloading, is practical.

4.5.2.1 Solar microcell energy harvesting

Solar harvesting typically provides one of the highest average energy densities among ambient energy sources:

$$P_{\text{solar}} \approx 100\text{--}1000\ \mu\text{W/cm}^2,$$

while indoor photovoltaic harvesting may yield:

$$P_{\text{solar,indoor}} \approx 10\text{--}50\ \mu\text{W/cm}^2.$$

This modality is well-suited to agricultural IoT, environmental monitoring, smart-city deployments, and building automation. In IDS contexts, solar availability enables higher duty cycles during daylight windows, allowing more frequent anomaly scoring, richer feature extraction, and short bursts of heavier analysis while preserving long-term autonomy through energy-neutral scheduling.

4.5.2.2 Vibration and piezoelectric harvesting

Mechanical vibration harvesting can be modeled as:

$$P_{\text{vib}} = \frac{1}{2} m\omega^2 A^2 \eta,$$

where m is mass, A vibration amplitude, ω frequency, and η conversion efficiency. This modality is common in industrial machinery, railway infrastructure, and structural health monitoring. Because harvested power is frequently bursty and context-dependent, IDS activation follows event-driven patterns, with intermittent, higher-fidelity detection triggered when vibration energy spikes coincide with elevated operational risk.

4.5.2.3 RF energy harvesting

RF harvesting draws energy from ambient radio sources and can be approximated by:

$$P_{\text{RF}} = \eta \cdot \frac{G_t G_r \lambda^2 P_t}{(4\pi R)^2},$$

often yielding:

$$P_{\mathrm{RF}} \approx 1\text{–}20\ \mu\mathrm{W}.$$

It is suitable for passive RFID, UHF, and microwave-powered devices, near-field medical implants, and ultra-low-power beacons. Since RF harvesting is typically low-power and more continuous in dense RF environments, it favors ultra-lightweight IDS modes such as statistical micro-IDS, sketch-based features, and sparse thresholding over compute-intensive inference.

4.5.2.4 Thermal (Seebeck) harvesting

Thermal harvesting is commonly modeled by:

$$P_{\mathrm{thermal}} = \alpha \Delta T^2 R_{\mathrm{load}},$$

and is well-suited for industrial pipes, power electronics, and wearables that use human body heat. Its relatively slow dynamics and lower variance enable steady low-rate monitoring with stable duty cycles, supporting predictable IDS sampling schedules under energy-neutral constraints.

4.5.3 Energy storage dynamics

Harvested energy is stored in capacitors, super capacitors, together with rechargeable micro-batteries. Storage dynamics follow:

$$E_{t+1} = \min(E_{\max}, E_t + E_h - E_c),$$

and when storage drops below a minimum operational threshold, the device enters a low-power sleep regime:

$$\text{if } E_{t+1} < E_{\min}, \text{ device enters sleep mode.}$$

For IDS-enabled systems, storage is not merely a power buffer; it determines whether detection can remain continuous, whether the node must degrade to low-cost monitoring, and whether radio communication is affordable. Table 4.2 summarizes the storage technologies that shape these harvesting-driven scheduling decisions. Therefore, IDS scheduling must track storage trends and allocate energy budgets across sensing, inference, and communication to avoid oscillations and prevent sustained deficits.

4.5.4 Harvesting-aware IDS duty cycling

Since IDS computation and communication consume energy comparable to the harvested inflow in many environments, the IDS duty cycle must be explicitly constrained by energy neutrality. Let

$$D_{\mathrm{IDS}}(t) = \frac{\Delta t_{\mathrm{IDS}}}{\Delta t}.$$

Table 4.2 Comparison of energy storage technologies for IDS-enabled IoT nodes, highlighting capacity limits, charge dynamics, and longevity implications for harvesting-driven scheduling.

Storage Type	Capacity	Charge Rate	Lifetime
Capacitor	1–5 mJ	Very Fast	Short
Supercapacitor	5–500 mJ	Fast	Medium
Thin-film Li-ion	100–2000 mJ	Slow	Long
Solid-state microbattery	50–800 mJ	Slow	Long

A minimal sustainability condition is

$$E_{\text{harvested}}(t) - E_{\text{IDS}}(t) \geq 0,$$

ensuring that the DS operation does not systematically drain storage over time. More advanced models use predictive scheduling to incorporate short-term energy forecasts and threat risk:

$$D_{\text{IDS}}(t+1) = f\left(E_t, \hat{E}_{t+1}, R_t\right),$$

where R_t denotes estimated risk. This coupling is critical because under low risk, a node can preserve energy by reducing IDS sampling, while under elevated risk, it can temporarily increase detection frequency when energy budgets permit, thereby maintaining responsiveness without triggering long-term depletion.

4.5.5 Harvesting-aware IDS pipeline and system implications

Fig. 4.6 illustrates the architecture of a harvesting-aware intrusion detection pipeline designed for sustainable IoT operation. The diagram integrates three tightly coupled subsystems: an energy acquisition and storage subsystem that converts stochastic ambient energy into buffered reserves; an energy management controller that forecasts short-term harvesting opportunities and allocates operational budgets; and an IDS subsystem whose inference mode dynamically adapts to both energy availability and threat context.

The architecture emphasizes treating detection as an energy-scheduled workload rather than a continuously active service. When stored energy declines and harvesting forecasts indicate scarcity, the IDS transitions toward lightweight statistical monitoring and reduced sampling frequency to preserve the baseline observability while preventing energy collapse. Conversely, during periods of surplus, particularly when forecasts predict continued replenishment, the system enables richer feature extraction, higher sampling rates, deeper inference models, and optional offloading for correlation and retraining. This adaptive degradation and escalation mechanism ensures long-term sustainability without sacrificing security responsiveness.

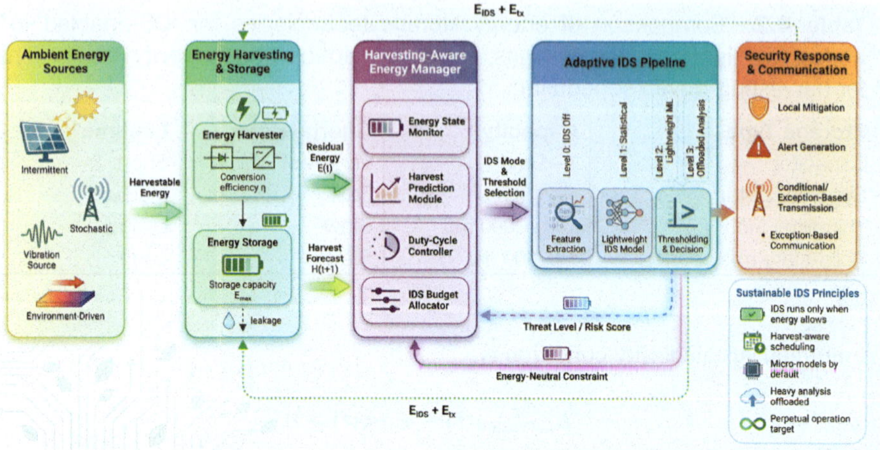

FIGURE 4.6

Harvesting-aware IDS pipeline integrating stochastic energy conversion, storage dynamics, predictive budget allocation, and energy-conditioned mode switching to sustain monitoring under intermittent power availability.

4.5.6 Energy prediction models for IDS activation

To maintain sustainable IDS operation, nodes must predict future harvested energy, expected IDS energy consumption, and environmental availability cycles. A simple linear predictor is:

$$\hat{E}_{t+1} = \alpha E_t + (1 - \alpha) E_{t-1},$$

and a Bayesian predictor can be modeled as:

$$p(E_{t+1} \mid E_t) = \mathcal{N}(\mu(E_t), \sigma^2).$$

These predictors feed scheduling decisions that reduce oscillatory behavior, limit frequent mode switching, and keep IDS duty cycling aligned with likely near-future energy availability rather than reacting myopically to instantaneous storage fluctuations.

4.5.7 Harvesting-aware anomaly detection

IDS behavior must adapt to energy conditions. A category sampling model is:

$$f_{\text{IDS}}(t) = \begin{cases} f_{\text{high}}, & E_t > T_{\text{high}}, \\ f_{\text{medium}}, & T_{\text{low}} < E_t \leq T_{\text{high}}, \\ f_{\text{low}}, & E_t \leq T_{\text{low}}. \end{cases}$$

This structure preserves sustainability by maintaining baseline coverage under scarce energy while enabling richer monitoring only when energy buffers exceed safe thresholds, thereby aligning detection intensity with feasible workload execution.

4.5.8 Mathematical model of sustainable IDS throughput

Effective IDS throughput is:

$$\Theta_{\text{IDS}} = \int 0^T f\text{IDS}(t), dt,$$

subject to the sustainability constraint:

$$\int 0^T E\text{IDS}(t), dt \leq \int 0^T E\text{harvested}(t), dt.$$

This inequality formalizes perpetual operation: over the long run, the energy consumed by IDS must not exceed the energy harvested, ensuring that detection remains viable without exhausting storage. Table 4.3 reports the harvesting-compatible IDS scheduling modes used to adapt monitoring intensity under storage constraint

Table 4.3 Harvesting-compatible IDS scheduling modes that adjust monitoring intensity to storage level to preserve sustainability while maintaining a minimum security observability floor.

Mode	Activation Condition	Energy Impact
Continuous Monitoring	$E_t > 0.7E_{\max}$	High
Periodic Sampling	$0.4E_{\max} < E_t \leq 0.7E_{\max}$	Medium
Event-Driven IDS	$E_t \leq 0.4E_{\max}$	Low
Intermittent Micro-IDS	$E_t \leq 0.2E_{\max}$	Very Low

4.5.9 Sustainable IDS design for intermittent computing

In highly intermittent environments, nodes may frequently lose power:

$$\exists t : E_t = 0.$$

Therefore, IDS design must support checkpointing, micro-epochs of computation, non-volatile memory caching, and restart-safe state machines. A minimal state evolution model is:

$$S_{t+1} = \begin{cases} F(S_t, x_t), & E_t > E_{\min}, \\ S_t, & E_t \leq E_{\min}. \end{cases}$$

This ensures that IDS logic does not corrupt the internal state across power cycles and that detection can resume reliably when energy returns, preserving continuity of monitoring despite intermittent execution.

4.5.10 Integrated sustainable IDS architecture and design implications

An integrated sustainable IDS architecture explicitly couples energy-harvesting dynamics with adaptive intrusion-detection control. Energy-state monitoring, short-term harvesting prediction, and IDS budget allocation operate under an energy-neutral constraint, transforming detection into a scheduled and budgeted workload rather than a continuously active service. Within this architecture, communication is event-driven and conditioned on both anomaly confidence and available energy to minimize radio usage, which remains the dominant source of device-level consumption. Detection complexity is dynamically scaled based on residual storage and assessed risk, allowing transitions among statistical monitoring, lightweight machine learning inference, and offloaded high-fidelity analysis. By aligning inference intensity with energy inflow and threat conditions, the system supports graceful degradation during scarcity and opportunistic strengthening during surplus. This design is particularly suited to long-lived, hard-to-access deployments where battery replacement and manual maintenance are impractical. Sustainability is achieved not by reducing security guarantees, but by coordinating detection behavior with harvesting variability and storage constraints. Fig. 4.7 presents this integrated sustainable IDS architecture.

4.6 Cross-layer energy optimization for secure IoT networks

Cross-layer optimization provides a unified approach to energy-efficient, security-aware IoT network design by treating the physical, MAC, and network, application, and IDS layers as an integrated multi-objective system. Classical network engineering optimizes these layers independently; however, in resource-limited IoT networks, energy consumption, communication reliability, and IDS performance are tightly coupled. Reducing communication frequency may extend the lifetime while simultaneously reducing IDS observability and degrading statistical confidence; increasing IDS computation may improve detection while accelerating CPU energy depletion, physical-layer noise, and channel variability directly impact feature quality, model uncertainty, and false-alarm behavior, which subsequently reshape retransmission patterns and reporting loads. Cross-layer optimization explicitly models these dependencies and turns them into coordinated control decisions that are consistent across the stack, rather than isolated per-layer heuristics that can conflict under tight energy budgets.

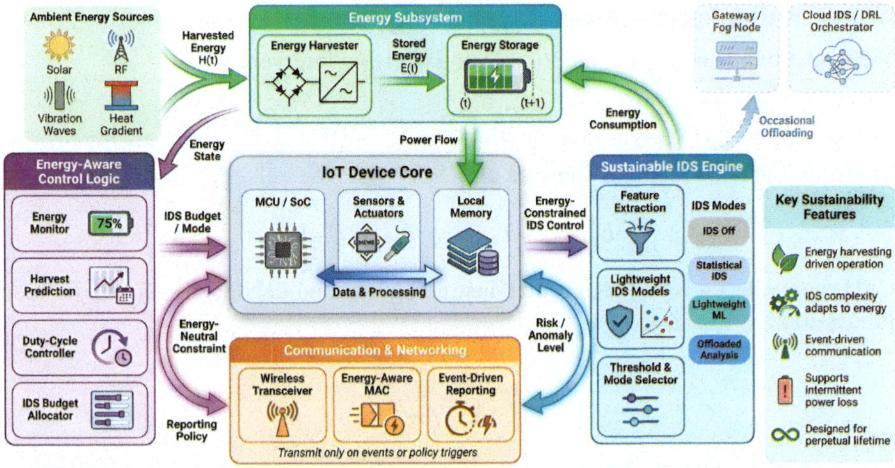

FIGURE 4.7

Integrated sustainable IDS architecture coupling energy harvesting, storage monitoring, predictive budgeting, and adaptive detection mode control under an energy-neutral operation constraint.

4.6.1 Motivation for cross-layer security–energy co-design

Traditional IoT protocol stacks assume fixed security parameters and static IDS behavior. In practice, this assumption is inefficient because 1) cryptographic costs may be unnecessary under low-risk contexts, 2) IDS may sample and infer too frequently, prematurely draining energy buffers, 3) routing protocols may select paths without anticipating IDS-triggered bursts of alert traffic, and 4) MAC layers may remain at conservative high duty cycles even when the inferred threat likelihood is low, thereby wasting energy on idle listening. These inefficiencies become critical in harvesting-driven and coin-cell devices where the feasible operating region is narrow, and the cost of misconfiguration is rapid energy collapse. Energy and security interact through feedback loops that couple all layers:

$$E_{\text{total}} = E_{\text{PHY}} + E_{\text{MAC}} + E_{\text{NET}} + E_{\text{APP}} + E_{\text{IDS}}.$$

A meaningful optimizer must therefore jointly minimize energy while satisfying minimum security and detection constraints:

$$\min E_{\text{total}} \quad \text{subject to:} \quad S \geq S_{\min}, \quad P_{\text{det}} \geq P_{\min},$$

where S denotes cryptographic strength and P_{det} denotes IDS probability. These constraints are dynamic rather than static: $S_{\min}$ and $P_{\min}$ tighten under elevated risk, while energy constraints tighten under harvesting scarcity and buffer depletion, motivating cross-layer policies that scale security intensity, observability, and reporting overhead as a function of both risk and energy state.

4.6.2 Mathematical cross-layer energy model

We model total energy consumption over a decision interval as:

$$E_{\text{tot}} = E_{\text{tx}} + E_{\text{rx}} + E_{\text{cpu}} + E_{\text{crypt}} + E_{\text{IDS}}.$$

Transmission and reception energies are:

$$E_{\text{tx}} = P_{\text{tx}} T_{\text{tx}}, \qquad E_{\text{rx}} = P_{\text{rx}} T_{\text{rx}}.$$

CPU energy depends on the executed instruction mix, model operations, and protocol processing:

$$E_{\text{cpu}} = \sum_{i=1}^{N_{\text{instr}}} e_i.$$

Cryptographic energy depends on algorithmic parameters and implementation specifics:

$$E_{\text{crypt}} = f(k, b, r),$$

where k is key size, b is block size, and r is the number of rounds. IDS energy is decomposed into feature extraction, inference, and communication:

$$E_{\text{IDS}} = E_{\text{feat}} + E_{\text{model}} + E_{\text{comm}}.$$

The cross-layer insight is that E_{comm} depends on IDS design together with MAC duty cycling, routing hop count, PHY packet error rate, and retransmission behavior; E_{feat} depends on sampling rate and application-layer compression; E_{model} depends on model scaling, quantization decisions, and optional offloading. These dependencies imply that tuning IDS parameters in isolation can be suboptimal, because small changes in sampling and thresholding can trigger large shifts in channel utilization, retransmissions, and multi-hop forwarding load.

4.6.3 Cross-layer optimization objective

We define a composite cost:

$$J = w_1 E_{\text{tot}} + w_2 D + w_3 (1 - P_{\text{det}}) + w_4 (1 - R),$$

where D is end-to-end delay, R is delivery reliability, and P_{det} is IDS detection performance. Weights w_i tune the trade-off between lifetime, QoS, and security. The cross-layer optimization problem is:

$$\min_{\theta_{\text{PHY}}, \theta_{\text{MAC}}, \theta_{\text{NET}}, \theta_{\text{IDS}}, \theta_{\text{APP}}} J,$$

subject to feasibility constraints induced by hardware limits, such as maximum transmit power, memory, CPU cycles, and energy buffer; protocol constraints such as duty-cycle bounds and channel plans; and security constraints such as minimum authentication strength and acceptable false positive rates. The optimizer is typically implemented as a feedback controller, with policy parameters updated from observed outcomes, and as a DRL policy when the environment is high-dimensional, stochastic, and non-stationary.

4.6.4 Cross-layer architectural stack and design implications

Cross-layer energy optimization for secure IoT networks is structured around a unified optimization engine that continuously observes three categories of state variables: energy state and buffer evolution, network dynamics such as congestion and link quality, and security context, including anomaly scores, IDS confidence, and alert frequency. Fig. 4.8 presents this architectural structure.

Based on these observations, the optimization engine generates coordinated control actions that span multiple layers of the protocol stack. At the physical layer, transmission power and modulation parameters are adjusted to reduce unnecessary radio expenditure. At the MAC layer, duty cycle and backoff behavior are adapted to balance observability and energy savings. At the network layer, routing weights are modified to reflect residual energy and trust penalties. At the application layer, the sampling rate and compression are scaled based on risk and resource constraints. At the IDS layer, model complexity, and anomaly thresholds are dynamically selected to maintain detection guarantees within the available energy budget. The central architectural implication is that IDS is not treated as an isolated application module. Instead, IDS outputs become control signals that reshape network behavior. Risk-conditioned duty cycles, trust-aware routing penalties, and adaptive sampling are triggered by detection feedback, while energy state and QoS constraints bound IDS aggressiveness to prevent cascade effects that could destabilize device lifetime. The figure, therefore, captures the transformation from layered optimization to fully integrated cross-layer control.

4.6.5 Physical layer optimization

At the physical layer, transmission power control and modulation selection directly impact battery consumption and packet error behavior. A simplified relationship between transmit power and received power is:

$$P_{\text{tx}} = \frac{(4\pi R)^2}{G_t G_r \lambda^2} P_{\text{rx}}.$$

Lower-power modulations such as OOK and BPSK can reduce PHY energy and radio-on time while potentially increasing BER on noisy channels, thereby increasing retransmissions and degrading the IDS feature quality through missing packets and distorted temporal statistics. PHY decisions must therefore be coordinated with MAC retransmission limits and with IDS tolerance to missing observations, since link-layer recovery policies can amplify energy use under fading and interference.

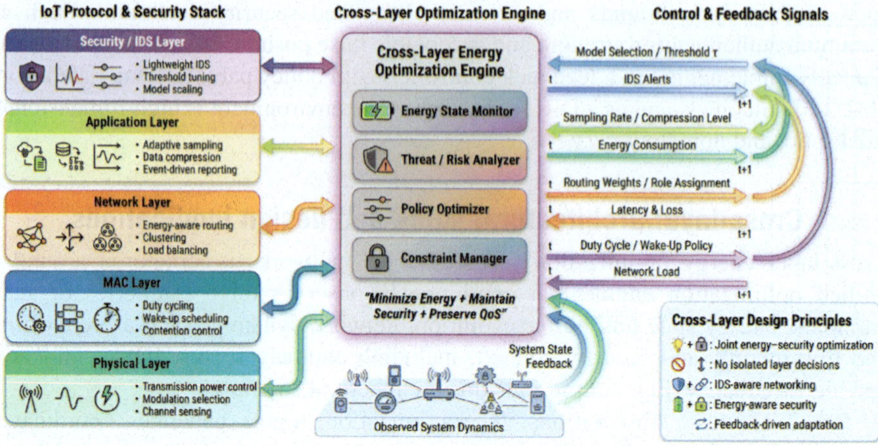

FIGURE 4.8

Cross-layer energy optimization architecture for secure IoT networks, illustrating unified monitoring of energy, network, and security state variables with coordinated adaptation across PHY, MAC, routing, application, and IDS layers.

4.6.6 MAC layer optimization

MAC duty cycling controls radio wake-ups and dominates idle listening costs:

$$D_{\text{MAC}} = \frac{T_{\text{active}}}{T_{\text{frame}}}.$$

A cross-layer IDS-aware MAC reduces the duty cycle when the inferred anomaly likelihood is low and increases it when risk rises, and when the network requires richer observability:

$$D_{\text{IDS-aware}} = g(P_{\text{risk}}, E_{\text{store}}, Q, L),$$

where P_{risk} is risk level, E_{store} is stored energy, Q is queue pressure, and L is link quality. This structure prevents wasting energy on high-duty operations during low-risk, low-traffic periods, while ensuring that monitoring coverage does not collapse when threats emerge, and timely alert delivery becomes essential.

4.6.7 Network layer optimization

IDS-aware routing integrates energy cost, delay, and security context into path selection:

$$C_{\text{route}} = \alpha E_{\text{hop}} + \beta\left(1 - P_{\text{det}}^{\text{hop}}\right) + \gamma L_{\text{delay}} + \xi\, \mathcal{R}_{\text{trust}},$$

where $\mathcal{R}_{\text{trust}}$ is a trust and risk penalty derived from IDS outputs such as anomaly score and reputation. Nodes exhibiting suspicious behavior receive higher penalties, reducing their routing priority and limiting their impact on traffic forwarding. This coupling is especially important in multi-hop IoT, where compromised relays can amplify energy consumption through selective forwarding, replay attacks, and induced retransmissions that force repeated transmissions across several hops.

4.6.8 Application layer optimization

Sampling, compression, and data-rate control reduce energy while preserving IDS observability. Let sampling frequency be:

$$f_s(t) = f_{\min} + (f_{\max} - f_{\min}) P_{\text{risk}}(t),$$

which increases feature density when risk rises while preserving energy during benign periods. Compression ratio and feature dimensionality can be similarly adapted, enabling micro-feature reporting under scarce energy and richer feature sets when buffers are healthy and when the network can afford increased observability.

4.6.9 IDS layer optimization

Cross-layer-aware IDS adjusts model size, thresholds, feature sets, and communication frequency as a function of energy state, MAC duty cycle, and risk:

$$\theta_{\text{IDS}}(t) = h(E_t, P_{\text{risk}}(t), D_{\text{MAC}}, L, Q).$$

This includes switching among multiple IDS modes, such as statistical detection, lightweight ML inference, and offloaded analysis, together with enforcing event-driven alerts to minimize E_{comm}. The central constraint is sustainability: detection must not induce a cascade of transmissions that collapses energy buffers under intermittent harvesting, and mode switching must avoid instability induced by frequent threshold oscillations.

4.6.10 Joint cross-layer optimization algorithm

We model joint optimization as a sequential decision process:

$$V(s_t) = \min_{a_t} \left[J(s_t, a_t) + \gamma V(s_{t+1}) \right],$$

with state:

$$s_t = (E_t, P_{\text{risk}}, \text{RSSI/SNR}, D_{\text{MAC}}, C_{\text{route}}, Q, \text{loss rate}),$$

and action:

$$a_t = (\theta_{\text{PHY}}, \theta_{\text{MAC}}, \theta_{\text{NET}}, \theta_{\text{APP}}, \theta_{\text{IDS}}).$$

This formulation supports dynamic programming in small state spaces while naturally extending to DRL policies in high-dimensional, stochastic, and non-stationary environments, thereby enabling adaptive cross-layer control under uncertain harvesting, fading, mobility, and adversarial drift.

4.6.11 Cross-layer optimization

Cross-layer optimization relies on coordinated design choices across the physical, MAC, network, application, and IDS layers of the IoT protocol stack. These choices jointly shape system sustainability and detection performance rather than acting as isolated energy-efficiency or intrusion-detection mechanisms. Changes at lower layers, such as transmission power and duty cycling, directly affect radio energy consumption and observability, while higher-layer adaptations regulate feature density, alert frequency, and inference complexity. Excessive optimization at any single layer can impose unintended costs on others, such as increased retransmissions and alert traffic. This motivates the need for coordinated cross-layer control policies, particularly under strict energy budgets and dynamic threat conditions. Table 4.4 summarizes the key optimization levers available at each layer of the IoT protocol stack and highlights their coupled energy-security implications.

Table 4.4 Cross-layer optimization parameters and their coupled energy–security effects across the IoT protocol stack.

Layer	Optimization Parameter	Energy–Security Effect
PHY	Transmission power, modulation, and coding	Reduces transmission energy; alters BER and IDS feature fidelity; impacts retransmissions and multi-hop forwarding cost.
MAC	Duty cycling, backoff, and retry limits	Saves radio energy; affects observability, latency, and alert delivery under elevated risk conditions.
Network	Energy-aware and trust-aware routing	Balances battery depletion; penalizes suspicious relays; modifies hop-dependent IDS telemetry and alert overhead.
Application	Adaptive sampling and compression	Reduces sensing and CPU cost; controls feature density available to IDS and limits uplink traffic during energy scarcity.
IDS	Dynamic model scaling and thresholding	Preserves detection accuracy under energy constraints; prevents energy collapse due to excessive alerting and high-frequency inference.

4.6.12 Integrated optimization example

Assume an energy budget for the next decision interval:

$$E_{\text{available}} = 120\ \mu\text{J}.$$

Within this constraint, a cross-layer optimizer jointly selects parameters across the protocol stack to satisfy both sustainability and security requirements. At the physical layer, minimum transmission power is chosen to reduce radio energy while preserving link reliability. At the MAC layer, a conservative duty cycle limits idle listening and contention overhead. Routing decisions favor energy improvement and trusted relays to avoid premature battery depletion and excessive retransmissions, while application-layer compression reduces feature dimensionality and uplink traffic volume. Formally, the selected configuration is:

$$\theta_{\text{PHY}} = P_{\min}, \quad \theta_{\text{MAC}} = 5\% \text{ duty}, \quad \theta_{\text{NET}} = \text{energy- and trust-aware routing},$$
$$\theta_{\text{APP}} = \text{compressed sampling},$$

combined with a low-cost IDS model:

$$\text{Micro-Autoencoder, 8 neurons,}$$

replacing a more computationally intensive alternative:

$$\text{GRU-64.}$$

Under this coordinated configuration, the system achieves substantial energy savings while maintaining baseline intrusion-detection coverage:

$$E_{\text{savings}} \approx 78\%.$$

Critically, these savings are not solely attributable to reducing IDS model complexity. Instead, they arise from the compounded effect of cross-layer coordination: reduced radio-on time at the MAC layer, fewer retransmissions enabled by PHY-aware parameter selection, lower alert hop cost through energy-aware routing, and decreased feature transmission rate through application-layer compression. This example illustrates how holistic cross-layer optimization outperforms isolated, single-layer tuning under strict energy budgets.

4.6.13 Closed-loop cross-layer energy-security control and system implications

The complete closed-loop cross-layer energy-security optimization architecture formalizes the interaction between harvesting dynamics, network behavior, and intrusion detection analytics within a unified feedback control system. At the sensing stage, residual energy $E(t)$, harvested energy $H(t)$, and short-term harvesting forecasts $H(t+1)$ define the sustainability state of the device. Simultaneously, IDS analytics provide a security state variables, including anomaly scores, detection confidence, and alert frequency. These signals are jointly processed by a multi-objective optimizer that minimizes a cost function combining energy expenditure, latency,, and reliability degradation, and security risk, subject to operational

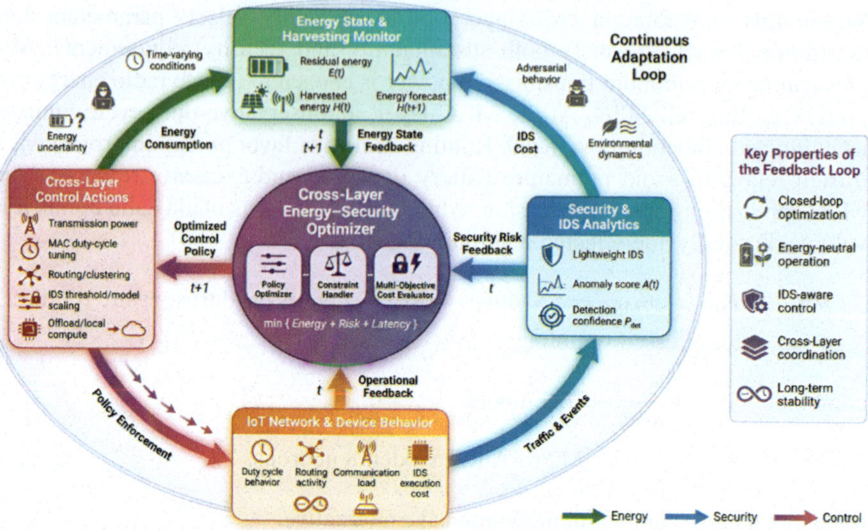

FIGURE 4.9

Closed-loop cross-layer energy-security optimization architecture integrating harvesting dynamics, network state, and IDS analytics into a unified feedback controller with coordinated adaptation across protocol layers.

constraints.The resulting control policy adapts parameters across the protocol stack: transmission power at the physical layer, duty cycling at the MAC layer, routing and clustering behavior at the network layer, sampling, and compression at the application layer, and IDS thresholds together with model complexity at the detection layer. Offloading decisions are also governed by this policy when local energy and risk conditions justify delegation. Crucially, observed outcomes, e.g., packet loss, energy drain rate, detection accuracy, and alert stability, are fed back into the optimizer, forming a closed-loop control structure. This feedback mechanism stabilizes system performance under workload fluctuations, environmental intermittency, and adversarial activity, preventing oscillatory duty cycles, routing instability, and energy collapse. Fig. 4.9 illustrates this complete closed-loop cross-layer energy-security optimization architecture.

4.7 Carbon-aware and green network optimization for IoT networks

As global-scale IoT networks scale toward tens of billions of devices, their cumulative energy demand and associated carbon footprint become material sustainability constraints rather than secondary design considerations. Individual IoT operations often consume only microjoules to millijoules. however, when aggregated across dense wireless infrastructures, gateways, fog nodes, and cloud backends, the combined energy use of radio transmissions, protocol overhead, IDS inference, logging, model updates, and correlation analytics translates into non-trivial greenhouse gas emissions. This motivates *carbon-aware network optimization*, which extends energy efficiency by explicitly accounting for *time-varying carbon intensity* of electricity, *renewable availability*, and *location-dependent* compute footprints at the edge and in the cloud. In this setting, the objective is not limited to minimizing joules; the objective expands to minimizing *grams of* CO_2e while preserving reliability, latency, and security constraints that define operational feasibility in real deployments.

4.7.1 Carbon footprint of IoT networks

Let the total carbon footprint of an IoT network over an observation window T be:

$$C_{\text{tot}} = C_{\text{dev}} + C_{\text{net}} + C_{\text{edge}} + C_{\text{cloud}} + C_{\text{IDS}}.$$

Here, C_{dev} accounts for device-side sensing and computation, C_{net} reflects the communication infrastructure footprint including access points, relays, and network services, C_{edge} captures fog and edge processing emissions, C_{cloud} captures backend analytics and storage emissions, and C_{IDS} captures the incremental carbon attributable to intrusion detection workloads such as inference, correlation, alerting, and retraining. Given energy consumption E and carbon intensity κ (gCO_2/kWh), carbon emissions are:

$$C = E \cdot \kappa.$$

Because κ varies with grid mix, renewable penetration, congestion, and time of day, carbon-aware IoT networks must ingest real-time and predicted $\kappa(t)$, combine it with energy models, and decide *when* and *where* to compute, transmit, and detect. This implies that a low-energy decision is not guaranteed to be a low-carbon decision when the same joule is produced during a high-intensity interval.

4.7.2 Dynamic carbon-intensity modeling

We model carbon intensity as a time-varying signal:

$$\kappa(t) = \kappa_{\text{base}} + \kappa_{\text{var}}(t),$$

where $\kappa_{\text{var}}(t)$ captures diurnal patterns and stochastic variation. An operation executed at time t incurs:

$$C(t) = E(t)\,\kappa(t).$$

Solar-dominant grids tend to exhibit lower $\kappa(t)$ around midday, wind-driven low-carbon intervals can occur irregularly, and high-carbon peaks often appear during demand surges when fossil generation ramps up, and elevated night-time intensity can occur when renewables drop and fossil baseload dominates. These variations motivate the temporal shifting of delay-tolerant operations to low-$\kappa(t)$ windows, while enforcing conservative operation when $\kappa(t)$ spikes, particularly for background telemetry and periodic security audits that are not strictly real-time.

4.7.3 Carbon-aware transmission scheduling

Energy-aware IoT networks already reduce transmission frequency; carbon-aware systems additionally schedule transmissions when the *carbon cost of sending* is minimal. Let $\mathcal{T}$ be the set of feasible transmission times within a deadline constraint. The carbon-optimal schedule is:

$$\mathcal{T}^* = \arg\min_{\mathcal{T}} \int_{\mathcal{T}} \kappa(t)\, E_{\text{tx}}(t)\, dt,$$

subject to application deadlines and queue stability. A practical threshold policy is:

$$\text{Transmit if } \kappa(t) \le \kappa_{\text{th}}, \qquad \text{else delay up to } \Delta_{\max},$$

which yields carbon savings for delay-tolerant telemetry, periodic reporting, and batch IDS summaries, while preserving strict real-time traffic when required. In operational terms, this policy shifts background reporting to renewable-heavy intervals, reducing the carbon impact of the same number of transmitted bytes without requiring additional compression.

4.7.4 Carbon-aware MAC duty cycling

Duty cycling should be modulated by both energy state and carbon intensity:

$$D_{\text{carbon}}(t) = f\big(E_{\min}, \kappa(t), \text{QoS}, P_{\text{risk}}(t)\big).$$

A carbon-modulated duty cycle can be written as:

$$D(t) = D_{\min} + \big(D_{\max} - D_{\min}\big)\,\phi(t), \qquad \phi(t) = \exp\big(-\lambda\kappa(t)\big),$$

so that duty cycle decreases as $\kappa(t)$ increases. In a security-aware setting, $\phi(t)$ must respect risk; the duty cycle should not drop below a monitoring floor when $P_{\text{risk}}(t)$ is elevated, since a carbon-optimal sleep decision can create observability blind spots that raise long-term risk and may increase emissions later through incident response, reconfiguration, and recovery traffic.

4.7.5 Carbon-aware routing optimization

Routing should incorporate carbon cost in addition to energy, reliability, latency, and IDS-driven risk. Define carbon cost for traversing link (i, j) at time t as:

$$C_{ij}(t) = E_{ij}(t)\,\kappa(t),$$

where $E_{ij}(t)$ includes transmission energy and expected retransmissions due to loss. The carbon-minimizing path is:

$$\min_{\mathcal{P}} \sum_{(i,j)\in\mathcal{P}} C_{ij}(t),$$

subject to:

$$P_{\text{det}} \geq P_{\min}, \qquad R \geq R_{\min}, \qquad D \leq D_{\max}.$$

This formulation yields routing that preferentially uses links and relays that reduce expected energy and retransmissions during high-carbon intervals, while preserving detection coverage and QoS constraints. The model also aligns with cross-layer design because the expected retransmission term couples PHY conditions, MAC retry limits, and routing decisions into a single carbon-valued metric.

4.7.6 Carbon-aware data compression and sampling

Application-layer sampling and compression can be adapted to carbon intensity:

$$f_s(t) = f_{\min} + (f_{\max} - f_{\min})\, \psi\big(\kappa(t)\big), \qquad \psi\big(\kappa(t)\big) = \frac{1}{1 + \alpha\kappa(t)}.$$

When $\kappa(t)$ is high, sampling approaches $f_{\min}$ and features can be compressed more aggressively; when $\kappa(t)$ is low during renewable peaks, the system can increase sampling for richer observability, periodic audits, and model refresh tasks that improve long-term security posture. This schedule is most effective when combined with deadline-aware buffering, thereby improving data quality during low-carbon windows without violating application constraints.

4.7.7 Green IDS models

Carbon-aware IDS extends energy-aware IDS by explicitly considering $\kappa(t)$ in mode selection:

$$\theta_{\text{IDS}}(t) = h\big(E(t), \kappa(t), P_{\text{risk}}(t)\big).$$

Operationally, this means using extremely low-cost micro-models such as EWMA, Manhattan distance, sketch-based detectors, and sparse thresholding when $\kappa(t)$ is high and energy is scarce, while enabling richer anomaly models, deeper feature extraction, and periodic calibration when $\kappa(t)$ is low and energy is abundant. Security cannot be reduced without bounds; the IDS must maintain a minimum monitoring floor, with risk-driven overrides that enforce higher vigilance even during high-carbon periods.

4.7.8 Carbon-aware IDS inference modes

We define three IDS operating modes:

$$M(t) \in \{\text{Low-Carbon Mode, Balanced Mode, High-Renewable Mode}\}.$$

Low-Carbon Mode employs minimal model complexity, reduced sampling, sparse alerting, and no retraining; it is optimized for minimal carbon cost per unit time while retaining baseline coverage. Balanced Mode uses mid-complexity models and normal sampling for standard operation. High-Renewable Mode enables feature-rich models, increased sampling, and optional retraining and calibration, exploiting low-$\kappa(t)$ windows for security hardening and reducing long-term risk. These modes provide a structured control interface that can be implemented in rule-based scheduling and learned by a DRL agent that treats carbon intensity as a first-class state variable.

4.7.9 Carbon-aware cloud offloading

Offloading decisions must consider carbon at both ends: uplink transmission at time t and cloud and edge execution, each with its own carbon intensity. Let κ_{cloud} denote the effective carbon intensity of the chosen execution site. The carbon cost of offloading is:

$$C_{\text{offload}}(t) = E_{\text{uplink}}(t)\,\kappa(t) + E_{\text{cloud}}\,\kappa_{\text{cloud}}.$$

The system should offload when:

$$C_{\text{local}}(t) > C_{\text{offload}}(t),$$

where $C_{\text{local}}(t) = E_{\text{local}}(t)\,\kappa(t)$ includes device-side compute and any additional retransmissions and MAC overhead. This criterion supports shifting heavy IDS correlation and retraining toward low-carbon compute regions and low-$\kappa(t)$ time windows while preserving near-real-time detection through local micro-IDS monitoring.

4.7.10 Multi-layer carbon optimization framework and architectural implications

We define a unified carbon-aware objective:

$$J_{\text{carbon}} = w_1 C_{\text{tx}} + w_2 C_{\text{cpu}} + w_3 C_{\text{route}} + w_4 C_{\text{IDS}} + w_5(1 - R) + w_6(1 - P_{\text{det}}),$$

subject to energy, latency, and protocol feasibility constraints. The optimization variables span cross-layer controls: PHY transmit power and coding, MAC duty cycle and retry policies, network routing weights and role assignment, application sampling and compression, IDS threshold and model scaling, and offloading location and timing. The critical systems implication is that carbon awareness becomes a first-class signal, comparable to residual energy and risk, and must be integrated into the same closed-loop controller or DRL policy that governs energy and security.

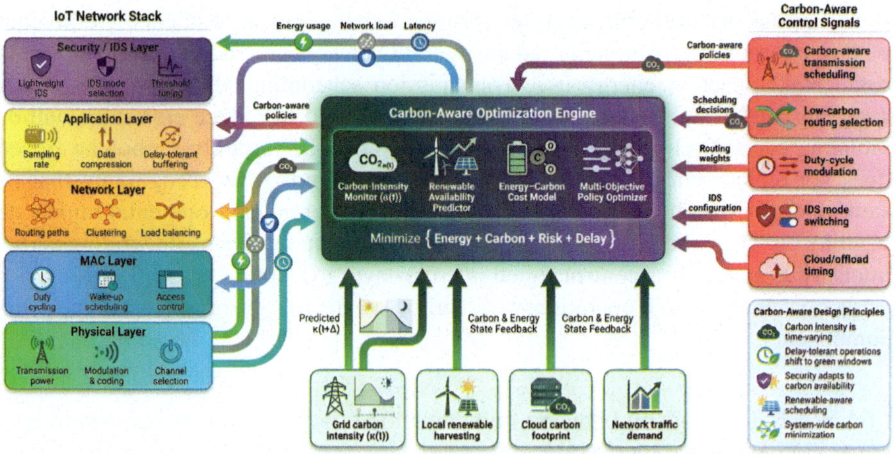

FIGURE 4.10

Carbon-aware cross-layer optimization architecture integrating time-varying carbon intensity and renewable forecasts into coordinated adaptation of transmission scheduling, duty cycling, routing, IDS operation, and offloading decisions.

Fig. 4.10 illustrates how carbon-awareness is integrated into the IoT cross-layer control loop. The diagram extends the energy- and security-aware optimization architecture by incorporating time-varying carbon intensity, renewable availability forecasts, and compute-site carbon footprints as explicit control inputs. Carbon intensity $\kappa(t)$, predicted renewable windows, and edge or cloud execution footprints are ingested alongside residual energy state and IDS-derived risk indicators. These signals are processed by a carbon-aware optimization engine that minimizes a joint objective over energy consumption, carbon emissions, latency, reliability, and detection performance. The resulting policy coordinates transmission scheduling, MAC duty cycling, routing weight adjustment, adaptive sampling, IDS mode selection, and offloading timing. A key operational implication illustrated by the figure is temporal workload shifting. Delay-tolerant operations, such as batch telemetry aggregation, periodic IDS summaries, model calibration, and retraining, are deferred to low-carbon intervals when renewable penetration is high. In contrast, time-critical security responses remain preemptive and are executed immediately when threat conditions require intervention, regardless of carbon intensity. The architecture, therefore, preserves security guarantees while systematically reducing lifecycle emissions through carbon-aware scheduling.

4.7.11 Table: carbon-aware vs. Traditional IoT networks

Carbon-aware IoT design extends conventional energy-efficient operation by incorporating time-varying carbon intensity into system-level decision-making. Traditional approaches primarily optimize for functionality and, at best, energy efficiency, whereas carbon-aware systems adapt operational behavior according to the environmental impact of energy use. Transmission scheduling, duty cycling, routing, sampling, and IDS behavior are dynamically adjusted to reduce emissions without violating latency, reliability, and security constraints. Importantly, carbon awareness does not replace energy optimization; rather, it extends it by recognizing that the same energy expenditure can have a significantly different environmental impact depending on when and where it occurs. This comparison motivates integrating carbon intensity as a first-class control signal in cross-layer IoT optimization. Table 4.5 contrasts conventional IoT operation with carbon-aware IoT design across key system components.

Table 4.5 Comparison between traditional IoT operation and carbon-aware IoT operation across protocol stack components.

Component	Traditional IoT	Carbon-Aware IoT
Transmission Timing	Fixed periodic and event-driven	Scheduled to low-carbon windows when delay-tolerant and deadline-feasible
MAC Duty Cycle	Static and energy-only adaptation	Dynamic, modulated by time-varying carbon intensity $\kappa(t)$ and risk with a monitoring floor
Routing Metric	Hop count and residual energy	Carbon cost combined with expected retransmissions, trust level, and risk penalties
Sampling Rate	Static per application profile	Green-adaptive sampling tied to $\kappa(t)$, deadlines, and observability requirements
IDS Mode	Always-on and energy-aware only	Carbon-aware mode switching with minimum monitoring floor and risk-driven override
Cloud Offloading	Static policies	Carbon-cost-optimized by execution time and compute region with uplink–carbon coupling

4.7.12 Case study: 65% carbon reduction via green scheduling

Assume peak and renewable-heavy carbon intensities:

$$\kappa_{\text{peak}} = 950\,\text{gCO}_2/\text{kWh}, \qquad \kappa_{\text{renew}} = 180\,\text{gCO}_2/\text{kWh}.$$

By shifting delay-tolerant transmissions from peak to renewable windows, the carbon savings for a single node with transmission energy E_{tx} are:

$$\Delta C = E_{\text{tx}}\left(\kappa_{\text{peak}} - \kappa_{\text{renew}}\right).$$

For a fleet-scale deployment, the proportional reduction approaches:

$$\frac{\kappa_{\text{peak}} - \kappa_{\text{renew}}}{\kappa_{\text{peak}}} = \frac{950 - 180}{950} = \frac{770}{950} \approx 0.81,$$

yet after accounting for operational constraints such as deadlines, connectivity availability, and unavoidable peak-time traffic, a conservative operational reduction on the order of:

$$\Delta C_{\text{fleet}} \approx 65\%$$

is achievable in many delay-tolerant telemetry workloads, particularly when combined with carbon-aware duty cycling and adaptive sampling.

4.8 Full integration framework for energy-efficient and carbon-aware IoT networks

The preceding sections examined several dimensions of energy and carbon optimization in IoT networks, including physical-layer energy efficiency, MAC-layer duty-cycle control, network-layer green routing, application-layer adaptive sampling, energy harvesting integration, and carbon-aware operational policies. These components are unified here into a comprehensive cross-layer architecture capable of supporting large-scale IoT networks with minimal energy consumption and reduced carbon footprint, while preserving reliability, responsiveness, and security through integrated lightweight and AI-enhanced IDS systems.This integration framework represents the culmination of Chapter 4. It provides a conceptual, mathematical, and architectural foundation for the construction of holistic, energy-efficient IoT networks. The framework integrates energy modeling and optimization across device, network, and cloud layers; carbon-intensity-aware adaptation of communication, routing, and computation; sustainable IDS deployment using lightweight, duty-cycled, and DRL-enhanced models; renewable energy harvesting and storage-aware operational scheduling, and cross-layer feedback loops enabling multi-objective optimization over long-term IoT operation.

4.8.1 Unified multi-layer optimization model

We define a unified optimization model that captures cost and performance metrics across all interacting layers of the IoT stack. Rather than treating physical transmission, MAC scheduling, routing, application sampling, security processing, and cloud orchestration as independent subsystems, the framework models them as components of a single coupled control problem. Let

$$\mathcal{L} = \{\text{PHY}, \text{MAC}, \text{NET}, \text{APP}, \text{SEC}, \text{CLOUD}\}$$

denote the set of layers participating in joint optimization. Each layer contributes decision variables and induces both resource consumption and performance outcomes. We define a global parameter vector

$$\Theta = \{\theta_{\text{PHY}}, \theta_{\text{MAC}}, \theta_{\text{NET}}, \theta_{\text{APP}}, \theta_{\text{SEC}}, \theta_{\text{CLOUD}}\},$$

where each component represents tunable parameters such as transmission power, duty cycle, routing weights, sampling frequency, IDS mode selection, threshold configuration, and offloading strategy. The total energy expenditure induced by Θ is modeled as

$$E_{\text{tot}}(\Theta) = E_{\text{tx}} + E_{\text{rx}} + E_{\text{comp}} + E_{\text{idle}} + E_{\text{IDS}} + E_{\text{cloud}},$$

while the corresponding carbon footprint is

$$C_{\text{tot}}(\Theta) = C_{\text{tx}} + C_{\text{rx}} + C_{\text{edge}} + C_{\text{cloud}} + C_{\text{IDS}}.$$

Performance metrics are represented by the end-to-end delay

$$D_{\text{delay}}(\Theta),$$

delivery reliability

$$R(\Theta),$$

and detection probability

$$P_{\text{det}}(\Theta).$$

The global multi-objective optimization problem is therefore formulated as

$$\min_{\Theta} \left(w_E E_{\text{tot}}(\Theta) + w_C C_{\text{tot}}(\Theta) + w_D D_{\text{delay}}(\Theta) + w_R \left(1 - R(\Theta)\right) + w_S \left(1 - P_{\text{det}}(\Theta)\right) \right),$$

subject to feasibility constraints imposed by hardware limits, protocol standards, energy availability, carbon budgets, and minimum security guarantees. This formulation provides the analytical foundation for the integrated cross-layer controller developed in the remainder of this chapter.

4.8.2 Cross-layer integration architecture

We design four primary control loops. The Energy Control Loop extends device longevity through duty cycling, adaptive transmission power, and budgeting that accounts for harvesting. The carbon control loop adjusts operational intensity based on real-time carbon intensity and renewable energy forecasts. The security control loop scales IDS complexity, thresholding, and offloading based on risk and observability requirements. The QoS and performance loop maintains guarantees on latency, reliability, and throughput. The interaction among these control loops must avoid instability and contradictory policies; therefore, the integrated system employs hierarchical control expressed as Carbon Loop → Energy Loop → QoS Loop → Security Loop. This precedence ensures that sustainability constraints dominate, followed by energy feasibility, then performance preservation, and finally adaptive security scaling within the feasible operational region.

4.8.3 Full stack integration diagram

The full integration architecture operationalizes the previously defined mathematical model across device, edge, and cloud layers. At the lowest category, IoT devices continuously monitor residual energy $E_{\text{res}}(t)$, harvested energy rate $H(t)$, instantaneous carbon intensity $\kappa(t)$, traffic load $\lambda * \text{net}(t)$, and security risk index $P * \text{risk}(t)$. These state variables are locally processed to determine device-level control actions such as adaptive duty cycling, transmission power scaling, lightweight IDS mode selection, and conditional communication. Devices transmit compressed telemetry and anomaly indicators to the edge layer to minimize radio energy consumption and reduce carbon cost under high-intensity grid intervals.

At the intermediate category, edge gateways aggregate multi-device telemetry, perform cluster-level anomaly correlation, execute more computationally intensive IDS inference models, and evaluate routing load balancing under carbon and energy constraints. Edge nodes serve as regional optimization agents that enforce cross-layer policies while preventing energy hotspots and carbon-intensive multi-hop forwarding bursts caused by unstable duty cycles and retransmission cascades.

At the top category, cloud orchestration integrates long-term carbon intensity forecasts $\kappa_{\text{pred}}(t+\tau)$, renewable availability models, federated IDS updates, and DRL-based policy learning. Heavy retraining tasks, firmware updates, and global correlation analytics are scheduled during predicted low-carbon windows to minimize emissions. Optimized policy parameters are propagated downward across layers, forming a continuous bidirectional feedback loop. This hierarchical and recursive control structure ensures that device-level decisions remain aligned with sustainability, carbon reduction, and security objectives across time horizons ranging from seconds to days. Fig. 4.11 illustrates this complete energy–carbon–security integration architecture.

4.8.4 Inter-layer signaling and feedback

We define the following shared state signals:

$$s_E(t) = \text{energy state}, \quad s_C(t) = \text{carbon intensity}, \quad s_Q(t) = \text{QoS state},$$
$$s_S(t) = \text{security risk state}.$$

Layer decisions follow:

$$a_{\text{layer}}(t) = \pi_{\text{layer}}(s_E, s_C, s_Q, s_S),$$

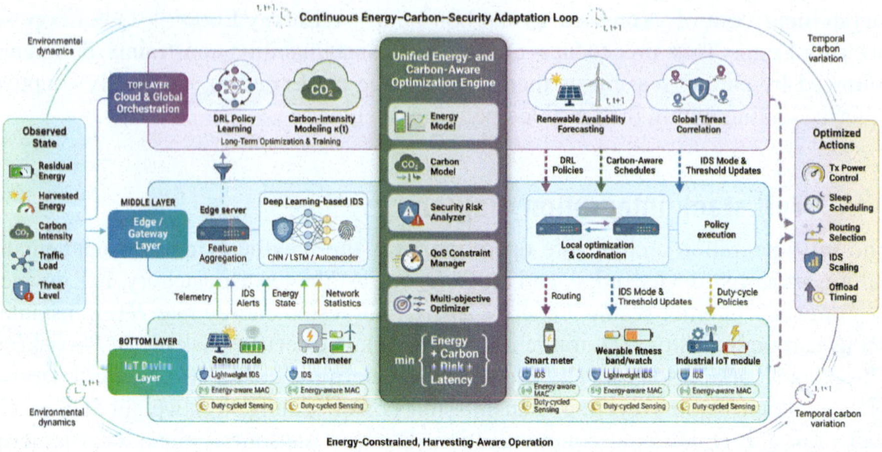

FIGURE 4.11

Complete integration architecture for energy-efficient and carbon-aware IoT networks, illustrating a unified energy–carbon–security feedback loop spanning device, edge, and cloud layers with hierarchical control and bidirectional policy propagation.

which ensures coordinated adaptation rather than isolated per-layer optimization. The practical interpretation is that a routing decision can be conditioned on both carbon intensity and risk, while duty cycling remains aware of the observability requirements imposed by the IDS.

4.8.5 Integrated energy and carbon state representation

A unified state representation is essential:

$$s(t) = \left[E_{\text{res}}(t), H(t), \kappa(t), \kappa_{\text{pred}}(t+\tau), \lambda_{\text{net}}(t), r_{\text{loss}}(t), P_{\text{risk}}(t)\right].$$

This state vector jointly captures sustainability, performance, and threat conditions, enabling DRL-based cross-layer decision-making that is proactive rather than reactive, as it includes forecasted carbon intensity and harvested energy inflow.

4.8.6 Green DRL-based control engine

A DRL controller optimizes global decisions with action variables that include duty cycle, routing path, sampling frequency, IDS mode, and offloading timing. The reward is defined as:

$$R(t) = -\left(\alpha E_{\text{tot}} + \beta C_{\text{tot}} + \gamma D_{\text{delay}} - \delta R - \eta P_{\text{det}}\right),$$

so that maximizing expected cumulative reward yields long-term, sustainable, and secure operation. This reward structure reflects the view that carbon is not an external constraint; it is treated as a measurable cost signal coupled to energy and performance, with security enforced through detection-dependent terms.

4.8.7 Integrated green routing and IDS model

Each routing decision simultaneously considers carbon cost and security performance:

$$\mathcal{P}^* = \arg\min_{\mathcal{P}} \left(\sum_{(i,j)\in\mathcal{P}} E_{ij}\kappa(t) + \eta \cdot \frac{1}{P_{\text{det}}(\mathcal{P})} \right).$$

Routes are therefore selected based on joint sustainability and detectability criteria, where the detectability term discourages routing that reduces IDS coverage through trusted-path collapse, reduced diversity, and persistent selection of low-observability links.

4.8.8 Multi-hour and multi-day carbon forecast integration

Carbon forecasts are modeled as:

$$\hat{\kappa}(t+\tau) = f(\kappa(t), w, s),$$

where w and s represent weather and seasonal variables. Predictive scheduling aligns transmissions, retraining, and high-complexity IDS activation with renewable-dominant intervals, reducing emissions while improving the security posture by concentrating calibration and audit workloads into low-carbon windows.

4.8.9 Evaluation metrics for integrated framework

Sustainability-focused metrics include Carbon Reduction Ratio:

$$\text{CRR} = 1 - \frac{C_{\text{tot,new}}}{C_{\text{tot,baseline}}},$$

Energy Savings Ratio:

$$\text{ESR} = 1 - \frac{E_{\text{tot,new}}}{E_{\text{tot,baseline}}},$$

Green Security Efficiency:

$$\text{GSE} = \frac{P_{\text{det}}}{E_{\text{IDS}} + C_{\text{IDS}}},$$

and Green-Lifetime Extension:

$$\text{GLE} = \frac{L_{\text{new}}}{L_{\text{baseline}}}.$$

These metrics jointly quantify whether an IoT system reduces emissions without silently degrading detection coverage and shortening its lifetime under harvesting intermittency.

CHAPTER

5 Green-ML-based IDS mechanisms

5.1 Introduction

Energy sustainability and computational efficiency have emerged as foundational constraints in modern IoT security engineering. As IoT networks expand from hundreds of nodes to planetary-scale infrastructures comprising billions of heterogeneous devices distributed across smart cities, industrial control systems, precision agriculture, medical monitoring platforms, environmental telemetry grids, and autonomous sensing networks, the cumulative energy overhead induced by continuous IDS transforms from a secondary optimization concern into a primary architectural determinant. In large-scale deployments, the energy consumed by embedded security mechanisms directly affects operational costs, device lifetimes, carbon footprints, maintenance cycles, and overall system resilience. Consequently, IDS cannot be designed independently of energy dynamics. Instead, energy must be embedded into the mathematical core of IDS architecture as a strict feasibility constraint. In realistic IoT networks, nodes frequently operate under ultra-low-power conditions characterized by constrained battery capacity, stochastic harvesting inflow, duty-cycled execution patterns, non-volatile memory persistence overhead, and limited thermal dissipation envelopes. These devices typically rely on microcontrollers operating at sub-100 MHz, SRAM[1] capacities measured in tens of kilobytes, the absence of hardware floating-point acceleration, and radios whose transmission energy dominates computational arithmetic by orders of magnitude. Under such conditions, conventional full-capacity IDS paradigms, whether signature-based, ML-driven, deep neural network-based, or RL-based, impose computational and communication overhead that violates embedded feasibility constraints. The classical IDS objective of maximizing detection strength while ignoring long-term energy sustainability becomes incompatible with the realities of embedded deployment.

Green-ML-based IDS, therefore, emerges not as incremental optimization but as a structural redesign discipline. It integrates energy-aware systems engineering, lightweight algorithm design, hardware-conscious model compression, adaptive scheduling theory, distributed coordination, and cyber-physical control. The motivation for Green-ML-based IDS arises from five structural constraints inher-

[1] SRAM, or static random-access memory, is a fast volatile memory technology commonly used in microcontrollers for temporary data storage during program execution.

Green Intrusion Detection Systems for IoT. https://doi.org/10.1016/B978-0-44-344249-0.00012-0

ent to IoT networks. First, finite battery capacity imposes strict lifetime budgets measured across multi-year deployment horizons in remote agricultural fields, industrial pipelines, critical infrastructure corridors, and unattended sensing regions. IDS workloads must remain bounded within cumulative lifetime energy envelopes to prevent premature node exhaustion. Second, energy harvesting from solar radiation, radio-frequency scavenging, thermal gradients, and mechanical vibration introduces stochastic temporal variability, thereby requiring security mechanisms that scale proportionally with instantaneous reserves rather than assuming a stationary supply. Third, wireless communication incurs disproportionately high energy cost relative to local arithmetic, since radio transmission cycles demand substantial current draw and extended active duty windows; therefore, alert broadcasting without suppression rapidly depletes residual energy. Fourth, memory and compute resources remain severely limited; embedded microcontrollers with SRAM below 64 kB and fixed-point arithmetic pipelines cannot sustain high-parameter neural agents. Fifth, device density at a global scale implies that even microjoule inefficiencies per node aggregate into a measurable carbon impact across billions of endpoints. These constraints necessitate cross-layer co-design across sensing, modeling, communication, and control.

The proposed Green-ML-based IDS establishes a unified cross-layer security architecture that integrates IDS, distributed coordination, FL, and carbon-aware optimization within a closed-loop control paradigm. Unlike conventional IoT-based IDS frameworks that prioritize detection accuracy alone, Green-ML-based IDS introduces energy- and carbon-intelligent orchestration as first-class optimization objectives. As illustrated in Fig. 5.1, the architecture spans four hierarchical computational strata: IoT sensing layer, edge gateways, fog/regional intelligence nodes, and cloud-level global orchestration. At the IoT layer, ultra-lightweight TinyML models perform low-power feature extraction and preliminary anomaly detection under strict energy constraints. Edge gateways aggregate local alerts, execute lightweight distributed inference, and perform adaptive scheduling based on instantaneous carbon intensity and energy availability. At the fog layer, regional coordinators enable distributed anomaly consensus and model synchronization, while the cloud layer governs global FL, carbon-aware scheduling policies, and long-term optimization objectives. The entire framework operates under a feedback-driven control loop in which detection confidence, energy consumption, carbon footprint, and communication overhead jointly impact subsequent operational decisions. This holistic integration transforms IDS from a static classification task into a sustainable cyber-physical intelligence system that simultaneously optimizes security robustness, energy efficiency, and environmental impact.

5.1.1 Energy-driven security: formal paradigm

The conceptual shift from conventional IDS to Green-ML-based IDS redefines energy as a primary constraint variable in optimization. IDS design becomes a multi-

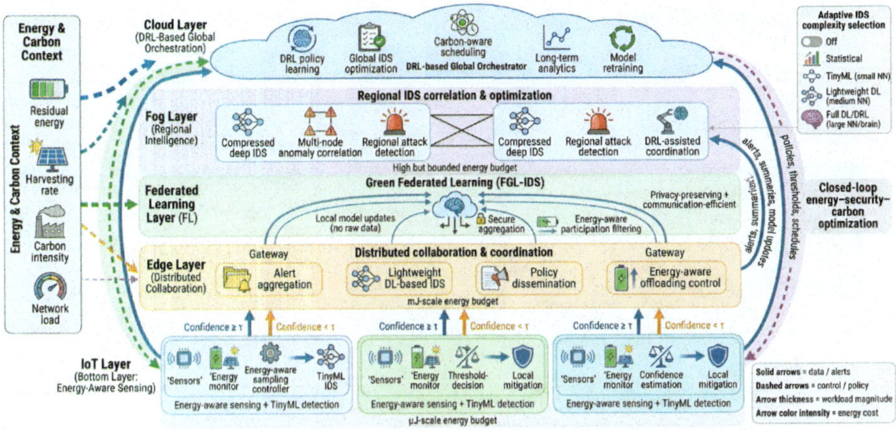

FIGURE 5.1

The architecture unifies IoT sensing, edge intelligence, fog-level coordination, and cloud-based FL under a carbon-aware closed-loop control mechanism. Security decisions are jointly optimized with energy consumption and carbon-intensity metrics, enabling sustainable, distributed cyber defense across heterogeneous IoT networks.

objective constrained optimization problem expressed as

$$\min_{M,P,\Pi} \left(E_{\text{comp}}(M) + E_{\text{comm}}(P) + E_{\text{monitor}}(\Pi)\right)$$

subject to

$$\text{Security}(M, P, \Pi) \geq S_{\min}.$$

In this formulation, M denotes the selected detection model, P represents the communication policy, and Π denotes the monitoring schedule parameters, including sampling rate and activation windows. Energy terms decompose computational cost, radio overhead, and sensing expenditure into separable but coupled variables. Security is defined as a composite function of detection rate, false-alarm behavior, mitigation latency, and robustness to adversarial drift. This formulation transforms IDS design into a constrained control problem in which model complexity, communication rate, and monitoring intensity adapt dynamically to maintain feasibility. To ground this abstraction in measurable hardware quantities, computational energy can be parameterized as

$$E_{\text{comp}} = N_{\text{cycles}} \cdot \epsilon_{\text{cycle}} + N_{\text{mem}} \cdot \epsilon_{\text{mem}},$$

where ϵ_{cycle} denotes per-instruction energy and ϵ_{mem} denotes per-memory-access energy. Communication energy can be modeled as

$$E_{\text{comm}} = N_{\text{TX}} \cdot E_{\text{TX}} + N_{\text{RX}} \cdot E_{\text{RX}},$$

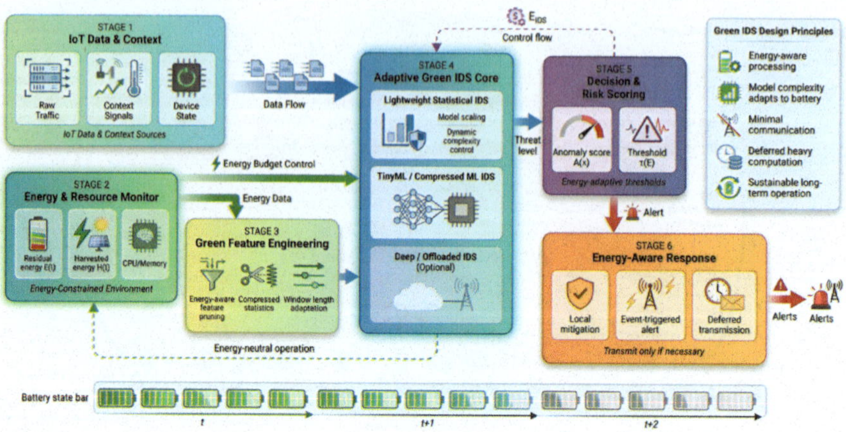

FIGURE 5.2

The architecture integrates sensing, real-time energy estimation, adaptive feature engineering, scalable inference selection, anomaly scoring with dynamic thresholds, and controlled mitigation under strict energy feasibility enforcement. The feedback path ensures long-term stability of the energy state and sustained detection capability.

with E_{TX} and E_{RX} determined by radio transceiver power states and modulation duration. Monitoring energy is governed by sensor activation frequency and ADC sampling cost.

5.1.2 Green-ML-based IDS processing pipeline

The Green-ML-based IDS processing pipeline embodies a closed-loop architecture in which energy monitoring governs detection behavior at every stage. The pipeline begins with raw traffic acquisition and contextual telemetry capture. Immediately after sensing, an energy estimation module continuously computes residual storage energy, the harvested inflow rate, the predicted depletion trajectory, and the instantaneous energy budget available for IDS execution. This energy state feeds into adaptive feature engineering, where dimensionality reduction, window-size compression, statistical aggregation, and integer-only transformation techniques bound arithmetic costs. The inference stage selects a feasible detection model according to residual energy thresholds. Anomaly scoring then computes risk metrics using adaptive thresholds scaled according to the available budget. Additionally, mitigation and communication actions are executed only after verifying feasibility within the energy envelope. Feedback from anomaly outcome and energy accounting loops back to adjust feature set size, model selection, and sampling frequency, thereby forming a sustainable cyber-physical control cycle. Fig. 5.2 illustrates this Green-ML-based IDS processing pipeline.

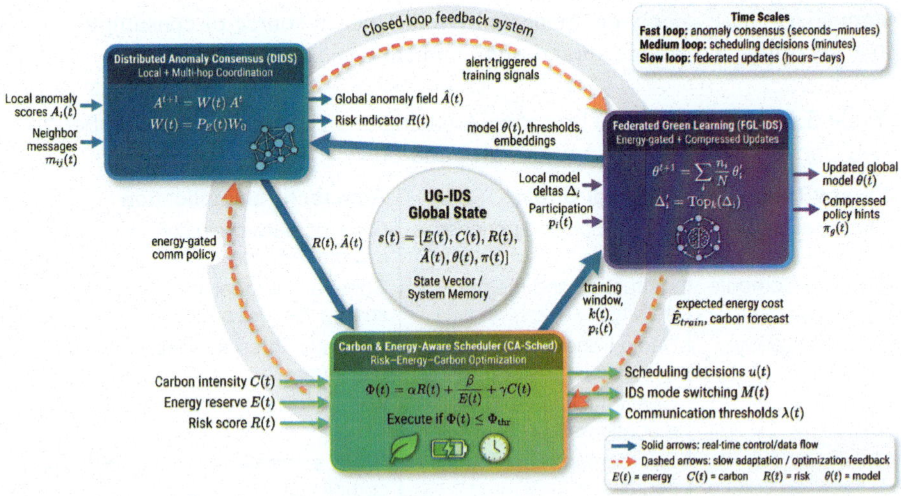

FIGURE 5.3

Closed-loop control structure governing long-term adaptation of the Green-ML-based IDS. The control loop integrates anomaly feedback, energy dynamics, and scheduling decisions to regulate detection intensity and model complexity over time.

While the processing pipeline describes the sequential execution of sensing, inference, and mitigation under instantaneous energy constraints, the long-term behavior of the Green-ML-based IDS is governed by a higher-level closed-loop control structure. In this control loop, anomaly feedback, residual energy dynamics, and scheduling decisions are continuously integrated to regulate detection intensity, model complexity, and communication behavior over time. This mechanism enables the system to adapt to evolving threat conditions and fluctuating energy availability, ensuring sustained IDS performance without compromising long-term energy feasibility. Fig. 5.3 illustrates this higher-level closed-loop control structure.

5.1.3 Energy taxonomy and lifecycle modeling

Energy consumption within embedded IDSs can be decomposed into static baseline power, dynamic computational energy, communication expenditure, mitigation overhead, and duty-cycle transition cost. Static baseline energy reflects MCU clock operation and peripheral readiness are independent of workload. Dynamic energy scales with arithmetic operations, multiply-accumulate count, and memory access frequency. Communication energy dominates in radio-intensive deployments and scales with transmission duration and packet size. Mitigation energy depends on reconfiguration actions such as channel switching, flow isolation, and packet dropping. Duty-cycle transitions introduce overhead during wake-sleep state changes. Table 5.1

summarizes these energy components by linking each source of consumption to its physical origin and architectural design implications.

Table 5.1 Granular energy taxonomy enabling analytical modeling of embedded IDS lifecycle consumption and design trade-offs.

Energy Type	Physical Origin	Architectural Implication
Static Baseline	MCU clock and peripherals	Governs duty-cycle scheduling and idle optimization
Dynamic Compute	Instruction and memory activity	Constrains model size, precision scaling, feature count
Communication	Radio transmission cycles	Motivates threshold adaptation and batching
Mitigation	Control actions and reconfiguration	Requires rate-limited execution policies
Harvest Inflow	Environmental energy sources	Drives adaptive scaling of IDS complexity

5.2 Energy-constrained IDS theory

Energy-constrained IDS operation treats energy not as a static deployment constraint, but as a dynamic state variable within a discrete-time cyber-physical security system. Let $E(t)$ denote the residual energy available at time t. The energy evolution of an IDS-enabled IoT node can be expressed as

$$E(t+1) = E(t) + E_{\text{harvest}}(t) - E_{\text{IDS}}(t).$$

In this formulation, $E_{\text{harvest}}(t)$ represents the energy replenished through harvesting or recharging, whereas $E_{\text{IDS}}(t)$ denotes the total energy consumed by intrusion-detection operation during the same interval. The IDS energy term decomposes into feature extraction, model inference, communication, and mitigation costs:

$$E_{\text{IDS}}(t) = E_{\text{feat}}(t) + E_{\text{inf}}(t) + E_{\text{comm}}(t) + E_{\text{mit}}(t).$$

This decomposition is important because each component is controlled by a different design lever. Feature extraction depends on sampling frequency and feature dimensionality; inference depends on model complexity; communication depends on alert frequency and reporting policy; and mitigation depends on the selected response action. Therefore, sustainable IDS operation requires joint control over the entire detection pipeline rather than isolated optimization of a single module.

At every decision interval, IDS execution must satisfy the basic energy feasibility condition

$$E_{\text{IDS}}(t) \leq E(t),$$

ensuring that the node does not allocate more energy to detection than is currently available. However, energy feasibility alone is insufficient, because an IDS that saves energy by disabling detection would fail its security objective. The system must also maintain minimum detection quality, which can be expressed as

$$\mathrm{TPR}(t) \geq T_{\mathrm{min}}, \quad \mathrm{FPR}(t) \leq F_{\mathrm{max}}.$$

Here, T_{min} defines the minimum acceptable true-positive rate, while F_{max} defines the maximum tolerable false-positive rate. The resulting optimization problem seeks to minimize IDS energy consumption while preserving both energy feasibility and detection guarantees:

$$\min_{F(t),M(t),P(t)} \quad E_{\mathrm{IDS}}(t),$$

subject to energy-budget constraints and security-performance bounds. In this expression, $F(t)$ denotes the selected feature set or feature-compression policy, $M(t)$ denotes the active detection model, and $P(t)$ denotes the communication or reporting policy.

This formulation provides the mathematical basis for the Green-ML-based IDS architecture introduced in this work. The architecture vertically integrates energy foundations, green networking, lightweight security primitives, ultra-lightweight detection, green intelligence, and global orchestration into a single energy-aware security stack. Rather than treating intrusion detection as an always-on software function, the Green-ML-based IDS treats detection as a scheduled, budgeted, and adaptive workload whose operating mode changes according to residual energy, harvesting availability, traffic intensity, and security risk. Fig. 5.4 provides an overview of this Green-ML-based IDS architecture. While this layered architecture captures the internal organization of an energy-aware IDS, practical IoT deployments also require distributed coordination across geographically dispersed and resource-heterogeneous nodes. A single-node IDS cannot provide sufficient visibility in multi-hop networks, where attacks may propagate through relays, gateways, and clustered edge regions. For this reason, the Green-ML-based IDS extends the energy-constrained control model to a distributed coordination topology. In this model, lightweight IDS agents perform local anomaly scoring, neighbor-level correlation, and compressed evidence exchange, while relay and gateway nodes perform multi-hop fusion, consensus formation, and policy dissemination. Communication links are activated only when residual energy and risk conditions justify transmission, preventing unnecessary radio use and preserving network lifetime. Fig. 5.5 illustrates this multi-hop distributed IDS coordination model. Building on distributed coordination, the Green-ML-based IDS further adopts a hierarchical–swarm hybrid architecture to improve scalability and resilience. The hierarchical component provides global organization through gateways, edge controllers, and orchestration layers, while the swarm component enables localized, self-organizing cooperation among lightweight IDS agents. Local agents exchange compact anomaly evidence through gossip-based communication, allowing clusters to reach consensus before escalating events to higher layers. This

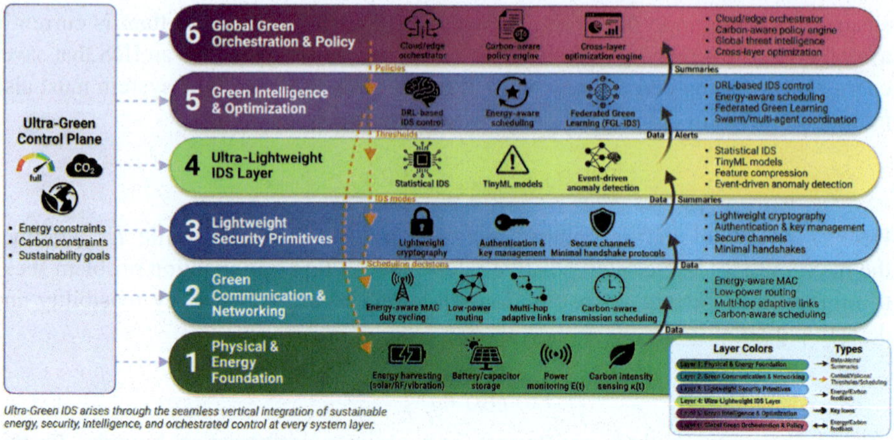

FIGURE 5.4

The architecture of the Green-ML-based IDS, illustrating the vertical integration of energy foundations, green networking, lightweight security primitives, ultra-lightweight detection, green intelligence, and global orchestration.

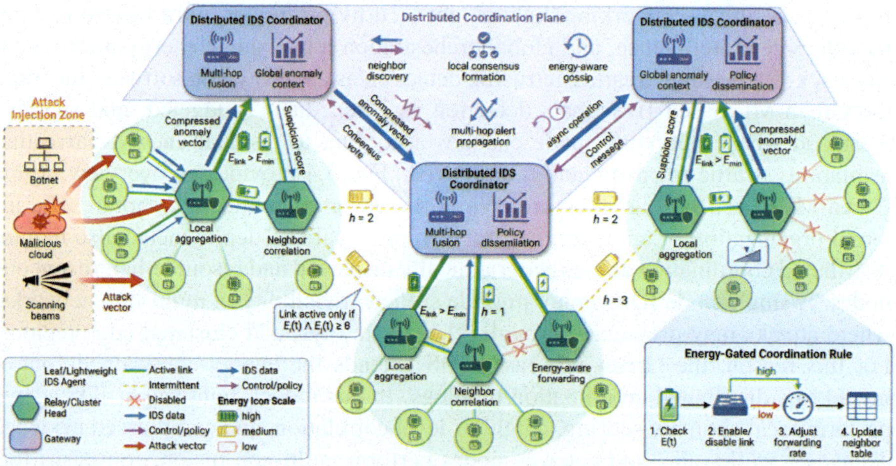

FIGURE 5.5

Multi-hop distributed IDS coordination topology with energy-gated communication links. Lightweight IDS agents perform local aggregation and neighbor correlation, while relay and gateway nodes execute multi-hop fusion, consensus formation, and policy dissemination. Communication links are dynamically enabled and disabled based on residual energy thresholds to ensure sustainable distributed IDS.

reduces redundant reporting, limits energy-expensive uplink traffic, and improves robustness when individual controllers fail or become temporarily unavailable. The

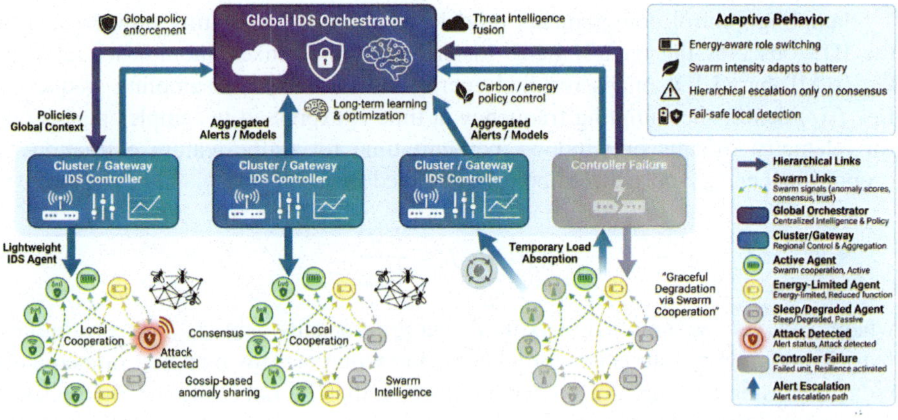

FIGURE 5.6

Hierarchical–swarm hybrid IDS architecture. The system combines global orchestration with swarm-based local intelligence, enabling scalable, resilient, energy-aware, and self-organizing IDS in large-scale IoT networks.

resulting architecture supports graceful degradation: if a cluster controller is compromised, depleted, or disconnected, neighboring agents can continue local detection and partial coordination until higher-level control is restored. Fig. 5.6 illustrates this hierarchical–swarm hybrid IDS architecture.

5.2.1 Model switching under energy constraints and threshold control

Model switching is the central mechanism through which the Green-ML-based IDS adapts detection complexity to the available energy budget. Let $\{M_1, M_2, M_3, M_4\}$ denote a set of increasingly complex detection models, where M_1 represents the lightest statistical or rule-based detector and M_4 represents the most expressive, computation-intensive model. Their energy costs satisfy

$$c_1 < c_2 < c_3 < c_4.$$

The model-selection policy $\pi(E(t))$ maps the current energy state to an active detector:

$$M(t) = \pi(E(t)).$$

This policy enforces piecewise feasibility thresholds so that higher-cost models are activated only when sufficient energy is available, while lower-cost models preserve baseline security coverage during scarcity. The Green-ML-based IDS therefore behaves as a hybrid dynamical system in which the detection state changes when residual energy crosses predefined operating boundaries.

Sampling control complements model switching by regulating how frequently the IDS observes the environment. Instead of using a fixed monitoring rate, the Green-ML-based IDS maps residual energy into an adaptive sampling frequency. Let $f_s(t)$ denote the sampling frequency at time t, expressed in samples per second for telemetry streams or windows per unit time for traffic-feature extraction. A proportional energy-normalized policy is defined as

$$f_s(t) = f_{\max} \frac{E(t)}{E_{\max}},$$

where $E_{\max}$ is the nominal maximum energy capacity and $f_{\max}$ is the highest feasible monitoring rate under fully charged conditions. This mapping immediately reduces sensing pressure during energy scarcity, thereby bounding the energy spent on sensing, feature extraction, and inference.

In practice, strict proportional control should be stabilized using saturation limits. A feasible implementation is

$$f_s(t) = \mathrm{clip}\left(f_{\min},\ f_{\max} \frac{E(t)}{E_{\max}},\ f_{\max} \right),$$

where clip$(\cdot)$ constrains the sampling rate to a safe interval, $f_{\min}$ preserves minimum situational awareness, and $f_{\max}$ prevents excessive monitoring under full-energy conditions. Since many IoT nodes operate using duty-cycled execution, this sampling policy can also be implemented through the inter-sample period

$$\Delta(t) = \frac{1}{f_s(t)},$$

which schedules sleep–wake transitions and links monitoring frequency directly to platform-level energy consumption.

The effect of sampling on IDS energy can be made explicit. Let e_{feat} denote the average energy per sampling step for sensing and feature computation, and let e_{inf} denote the average inference energy per decision. If detection is executed on every sample, the expected IDS energy rate becomes

$$\dot{E}_{\mathrm{IDS}}(t) \approx f_s(t)\big(e_{\mathrm{feat}} + e_{\mathrm{inf}}\big) + \dot{E}_{\mathrm{base}},$$

where $\dot{E}_{\mathrm{base}}$ captures static baseline power and peripheral readiness overhead. This relation shows that reducing $f_s(t)$ produces an approximately linear reduction in compute energy, while also indirectly reducing communication energy by decreasing the number of threshold evaluations and alert opportunities per unit time.

Threshold control complements sampling control by regulating communication behavior, which remains one of the dominant energy drains in many IoT devices. Let $A(t)$ denote the anomaly score produced by the detector at time t, with larger values indicating greater deviation from normal behavior. An alert decision is made according to

$$\text{SendAlert}(t) = \mathbb{I}\big[A(t) \geq \lambda(t)\big],$$

where $\mathbb{I}[\cdot]$ is the indicator function and $\lambda(t)$ is a dynamic threshold. A simple energy-adaptive threshold law is given by

$$\lambda(t) = \lambda_0 + \alpha\left(1 - \frac{E(t)}{E_{\max}}\right),$$

where λ_0 is the baseline detection threshold calibrated under nominal energy availability, and α is a sensitivity coefficient controlling how aggressively communication is suppressed as energy declines. This control law raises the alert threshold when energy reserves fall, requiring stronger anomaly evidence before activating the radio. The mechanism protects long-term sustainability by preserving residual energy for continued monitoring rather than spending it on frequent low-confidence alerts.

To make the coupling between thresholding and communication energy explicit, let e_{tx} denote the energy per alert transmission and let $p_\lambda(t) = \Pr\big(A(t) \geq \lambda(t)\big)$ denote the probability that an alert is triggered under threshold $\lambda(t)$. The expected communication energy per unit time can be approximated as

$$\dot{E}_{\text{comm}}(t) \approx f_s(t)\, p_\lambda(t)\, e_{\text{tx}} + \dot{E}_{\text{rx}}(t),$$

where $\dot{E}_{\text{rx}}(t)$ models reception overhead and beacon listening cost. Since $p_\lambda(t)$ is monotonically decreasing with $\lambda(t)$ for typical anomaly-score distributions, the combined control of $f_s(t)$ and $\lambda(t)$ yields multiplicative suppression of communication expenditure. This provides a principled justification for jointly adapting sampling and thresholds: sampling bounds compute frequency, while thresholding bounds radio utilization conditional on anomaly evidence.

For stability under noisy energy measurements and non-stationary traffic, a hysteresis-based threshold controller can be used. Define two energy boundaries E_{high} and E_{low}, with $E_{\text{low}} < E_{\text{high}}$. The system increases the alert threshold only when $E(t) \leq E_{\text{low}}$ and decreases it only when $E(t) \geq E_{\text{high}}$. This hysteresis mechanism prevents rapid switching between detection modes, reduces duty-cycle transition overhead, and produces smoother long-term behavior in intermittent harvesting systems.

Fig. 5.7 illustrates the energy- and carbon-aware scheduling and model-switching logic of the Green-ML-based IDS. Residual energy levels, harvesting dynamics, and risk indicators jointly determine the active detection mode. By enforcing energy-dependent thresholds, the system ensures that higher-complexity models are activated only when sufficient energy is available, while lightweight detection modes preserve security coverage under constrained conditions.

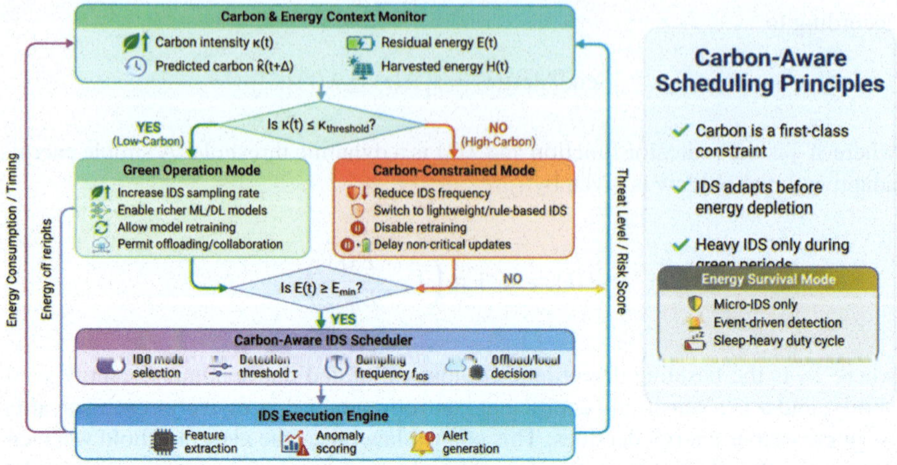

FIGURE 5.7

Energy and carbon-aware scheduling and model switching logic of the Green-ML-based IDS. Detection modes are dynamically selected based on residual energy thresholds, risk levels, and sustainability constraints to balance security effectiveness and long-term energy feasibility.

5.2.2 Feature activation under energy budget

Feature activation is the principal mechanism through which Green-ML-based IDS reduces dynamic compute cost while retaining sufficient discriminative information for robust detection. Let the full feature universe be $\mathcal{F} = \{f_1, f_2, \ldots, f_d\}$, where each feature f_i has an associated computation energy cost $\kappa(f_i)$ that captures sensing, arithmetic, and memory access overhead required for extraction. Let $F(t) \subseteq \mathcal{F}$ denote the active feature subset at time t. The objective is to select a subset that minimizes instantaneous compute energy while guaranteeing a minimum level of retained information needed for detection:

$$\min_{F(t)} \sum_{f_i \in F(t)} \kappa(f_i) \quad \text{s.t.} \quad I(F(t)) \geq G_{\min}.$$

Here, $I(F(t))$ is an information retention functional that quantifies the detection utility of the chosen features, and $G_{\min}$ defines the minimum acceptable discriminative content required to satisfy security constraints. In practice, $I(F(t))$ can be instantiated using mutual information with the attack label, the Fisher score[2], entropy reduction, correlation-based relevance, and empirical proxies such as the validation-set contribution to the true positive rate under constrained inference. The computational

[2] The Fisher score is a supervised feature-ranking criterion that measures how well a feature separates different classes by comparing between-class variation with within-class variation.

feasibility of a feature set depends on both feature cardinality and per-feature energy asymmetry. Some features require only incremental counters and integer additions, while others require expensive operations, e.g., FFT[3] transforms, histogram maintenance, and multi-pass aggregation windows. This motivates explicitly modeling the feature extraction energy:

$$E_{\text{feat}}(t) = \sum_{f_i \in F(t)} \kappa(f_i) n_i(t),$$

where $n_i(t)$ denotes the number of times feature f_i is computed within the sampling window, which depends on window length, packet rate, and aggregation policy. Under duty-cycled execution, $n_i(t)$ is itself controlled by $f_s(t)$ and by window sizing, producing a coupled resource-allocation problem across sensing and computation. Binary feature activation can be expressed by introducing indicator variables $z_i(t) \in \{0, 1\}$ such that $z_i(t) = 1$ implies feature f_i is active at time t. The energy objective becomes

$$\min_{\mathbf{z}(t)} \sum_{i=1}^{d} z_i(t)\kappa(f_i) \quad \text{s.t.} \quad I(\mathbf{z}(t)) \geq G_{\min}.$$

A feasible energy-proportional activation rule enforces activation only for features whose cost lies below an energy-scaled bound. Let $B(t)$ be the instantaneous compute budget allocated to feature extraction after reserving energy for inference and mandatory system functions. A simple activation mechanism is

$$z_i(t) = \mathbb{I}\big[\kappa(f_i) \leq \tau(t)\big], \qquad \tau(t) = \beta \frac{B(t)}{d},$$

where β controls conservativeness. This rule activates low-cost features preferentially in times of scarcity, while high-cost features become available only as budgets increase. Since naive thresholding may discard features that are moderately expensive but highly informative, a utility-aware activation mechanism can be used to weight each feature according to its benefit-cost ratio. Let u_i denote the offline utility score of feature f_i, estimated during profiling using mutual information, SHAP[4] contribution, permutation importance, or validation-set performance gain. Runtime selection then prioritizes features with high $u_i/\kappa(f_i)$, thereby retaining the maximum discriminative information per unit of energy. To align feature activation with detection guarantees, the constraint $I(F(t)) \geq G_{\min}$ can be operationalized through accuracy surrogates. Let $\widehat{\text{TPR}}(F(t))$ and $\widehat{\text{FPR}}(F(t))$ denote predicted detection performance under the active feature set obtained from calibration curves built during

[3] FFT, or fast Fourier transform, is an efficient algorithm for computing the discrete Fourier transform and is commonly used to extract frequency-domain features from signals.

[4] SHAP, or Shapley additive explanations, is an explainability method that estimates how much each feature contributes to a model prediction based on concepts from cooperative game theory.

profiling. The constraint becomes

$$\widehat{\mathrm{TPR}}(F(t)) \geq T_{\min}, \qquad \widehat{\mathrm{FPR}}(F(t)) \leq F_{\max},$$

thereby ensuring that energy-driven feature pruning does not collapse security guarantees. This produces a principled runtime procedure in which the device first proposes a low-energy feature set, then validates feasibility against calibrated security bounds, then expands the set only when constraints are violated. Feature activation is therefore not an isolated compression trick; it is a control variable embedded into the same closed-loop energy regulator that governs sampling and threshold adaptation. When integrated with model switching, sampling control, and communication throttling, feature activation enables graceful degradation under scarcity and controlled expansion under abundance, ensuring that the IDS remains operational across intermittent energy profiles while preserving minimum security guarantees.

5.2.3 Control-theoretic architecture

Energy-constrained IDS can be rigorously modeled as a feedback-regulated cyber-physical control system, with residual energy serving as a state variable that governs permissible detection behavior. The architectural abstraction illustrated in Fig. 5.8 formalizes this perspective by structuring the IDS as a closed-loop controller that continuously senses energy state, computes feasible control actions, executes adaptive detection operations, and updates future energy dynamics through feedback coupling. Rather than treating detection as an isolated inference task, the architecture embeds IDS execution within a dynamical system whose stability depends upon bounded energy evolution. Let the system state at time t be defined as the vector

$$\mathbf{x}(t) = \begin{bmatrix} E(t) \\ A(t) \\ \Theta(t) \end{bmatrix},$$

where $E(t)$ denotes residual energy, $A(t)$ denotes anomaly score statistics, and $\Theta(t)$ represents configuration parameters including sampling frequency, feature subset size, model index, and communication threshold. The controller computes a control vector

$$\mathbf{u}(t) = \begin{bmatrix} f_s(t) \\ M(t) \\ F(t) \\ \lambda(t) \end{bmatrix},$$

which determines the monitoring rate, the active detection model, the feature activation mask, and the anomaly threshold, respectively. These control actions are constrained by the feasibility condition

$$E_{\mathrm{IDS}}(t) \leq E(t),$$

which ensures that instantaneous execution does not violate physical energy limits.

The architecture depicted in Fig. 5.8 consists of four tightly coupled planes. The first plane performs continuous energy-state estimation via ADC[5] sampling of the battery voltage, inflow measurement, and predictive depletion modeling. This state estimator produces $\widehat{E}(t)$, a filtered energy estimate that compensates for sensor noise and transient fluctuations. The second plane constitutes the decision controller, which solves a constrained optimization problem at each control interval. Given $\widehat{E}(t)$ and recent anomaly statistics, the controller computes a feasible configuration $\Theta(t)$ that satisfies detection constraints while minimizing projected energy expenditure. The third plane runs the adaptive IDS engine, which includes feature extraction, inference, anomaly scoring, and mitigation logic, as specified by the selected configuration. The fourth plane updates the energy state through the dynamical equation

$$E(t+1) = E(t) + E_{\text{harvest}}(t) - E_{\text{IDS}}(t),$$

thereby closing the loop.

A fundamental objective of this control-theoretic formulation is long-horizon energy stability. Let $E_{\min}$ denote a safety threshold below which device operation becomes unsafe. Stability requires that

$$E(t) \geq E_{\min}, \quad \forall t.$$

A sufficient condition for boundedness is that expected harvested energy equals and exceeds expected IDS expenditure over a sliding horizon:

$$\mathbb{E}[E_{\text{harvest}}(t)] \geq \mathbb{E}[E_{\text{IDS}}(t)].$$

When harvesting becomes intermittent, the controller compensates by reducing feature dimensionality, lowering the sampling rate, increasing the anomaly threshold, and selecting lower-complexity models, thereby decreasing $E_{\text{IDS}}(t)$ until equilibrium is restored. This feedback mechanism transforms IDS into a self-regulating energy-aware controller. Detection output impacts future energy allocation via adaptive mitigation-cost modeling. High anomaly intensity increases short-term energy expenditure due to mitigation actions and potential communication bursts. The controller, therefore, incorporates anomaly-persistence statistics into its cost projection. Let $\rho(t)$ denote a smoothed anomaly persistence metric. The projected future energy requirement becomes

$$\widehat{E}_{\text{future}}(t) = \sum_{k=0}^{H} \widehat{E}_{\text{IDS}}(t+k \mid \rho(t)),$$

[5] ADC, or analog-to-digital converter, is a circuit that converts continuous analog signals, such as battery voltage, into digital values that can be processed by a microcontroller.

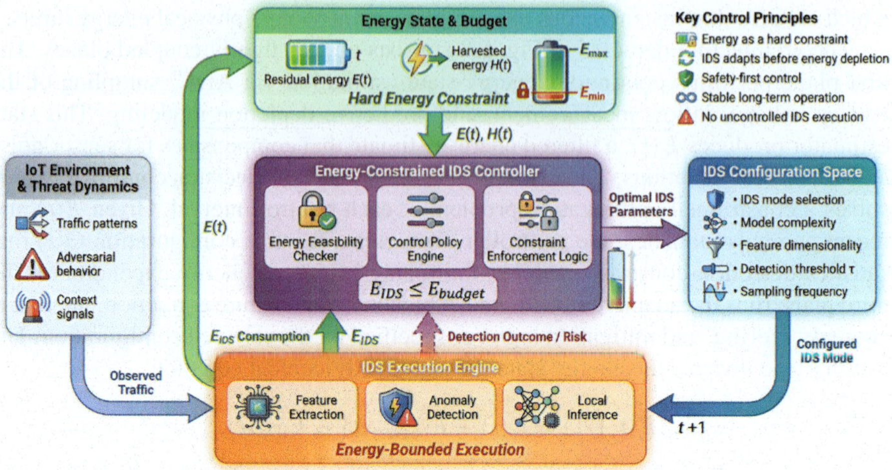

FIGURE 5.8

Control-theoretic Green-ML-based IDS architecture formulated as a feedback-regulated cyber-physical system. Residual energy estimation feeds a constrained decision controller that computes adaptive configuration parameters, including sampling rate, feature activation, model scaling, and communication threshold. Detection and mitigation actions update the energy state through a discrete-time dynamical equation, ensuring long-horizon boundedness and sustainable IDS under time-varying energy availability.

where H is a planning horizon. Configuration updates are selected to maintain

$$\widehat{E}_{\text{future}}(t) \leq \widehat{E}_{\text{budget}}(t),$$

ensuring sustainable operation under elevated threat levels.

Fig. 5.8 visually captures this architecture by positioning the energy estimator at the input of the decision controller, illustrating adaptive parameter computation prior to inference execution. The feedback arrow from the detection output to energy accounting emphasizes that mitigation and communication impact the subsequent residual energy. The architecture demonstrates that security strength and energy trajectory evolve jointly rather than independently. The energy complexity of individual subsystems within this architecture can be comparatively analyzed through dominant energy drivers and controllable parameters. Table 5.2 categorizes these components and identifies primary optimization levers available to the controller. This control-theoretic abstraction establishes a unifying framework in which sampling control, threshold scaling, feature activation, model switching, mitigation regulation, and energy estimation operate as coordinated actuators within a constrained dynamical system. By embedding feasibility directly into the controller's decision space, Green-ML-based IDS achieves sustainable detection capability across intermittent harvesting system, extended deployment lifetimes, and large-

Table 5.2 Energy complexity distribution across IDS subsystems within the control-theoretic Green-ML-based IDS architecture.

Subsystem	Relative Energy Cost	Dominant Variable	Optimization Lever
Feature Extraction	Low-Moderate	Dimensionality and sampling rate	Adaptive pruning and window scaling
Model Inference	Moderate	Multiply-accumulate count and precision	Quantization and model compression
Communication	Very High	Radio duty cycle and packet size	Threshold adaptation and transmission batching
Mitigation	Moderate	Action frequency and reconfiguration overhead	Rate limiting and deferred enforcement
Energy Monitoring	Minimal	Measurement interval and ADC cost	Sparse estimation and predictive filtering

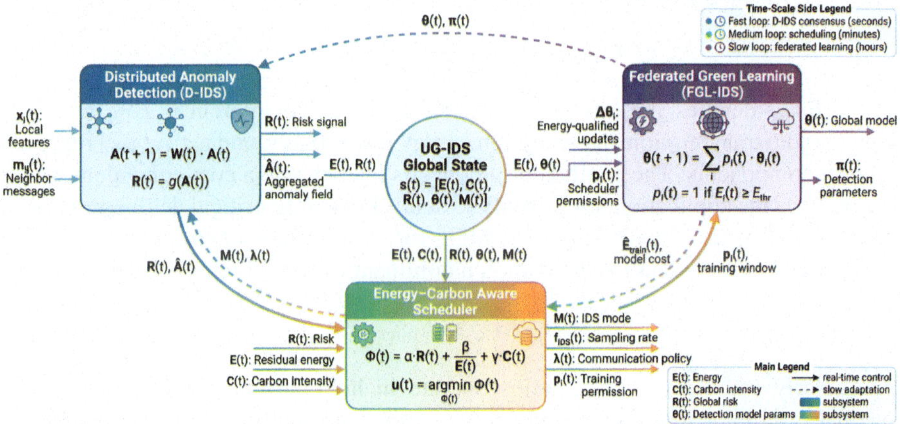

FIGURE 5.9

Control-Theoretic Architecture for Green-ML-based IDS. This architecture defines feedback loops between detection, decision-making, and energy control to optimize security and energy consumption.

scale device populations while preserving minimum security guarantees defined by the application domain. The Green-ML-based IDS framework incorporates control-theoretic principles to dynamically adjust detection thresholds and offloading decisions in response to environmental conditions. This closed-loop feedback system optimizes both energy consumption and security, as illustrated in Fig. 5.9. It depicts the feedback loops among the detection system, decision-making layer, and energy management components, enabling the system to adaptively respond to changing network conditions and energy constraints.

5.2.4 Energy-aware learning: on-device vs offloading

Energy-aware learning in Green-ML-based IDS extends beyond inference efficiency and enters the domain of distributed resource allocation across device, edge, and cloud categorys. The fundamental decision is whether to execute inference, adaptation, model update, and feature aggregation locally within the embedded node and then transmit the results to a more capable computational category This decision is governed by a comparative cost model that incorporates energy, latency, reliability, and exposure to security risks. The cost comparison can be formalized as:

$$C_{\text{local}} \overset{?}{<} C_{\text{offload}},$$

where the local execution cost is

$$C_{\text{local}} = E_{\text{infer}} + \gamma\, t_{\text{local}},$$

and the offloading cost is

$$C_{\text{offload}} = E_{\text{TX}} + E_{\text{RX}} + \gamma\, t_{\text{cloud}}.$$

Here, E_{infer} denotes the energy required for on-device inference, E_{TX} and E_{RX} denote radio transmission and reception energy respectively, and t_{local}, t_{cloud} represent latency components. The coefficient γ converts latency into a cost-equivalent weight that reflects the application's sensitivity to delay. For safety-critical deployments such as industrial control monitoring, γ is high; for long-horizon environmental sensing, γ is lower. In embedded IoT hardware, a dominant empirical regime holds:

$$E_{\text{TX}} \gg E_{\text{infer}},$$

particularly when low-power radios operate in high-current transmit states. This inequality implies that transmitting raw features and inference requests frequently consumes more energy than executing compact on-device models. Consequently, Green-ML-based IDS adopts a local-first inference principle, in which micro-models operate continuously while offloading is triggered selectively under specific conditions. A refined offloading trigger can be defined using a confidence-based gating function. Let $\hat{y}(t)$ denote model output and let $c(t)$ represent confidence magnitude derived from the decision margin. Define a confidence threshold τ_c. Offloading occurs when:

$$\text{Offload}(t) = \mathbb{I}\left[c(t) \le \tau_c\right] \cdot \mathbb{I}\left[E(t) \ge E_{\text{tx,min}}\right],$$

where $E_{\text{tx,min}}$ is the minimum safe energy reserve required for transmission. This dual condition ensures that low-confidence events escalate to more powerful edge and cloud models while preventing energy collapse under scarcity.

A key feature of Green-ML-based IDS is its ability to offload computational tasks based on real-time energy and carbon intensity metrics. As depicted in Fig. 5.10,

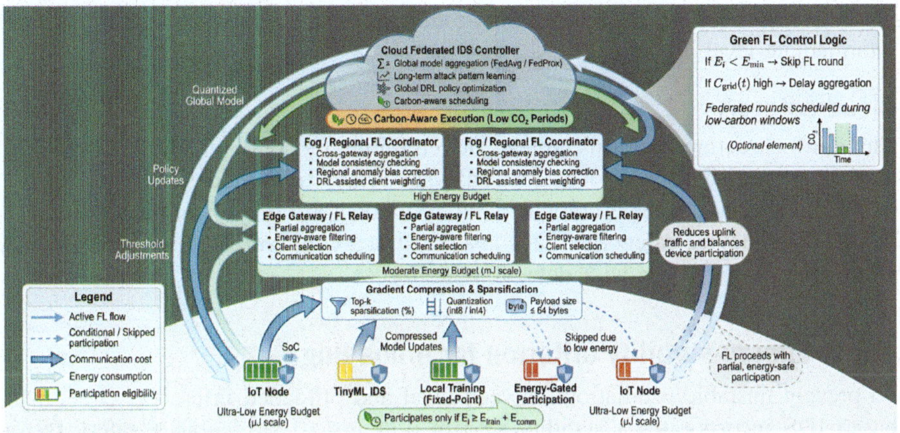

FIGURE 5.10

Cloud–Fog–Edge Carbon-Aware Execution and Offloading Mechanism.

anomaly detection tasks can either remain on-device, be offloaded to edge devices, and be forwarded to cloud infrastructure depending on task complexity, residual energy, and environmental conditions. This dynamic offloading ensures minimal energy consumption while maintaining real-time performance. The offloading decisions are made dynamically based on a joint optimization function that accounts for energy availability, computation cost, and carbon footprint.

5.2.5 Categoryed Green learning strategy

Green-ML-based IDS therefore, implements a hierarchical learning strategy composed of three coordinated categories:

Device category

The device executes compact quantized models such as Green Logistic Regression, shallow trees, and sparse Micro-NNs[6]. These models operate under strict energy budgets and provide baseline anomaly detection with predictable latency and minimal memory footprint. Feature compression and quantization are enforced to maintain fixed-point arithmetic feasibility.

Edge category

Gateways aggregate summaries from multiple devices and execute higher-capacity compressed deep models. Edge nodes possess greater memory and computational throughput, enabling more sophisticated drift detection, cross-device correlation, and

[6] Micro-NNs, or micro neural networks, are very small neural network models designed for memory- and energy-constrained devices, typically using few layers, few parameters, and low-precision arithmetic.

federated aggregation. Edge processing reduces cloud communication and provides intermediate-level intelligence.

Cloud category

Cloud infrastructure performs large-scale retraining, model distillation, global threat modeling, and adversarial robustness analysis. Heavy training costs are absorbed in this category, and distilled compact student models are periodically transmitted to the edge and device categories. This layered strategy minimizes device-level energy while preserving system-wide detection fidelity.

5.2.6 Energy-stability criterion for offloading

To prevent unstable oscillation between local and offloaded inference, Green-ML-based IDS incorporates a stability margin. Let $\eta \in (0, 1)$ denote a safety factor. Offloading is permitted only if:

$$E_{\mathrm{TX}} \leq \eta E(t).$$

This inequality requires that transmission cost consume only a bounded fraction of the residual energy. The safety margin prevents rapid depletion during bursts of anomalous activity. Additionally, cumulative offloading energy over a sliding window of length T must satisfy:

$$\sum_{k=t-T}^{t} E_{\mathrm{TX}}(k) \leq \eta_T \sum_{k=t-T}^{t} E_{\mathrm{harvest}}(k),$$

which guarantees long-horizon sustainability when harvesting is intermittent.

5.2.7 Communication-optimized update mechanisms

Model updates from edge to device are also energy-optimized. Instead of transmitting full parameter matrices, Green-ML-based IDS employs delta updates:

$$W_{\mathrm{new}} = W_{\mathrm{old}} + \Delta W,$$

where ΔW contains only changed parameters above a magnitude threshold. Compression of ΔW through run-length encoding, entropy coding, or structured sparsity further reduces transmission cost. Since update energy contributes to E_{comm}, infrequent batched updates are favored over frequent micro-updates.

Fig. 5.11 illustrates the energy-optimized ML-based IDS architecture with an explicit energy control plane. The energy monitor feeds both feature extraction and model inference modules, dynamically allocating budget across categories. Device-level inference operates continuously under tight constraints, while escalation to the edge and the cloud is governed by confidence and energy constraints. The architecture embodies a resource-aware pipeline rather than a static classifier. Fig. 5.12 further

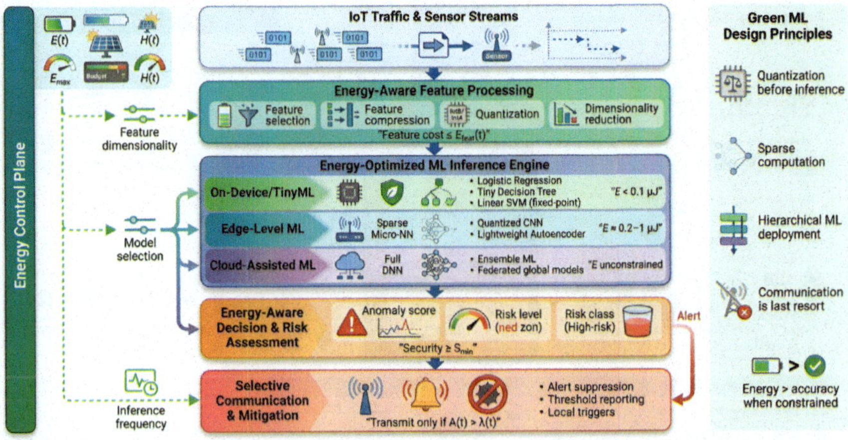

FIGURE 5.11

Energy-optimized Green-ML-based IDS with hierarchical execution across device, edge, and cloud categories. The energy control plane allocates budget for feature extraction, inference, and communication. Escalation decisions are governed by confidence metrics and residual energy feasibility constraints.

details the layered execution logic. The diagram separates inference complexity scaling from communication gating. Sampling frequency adapts according to residual energy; feature dimensionality scales under compute budget; model depth adjusts under inference constraints; communication is triggered only when anomaly confidence exceeds energy-shaped thresholds. This structured adaptation ensures graceful degradation: as energy decreases, ensembles reduce to sparse Micro-NNs, then to shallow trees, and additionally to statistical detectors. Detection continuity is preserved while preventing energy exhaustion.

5.2.8 Energy-accuracy Pareto category

Green-ML-based IDS model selection can be interpreted using an energy–accuracy Pareto category. Let $\mathcal{M}$ denote the candidate model set. Each model M_i has an associated pair:

$$(E_{\text{infer}}(M_i),\ \text{Accuracy}(M_i))\,.$$

The Pareto-optimal set[7] consists of models for which no other candidate achieves higher accuracy with lower energy. Runtime switching selects among Pareto-efficient candidates are subject to residual energy. This view clarifies that Green-ML-based

[7] A Pareto-optimal set contains solutions for which no objective can be improved without worsening at least one other objective. In this context, a model is Pareto-optimal if no alternative model provides higher accuracy with lower energy consumption.

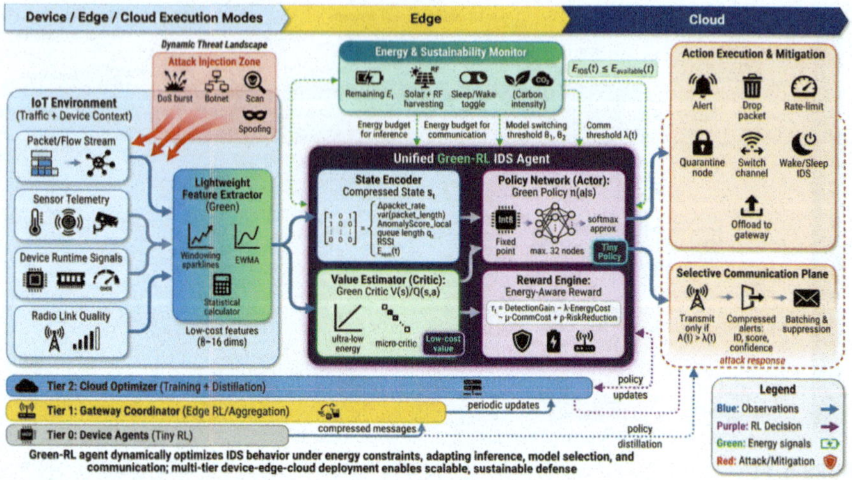

FIGURE 5.12

Refined runtime adaptation logic for Green-ML-based IDS The figure illustrates hierarchical model scaling, adaptive sampling, feature compression, and energy-gated communication under bounded embedded budgets. The system transitions smoothly across complexity levels as residual energy evolves.

IDS does not aim to minimize energy in absolute terms; instead, it seeks optimal trade-offs under strict feasibility constraints.

Fig. 5.13 illustrates the process of distributed anomaly detection in Green-ML-based IDS. Each layer of the system, from IoT devices to the fog layer, participates in detecting anomalies while considering local energy constraints. This distributed approach minimizes energy consumption while maintaining the system's ability to detect intrusions in real time. Table 5.3 provides a structured comparison of representative Green-ML-based IDS models under embedded constraints, highlighting their memory footprints, energy costs, latencies, and architectural advantages.

5.2.9 Security utility per Joule

The defining metric for Green-ML-based IDS can be formalized as security utility per unit energy:

$$U_E = \frac{\text{TruePositiveRate} - \lambda\,\text{FalsePositiveRate}}{E_{\text{infer}} + E_{\text{comm}}},$$

where λ penalizes false alarms. Maximizing U_E aligns detection performance with energy accountability. This metric provides a principled evaluation framework that captures the essence of Green-ML-based IDS: achieving robust IDS within physically bounded embedded systems.

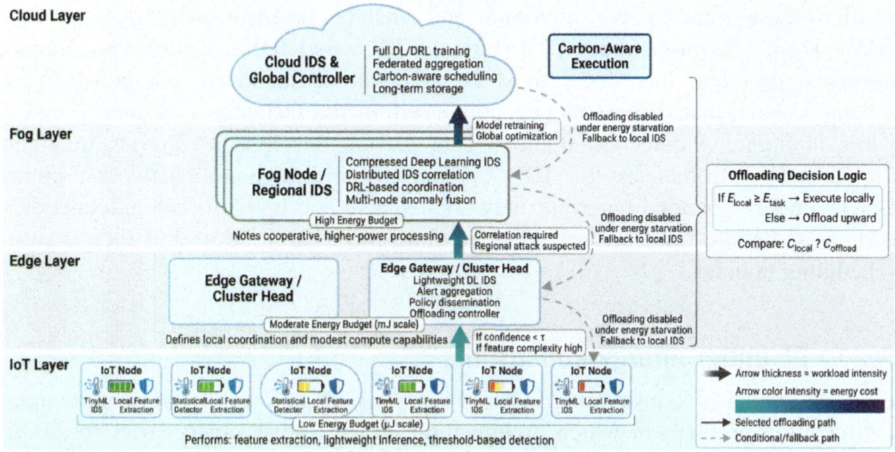

FIGURE 5.13

Distributed Anomaly Detection for Green-ML-based IDS. The system dynamically distributes computational tasks across the network layers, balancing energy efficiency and detection accuracy.

Table 5.3 Energy-latency-memory comparison of representative Green-ML-based IDS models across embedded and edge categories. Values are indicative and hardware-dependent, but they illustrate relative scaling trends.

Model	Memory (Bytes)	Energy per Inference (μJ)	Latency (μs)	Strengths
Green Logistic Regression	128-256	0.05	10-20	Deterministic, ultra-low energy
Green Tiny Decision Tree	200-400	0.10	15-25	Interpretable, fixed execution path
Sparse Micro-NN	512-4096	0.15-0.35	30-50	Nonlinear capacity with bounded cost
Green Ensemble	1024-6144	0.25-0.65	50-90	Robust under drift
Compressed DNN (Gateway)	8-32 kB	0.75-1.8	100-200	High detection strength at edge category

5.3 Green DL-based IDS models

DL provides the highest-capacity class of IDS methods for heterogeneous IoT traffic, particularly under non-linear, temporally structured, and high-noise conditions where feature interactions are complex. However, conventional DL architectures (large CNNs, LSTMs/GRUs, dense autoencoders, and Transformers) are fundamentally misaligned with the energy, memory, and arithmetic constraints of embedded IoT nodes and even many edge gateways. Their reliance on floating-point computation, dense matrix multiplication, high activation memory and frequent memory movement yield excessive energy per inference and unstable latency under duty cycling. Green Deep Learning (Green-DL) reframes DL-based IDS as an energy-bounded inference problem: the model must be architected, quantized, compressed, and scheduled such that it remains executable within the instantaneous energy budget while maintaining detection fidelity. This section develops a rigorous treatment of Green-DL mechanisms for IDS, spanning quantized neural networks, micro-CNNs, energy-bounded recurrent networks, sparse and bottlenecked autoencoders, compressed micro-transformers, adaptive multi-model arbitration, and energy-aware scheduling policies.

5.3.1 DL under energy constraints

DL under energy constraints reframes network design as a hardware-coupled optimization problem in which architectural choices must satisfy strict feasibility envelopes dictated by microcontroller execution windows, memory hierarchy behavior, and radio-dominated energy budgets. Let a deep network M comprise a layer set $\mathcal{L}$ in which each element $l \in \mathcal{L}$ denotes a computational block, such as a convolutional layer, a fully connected layer, an attention block, a normalization stage, a pooling operator, and a residual module. The total inference energy is naturally modeled as an additive accumulation over layers:

$$E_{\mathrm{DL}}(M) = \sum_{l \in \mathcal{L}} E_l.$$

For embedded and edge devices, the per-layer energy E_l is dominated by two physical contributors, arithmetic activity and memory movement, since the energy required to toggle transistors during multiply-accumulate execution scales with the number of active operations, while the energy required to move data across memory hierarchy scales with reads, writes, and buffer transfers. A practical layer-energy abstraction, therefore, takes the form

$$E_l = \alpha \cdot \mathrm{MACs}_l + \beta \cdot \mathrm{MemOps}_l,$$

where MACs_l is the multiply-accumulate count and MemOps_l is the number of memory operations required to fetch weights, read activations, write intermediate buffers, and commit outputs. The coefficients α and β encode hardware-dependent energy per MAC and energy per memory access, while also implicitly reflecting the precision (int8, int4, mixed precision), memory type (SRAM, flash, external RAM), access locality, cache behavior, DMA transfers, and pipeline stalls. This decomposition is central to Green's DL because two networks with comparable MAC counts can exhibit sharply different energy profiles when activation footprints differ, when weight reuse patterns change, when buffer lifetimes extend across residual paths, and when intermediate tensors exceed on-chip SRAM limits, forcing external memory traffic. To expose the memory component more explicitly, MemOps_l can be decomposed as

$$\text{MemOps}_l = R_l^{(W)} + R_l^{(A)} + W_l^{(A)} + R_l^{(B)} + W_l^{(B)},$$

where $R_l^{(W)}$ counts weight reads, $R_l^{(A)}$ counts activation reads, $W_l^{(A)}$ counts activation writes, and $R_l^{(B)}$, $W_l^{(B)}$ represent auxiliary buffer operations for im2col transforms, attention key-value caches, batch-norm statistics, and residual merges. This breakdown is useful because Green-DL optimization differs depending on which terms dominate. Convolution-heavy networks often reuse weights efficiently while producing large intermediate activations, whereas attention blocks tend to exhibit large activation persistence, particularly in key-value storage, even when weight size remains moderate. In constrained SRAM, activation movement dominates energy consumption through repeated reads and writes, motivating activation checkpointing, operator fusion, and memory-aware scheduling. Operational feasibility differs substantially across categories. On IoT devices, the per-layer operation envelope is typically constrained by short execution windows, limited MAC throughput, and strict duty-cycle constraints. A practical bound can be stated as

$$\text{MACs}_l \leq \text{few} \times 10^3,$$

which reflects realistic constraints for always-on tasks that must complete within millisecond-scale active windows at low clock rates while preserving time for sensing, communication, and sleep transitions. On edge gateways, higher throughput and larger memory budgets expand the feasible region:

$$\text{MACs}_l \leq 10^6 \text{ to } 10^7,$$

which enables moderately sized CNN backbones, compressed transformer blocks with reduced head dimension, and micro-transformers with constrained sequence length. In the cloud, arithmetic feasibility can scale to very high operation counts:

$$\text{MACs}_l \approx 10^9+,$$

Yet cloud execution remains constrained by communication energy, latency, privacy risk, and operational cost. In many IoT networks, the dominant feasibility limiter for cloud inference is not compute but the act of transmitting sufficient data to justify offloading, since radio transmission energy can exceed multiple local inference cycles. Green-DL therefore restructures deep architectures by jointly minimizing compute density, memory traffic, model size, and activation precision, thereby pushing the design into an energy-feasible region for the target category. This design objective is captured by a multi-criteria minimization:

$$\min\left(\text{MACs, MemOps, ModelSize, ActivationPrecision}\right),$$

subject to embedded feasibility constraints that are physically meaningful. Let $M_{\max}$ denote an available memory budget, including code, stacks, buffers, and model parameters, and let $L_{\max}$ denote a maximum allowable latency per inference window. Feasibility can then be enforced using

$$\text{ModelSize}(M) \leq M_{\max}, \qquad T_{\text{infer}}(M) \leq L_{\max}, \qquad E_{\text{DL}}(M) \leq E_{\text{budget}}(t).$$

The activation precision term is included because the activation bit-width governs both arithmetic energy and memory traffic, and in many embedded accelerators, activation bandwidth becomes the dominating bottleneck. Lowering activation precision reduces MemOps_l energy cost indirectly by shrinking the bytes moved per operation, which can be represented by a byte-aware memory energy expression:

$$E_l^{\text{mem}} = \beta \cdot \text{BytesMoved}_l \quad \text{with} \quad \text{BytesMoved}_l \propto \text{MemOps}_l \cdot b_l,$$

where b_l is the bit-width used for weights and activations. This relationship provides a direct justification for mixed-precision pipelines, operator fusion, and activation recomputation strategies in Green-DL. From an IDS perspective, deep models must satisfy not only resource constraints but also security and reliability under distribution shifts, adversarial perturbations, and noisy telemetry. As a result, Green-DL does not merely shrink networks; it constructs category-specific deep IDS designs that maintain robust decision margins under compression. This motivates additional constraints expressed through detection guarantees, such as minimum true positive rate, bounded false positive rate, and bounded drift sensitivity, while remaining executable within the energy-state-dependent budget. Consequently, Green-DL becomes a disciplined co-design problem spanning architecture, quantization, memory scheduling, and runtime energy control, ensuring deep inference remains sustainable across heterogeneous IoT networks.

5.3.2 Green CNN models (micro-CNNs)

Classical convolutional neural networks exhibit high arithmetic density and large intermediate activation footprints due to dense spatial convolution and channel expansion. In embedded IoT settings, both multiply-accumulate (MAC) operations and activation storage dominate inference energy, because arithmetic cost scales with MACs while memory cost scales with tensor size and access frequency. Green CNN models, referred to here as Micro-CNNs, redesign the convolutional pipelines so that arithmetic intensity and memory movement remain bounded within MCU-class feasibility envelopes. The design principles include replacing dense convolutions with depthwise-separable convolutions and grouped operators, aggressively quantizing kernels and activations, reducing channel widths, constraining spatial resolution, and minimizing intermediate buffer lifetimes. The objective is a simultaneous reduction of MACs and MemOps so that both compute energy ($\alpha \cdot \text{MACs}$) and memory energy ($\beta \cdot \text{MemOps}$) decrease.

5.3.2.1 Depthwise-separable convolution

Consider an input tensor of spatial resolution $H \times W$ with C_{in} channels and output channels C_{out}, using kernel size $k \times k$. The multiply-accumulate count for a standard convolution is

$$\text{MACs}_{\text{std}} = HWC_{\text{in}}C_{\text{out}}k^2.$$

This expression reflects that each output activation requires accumulation across all input channels and spatial kernel elements. The associated memory footprint includes reading $C_{\text{in}}C_{\text{out}}k^2$ weights and storing HWC_{out} output activations, which amplifies memory traffic. Depthwise-separable convolution decomposes this operation into two stages: a depthwise stage that performs spatial filtering independently per channel, followed by a pointwise stage that mixes channels using 1×1 kernels. The resulting multiply-accumulate count becomes

$$\text{MACs}_{\text{dw}} = HWC_{\text{in}}k^2 + HWC_{\text{in}}C_{\text{out}}.$$

The reduction factor is therefore

$$\frac{\text{MACs}_{\text{std}}}{\text{MACs}_{\text{dw}}} = \frac{C_{\text{out}}k^2}{k^2 + C_{\text{out}}},$$

which grows with channel count and kernel size. For common IDS-relevant configurations where $k = 3$ and $C_{\text{out}} \geq 32$, this ratio yields substantial savings. Importantly, the reduction is not solely arithmetic; the depthwise stage reduces the weight tensor size dramatically, and the pointwise stage accesses contiguous memory with improved locality, which lowers MemOps. The combined effect explains empirical reductions in the range

$$\text{Reduction} \approx 8\text{–}15\times,$$

depending on channel configuration and spatial resolution. From an energy perspective, the new layer energy becomes

$$E_{\text{dw}} = \alpha \cdot \text{MACs}_{\text{dw}} + \beta \cdot \text{MemOps}_{\text{dw}},$$

which can be significantly smaller than E_{std} even when MACs reduction appears moderate, since memory traffic often dominates embedded energy cost.

5.3.2.2 Green micro-CNN architecture

A representative Micro-CNN pipeline for IDS feature streams is

$$\text{Conv}_{\text{dw}} \rightarrow \text{Conv}_{\text{pw}} \rightarrow \text{ReLU} \rightarrow \text{Pooling} \rightarrow \text{FC-int4}.$$

Depthwise and pointwise kernels are typically quantized to int8. Final fully connected weights may be int4 to reduce parameter storage and memory fetch cost. Activations are clipped to bounded integer ranges to prevent overflow and stabilize quantized accumulation. Clipping constrains dynamic range, reducing buffer width, and lowering activation storage cost in SRAM. The total inference energy can be approximated as

$$E_{\text{microCNN}} = \sum_{l \in \mathcal{L}} \left(\alpha \cdot \text{MACs}_l + \beta \cdot \text{MemOps}_l\right),$$

where $\mathcal{L}$ includes depthwise, pointwise, pooling, and fully connected layers. In embedded configurations with channel widths below 32 and spatial maps below 16×16, practical energy falls in

$$E_{\text{microCNN}} \in [0.15, 0.40]\ \mu\text{J}.$$

The dominant determinants are channel count per block, activation map size, quantization bit-width, and memory locality. Since activation maps often dominate MemOps, pooling and stride selection become critical levers for reducing memory energy.

5.3.3 Green recurrent networks (micro-RNN, LSTM-lite, GRU-lite)

Temporal anomaly detection requires modeling sequential dependencies in telemetry and traffic windows. Standard recurrent architectures exhibit quadratic scaling with respect to the hidden dimension because each time step involves matrix multiplications over hidden-state transitions. A canonical recurrence is

$$h_t = f(W_h h_{t-1} + W_x x_t),$$

with $W_h \in \mathbb{R}^{n \times n}$ and $W_x \in \mathbb{R}^{n \times d}$. The hidden transition multiplication dominates cost with complexity proportional to n^2. Embedded feasibility requires reducing this quadratic term.

5.3.3.1 Low-rank Green-RNN

Factorization of the recurrent matrix into low-rank form

$$W_h = U V^T,$$

with $U, V \in \mathbb{R}^{n \times r}$ and $r \ll n$, reduces the transition computation from n^2 MACs to approximately $2nr$ MACs. The reduction ratio

$$\frac{2nr}{n^2} = \frac{2r}{n}$$

demonstrates linear scaling in rank. When $r = n/8$, the reduction becomes approximately $1/4$, yielding substantial energy savings. Quantization further reduces α by lowering arithmetic precision. Sparse masks on U and V reduce memory fetch cost.

5.3.3.2 Gate-reduced LSTM (LSTM-lite)

Standard LSTM architecture computes four gates at each time step, each requiring affine transformations and nonlinear activations. Removing selected gates simplifies the recurrence to a reduced form, such as retaining only input and candidate gates. Eliminating two gates reduces the number of matrix multiplications per step and the storage required for activations. Empirical reductions in the multiply-accumulate count are typically

$$\text{MACs reduction} \approx 40\text{–}55\%.$$

Since nonlinearities, e.g., sigmoid and tanh, are expensive in low-precision environments, approximating them with piecewise linear functions further reduces arithmetic energy.

5.3.4 Green autoencoders for unsupervised IDS

Autoencoders detect anomalies through reconstruction error

$$A(x) = \|x - \hat{x}\|_p,$$

where $\hat{x}$ is the decoder output. In Green-AE design, the encoder and decoder are quantized, sparsified, and compressed. The encoder aggressively reduces dimensionality to shrink the latent representation size, thereby limiting activation memory and MAC count. A Green-AE pipeline can be expressed as

$$x \to \text{int8-linear} \to \text{Sparse Bottleneck} \to \text{int4-decoder} \to \hat{x}.$$

The sparse bottleneck ensures that the latent code has minimal dimension and minimal memory footprint. Decoder pruning is aggressive since exact reconstruction fidelity is less critical than anomaly separation margin. Energy typically lies within

$$E_{\text{greenAE}} \in [0.3, 0.8]\ \mu\text{J}.$$

Under severe energy scarcity, partial decoding can approximate $A(x)$ by reconstructing only dominant feature subsets, thereby reducing MACs and MemOps at the expense of fine-grained sensitivity.

5.3.5 Green transformers (micro-transformers)

Self-attention models compute

$$\text{Attention}(Q, K, V) = \text{softmax}\left(\frac{QK^T}{\sqrt{d}}\right)V,$$

where quadratic interaction in sequence length T leads to $\mathcal{O}(T^2 d)$ complexity. This scaling is infeasible for the MCU-class hardware. Green Transformers reduce complexity by adopting linearized attention:

$$A(Q, K, V) = \phi(Q)\left(\phi(K)^T V\right),$$

which leverages associativity to achieve linear scaling in T under appropriate kernel feature maps $\phi(\cdot)$. Token compression reduces sequence length before attention, lowering both arithmetic and memory requirements. Low-rank projection matrices reduce the parameter count and the storage required for weights. Replacing softmax with ReLU-based normalization avoids exponentials, enabling efficient integer implementation. The total energy becomes

$$E_{\text{microTR}} = \alpha \cdot \text{MACs}_{\text{linAttn}} + \beta \cdot \text{MemOps}_{\text{linAttn}},$$

with practical energy in

$$E_{\text{microTR}} \in [0.5, 1.5]\ \mu\text{J}.$$

Such models are typically suitable for gateway-category IDS, where moderate energy envelopes permit stronger contextual modeling.

5.3.6 Unified Green-DL pipeline

The architecture in Fig. 5.14 should be interpreted as an energy-regulated inference ecosystem rather than a single deep model instance. The pipeline integrates heterogeneous telemetry streams, compressed representations, hierarchical micro-models, adaptive fusion, and energy-gated communication under closed-loop control. The central organizing principle is that each computational stage consumes a portion of a bounded energy budget; consequently, inference must be dynamically orchestrated to preserve feasibility across duty cycles and harvesting fluctuations. The pipeline begins with heterogeneous traffic statistics, device telemetry signals, protocol metadata, and temporal counters. These inputs pass through a green preprocessing layer that enforces numeric range constraints using fixed-point scaling, reduces entropy through binning and temporal aggregation, and maps floating-point features into integer formats such as int8 and int4. Let $x \in \mathbb{R}^d$ denote raw features and let $T(\cdot)$ represent preprocessing. The transformed representation becomes

$$x' = T(x),$$

where T enforces bounded dynamic range:

$$x_i' = \text{clip}(\lfloor s_i x_i \rfloor, -Q_{\max}, Q_{\max}),$$

with scaling coefficient s_i and quantization bound $Q_{\max}$ determined by bit-width. This transformation reduces memory traffic because activations are stored in low-bit form, and reduces arithmetic energy because integer multiply-accumulate operations replace floating-point arithmetic. The inference engine is multi-modal. Micro-CNN blocks extract localized spatial correlations in traffic feature windows. Micro-RNN and LSTM-lite modules capture short-term sequential anomalies such as bursty scans and periodic deviations. Sparse autoencoders compute reconstruction-based deviation scores for unsupervised detection. Micro-transformers, typically gateway-executed, capture contextual dependencies across longer windows when energy budget permits. Let the set of active models at time t be $\mathcal{M}(t)$. The instantaneous inference energy becomes

$$E_{\text{infer}}(t) = \sum_{M_i \in \mathcal{M}(t)} E_i.$$

Model arbitration is therefore critical. Instead of executing all models at full rate, the controller solves a constrained mixture problem that minimizes expected energy while preserving detection strength. Let $y_i(x')$ denote model outputs and let $w_i(t)$ denote adaptive fusion weights satisfying

$$\sum_i w_i(t) = 1, \quad w_i(t) \geq 0.$$

The ensemble output becomes

$$y(t) = \sum_i w_i(t) y_i(x').$$

The weights are energy- and confidence-dependent:

$$w_i(t) = g_i(E(t), C_i(t)),$$

where $C_i(t)$ is model-specific confidence. Under energy scarcity, $w_i(t)$ concentrates on low-cost models; under abundance, weight shifts toward higher-capacity components. The expected inference energy becomes

$$\mathbb{E}[E_{\text{infer}}(t)] = \sum_i w_i(t) E_i,$$

which can be bounded by controlling $w_i(t)$. Selective communication further constrains operational cost. Let $A(t)$ denote the fused anomaly score. Transmission occurs only when

$$A(t) \geq \lambda(t),$$

with $\lambda(t)$ shaped by energy state. Communication energy E_{TX} is therefore incurred selectively, preventing radio dominance under benign traffic. An energy-aware controller closes the loop by regulating model activation set $\mathcal{M}(t)$, precision level, inference frequency, and fusion weights according to residual energy $E(t)$, and harvested energy $H(t)$, and duty-cycle state $D(t)$. The energy evolution obeys

$$E(t+1) = E(t) + H(t) - E_{\text{total}}(t),$$

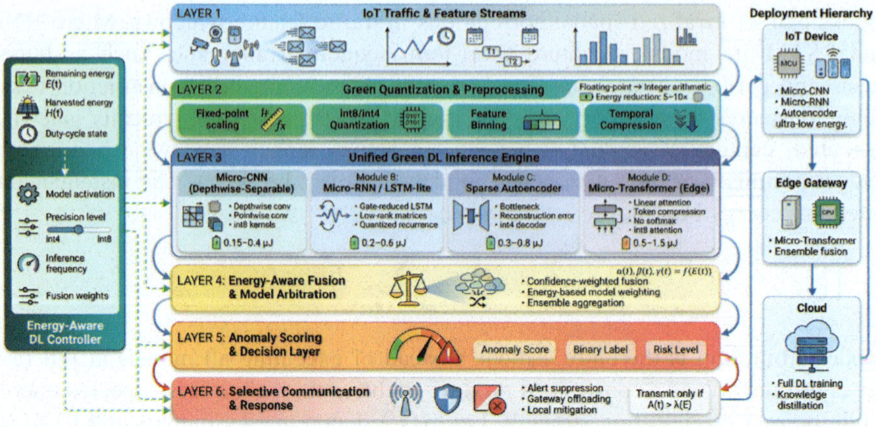

FIGURE 5.14

Unified Green-DL IDS pipeline formulated as an energy-controlled inference ecosystem. Heterogeneous telemetry undergoes fixed-point preprocessing and compression before hierarchical micro-model inference. Energy- and confidence-aware fusion minimizes expected inference cost. Selective communication limits radio overhead. A closed-loop energy controller regulates model activation, precision, and frequency based on the dynamics of residual and harvested energy.

where

$$E_{\text{total}}(t) = E_{\text{feat}}(t) + E_{\text{infer}}(t) + E_{\text{comm}}(t).$$

The architecture depicted in Fig. 5.14 illustrates this closed-loop structure: preprocessing constrains representation cost; hierarchical inference adapts complexity; fusion balances accuracy and energy; communication gating prevents radio overuse; and the energy controller ensures a bounded residual trajectory.

5.3.7 Mathematical optimization for Green-DL IDS

Let θ denote model parameters including weights, biases, quantization scales, sparsity masks, and structural hyperparameters. The energy of memory movement requires minimal inference energy subject to detection constraints:

$$\min_{\theta} E_{\text{infer}}(\theta) \quad \text{s.t.} \quad A(\theta) \geq A_{\min}.$$

Inference energy is decomposed into interpretable penalties:

$$E_{\text{infer}}(\theta) = \lambda_1 \text{MACs}(\theta) + \lambda_2 \text{Memory}(\theta) + \lambda_3 \text{PrecisionLoss}(\theta).$$

The first term measures arithmetic intensity. The second measures the effective parameter count and activation footprint, capturing the energy used for memory movement. The third penalizes accuracy degradation due to low-bit quantization and compression. Let

$$\epsilon_l = \mathbb{E}\left[\left|a_l^{\text{fp}} - a_l^{\text{quant}}\right|\right]$$

represent layer-wise quantization error. A compact surrogate becomes

$$\theta^* = \arg\min_{\theta} \left(\lambda_1 \sum_l \text{MACs}_l + \lambda_2 \|W\|_0 + \lambda_3 \sum_l \epsilon_l \right).$$

This formulation formalizes Green-DL practice: redesign layers to reduce MACs_l, prune to reduce $\|W\|_0$, calibrate quantization to reduce ϵ_l.

5.3.8 Hierarchical Green-DL execution model

Green-DL execution is category-dependent due to heterogeneous energy envelopes.

On-device category

Feasible inference satisfies

$$E_{\max} < 0.5\ \mu\text{J}.$$

This constraint implies shallow micro-CNNs, GLR-like heads, and short-window micro-RNN modules with bounded activation footprint.

Edge Gateway category

The envelope expands:

$$E_{\max} < 5\ \mu\text{J}.$$

This permits compressed deep CNNs, sparse transformers with token compression, and higher-dimensional embeddings.

Cloud category

Compute energy is effectively unconstrained locally:

$$E_{\max} \approx \infty,$$

Yet communication energy, privacy constraints, and latency govern offloading decisions. The runtime switching rule selects the highest-utility feasible level:

$$\text{ExecutionLevel}(t) = \arg\max_{\ell} \left\{ U_\ell : E(t) \geq E_{\text{required}}(\ell) \right\},$$

where utility U_ℓ incorporates detection strength and confidence stability.

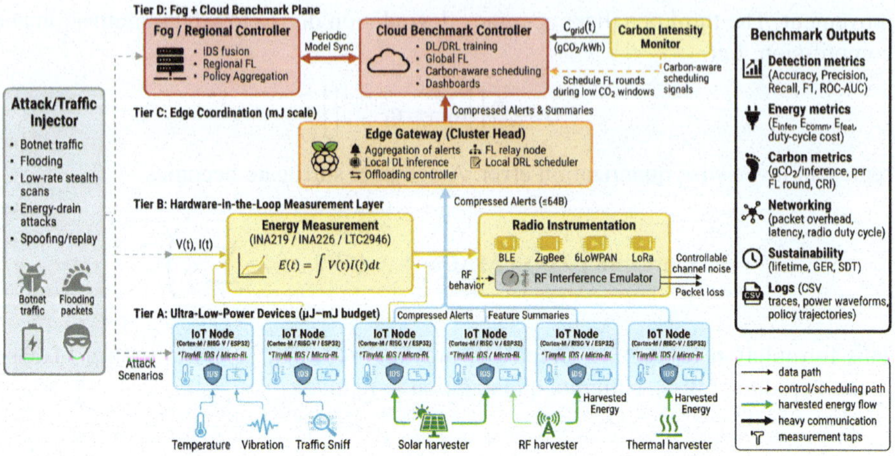

FIGURE 5.15

Hierarchical–Swarm IDS Hybrid Architecture.

5.3.9 Energy-accuracy envelope of Green-DL models

The feasible designs lie on a Pareto category:

$$\mathcal{P} = \{(E, A) \mid \nexists (E', A') \text{ with } E' < E \wedge A' > A\}.$$

This formalizes irreducible trade-offs. Let $U_E = A/E$ denote energy-normalized utility. Green-DL models are selected to maximize U_E within feasibility bounds.

To balance scalability and resilience, Green-ML-based IDS adopts a hybrid hierarchical–swarm coordination paradigm. In contrast to purely centralized and decentralized models, this hybrid approach minimizes bottlenecks, ensures fault tolerance, and reduces communication overhead. As shown in Fig. 5.15, IoT devices are grouped into local swarms that perform cooperative voting and anomaly detection. The local results are aggregated by edge gateways, which supervise multiple swarms and synchronize information across regional clusters. This decentralized coordination allows for more efficient processing and faster decision-making, especially in resource-constrained environments.

5.3.10 Green multi-model ensemble

The ensemble fusion is defined as

$$y(t) = \alpha(t) y_{\text{cnn}} + \beta(t) y_{\text{rnn}} + \gamma(t) y_{\text{ae}},$$

with

$$\alpha(t) + \beta(t) + \gamma(t) = 1.$$

Weights adapt according to residual energy:

$$[\alpha(t), \beta(t), \gamma(t)] = f(E(t)),$$

so that energy scarcity concentrates mass on low-cost models. Expected energy becomes

$$\mathbb{E}[E(t)] = \alpha(t)E_{\text{cnn}} + \beta(t)E_{\text{rnn}} + \gamma(t)E_{\text{ae}}.$$

This adaptive mixture ensures bounded average cost.

5.3.11 Green-DL training and distillation

Training occurs at the gateway and in the cloud to avoid infeasibility on devices. Quantization-aware training optimizes low-bit parameters directly. Knowledge distillation transfers representations from teacher T to student S through

$$\mathcal{L} = \lambda_1 \mathcal{L}_{\text{CE}}(S(x), y) + \lambda_2 \mathcal{L}_{\text{KD}}(S(x), T(x)).$$

Distillation compresses decision geometry into micro-models while preserving detection capability. The resulting student satisfies

$$E_{\text{student}} \ll E_{\text{teacher}},$$

Yet it approximates teacher accuracy within an acceptable margin. Unified Green-DL is therefore an energy-aware framework in which preprocessing, hierarchical inference, fusion, communication gating, and control are tightly integrated. The system does not deploy DL statically; it continuously negotiates energy, accuracy, latency, and memory to maintain sustainable IDS across heterogeneous IoT categories.

5.4 Green RL-based IDS models

RL introduces autonomous, adaptive, and sequential decision-making into IoT IDS by explicitly optimizing *actions over time* rather than static classification decisions. This capability is essential in operational IoT networks where threats evolve, benign traffic exhibits non-stationarity, devices' duty cycle, links fluctuate, and mitigation actions incur different energy and availability costs. However, conventional DRL algorithms (DQN, PPO, A3C, DDPG) are computationally intensive, memory hungry, and update-heavy, which conflicts with the strict energy envelopes of embedded nodes and even many edge gateways. Green RL (Green-RL IDS), therefore, reformulates RL for IDS as an *energy-bounded control problem*: the agent must learn policies that maximize long-horizon detection and mitigation utility while guaranteeing feasibility under limited computing, memory, and communication resources energy. The Green-RL IDS design space includes

1) state-space compression and low-cost sensing, 2) compact policy and value representations (quantized and sparse), 3) hierarchical and hybrid agents that degrade gracefully under energy scarcity, 4) selective communication and coordination, and 5) scheduling policies that explicitly decide *when* IDS mechanisms should run. Beyond these core elements, Green-RL IDS additionally requires stability-aware exploration, cost-constrained learning, and cross-category training workflows that prevent update overhead from dominating the device energy budgets.

5.4.1 RL for IDS: problem formulation

The IoT IDS is modeled as a MDP:

$$\mathcal{M} = (\mathcal{S}, \mathcal{A}, P, R, \gamma),$$

where $\mathcal{S}$ is the (compressed) device and network state, $\mathcal{A}$ is a compact action set encoding IDS decisions, $P(s'|s, a)$ is the transition kernel capturing how traffic and device state evolve under actions, $R(s, a)$ is the reward that must incorporate both security utility and energy expenditure, and $\gamma \in (0, 1)$ discounts future outcomes. The MDP abstraction is appropriate because IDS actions (e.g., rate limiting, channel switching, sleep and wake decisions) alter the future traffic distribution and the device's energy trajectory, making the objective intrinsically sequential. In practice, IoT observations are often partial, since a node cannot continuously observe the full network context. The operational setting can therefore be interpreted as a partially observed MDP in which the agent maintains a compact belief proxy computed from low-cost statistics, yet the policy remains implementable as a function of the compressed state vector to preserve feasibility. Because IoT nodes cannot afford high-dimensional telemetry, the state must be constrained:

$$\dim(\mathcal{S}_{\text{IoT}}) \leq 8\text{–}16,$$

which is not merely an implementation preference; it is a feasibility constraint that ensures the feature pipeline and policy evaluation remain within the per-decision energy budget. The action set is similarly compact:

$$\mathcal{A} = \{\text{Alert, Drop Packet, Rate-Limit, Switch Channel, Wake IDS,}\\ \text{Sleep IDS, Update Thresholds}\}.$$

Each action has a distinct energy footprint and risk implication. For example, `Alert` and `Switch Channel` typically incur high communication and radio reconfiguration energy, whereas `Update Thresholds` is mostly compute-local and thus cheaper. A Green-RL IDS formulation treats actions as control actuators that change both cyber state and physical energy state. This yields a coupled cyber-physical transition model:

$$P(s', E' \mid s, E, a) = P(s' \mid s, a)\, P(E' \mid E, a, H),$$

where H denotes harvested inflow statistics. This coupling is central because the same action can be feasible under different conditions, depending on residual energy and harvesting context. The reward must explicitly penalize energy usage while preserving detection utility:

$$R(s,a) = R_{\text{det}}(s,a) - \lambda E(a),$$

where $R_{\text{det}}(s,a)$ encodes security benefit (e.g., correct mitigation, reduced compromise probability, improved time-to-detect) and $E(a)$ encodes the energy cost of executing a. The coefficient λ converts energy units into reward units, thereby controlling the system's aggressiveness. The discrete energy-cost illustration:

$$E(a) \in \{0.01, 0.1, 1.0\}\ \mu\text{J}$$

captures the reality that some actions are essentially "free" (local parameter updates), some are moderate (local mitigation), and some are expensive (radio transmission and channel changes). In operational deployments, $E(a)$ can be replaced by measured per-action profiles obtained from profiling traces, yet the Green-RL IDS principle remains the same: the optimal policy must internalize the energy budget via reward shaping and hard feasibility gates. A stronger constrained formulation models this as a constrained MDP (CMDP) with a cost function $C(s,a) = E(a)$:

$$\max_{\pi} \mathbb{E}_{\pi}\left[\sum_{t=0}^{\infty} \gamma^t R_{\text{det}}(s_t, a_t)\right] \quad \text{s.t.} \quad \mathbb{E}_{\pi}\left[\sum_{t=0}^{\infty} \gamma^t C(s_t, a_t)\right] \le \bar{C},$$

where $\bar{C}$ denotes a long-horizon energy budget. This CMDP view is important because it separates utility maximization from cost feasibility, preventing reward-scale choices from unintentionally encouraging energy collapse.

5.4.2 Green RL state space compression

IoT devices cannot maintain high-dimensional states due to 1) feature extraction energy, 2) memory footprint for buffering, and 3) the downstream cost of policy and value evaluation. Green state design, therefore, prioritizes low-cost sufficient statistics that preserve discriminative information for both detection and mitigation control. A representative compressed state is:

$$s_t = \left[\Delta p_t,\ \text{var}(L_t),\ \text{RSSI}_t,\ \text{AnomScore}_t,\ q_t,\ E_{\text{rem},t}\right],$$

where Δp_t captures abrupt traffic-rate changes that often accompany scans and floods, $\text{var}(L_t)$ captures packet-size dispersion associated with attack tools and protocol misuse, RSSI_t provides a low-cost proxy for link reliability (affecting both detection quality and the cost-benefit of communication), AnomScore_t is the output of a lightweight statistical detector (serving as a cheap teacher signal and reducing RL sample complexity), q_t approximates congestion and device workload, and $E_{\text{rem},t}$ is the remaining energy reserve which is the primary feasibility variable. This construction is deliberately hybrid: it couples low-level network statistics with system-level energy state, so the policy can trade off security actions against survivability.

To align compression with energy modeling, each state component can be associated with an extraction cost κ_i, yielding feature energy

$$E_{\text{state}}(t) = \sum_{i=1}^{d} \kappa_i \, \mathbb{I}[s_t^{(i)} \text{ computed}],$$

which allows the controller to disable expensive features under scarcity while preserving minimal situational awareness. This yields a two-level decision: first decide the state subset to compute, then decide the action using the resulting compressed state. Such co-design prevents the RL loop from assuming a fixed observation pipeline that becomes infeasible at low energy.

5.4.3 Green policy networks

The policy $\pi(a|s)$ must be small enough to 1) fit in limited RAM and flash, 2) execute in low-bit integer arithmetic, and 3) maintain predictable latency under duty cycling. A compact policy network is:

$$\pi(a|s) = \text{softmax}(W_2 \, \sigma(W_1 s)),$$

where W_1 and W_2 are small matrices and $\sigma(\cdot)$ is a cheap nonlinearity. In Green-RL IDS, the above form is retained but engineered for embedded feasibility: W_1, W_2 are quantized to int8 (and potentially int4 for final layers), the hidden dimension is bounded (e.g., ≤ 32) to control MACs, and expensive operations (softmax, floating-point activations) are replaced with integer-friendly approximations. Specifically, replacing softmax with hardmax and a linear normalizer avoids exponentials and improves determinism, while using integer ReLU6 clips activations to a bounded range, stabilizing quantized inference. These constraints yield:

$$\|\pi\|_{\text{mem}} < 8 \text{ kB}, \qquad E_\pi < 0.08 \ \mu\text{J},$$

where the memory bound ensures deployability on microcontroller-class hardware and the energy bound ensures the policy evaluation does not dominate the IDS decision budget. The key Green-RL IDS insight is that policy expressiveness must be matched to the state compression; if S is low-dimensional and structured, a small policy can achieve robust control without deep networks. In addition, exploration must be energy-aware. A practical exploration schedule uses an energy-gated ϵ-greedy policy:

$$\epsilon(t) = \epsilon_{\min} + (\epsilon_{\max} - \epsilon_{\min}) \frac{E(t)}{E_{\max}},$$

So exploratory actions become rarer as residual energy declines, reducing the probability of expensive missteps.

5.4.4 Green value estimators (Q, V)

Value estimation frequently dominates computational overhead in actor-critic and value-based deep RL architectures because critics are typically implemented as multi-layer neural networks that require repeated forward and backward passes. In embedded IoT IDS, such architectures violate energy feasibility constraints. Green-RL IDS therefore re-engineers value estimation around linear and sparse approximators whose computational complexity scales linearly with state dimension and whose memory footprint remains tightly bounded. A Green linear Q-function is defined as

$$Q(s,a) \approx w_a^T s,$$

where each action a is associated with a parameter vector $w_a \in \mathbb{R}^d$. Evaluation reduces to a dot product between the compressed state s and the corresponding weight vector. Under integer quantization (int8 and int16), this computation requires d multiply–accumulate operations and one argmax over actions. The resulting energy remains minimal:

$$E_{\text{Q-linear}} \approx 0.02\ \mu\text{J},$$

which is compatible with high-frequency scheduling loops and duty-cycled execution. To further reduce arithmetic density, sparsity is introduced at the critic level:

$$Q(s,a) = \sum_{i \in \mathcal{I}} w_{ai} s_i, \qquad |\mathcal{I}| \ll d.$$

Only a subset $\mathcal{I}$ of state indices contributes materially to control decisions. The effective MAC reduction factor becomes

$$\frac{d}{|\mathcal{I}|},$$

implying that when only 4-6 state components dominate policy-relevant variance, arithmetic cost can drop by a factor of two to four without measurable degradation in control quality. This sparsity is particularly valuable when the RL loop executes at a high rate for tasks such as IDS wake-sleep decisions, threshold tuning, and sampling-rate adaptation. Stability under low-precision arithmetic requires bounding the temporal-difference (TD) error:

$$\delta \leftarrow \text{clip}(\delta, -\delta_{\max}, \delta_{\max}),$$

which prevents quantization-induced amplification of large residuals. Without clipping, fixed-point representations can cause unstable parameter oscillation due to overflow and scale mismatch. Thus, clipping acts as an embedded stability constraint.

5.4.5 Green DQN (Q-learning with micro-networks)

Deep Q-Network (DQN) learning traditionally relies on deep critics, replay buffers, and target networks. Each component increases the memory footprint and the complexity of updates. Green-DQN modifies this structure to enforce strict embedded feasibility. The canonical update

$$Q(s,a) \leftarrow Q(s,a) + \alpha \left(R + \gamma \max_{a'} Q(s',a') - Q(s,a) \right)$$

remains structurally intact; however, the approximator is reduced to a micro-network with a single hidden layer of width less than 32 neurons and quantized weights. Target networks are removed to eliminate duplicated parameter storage, and stability is preserved through reduced learning rates and TD clipping rather than architectural redundancy. Replay memory is compressed by storing quantized states $\tilde{s}$ and state deltas rather than raw floating-point vectors:

$$\text{ReplayBytes} \approx B \cdot (\text{Bytes}(\tilde{s}) + \text{Bytes}(a) + \text{Bytes}(r) + \text{Bytes}(\Delta\tilde{s})).$$

Here B denotes buffer length. Delta encoding exploits temporal correlation to reduce energy consumption for memory movement. Since memory access often costs as much as arithmetic in embedded systems, this compression has a tangible energy impact. Update execution is energy-gated:

$$\text{Update}(t) = \mathbb{I}[E(t) \geq E_{\text{upd,min}}] \cdot \mathbb{I}[t \bmod K = 0].$$

Weight updates, therefore, occur only when residual energy exceeds a safety threshold and only at sparse intervals. This converts learning into a conditional operation rather than a constant background load. The resulting update energy remains bounded:

$$E_{\text{GDQN}} \in [0.09, 0.25] \ \mu\text{J}.$$

This range reflects device-category versus gateway-category updates and compressed state dimensionality.

5.4.6 Green actor-critic (AC-lite)

Actor-critic architectures naturally separate policy and value estimation. In Green AC-lite, this separation is exploited to minimize computational burden while preserving stability. The critic remains linear:

$$V(s) = w^T s.$$

The TD error

$$\delta = r + \gamma V(s') - V(s)$$

is computed with minimal arithmetic, and the critic update

$$w \leftarrow w + \alpha \delta s$$

scales linearly with state dimension. The actor update is performed using a quantized policy gradient:

$$\theta \leftarrow \theta + \eta \delta \nabla_\theta \log \pi_\theta(a|s).$$

The gradient computation is bounded because the policy network is shallow and quantized. The total inference energy

$$E_{\text{AC-lite}} \approx 0.12 \ \mu\text{J}$$

remains predictable and suitable for continuous control tasks such as rate limiting and threshold modulation. To improve robustness under traffic drift, a forgetting factor is incorporated:

$$w \leftarrow (1 - \rho)w + \rho(w + \alpha \delta s).$$

This exponentially decays stale value estimates, preventing long-term bias accumulation.

5.4.7 Green PPO-lite

Proximal Policy Optimization (PPO) introduces conservative updates via clipping:

$$L = \mathbb{E}\left[\min\left(r_t(\theta)A_t,\ \text{clip}(r_t(\theta), 1 - \epsilon, 1 + \epsilon)A_t\right)\right].$$

Standard PPO is batch-intensive and memory-heavy. Green PPO-lite restricts ϵ, batch size, and epoch count. Advantage estimation uses the linear critic rather than long-horizon estimators, and all arithmetic is quantized. Training is harvested-energy gated:

$$\text{Train}(t) = \mathbb{I}[H(t) \geq H_{\text{min}}] \cdot \mathbb{I}[E(t) \geq E_{\text{train,min}}].$$

Thus, training is opportunistic rather than continuous. Inference energy remains feasible:

$$E_{\text{PPO-lite}} \approx 0.25 \ \mu\text{J}.$$

5.4.8 Hybrid Green DRL for IoT IDS

Graceful degradation ensures that control complexity adapts to residual energy:

$$\text{Action}(t) = \begin{cases} \text{Green-DQN}(s_t), & E_{\text{rem}} > T_1, \\ \text{AC-lite}(s_t), & T_2 < E_{\text{rem}} \le T_1, \\ \text{Q-linear}(s_t), & E_{\text{rem}} \le T_2. \end{cases}$$

Threshold hysteresis prevents oscillatory switching:

$$T_1^{\uparrow} > T_1^{\downarrow}, \qquad T_2^{\uparrow} > T_2^{\downarrow}.$$

This structure transforms algorithm selection into an energy-aware supervisory controller that guarantees a bounded energy trajectory while preserving minimum detection capability.

5.4.9 Green-RL IDS adaptive IDS scheduling

Scheduling is formulated as a control problem over the sampling rate:

$$f_{t+1} = f_t + \Delta f(a).$$

Average energy becomes

$$E_{\text{avg}} = f\,E_{\text{feat}} + E_{\pi}.$$

The RL agent increases f only when the expected marginal detection benefit exceeds the marginal feature cost. Energy-proportional IDS operation emerges naturally from this formulation. Near-depletion penalty shaping:

$$R'(s,a) = R(s,a) - \lambda E(a) - \lambda_b \mathbb{I}[E(t) \le E_{\min}]$$

ensures avoidance of unsafe low-energy states.

5.4.10 Green multi-agent RL (GMARL)

For distributed networks with N agents:

$$R = \sum_{i=1}^{N} \left(R_{\text{det}}^{i} - \lambda E_i(a_i) \right).$$

Communication is the dominant system-level cost. Sparse event-driven coordination ensures:

$$E_i(a_i) \le 0.2\ \mu\text{J}, \qquad E_{\text{comm}} \le 15\text{–}40\ \mu\text{J}.$$

Compressed message design:

$$\text{msg} = \left[\text{nodeID, AnomFlag, } p_{\text{confidence}}\right]$$

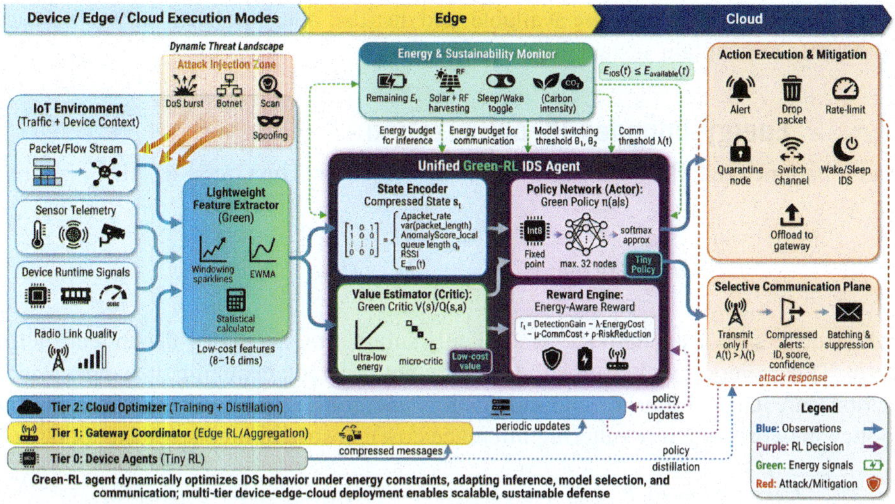

FIGURE 5.16

Cross-category Green-RL IDS control architecture integrating compressed state construction, energy-feasible policy, and value inference, event-driven coordination, and selective escalation for mitigation and training under strict device energy budgets. The design emphasizes feasibility gating to prevent communication-dominated energy collapse while preserving long-horizon detection utility.

minimizes radio overhead while enabling correlation at gateways. Energy-gated transmission:

$$\mathrm{SendMsg}_i(t) = \mathbb{I}\left[A_i(t) \ge \lambda_i(t)\right]$$

5.4.11 Green-RL IDS architecture

The system in Fig. 5.16 should be interpreted as a cross-category control architecture that separates 1) low-cost sensing and feature extraction, 2) energy feasibility monitoring, 3) compact policy and value inference, and 4) selective escalation to higher categorys for heavy mitigation and training. The device layer produces compressed state features and local anomaly cues; an energy monitor enforces feasibility by gating whether RL decisions can trigger compute-intensive IDS modes and communication-intensive alerts. The Green-RL IDS agent then maps the compressed state into actions using a fixed-point low-bit policy and an ultra-light critic, explicitly optimizing detection utility minus energy and communication penalties. The selective communication plane is essential: it prevents the system from collapsing into a radio-dominated energy consumption by transmitting every anomaly score; instead, it transmits only when the energy-adaptive threshold indicates that the expected risk reduction justifies the radio cost. Gateway and cloud layers provide coordination, policy refinement, and distillation: training and aggregation occur where energy and compute are available, and distilled micro-policies are pushed back to devices to maintain sustainable local autonomy.

5.4.12 Energy-bounded RL optimization

Let θ parameterize the policy and value approximator. The Green-RL IDS objective is:

$$\theta^* = \arg\max_{\theta} \mathbb{E}\left[\sum_t \gamma^t \left(R_t - \lambda E_\theta(s_t, a_t)\right)\right],$$

which differs from standard RL by explicitly subtracting the policy-dependent energy term. This is important because $E_\theta(s_t, a_t)$ is not constant: changing θ changes which actions are taken (altering communication and mitigation cost) and changes the policy network structure (altering inference cost). A structured energy model is:

$$E_\theta(s_t, a_t) = \omega_1 E_\pi(s_t) + \omega_2 E_{\text{feat}}(s_t) + \omega_3 E_{\text{comm}}(a_t) + \omega_4 E_{\text{mit}}(a_t),$$

where $E_\pi(s_t)$ is the inference energy for policy evaluation, $E_{\text{feat}}(s_t)$ is the energy required to compute the compressed state, $E_{\text{comm}}(a_t)$ is the action-dependent communication cost, and $E_{\text{mit}}(a_t)$ captures mitigation overhead. The weights ω_1, ω_2, ω_3, ω_4 map each energy component into a unified penalty scale consistent with R_t. Operationally, the policy must satisfy a long-horizon energy budget:

$$E_{\text{daily}} \leq E_{\text{budget}}, \qquad E_{\text{budget}} \in [1, 5]\ \text{mJ}.$$

This constraint prevents policies that appear locally optimal (e.g., frequent alerting) but are globally infeasible because they drain the device over operational timescales. A standard enforcement mechanism uses a Lagrangian multiplier that adapts online:

$$\max_{\pi} \mathbb{E}_\pi\left[\sum_t \gamma^t R_{\text{det}}(s_t, a_t)\right] - \lambda(t)\left(\mathbb{E}_\pi\left[\sum_t \gamma^t C(s_t, a_t)\right] - \bar{C}\right),$$

with multiplier update

$$\lambda(t+1) = \left[\lambda(t) + \eta_\lambda \left(C_t - \bar{c}\right)\right]_+,$$

where $[\cdot]_+$ clamps to non-negative values, C_t is observed energy cost, and $\bar{c}$ is a per-interval budget. This approach increases $\lambda(t)$ when energy overspend occurs, making expensive actions less attractive and restoring feasibility.

Table 5.4 presents a comparative feasibility envelope of representative Green-RL IDS algorithms across three dominant embedded resource dimensions: per-decision energy consumption, memory footprint, and inference latency. The table should be interpreted as a structural comparison between algorithmic families under quantized micro-policy implementations rather than as hardware-specific constants, since absolute values vary with MCU architecture, clock frequency,

SRAM organization, and precision configuration. Despite this variability, the relative ordering reflects inherent computational structure and therefore remains stable across typical embedded IoT platforms.

Per-decision energy directly determines whether an RL controller can execute within tight microjoule-scale budgets imposed by duty-cycled sensing nodes. Green Q-learning exhibits the lowest energy requirement (0.02-0.05 μJ) because action selection reduces to a small number of integer operations in a tabular and sparse linear approximation. Such minimal arithmetic makes it appropriate for ultra-tiny endpoints and embedded schedulers where policy evaluation must not consume excessive system resources. Green DQN increases energy demand (0.09-0.25 μJ) due to micro-network forward passes and limited parameter updates, though strict control of hidden-layer width and low-bit quantization preserves feasibility. AC-lite occupies a similar range (0.12-0.20 μJ) because it combines a compact actor with a linear critic; the resulting dual evaluation remains predictable and bounded, making it well-suited for continuous control tasks such as traffic shaping and threshold adaptation. Green PPO-lite requires higher energy (0.25-0.40 μJ) owing to conservative policy updates and ratio computations, yet remains compatible with gateway-class embedded systems when updates are intermittently scheduled. GMARL reports energy on a per-agent basis (0.15-0.30 μJ), reflecting that each node performs local inference while coordination energy, which is primarily communication-driven, is managed separately through sparse messaging. Memory footprint governs deployability on microcontroller-class hardware where SRAM is typically limited. Green Q-learning requires only 2–4 kB due to its compact representation. Green DQN expands this requirement to 4–10 kB to accommodate micro-network parameters and minimal transition storage. AC-lite ranges from 6–12 kB because both actor and critic parameters must be retained, though the critic remains linear. Green PPO-lite occupies 10–20 kB, reflecting the need to store policy parameters along with limited rollout buffers during conservative updates. GMARL spans 14-40 kB per agent, since multi-agent coordination and additional metadata storage increase local memory demands, especially when compressed messaging and aggregation buffers are maintained. Latency represents the wall-clock time required to map a compressed state into an action under integer-friendly inference. Lower latency directly improves responsiveness to fast-moving threats while reducing active CPU time. Green Q-learning achieves the smallest latency window (20–40 μs) because evaluation is computationally minimal. Green DQN increases latency (40–80 μs) due to forward propagation through a micro-network. AC-lite extends latency slightly further (60–120 μs) because both actor inference and critic evaluation are performed. Green PPO-lite reaches 100–150 μs when conservative update logic is active. GMARL displays 100–180 μs per agent, while end-to-end coordination latency depends on sparse communication intervals rather than purely local inference. Collectively, Table 5.4 reveals a clear scaling principle: as representational capacity and adaptability increase, energy, memory, and latency grow accordingly. Green Q-learning occupies the ultra-low-resource corner, making it suitable for minimal scheduling control. Green DQN and AC-lite balance expressiveness with embedded feasibility. Green PPO-lite targets adaptive control under drift within moderate energy budgets. GMARL enables distributed intelligence provided that communication remains sparse and event-driven. This layered spectrum supports the central thesis of Green-RL IDS: RL for IoT IDS must be engineered as an energy-proportional control mechanism whose algorithmic complexity matches the physical resource envelope of the deployment category

Table 5.4 Energy-memory-latency envelope of Green-RL IDS algorithms under embedded feasibility constraints. Values reflect relative scaling trends under quantized micro-policies, sparse critics, and energy-gated updates.

Green RL Method	Energy (μJ)	Memory (kB)	Latency (μs)	Use Case
Green Q-Learning	0.02-0.05	2-4	20-40	Ultra-tiny endpoints and schedulers
Green DQN (GDQN)	0.09-0.25	4-10	40-80	IDS activation and mitigation control
AC-lite	0.12-0.20	6-12	60-120	Traffic shaping and threshold tuning
Green PPO-lite	0.25-0.40	10-20	100-150	Adaptive sampling under drift
GMARL (multi-agent)	0.15-0.30 per agent	14–40	100-180	Distributed IDS with sparse coordination

5.5 Toward a unified Green-ML-based IDS architecture: models, algorithms, frameworks, and energy-optimal deployment

The design of a truly "green" IDS for IoT networks requires a convergence of multiple domains that have traditionally evolved separately: energy-aware ML, carbon-optimized network engineering, lightweight cryptography, secure distributed system, and RL for adaptive mitigation. This section presents a comprehensive, mathematically rigorous, and operationally detailed blueprint for a unified Green-ML-based IDS architecture, a next-generation IDS paradigm explicitly engineered for ultra-low-power IoT devices, energy-harvesting nodes, and large-scale deployments aiming to reduce both operational energy consumption and associated carbon footprint. A central premise is that sustainability constraints must be treated as design-time invariants and runtime control signals, meaning that feasibility is maintained under heterogeneous hardware, intermittent energy inflows, bursty traffic systems, and time-varying grid carbon intensity, with detection guarantees retained as explicit constraints rather than implicit expectations.

Unlike prior sections, which treated Green-ML-based IDS components in isolation (e.g., lightweight ML, FL, DRL-based IDS mitigation), the unified Green-

ML-based IDS agent integrates them within a cohesive, system-level, multi-layered architecture. The ambition of a unified Green-ML-based IDS agent is not merely efficient detection, but a holistic model of *sustainable security orchestration*, including: 1) minimization of compute energy, 2) reduction of communication overhead, 3) alignment with carbon-aware scheduling, 4) multi-node cooperative IDS sharing, 5) green-optimized classification, feature extraction, and learning, 6) lightweight cryptographic layers bound to energy budgets, 7) DRL-coordinated adaptation across heterogeneous energy sources, and 8) end-to-end life-cycle sustainability of IDS models. In operational terms, the unified Green-ML-based IDS agent treats the IDS stack as a cyber-physical service whose intensity is continuously shaped by residual energy, harvested energy forecasts, carbon intensity forecasts, and real-time security risk, thereby preventing a pathological system in which frequent alerts, continuous retraining, and heavy offloading collapse device lifetime.

This section is structured as follows. We begin with a formal definition of the *Green-ML-based IDS Objective Function*, which unifies energy, accuracy, latency, sustainability, and life-cycle considerations into a single multi-term optimization target. We then derive computational and energy models suitable for microcontroller- and gateway-class execution, and we construct a unified Green-ML-based IDS pipeline spanning device, edge, and cloud categories. Next, we define a multi-layer, federated, distributed, DRL-hybrid coordination plane in which gateways and edge servers collaborate with device-level micro-IDS agents under strict energy constraints. Multiple large tables summarize model footprints, inference costs, energy scaling properties, carbon intensities, sustainability ratios, mitigation efficiency, distributed workload allocation, and adaptive DRL state-action policies. Additionally, we specify the Green IDS Protocol (GIDP), a protocol designed to jointly coordinate detection, reporting, federated updates, mitigation, energy gating, and carbon-aware scheduling. The unified Green-ML-based IDS agent. Narrative, therefore, progresses from objective definition to feasible computation to cross-category orchestration to protocol-level enforcement, ensuring that the framework is implementable on real IoT stacks rather than remaining a conceptual abstraction.

The Green-ML-based IDS is a hierarchical, six-layer architecture designed to optimize both security and sustainability. As shown in Fig. 5.17, the architecture comprises six functional layers, each responsible for a specific aspect of IDS operation and energy management. The architecture spans from the sensing layer, where lightweight anomaly-detection models run on IoT devices, to the edge and fog layers, where more complex decision-making occurs. The top layers of the system perform global orchestration, integrating ML-based decision support and FL for continuous model improvement. The system is designed to ensure scalability, energy efficiency, and real-time anomaly detection.

5.5.1 Formal definition of the Green-ML-based IDS objective

We define the Green-ML-based IDS design objective as a multi-term constrained optimization over an admissible parameter space Θ (model parameters, feature masks,

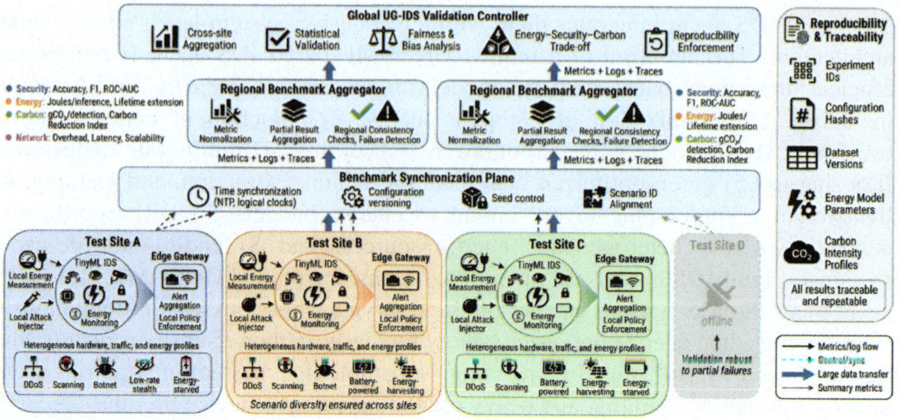

FIGURE 5.17

Integrated Six-Layer Green-ML-based IDS Architecture.

protocol timers, DRL weights, duty-cycle policies, and deployment decisions). Let $\theta \in \Theta$ denote a full unified Green-ML-based IDS agent configuration. The unified objective is:

$$\min_{\theta \in \Theta} \Big(w_e E(\theta) + w_c C(\theta) + w_m M(\theta) + w_s S(\theta) + w_f F(\theta) - w_a A(\theta) \Big),$$

where $E(\theta)$ is the expected energy consumption per IDS decision cycle (including sensing, computation, and communication), $C(\theta)$ is the carbon contribution per cycle induced by the energy source mix and placement decisions, $M(\theta)$ is the memory footprint (flash + RAM) required by the IDS stack, $S(\theta)$ is the sustainability cost capturing life-cycle and operational replacement overheads, $F(\theta)$ measures communication frequency overhead (events, synchronization, federated updates), and $A(\theta)$ is detection utility (accuracy, threat coverage, and expected risk reduction). The weights $w_{\{.\}}$ tune system priorities across deployment contexts; for example, energy-harvesting nodes increase w_e and w_f to avoid battery depletion and radio-heavy operation, whereas infrastructure gateways increase w_a to prioritize detection coverage. In addition to these weights, the unified Green-ML-based IDS agent implicitly assumes that the objective must remain robust under temporal variability, meaning that θ is not a static setting chosen once, but a configuration that can be updated by the orchestration plane under feasibility gates, which motivates the later protocol-level control logic. To ensure operational feasibility, the objective is paired with hard constraints:

$$E(\theta) \le E_{\max}, \qquad M(\theta) \le M_{\max}, \qquad \mathbb{P}\big(A(\theta) \ge A_{\min}\big) \ge 1 - \delta,$$

where $E_{\max}$ and $M_{\max}$ are platform-dependent and δ bounds reliability degradation under non-stationary traffic. The probabilistic constraint is essential in IoT settings because traffic distributions evolve due to concept drift and adversarial adaptation, and a unified Green-ML-based IDS agent must maintain performance with a bounded failure probability rather than pointwise guarantees. A practical implementation also introduces a safety margin, $\eta \in (0, 1)$, to prevent energy collapse under bursty workloads, yielding an operational feasibility condition, $E(\theta) \leq \eta E_{\max}$, in critical deployments. For microcontrollers, the energy term decomposes as:

$$E(\theta) = E_{\text{comp}}(\theta) + E_{\text{mem}}(\theta) + E_{\text{comm}}(\theta) + E_{\text{misc}}(\theta),$$

where E_{comp} accounts for integer MACs and control logic, E_{mem} accounts for SRAM accesses and flash reads, E_{comm} accounts for radio transmit/receive, and E_{misc} captures sensing and peripheral overhead (timers, ADC reads, clock scaling). The separation between computation and memory is significant because, on many low-power MCUs, memory traffic becomes comparable to arithmetic energy, implying that compression and early quantization reduce both compute and memory costs simultaneously. The communication component is explicitly:

$$E_{\text{comm}} = P_{\text{tx}}\, t_{\text{tx}} + P_{\text{rx}}\, t_{\text{rx}},$$

showing that Green-ML-based IDS must control both transmission power states and airtime. In practice, t_{tx} and t_{rx} are driven by 1) alert rate, 2) protocol overhead (handshakes, beacons), 3) federated and coordination timers, and 4) neighbor collaboration frequency, which motivates protocol constraints on message size and rate later in the section. Carbon contribution depends on energy sources and placement:

$$C(\theta) = \lambda_{\text{grid}}(t)\, E_{\text{grid}}(\theta, t) + \lambda_{\text{harv}}(t)\, E_{\text{harv}}(\theta, t),$$

where $\lambda_{\text{grid}}(t)$ is the time-varying carbon intensity of the grid (gCO_2/kWh) and $\lambda_{\text{harv}}(t)$ is the effective carbon intensity of harvested energy (often close to zero at runtime but with embodied cost captured in $S(\theta)$). In the simplified operational model used throughout this chapter, when grid energy dominates:

$$C(\theta) \approx \lambda_{\text{grid}}\, E(\theta),$$

which makes carbon-aware scheduling equivalent to time-shifting and placement decisions that reduce λ_{grid} and reduce $E(\theta)$. A deployment-level interpretation is that the unified Green IDS agent reduces emissions through a dual strategy: decreasing joules per decision and scheduling heavier workloads into periods with lower carbon intensity, while preserving a minimum online detection service even during carbon-constrained windows.

5.5.2 Green feature extraction model

In microcontroller-class IDS, feature extraction often dominates energy because it requires repeated parsing, counting, buffering, and memory accesses. unified Green-ML-based IDS agent. Therefore, it defines a compositional, energy-bounded feature operator:

$$\phi(x) = \text{Quantize}(\text{Select}(x)),$$

which formalizes that 1) raw observations x are never fully processed if not needed, 2) only a subset of features are computed, and 3) the computed features are quantized early to reduce memory and downstream compute. Early quantization is particularly important in streaming IDS because intermediate buffers and sliding-window accumulators consume SRAM and induce repeated memory traffic; quantized feature streams reduce buffer width and enable integer-only downstream inference. The operator is subject to explicit feasibility constraints:

$$\dim(\phi(x)) \le d_{\max}, \qquad C(\phi(x)) \le C_{\max}, \qquad E(\phi(x)) \le E_{\max},$$

where $d_{\max}$ bounds the feature dimension to ensure a bounded policy/model compute, $C_{\max}$ bounds computational complexity (e.g., MAC count and memory operations), and $E_{\max}$ bounds the energy spent per window on feature extraction. These constraints imply that the feature operator is itself a controlled subsystem whose configuration can be adjusted by the orchestration plane, for example, by shrinking the window length, reducing parsing depth, disabling expensive entropy features, and switching to approximation-friendly counters. Feature selection is realized by a Green Feature Mask:

$$m_i = \begin{cases} 1 & \text{if } E_i < \tau_e \wedge I_i > \tau_i, \\ 0 & \text{otherwise,} \end{cases}$$

where E_i is per-feature extraction energy and I_i is information gain (or a proxy such as mutual information with attack labels, Fisher score, and contribution to anomaly score variance). The conjunction $E_i < \tau_e \wedge I_i > \tau_i$ ensures that unified Green IDS agent. prioritizes "high-value, low-cost" features. Under energy scarcity, τ_e is tightened, and τ_i is raised, shrinking the active feature set; under energy abundance, the mask expands to improve detection coverage. A practical interpretation is that the feature mask implements a constrained knapsack selection under an energy budget, but in a form that can be implemented via threshold comparisons rather than the expensive combinatorial optimization. To prevent unstable feature oscillation across windows, the unified Green-ML-based IDS agent enforces hysteresis:

$$m_i(t) = \begin{cases} 1 & \text{if } E_i < \tau_e^{\uparrow} \wedge I_i > \tau_i^{\uparrow}, \\ 0 & \text{if } E_i > \tau_e^{\downarrow} \vee I_i < \tau_i^{\downarrow}, \\ m_i(t-1) & \text{otherwise,} \end{cases}$$

with $\tau^{\uparrow} \neq \tau^{\downarrow}$ to avoid chattering. This makes feature selection stable under noisy energy and traffic conditions and prevents energy spikes due to repeated feature reconfiguration. A system-level benefit is that hysteresis reduces the variance of

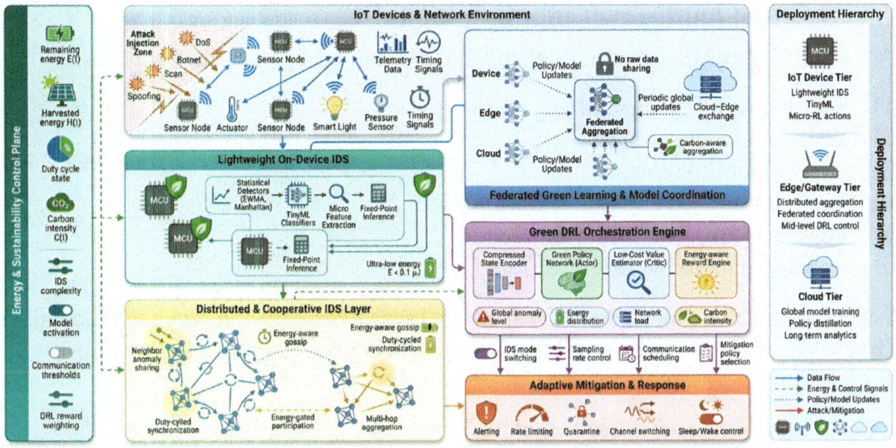

FIGURE 5.18

Green-ML-based IDS Architecture integrating on-device micro-IDS, distributed collaboration, federated intelligence, and DRL-based IDS IDS sustainability orchestration under joint energy and carbon constraints.

$E(\phi(x))$ across windows, which simplifies budget allocation in subsequent pipeline layers and improves the predictability of duty-cycle behavior.

5.5.3 Unified Green-ML-based IDS architecture

The proposed architecture connects local detection, neighbor collaboration, federated aggregation, and DRL-based IDS adaptation through explicit energy-feasibility gates. This structure ensures that high-cost coordination functions activate only when residual energy and carbon conditions support sustainable execution. Fig. 5.18 corresponds to the full unified Green-ML-based IDS agent system graph: 1) a device-category micro-IDS plane, 2) a distributed neighbor collaboration plane, 3) an FL and policy aggregation plane, and 4) a DRL plane that adapts IDS modes, sampling, communication, and mitigation. The key design principle is *energy feasibility as a gate* between planes. The sustainability control plane observes residual energy $E(t)$, harvested energy $H(t)$, duty-cycle state, carbon intensity $C(t)$, and current IDS complexity; it then constrains which functions are allowed to execute, and at what rate, by selecting feature masks, quantization levels, and model categories (TinyML and gateway inference), and communication thresholds. This ensures that expensive actions, including offloading, federated participation, and mitigation, occur only when both energy and carbon conditions justify them, preventing radio-dominated operation and preserving long-lived sensing. Fig. 5.18 should therefore be read as a control graph in which sensing and micro-inference remain continuously available, whereas collaboration, federation, and DRL refinement activate conditionally under explicit feasibility gates.

5.5.4 Green multi-layer pipeline model

A unified Green-ML-based IDS agent is implemented as a six-layer pipeline:

1) Energy-aware sensing and pre-filtering,
2) Green feature encoding,
3) Lightweight inference,
4) Energy-optimized communication plane,
5) Federated–distributed coordination,
6) Global sustainability optimization.

Let E_ℓ denote the expected energy spent by layer ℓ per decision window. The unified Green-ML-based IDS agent enforces the following budget allocation model:

$$E_\ell \leq \beta_\ell E_{\text{budget}}, \qquad \sum_{\ell=1}^{6} \beta_\ell \leq 1,$$

where β_ℓ are layer-specific multipliers controlling budget partitioning. This formalization is critical: it prevents "budget theft" by communication and coordination layers and ensures that core sensing and local detection remain functional even when higher layers are disabled. In practice, β_ℓ are adaptively tuned based on threat level and energy abundance:

$$\beta_\ell(t) = \beta_\ell^{(0)} + \Delta\beta_\ell\big(\text{Risk}(t), E(t), C(t)\big),$$

so that during high-risk periods, the unified Green-ML-based IDS agent shifts budget from coordination and reporting toward local detection and mitigation, while during low-risk periods it shifts budget toward sporadic federated updates and model maintenance. The budget partitioning also stabilizes system behavior under intermittent harvesting, since the controller can reduce β_4 and β_5 to suppress communication and federation during scarcity while preserving a minimal sensing and inference service under β_1–β_3.

5.5.5 Green-ML-based IDS algorithm (GIDSA)

Algorithm 5.1 operationalizes a unified Green-ML-based IDS agent at the device category by combining 1) energy estimation, 2) energy-feasible feature extraction, 3) quantized inference, 4) confidence-based escalation, 5) DRL-driven mitigation, and 6) continuous energy model updates. The variable E_{rem} is treated as a stateful constraint that is updated each window and controls whether to (a) enter micro-sleep, (b) run only micro-IDS, (c) escalate to gateway inference, and (d) transmit alerts. Confidence gating ensures that offloading is used only when local inference uncertainty is high and the expected accuracy gain justifies radio cost. A practical implementation also includes an escalation hysteresis buffer to prevent frequent transmissions when conditions are borderline, thereby preventing instability in E_{comm} under fluctuating traffic.

Algorithm 5.1 Green-ML-based IDS pipeline.

Input: raw packet stream X, energy budget E_b
$E_{\text{rem}} \leftarrow E_b$
for each time window t **do**
  Estimate available energy: $E_a \leftarrow \text{Harvest}(t) + \text{Battery}(t)$
  if $E_a < \tau_{\min}$ **then**
    Enter micro-sleep mode; continue
  end if
  Extract green features ϕ_t under E_{rem}
  Perform quantized inference $y_t = f_Q(\phi_t)$
  if $\text{Confidence}(y_t) < \eta$ **then**
    Request gateway inference
    Deduct communication energy
  end if
  if y_t indicates anomaly **then**
    Trigger DRL policy action a_t
  end if
  Update energy model
end for

5.5.6 Green FL formalism

In addition to feasibility-constrained optimization, the local loss can incorporate structural regularization to explicitly promote energy-efficient parameterizations:

$$L_i^{\text{green}}(\theta_i) = L_i(\theta_i) + \lambda_E E_i(\theta_i) + \lambda_S \|\theta_i\|_0,$$

where $\|\theta_i\|_0$ approximates the number of active parameters after pruning and masking. This term favors sparse updates that reduce both local compute cost and global communication payload. The communication energy component can be further modeled as:

$$E_{\text{comm},i} = P_{\text{tx}} \cdot t_{\text{tx}} + P_{\text{rx}} \cdot t_{\text{rx}},$$

with transmission time approximately proportional to the compressed update size:

$$t_{\text{tx}} \propto k(t) \cdot b_q,$$

where b_q is the number of bits per quantized coordinate. Consequently, adaptive sparsification jointly reduces airtime and radio energy. To explicitly couple energy and carbon dimensions, the participation weight modifiers can be defined as smooth scaling functions:

$$\rho(E_i) = \min\left(1, \frac{E_i}{E_{\text{safe}}}\right), \qquad \xi(C_i) = \exp(-\beta_C C_i),$$

where E_{safe} denotes a stability threshold and C_i represents local carbon intensity. This continuous weighting prevents abrupt discontinuities in participation while still prioritizing stable, low-carbon contributors. Under intermittent availability, the global update variance becomes:

$$\text{Var}(\theta^{(t+1)}) = \eta^2 \sum_i p_i(t)\alpha_i^2 \text{Var}(\nabla L_i(\theta)),$$

which shows that aggressive sparsification and low participation can amplify variance. Therefore, the unified Green-ML-based IDS agent balances compression aggressiveness against statistical stability by constraining:

$$k(t) \geq k_{\min} \quad \text{whenever} \quad \sum_i p_i(t)\alpha_i < \tau_{\text{high}},$$

ensuring that the effective signal does not collapse below a minimum level required for convergence. From a long-horizon sustainability perspective, the cumulative training energy per device must satisfy:

$$\sum_{t=0}^{T} E_i^{\text{train}}(t) \leq E_{i,\text{budget}},$$

which prevents excessive training bursts from draining battery resources. In deployment, this constraint is enforced through adaptive local epoch scaling:

$$\text{Epochs}_i(t) = \left\lfloor \text{Epochs}_{\max} \frac{E_i(t)}{E_{i,\max}} \right\rfloor,$$

so that training intensity scales proportionally with instantaneous energy availability. Additionally, convergence under energy-aware weighting can be characterized by the effective learning rate:

$$\eta_{\text{eff}}(t) = \eta \sum_i p_i(t)\alpha_i,$$

implying that sustainable convergence requires bounded decay of $\eta_{\text{eff}}(t)$ across rounds. If $\eta_{\text{eff}}(t)$ drops below a stability threshold, aggregation frequency must be reduced and sparsification relaxed to maintain statistical progress without violating energy constraints.

Fig. 5.19 depicts the process of energy-aware FL in Green-ML-based IDS. By allowing devices to collaboratively update their detection models without sharing sensitive data, the system reduces communication costs and minimizes energy consumption during learning. This approach enhances privacy and optimizes the training process across the network.

Building on the concept of distributed coordination, Fig. 5.20 illustrates the architecture of Federated Green Learning (global FL-IDS) with energy-aware

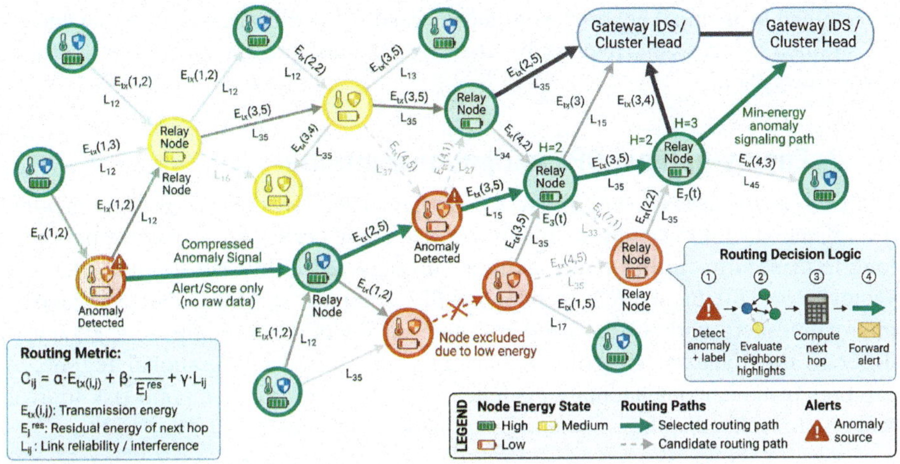

FIGURE 5.19

Energy-Aware FL for Green-ML-based IDS. FL allows devices to collaborate in model training while minimizing energy consumption and preserving privacy.

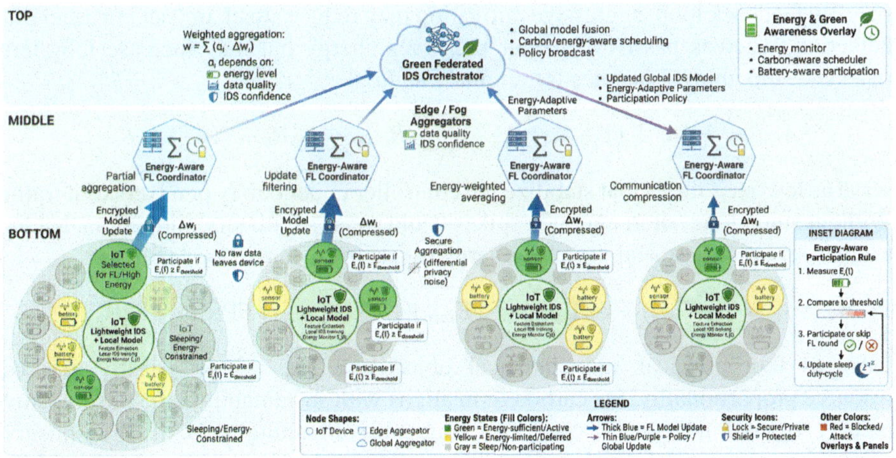

FIGURE 5.20

Federated Green Learning (global FL-IDS) with energy-aware participation. This model aggregates updates from IoT devices, with each node's participation determined by residual energy levels and harvesting dynamics, ensuring sustainable learning without depleting device resources.

participation. In this model, IoT devices participate in the FL process based on their energy status. The system aggregates encrypted model updates from multiple IoT nodes, weighted by their energy availability, to create a global model. Participation is determined by residual energy levels and harvesting conditions, ensuring that energy-constrained devices contribute only when feasible and preserving energy efficiency across the system.

5.5.7 Energy-optimal DRL mitigation controller

The DRL controller is formulated as a constrained Markov decision process in which the objective is not merely to maximize detection performance, but to maximize long-term security utility under explicit physical feasibility constraints. The state vector $s_t = (E_t, B_t, A_t, R_t)$ is intentionally compact so it can be evaluated on microcontrollers without the need for state encoders. Each component encodes a different control axis: E_t governs feasibility, B_t encodes operational regime, A_t captures instantaneous anomaly evidence, and R_t aggregates temporal risk to avoid reacting to isolated spikes. The energy transition equation

$$E_{t+1} = E_t - E(a_t) + H_t$$

establishes that every mitigation action directly reshapes future feasibility. In contrast to classical IDS controllers, which affect only the network state, here actions reshape the device's physical energy state. This coupling introduces a resource-security feedback loop: aggressive mitigation may reduce attack impact but accelerate depletion, whereas passive behavior preserves energy but may increase long-term risk. The smoothing dynamics for anomaly and risk

$$A_{t+1} = \lambda_A A_t + (1 - \lambda_A)\hat{A}_{t+1}, \qquad R_{t+1} = \lambda_R R_t + (1 - \lambda_R)\hat{R}_{t+1}$$

serve as low-pass filters that stabilize the controller under bursty or adversarial traffic. Without smoothing, short anomaly spikes could cause oscillatory mitigation,, leading to excessive radio use and unstable energy trajectories. The reward structure

$$r_t = -\alpha E(a_t) - \alpha_b \mathbf{1}[E_{t+1} < E_{\min}] + \beta C(a_t) - \gamma \mathrm{FPR}_t + \delta \mathrm{TPR}_t$$

balances four physical and statistical objectives. The energy penalty enforces resource proportionality; the carbon term aligns with sustainability; the false-positive penalty discourages unnecessary blocking and offloading; and the true-positive reward encourages risk suppression. The additional barrier penalty, α_b, introduces a soft safety constraint, ensuring that the controller learns to avoid a near-depletion system even when short-term rewards appear favorable. The carbon budget evolution

$$B_{\mathrm{CO2}}^{(t+1)} = B_{\mathrm{CO2}}^{(t)} - C(a_t)$$

elevates carbon-awareness from a passive monitoring variable to a controllable resource. As B_{CO2} shrinks, the adaptive scaling

$$\beta_t = \beta\left(1 + \frac{1}{B_{\mathrm{CO2}}^{(t)} + \epsilon}\right)$$

progressively increases carbon sensitivity, ensuring that the controller shifts heavy mitigation and offloading into lower-carbon intervals whenever security conditions permit. The expected return

$$J(\pi) = \mathbb{E}_\pi \left[\sum_{t=0}^{\infty} \gamma_d^t r_t \right]$$

Therefore, it encodes long-horizon sustainability. A high discount factor, γ_d, promotes conservative policies that prioritize future feasibility rather than short-term bursts of detection performance. The policy parameterization

$$\pi_\theta(a \mid s) = \mathrm{softmax}(Ws + b)$$

is intentionally linear to ensure predictable inference cost and integer-only execution on constrained hardware. The advantage-based update

$$\nabla_\theta J(\pi_\theta) = \mathbb{E}_\pi \left[\nabla_\theta \log \pi_\theta(a_t \mid s_t) \hat{A}_t \right]$$

maintains statistical efficiency while avoiding deep critic networks that would violate energy feasibility. The feasibility projection

$$a_t^{\mathrm{exec}} = \Pi_{\mathcal{A}_{\mathrm{feas}}(t)}(a_t)$$

transforms the controller from a purely learned system into a safety-aware hybrid controller. Even if the learned policy proposes an infeasible action, the projection guarantees that the executed action respects instantaneous resource constraints. This mechanism prevents catastrophic exploration during early training and ensures hard energy compliance at runtime. Additionally, the dual-variable adaptation

$$\alpha_{t+1} = \left[\alpha_t + \eta_\alpha \left(\mathbb{E}_\pi[E(a_t)] - \bar{E} \right) \right]_+$$

introduces self-regulation. If average energy consumption exceeds the desired bound $\bar{E}$, the penalty weight α increases automatically, pushing the controller toward cheaper actions. This converts the DRL controller into a primal–dual optimization system that dynamically enforces sustainability without manual retuning. Collectively, these mechanisms ensure that mitigation is not only detection-effective but physically sustainable, carbon-aligned, and provably bounded under a fluctuating energy system.

5.5.8 Energy profiles of IDS components

Table 5.5 provides a component-level resource profile that clarifies which unified Green-ML-based IDS agent functions dominate device energy consumption, and which functions must therefore be aggressively gated. The Green feature extractor remains in a sub-microjoule regime due to quantized counters and approximate filtering, enabling continuous operation. The TinyML classifier remains feasible due to low-bit parameter storage and bounded MAC counts, supporting frequent local decisions. The micro-DRL agent incurs higher per-step energy because it evaluates a policy and a value estimate in the same window, yet it remains feasible when invoked conditionally based on anomaly evidence rather than continuously. The energy model update remains negligible, which motivates its role as a persistent supervisory signal. Federated update preparation is orders of magnitude more expensive because of gradient formation, sparsification, and serialization require multiple passes over data and buffers, implying that federated participation must be scheduled intermittently and, when possible, shifted to gateways. Edge offload transmission dominates the profile, since radio airtime and power state transitions often exceed inference energy by one to two orders of magnitude; this observation motivates confidence gating, threshold adaptation, and strict message size constraints in GIDP to prevent the device from collapsing into a radio-dominated energy regime.

Table 5.5 Energy and resource profile of unified Green-ML-based IDS agent. Components under embedded feasibility constraints.

Component	Energy (μJ)	Latency (ms)	Memory (kB)	Notes
Green Feature Extractor	0.12	0.08	0.5	Quantized, low-pass filtering
TinyML Classifier	0.20	0.15	2.0	8-bit weights
Micro-DRL Agent	0.35	0.20	3.5	Q-learning and SARSA
Energy Model Update	0.05	0.05	0.25	Battery + harvester
Federated Update Prep	5.2	10.0	8.0	Sparse gradients
Edge Offload Transmission	22-45	1.0	—	Dominant cost factor

5.5.9 Green-ML-based IDS deployment across network layers

This deployment view clarifies how the unified Green-ML-based IDS distributes sensing, collaboration, federated updating, and DRL-based IDS control across resource tiers. It emphasizes that higher-cost coordination functions remain conditional on explicit energy and carbon feasibility checks. Fig. 5.21 complements Fig. 5.18 by emphasizing deployment and control flow across categories. The device category performs continuous ultra-light monitoring and escalates only sporadically. The collaboration layer enables neighbor-based evidence sharing with energy-gated participation, improving robustness to localized attacks and maintaining bounded communication. The federated layer coordinates periodic model and policy updates without raw data exchange, using sparse deltas and energy-carbon-aware participation. The DRL orchestration layer uses compressed states and energy-aware rewards to adapt IDS mode, sampling rate, communication schedule, and mitigation actions. Across all categories, the sustainability control plane enforces feasibility by gating expensive

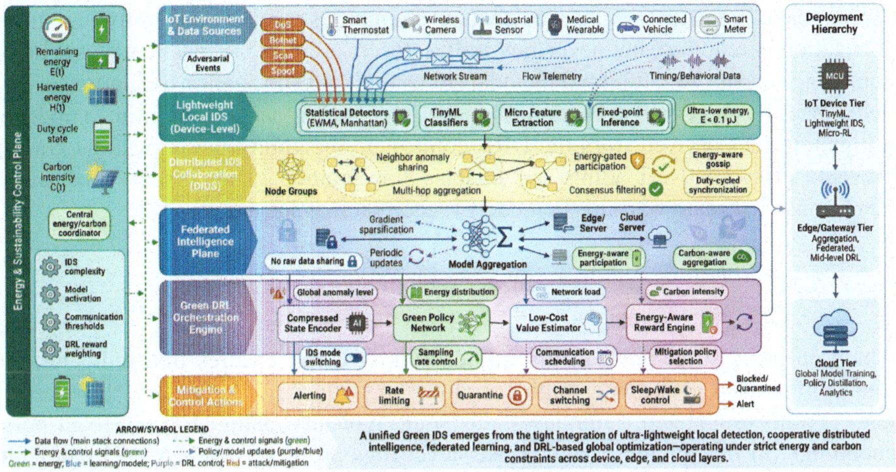

FIGURE 5.21

Unified Green-ML-based IDS agent, deployment across device, edge, and cloud categories with energy-gated collaboration, FL, and DRL orchestration for sustainable IDS and mitigation.

operations, ensuring that radio transmissions and federated updates do not dominate the device energy envelope.

5.5.10 Green-ML-based IDS protocol (GIDP)

GIDP coordinates energy-aware IDS behavior across devices, neighbors, gateways, and cloud services. Rather than treating communication as a transparent transport layer, GIDP elevates orchestration to a resource-constrained control function that explicitly regulates what information is exchanged, when it is exchanged, and under what conditions it is feasible. The protocol is designed for intermittently powered, carbon-sensitive IoT networks in which excessive coordination can easily dominate the total energy budget. Therefore, GIDP enforces bounded message semantics, compact payloads, and state-aware transmission policies. GIDP defines five message types:

1) `GIDP-HELLO` (energy beacons),
2) `GIDP-FEAT` (quantized feature summaries),
3) `GIDP-ALERT` (event reporting),
4) `GIDP-MODEL` (model deltas),
5) `GIDP-POLICY` (DRL mitigation rules).

Each message type serves a distinct control-layer purpose. `GIDP-HELLO` packets advertise residual energy, duty-cycle state, and lightweight health indicators, allowing neighbors and gateways to construct an energy-feasible coordination graph. `GIDP-`

FEAT packets transmit compressed feature summaries when collaborative anomaly correlation is required, but never raw traffic traces. GIDP-ALERT packets report high-confidence events with minimal metadata to enable rapid mitigation escalation. GIDP-MODEL packets carry sparse FL deltas, and GIDP-POLICY packets disseminate updated mitigation rules derived from the DRL controller. Separating these message classes prevents protocol overloading and enables fine-grained gating under constrained conditions. To bound transmission energy, each message is constrained:

$$\text{Size} \leq 64 \text{ bytes},$$

which enforces strict payload discipline. This size cap ensures that radio airtime remains bounded even under high coordination frequency. Practically, this implies that 1) only quantized summaries are sent, typically using 4-8 bit fixed-point encodings, 2) full telemetry and packet-level logs are never exchanged by default, and 3) federated updates and policy refreshes are transmitted as sparse coordinate-value pairs rather than dense tensors. Because radio transmission energy scales approximately linearly with packet size and airtime, this hard constraint directly limits worst-case communication energy. In the unified Green-ML-based IDS agent, the protocol layer also inherits energy gating from the local controller. If residual energy $E(t)$ falls below a predefined safety threshold, protocol behavior degrades gracefully: the frequency of HELLO beacons is reduced, periodic FEAT exchanges are disabled, and only high-priority ALERT packets are permitted. This design prevents low-utility coordination chatter from draining energy reserves during the survival system. The gating mechanism effectively transforms the communication stack into an energy-proportional service, where coordination intensity scales with the task's feasibility. At the gateway layer, GIDP further incorporates carbon-aware orchestration. MODEL aggregation rounds and POLICY dissemination cycles are not executed immediately upon receipt; instead, they can be deferred to intervals of lower grid carbon intensity provided that system risk remains below a critical threshold. This deferral strategy decouples latency-sensitive detection from delay-tolerant optimization tasks, allowing the system to reduce carbon emissions without degrading minimum security guarantees. Morever, GIDP functions as a sustainability-aware control plane for distributed IDS. It ensures that cooperation remains communication-sparse, energy-bounded, and carbon-aligned while preserving detection continuity and coordination integrity across device, gateway, and cloud categories.

5.5.11 Sustainability score for IDS

We define a sustainability score that normalizes detection utility by multi-dimensional cost:

$$\text{SUS} = \frac{A - \lambda E - \mu C - \nu F}{L},$$

where A is accuracy and detection utility, E is energy consumption, C is carbon contribution, F is communication overhead, and L is life-cycle cost, capturing deployment, maintenance, and replacement. The numerator expresses net "useful security" after subtracting operational energy/carbon/communication penalties, while dividing by L enforces that solutions requiring frequent battery replacement, high-maintenance hardware, and short-lived deployments are penalized even if their runtime energy is low. unified Green-ML-based IDS agent. requires:

$$\text{SUS} \geq 1.0,$$

as a deployment-level admissibility criterion; in practice, this threshold is tuned by application domain (e.g., medical, agricultural, and industrial) and threat criticality. A further operational interpretation is that SUS[8] enables cross-deployment comparison by translating heterogeneous constraints into a single ratio. This supports policy decisions about whether to prioritize increased detection coverage or extended device lifetime under sustainability targets. The sustainability score SUS can be interpreted as a constrained efficiency function that unifies three traditionally separate design axes: detection utility, operational externalities, and lifecycle burden. In conventional IDS evaluation, A is frequently treated as the dominant performance objective, while energy, communication, and carbon footprint are either reported descriptively and relegated to secondary ablation. In Green-ML-based IDS settings, this separation becomes mathematically misleading because energy depletion, carbon intensity fluctuations, and communication-induced duty-cycle expansion jointly determines the long-run survival of the security function. The score, therefore, enforces an integrated perspective by penalizing each incremental unit of operational resource use with weighting coefficients (λ, μ, ν), which are interpretable as shadow prices reflecting the marginal sustainability cost of energy draw, carbon emission intensity, and network burden. Within this interpretation, λ encodes battery scarcity, μ encodes carbon budget scarcity, and ν encodes spectrum and neighbor burden, thereby creating a tunable mechanism for domain-driven sustainability priorities.

From a deployment engineering perspective, the denominator L plays a decisive role because embedded security solutions frequently shift runtime energy costs into maintenance intensity and replacement frequency. A design that achieves low E through aggressive duty cycling might still impose substantial lifecycle costs if it relies on fragile energy-harvesting hardware, periodic calibration, frequent battery swaps, and short-lived components. Including L ensures the score remains robust against such pathological cases by compressing all non-runtime sustainability liabilities into a single penalty factor. Formally, L can be instantiated as a weighted sum of expected technician visits, expected battery replacement events, amortized hardware replacement, and associated operational downtime. With this structure, the constraint SUS ≥ 1.0 becomes a direct admission rule: the system is rejected if its

[8] SUS denotes the Sustainability Utility Score, a composite ratio used to compare security utility against energy or sustainability cost across heterogeneous deployments.

sustainability-normalized security output fails to exceed its normalized sustainability burden.

The admissibility threshold can be further refined into categorized operational modes, where high-criticality deployments enforce stricter minimum SUS margins to prevent hidden sustainability debt from accumulating silently. Medical infrastructure, safety-critical industrial control, and remote monitoring in inaccessible regions may warrant higher SUS thresholds, given the severe replacement costs and consequences of failure. Agricultural and consumer smart-home deployments may accept lower thresholds while maintaining broader coverage. Importantly, the score supports cross-deployment comparisons by mapping heterogeneous constraints into a single scale-free ratio, enabling governance decisions that trade marginal detection improvements against extended system lifetime under sustainability targets.

5.5.12 Unified energy-carbon feasibility region

To formally characterize the operational envelope of Green-ML-based IDS, we define a joint feasibility region over energy, carbon intensity, and detection quality. Let the triplet state be:

$$\chi(t) = \big(E(t), C(t), A(t)\big),$$

where $E(t)$ is residual energy, $C(t)$ is grid carbon intensity, and $A(t)$ is achieved detection utility. The admissible operating region is:

$$\mathcal{R}_{\text{UG}} = \Big\{\chi : E(t) \geq E_{\min},\ C(t) \leq C_{\max}^{\text{eff}},\ A(t) \geq A_{\min}\Big\}.$$

Here, $C_{\max}^{\text{eff}}$ is not a fixed carbon threshold but an effective bound derived from the system carbon budget:

$$C_{\max}^{\text{eff}} = \frac{B_{\text{CO2}}^{\text{rem}}}{P_{\text{IDS}}(t)\,\Delta t}.$$

This formulation ensures that the IDS respects cumulative carbon budgets rather than instantaneous carbon only. The controller thus enforces:

$$\chi(t) \in \mathcal{R}_{\text{UG}} \quad \forall t.$$

Violating any constraint triggers a mode transition and workload deferral. The feasibility region $\mathcal{R}_{\text{UG}}$ defines a cyber-physical admissibility set for Green-ML-based IDS, in which energy resilience, carbon compliance, and security quality are treated as simultaneous hard constraints rather than loosely coupled objectives. The state $\chi(t)$ explicitly binds together three quantities that are often evaluated independently: energy reserve $E(t)$ captures survivability under constrained power, carbon intensity $C(t)$ captures the environmental externality associated with computation and communication, and detection utility $A(t)$ captures protection efficacy. Constraining $\chi(t)$ to remain within $\mathcal{R}_{\text{UG}}$ transforms IDS operation into a constrained dynamical system, where the controller must adapt model complexity, sampling rate, communication frequency, and participation level to prevent state escape.

A key technical contribution of this formulation is the definition of $C_{\max}^{\text{eff}}$ as a time-varying effective constraint derived from remaining carbon budget $B_{\text{CO2}}^{\text{rem}}$, IDS power draw $P_{\text{IDS}}(t)$, and decision horizon Δt. This prevents the common pitfall of using static carbon thresholds that ignore cumulative budget depletion. In practice, if $P_{\text{IDS}}(t)$ increases due to heavier inference and higher communication duty, the effective admissible carbon intensity decreases, tightening the constraint automatically. This yields a budget-consistent mechanism that enforces carbon feasibility at the system level rather than at instantaneous snapshots. The enforcement condition $\chi(t) \in \mathcal{R}_{\text{UG}}$ for all t can be implemented as a barrier-certificate style controller, where safety filters project proposed actions back into the feasible set. When constraints are violated, mode transition and workload deferral become mandatory responses, thereby preventing energy collapse and a runaway carbon budget.

5.5.13 Energy-communication tradeoff surface

Communication dominates embedded IDS energy. Let:

$$E_{\text{total}} = E_{\text{local}} + E_{\text{comm}},$$

with

$$E_{\text{comm}} = N_{\text{tx}} \cdot E_{\text{pkt}}.$$

Detection gain from cooperation is modeled as:

$$\Delta A = g(N_{\text{neighbors}}, d),$$

where d is the aggregation depth. The system therefore optimizes:

$$\max_{d, N_{\text{neighbors}}} \left(\Delta A - \lambda E_{\text{comm}}\right).$$

The optimal cooperation radius d^* satisfies:

$$\frac{\partial \Delta A}{\partial d} = \lambda \frac{\partial E_{\text{comm}}}{\partial d}.$$

This establishes a principled stopping rule for multi-hop expansion, preventing energy-dominant coordination. The trade-off surface formalizes a central physical reality in distributed IDS deployments: network collaboration improves detection quality but incurs disproportionate energy overhead due to radio activity. The decomposition $E_{\text{total}} = E_{\text{local}} + E_{\text{comm}}$ isolates computation from communication and exposes the dominant term in many low-power radios. Since E_{comm} scales linearly with packet count N_{tx} and per-packet cost E_{pkt}, collaboration mechanisms that scale neighbor interaction without bound lead to quadratic growth in network burden at scale. The detection gain function $\Delta A = g(N_{neighbors}, d)$ captures diminishing returns since additional neighbors often contribute correlated information, while deeper aggregation can induce redundancy and latency.

The objective $\max(\Delta A - \lambda E_{comm})$ introduces an explicit energy-penalized cooperation criterion, where λ represents the marginal energy value of a unit detection gain. The first-order condition defining d^* equates marginal detection improvement with marginal communication cost under the energy valuation λ. This yields a principled stopping rule: multi-hop expansion continues only while incremental cooperation yields a detection increase sufficient to offset its energy and carbon consequences. In practice, this criterion induces adaptive neighbor selection, adaptive hop-depth truncation, and opportunistic aggregation during low-carbon, high-energy states, while suppressing coordination under scarcity. The result is a sustainability-preserving cooperative IDS that avoids a coordination system dominated by radio energy.

5.5.14 Carbon-aware federated participation dynamics

Let participation indicator:

$$z_i(t) \in \{0, 1\}.$$

Define participation probability:

$$\Pr(z_i(t) = 1) = \sigma\left(\alpha_E E_i(t) - \alpha_C C(t)\right),$$

where $\sigma(\cdot)$ is logistic. This continuous participation model smooths federated availability and prevents oscillatory engagement. The expected effective client mass becomes:

$$\mathbb{E}[N_{active}] = \sum_i \Pr(z_i(t) = 1).$$

To maintain convergence:

$$\mathbb{E}[N_{active}] \geq N_{crit}.$$

Thus, carbon-aware deferral is allowed only when convergence stability remains preserved. Carbon-aware federated participation reframes FL from a purely availability-driven process into a sustainability-aware control mechanism. The binary indicator $z_i(t)$ captures whether client i participates in the current federated round. Instead of deterministic scheduling, participation is modeled probabilistically via a logistic function of residual energy $E_i(t)$ and carbon intensity $C(t)$, with coefficients α_E and α_C controlling sensitivity. This yields a smooth participation law that avoids abrupt transitions between full participation and full deferral, thereby reducing oscillations that can destabilize convergence dynamics and induce bursty communication overhead.

The expected number of active clients becomes $\mathbb{E}[N_{\text{active}}] = \sum_i \Pr(z_i(t) = 1)$, which enables direct coupling between sustainability constraints and convergence conditions. The requirement $\mathbb{E}[N_{\text{active}}] \geq N_{\text{crit}}$ is critical because federated optimization stability depends on sufficient client mass to maintain gradient diversity and reduce estimator variance. Carbon-aware deferral is therefore constrained by a convergence floor: the system may reduce participation during high-carbon periods only to the extent that the expected client mass remains above the critical threshold. This ensures sustainability-aware scheduling does not collapse learning stability, thereby aligning carbon goals with the statistical feasibility of model training.

5.5.15 Multi-timescale Lyapunov stability

Let the energy trajectory be:

$$E(t+1) = E(t) - u(t) + h(t),$$

where $u(t)$ is IDS consumption and $h(t)$ harvested energy. Define Lyapunov candidate:

$$V(t) = \frac{1}{2}(E(t) - E^*)^2.$$

Drift:

$$\Delta V(t) = (E(t) - E^*)\big(-h(t) + u(t)\big).$$

Stability requires:

$$\mathbb{E}[\Delta V(t)] < 0 \quad \text{whenever } E(t) > E^*.$$

This ensures bounded energy oscillation under adaptive workload control. Carbon scheduling modifies $u(t)$ to maintain a negative drift expectation. Multi-timescale Lyapunov stability provides a rigorous control-theoretic guarantee that Green-ML-based IDS energy dynamics remain bounded despite stochastic harvesting, bursty threat processes, and adaptive workload scheduling. The energy recursion $E(t+1) = E(t) - u(t) + h(t)$ defines a discrete-time stochastic system where $u(t)$ represents control-dependent consumption and $h(t)$ represents stochastic inflow. The Lyapunov candidate $V(t) = \frac{1}{2}(E(t) - E^*)^2$ quantifies deviation from the desired operating energy setpoint E^*, which represents the sustainable equilibrium region where the IDS can maintain baseline monitoring while retaining resilience against threat surges.

The drift expression $\Delta V(t) = (E(t) - E^*)(-h(t) + u(t))$ captures whether the energy trajectory is being pushed away from equilibrium and pulled back toward it. The condition $\mathbb{E}[\Delta V(t)] < 0$ whenever $E(t) > E^*$ enforces negative drift above the setpoint, thereby preventing runaway energy accumulation that could lead to wasteful over-activation, while also implying that the controller modulates $u(t)$ to remain aligned with available inflow and sustainability budgets. On a slower timescale, carbon-aware scheduling adjusts $u(t)$ not only based on $E(t)$ and $h(t)$ but also based on carbon intensity $C(t)$ through workload deferral, model downgrading and participation suppression, thereby maintaining negative drift expectation under joint energy-carbon constraints. This yields a two-timescale stability logic: short-horizon energy control maintains immediate feasibility, while long-horizon carbon control maintains cumulative sustainability compliance. Furthermore, these guarantees establish that Green-ML-based IDS can operate indefinitely under adaptive control without energy collapse, without carbon budget violation, and with preserved detection admissibility.

5.5.16 Ultra-Green control as constrained Markov decision process

The full Green-ML-based IDS scheduler can be modeled as a constrained MDP:

$$\mathcal{M} = (\mathcal{S}, \mathcal{A}, P, R, \mathcal{C}),$$

with constraints:

$$\mathbb{E}[E(a_t)] \leq E_{\max}, \quad \mathbb{E}[C(a_t)] \leq C_{\max}.$$

Optimization becomes:

$$\max_{\pi} \mathbb{E}\left[\sum_t \gamma^t R_t\right] \quad \text{s.t.} \quad \mathbb{E}[C_t] \leq C_{\max}, \quad \mathbb{E}[E_t] \leq E_{\max}.$$

Using Lagrangian relaxation:

$$\mathcal{L} = \mathbb{E}\left[\sum_t \gamma^t \left(R_t - \lambda_E E_t - \lambda_C C_t\right)\right].$$

This formalizes sustainability as a dual-penalized optimization problem embedded within policy learning. The Green-ML-based IDS scheduler is fundamentally a constrained sequential decision system in which sustainability constraints are treated as hard constraints on policy trajectories rather than post-hoc evaluation metrics. The state space $\mathcal{S}$ encapsulates residual energy, harvested inflow prediction, grid carbon intensity, threat context, recent anomaly scores, communication backlog, and model configuration status. The action space $\mathcal{A}$ includes model switching, sampling rate scaling, communication throttling, cooperative radius selection, mitigation aggressiveness, federated participation decisions, and inference placement transitions across device, edge, and cloud categories. The transition kernel P captures both physical energy evolution and stochastic threat dynamics, thus coupling cyber processes with environmental stochasticity. The reward R_t must be interpreted not as raw detection accuracy but as a composite utility functional integrating detection gain, false alarm penalties, mitigation timeliness, and resilience under adversarial perturbation. The constraint set $\mathcal{C}$ includes energy and carbon budget compliance, thereby converting classical RL into a constrained Markov decision process in which feasibility is preserved across expected trajectories. The Lagrangian relaxation introduces dual multipliers λ_E and λ_C, which acquire a direct economic interpretation as marginal sustainability prices. These multipliers dynamically adjust during policy optimization, shaping the tradeoff surface between detection intensity and sustainability cost. A rise in λ_E compresses high-energy actions, while a rise in λ_C suppresses carbon-intensive operations such as heavy inference during peak grid intensity. This transforms sustainability from an external auditing metric into an intrinsic shaping force embedded within the policy gradient itself. The resulting dual ascent formulation allows stable convergence toward policies that maximize long-horizon discounted utility while maintaining expected feasibility under energy and carbon constraints.

5.5.17 Global carbon elasticity coefficient

Define Carbon Elasticity of IDS workload:

$$\varepsilon_C = \frac{\partial \log P_{\text{IDS}}}{\partial \log C(t)}.$$

If:

$$\varepsilon_C < 0,$$

The system reduces workload under high carbon, satisfying sustainability responsiveness. Green-ML-based IDS aims for:

$$|\varepsilon_C| \geq 0.5,$$

indicating significant carbon elasticity without destabilizing detection performance. The carbon elasticity coefficient quantifies how sensitively IDS power draw reacts to variations in carbon intensity. Here P_{IDS} denotes instantaneous power allocated to inference, communication, sensing, and cooperation. Taking the logarithmic derivative normalizes both axes, producing a scale-invariant measure that remains interpretable across heterogeneous deployments. A negative elasticity indicates that workload contracts as carbon intensity increases, demonstrating sustainability responsiveness. A magnitude near zero would imply carbon-indifferent behavior, thereby violating Ultra-Green principles.

The target condition $|\varepsilon_C| \geq 0.5$ reflects a balanced responsiveness system. A value below this magnitude indicates insufficient adaptation, meaning the IDS continues to operate at a heavy workload during high-carbon intervals. An excessively large magnitude would induce abrupt workload suppression, potentially degrading detection stability and convergence in federated settings. Therefore, the elasticity coefficient acts as a tunable control invariant that regulates how aggressively the workload reacts to environmental carbon signals. It effectively operationalizes sustainability reactivity as a measurable system property rather than a qualitative aspiration.

5.5.18 Sustainability-constrained optimal deployment problem

Deployment across categories is solved as:

$$\min_{\theta_{\text{device}},\theta_{\text{edge}},\theta_{\text{cloud}}} \sum_{k\in\{\text{device,edge,cloud}\}} w_k\left(E_k+\lambda C_k\right)$$

subject to:

$$A_{\text{global}} \geq A_{\text{min}}.$$

category allocation satisfies:

$$\theta_{\text{device}} \subset \theta_{\text{edge}} \subset \theta_{\text{cloud}},$$

ensuring monotonic capability scaling. The solution determines model partitioning and inference placement under sustainability constraints. The sustainability-constrained deployment problem formalizes architectural partitioning as an optimization over inference-placement variables θ_k, which represent parameter subsets, feature extractors, compression modules, and coordination mechanisms assigned to each category The weighting coefficients w_k reflect deployment priorities such as energy scarcity at the device category, carbon sensitivity in the cloud category and in the edge category with bandwidth constraints. By minimizing the weighted sum of energy and carbon costs while enforcing global detection performance, the formulation balances workload across hierarchical layers in a principled manner.

The inclusion relation $\theta_{\text{device}} \subset \theta_{\text{edge}} \subset \theta_{\text{cloud}}$ enforces monotonic capability expansion, meaning that higher categories possess strictly greater modeling capacity and contextual aggregation capability. This structural constraint guarantees that migration upward in the hierarchy never reduces representational power, thereby preserving detection monotonicity. The solution yields optimal model partitioning that respects device limitations while leveraging higher-category resources during sustainable operating intervals. In practice, this results in compressed TinyML modules executing at endpoints, intermediate-aggregation models operating at gateways, and full-scale adaptive agents residing in cloud infrastructure, each activated by carbon-aware scheduling logic.

Fig. 5.22 illustrates the evaluation pipeline for Green-ML-based IDS performance. It shows the stages involved in experimental execution, metrics extraction, and robustness validation. This pipeline ensures a comprehensive analysis of energy efficiency, detection accuracy, and carbon footprint.

5.5.19 Theoretical sustainability bound

Assume average detection utility $\bar{A}$ and average energy $\bar{E}$. Sustainability index:

$$\text{SUS} = \frac{\bar{A}}{\bar{E}\cdot\bar{C}}.$$

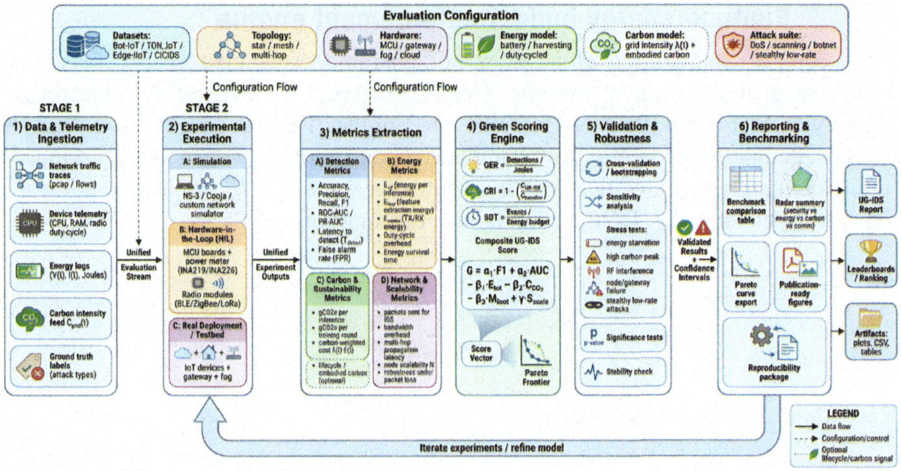

FIGURE 5.22

Evaluation Pipeline for Green-ML-based IDS Performance. This pipeline includes data ingestion, experimental execution (either simulation and real deployment), and metric extraction for performance assessment. It also includes validation steps for robustness and sustainability.

For long-term viability:

$$\lim_{T\to\infty} \frac{1}{T} \sum_{t=1}^{T} \frac{A_t}{E_t C_t} \geq \kappa,$$

for threshold κ determined by deployment policy. This bound links detection, energy, and carbon multiplicatively, underscoring the need for joint optimization. The multiplicative sustainability index expresses the intuition that detection performance must scale proportionally with both energy and carbon expenditure. Unlike additive penalty formulations, the ratio $\bar{A}/(\bar{E}\bar{C})$ enforces strict coupling: if either energy consumption and carbon intensity rise without a commensurate increase in detection gain, the sustainability index deteriorates sharply. This multiplicative coupling discourages a pathological system where detection utility increases marginally at disproportionate environmental cost.

The asymptotic condition establishes long-run sustainability as a time-averaged inequality over the operational horizon T. The threshold κ encodes deployment-level sustainability policy, potentially derived from regulatory carbon caps, battery lifetime guarantees, and infrastructure-level sustainability mandates. Maintaining the inequality ensures that over an arbitrarily long time horizon,s the system generates sufficient detection utility per unit energy-carbon product to justify continued operation. This transforms sustainability into a provable performance guarantee rather than a qualitative design goal.

5.5.20 Runtime energy budget enforcement engine

Architectural optimization alone does not guarantee sustained energy feasibility. enforcement must occur at runtime. Green-ML-based IDS, therefore, incorporates a lightweight Energy Budget Enforcement Engine (EBEE) embedded within the MCU scheduler. EBEE monitors cumulative consumption within sliding windows and dynamically throttles IDS activity when necessary. Let $E_{\text{budget}}^{\Delta}$ be the allowable energy per window Δt. Define cumulative consumption:

$$E_{\text{used}}(t) = \sum_{\tau=t-\Delta t}^{t} E_{\text{IDS}}(\tau).$$

Execution remains admissible only if:

$$E_{\text{used}}(t) \leq E_{\text{budget}}^{\Delta}.$$

If violated, EBEE triggers adaptive degradation:

$$\text{Mode}(t+1) = \begin{cases} \text{ReduceSampling}, & \text{if } E_{\text{used}} > E_{\text{budget}}^{\Delta} \\ \text{MicroModel}, & \text{if sustained overload} \\ \text{Sleep}, & \text{if critical threshold crossed} \end{cases}$$

This transforms energy from a passive measurement into an active scheduling constraint. The EBEE functions as a hard real-time supervisory controller that enforces feasibility constraints independent of higher-level policy optimization. While architectural design, carbon-aware scheduling, and constrained MDP optimization operate at design-time and learning-time scales; EBEE operates at microsecond-to-second granularity within the firmware scheduler. The sliding-window accounting mechanism ensures that short bursts of activity do not accumulate silently into long-term depletion. The window parameter Δt defines the temporal granularity of enforcement, allowing deployment engineers to tune responsiveness against measurement overhead.

The inequality $E_{\text{used}}(t) \leq E_{\text{budget}}^{\Delta}$ defines a strict safety barrier. Once violated, EBEE initiates graded degradation rather than abrupt shutdown. The first-level response reduces sampling intensity, thereby shrinking feature extraction and inference cost. If overload persists across multiple windows, the scheduler demotes the active detection model to a micro-model variant with reduced parameter footprint and arithmetic intensity. If residual energy approaches the critical threshold, full sleep is enforced to protect battery integrity and prevent brownout instability. This graded response strategy prevents catastrophic energy collapse while preserving minimal situational awareness. By embedding enforcement directly into MCU-level scheduling, energy transitions from a diagnostic metric into an executable constraint.

5.5.21 Fine-grained memory traffic minimization

On MCUs, SRAM accesses often consume more energy than arithmetic operations. Let:

$$E_{\text{mem}} = N_{\text{rd}}E_{\text{rd}} + N_{\text{wr}}E_{\text{wr}}.$$

Green-ML-based IDS minimizes N_{rd} and N_{wr} through coordinated micro-architectural strategies applied at data layout, buffer management, allocation discipline, and loop scheduling levels. First, feature buffers are organized using a struct-of-arrays (SoA) layout rather than an array-of-structs representation, thereby aligning homogeneous feature values contiguously in memory. This alignment improves spatial locality, reduces cache-line fetch redundancy, and minimizes pointer arithmetic overhead, ultimately decreasing the number of memory read transactions required for sequential feature processing. Second, double-buffer elimination is achieved by in-place transformation of feature vectors, ensuring that intermediate tensors are not copied redundantly into temporary buffers. This directly reduces write traffic and prevents unnecessary memory duplication that would otherwise inflate N_{wr}.

Third, static allocation replaces dynamic heap-based memory management, thereby eliminating fragmentation, allocation metadata overhead, and unpredictable energy spikes during heap traversal. Static allocation ensures deterministic memory layout and stable access patterns, both of which contribute to reduced dynamic power consumption and improved long-term firmware reliability. Fourth, loop fusion merges consecutive passes over feature arrays into a single traversal, collapsing multiple read-compute-write cycles into a unified memory sweep. By minimizing repeated memory traversals, instruction dispatch overhead, and bus toggling frequency, these overheads are significantly reduced. If baseline SRAM traffic is T_0, optimized traffic becomes:

$$T_{\text{opt}} = T_0(1 - \gamma),$$

where empirical γ ranges between 0.25 and 0.45 depending on workload locality. The reduction coefficient γ quantifies the proportion of memory transactions eliminated by architectural restructuring. Because dynamic memory energy scales approximately linearly with transaction count, a 25% to 45% reduction in traffic translates into a proportional decrease in memory subsystem energy draw. In ultra-low-power nodes, where SRAM and bus toggling may account for a significant share of inference energy, such reductions materially impact total consumption. The importance of memory traffic optimization is further amplified by the fact that write operations often incur higher energy per transaction due to charge injection and peripheral synchronization overhead, meaning reductions in N_{wr} can produce disproportionate savings.

Consequently, fine-grained memory optimization is not merely an implementation refinement but a primary sustainability lever. Since inference arithmetic may already be quantized and compressed, memory movement frequently becomes the dominant marginal cost. By explicitly minimizing read and write counts at the firmware level, Green-ML-based IDS aligns micro-architectural efficiency with system-level sustainability objectives, reinforcing that energy-aware design must encompass not only model compression but also data movement discipline within the memory hierarchy.

Fig. 5.23 presents the MCU-level optimization pipeline, which is designed to meet the constraints of limited processing power and energy budgets in Green-ML-based IDSs. This pipeline consists of several stages, including register-centric optimization, memory management, fixed-point arithmetic, and energy-aware execution.

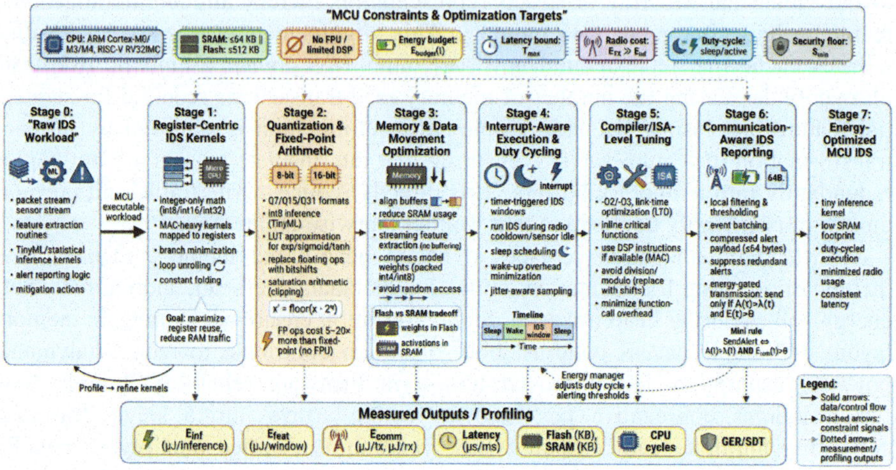

FIGURE 5.23

MCU-level Optimization Pipeline for Green-ML-based IDS. The figure shows the various optimization stages for an energy-efficient IDS on MCU platforms, considering energy, latency, and computational constraints.

5.5.22 Wake–sleep duty cycle optimization

Deep sleep transitions provide the largest single energy savings in IoT devices. Let:

$$E_{\text{active}}, \quad E_{\text{sleep}}, \quad t_{\text{active}}, \quad t_{\text{sleep}}$$

define state energies and durations. Average power becomes:

$$P_{\text{avg}} = \frac{E_{\text{active}} t_{\text{active}} + E_{\text{sleep}} t_{\text{sleep}}}{t_{\text{active}} + t_{\text{sleep}}}.$$

Green-ML-based IDS adjusts t_{active} adaptively:

$$t_{\text{active}}(t+1) = t_{\text{active}}(t) \cdot \frac{R(t)}{R_{\text{nominal}}}.$$

Thus, higher risk increases monitoring window length, while low-risk intervals allow aggressive sleep expansion. This proportional adjustment preserves responsiveness without fixed duty cycles. Duty-cycle optimization exploits the substantial asymmetry between active-state energy consumption and deep-sleep leakage. In typical microcontroller architectures, E_{sleep} is several orders of magnitude smaller than E_{active}, meaning that incremental increases in t_{sleep} yield disproportionately large reductions in P_{avg}. The average power expression formalizes this relationship by weighting the state energy by the temporal duration. Because battery lifetime scales inversely with P_{avg}, optimizing temporal allocation directly translates into extended operational longevity. Static duty cycles, however, fail to account for temporal variability in threat intensity, communication bursts, and harvest conditions. A fixed ratio between t_{active} and t_{sleep} may either underutilize monitoring capacity during high-risk intervals and waste energy during benign periods. The adaptive scaling rule introduces a proportional controller driven by real-time risk signal $R(t)$ normalized against a nominal baseline R_{nominal}. When anomaly likelihood increases, t_{active} expands proportionally, increasing sampling density and inference frequency. When environmental risk subsides, the active window contracts, extending sleep duration and conserving energy.

This formulation can be interpreted as a continuous gain modulation mechanism, in which risk serves as the control input that regulates surveillance intensity. Because the update rule scales multiplicatively rather than switching discretely between predefined modes, abrupt oscillations are avoided, and temporal transitions remain smooth. The controller, therefore, behaves as a first-order adaptive regulator that tracks threat intensity without introducing instability associated with binary toggling. When combined with the Energy Budget Enforcement Engine, adaptive duty cycling operates within a constrained envelope. EBEE guarantees that expanded active windows do not violate sliding energy budgets, while risk-proportional scaling ensures that security responsiveness remains preserved. This interaction yields a self-regulating temporal allocation strategy in which monitoring effort increases precisely when justified by threat conditions and contracts automatically when risk diminishes. The resulting system aligns energy expenditure with both adversarial dynamics and sustainability objectives, achieving responsive security without compromising long-term energy feasibility.

5.5.23 Carbon-aware compilation and deployment profiles

Energy optimization must extend to build-time configuration. Green-ML-based IDS defines deployment profiles:

$$\mathcal{P} \in \{\text{Ultra-Low-Power, Balanced, High-Security}\}.$$

Each profile configures model depth and quantization level, sampling frequency bounds, federated participation interval, offloading threshold, and compiler flags, including link-time optimization aggressiveness. Carbon-aware builds further adjustments:

$$\text{Profile}(t) = \arg\min_{\mathcal{P}} \left(E_{\mathcal{P}} + \lambda C_{\mathcal{P}} \right)$$

subject to detection constraint $A \geq A_{\text{min}}$. Deployment profiles function as a discrete sustainability system that defines the feasible operational envelope prior to firmware execution. Rather than treating sustainability exclusively as a runtime concern, Green-ML-based IDS embeds environmental awareness into the compilation pipeline, thereby influencing binary layout, instruction selection, quantization parameters, and scheduling limits before the system is deployed. Each profile $\mathcal{P}$ corresponds to a parameterized configuration vector containing architectural depth, fixed-point precision scaling, sampling ceilings, aggregation periodicity, offloading sensitivity, and compiler optimization directives. These parameters directly impact energy per inference, memory footprint, radio duty cycle, and execution latency.

The Ultra-Low-Power profile enforces aggressive quantization, shallow inference graphs, narrow sampling windows, extended synchronization intervals, and maximal static compiler optimization. Balanced configuration relaxes certain compression constraints to preserve detection fidelity while maintaining bounded overhead. High-Security configuration increases representational capacity and monitoring intensity within a predefined sustainability envelope, accepting elevated energy draw in exchange for stronger detection robustness. Importantly, these profiles are not heuristic presets but formally characterized energy-carbon tradeoff points within the sustainability objective space. The optimization rule

$$\text{Profile}(t) = \arg\min_{\mathcal{P}} \left(E_{\mathcal{P}} + \lambda C_{\mathcal{P}} \right)$$

introduces carbon-weighted selection at deployment time. Here $E_{\mathcal{P}}$ denotes expected per-cycle energy under profile $\mathcal{P}$, while $C_{\mathcal{P}}$ represents the associated carbon impact, computed via projected energy consumption under current grid intensity. The Lagrange multiplier λ reflects the relative priority of carbon valuation versus energy minimization. The constraint $A \geq A_{\text{min}}$ guarantees that sustainability adaptation does not degrade detection utility below an admissible threshold.

This formulation elevates compilation from a static code-generation step to a sustainability-aware optimization phase. During periods of elevated carbon intensity, such as peak fossil-fuel grid intervals, the deployment pipeline may automatically select lower-impact profiles. During low-carbon windows, higher-capacity builds may be permitted within carbon budgets. The decision boundary thus becomes temporally adaptive, aligning binary configuration with environmental context. Furthermore, compiler-level directives, such as instruction scheduling, dead-code elimination, loop unrolling suppression, and link-time inlining, affect instruction density, memory locality, and execution path determinism. These low-level decisions indirectly alter energy and carbon footprints by affecting cycle count and memory traffic. Embedding sustainability criteria into these build parameters ensures that optimization is applied holistically across the software lifecycle.

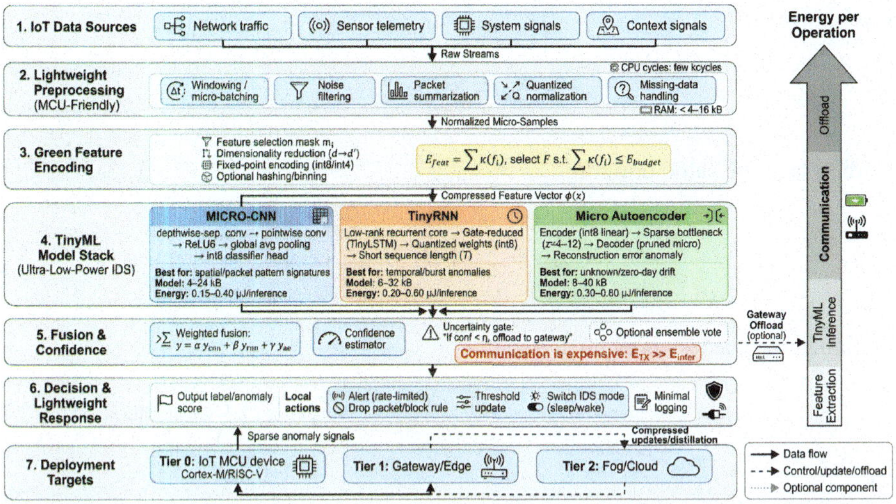

FIGURE 5.24

Energy-Carbon Aware Optimization for Task Allocation. The system dynamically adjusts detection task allocation based on energy consumption and carbon intensity, minimizing environmental impact.

By integrating carbon-aware profile selection into build-time processes, Green-ML-based IDS extends sustainability governance across three temporal layers: design-time architectural choice, compile-time configuration, and runtime adaptation. This tri-layer integration ensures that environmental constraints are continuously respected rather than evaluated retroactively. Sustainability therefore becomes an intrinsic property of the compiled artifact itself, aligning software engineering practice with carbon accountability and energy feasibility from inception through deployment.

As shown in Fig. 5.24, Green-ML-based IDS employs optimization algorithms that account for both energy consumption and carbon intensity when allocating resources for detection tasks. This dynamic optimization ensures the system minimizes environmental impact while maintaining high intrusion-detection accuracy. By considering both energy and carbon metrics, Green-ML-based IDS contributes to sustainable computing.

5.5.24 End-to-end energy accounting model

To ensure measurable optimization, Green-ML-based IDS maintains per-component accounting:

$$E_{\text{cycle}} = E_{\text{feat}} + E_{\text{model}} + E_{\text{comm}} + E_{\text{sched}}.$$

Over horizon T:

$$E_{\text{total}} = \sum_{t=1}^{T} E_{\text{cycle}}(t).$$

Carbon over the same horizon:

$$C_{\text{total}} = \sum_{t=1}^{T} C(t) \cdot E_{\text{cycle}}(t).$$

Optimization success is evaluated via:

$$\Delta E = \frac{E_{\text{baseline}} - E_{\text{Green-ML-based IDS}}}{E_{\text{baseline}}}, \quad \Delta C = \frac{C_{\text{baseline}} - C_{\text{Green-ML-based IDS}}}{C_{\text{baseline}}}.$$

The end-to-end accounting framework transforms sustainability from a qualitative objective into a quantitatively verifiable system invariant. The per-cycle decomposition E_{cycle} isolates the energy contributions of feature extraction, model inference, communication activity, and scheduler overhead, thereby enabling granular attribution of consumption to architectural subsystems. This decomposition is essential because energy reduction achieved in one subsystem may be partially offset by overhead introduced elsewhere, such as additional scheduling logic and compression stages. Without per-component visibility, such compensatory effects remain hidden.

By aggregating $E_{\text{cycle}}(t)$ over operational horizon T, the formulation produces E_{total}, a cumulative measure that captures both steady-state consumption and transient burst behavior. This temporal integration is critical in adaptive systems where workload varies with threat intensity, harvest conditions, and carbon-aware scheduling policies. Short-term measurements can underestimate cumulative cost, whereas long-horizon integration reveals sustained efficiency gains. Carbon accumulation is modeled through weighted integration of instantaneous energy with carbon intensity $C(t)$, yielding C_{total}. This formulation explicitly captures time-varying carbon signals, such as grid fluctuations and renewable intermittency. A joule consumed during high-carbon intensity contributes more heavily to C_{total} than an equivalent joule consumed during low-carbon intervals. Consequently, this metric incentivizes temporal shifting of workload toward low-carbon windows when feasible, thereby aligning energy scheduling with environmental impact minimization.

The improvement ratios ΔE and ΔC provide normalized sustainability indicators relative to a baseline IDS configuration executed under identical hardware and workload conditions. These ratios enable reproducible benchmarking across deployments, firmware versions, and architectural variants. A positive ΔE indicates a fractional energy reduction, while a positive ΔC indicates fractional carbon reduction. Because both metrics are normalized, they remain comparable across heterogeneous devices and deployment scales.

The accounting model, therefore, provides three critical guarantees: traceability, reproducibility, and accountability. Traceability ensures that each subsystem's energy contribution can be inspected independently. Reproducibility ensures that reported gains can be validated under controlled experimental conditions. Accountability ensures that sustainability claims correspond to measured hardware-level data rather than theoretical projections. In large-scale IoT networks, such as end-to-end accounting, become indispensable for regulatory compliance, fleet-wide optimization, and lifecycle carbon auditing. By embedding this accounting framework directly into Green-ML-based IDS' runtime logging infrastructure, sustainability transitions from an aspirational design property into a measurable, enforceable operational characteristic.

5.5.25 Predictive harvest-aware adaptation

For energy-harvesting nodes, predictive scheduling improves sustainability. Let $\hat{H}(t+\Delta)$ be predicted harvest. IDS activation condition becomes:

$$E(t) + \hat{H}(t+\Delta) \geq E_{\text{req}}.$$

This allows temporary energy borrowing during replenishment, increasing detection coverage without long-term depletion. Harvest-aware adaptation integrates forecasting into scheduling decisions. If the predicted inflow $\hat{H}(t+\Delta)$ indicates imminent replenishment; the controller may temporarily elevate the workload beyond the instantaneous reserve, relying on anticipated recovery. This forward-looking logic prevents underutilization during periods of renewable availability while avoiding sustained depletion. Prediction can be implemented via lightweight regression on historical solar cycles and environmental sensors. Integrating the forecast into the activation condition shifts scheduling from reactive throttling to anticipatory control. Predictive harvest-aware adaptation extends the sustainability framework from reactive constraint enforcement to anticipatory energy control. The inequality

$$E(t) + \hat{H}(t+\Delta) \geq E_{\text{req}}$$

formalizes a forward-feasibility condition in which present activation decisions incorporate expected near-term replenishment. Here $E(t)$ represents instantaneous stored energy, while $\hat{H}(t+\Delta)$ captures forecasted inflow over horizon Δ. The requirement E_{req} denotes the energy needed to sustain the proposed IDS workload for the upcoming decision interval. When the inequality holds, the scheduler may allocate workload intensity that would otherwise appear infeasible under instantaneous energy accounting alone.

This mechanism can be interpreted as bounded energy borrowing with guaranteed repayment under a predicted harvest. In contrast to unrestricted borrowing, which risks cumulative depletion, the predictive condition ensures that any temporary increase in consumption is offset by expected inflows within the forecast horizon. The quality of prediction directly impacts the risk of over-allocation. Let the prediction error be $\epsilon_H(t) = H(t + \Delta) - \hat{H}(t + \Delta)$. To maintain robustness, the controller may enforce a safety margin such that

$$E(t) + \hat{H}(t + \Delta) - \eta\sigma_H \geq E_{\text{req}},$$

where σ_H represents forecast variance and η defines a confidence coefficient. This probabilistic adjustment ensures that activation decisions remain resilient against forecast uncertainty. Forecast models can be implemented using lightweight autoregressive estimators, exponentially weighted moving averages, seasonal regression tied to diurnal solar cycles, or sensor-fusion predictors that integrate light intensity, temperature gradients, and historical harvest traces. Since embedded nodes cannot sustain heavy computational load for forecasting, prediction algorithms must remain computationally inexpensive while maintaining acceptable accuracy. The transition from purely reactive throttling to anticipatory scheduling introduces a model predictive control interpretation of Green-ML-based IDS. The scheduler now evaluates not only current energy feasibility but also projected near-term dynamics. During anticipated high-harvest intervals, such as midday solar peaks, IDS monitoring windows may expand, sampling frequency may increase, and cooperative aggregation may intensify. During a predicted low-harvest periods, workload contraction occurs preemptively to prevent abrupt enforcement by the Energy Budget Enforcement Engine.

This anticipatory logic improves sustainability along three axes. First, it increases detection coverage during renewable abundance, reducing missed anomaly windows. Second, it prevents conservative under-utilization that would otherwise leave harvest energy unused. Third, it stabilizes energy trajectory by smoothing transitions between active and throttled states. By embedding predictive harvest models into activation conditions, Green IDS elevates sustainability control from reactive budget enforcement to forward-looking adaptive governance, aligning security intensity with renewable availability in a mathematically grounded manner.

5.5.26 Stability of adaptive implementation policies

Adaptive sampling, offloading, and mode switching must avoid oscillation. Define mode variable $m(t)$ and transition thresholds:

$$E_{\uparrow} > E_{\downarrow}.$$

Mode switch occurs only if:

$$E(t) > E_{\uparrow} \quad \text{or} \quad E(t) < E_{\downarrow}.$$

This hysteresis band ensures bounded switching frequency:

$$\text{SwitchRate} \leq \frac{1}{\Delta_{\min}}.$$

Stability in the presence of fluctuating harvest and traffic, therefore, remains guaranteed. Hysteresis introduces a separation margin between upward and downward transition thresholds, preventing rapid toggling between operational modes under minor energy fluctuations. The inequality $E_{\uparrow} > E_{\downarrow}$ defines a deadband region where no transition occurs, thus dampening oscillatory behavior. The minimum dwell time Δ_{min} bounds the switching frequency, ensuring that the computational overhead of reconfiguration does not negate energy savings. This control-theoretic stabilization preserves smooth workload adaptation even under highly stochastic harvest patterns.

CHAPTER

Addressing IoT vulnerabilities

6

6.1 Introduction

As shown in earlier chapters, the Internet of Things (IoT) has become a major technological paradigm, interconnecting vast numbers of heterogeneous devices across application domains such as smart homes, healthcare, industrial automation, transportation, and smart cities. By integrating environmental sensing, computation, and communication, IoT systems support continuous data collection and enable informed, real-time decision-making. For all these advantages, the rapid adoption of IoT has also sharply increased the security risks that threaten system dependability, data integrity, and personal privacy. Most IoT devices offer far less performance, energy capacity, and computational power than conventional computing platforms, and they are frequently deployed in physically accessible environments. As a result, security has often been treated as a secondary or incidental design goal rather than a necessity; a trade-off that has fueled the proliferation of vulnerabilities across IoT systems.

IoT security vulnerabilities arise at multiple levels of the system architecture. Weak or absent authentication, insecure communication protocols,[1] defective software and firmware, inadequate physical protection, and poor management of the device lifecycle are all common. By exploiting these weaknesses, attackers can gain unauthorized access, alter information transmitted between devices, and compromise large numbers of devices simultaneously. Often, compromised IoT devices are used to create botnets or launch large-scale distributed denial-of-service attacks. The situation is further aggravated by the heterogeneity of IoT technologies and the absence of consistent security standards, leading to uneven, fragmented protection across platforms and vendors.

To minimize these risks, it is important to adopt a holistic, security-by-design approach that spans the entire lifecycle and the full range of components associated with appropriate IoT activities. This involves hardened hardware, secure firmware implementation, consistent communication systems, and continuous maintenance. At the same time, it is important to adopt lightweight cryptographic algorithms, secure update mechanisms, intrusion detection, and AI-based security systems to enhance

[1] A protocol is a defined set of rules and formats that governs how devices or systems exchange data, ensuring they can communicate reliably and understand one another.

Green Intrusion Detection Systems for IoT. https://doi.org/10.1016/B978-0-44-344249-0.00013-2

resilience in IoT systems. Nonetheless, such solutions should be tailored to remain within IoT-specific limitations, so that they do not add further complexity to the system or create new attack vectors. As a result of this, the challenge of protecting IoT is an open research problem, which will need structural, technical and regulatory efforts.

6.1.1 Definition of IoT vulnerability

Let an IoT system be represented as a set of components:

$$S = d_1, d_2, ..., d_n \tag{6.1}$$

where each d_i represents an IoT component (device, protocol, firmware, service), labeled as i. For a given component d_i, its vulnerability score $V(d_i)$ can be modeled as:

$$V(d_i) = P_e \times I(d_i) \tag{6.2}$$

where, $P_e(d_i)$ represents the probability of the vulnerability in d_i can be exploited and $I(d_i)$ represents the impact of exploitation in the system.

The probability of exploitation depends on multiple factors, including the likelihood of an attack on the IoT system, the complexity of the exploitation, and the attacker's capabilities and resources. This can be modeled as the following equation:

$$P_e(d_i) = f(A_i, C_i, E_i) \tag{6.3}$$

where A_i represents the security breach attack that exposes the IoT system, such as open ports, wireless access, botnet attacks, and so on. In addition, C_i represents the attack's complexity, and E_i represents its capability and resources for breaching security. In IoT systems, A_i is often high due to always-on connectivity, while C_i is low due to weak authentication and insecure protocols.

On the other hand, the impact of IoT security attack exploitations can be modeled over the security objectives with the following equations:

$$I(d_i) = w_C C_i + w_{In} In_i + w_{Av} Av_i + w_{Pr} Pr_i \tag{6.4}$$

Here, C_i denotes the loss of confidentiality, In_i represents the loss of data or system integrity, Av_i corresponds to the loss of availability, and Pr_i captures the loss of privacy associated with IoT device i. The coefficients w_* are weighting factors that quantify the relative severity or importance of each loss dimension, allowing the impact function to be tailored to the specific operational context and application requirements of the IoT system. Across different IoT systems and frameworks, the values of the weighting coefficients may vary. For example, in healthcare IoT, w_{Pr} and w_{In} may be higher than w_{Av} due to sensitive patient data and safety implications, whereas in industrial IoT, w_{Av} and w_{In} may dominate due to production continuity and system reliability requirements. On the other hand, in smart home environments,

w_C and w_{Pr} are often prioritized due to risks of personal data exposure. In addition, the losses resulting from IoT security breach attacks, as stated in equation 6.4, are defined as follows:

- **Confidentiality Loss** (C_i): Confidentiality loss means divulging sensitive information created, stored, or transferred by the IoT devices. This comprises sensor measurements, user personal data, operation parameters, and context. It is often discussed that insecure communication protocols, weak authentication, and inadequate encryption enable attackers to intercept IoT traffic or steal data from targeted devices, thereby exposing sensitive information.
- **Integrity Loss** In_i: Loss of integrity occurs when data, firmware, or control logic of the IoT is altered without permission, with or without intent. Integrity breaches can result from firmware manipulation, malicious code injection, routing modification, or false data injection. These trade-offs undermine the trustworthiness of IoT systems by leading to incorrect sensing, actuation, or analytics, especially in safety-critical domains such as healthcare and industrial automation.
- **Availability Loss** Av_i: Availability loss signifies the inability of IoT devices or services to function according to requirements. Such a loss is typically linked with denial of service attacks, jamming, flooding, resource spamming, or, device failures due to a cyber or physical attack. It is often considered by practitioners that IoT systems are vulnerable to availability disruptions due to limited computational and energy capabilities, making them particular targets for massive-scale distributed denial-of-service attacks and network-wide intrusions.
- **Privacy Loss** Pr_i: Privacy loss is the unauthorized deriving, collecting, or misuse of personal or contextual data pertaining to individuals, places or actions in the realm of the IoT. In contrast to the loss of confidentiality, privacy loss can occur when data are not openly provided, for example, in traffic-analysis-based data aggregation or AI-based inference. IoT systems amplify privacy risks through their ongoing data collection, the limited understanding many users have of that collection, and the incorporation of smart analytics, all of which can lead to breaches of data, location, and model privacy.

It is important to note that IoT systems are interdependent and operate in a coordinated manner rather than in isolation. Thus, each IoT system vulnerability is aggregated as follows:

$$V(S_{IoT}) = \sum_{i=1}^{n} V(d_i) + \sum_{i \neq j} \delta_{ij} \tag{6.5}$$

in which the propagation risk is represented by the value of δ_{ij}, representing the effect of an infected node that allows the creation of a lateral movement or a botnet. This is why IoT vulnerabilities are commonly associated with major failures, such as botnets and distributed denial-of-service attacks.

6.2 Types of IoT vulnerabilities

IoT systems are exposed to a wide range of vulnerabilities. In this section, these vulnerabilities are briefly discussed with examples.

6.2.1 Weak authentication and authorization

Weak authentication is a common IoT vulnerability. The vulnerability results from the use of default credentials, static passwords and lack of mutual authentication between the device and servers. The ability of attackers to impersonate legitimate devices or users with minimal effort stems from the lack of proper access-control mechanisms in many IoT devices. Identity spoofing, Sybil attacks[2], and unauthorized access to devices are common in IoT applications due to a lack of strong cryptographic authentication and design decisions driven by cost considerations.

6.2.2 Insecure communication protocols

IoT systems often use lightweight communication protocols optimized for low latency and energy savings rather than security. Protocols like MQTT[3], CoAP[4], RPL[5] and 6LoWPAN[6] are established without necessarily having to encrypt or exchange secure keys, making the information subject to eavesdropping, replay and MITM[7]. IoT systems are a significant facilitator of large-scale attacks, such as IoT botnets and distributed denial-of-service attacks, by enabling attackers to intercept or alter data in transit.

6.2.3 Firmware and software vulnerabilities

Vulnerabilities in firmware can be exposed by insecure boot processes, the absence of verification of firmware integrity and unsafe firmware update systems. A large number of IoT devices fail to verify the integrity of the firmware they provide and offer no secure method for updating it over the air, allowing attackers to install

---

[2] A Sybil attack is one in which a single adversary creates and operates multiple fake identities to gain disproportionate influence over a network, subverting trust, voting, or reputation mechanisms. For additional informaiton, Douceur, J.R., 2002, March. The sybil attack. In International workshop on peer-to-peer systems (pp. 251-260). Berlin, Heidelberg: Springer Berlin Heidelberg.

[3] MQTT is a lightweight publish-subscribe messaging protocol designed for resource-constrained devices and low-bandwidth, high-latency networks, making it widely used in IoT communication.

[4] CoAP is a lightweight web-transfer protocol that adapts a REST-style request/response model over UDP for resource-constrained IoT devices and networks.

[5] RPL is an IPv6 routing protocol that organizes nodes into a destination-oriented directed acyclic graph (DODAG) to enable efficient routing in constrained, unreliable IoT networks.

[6] 6LoWPAN is an adaptation layer that compresses and fragments IPv6 packets so they can be transmitted over low-power, low-bandwidth wireless links such as IEEE 802.15.4.

[7] MITM attack is one in which an adversary secretly intercepts and possibly alters the communication between two parties who believe they are communicating directly with each other.

malicious firmware and retain long-term control over devices. Since firmware has limited implementation, these attacks may bypass higher-level security measures and persist long enough to be highly hazardous in large-scale IoT systems.

6.2.4 Physical device vulnerabilities

IoT devices are frequently deployed in unprotected or public settings, which means they could be exposed to physical attacks. Opponents may use a debug interface, modify firmware, manipulate sensors or simply alter hardware pads. Physical access enables attackers to compromise logic controls and bypass them entirely, leading to device cloning, permanent malware, or the injection of fake sensor data, which can delegitimize the reliability of the whole IoT system.

6.2.5 Resource constraint-induced vulnerabilities

IoT devices have their security severely limited by a lack of processing power, memory, and energy. These limitations preclude the use of strong cryptography, real-time monitoring, or intrusion detection. Consequently, most of the IoT systems are weakly protected and therefore susceptible to both passive and active attacks.

6.2.6 Network and routing vulnerabilities

Weak routing protocols and dynamic network structures make IoT networks vulnerable to routing attacks and topology attacks. Examples of attacks that can disrupt the delivery of data, degrade the network, or even completely terminate service include sinkhole[8], wormhole[9], blackhole[10], jamming[11], and flooding[12]. The weaknesses have a direct effect on availability and reliability, critical safety-critical and IIoT requirements.

6.2.7 Data integrity and confidentiality vulnerabilities

IoT devices constantly generate and transmit sensitive data, which is often not properly secured with respect to integrity and confidentiality. Attackers can alter sensor readings, introduce false information or capture private information being

---

[8] a compromised node advertises a falsely attractive route to lure surrounding traffic toward itself, allowing it to intercept, drop, or manipulate the data passing through

[9] two colluding attackers create a private out-of-band tunnel between distant points in the network, replaying captured packets to distort routing and topology perception

[10] a malicious node attracts traffic by advertising itself as having the best route, then silently drops all packets instead of forwarding them

[11] an adversary deliberately transmits interfering signals on the wireless channel to disrupt legitimate communication and degrade or deny network availability

[12] an attacker overwhelms a node or network with a high volume of bogus or excessive traffic to exhaust resources and deny service to legitimate users

transferred or stored. Weakened data integrity may result in erroneous actuations, failure of systems or risk to people, particularly in areas of health, smart grids, and fortified automation.

6.2.8 Privacy vulnerabilities

Exposure to privacy vulnerabilities occurs when the IoT systems collect, analyze, and transmit personal or situational information without adequate precautions. Hackers may use unauthorized access to IoT data to expose sensitive information, including user behavior, location, or health status, or users' credentials. In IoT systems using AI, privacy concerns are also magnified by data aggregation and model inference, resulting in data, location, and model privacy leakage that is not confined to isolated devices but is a societal issue.

6.2.9 Botnet and large-scale exploitation vulnerabilities

Weak IoT devices are often used on an extensive scale and integrated into botnets. Poor authentication and a lack of proper communication enable malware to spread within thousands or millions of devices in a short period of time. Large-scale DoS attacks are then initiated using these botnets, increasing the vulnerabilities of localized devices and amplifying them into global vulnerabilities that impact critical internet infrastructure and services.

6.2.10 IoT system lifecycle and maintenance vulnerabilities

IoT security typically degrades over time due to poor lifecycle management. Numerous devices are supplied with little or no firmware updates and vendors can end up giving up on products soon after their deployment. Unfixed vulnerabilities accumulate, leaving devices permanently exposed to known attacks. This long-term maintenance gap results in an increasing number of unsecured legacy devices in IoT environments.

6.2.11 Human and usability vulnerabilities

Human factors also contribute to the insecurity of the IoT. The default settings are often left unchanged, updates are not implemented, and security choices are not configured due to a lack of awareness or poor usability. Flexible or non-intuitive security interfaces also discourage secure behavior and introduce socio-technical vulnerabilities that intensify the technical vulnerabilities.

6.2.12 AI-specific vulnerabilities in intelligent IoT

With Intelligent IoT systems, AI introduces new types of vulnerabilities, such as data poisoning, adversarial inputs, and model theft. Hacked devices can introduce malicious data that misleads ML models and attackers could use model inference to recover sensitive information. Even though AI can improve detection and automation, it can also introduce complications in the system and expand the attack surface unless integrated securely.

6.3 Security risks in IoT infrastructure

Practitioners tend to regard the vulnerabilities of IoT systems as systemic weaknesses rather than isolated flaws, and for good reason: any IoT deployment knits together a range of components whose security capabilities differ markedly. At one end sit resource-constrained edge devices, in the middle lie heterogeneous networking technologies, and at the other end reside cloud or middleware backends together with the user-facing applications they support. Because security controls are rarely applied with equal rigor across this end-to-end architecture, risk does not distribute itself evenly. Instead, it accumulates at the seams where devices meet gateways, where gateways meet cloud services, and where cloud platforms meet applications. The same concentration appears at critical moments in a device's lifecycle, particularly during bootstrapping, onboarding, and over-the-air updates. It is precisely at these junctures, when trust relationships are forged and cryptographic keys exchanged, that devices tend to operate with the least protection. Practitioners illustrate the point starkly, noting that the sensors and actuators of the sensing layer may have little or no built-in security, and that data passing through the network layer can lose its trustworthiness entirely when the appropriate safeguards are absent.

The threats facing IoT systems vary considerably from one network layer to the next. Various existing frameworks map security threats by network layer. The most common divides the system into three layers: perception, network, and application, while other treatments insert a middleware, or support layer, between the network and application tiers to yield a four-layer model. More sophisticated analyses adopt a five-layer architecture inspired by the OSI stack, spanning the physical, MAC, network, transport, and application layers. This finer-grained view is especially useful for showing how particular protocols can be exploited at distinct stages of communication. This section examines the security risks inherent in each layer of the IoT infrastructure and considers their implications for the secure and uninterrupted operation of IoT systems.

6.3.1 Perception (sensing/physical) layer security risks

The perception layer is considered the first layer of any IoT architecture, as shown in Fig. 6.1. This layer includes sensors, actuators, RFID tags, embedded controllers, and other physical devices that interact directly with the external environment. Because these components are often deployed in exposed, unattended, and minimally protected locations, the perception layer is highly vulnerable to physical compromise, firmware abuse, sensor manipulation, and device-level disruption. The main security risks at this layer are described below.

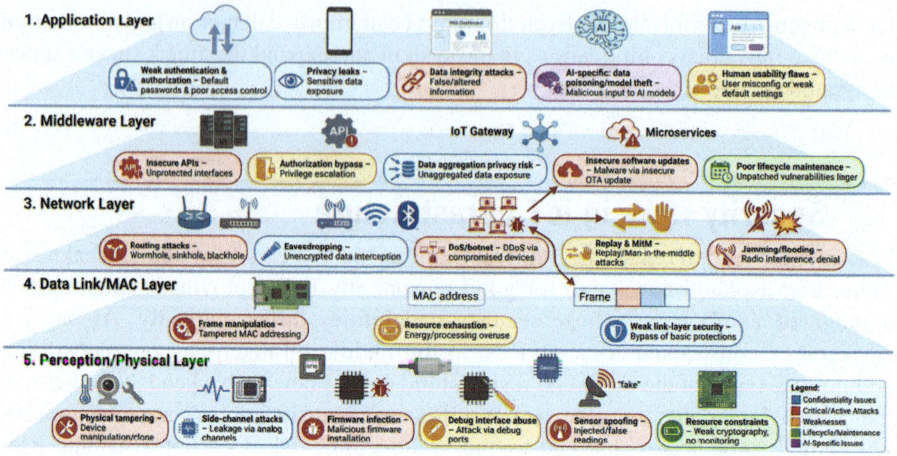

FIGURE 6.1

Security risks in different IoT infrastructure layers.

6.3.1.1 Physical capture and tampering

Physical exposure of IoT devices is a significant weakness at the perception level. These devices are often deployed in unprotected or minimally secured locations and as such are vulnerable to theft and manipulation. Various sources state that if an attacker gains physical access to a node, they can retrieve stored information and spy on ongoing interactions. In other instances, the attacker can alter memories or steal cryptographic keys, which can result in a rootkit of the whole system. Physical compromise usually leads to stealthy and prolonged control of the machine. Attackers can gain permanent access without being detected or flagged as intruders by modifying hardware (firmware) or switching to hidden debug interfaces. This kind of low-level alteration is hard to detect, as a single software monitoring tool cannot be active long enough to detect it.

Another concern is that higher-level security mechanisms are easily evaded by physical attacks. Cryptography schemes, authentication methodologies and secure communication systems are rendered useless when an attacker can have direct access to hardware components. In such a case, the device makes it easy to extract the secrets and keys, rendering top-layer protection largely meaningless. The effects of physical compromise may extend far beyond the compromised node to the entire network. An infected device may be exploited to launch attacks on a wider scale, such as creating botnets and launching DDoS[13] attacks. Additionally, compromised nodes can issue malicious requests or insert false or manipulated data, undermining system availability and data integrity. These impacts lead to a rise in localized

[13] A DDoS attack is one in which an attacker uses many compromised devices to simultaneously flood a target system with traffic, exhausting its resources and making it unavailable to legitimate users.

physical access to system-wide breakdowns. Several real-life incidents have shown that the impact of physical attacks in IoT systems is especially severe in safety-related sectors. The medical and automotive IoT systems provide examples illustrating how compromised devices can endanger human safety, not just data security. Attackers can gain malicious control or alter sensor data in such environments, leading to incorrect actuation, unsafe system operation, or even fatal consequences.

From the discussions above, it can be concluded that perception-layer devices themselves can be resource-constrained and no longer highly safeguarded. These vulnerabilities render them physically vulnerable to attacks and allow attackers to steal honest nodes or replace them with malicious ones, gaining a foothold for more severe attacks across the entire IoT architecture.

6.3.1.2 Firmware/OTA update abuse at the edge IoT device

Perception-layer compromises are directly correlated with insecure firmware and the process of software updates. Specifically, real-world attack incidents show that the over-the-air (OTA) update capability can be abused to install malicious or falsified code on IoT devices. The attacks facilitate the malicious injection of code and false data into the sensing layer and, in this way, conveniently penalize compromised nodes for acting incorrectly, even when they may appear correct. Once a device has been infected with malicious code, the impacts are usually difficult to eradicate. Hacked nodes may be repurposed for unintended operations such as creating false information, controlling system behavior, and, in certain circumstances, hijacking part or all of the IoT systems. Inaccurate data generated at the device level can also be transmitted to gateways or cloud services, leading to inaccurate analytics outputs and overall system faultiness.

In many cases, practitioners underscore the necessity of OTA updates to facilitate maintenance and vulnerability patching, especially when deployments are at large scale, while noting that insecure update mechanisms can have dire consequences for the integrity and availability of the update process. Even without direct physical access to a device, it is possible to use OTA channels with weak validation, weak authorization, or weak integrity checks, allowing attackers to use the IoT device-provided services. As a result, the OTA updates have become a highly leveraged attack surface rather than a protective mechanism. An important practical issue that is brought to the fore is the role of gateways during the update process. Most IoT devices lack the capability to verify or install firmware updates independently; instead, they rely on gateways to mediate updates. In this case, gateways typically perform a set of simple validity checks such as hash checksum validation. Because the gap between gateway and validation is low or exposes cryptographic keys, a gateway is a major failure point and can be used to compromise systems on a large scale. The threat posed by OTA updates also becomes increasingly significant as the system's size and heterogeneity grow. Real-world industrial and large-scale IoT systems report that applying updates to large numbers of heterogeneous devices is complex due to limited inter-device interaction, power constraints, sleep states, protocol heterogeneity, and multi-vendor interactions. These variables complicate the establishment of standardized, safe update processes across the entire system.

Overall, the above discussion emphasizes the structural and economic constraints that intensify the limitations on the abuse of Firmware/OTA updates. In the cheapest IoT implementation, firmware is not always upgradeable, and timely patch management is neither feasible nor possible. In other situations, devices may have delicate firmware resources, debug interfaces, and manufacturer-added components that, when disclosed, can lead to a devastating, protracted compromise. These can all be used to explain why insecure update mechanisms have long been a fundamental cause of IoT vulnerabilities and cannot be attributed solely to implementation flaws.

6.3.1.3 Sensor spoofing

A commonly known perception-layer integrity threat in an IoT system is sensor spoofing. In such an attack, one of the adversaries causes the system to accept fabricated measurements or a falsified sensor identity as valid. There are two similar points of view of sensor spoofing. At first, spoofing may be at the signal level or at the measurement level. Attackers in this case interfere with the sensing process by providing false stimuli or saturating sensors with spurious signals. Due to this, the device captures and documents skewed measurements. Such behavior is commonly referred to as sensor overload, in which sensors are flooded with spurious signals or messages, causing them to behave abnormally. In more sophisticated versions of this attack, instead of introducing grossly incorrect values, the attackers put a small, well-calibrated modification on sensor responses. This is mostly observed in large industrial environments. The false values are never outside the normal noise range, which is why they are hard to identify using conventional anomaly detection methods. This tactic suggests sensor spoofing is not necessarily a crude manipulation of data; it may be a subtle technique that causes the control to make decisions without attention.

Second, sensor spoofing is also mentioned at the identity and data-collection interface in RFID-based and tag-based sensing systems, which belong to the perception layer. Attackers could also use other permitted tags that could gain access to the same permissions and services within such environments. In this way, the attackers can insert useless observations into the collected data that appear legitimate to the system. Sensor spoof attacks may mislead RFID readers into accepting spoofed information. In addition to integrity breaches, system availability and energy efficiency can be compromised by identity-based spoofing. Spoofed messages can lead to packet loss, retransmissions, and unnecessary network traffic, and can even drain batteries in resource-constrained devices. These secondary effects point out that the concept of spoofing does not affect data accuracy alone.

Overall, sensor spoofing provides a direct perception-layer pathway to false data injection and degraded decision-making performance. Depending on how the attack is executed, it may also lead to availability issues for sensors and IoT components due to congestion, retries, and prolonged device operation.

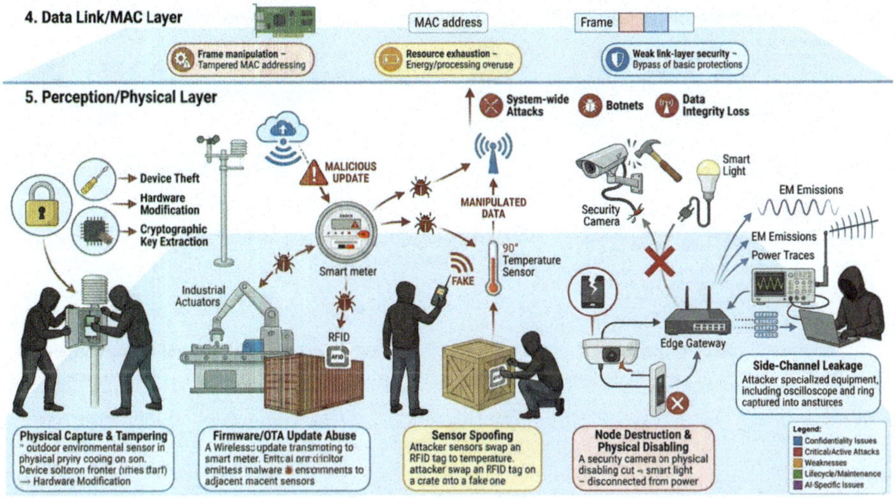

FIGURE 6.2

Security vulnerabilities in the network layer of IoT systems.

6.3.1.4 Node destruction and physical disabling

Node destruction and physical disabling are considered among the major threats to the availability of IoT devices in an IoT-connected system. This is a key threat on the perception layer. Unlike sensor spoofing or firmware manipulation, they rely on physical damage, disabling, or removal of sensors and actuators in their deployment areas. There are many IoT devices deployed in unattended or open areas, such as outdoor infrastructure, industrial plants, and community areas. In these environments, attackers can cut the power supply or damage or destroy equipment, which, in most cases, causes permanent or long-term service disruption. Infected devices may not be repairable with software recovery and may need to be replaced or repaired. A small number of lost nodes may have severe consequences for a system's performance. For example, the destruction of an IoT system node can reduce sensing coverage, disrupt routing paths, or impair overall system reliability. These kinds of situations are particularly evident in IoT networks that are resource-limited or have few deployed nodes. Consequently, it is common knowledge that physical disabling is a simple but effective attack vector. It also exploits the exposed nature of devices at the perception layer, potentially causing cascading failures that propagate to deeper layers of the IoT architecture.

6.3.1.5 Side-channel leakage from physical devices

Side-channel leakage is considered a physical-layer threat in IoT systems. Attackers can use this threat when they can see innocent information emitted by devices during normal operation without proper monitoring or embedding. Assailants can detect the power consumption and time behavior of the gadgets, or electromagnetic radiation,

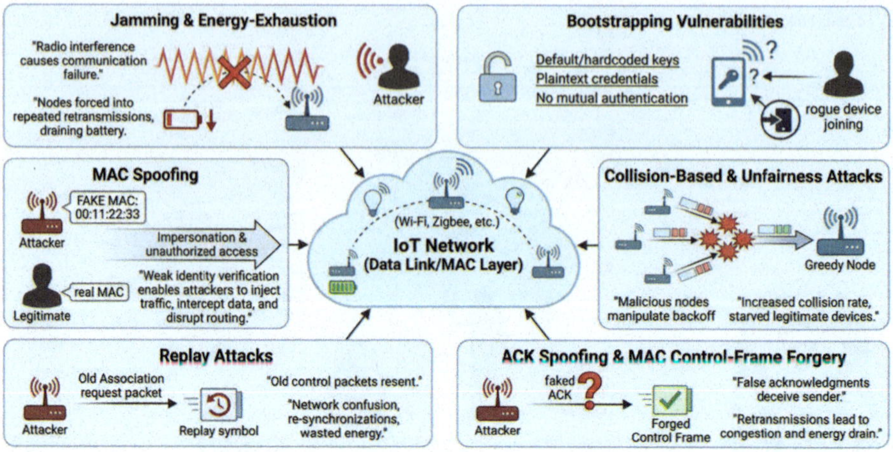

FIGURE 6.3

IoT vulnerabilities present in the Data Link Layer.

through physical proximity to the devices. Based on them, they can deduce sensitive internal data, including security-related parameters or cryptographic keys. Most IoT devices are resource-constrained and lack advanced shielding or noise masking. Consequently, the signals generated during the computations can often be observed and analyzed more easily than in conventional computing systems. It is also noted that side-channel attacks do not require direct access to device memory or firmware. Rather, they exploit the material capabilities of computation, enabling attackers to dodge logical security measures altogether. Although side-channel leakage is not as widely debated as other threats (e.g., node capture or sensor spoofing), it remains a real-world threat in IoT ecosystem. This is particularly easy to exploit when attackers can maintain a sustained physical distance from the gadgets. These remarks support the broader assumption that physical exposure is a root vulnerability in perception-layer IoT deployments.

Fig. 6.2 shows the IoT vulnerabilities and attacks present in the perception layer.

6.3.2 Data link/mac layer security risks

In this section, we address the security risks and vulnerabilities that are likely to affect IoT-deployed systems at the Data Link/MAC Layer. Fig. 6.3 shows the IoT vulnerabilities and attacks present in the Data Link/MAC layer.

6.3.2.1 Jamming and energy-exhaustion

Jamming and energy-exhaustion attacks are often considered closely related to IoT device availability threats that primarily occur at the data link (MAC) layer in IoT systems. Even though jamming is caused by physical radio interference, its effects on the network are most felt at the MAC layer, where interference hinders devices' access to the shared wireless channel because they cannot reliably sense, reserve, or harness it. To transmit interference on the control frame, attackers can corrupt it, introduce collisions, and trigger repeated carrier sensing or acknowledgment cycles. Such an action compels nodes to repeatedly back off and unnecessarily retransmit, ultimately causing a communication system to break down. Moreover, attackers can exploit MAC-layer power management capabilities to execute energy-exhaustion or sleep-deprivation attacks. Attackers can cause a progressive drain of battery resources by keeping nodes inactive with repeated bogus requests, keeping them awake, or causing never-ending contention and retransmission, without necessarily putting communication resources at risk. This is especially harmful since such attacks are simulated to resemble normal traffic patterns and, as such, they are hard to counter. IoT MAC protocols are particularly susceptible to jamming and energy-draining attacks due to low-power radios, minimal contention-based schemes, and excessive duty-cycle activity, yet lack strong anti-jamming or energy-conscious defensive techniques. Consequently, low-effort or intermittent attacks can cause substantial degradation of throughput, network coverage, and system partitioning over the long term. Generally, the existing reports and studies present MAC-layer jamming and energy exhaustion as viable, ongoing DoS threats whose design hinges on efficiency-focused protocol structures and finite resource usage, and that disrupt IoT networks without any issues with device firmware or upper-layer protocol vulnerabilities.

6.3.2.2 Bootstrapping

Bootstrapping refers to the process by which a new IoT device joins a network, establishes trust, obtains cryptographic credentials, and configures communication parameters. In IoT deployments, bootstrapping often occurs automatically and wirelessly, particularly in smart-home, industrial IoT, and sensor-network environments. However, insecure bootstrapping mechanisms are among the most critical vulnerabilities at the MAC/Data-Link layer. Common bootstrapping weaknesses include:

- Use of default or hardcoded network keys
- Transmission of credentials in plaintext
- Lack of mutual authentication during association
- Weak out-of-band verification
- Acceptance of devices without identity validation

An adversary exploiting these weaknesses can introduce rogue devices, perform man-in-the-middle attacks during association, inject malicious keys, or impersonate coordinators.

6.3.2.3 MAC spoofing

Among the vulnerabilities in the data link (MAC) Layer, MAC spoofing is one, although it is sometimes classified as a Perception Layer vulnerability. In such attacks, an intruder will forge or counterfeit the MAC address of an authorized device to gain unauthorized access and disrupt network behavior. IoT systems use a MAC address (or a lightweight identifier) to identify a device, rather than strong cryptographic authentication to validate that device. Due to the low overhead and energy-efficient design of MAC-layer protocols, identity verification in access, association, and neighbor discovery processes is usually weak, or even non-existent, by the device and other entities in the IoT network. In this regular setup, attackers may be able to impersonate trusted nodes by replying to, or forging, MAC-layer identifiers and may join the network, inject malicious frames, or intercept traffic. The danger is particularly acute during the bootstrapping and re-association phases, when devices receive MAC-layer control messages that are only minimally validated to minimize latency and save power. As a consequence, MAC spoofing can lead to broader system-wide failure of an IoT system. Attackers can induce routing inconsistencies, increase collisions, and cause unfair channel access by masquerading as multiple devices or nodes of strategic interest, thereby degrading network availability. When dense deployment is also off the table, there is also the possibility of flooding the network with bogus control or data frame setups, spoofing identities to amplify retransmissions and hasten battery drain in true hosts. MAC-layer spoofing can also introduce false data injection and sensor impersonation, where the identity is loosely tied to hardware or cryptographic credentials; attackers can replace or clone nodes without interruption and still utilize a legitimate MAC identity. This enables covert, slow, and subversive attacks that undermine confidence in sensor-collected information and control decisions at higher levels of the IoT network. In general, MAC spoofing is presented as a potential attack that exploits loose identity assumptions at the data link layer and exacerbates the threat of DoS, energy exhaustion, and data corruption attacks across the IoT stack.

6.3.2.4 Collision-based and unfairness attacks

Collision-based and unfairness attacks are another kind of MAC-Layer attack that primarily affect network availability and violate system or device access regulations in IoT protocols. These attacks involve the deliberate breach of fairness mechanisms by adversaries, such as the backoff timing or the contention protocol, to gain unfair access to the wireless channel. In contrast to jamming attacks, malicious nodes use valid MAC frames and do not elicit responses to malicious actions, but they obey the general structure of protocols, making their behavior hard to distinguish from legitimate communication. Attackers can starve legitimate devices, increase the collision rate, and considerably reduce network throughput by transmitting more aggressively or manipulating backoff behavior. Such actions are commonly denoted as MAC misbehavior, greedy channel access, or backoff manipulation. Even though such attacks resemble jamming-based DoS, they are often considered a separate vulnerability of the MAC layer because they rely on protocol design assumptions rather than direct radio interference.

6.3.2.5 Replay attacks

Replay attacks at the MAC layer are techniques that aim to control IoT systems and the timing of messages during device boot, re-association, and other events. In such attacks, attackers steal legal MAC-layer packets, such as association requests, acknowledgments, or synchronization packets, and later re-send them to the target devices. Receiving messages repeatedly can disrupt the network state, confuse synchronization, and cause devices to rejoin or resynchronize with the network. This behavior can also result in needless power-ups in energy-restricted IoT setups and use additional power. Replay attacks should be discussed as a closely related issue, though they may not always be identified as a separate threat category. Rather, they have been widely accepted as mechanisms that exploit vulnerabilities in the MAC layer's initialization and state management processes, leading to instability and reduced availability.

6.3.2.6 ACK spoofing and MAC control-frame forgery

ACK Spoofing and MAC Control-Frame Forgery are MAC-layer techniques for compromising trustworthy communication among IoT devices. In such attacks, attackers send forged acknowledgment frames or other control messages to deceive legitimate nodes into believing the message has been received. False acknowledgments can lead the sender to believe that data has been received when, in reality, it has not, whereas forged control frames may cause retransmissions to occur inappropriately or lead to basic channel congestion. These attacks do not necessarily involve impersonation of a specific local device identity, unlike full MAC spoofing. They exploit a lack of validation of MAC control frames and an underweight design of most IoT protocols instead. The resulting effect encompasses poor availability, increased rate of collisions and accelerated energy loss. Based on this, ACK spoofing is generally considered a type of MAC-layer control abuse that complements identity and denial-of-service attacks, rather than as a separate vulnerability.

6.3.3 Network layer security risks

Network-layer threats in IoT systems exploit routing decisions, weak transport protection, and constrained node resources to disrupt data forwarding and compromise service availability. These attacks are particularly critical because compromised nodes can manipulate paths, inject false routing information, flood constrained devices, and expose communication channels.

Fig. 6.4 illustrates the main vulnerabilities present at the network layer of IoT systems. The figure summarizes four major threat classes: routing manipulation and topology attacks, control-plane abuse in RPL-based routing protocols, DDoS and botnet-driven flooding, and insecure communication protocols with weak transport protection. Routing attacks include sinkhole, wormhole, fake-route announcement, and data loss manipulation, each of which can redirect traffic, isolate nodes, and corrupt forwarding behavior. RPL-focused attacks target control messages and routing state by exploiting excessive control fields, spoofed nodes, rank manipulation, and resource-draining behavior. DDoS and botnet-based flooding overload constrained IoT devices through coordinated traffic bursts, causing service disruption, weak authentication exposure, and device compromise. The final panel highlights insecure communication protocols, where unencrypted MQTT,

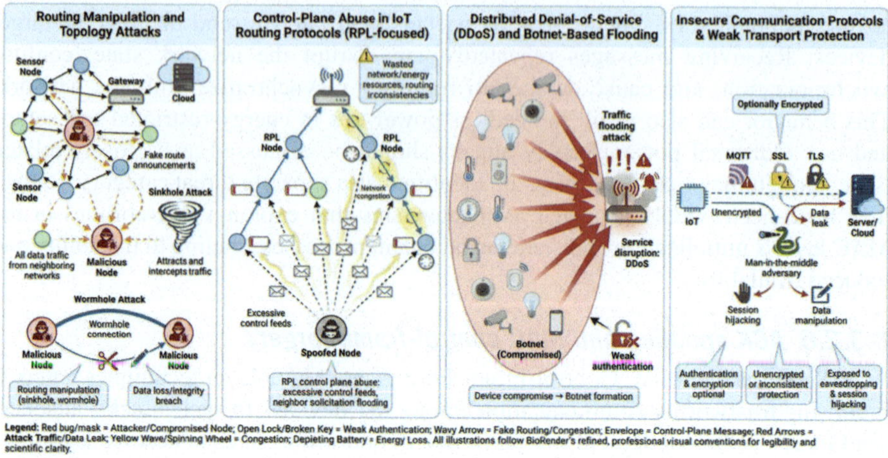

FIGURE 6.4

IoT vulnerabilities present in IoT Network Layer.

weak SSL/TLS use, exposed credentials, session hijacking, and man-in-the-middle attacks can compromise data confidentiality, integrity, and availability. Together, these vulnerabilities show that IoT network-layer security requires secure routing, authenticated control messages, encrypted communication, traffic rate control and lightweight intrusion detection mechanisms.

6.3.3.1 Routing manipulation and topology attacks

Routing Manipulation and Topology Attacks are widely considered as network-layer weaknesses in IoT systems. In these attacks, security breakers and attackers will manipulate routing decisions to redirect data, intercept it, or block its transmission. Typical cases are sinkhole and wormhole attacks, in which adversarial nodes publicly claim invalid routing information or form fake low-latency connections that rearrange the network topology. After attracting traffic to compromised nodes, attackers can either selectively drop packets, modify transmitted data, or perform traffic analysis. These interventions compromise data integrity and network availability. IoT networks are vulnerable to routing manipulation due to their dynamic topologies, limited authentication of routing updates, and the use of lightweight routing protocols tailored for constrained devices.

6.3.3.2 Control-plane abuse in IoT routing protocols

In addition to general routing manipulation, IoT systems exhibit protocol-specific vulnerabilities, particularly in the Routing Protocol for Low-Power and Lossy Networks (RPL). Attackers may use RPL management messages to control routing state via routing solicitations or neighbor discovery messages, or to cause excessive control feeds. This abuse may cause routing inconsistencies, overhead, and waste of limited network and energy resources. From a practitioner's perspective, RPL is designed to trade off high security implementation for efficiency and flexibility. As a result, control-plane mechanisms can be abused by compromised or spoofed nodes, degrading network performance and reliability.

6.3.3.3 DDoS and botnet-based flooding

Distributed denial-of-service (DDoS) attacks are consistently reported as among the most harmful network-layer threats in both regular networking systems and IoT environments. Attackers utilize these attacks to saturate devices, gateways or reverse services with enormous amounts of traffic, and block out legitimate traffic. One of the key characteristics of DDoS attacks related to the IoT is the involvement of compromised IoT devices in botnets. In a regular setup, due to weak authentication, insecure communication practices, and always-on connectivity, most IoT devices can be easily recruited to generate a DDoS attack. As they become compromised, these devices can collectively generate large-scale traffic floods, increasing availability threats not only to the network but also to the entire IoT domain.

6.3.3.4 Insecure communication protocols and weak transport protection

Another major contributor to network-layer risk is the utilization of insecure or poorly secured communication protocols. It is evident from the practitioner's perspective that popular IoT messaging protocols, such as MQTT, lack default security. In these messaging protocols, authentication, encryption, and integrity protection are typically optional. Even where transport-layer protections such as SSL or TLS are brought to bear, the practical difficulties are far from resolved: certificate management, key distribution, performance overhead, and the sheer challenge of achieving compatibility across heterogeneous devices all stand in the way. These are certificate management, key distribution, performance overhead and compatibility of heterogeneous devices. The cumulative effect is that most IoT implementations end up either non-encrypted or only inconsistently encrypted, leaving their data exposed to eavesdropping, manipulation, and session hijacking.

6.3.4 Security risks and vulnerabilities at the middleware / support layer

The IoT support layer introduces security risks associated with service, message brokering, API exposure, tenant isolation, and database interaction. Because this layer connects IoT devices to application services, attacks against it can propagate across middleware components and cloud-facing endpoints.

Fig. 6.5 shows the security risks and attack vulnerabilities present in the IoT support layer. The figure groups these threats into six main categories: cloud flooding attacks, cloud malware injection, signature wrapping attacks against messaging services, SQL injection and database exploitation, middleware broker compromise, and weak API authentication and authorization. Cloud flooding attacks exhaust computational resources by generating malicious traffic streams, causing service

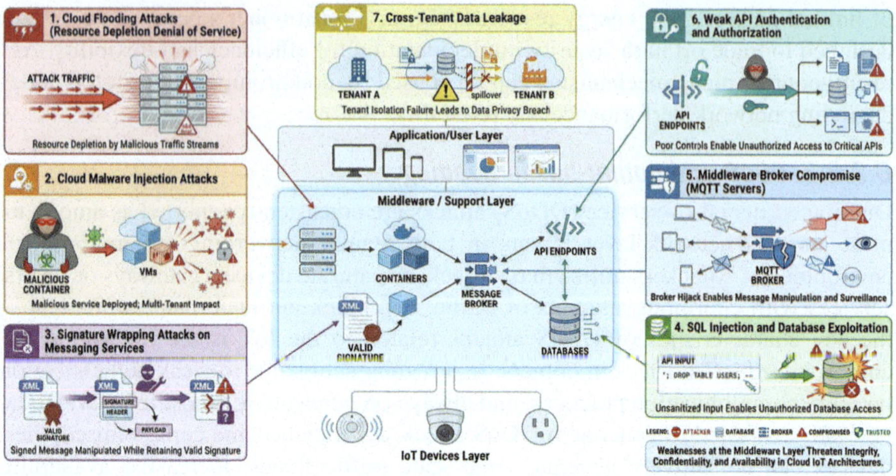

FIGURE 6.5

Security risks and Attack vulnerabilities present in the IoT support layer.

degradation and DoS. Malware injection attacks compromise virtual machines, containers, and cloud-hosted services, enabling multi-tenant impact. Signature wrapping attacks manipulate XML-based messages by retaining a valid signature while altering the structure of the signed content. SQL injection attacks exploit weaknesses in input validation and database interfaces to gain unauthorized access to data. Middleware broker compromise targets MQTT brokers and message-routing components, enabling message manipulation, broker hijacking, and surveillance. Weak API authentication exposes endpoints to unauthorized access, abuse of privileges, and control over critical IoT services. In addition, these risks show that the IoT support layer requires authenticated APIs, secure message brokers, tenant isolation, input validation, signature verification, and continuous monitoring across cloud and middleware services.

6.3.4.1 Cloud flooding attacks (resource depletion denial of service)

Cloud flooding attacks, a form of resource-depletion denial-of-service, target the middleware and cloud layers on which most large-scale IoT deployments ultimately depend. Because IoT architectures funnel data from vast numbers of sensors and devices toward centralized cloud services for aggregation, storage, and analysis, these services become an attractive choke point for adversaries. In a flooding attack, the attacker overwhelms cloud servers, brokers, or application interfaces with an immense volume of requests, connection attempts, data uploads, API calls, or authentication queries until the system's legitimate processing capacity is exhausted. The objective is not to breach confidentiality or alter data, but to consume finite resources such as CPU cycles, memory, bandwidth, and connection pools so thoroughly that genuine devices and users are denied service. The IoT setting makes this threat especially acute. Compromised devices, often recruited into botnets after weak authentication or unpatched firmware is exploited, can be marshaled into massive distributed denial-of-service campaigns that direct coordinated traffic at a single cloud endpoint, as the Mirai botnet notoriously demonstrated. Moreover, because cloud platforms frequently serve many tenants and applications simultaneously, the depletion of shared resources can cascade well beyond the intended target, degrading or disabling services for numerous unrelated users. The consequences extend beyond mere unavailability: when time-sensitive IoT systems such as healthcare monitors, industrial controllers, or traffic-management infrastructure lose access to their cloud backend, the resulting disruption can pose safety and operational risks rather than mere inconvenience. Defending against cloud flooding therefore depends on layered measures-rate limiting, traffic filtering, anomaly-based detection of abnormal request patterns, elastic resource scaling, and the early isolation of compromised devices; since prevention alone cannot fully guarantee that the cloud layer will remain reachable under a determined, distributed assault.

6.3.4.2 Cloud malware injection attacks

Cloud malware injection attacks exploit the middleware level by placing malicious virtual machines, containers, or service elements within the cloud. Attackers can disguise these compromised components as legitimate services, allowing them to be deployed without arousing suspicion. Once injected, such malicious services may intercept data, alter system operations, or extract the sensitive information the cloud is processing. The impact is especially severe for multi-tenant IoT platforms, where a single compromised service can affect tens or hundreds of users or applications at once. Weak validation of service images and insufficient separation between cloud elements make these attacks feasible, thereby posing a significant threat to both integrity and confidentiality.

6.3.4.3 Signature wrapping attacks on middleware messaging services

Signature wrapping attacks[14] are addressed as a vulnerability at the message level because they target middleware services that rely on XML- or interface-based communication. Deviations in these attacks occur when the adversary modifies the structure of a signed message by shifting or copying signed parts whilst preserving the initial cryptographic signature. This can cause the middleware to treat a manipulated message as a valid one despite the change in meaning. This vulnerability enables attackers to evade integrity checks and carry out unauthorized operations without compromising encrypted data. The attacks demonstrate weaknesses stemming from protocol complexity and a loss of trust in middle-level security mechanisms.

[14] A Signature Wrapping attack is one in which an adversary exploits the separation between signature verification and message processing in XML/SOAP-based services, restructuring a signed document to inject malicious content while keeping the original signature valid.

6.3.4.4 SQL injection and backend database exploitation

SQL injection[15] remains a persistent middleware-layer vulnerability in IoT systems that rely on backend databases to store, analyze, and manage device data. Many middleware applications fail to validate or sanitize inputs from devices or external APIs, allowing attackers to exploit this gap to execute unauthorized database queries that read, modify, or destroy stored data. Because middleware databases frequently hold sensitive operational or personal information, a successful injection can lead to large-scale data breaches and a loss of integrity. Although SQL injection is a familiar problem in web security, it continues to affect IoT middleware in particular, owing to compressed development cycles and the limited security testing such systems typically undergo.

6.3.4.5 Middleware broker compromise (e.g., MQTT servers)

MQTT servers are considered middleware and are essential, high-value targets of attack. These brokers transport publish-subscribe traffic between applications and devices in the IoT and serve as centralized coordination points. Should a broker be compromised, propaganda through message routes, the introduction of false information, the suppression of genuine messages, or surveillance of the scope of communications can be carried out. Since brokers are usually on large-scale systems, a single breach can disrupt entire IoT systems. From a practitioner's perspective, ineffective authentication, improper access controls, and insufficient monitoring are significant risks of Middleware broker compromise.

6.3.4.6 Weak API authentication and authorization

Weak API authentication and authorization on middleware APIs are consistently cited as one primary security problem in IoT systems. Middleware platforms offer APIs to manage devices, access data, and integrate with applications, and insecurely exposed interfaces can create opportunities for abuse. According to different sources, sensitive credentials are hard-coded, token management is weak, and coarse-grained access control is used, thereby enabling attackers to have unauthorized access. The flaws allow hacking of backend services, disclosure of sensitive information, and execution of unauthorized customer commands. Moreover, compromised APIs are frequently used to establish an initial foothold, allowing the attacker to move laterally within the IoT infrastructure; thus, API security is an ancillary requirement at the middleware level.

6.3.4.7 Cross-tenant data leakage in cloud-based IoT platforms

Cross-tenant data leakage is addressed as a major privacy threat of cloud-based IoT infrastructure serving more than two users (or applications). Such environments also share resources among tenants, and a lack of isolation may

[15] SQL injection is a web-based attack in which an adversary inserts malicious SQL code into input fields or queries to manipulate a database, allowing unauthorized access, modification, or extraction of data

result in unintentional data exposure. Configuration errors in Cloud-IoT architecture, virtualization vulnerabilities, or vulnerabilities in middle- or shared-middleware functions can enable data leakage between tenants. This may disclose sensitive sensor data, user activity data, or trade secrets. This risk is especially acute in industrial, healthcare, and smart-city applications, where data separation is strictly governed by privacy, safety, and regulatory concerns.

6.3.5 Security risks at application layer of IoT systems

The application layer is a high-risk surface because it connects user-facing services, device commands, authentication logic, and data-handling functions. Attacks at this layer can compromise user privacy, disrupt service availability, and expose IoT systems to unauthorized control.

Fig. 6.6 presents vulnerabilities and attacks at the application layer of IoT architecture. The figure highlights five major risk categories: unauthorized access and code-level vulnerabilities, data theft and sniffing, insecure application configuration and data handling, access-control weaknesses with weak authentication, and service interruption through application-level DoS attacks. Code-level weaknesses such as injection flaws, buffer overflows, malware, viruses, Trojans, and spyware can compromise the application logic and enable unauthorized control. Data theft and sniffing expose sensitive information through weak encryption, protocol translation leakage, and insecure data flows. Misconfiguration risks include default settings, poor session management, unencrypted storage, and excessive data retention. Weak authentication and poor role management can lead to privilege escalation. Application-level DoS attacks can exhaust resources through invalid requests, excessive traffic, and service overload. Together, these vulnerabilities show that IoT application-layer security requires secure coding, strong authentication, role-based access control, encrypted storage, careful data-retention policies, and continuous application monitoring.

6.3.5.1 Unauthorized access and code-level vulnerabilities

Unauthenticated access is always termed as a significant security threat in IoT systems at the application layer. The attacker usually exploits existing software vulnerabilities, such as code injection, buffer overflows, and poor input validation, to circumvent application procedures. After gaining unauthorized access, attackers can interfere with application behavior, steal confidential data, or send malicious instructions to other connected devices. Other types of application-layer malware, such as viruses, worms, trojans, and spyware, always pose a severe threat in the IoT infrastructure. This malware enables sustained surveillance, data theft, and rogue control of an IoT service, directly undermining integrity and trust in the systems.

6.3.5.2 Access control weaknesses and weak authentication

Weak access control is a recurrent vulnerability, often considered a fundamental vulnerability at the application layer. The presence of inadequate authentication,

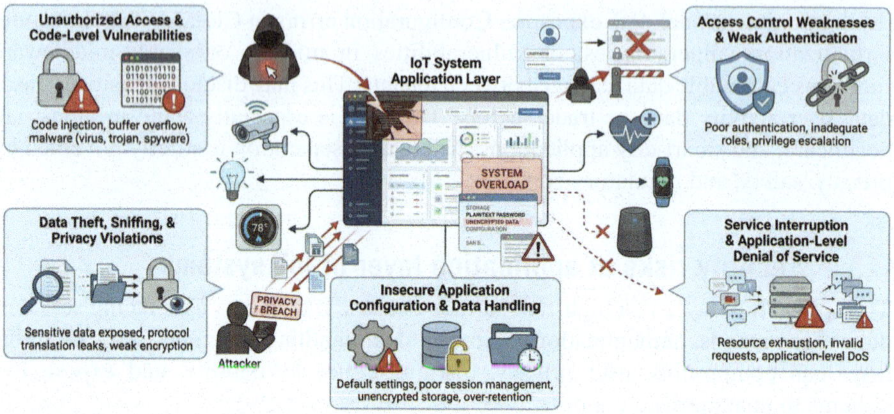

FIGURE 6.6

Vulnerabilities present at Application Layer of IoT Architecture.

inappropriate authorization protocols, and the absence of role distinction enable any attacker to raise privileges once the application interface is breached. Since the application layer is the first touchpoint for both users and administrators, access control failures can render the entire IoT system vulnerable. When verification checks are evaded at this level, attackers may gain unhindered access to data, services, and device management capabilities. Consequently, access control remains a key concern in application-layer security.

6.3.5.3 Data theft, sniffing, and privacy violations

Another key risk with the application layer is data theft and privacy breaches. In an IoT architecture, the application layer is responsible for processing or storing personal information, user records, and data usage patterns, i.e., sensitive data. Even without complete integration failure, attackers may get access to the system and readily decode sensitive information due to weakened encryption, poor management of keys, or direct storage of text (plaintext). It has been reported in various cases that application-layer sniffing is more likely when protocol translation is performed by decrypting and re-encrypting traffic at the gates. It is at these intermediate processing points that data interception or unauthorized access can occur, making the application layer a point of attack for privacy.

6.3.5.4 Service interruption and application-level denial of service

Service interruption attacks, similar to DoS attacks, also threaten the application layer. These attacks are a type of security breach in which attackers exploit application-level logic flaws, make resource-intensive requests, or provide invalid input to overload application services. However, instead of overloading network bandwidth, these attacks overload processing, memory, or database resources at the application level. Since IoT applications can manage or coordinate large numbers of devices, the failure of application-layer services can quickly spread and impact system behavior as a whole.

6.3.5.5 Insecure application configuration and data handling

Insecure application configuration is considered one of the most significant yet often-overlooked threats in the application layer of IoT architecture. Default encryption, high privileges, poor session management, and insecure storage can leave IoT applications vulnerable, even without attackers' use of advanced exploitation skills. Mishandling of data, including storing sensitive data without encryption and retaining data beyond the time of need, is another poor practice that may lead to data leakage. These operations elevate privacy risks in the long run and could contravene regulatory provisions. The security of the application layer relies not only on secure code but also on proper configuration and careful management of data content.

To put the overall discussion in a nutshell, the application layer is the most accessible and visible attack surface in IoT systems. In this layer, technical vulnerabilities directly affect user-facing services and sensitive data. Application-layer attacks may have immediate consequences, including breaches of privacy, loss of control, and outages. In contrast to lower-layer attacks, which might require physical presence or network proximity, numerous vulnerabilities in application layers can be remotely exploited. Because of this fact, application logic and strong access control must be secured and data handling process security mechanisms are required to provide trust and resilience to IoT implementations.

6.4 IoT vulnerabilities mitigation strategies & risk management frameworks

To address weaknesses in IoT systems and control the risks of unauthorized or abnormal access, while ensuring the proper security of the deployed IoT architecture, four security frameworks can be used. This section presents these frameworks in depth.

6.4.1 Prevention-Detection-Mitigation (PDM) as a proactive risk-control framework in IoT

The PDM framework is a structured, proactive approach to managing security risks in both WSNs and IoT systems. Defenses of IoT systems primarily focus on preventing external attackers from exploiting vulnerabilities in communication protocols, encryption schemes, or device configurations. Prevention is often described as the first line of defense, with the primary aim of minimizing the attack surface and the likelihood of a successful attack. At the perception layer, preventive measures aim to defend devices against unauthorized access and cyberattacks. They consist of cryptographic mechanisms with reduced weight to guarantee data confidentiality and integrity, key distribution using secure methods to regulate participation in the

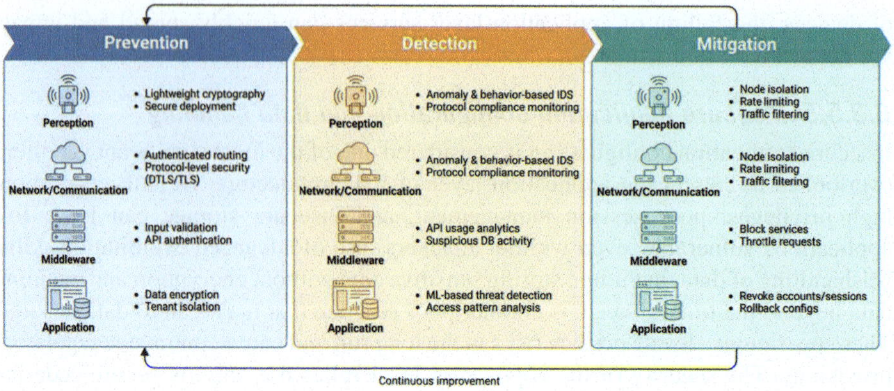

FIGURE 6.7

Prevention-Detection-Mitigation Pipeline for IoT Security in each layer.

network, and deployment planning that accounts for exposure to the physically insecure environment and associated risks. A basic block diagram of the PDM model is shown in Fig. 6.7. The main phases of this model are given as follows:

- **Prevention: Reducing the Attack Surface Before Compromise**
  During the prevention phase, practitioners aim to minimize vulnerability and restrict attackers' opportunities even before an attack occurs. Defenses of IoT systems primarily focus on preventing external attackers from exploiting vulnerabilities in communication protocols, encryption schemes, or device configurations. Prevention is always considered the first line of defense, with the main aim of minimizing the attack surface and the likelihood of a successful attack. At the perception layer, preventive measures aim to defend devices against unauthorized access and cyberattacks. They consist of cryptographic mechanisms with reduced weight to guarantee data confidentiality and integrity, key distribution using secure methods to regulate participation in the network, and deployment planning that accounts for exposure to the physically insecure environment and associated risks. Risk estimation for a deployment is itself a preventive measure, as equipment deployed to hostile or unguarded areas requires stronger protective strategies.
  At the network and communication layers, prevention is achieved through security measures in routing and communication processes. The authentication of involved nodes, protecting routing information, and applying protocol-level security where possible are the main prevention strategies, e.g., DTLS for limited application protocols or TLS-based protection for messaging systems. They actually come at the cost of overhead, but there are unavoidable trade-offs to eliminate eavesdropping, spoofing, and routing manipulation. Other aspects of prevention include implementing basic access control policies and device privileges to mitigate the effects of credential compromise.

At the middleware and application layers, prevention focuses on the API and the secure management of data in backend databases, as stored data and strict tenant isolation are defined as key prophylactic measures in cloud-based IoT platforms to secure software design and configuration. As part of prevention, it is important to validate input, implement strong authentication and authorization for the API, and securely manage data in backend databases to prevent attacks such as SQL injection, malware injection, and unauthorized access. Still, real-world case studies show that even when preventive methods are applied, threats can persist in IoT systems, primarily from insider attacks, node capture, and limited device resources. This limitation directly underscores the need for a strong attack-detection mechanism as a preventive measure.

Despite their value, prevention measures face a significant limitation in IoT environments. The constrained processing power, memory, and energy resources of many devices make it impractical to deploy robust security mechanisms uniformly across all of them. As a result, preventive controls are often lightweight, leaving certain attack surfaces exposed. Prevention alone is therefore argued to be insufficient, particularly against insider threats, node capture, and sophisticated protocol-level attacks. This shortcoming motivates the inclusion of detection and mitigation as core components of the PDM model.

- **Detection: Identifying Attacks That Bypass Preventive Controls**

  The second layer of defense is the detection phase, which is extremely important for attacks that cannot be prevented. IDS are among the primary mechanisms used to detect internal, current, or protocol-compliant attacks in IoT environments, employing constant monitoring of network traffic, node behavior, routing activity, and protocol compliance to detect deviations from expected behavior.

  In the MAC and network layers, detection is centered on detecting abnormal behavior like selective forwarding, manipulation of routing, unfair channel access, replay behavior or excessive retransmission. Such attacks are protocol-compliant and may compromise insider nodes, meaning that cryptographic prevention cannot stop them. This leads to a focus on behavior- and anomaly-based detection techniques. The IDS modeling process involves gathering data, identifying features, and detecting anomalies or misuse, treating detection as an ongoing process rather than a final test.

  In the middleware and application layers, detection strategies include monitoring service usage patterns, API request rates, access behaviors, and database activity. Some examples of threats detected by these techniques include cloud flooding, unauthorized access via API, and suspicious queries. ML-based detection methods are a promising direction for managing scale and heterogeneity, though they are still better described as a recent adoption than as a broadly established system.

  Across all layers, detection is described as proactive by design. It is necessary for systems to determine profiles of normal behavior and detection indicators in advance, rather than detecting attacks only after they have caused significant damage. Detection is, hence, the link between mitigation and prevention.

- **Mitigation: Limiting the Impact of Detected Attacks**

Mitigation involves an IoT system's response to malicious activity after it occurs, designed to minimize or avoid harm and maintain system operations, with systems determining profiles of normal behavior and detection indicators in advance. Mitigation in an IoT environment is not focused on full recovery but should manage impact under limited conditions. At the device and network levels, mitigation measures would involve isolating infected nodes, revoking their credentials, and rerouting to avoid malicious components. Given the physical inaccessibility of compromised nodes (which is often the case), logical isolation is proposed as the most sensible response. Rate limiting and traffic filtering can mitigate the effects of denial-of-service behavior and eliminate the possibility of further resource exhaustion.

Activities that can be performed at the middleware layer to mitigate attacks include blocking malicious service instances, throttling excessive requests during cloud-flooding attacks, and shutting down compromised brokers or API endpoints. Mitigation strategies in this case focus on preventing localized compromises from growing into system-wide failures, since the middleware services serve as consolidation points. At the application layer, mitigation involves disabling compromised accounts, revoking user sessions, rolling back secure configurations, and implementing stricter access controls once unauthorized access is identified. From a practitioner's point of view, mitigation measures should be thoughtful and lightweight, as inadequately developed solutions can introduce further instability or overhead in an already limited system.

Altogether, prevention, detection, and mitigation are the components of a complete and realistic security framework for IoT systems. This framework performs as a friendly risk-management ethos rather than a negative response to countermeasures. The designers would be urged to forecast the types of attacks to be encountered when designing a system, specify visible codes to identify the attacks, and strategize response measures that can be implemented effectively within the limited resources of the IoT architecture. By explicitly combining all three phases, PDM acknowledges the imperfect nature of security controls in the IoT space and provides a formalized means of risk assessment rather than an elementary mechanism for establishing the absence of risk.

6.4.2 Defense-in-depth & secure lifecycle thinking

In the AI era, IoT security increasingly calls for a defense-in-depth philosophy alongside secure lifecycle thinking. The guiding argument is that IoT security should be conceived as an ongoing threat-mitigation process rather than a one-off control implemented at a single point in the stack. The concept of security in AI-era IoT systems is understood to span the design, development, deployment, operation, and evolution phases with numerous overlapping protective mechanisms at each layer of the architecture. This view is driven by the ubiquity of heterogeneity, the physical exposure of IoT devices, limited resources, long deployment lifespans, and the growing demands of AI/analytics, which broaden capabilities as well as the attack surface. It is often recommended to have multiple layers of controls that reduce exposure, identify deviations, and remediate damage over the long term. To summarize, a defense-in-depth strategy in IoT systems connects to (a) secure software development models, (b) secure data management, (c) predictive/AI-assisted security analytics, and (d) security testing in the continuous minimization of IoT weaknesses and device exposure in the following way:

- **Secure Software Development Practices** Secure software development is considered one of the cornerstones of defense-in-depth. Insecure code, misconfiguration, and insufficient input validation are root causes of attacks such as SQL injection, malware injection, and unauthorized access, and can occur in middleware layers. The suggested posture is a preventive, lifecycle-based approach that involves creating applications with appropriate validation, least-privilege access, and secure configuration defaults, and ensuring these characteristics are preserved through updates and maintenance. Furthermore, secure software development practices with lifecycle thinking emphasize that software security must be pursued throughout the system lifecycle, not as a hardening effort at deployment.
- **Secure Data Management** In IoT system, secure data management is handled as a cross-cutting layer of defense that aids in terms of confidentiality, integrity, and privacy across a system lifetime. On the middleware/support layer, the cloud is linked to a centralized high-value focus to have cloud data secured (e.g., encrypted, access-controlled) in order to minimize the possibility of large-scale data theft and cross-tenant leakage. Inappropriate handling of sensitive data (plaintext) and excessive retention of sensitive data are identified as contributors to privacy risk at the application layer. Secure lifecycle thinking restates such fears as continuous obligations: data protection should occur when collecting, combining, storing, performing analytics, and sharing data, particularly as AI-powered processing increases the likelihood of inference and misuse of secondary data.
- **Predictive and AI-Driven Security Analytics** Predictive and AI-driven security analytics have emerged as the next stage in defense-in-depth, particularly within the detection layer. In IDS/IDPS pipelines, these techniques span data collection, preprocessing, feature extraction, and anomaly detection. ML methods, in particular, are being actively explored to cope with the scale, heterogeneity, and continually evolving attack patterns characteristic of IoT environments. Within these pipelines, AI-based analytics are best understood as an extension of monitoring rather than a replacement for foundational, baseline controls. More recently, predictive and AI-driven analytics have come to be regarded as a principle of the secure lifecycle process, in which models must be trained, updated, and validated as environments change, enabling deviations to be detected as early as possible across the MAC, network, middleware, and application layers.
- **Security Testing, Validation, and Continuous Assessment** Another recurring theme is the treatment of security testing and validation as lifecycle processes.

During development, IoT systems should be tested against known vulnerabilities and attack categories, and once operational, they must be reassessed as configurations, software, and the threat landscape evolve. This includes verifying communication security (e.g., protocol protections) as well as application logic and data flows. From a defensive standpoint, testing reinforces both prevention and detection by exposing weaknesses before attackers can exploit them, and by confirming that layered controls continue to function as intended following a scaling or update event.

6.4.3 Risk estimation at deployment and end-to-end security planning in IoT systems

It is often observed that IoT system development and maintenance practitioners emphasize that IoT security should not be addressed only after an attack; it should be addressed prior to deployment by estimating risks and planning end-to-end. Regarding the security requirements of IoT systems, security assessment directly involves estimating risk based on the device's location during deployment, recognizing that IoT devices' threat exposure is inherently dependent on the physical and operational environment. Devices used in open, unattended, or hostile environments are at greater risk of being physically captured, tampered with, jammed, and subjected to energy-exhaustion attacks than those deployed in controlled environments. IoT system architects, therefore, treat deployment-time risk assessment as a proactive measure that informs the level of protection required, which implementation mechanisms are feasible, and where security investments should be concentrated.

Fig. 6.8 presents an interaction block diagram between early risk estimation when the IoT system is deployed and end-to-end security planning and potential attack mitigation strategies, which are expected to be modified across various layers of the IoT system to apply this framework.

Security applied at a single level or to an isolated component is rarely sufficient for the sound operation of IoT systems. Effective architectural strategies must instead secure the network end-to-end, spanning the perception, communication, middleware, and application layers as a continuous whole. This holistic perspective is dictated by the very nature of IoT attacks, which seldom confine themselves to one layer: a single compromised device may inject counterfeit data, hijack routing decisions, overwhelm cloud services, and ultimately erode privacy at the application level. For this reason, the literature stresses that risk must be assessed in light of the interdependencies among layers, rather than by rating individual threats in isolation. Such reasoning aligns precisely with proactive security planning, in which architects anticipate how a weakness in one layer may cascade through the system as a whole.

Proactive planning naturally extends to cryptographic decisions that are sensitive to both the network layer and the vulnerability. There is no single cryptographic method suited to every situation; rather, encryption and authentication schemes must be chosen based on the threat profile, resource constraints, and the function of each

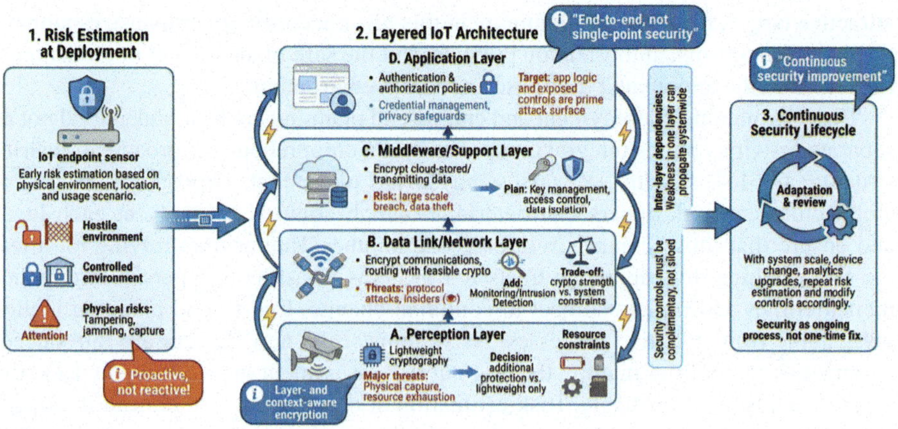

FIGURE 6.8

Working topology for early risk estimation and end-to-end security planning pipeline for IoT systems.

layer. This approach acknowledges that IoT systems are inherently heterogeneous, and that the cryptographic overhead tolerable at one level may be wholly impractical at another. At the perception layer, where energy, computation, and memory are severely limited, lightweight cryptographic primitives are essential. Here, cryptography serves as a primary means of providing a baseline for confidentiality, integrity, and authentication, while physical exposure and node capture remain residual risks that it cannot fully address. Evaluating whether devices are vulnerable, whether through easy physical access by intruders or through the inherent weaknesses of lightweight schemes, helps determine whether additional protective measures are warranted, or whether lightweight cryptography alone will suffice.

At the data link and network layers, planning focuses on encrypting communication and routing whenever practical, while recognizing that insider and protocol-level attacks cannot be defeated by cryptography alone. Cryptographic planning at these layers is therefore typically paired with monitoring and detection. The result is best understood as a design trade-off: stronger cryptography mitigates spoofing and eavesdropping, but a detector remains necessary to address routing manipulation and malicious channel behavior. At the middleware and support layer, cryptographic planning aims to secure the points where data is aggregated and stored in the cloud. Because cloud services act as centralized repositories, both stored data and data in transit should be encrypted in order to minimize large-scale data theft and privacy breaches. Where multi-tenancy and shared infrastructure are involved, risk assessment guides decisions about access control, key management, and data isolation. At the application layer, cryptographic and security planning become tightly interwoven with access control and identity management. Application interfaces expose sensitive information and control functions directly, which places them among the most attractive targets for attackers. Planning at this layer accordingly emphasizes authentication mechanisms, authorization policies, and the safe management of credentials, calibrated to the anticipated user base and threat environment.

Risk estimation at deployment and end-to-end planning are best understood not as separate activities but as integral components of a comprehensive, proactive security structure for IoT systems. By assessing device placement, exposure, and system architecture early, designers can determine which controls to apply at each layer and ensure that those controls reinforce one another. Rather than relying on after-the-fact patching, this approach treats IoT systems as assets that persist throughout their lifetimes and remain subject to continual change. End-to-end planning is thus inseparable from adaptive processes. As systems scale, new devices are introduced, or analytics capabilities mature, the original risk assessment must be revisited and the controls adjusted accordingly. Risk estimation at deployment is therefore no longer a one-time exercise but the starting point of a continuous security lifecycle; one that keeps the protective measures at each layer coherent with one another.

In a nutshell, risk estimation during IoT system deployment, together with end-to-end planning, can be considered a cornerstone of security management for IoT devices. This framework identifies physical context, architectural dependencies, and resource constraints as vulnerabilities that need to be controlled, and that successful security requires coordination across all layers. By choosing cryptographic support and prevention strategies tailored to layer-related risks, and by adopting a holistic approach to security rather than implementing security by bits, the literature offers a preventive direction for minimizing exposure, suppressing spread, and maintaining trust in large-scale IoT implementations.

6.4.4 IDS/IDPS pipeline as proactive monitoring in IoT security

IDS and IDPS are considered strong, proactive security mechanisms by various practitioners. As explained in earlier sections, no preventive controls, such as access control or cryptography, will ensure the security of IoT on their own. Rather, it depends on the constant monitoring, analysis, and feedback of IoT systems. Existing works note that IoT spaces are dynamic, heterogeneous, and often exposed, and that it is impossible to presuppose that every attack can be prevented in advance. Because of this, IDS is introduced as an operational model to continuously monitor system activity, identify abnormal activity, and intervene in a timely manner before local attacks can spread to system-wide activity. Practitioners also view IDS as a multi-stage pipeline rather than a single detection component. This pipeline generally involves data gathering, preprocessing, feature mining, identification or analysis, and response. The first phase is data collection, which involves gathering information across different components of the IoT system. Some of the common data sources are network traffic, routing control messages, MAC-layer events and application-level logs. A sound IDS places greater emphasis on ensuring this step balances visibility with resources, as IoT devices often generate large volumes of data and have tight energy and storage constraints. This is the reason why data is often selective, distributed, or offloaded to gateway and edge components.

Preprocessing and feature extraction serve as important intermediate steps that transform raw data into a representation an analyst can work with. Preprocessing may involve noise reduction, event consolidation, or normalization of traffic patterns, while feature extraction focuses on identifying behavioral traits that distinguish normal operation from malicious activity. Because IoT data is exceptionally diverse and noisy, poorly implemented preprocessing or feature selection can produce high false-positive or missed-detection rates. Sound preprocessing is therefore indispensable for efficient IDS operation under IoT constraints, allowing a reasonable level of detection performance to be maintained.

Detection itself forms the central component of the IDS pipeline. Two broad approaches are commonly distinguished: signature-based and anomaly-based detection. Signature-based strategies rely on recognizable attack patterns and perform well against previously encountered threats. Anomaly-based detection, by contrast, establishes a model of normal operation and flags deviations from that baseline. The latter is especially relevant in IoT settings, which are frequently subject to novel, emerging, or protocol-conforming attacks that signature-based methods are ill-equipped to catch. ML techniques for anomaly detection are particularly promising for managing scale and diversity, though many remain at the research stage, with practical deployment still largely unrealized.

The IDS and IDPS also differ in the response stage. Whereas IDS aims to detect and generate alerts, IDPS takes it a notch higher by enabling automated or semi-automated responses. These actions can include blocking malicious traffic, isolating compromised nodes, throttling suspicious activity, or inducing reconfiguration. Prevention mechanisms are often considered insufficient to address insider threats or attacks that meet the protocol's requirements. On the contrary, IDS and IPS can act dynamically after malicious behavior is identified. In measuring performance, several indicators stand out: detection accuracy, false-positive rate, response latency, and resource overhead-all of which are essential to operational IoT deployments.

IDS are deployed at various levels of an IoT system to provide adequate protection and operational support. At the perception layer, IDS solutions primarily aim to detect abnormal sensing behavior, node compromise, or data injection. Because the devices are physically vulnerable and resource-constrained, sensor readings and behavioral consistency are typically monitored in a lightweight manner at this layer, often with assistance from neighboring devices or gateways. Here, prevention remains essential, since detection alone does little to discourage physical capture or tampering. At the network layer, IDS solutions focus on detecting routing anomalies such as sinkhole, wormhole, and selective-forwarding attacks, as well as RPL control-plane abuse. Monitoring routing updates, packet-forwarding behavior, and topology changes provides useful signals that the IDS pipeline can use to identify activity that deviates from expected patterns. Network-layer detection is particularly valuable for exposing insider attacks that alter routing while otherwise appearing legitimate. At the middleware and cloud platform, IDS operates at the service-monitoring level,

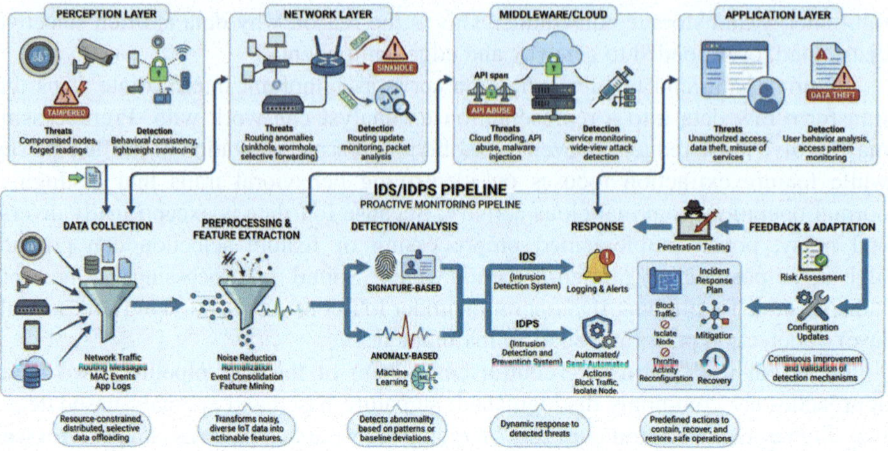

FIGURE 6.9

A generic pipeline and its interrelated components of IDS and IDPS.

identifying cloud flooding, abnormal broker behavior, unauthorized API access, or malware injection. Because the middle layer aggregates information and services, an IDS running here gains a broad vantage point from which to recognize large-scale or coordinated attacks that cannot be detected at the lower layers. Finally, at the application layer, IDS methods concentrate on analyzing user behavior, monitoring access patterns, and identifying anomalies in service usage. Application-layer detection is especially important for catching unauthorized access, data loss or theft, and the misuse of application services, particularly in systems that handle sensitive personal or operational information.

To meaningfully justify the IDS performance of a deployed IoT system, penetration testing should be operationalized as a regular security activity within the IDS pipeline. Rather than treating it as a one-off compliance exercise, the pipeline incorporates penetration testing as a recurring means of validating risk assumptions and security controls over the long term. Through realistic attack simulation, penetration testing can expose vulnerabilities that configuration inspection, passive monitoring, and anomaly detection cannot reveal. From the perspective of the IDS pipeline, it functions as an external feedback mechanism: the results can be used to refine detection models, improve features, and update attack signatures or anomaly baselines. In this way, penetration testing reinforces the IDS's proactive nature, keeping detection mechanisms aligned with an evolving threat landscape. Treated as an iterative process attuned to an organization's particular circumstances, such validation helps uncover weak points before attackers can exploit them and strengthens the overall effectiveness of the monitoring pipeline.

It is equally important to extend the IDS pipeline with clearly defined incident response, mitigation, and recovery operations. Once malicious activity is detected, response actions must be organized so as to prevent further damage and keep systems available. Such a response should not be ad-hoc; it must instead be guided by predefined procedures that remain practical under the constraints typical of IoT environments. Within the pipeline, mitigation aims to contain the effects of a detected attack by isolating compromised devices, filtering offending traffic, reconfiguring network routes, or shutting down compromised services. These measures help prevent cascading failures among interconnected IoT elements, an especially pressing concern where centralized middleware or critical applications are involved. Here the capabilities of an IDPS become significant, since they enable automated or semi-automated responses that complement detection. Recovery and continuity planning likewise belong to the response phase, which emphasizes restoring systems to a safe operational state with the minimum set of required services. Lessons drawn from security incidents then feed back into continuous risk assessment, IDS configuration, and penetration testing, giving the security framework the capacity to evolve over time and to remain effective as system architectures, workloads, and threat environments change. Fig. 6.9 shows a generic IDS pipeline commonly used to secure IoT systems after deployment.

6.5 Vulnerability mitigation in different IoT architecture layers

In previous sections, we discussed the different layers in an IoT architecture and their functionalities. In this section, we discuss what security techniques and vulnerability mitigation approaches can be applied in different IoT architecture layers.

6.5.1 IoT vulnerability mitigation strategies in perception/physical layer

A range of security-enhancing techniques, models, and approaches already exist for the perception layer and operate effectively in detecting and mitigating potential IoT vulnerabilities. Even so, there remains room to refine these methods and make them more robust. A number of effective security frameworks and pipelines have been developed for the IoT perception layer, and these too leave scope for further improvement. The sections that follow discuss them in brief.

6.5.1.1 Secure firmware handling, deployment awareness, and edge protection as preventive foundations

Securing firmware and software updates ranks among the most impactful preventive controls in IoT systems. Although update mechanisms are vital to long-term maintainability, the very channels that deliver updates can become vectors for lasting compromise if they are not handled properly. Over-the-air update functionality at the perception layer is a particular concern: an attacker who can exploit it may inject malicious or counterfeit code, manipulate a device's behavior over the long term, and corrupt data at its source. The implication is clear: update mechanisms must guarantee strong authenticity and integrity rather than relying on weak or unauthenticated validation procedures. Because firmware updates are frequently relayed through gateways that perform only minimal validation checks, update validation should be treated as a core security control rather than a peripheral feature. A trusted secure update manager is best understood not as a one-time configuration within software and update management, but as a lifelong safeguard that continually guards against the introduction of vulnerabilities throughout a device's operational life.

6.5.1.2 Physical exposure and risk estimation by deployment location

Physical exposure is another recurring concern that shapes preventive design at the perception layer. IoT devices are frequently deployed in locations where attackers can reach them to extract device information, tamper with hardware, or destroy nodes outright. These threats are compounded by the limited computational and energy resources of most devices, which constrain the elaborate defenses that might otherwise be applied. For this reason, estimating risk by deployment location is a genuine security requirement. Devices placed in open, unattended, or hostile environments call for considerably more robust defensive planning than those operating in controlled indoor settings.

6.5.1.3 Device and tag authentication to prevent cloning, spoofing, and unauthorized access

Authentication at the device and tag levels is another primary preventive measure. Weak or absent authentication opens the door to basic attacks on sensing identifiers, particularly in RFID[16]-based systems. Tag cloning, unauthorized access, and spoofing all become feasible when identifiers can be recovered through reverse engineering or simply observed in the field. Authentication and identity validation should therefore be treated as requirements for every hardware element at the perception layer, guarding against tag cloning, eavesdropping, the injection of fabricated data, and denial-of-service amplification attacks. Based on this, it can easily be said that authentication is not merely an access-control mechanism but the engineering precondition for trusting sensed data in the first place.

6.5.1.4 Cryptographic building blocks used as practical safeguards at the edge

Cryptographic mechanisms are best regarded as functional building blocks rather than unified, one-size-fits-all solutions. Cryptographic primitives should be selected based on the threats and constraints specific to each layer. Symmetric ciphers

[16] RFID is a wireless technology that uses radio waves to automatically identify and track tags attached to objects, transmitting stored data to a reader without requiring physical contact or line of sight

(such as AES[17] and 3-DES[18]), public-key cryptography (such as RSA[19]), digital signatures, and hash functions[20] (such as SHA-256 and hash chains) are common methods for ensuring the confidentiality and integrity of information at the edge and in communications between devices and the backend. Yet effective cryptography depends just as much on sound key management, the generation, distribution, updating, and revocation of keys, as on the choice of primitive itself. This is especially true at the perception layer, where constrained devices and components often operate in dynamic conditions. Cryptographic planning is thus closely tied to deployment context and each device's capabilities, rather than applied uniformly across the system.

6.5.1.5 Secure hardware and trusted boot as perception-layer hardening

Perception-layer security can also be framed as the hardware trust problem. Purpose-built hardware features tamper-resistant components, secure elements, and trusted-boot mechanisms which provide a foundational level of protection. Secure boot, for instance, ensures that only trusted firmware can execute, even under physically exposed conditions. Because this model of trust is anchored in hardware rather than software alone, it can withstand the close physical proximity of attackers and the resource constraints that limit what device updates can accomplish and limitations that a purely software-based approach cannot overcome on its own. Trusted hardware is therefore regarded as a cornerstone of stronger protection rather than a supplementary feature.

6.5.1.6 Addressing side-channel, boot-time, and power constraints at the edge

Several other edge-layer realities also shape preventive decisions; among them, side-channel leakage, boot-time exposure, and power limitations are main factors. Side-channel attacks that exploit power consumption, timing, or electromagnetic emissions are practicable under certain conditions, and the phases of the boot process represent sensitive intervals during which security controls may not yet be fully enforced. Devices are likewise vulnerable to sleep-deprivation attacks that drain their limited energy reserves. While such concerns do not always have definitive countermeasures, they strongly influence design constraints. Taken together, they motivate hardened startup procedures, secure configuration practices,

---

[17] AES is a widely adopted symmetric-key block cipher that encrypts data in fixed 128-bit blocks using key sizes of 128, 192, or 256 bits, valued for its strong security and efficiency.

[18] 3-DES is a symmetric-key block cipher that applies the older DES algorithm three times in succession to each data block, strengthening security over single DES but now largely deprecated in favor of AES.

[19] RSA is a widely used asymmetric (public-key) cryptographic algorithm that relies on the difficulty of factoring large prime products to enable secure encryption and digital signatures.

[20] a one-way mathematical function that maps input data of arbitrary size to a fixed-size output, such that the same input always yields the same output and the original input cannot feasibly be recovered.

and lightweight, deployment-aware protections that operate under stringent energy budgets.

6.5.1.7 Reinforcing wireless edge protection with authentication and key updates

Node capture and physical tampering represent genuine threats at the physical layer. An intruder who gains physical access to a device may read any data stored on it, intercept ongoing traffic, or alter internal hardware such as wiring or memory contents. Such actions can directly compromise device integrity and erode trust in the system as a whole. Physical-layer measures alone are not sufficient to secure wireless IoT deployments; rather, several basic practices are essential, including device verification, use of sufficiently strong cryptographic key sizes, and frequent key rotation. These measures provide necessary protection for perception-layer devices that rely on wireless communication and are exposed to insertion, impersonation, or manipulation by attackers. Taken together, these considerations justify integrating physical protection with cryptographic and key-management procedures, strengthening security at the perimeter where individual devices connect into the wider IoT system.

6.5.2 IoT vulnerability mitigation strategies in MAC/data-link layer

The Data Link layer, particularly the MAC sublayer, plays a foundational role in IoT communication by managing frame transmission, medium access coordination, link-layer authentication, and local error detection. Because most IoT deployments rely on wireless communication technologies such as IEEE 802.15.4[21], ZigBee[22], Bluetooth Low Energy[23], Wi-Fi[24], LoRaWAN[25], and 6TiSCH[26], the MAC layer operates in open, interference-prone, and physically accessible environments.

[21] IEEE 802.15.4 is a foundational standard that defines the physical (PHY) and medium access control (MAC) layers for low-rate, low-power wireless personal area networks, serving as the basis for many higher-level IoT protocols

[22] ZigBee is a low-power, low-data-rate wireless networking protocol built on top of IEEE 802.15.4 that supports mesh networking, enabling reliable short-range communication for home automation, smart energy, and industrial IoT applications

[23] Bluetooth Low Energy (BLE) is a power-efficient variant of the Bluetooth standard designed for short-range communication between devices that exchange small amounts of data intermittently, widely used in wearables, sensors, and smart-home devices

[24] Wi-Fi is a wireless networking technology based on the IEEE 802.11 family of standards that provides high-throughput, medium-range communication, commonly used to connect devices to local networks and the internet

[25] LoRaWAN (Long Range Wide Area Network) is a low-power, long-range wireless protocol built on LoRa modulation that enables small-data-rate communication over distances of several kilometers, designed for battery-powered IoT devices in wide-area deployments

[26] 6TiSCH (IPv6 over the TSCH mode of IEEE 802.15.4e) is a networking standard that combines IPv6 connectivity with the Time-Slotted Channel Hopping (TSCH) MAC mode to provide deterministic, reliable, and low-power communication for industrial IoT applications

As a result, it becomes a primary target for adversaries attempting to disrupt availability, impersonate legitimate devices, inject malicious frames, or exhaust energy-constrained nodes.

Common MAC-layer vulnerabilities include replay attacks, spurious frame injection, MAC spoofing, collision-based DoS attacks, exhaustion attacks, insecure association procedures, and denial-of-sleep[27] behavior. Since IoT nodes are typically constrained in terms of computational capability, battery capacity, and memory, mitigation mechanisms at this layer must be lightweight, energy-aware, and compatible with heterogeneous network protocols. The following subsections present comprehensive mitigation strategies tailored to IoT MAC/Data-Link environments.

6.5.2.1 Hash-chain defenses for replay and spurious MAC-layer traffic

One of the most effective lightweight mechanisms for preventing MAC-layer replay attacks and forged frame injection is the use of one-way hash-chain constructions. Replay attacks occur when an adversary captures a legitimate frame and later retransmits it to trigger unintended behavior. Similarly, spurious traffic injection involves transmitting forged frames to induce retransmissions, contention, state confusion, or energy depletion. Traditional countermeasures such as frame counters and timestamps provide some protection; however, they may be insufficient in environments where counters are improperly managed, or synchronization mechanisms are weak.

A hash-chain mechanism strengthens freshness guarantees by binding each transmitted MAC frame to a cryptographically verifiable sequence. In this design, a device generates a secret seed value and repeatedly applies a one-way hash function to produce a chain of values. The final value in the chain acts as an anchor or commitment. During device commissioning or secure association, the sender shares the anchor (or a secure commitment derived from it) with the gateway or coordinator.

During operation, each outgoing MAC frame carries the next undisclosed hash value from the chain, along with an integrity tag computed over the frame contents using the current hash element. Upon receiving a frame, the gateway verifies that the provided hash value links correctly to the previously stored value by applying the hash function forward. Because one-way hash functions are computationally irreversible, an attacker cannot generate valid future chain values. Furthermore, once a hash token has been accepted, it is recorded as used, preventing replay of previously valid frames. This approach offers several advantages for IoT environments:

- Freshness verification requires only lightweight hash computations.
- No expensive public-key cryptography is needed for each frame.
- Replay attempts are rejected before triggering retransmission or contention mechanisms.

[27] A denial-of-sleep attack is one in which an adversary repeatedly forces a battery-powered IoT or sensor device to stay awake; by triggering unnecessary communication, processing, or radio activity, so as to rapidly drain its energy reserves and shorten its operational lifetime.

- Spurious frames lacking valid chain tokens are discarded early, minimizing energy waste.

In addition, hash-chaining principles can be extended to fragmented packet transmission, ensuring that individual fragments cryptographically link to the original frame sequence. This prevents attackers from injecting forged fragments into reassembly buffers, which could otherwise lead to state corruption or memory exhaustion. By integrating hash-chain defenses at the MAC layer, IoT systems significantly reduce the feasibility of replay attacks and the generation of forged control frames, as well as energy-draining retransmission triggers.

6.5.2.2 Strong link-layer authentication and identity binding

MAC spoofing remains a major threat in IoT systems. Attackers can impersonate legitimate devices by altering MAC addresses, thereby gaining unauthorized access or injecting malicious traffic. To mitigate this risk, cryptographic binding between device identity and MAC-layer authentication must be enforced. During device provisioning, each IoT node should be assigned unique cryptographic credentials. Lightweight mutual authentication protocols, such as EAP-based methods adapted for constrained environments, can ensure that both the device and the gateway verify each other before establishing link-layer communication. Furthermore, MAC addresses should not be treated as sole identity indicators. Instead, they must be associated with cryptographic credentials stored securely in tamper-resistant memory.

Based on practitioners' perspective, disabling default credentials, enforcing secure onboarding, and preventing open association mechanisms are essential steps. By strengthening MAC-layer authentication, attackers are prevented from joining networks via simple address impersonation.

6.5.2.3 Lightweight encryption and integrity protection

Wireless MAC-layer frames are inherently susceptible to eavesdropping and manipulation. Even when confidentiality is not the primary concern, integrity and authenticity remain critical. IoT protocols such as IEEE 802.15.4 provide built-in security features including AES-CCM encryption and message authentication codes. However, misconfiguration or the disabling of security modes leaves networks vulnerable. To mitigate these vulnerabilities, the practice needs to be:

- Confidentiality and integrity protections must be enabled by default.
- Frame counters should be properly maintained to prevent replay.
- Nonce values must be unique and synchronized.
- Cryptographic integrity checks must supplement CRC error detection.
- Link-layer keys should be periodically rotated.
- Secure storage mechanisms must protect symmetric keys from extraction.

When properly implemented, these measures prevent passive sniffing, tampering, and unauthorized frame modification while incurring only moderate computational overhead.

6.5.2.4 Anti-jamming and collision-resilient MAC design

Jamming and collision-based DoS attacks directly target availability by overwhelming the wireless channel. Because IoT nodes rely on limited battery capacity, repeated retransmissions in the presence of interference can rapidly drain resources. Mitigation requires adaptive medium access mechanisms. FHSS and channel agility reduce the predictability of transmission channels, making sustained jamming more difficult. Time-slotted channel access mechanisms, such as TDMA or TSCH , further limit channel abuse by assigning bounded transmission windows to each node. Under such scheduling, attackers cannot continuously monopolize the medium. Adaptive duty cycling reduces the duration nodes remain actively listening, thereby limiting their exposure to interference. Monitoring collision rates and transmission failures can help detect abnormal interference patterns. When anomalies are detected, channel switching, backoff adjustment, or coordinated schedule reconfiguration can be triggered. These controls enhance availability while preserving energy efficiency.

6.5.2.5 Rate limiting and energy-aware admission control

Exhaustion and denial-of-sleep attacks exploit MAC-layer retransmission mechanisms and association handshakes to drain device batteries. Attackers may repeatedly initiate handshake requests, send malformed frames, or trigger collisions to force retransmissions. To mitigate this, the MAC layer should incorporate energy-aware defensive controls as follows:

- Limit the number of association or handshake attempts per time window.
- Enforce request rate caps for individual device identities.
- Apply challenge-response validation before allocating significant resources.
- Drop unauthenticated frames at early processing stages.
- Activate defensive low-power modes under suspicious traffic conditions.

These mechanisms act as an ENERGY-PRESERVING GATE, preventing attackers from repeatedly consuming airtime and processing cycles.

6.5.2.6 Robustness through error detection and correction

Collision-based attacks may corrupt even a single byte of a frame, forcing retransmission and increasing energy consumption. While cyclic redundancy checks (CRC) detect errors, they do not correct them. Incorporating forward error correction (where feasible) reduces retransmission frequency under burst interference conditions. By minimizing repeated transmissions, the MAC layer reduces the attacker's ability to exploit retransmission overhead as an energy-draining strategy. Stronger link-layer robustness therefore functions not only as a reliability enhancement but also as a defensive mechanism against exhaustion-based attacks.

6.5.2.7 MAC-layer anomaly detection and distributed monitoring

Early detection of denial-of-sleep or flooding attacks can significantly reduce damage. MAC-layer anomaly detection focuses on metrics such as:

- Sudden increases in retransmission counts
- Abnormal collision rates
- Repeated association requests
- Excessive handshake traffic
- Unexpected traffic bursts

Lightweight feature extraction at nodes, combined with more sophisticated analysis at gateways or edge devices, enables distributed situational awareness. Cooperative anomaly detection allows neighboring nodes to share abnormality indicators, facilitating coordinated mitigation actions such as rate limiting, isolation, rekeying, or schedule modification. This proactive approach prevents resource depletion before upper-layer intrusion detection systems are triggered.

6.5.2.8 Fairness enforcement and damage containment

Unfair channel capture and greedy transmission behavior may cause intermittent service denial even without full network compromise. MAC-layer fairness mechanisms, such as limiting frame size or enforcing airtime quotas, restrict the duration any single node can occupy the channel. Even when perfect detection is not possible, protocol-level fairness constraints limit the damage a misbehaving node can cause within a given timeframe. This damage containment principle enhances overall network resilience.

6.5.2.9 Integration into security-by-design

MAC/Data-Link layer mitigation strategies must not operate in isolation. Secure link-layer encryption should align with network-layer secure routing. Anomaly detection at MAC should integrate with intrusion detection systems. Key management policies must coordinate with device lifecycle management and secure firmware updates. Because vulnerabilities at lower layers propagate upward through the IoT stack, strengthening the MAC/Data-Link layer significantly reduces the overall attack surface. When combined with secure commissioning, key rotation, anomaly detection, and energy-aware controls, MAC-layer defenses form the first robust barrier against IoT compromise.

6.5.2.10 Secure bootstrapping mitigation in the MAC/data-link layer

Secure bootstrapping is a foundational requirement for protecting IoT systems at the Data Link and MAC layers, as it establishes the initial trust relationship between a device and the network. In many IoT deployments, devices join networks automatically and wirelessly, which creates opportunities for adversaries to exploit weak onboarding procedures. If bootstrapping relies on default credentials, shared global keys, or unauthenticated association processes, an attacker can introduce rogue devices, intercept key exchanges, or manipulate session parameters during commissioning. To mitigate these risks, IoT systems must adopt authenticated and identity-bound bootstrapping mechanisms.

A secure bootstrapping process begins by provisioning each device with a unique cryptographic identity during manufacturing. This identity may consist of a device-specific key pair, a manufacturer-signed certificate, or a hardware-rooted secret stored in secure memory. When the device attempts to join the network, it should perform mutual authentication with the gateway or coordinator, ensuring that both parties verify each other's legitimacy before proceeding. Rather than transmitting network keys directly, the system should implement authenticated key exchange protocols, such as elliptic-curve Diffie-Hellman-based mechanisms, to derive session keys dynamically. This prevents attackers from learning usable encryption keys even if they intercept communication during the association phase.

Additionally, secure bootstrapping should incorporate freshness guarantees by using nonces, timestamps, or single-use association tokens. These measures prevent replay of previously valid commissioning messages. In consumer or industrial environments where feasible, out-of-band verification methods, such as QR code scanning, NFC pairing, or physical button confirmation, can further strengthen onboarding security by requiring physical proximity or user confirmation. By ensuring strong identity verification, encrypted key establishment, and replay-resistant association procedures, secure bootstrapping prevents unauthorized devices from gaining network access and blocks attackers from compromising the system at its most vulnerable stage.

6.5.2.11 MAC spoofing attack mitigation in the data link layer

MAC spoofing remains a persistent threat in IoT environments because traditional networks often treat MAC addresses as identity markers, even though they can be easily forged. An attacker who successfully spoofs a legitimate MAC address may gain unauthorized access, inject malicious frames, bypass access control rules, or impersonate trusted devices. In resource-constrained IoT systems, where link-layer authentication is sometimes minimal, this attack can significantly undermine integrity and availability. Effective mitigation, therefore, requires eliminating reliance on MAC addresses as standalone identifiers and replacing address-based trust with cryptographic identity verification.

The most robust defense against MAC spoofing is to bind each MAC address to a unique cryptographic credential. During network operation, every MAC-layer frame should include an authentication tag computed using a device-specific secret or private key. Upon reception, the gateway validates not only the integrity of the frame but also that the cryptographic identity matches the registered MAC address. If a frame claims a legitimate MAC address but fails cryptographic verification, it is immediately rejected. This approach ensures that an attacker cannot simply modify the address field to impersonate another device.

Further protection can be achieved through secure re-authentication during network re-entry. Devices that disconnect and later attempt to rejoin should undergo fresh identity validation and key derivation to prevent reuse of stale credentials.

In more advanced deployments, anomaly detection techniques can monitor for duplicate MAC addresses that appear simultaneously across different signal profiles or physical locations. Radio-frequency fingerprinting methods may also help distinguish legitimate hardware from spoofed transmitters. By shifting from address-based identification to cryptographically enforced identity validation, IoT systems significantly reduce the feasibility of MAC spoofing and strengthen link-layer access control without imposing excessive computational overhead.

6.5.3 IoT vulnerability mitigation strategies in the network layer

The network layer in IoT architectures is responsible for routing, packet forwarding, addressing, fragmentation, and end-to-end data delivery across heterogeneous and resource-constrained environments. Because IoT systems frequently rely on multi-hop communication protocols such as RPL, 6LoWPAN, and IPv6, as well as various low-power wireless mesh networks, this layer becomes a primary target for adversaries seeking to disrupt availability, manipulate routing paths, intercept sensitive data, or inject malicious control traffic. The dominant threats at this layer include routing attacks, sinkhole and Sybil attacks, wormhole attacks, selective forwarding, fragmentation abuse, and denial-of-service conditions. Countering these vulnerabilities requires structured mitigation strategies that strengthen routing integrity, data confidentiality, and traffic resilience while respecting the resource constraints inherent in IoT devices.

6.5.3.1 Secure and authenticated routing protocols

One of the most critical mitigation strategies at the Network layer is implementing secure routing mechanisms to protect routing control messages from manipulation. In IoT mesh environments, protocols such as RPL construct routing trees based on exchanged control information. If routing messages are unauthenticated, attackers can advertise false routing metrics, create sinkholes, or redirect traffic through malicious nodes. To mitigate these vulnerabilities, routing control messages must be cryptographically authenticated and integrity-protected.

Secure RPL modes should be enabled so that routing advertisements include cryptographic signatures or message authentication codes. Each node in the routing topology should possess a cryptographic credential that enables verification of routing updates. Additionally, consistency checks must be enforced to validate routing metrics, such as rank, hop count, and link-quality indicators. Nodes should reject routing messages that violate expected logical relationships or exhibit abnormal metric fluctuations. By protecting routing advertisements and validating topology changes, the network prevents adversaries from inserting themselves into forwarding paths or manipulating data flow.

6.5.3.2 Protection against sinkhole and wormhole attacks

Sinkhole and wormhole attacks exploit routing mechanisms by attracting traffic toward malicious nodes or creating artificial shortcuts between distant nodes.

These attacks can severely compromise data confidentiality and integrity. Effective mitigation requires both structural and behavioral defenses.

First, route validation mechanisms should verify that advertised paths are plausible within known network constraints. Geographic consistency checks, hop-count validation, and latency profiling can detect abnormal routing shortcuts indicative of wormholes. Second, multipath routing strategies should be implemented to distribute traffic across multiple routes rather than relying on a single forwarding node. This reduces the impact of any single compromised router. Third, neighbor authentication and secure link establishment prevent unauthorized nodes from inserting themselves into routing tables. By combining authenticated neighbor discovery with path-plausibility analysis and redundancy, IoT networks significantly reduce their vulnerability to routing manipulation.tworks significantly reduce their vulnerability to routing manipulation.

6.5.3.3 Defense against sybil attacks

Sybil attacks occur when a malicious node claims multiple identities to influence routing decisions or overwhelm the network. Because IoT devices often rely on logical identities for routing and forwarding decisions, the absence of identity verification enables this attack.

Mitigation begins with strong identity binding at the Network layer. Each node must possess a unique cryptographic credential issued during secure bootstrapping. Network-level communication should verify that each logical identity corresponds to a validated cryptographic identity. Resource testing mechanisms can also be applied, where nodes must demonstrate computational or radio capabilities that are difficult to replicate across multiple fake identities simultaneously. Furthermore, monitoring for abnormal identity density within local neighborhoods can help detect potential Sybil behavior. By ensuring a one-to-one mapping between identity and cryptographic proof, IoT systems prevent attackers from amplifying their impact through identity forgery.

6.5.3.4 Secure fragmentation and reassembly controls

IoT networks frequently rely on 6LoWPAN fragmentation because low-power wireless technologies impose strict frame size limitations. However, fragmentation mechanisms introduce vulnerabilities, including buffer exhaustion, fragment replay, and fragment injection attacks. Attackers may send incomplete or malicious fragments to consume memory resources or manipulate packet reassembly. To mitigate these vulnerabilities, fragment authentication must be enforced. Each fragment should carry integrity protection linked to the original packet context. Reassembly buffers must enforce strict limits on the number of incomplete fragment chains allowed per source. Timeout mechanisms should automatically discard incomplete fragment sequences after defined intervals to prevent memory exhaustion. Additionally, fragment-identification fields must be validated to ensure consistency across all fragments in the same packet. These controls prevent attackers from abusing fragmentation logic to degrade network performance or corrupt reassembled data.

6.5.3.5 End-to-end confidentiality and integrity protection

While link-layer encryption protects local communication, Network-layer mitigation requires end-to-end security mechanisms to ensure that intermediate routing nodes cannot read or alter payload data. Protocols such as IPsec (adapted for constrained environments) or application-layer security overlays should be implemented to protect payload confidentiality across multiple hops. To mitigate data interception and tampering, encryption must be combined with message authentication codes and replay protection mechanisms at the Network layer. Sequence numbers or nonces must be validated to prevent replay of previously captured packets. Lightweight cryptographic suites tailored for IoT constraints should be selected to balance security strength and energy efficiency. By enforcing end-to-end confidentiality and integrity, IoT systems protect data even if intermediate routing nodes are compromised.

6.5.3.6 Rate limiting and flooding control

Flooding attacks at the Network layer can overwhelm routing tables and exhaust node resources. Attackers may generate excessive route requests, control messages, or data packets to saturate bandwidth and processing capacity. Mitigation requires rate limiting at both node and gateway levels. Each node should enforce thresholds on the number of control messages processed per time interval. Suspicious nodes exceeding defined thresholds should be temporarily isolated or deprioritized. Additionally, routing control message validation must discard malformed or inconsistent messages early in processing. Traffic shaping and prioritization mechanisms can ensure that critical data flows are preserved even under attack conditions. These measures reduce the feasibility of denial-of-service attacks targeting routing infrastructure.

6.5.3.7 Trust and reputation-based routing

Because IoT nodes may operate in distributed, unattended environments, trust evaluation mechanisms provide an additional layer of mitigation. Nodes can monitor their neighbors' forwarding behavior and assign trust scores based on packet delivery consistency, responsiveness, and anomaly detection. If a node exhibits selective forwarding or fails to propagate routing updates, its trust score decreases, and it may be excluded from routing decisions. Reputation systems must be carefully designed to prevent false accusation attacks; therefore, trust metrics should rely on aggregated observations rather than isolated events. By incorporating behavioral trust evaluation into routing selection, IoT networks reduce the impact of compromised forwarding nodes.

6.5.3.8 Network layer anomaly detection and intrusion monitoring

Modern IoT security architectures increasingly integrate anomaly detection mechanisms at the Network layer. Monitoring metrics such as routing update frequency, path changes, packet drop ratios, and traffic asymmetry can reveal abnormal activity indicative of routing manipulation or flooding. Lightweight intrusion detection components deployed at edge gateways can aggregate routing telemetry and detect deviations from normal traffic patterns. When anomalies are identified, automated mitigation actions such as route recalculation, node isolation, or re-keying procedures can be triggered. Because IoT devices are constrained, computationally intensive detection algorithms should be executed at gateways or edge servers rather than at individual nodes. Early detection prevents widespread propagation of routing-based attacks.

6.5.3.9 Secure neighbor discovery and address management

IPv6-based IoT deployments rely on neighbor discovery protocols for address resolution and topology maintenance. However, spoofed neighbor advertisements or duplicate address attacks can disrupt routing stability. Mitigation requires cryptographic protection of neighbor discovery messages. Secure Neighbor Discovery (SEND) mechanisms or equivalent lightweight authentication techniques should be implemented to validate address ownership. Duplicate address detection processes must verify cryptographic identity before accepting new addresses into routing tables. By protecting address management processes, IoT networks prevent impersonation and routing confusion at the Network layer.

6.5.3.10 Integration with security-by-design principles

Network-layer mitigation strategies must operate within a holistic security-by-design framework. Secure bootstrapping ensures valid identities; secure routing protects topology integrity; encryption ensures confidentiality; anomaly detection enhances resilience; and rate limiting preserves availability. These mechanisms must be coordinated with link-layer security and application-layer protections to avoid fragmented defense. Key management procedures should align with device lifecycle policies, including secure firmware updates and credential rotation. Routing security must be adaptable to heterogeneous deployments such as industrial IoT, smart cities, healthcare, and transportation systems, each with distinct risk profiles.

To summarize, the Network layer is a strategic control point in IoT architectures because it governs routing, multi-hop communication, and packet delivery. Vulnerabilities at this layer can compromise confidentiality, integrity, availability, and system reliability across the entire IoT stack. Effective mitigation requires authenticated routing protocols, protection against sinkhole and wormhole attacks, Sybil resistance, secure fragmentation management, end-to-end encryption, flooding control, trust-based routing evaluation, and anomaly detection mechanisms. When implemented systematically and tailored to IoT resource constraints, these mitigation strategies significantly reduce exposure to routing manipulation, denial-of-service conditions, identity abuse, and data interception. Strengthening the Network layer is, therefore, essential for building resilient, scalable, and trustworthy IoT ecosystems.

6.5.4 IoT vulnerability mitigation strategies in the middleware/support layer

The Middleware, often referred to as the Support layer, acts as the operational backbone of IoT ecosystems. It bridges the lower communication layers and the application layer by providing services such as data aggregation, device management, service orchestration, authentication services, cloud integration, edge analytics, storage management, and API exposure. Because this layer processes, stores, and distributes large volumes of IoT-generated data, it becomes a high-value target for adversaries. Vulnerabilities at this layer can lead to unauthorized data access, service disruption, privilege escalation, large-scale data breaches, and manipulation of IoT decision-making processes.

Unlike the constrained lower layers, the Middleware layer often runs on cloud or edge servers with higher computational capability. However, this expanded functionality introduces a broader attack surface. Common vulnerabilities include insecure APIs, improper access control, weak authentication mechanisms, insufficient encryption of stored data, insecure data aggregation processes, misconfigured cloud services, insecure containerization environments, and lack of monitoring of service orchestration mechanisms. Mitigating these vulnerabilities requires structured, multidimensional defensive strategies that combine identity management, secure service design, monitoring, and data governance.

6.5.4.1 Identity and access management enforcement

A primary mitigation strategy at the Middleware layer is implementing strong identity and access management (IAM) controls. Middleware platforms frequently expose APIs and dashboards that allow administrators, devices, and applications to interact with IoT services. If access controls are improperly configured or overly permissive, unauthorized actors may gain control over devices or extract sensitive data. To mitigate these risks, all users, services, and devices interacting with middleware components must be authenticated using robust mechanisms, such as multi-factor authentication, token-based authentication (e.g., OAuth 2.0), or certificate-based identity verification. Role-based access control (RBAC) or attribute-based access control (ABAC) policies should be enforced to ensure that each entity only receives the minimum privileges necessary for its function. Privilege escalation pathways must be eliminated by regularly auditing permission assignments and removing dormant accounts or excessive rights. In addition, session management should enforce expiration policies and detect abnormal session behavior. Token rotation and refresh mechanisms must be securely implemented to prevent token replay or session hijacking. By applying strict identity governance, the middleware layer reduces the likelihood of unauthorized administrative access and data misuse.

6.5.4.2 Secure API design and gateway protection

Middleware services rely heavily on APIs to enable communication among devices, applications, and cloud services. Insecure APIs are among the most significant attack vectors in IoT ecosystems. Attackers may exploit improper input validation, lack of rate limiting, or inadequate authentication to inject malicious commands or extract sensitive information. Mitigation begins with secure API design principles. All API endpoints must enforce authentication and authorization checks before processing requests. Input validation mechanisms should sanitize and verify incoming data to prevent injection attacks. Rate-limiting and throttling policies must be implemented to mitigate denial-of-service attacks targeting service endpoints.

API gateways should be deployed as protective layers between external traffic and internal services. These gateways can enforce security policies, filter traffic, validate tokens, and monitor anomalous request patterns. Logging and monitoring API usage are essential for detecting misuse or suspicious behavior. Secure API lifecycle management, including regular vulnerability testing and patching, ensures continuous protection against emerging threats.

6.5.4.3 Data encryption and secure storage management

The Middleware layer often stores aggregated sensor data, device metadata, logs, and analytics results. If stored data is left unencrypted or improperly protected, adversaries gaining access to the storage infrastructure may exfiltrate sensitive information. To mitigate this vulnerability, encryption must be applied both at rest and in transit. Data stored in databases, file systems, or cloud storage services should be encrypted with strong symmetric-key algorithms. Encryption keys must be managed securely using centralized key management services that enforce rotation and strict access controls.

Data classification policies should be implemented to identify sensitive information and apply appropriate levels of protection. Backup data must also be encrypted and stored securely to prevent exploitation through backup compromise. By protecting stored data and ensuring secure key management, the middleware layer maintains confidentiality and integrity even in the event of breaches of infrastructure components.

6.5.4.4 Secure data aggregation and integrity verification

Middleware components frequently aggregate data from multiple devices before forwarding it to applications or analytics engines. Without proper validation, malicious or corrupted data can influence aggregated outputs and compromise decision-making processes. Mitigation strategies include validating data integrity at the aggregation point using cryptographic signatures or message authentication codes. Middleware services should verify the authenticity of data before incorporating it into analytics pipelines. Data provenance tracking mechanisms can help trace the origin of each data element, ensuring accountability and tamper detection.

Anomaly detection systems can also analyze aggregated data patterns to identify anomalous device behavior. For example, sudden deviations in sensor readings that violate known environmental constraints may indicate compromised devices or data-injection attempts. By combining cryptographic verification with behavioral analysis, middleware services prevent malicious data from influencing system outcomes.

6.5.4.5 Secure cloud and edge infrastructure configuration

Many IoT middleware platforms operate within cloud or fog computing environments. Misconfigured cloud storage buckets, exposed management interfaces, or improperly isolated containers can create severe vulnerabilities. Mitigation requires secure configuration management practices. Cloud services should follow the principle of least privilege, ensuring that only necessary ports and services are exposed. Containerized middleware components must enforce isolation through proper namespace separation, access control lists, and runtime security policies. Regular configuration audits and automated compliance checks should verify adherence to security baselines. Intrusion detection systems at the cloud or edge level can monitor for unauthorized access attempts or suspicious process behavior. By securing the infrastructure hosting middleware services, IoT ecosystems reduce the risk of large-scale compromise.

6.5.4.6 Secure device management and update orchestration

The Middleware layer often manages firmware updates, device provisioning, and remote configuration. If update mechanisms are insecure, attackers may distribute malicious firmware or intercept configuration changes. Mitigation involves enforcing cryptographically signed firmware updates. Before installing any update, devices must verify the firmware's digital signature using the manufacturer's trusted keys. Secure update channels must use encrypted communication protocols to prevent interception or tampering.

Middleware services should maintain version-tracking and rollback mechanisms to detect unauthorized modifications. Access to device management dashboards must be strictly controlled, and all update operations should be logged for auditing purposes. By protecting update orchestration, IoT systems prevent attackers from introducing persistent backdoors.

6.5.4.7 Monitoring, logging, and incident response integration

Continuous monitoring is essential to detect abnormal activity within the Middleware layer. Logs should capture authentication attempts, API access patterns, configuration changes, data aggregation anomalies, and update operations. Security information and event management (SIEM) systems can aggregate logs from middleware services and perform correlation analysis to identify multi-stage attacks. Automated alerting mechanisms should notify administrators of suspicious behavior, such as repeated failed authentication attempts or unusual surges in API traffic.

Incident response plans must define procedures for isolating compromised services, revoking credentials, rotating encryption keys, and restoring secure configurations. Regular penetration testing and red-team exercises help evaluate the effectiveness of middleware security controls.

6.5.4.8 Privacy preservation and data governance controls

Because middleware platforms handle large volumes of user-generated and sensor-derived data, privacy preservation is a crucial mitigation objective. Unauthorized data exposure can lead to regulatory violations and loss of trust. Data minimization principles should be applied to collect only necessary information. Personally identifiable information must be anonymized or pseudonymized before storage or analytics processing. Access to sensitive datasets should be restricted and monitored.

Compliance with relevant data protection regulations must be ensured through policy enforcement and auditing mechanisms. Privacy-by-design principles should guide the middleware architecture by embedding privacy controls at every stage of data handling.

6.5.4.9 Integration within the IoT security architecture

Middleware mitigation strategies must be integrated with protections implemented at other layers. Secure bootstrapping at lower layers ensures authenticated device identities. Network-layer encryption protects data in transit. Application-layer controls manage user interactions. Together, these layers create a defense-in-depth model. Key management, identity verification, logging, and anomaly detection should be coordinated across layers to prevent fragmented defenses. A holistic security-by-design approach ensures that middleware protections support overall system resilience.

To summarize, the Middleware or Support layer serves as a critical control hub in IoT systems, managing data processing, device orchestration, service exposure, and analytics integration. Vulnerabilities at this layer can lead to systemic compromise, large-scale data breaches, and service disruption. Effective mitigation requires strong identity and access management, secure API design, encrypted storage, integrity validation, secure infrastructure configuration, protected firmware updates, continuous monitoring, and privacy-preserving data governance. When implemented consistently and maintained through regular auditing and monitoring, these strategies significantly reduce the attack surface of IoT middleware environments. Strengthening this layer ensures that the intelligence and automation capabilities of IoT systems remain secure, reliable, and trustworthy.

6.5.5 IoT vulnerability mitigation strategies in the application layer

The Application layer represents the highest level of the IoT architecture, where user-facing services, dashboards, analytics platforms, automation logic, and decision-making systems operate. Unlike lower layers that focus on connectivity and routing, the Application layer directly interacts with end users, enterprise systems, and business processes. Consequently, vulnerabilities at this layer can lead to data breaches, unauthorized device control, privacy violations, manipulation of automated decisions, and large-scale operational disruptions. Because IoT applications frequently integrate web interfaces, mobile applications, cloud services, APIs, and third-party platforms, the attack surface at this layer is extensive and continuously evolving.

Common vulnerabilities in the Application layer include weak authentication and authorization controls, insecure APIs, injection attacks, cross-site scripting, improper session management, insecure firmware update interfaces, inadequate input validation, lack of privacy protection, insufficient logging, and insecure integration with external services. Effective mitigation strategies must therefore combine secure coding practices, identity management, data governance, monitoring mechanisms, and regulatory compliance frameworks. The following subsections provide detailed mitigation approaches tailored specifically to IoT application environments.

6.5.5.1 Strong authentication and authorization controls

Weak or improperly configured authentication remains one of the most exploited vulnerabilities in IoT applications. Many IoT dashboards, mobile apps, and web portals rely solely on passwords, often without enforcing password complexity rules or requiring multi-factor authentication. Attackers who compromise user credentials may gain administrative access to devices, alter system configurations, or extract sensitive data. Mitigation begins with enforcing strong authentication mechanisms. Multi-factor authentication should be mandatory for administrative accounts and recommended for all users. Password policies must enforce complexity, uniqueness, and expiration rules. Account lockout mechanisms should limit repeated failed login attempts to reduce the feasibility of brute-force attacks. For device-to-application communication, certificate-based or token-based authentication mechanisms should replace static shared secrets.

Authorization controls must follow the principle of least privilege. Role-based access control (RBAC) or attribute-based access control (ABAC) should ensure that users and services only access the data and functions necessary for their roles. Administrative privileges must be separated from operational privileges, and critical functions, such as firmware updates or device resets, should require additional authorization checks. Regular audits of user permissions are necessary to prevent privilege creep.

6.5.5.2 Secure API development and protection

IoT applications rely heavily on APIs to enable communication among devices, middleware services, and user applications. Insecure APIs are among the most common entry points for attackers. Improper input validation, lack of authentication, insufficient rate limiting, and insecure error handling can allow injection attacks, data extraction, or service disruption. Mitigation requires adopting secure API development standards from the design phase. All API endpoints must enforce authentication and verify access tokens before processing requests. Input validation must be applied to all parameters to prevent SQL injection, command injection, and script injection attacks. Sensitive error messages should not expose internal implementation details that could assist attackers.

Rate-limiting and throttling mechanisms must restrict excessive requests to prevent API-based denial-of-service attacks. API gateways can serve as protective intermediaries, filtering traffic, validating credentials, and logging request patterns. Additionally, APIs should operate over secure communication protocols such as HTTPS with properly configured TLS to protect data in transit.

6.5.5.3 Secure coding practices and input validation

Application-layer vulnerabilities often arise from insecure coding practices rather than protocol weaknesses. Cross-site scripting (XSS), cross-site request forgery (CSRF), buffer overflows, and improper deserialization attacks can compromise IoT applications if secure development principles are not enforced. Mitigation begins with implementing secure coding standards throughout the development lifecycle. Input validation must be applied consistently across all data entry points, including web forms, device messages, configuration uploads, and API parameters. Data should be sanitized before processing or storage to eliminate malicious scripts or unexpected commands.

Static and dynamic code analysis tools should be integrated into the development pipeline to detect vulnerabilities before deployment. Regular penetration testing and security code reviews further strengthen application resilience. By embedding security into the software development lifecycle, IoT applications reduce exposure to common exploitation techniques.

6.5.5.4 Secure firmware and application update mechanisms

Many IoT applications include functionality to manage firmware updates and software patches. If update mechanisms are not properly secured, attackers may distribute malicious firmware, inject backdoors, or manipulate device behavior. Mitigation requires that all firmware and application updates be digitally signed using trusted manufacturer keys. Devices must verify the signature of updates before installation, rejecting any unauthorized or tampered firmware. Update delivery channels must be encrypted to prevent interception or modification during transmission.

Version control and integrity checks should ensure that devices cannot downgrade to vulnerable firmware versions without authorization. Logging update events enables administrators to track the distribution of updates and identify suspicious modifications. Secure update orchestration is critical to maintaining long-term device security and preventing persistent compromise

6.5.5.5 Data privacy and protection controls

IoT applications frequently process sensitive personal and operational data. Inadequate data protection at the Application layer can lead to privacy violations, regulatory noncompliance, and reputational damage. Mitigation strategies include implementing data minimization practices to collect only necessary information. Personally identifiable information should be anonymized or pseudonymized whenever possible. Encryption should protect sensitive data both in transit and at rest within application databases. Access to sensitive datasets must be restricted and logged. Privacy impact assessments should be conducted during application design to identify potential risks of data exposure. Compliance with data protection regulations requires clear data retention policies, user consent mechanisms, and transparent documentation of data use.

6.5.5.6 Secure session management

Session hijacking and improper session handling can allow attackers to impersonate legitimate users. Weak session tokens, predictable identifiers, or missing expiration mechanisms increase risk. Mitigation involves generating cryptographically strong session tokens and transmitting them only over encrypted channels. Sessions should automatically expire after a defined inactivity period. Sensitive actions may require re-authentication to prevent misuse of hijacked sessions. Token revocation mechanisms should allow administrators to invalidate compromised sessions immediately. By enforcing secure session management policies, IoT applications protect user identities and reduce the risk of unauthorized access.

6.5.5.7 Application-level logging and monitoring

Application-layer monitoring plays a crucial role in detecting abnormal behavior that may indicate exploitation. Without proper logging, attacks may remain undetected until significant damage occurs. Mitigation requires maintaining detailed logs of authentication attempts, configuration changes, API usage, firmware updates, and administrative actions. Logs should be stored securely and protected from tampering. Security information and event management (SIEM) systems can analyze log patterns to detect anomalies, such as repeated failed logins, unusual access times, or abnormal data-extraction behavior.

Automated alert systems should notify administrators of suspicious events in real time. Incident response procedures must define clear actions to isolate compromised accounts, rotate credentials, and restore secure configurations.

6.5.5.8 Secure integration with third-party services

IoT applications often integrate with external analytics platforms, payment gateways, cloud services, or automation engines. Each integration expands the attack surface. Mitigation requires vetting third-party services for security compliance and enforcing secure communication channels between systems. API keys and integration credentials must be stored securely and rotated periodically. Data shared with external services should adhere to strict access-control and encryption policies.

Dependency management is also critical. Outdated libraries or plugins can introduce vulnerabilities into otherwise secure applications. Regular updates and vulnerability scanning of third-party components reduce this risk.

6.5.5.9 Resilience against application-layer DoS

Application-layer denial-of-service attacks attempt to overwhelm processing logic or exhaust system resources by flooding the system with excessive requests or complex computations. Mitigation involves implementing rate limiting, request throttling, and traffic prioritization mechanisms. Load balancing and scalable cloud infrastructure can distribute traffic to prevent service interruption. Caching frequently requested data reduces processing overhead.

Application-layer firewalls can filter malicious request patterns before they reach core services. By combining traffic management with scalable architecture, IoT applications maintain availability under stress conditions.

6.5.5.10 Security-by-design integration

Application-layer mitigation strategies must integrate with protections implemented at lower layers. Secure bootstrapping ensures authenticated device identities; network-layer encryption protects communication; middleware access controls manage data processing. The Application layer must enforce consistent identity verification and logging across all interactions. Security should not be added as an afterthought. Instead, application design must embed authentication, authorization, encryption, validation, monitoring, and privacy controls from the outset. Continuous vulnerability assessments and patch management ensure long-term resilience.

To summarize, the Application layer serves as the interface between IoT systems and human or enterprise users. Because it directly exposes functionality and data to external interaction, it is a primary target for attackers seeking to manipulate devices, extract information, or disrupt services. Mitigating vulnerabilities at this layer requires strong authentication, secure API design, encrypted data handling, robust update mechanisms, privacy preservation, session protection, monitoring, and controlled integration with external services. When these mitigation strategies are implemented systematically and supported by continuous monitoring and secure development practices, IoT applications become significantly more resilient against exploitation. Strengthening the Application layer ensures that IoT ecosystems remain reliable, trustworthy, and aligned with security and privacy requirements.

CHAPTER

7 Integration of sustainable IDS in smart environments

7.1 Introduction

The rapid expansion of IoT technology across smart cities, transportation, renewable energy systems, industrial automation, and smart infrastructure has formed a densely interconnected digital ecosystem. This shift has improved operational efficiency and enabled real-time monitoring, but it has also considerably enlarged the cyberattack surface and increased the environmental cost of intelligent systems. Contemporary intrusion detection systems must therefore meet two essential demands at once: they must guarantee reliable run-time security while operating within stringent limits on energy and computational resources. This dual goal has given rise to the notion of Green IDS, in which cybersecurity mechanisms are designed to balance strong threat detection against resource efficiency.

A green IoT environment is a digital ecosystem in which connected devices, gateways, edge nodes, and cloud servers operate with lower energy use, better hardware management, and reduced carbon emissions. At the system level, four elements are closely interrelated within such an environment: intelligent algorithms and models, data collection and processing mechanisms, edge or gateway computing platforms, and cloud-level computational infrastructure. Sustainability in IoT is not confined to minimizing operational power; it also extends to lifecycle concerns such as hardware production, energy sourcing, workload allocation, and adaptive computation algorithms that vary processing intensity with system conditions.

Recent developments in IoT security show AI-based IDS being increasingly integrated alongside models built on DRL and edge-centric deployment schemes. Deploying lightweight detection models at gateways demonstrates that real-time protection can be provided while keeping CPU usage, latency, and energy consumption in check-qualities essential to sustainable smart systems. Challenges remain, however. Scaling up data analytics and retraining ever more complex models can impose heavy energy demands, and the environmental dimensions of computation, especially in distributed cloud-edge architectures, must be weighed within security design. Next-generation Green IDS should be built on adaptive, collaborative architectures that coordinate activity across the edge and the cloud, with security mechanisms that dynamically adjust their behavior based on available energy, workload density, and

Green Intrusion Detection Systems for IoT. https://doi.org/10.1016/B978-0-44-344249-0.00014-4

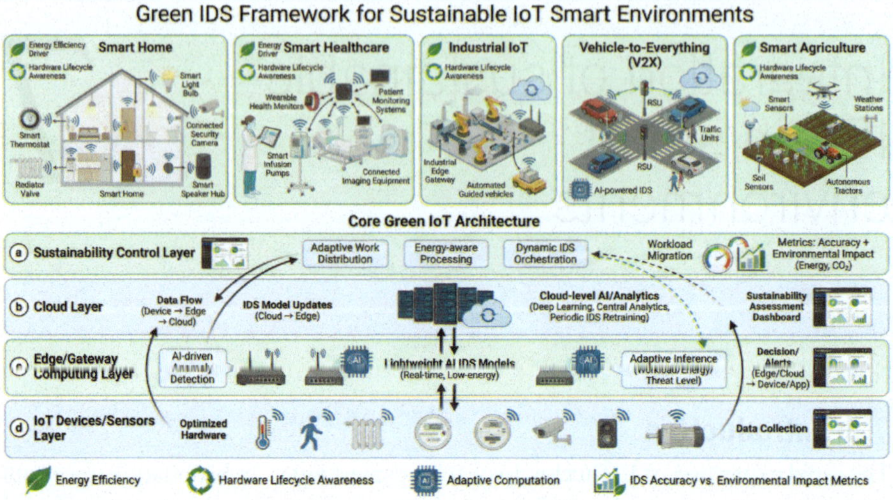

FIGURE 7.1

Components and primary architecture present in Green IoT system. In addition, the primary components and elements are present in smart environments where Green IDS needs to apply.

threat severity. Sustainability measures should likewise be folded into IDS evaluation, so that assessment captures environmental impact as well as detection accuracy. Fig. 7.1 shows the main components of the Green IoT framework, together with the IoT-enabled smart environments that depend on Green IDS for proper functioning.

This chapter draws on real-world case studies from smart cities, transportation networks, IoT for renewable energy, agricultural fields, and industrial automation. Its primary aim is to examine the sustainable implementation of IDS in smart environments supported by green IoT. It considers lightweight IDS deployments on low-power platforms and the trade-offs that such operation entails. Throughout the chapter, the principles of Green AI and long-term sustainable IoT, along with their frameworks, models, and techniques, are brought together to offer guidance for designing low-impact yet robust intrusion detection systems that support environmentally friendly smart infrastructures.

7.2 Sustainable IDS in smart cities

The fast development of the Internet of Things (IoT) has transformed the conventional city infrastructure as highly structured smart city ecosystems. Smart city ecosystems already in place include a variety of technologies, such as Wireless Sensor Networks, low-power sensing devices, Machine-to-Machine communication, edge computing, and cloud computing, which provide real-time services. Such ser-

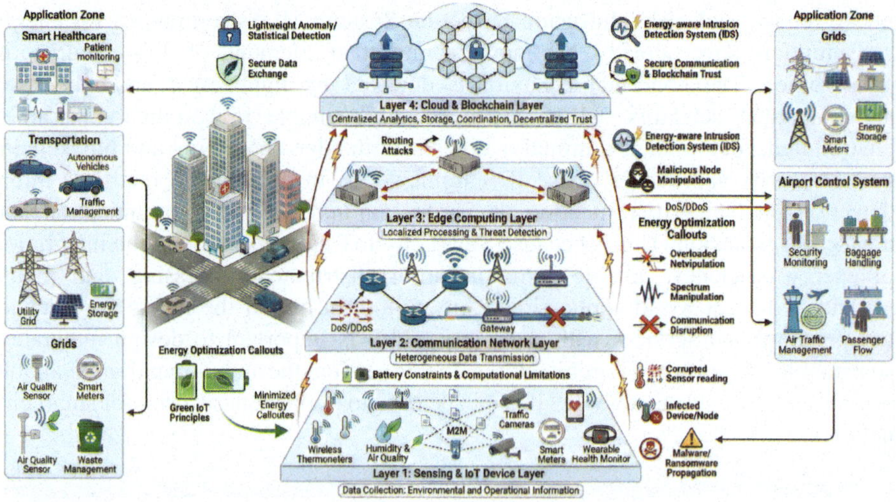

FIGURE 7.2

IoT layers present in smart cities and the potential of being affected by network attacks.

vices will be smart healthcare, smart transportation, smart grids, environmental monitoring, vehicle-to-everything, smart homes, an appropriately monitored airport and fleet management system, and automated public utilities and so forth. The smart city IoT architecture has several layers. Environmental and operational data is collected on the sensing layer. The communication layer provides information transmission by wireless and heterogeneous technologies. The edge computing layer enables processing data near devices in a low-latency manner. The cloud layer supports mass analytics and multi-year storage. Similarly, in recent years, blockchain-based mechanisms have been adopted to develop decentralized trust, secure data exchange, and efficient resource management in IoT-enabled smart city networks. The future of smart cities is based on IoT applications. By using data to inform decisions, they achieve common benefits such as energy optimization, better resource distribution, data-driven roles in smart transportation routing, and, overall, enhanced quality of life. The notion of green IoT also focuses more on energy-efficient communication and computation, since most IoT devices are subject to high degrees of battery, memory, and processing limitations. Regardless of these advantages, smart city IoT networks are distributed and heterogeneous, which subjects them to high cyber threats. Threats include botnet attacks (Mirai and BASHLITE), DoS attacks, flooding, data-injection attacks, malware propagation, routing attacks, malicious node manipulation, and spectrum manipulation in cognitive radio systems. These attacks can shut down services and reduce system reliability. They can also saturate computational and communication resources, thereby increasing energy consumption. Fig. 7.2 shows an image representation of IoT layers in smart cities and the potential security-breach attacks they are susceptible to.

To reduce such risks, Intrusion Detection Systems (IDSs) optimized for energy consumption have already become an important element of IoT security in smart cities. The abnormal behavior is detected by lightweight anomaly-based and statistical detectors, which are especially suitable in resource-constrained environments due to their minimal overhead. With edge computing and blockchain-based security approaches, these IDS frameworks, in turn, aid in real-time threat detection, data integrity protection, data reduction in redundant communication, and device life extension. This is because Smart city IoT networks require the integration of energy efficiency, reliable communication, distributed processing, and robust security with real-world applications. Any failure in one of the layers may impact to interconnected services within the city and it is important to design integrated, sustainable and secure IoT architectures. In this section, the author mentions available energy-efficient, sustainable IDS that can be used to implement security for smart city networks.

7.2.1 Statistical learning based Green IDS

Statistical learning methods have been used to derive network characteristics and build energy-efficient IDS. One such system is **IoTBoT-IDS**, a statistical learning-based anomaly detector that models the normal behavior of a healthy network and flags deviations as potential attacks. The methodology has three steps. In the first, informative network-flow features are derived from raw packet-capture data; rather than retaining all raw packet attributes, the data are reduced to eight key flow-level features, source and destination IP addresses, MAC addresses, ports, and packet sizes, and a statistical extraction mechanism then computes time-window statistics such as the mean, standard deviation, and packet count within one-second blocks, capturing behavioral patterns over time, including traffic surges associated with DDoS activity. The second step uses a Beta Mixture Model to estimate the probability density of legitimate traffic, with the Expectation-Maximization algorithm estimating the model parameters. In the final step, a Correntropy-based similarity measure compares the successive posterior-probability sequences produced by the mixture model; as new traffic observations arrive, dynamic thresholds are set using the Interquartile Range to determine whether an observation lies within normal limits or signals abnormal activity. Combining the Beta Mixture Model with the Correntropy measure enables the system to detect even subtle deviations in traffic behavior, improving its ability to identify previously unknown botnet variants. The framework was tested on three datasets: Kitsune, the IoT Network Intrusion Dataset, and the ISCX dataset. On the Kitsune and IoT Network Intrusion datasets, which span attack types such as SYN, SSDP, HTTP, and UDP flooding, scanning activity, and Mirai botnet variations, IoTBoT-IDS achieves a detection rate near 100% with a very low false-positive rate, while on the ISCX dataset its accuracy and precision reach roughly 99.93% and 99.88%, respectively. It also runs well on low-specification platforms such as Raspberry Pi devices, reflecting its lightweight design.

7.2.2 Green DL-based IDS

Although DL[1] methods are often assumed to be costly and energy-hungry, there is now clear evidence that they can be implemented efficiently enough to provide appropriate, inexpensive intrusion detection for the IoT-dependent communication of smart cities. Such networks need routing that draws minimal battery power at all times while maintaining strong security and communication availability. Intelligent and Secure Edge-Enabled Computing (ISEC) is a hybrid system that addresses this by pairing blockchain-supported security with DL-based routing intelligence. The network is arranged as a partial mesh in which IoT sensors transmit data to nearby edge servers, and a DL-based artificial NN makes routing decisions through a linear activation that ranks several metrics: node density, node cost (energy consumption together with bit error rate), and link response time derived from congestion measurements. Beyond intelligent routing, the system incorporates secure communication by modifying the Diffie-Hellman key-exchange protocol between communicating nodes: data are sent in a series of blocks under an XOR-based hashing scheme, each block carrying both its own hash and that of the preceding block, while a Distributed Hash Table at the edge layer manages secure key storage and retrieval, improving scalability and reducing lookup overhead.

The mechanism was tested in an NS-3 simulation with 200 sensor nodes, varying the number of attackers and edge servers, and evaluated for energy use, throughput, delay, route interruption, and network overhead. ISEC improved energy consumption by roughly 10-30% under various conditions, raised throughput by 11-18%, and reduced end-to-end delay by about 9-15%, while curbing increases in network overhead by 45-59% and cutting route interruptions by 26-45%, gains attributable to smart multi-metric routing, congestion-aware decision-making, and lightweight security. Energy consumption was estimated using the classical radio energy model to capture transmission and reception costs, and the system proved to save energy even as the number of attackers rose; by steering nodes away from unstable or overloaded neighbors, the DL routing extends network lifetime and balances overall energy use. The results thus show lower energy consumption, high throughput, and low latency, in keeping with the aims of sustainable Green IoT smart-city infrastructure.

7.2.3 Blockchain-based Green IDS

In IoT-enabled smart cities, individual IoT devices are commonly referred to as Wireless Sensor Nodes (WSNs), and their interconnected networks as Wireless Sensor Networks. WSN nodes are typically battery-powered, limited in memory and processing, and placed in unattended or open locations, all of which leaves them exposed to attacks such as node capture, replay, side-channel and false-data attacks,

[1] Deep learning is a subfield of machine learning that uses multi-layered (deep) artificial neural networks to automatically learn hierarchical representations and complex patterns directly from large volumes of raw data, without relying on manual feature engineering.

eavesdropping, spoofing, denial-of-service, phishing, unauthorized access, and malicious code injection. Traditional cryptographic methods are too resource-intensive to run on such constrained platforms, given their computational and storage demands, and centralized security architectures introduce single points of failure and trust-management difficulties. One way to address this is through a blockchain-based WSN architecture that leverages distributed ledger technology, cryptographic hashing, and decentralized validation. Sensors store their measurements in blockchain-style chunks, each containing a timestamp, the previous block's hash, a nonce, and a block index. Each block uses Merkle-tree digital signatures to ensure data immutability and prevent duplication. Elliptic Curve Cryptography securely generates keys, and SHA-256 hash functions chain the blocks together, so that altering any block changes its hash and is instantly detected by peer nodes through hash comparison.

The system is implemented in a cluster-based WSN framework, in which sensor nodes communicate with cluster heads and blockchain records are exchanged over a peer-to-peer network. To keep nodes synchronized and limit computational growth, a periodic blockchain reset mechanism refreshes the chain state at intervals. Because the architecture avoids the centralized verification authority of conventional designs, it gains both robustness and stronger trust. In testing, the blockchain approach processes slightly fewer data records in a given period, but the performance drop is very small and the system remains effective. More significantly, while the likelihood of data manipulation rises sharply in traditional WSNs as traffic grows, the blockchain-based implementation keeps the potential for tampering close to zero, since any modified block produces an immediate inconsistency under hash verification. By combining effective clustering with lightweight cryptography, the approach also conserves power and supports Green IDS aims: energy-efficient routing, such as LEACH-based clustering, lowers communication costs, and distributed storage relieves congestion at any single node. Blockchain operations add computation through hashing, nonce generation, and asymmetric cryptography, and processing time grows with the number of records-so, to contain this, the approach favors symmetric over asymmetric encryption, simplifies hash operations, and periodically resets the blockchain to manage block size growth.

A distributed blockchain-SDN-based architecture addresses the problems posed by centralized cloud services and SDN controllers. Traditional IoT designs depend on a central controller, cloud, or SDN, creating a single point of failure that introduces latency and resource waste and leaves the network vulnerable to denial-of-service and distributed denial-of-service attacks. At the same time, hundreds of thousands of heterogeneous IoT devices continuously produce vast volumes of unstructured data, complicating threat monitoring and control. SDN, though it improves network programmability, remains centralized, and while blockchain can strengthen data trust and integrity, it adds overhead. To reconcile these tensions, the architecture combines IoT, SDN, blockchain, and Network Function Virtualization into a distributed, energy-efficient, and secure design that delivers scalable, low-latency, attack-resistant operation in smart cities. It is structured into three tiers: a perception layer of IoT devices, an SDN or edge layer, and a cloud layer. At the perception layer, an energy-aware Cluster Head Selection algorithm selects cluster heads based on residual energy, proximity to the base station, and predefined energy thresholds, favoring the least-burdened nodes to reduce energy consumption and extend network lifetime. The SDN layer adopts a multi-controller architecture that separates the control and data planes, with dedicated controllers for security, packet forwarding, application services, and intrusion monitoring, and traffic managed through OpenFlow routing and Floodlight controllers alongside anomaly detection. An Ethereum-based blockchain with Proof-of-Work and smart contracts is also incorporated: IoT device identities are enrolled in the ledger to guarantee immutability, integrity, and access control, while NFV virtualizes functions such as routing and firewalling, lessening hardware dependence and improving load balancing. In testing, the cluster-head selection method yields more energy-balanced cluster heads, thereby improving efficiency and reducing power consumption compared with the standard LEACH and LEACH-Mobile protocols. Compared with baseline models, the architecture increases throughput-particularly under high transaction loads-and reduces response time; although blockchain energy use scales with transaction volume, it incurs no unmanageable cost. Under simulated distributed denial-of-service attacks, CPU utilization stabilizes more quickly, indicating greater resilience. NFV reduces reliance on specialized hardware and improves resource allocation, while distributed SDN controllers minimize retransmission. Blockchain operations do add computational cost to consensus and transaction processing, yet its decentralized certification structure curbs malicious traffic and enhances network stability. The architecture therefore achieves balanced energy consumption at the device level while keeping smart cities operating efficiently at the edge and cloud.

7.2.4 Green ML-based IDS

As IoT products and techniques are adopted ever more rapidly across smart cities and woven into an ever wider range of applications, they generate enormous, continuous volumes of wireless traffic. Older centralized, cloud-based IDS[2] architectures struggle to process this data, which is both complex and costly to handle in that manner; they tend to introduce substantial latency, congest the network, and create single points of failure. These shortcomings make them ill-suited to real-time detection in the resource-limited infrastructures of smart cities. Compounding the problem, wireless IoT networks operating over the common IEEE 802.11[3] standard are vulnerable to flooding, injection, and impersonation attacks. Many existing

[2] IDS denotes an IDS system, a security mechanism that monitors network, host, and application behavior to detect malicious activity.

[3] IEEE 802.11 is the family of wireless local-area networking standards commonly used by Wi-Fi networks.

ML[4]- and DL[5]-based IDS prioritize detection precision while neglecting scalability, and others are so computationally intensive that they cannot easily be distributed across fog and edge layers or replicated on edge IoT devices. To address these limitations, two IDS frameworks, a semi-distributed and a fully distributed model, can be built on a fog-edge collaborative processing scheme. The aim is a scalable design that delivers high detection performance, spreads computation across both fog and edge devices, and keeps resource requirements modest. The system uses the AWID dataset[6], which centers on impersonation and ordinary traffic. For feature engineering, a stacked autoencoder[7] with a 154:100:50 structure produces compact feature representations, which are then appended to the original features to enrich the data representation. The dataset is then split into three partitions to enable parallel processing. Several feature-selection methods are considered: wrapper approaches such as SVM[8] and J48,[9] and filter approaches such as Information Gain, OneR, and Correlation-based Feature Selection with the best features of each partition retained. In the semi-distributed architecture, feature selection is performed independently at the edge, after which the selected features are aggregated and classified by a Multi-Layer Perceptron[10] at the fog layer. In the fully distributed architecture, feature selection and MLP classification are carried out independently within each partition, and the final decision is obtained by combining the outputs of the parallel classifiers. Performance is assessed using accuracy, detection rate, false-alarm rate, F1 Score, Matthews Correlation Coefficient[11], and model-building time. The semi-distributed approach achieves very strong results, with an accuracy of 99.97% and a detection rate of 99.96%, along with a very low false-alarm rate and high correlation performance. The fully distributed model is marginally less accurate but builds far more quickly: roughly two and a half times faster than the semi-distributed version without sacrificing competitive detection capability.

A further approach is the Artificial Fish Swarm-driven weight-normalized AdaBoost (AF-WAdaBoost)[12] model, which sets out to build an adaptive, AI-

---

[4] ML denotes Machine Learning, a class of data-driven methods that learn patterns from data to support prediction, classification, and anomaly detection.

[5] DL denotes deep learning, a subset of ML that uses multi-layer neural networks to learn complex representations from data.

[6] AWID, the Aegean Wi-Fi Intrusion Dataset, contains IEEE 802.11 wireless traffic traces with normal traffic and attack traffic.

[7] A stacked AE is a neural network architecture composed of multiple AE layers that learn compact feature representations through reconstruction-based training.

[8] SVM denotes support vector machine, a supervised learning method that separates classes using a maximum-margin decision boundary.

[9] J48 is a Java implementation of the C4.5 decision-tree algorithm used for interpretable classification.

[10] A Multi-Layer Perceptron is a feedforward neural network with input, hidden, and output layers.

[11] Matthews Correlation Coefficient is a balanced classification metric that accounts for true positives, true negatives, false positives, and false negatives.

[12] AF-WAdaBoost combines Artificial Fish Swarm Optimization with a weight-normalized AdaBoost ensemble to improve adaptive IDS.

based, and computationally efficient threat-detection environment that strengthens security while supporting the sustainable operation of IoT. IoT devices typically combine limited processing power, limited bandwidth, and low intrinsic security, leaving them exposed to denial-of-service, distributed denial-of-service, malware injection, and network-layer intrusion attacks. Inefficient detection compounds the problem, as it can lead to frequent hardware replacement, high maintenance costs, and needless resource consumption- all of which undermine long-term sustainability. The process follows a familiar sequence of data gathering, preprocessing, model training, detection, and evaluation. During preprocessing, min-max normalization[13] scales each feature to a uniform range from 0 to 1, preventing bias from features with large numerical values. Artificial Fish Swarm Optimization[14] is then incorporated to dynamically adjust the classifiers' weights. This optimization method mimics the behavior of real fish-preying, swarming, and chasing: preying enables the exploration of new solution spaces, swarming draws the classifiers together toward beneficial states, and chasing has weaker classifiers follow the best-performing one, thereby improving the accuracy of the ensemble as a whole. Alongside this, a modified weight-normalized AdaBoost[15] mechanism combines weak learners into a stronger classifier, with the weight-update rule refined to prevent the extreme weight imbalances that would otherwise arise from repeatedly misclassified samples. By combining swarm-based optimization with weight-normalized boosting, the framework adapts to shifting attack patterns. In testing, AF-WAdaBoost outperforms several conventional ML techniques, achieving attack-detection rates of 98.5% on CICIDS2017, 97.3% on NSL-KDD, and 99.9% on UNSW-NB15. Its overall accuracy reaches 99.99%, with a precision of 99.4% and an F-measure of 99.7%; the high F-measure reflects strong precision and recall, indicating that the system markedly reduces both false positives and false negatives. These results confirm that the adaptive ensemble can raise detection capacity while remaining computationally efficient enough for an IoT setting. Fig. 7.3 shows the sustainable IDS mechanisms currently used in smart cities to support stable IoT application and architecture operation. Table 7.1 presents a comparative analysis of sustainable IDS techniques applied in smart-city IoT applications.

[13] Min–max normalization rescales numerical features into a fixed range, commonly between 0 and 1, to reduce scale-related bias during model training.

[14] Artificial Fish Swarm Optimization is a population-based optimization method inspired by fish behaviors such as preying, swarming, and chasing.

[15] AdaBoost, short for adaptive boosting, combines weak classifiers into a stronger ensemble by increasing the influence of difficult training samples.

Table 7.1 Comparative analysis of sustainable IDS techniques used in Smart City environments.

Technique Category	Model / Framework	Core Methodology	Dataset / Evaluation	Detection Performance	Energy Efficiency Contribution
Statistical Learning IDS	IoTBoT-IDS	Beta Mixture Model with Correntropy-based anomaly detection and statistical flow feature extraction	Kitsune, IoT Network Intrusion Dataset, ISCX dataset	~99.93% accuracy, 99.88% precision	Lightweight statistical computation suitable for Raspberry Pi–level hardware, low computational overhead
DL-based IDS	Intelligent and Secure Edge-enabled Computing (ISEC)	DL–based routing combined with blockchain-assisted communication and DHT-based key management	NS-3 simulation with 200 sensor nodes	Improved throughput (11–18%), reduced delay (9–15%), reduced route interruption (26–45%)	Energy consumption reduced by 10–30% through intelligent routing and congestion-aware decision-making
Blockchain-based IDS	Blockchain-integrated WSN security framework	Distributed ledger with Merkle tree authentication, ECC key generation, SHA-256 hashing	Simulation-based evaluation in clustered WSN environment	Near-zero probability of data tampering detection	Energy-efficient clustering and distributed storage reduce communication overhead
Blockchain + SDN IDS	Distributed IoT–SDN–Blockchain architecture	Cluster-head energy optimization, OpenFlow-based SDN control, Ethereum blockchain with smart contracts	Simulation with smart city IoT network scenarios	Improved throughput and reduced response time under attack conditions	Energy-balanced cluster-head selection and NFV-based resource optimization improve sustainability
ML IDS	Fog–Edge collaborative IDS architecture	Stacked AE feature extraction with distributed MLP classification	AWID dataset (WiFi intrusion dataset)	~99.97% accuracy, 99.96% detection rate	Distributed processing reduces latency and computational load across fog–edge infrastructure
Ensemble ML IDS	AF-WAdaBoost (Artificial Fish Swarm-driven AdaBoost)	Artificial Fish Swarm Optimization combined with a weight-normalized AdaBoost ensemble classifier	CICIDS2017, NSL-KDD, UNSW-NB15	Overall accuracy 99.99%, precision 99.4%, F-measure 99.7%	Optimization-based learning reduces computational cost while maintaining high detection accuracy

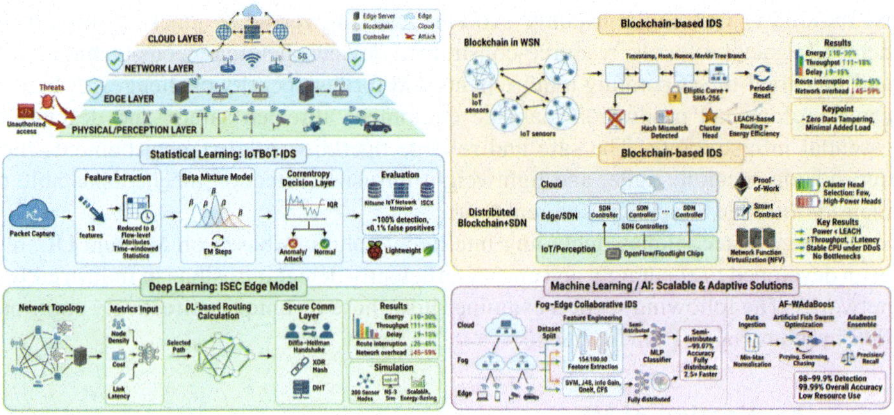

FIGURE 7.3

A block diagram of Sustainable IDS present in IoT architectures active in Smart City applications.

7.3 Sustainable IDS in IIoT

The **Industrial Internet of Things (IIoT)**[16] brings together industrial machines, sensors, controllers, communication networks, and data analytics infrastructure to form a connected cyber-physical environment in which industrial operations are automated, regulated, and streamlined for their application. It is widely deployed in critical sectors such as manufacturing, energy, transportation, and smart-factory systems, where sensors capture real-time data that are transmitted over industrial networks and analyzed at the edge, fog, or cloud to support intelligent decision-making and proactive maintenance. A typical IIoT system comprises sensing and communication equipment, edge and cloud computing resources, and control and supervisory devices such as SCADA[17]. Yet this connectivity also exposes the infrastructure to cyberattacks, including denial-of-service attacks[18], false data injection, malware, replay attacks, eavesdropping, unauthorized access, and large-scale botnet campaigns that can disrupt operations and endanger operators. Conventional signature-based[19] intrusion detection is ill-suited to such settings, since

[16] IIoT denotes the Industrial Internet of Things, a class of IoT systems that connect industrial machines, sensors, controllers, and analytics platforms for automation, monitoring, and control.

[17] SCADA denotes Supervisory Control and Data Acquisition, an industrial control architecture used to monitor and control physical processes through sensors, controllers, and operator interfaces.

[18] DoS denotes denial-of-service, an attack that disrupts service availability by overwhelming system resources, communication links, and processing capacity.

[19] A signature-based IDS detects attacks by matching observed activity against known attack patterns, rules, and signatures.

IIoT traffic is vast and constantly evolving, making zero-day attacks[20] difficult to detect. Legacy protocols, resource-constrained devices, heterogeneous technologies, and strict real-time operating requirements add further security challenges. A breach can therefore halt production, damage equipment, threaten safety, and destabilize essential infrastructure. The safe and reliable operation of IIoT environments thus depends on accurate, agile, and lightweight intrusion detection mechanisms able to identify multiple attack types in real time.

A range of techniques, including intelligent solutions based on ML and DL, has been developed to accurately and energy-efficiently detect intrusions in Industrial IoT networks. The following section examines how these techniques effectively carry out IDS in Industrial IoT environments.

7.3.1 Application of ML

One approach is a machine-learning-based intrusion-prevention firewall that automatically generates prevention rules while achieving zero false positives on IIoT edge devices. It introduces a new class of models, termed z-classifiers, together with an iterative training strategy that transforms an ordinary classifier into a zero-false-positive prevention model. The starting point is the observation that conventional classifiers, support vector machines among them, cannot be relied upon to reach zero false positives because of class imbalance and limitations in their cost functions. The proposed algorithm employs a removal-and-refinement procedure: false-positive samples are progressively removed from the training set, and false-alarm cases are emphasized during retraining, continuing until legitimate traffic is consistently classified. A decision-tree classifier (CART) serves as one instance of this scheme, since its learned decision boundary can be converted directly into usable firewall rules. The result is a proactive intrusion-prevention system that works in tandem with an intrusion detection system: the firewall blocks a portion of the attacks, while the remaining traffic is passed to the IDS for analysis. Tested on the SmartGrid Attack and KDD Cup ’99 datasets, the method consistently produced zero false positives across multiple runs. On the power-grid dataset the classifier achieved no false positives, with false negatives falling on average as training increased; on KDD Cup ’99 it identified a large volume of malicious traffic without raising false alarms, flagging more than two hundred thousand malicious records after full training. These findings indicate a framework that places a high premium on operational reliability while still delivering solid detection performance. A second approach is an ensemble learning method that combines three ML classifiers to improve predictive stability and reliability. Its first component uses the Pearson Correlation Coefficient to reduce the feature set by removing unimportant and redundant attributes, which lowers computational cost and training time. The second applies the Isolation Forest algorithm to detect and re-

[20] A zero-day attack exploits a previously unknown vulnerability before a patch, rule, and signature is available.

move abnormal samples, easing the problem of data imbalance. The processed data then passes to a Random Forest classifier, which renders the final intrusion classification. Because the feature selection and anomaly detection steps can be interchanged, two configurations arise: RF-PCCIF and RF-IFPCC. Evaluated on the Bot-IoT and NF-UNSW-NB15-v2 industrial-IoT security datasets, the framework shows strong detection performance. On Bot-IoT, it achieves roughly 99.98% accuracy for RF-PCCIF and 99.99% for RF-IFPCC, with prediction times of about six seconds; on NF-UNSW-NB15-v2, it reaches approximately 99.30% and 99.18% accuracy, with prediction times near seven seconds. The ensemble also markedly improves the detection of normal traffic in the imbalanced Bot-IoT dataset. By thinning the data in this way, the method reduces computational cost, eliminates unnecessary processing, and shortens prediction time, making it well-suited for lightweight execution in resource-constrained environments.

Zero-day attacks are a significant issue in IoT and Industrial IoT systems because they exploit previously unknown vulnerabilities before defensive signatures can be developed. To identify them, it is proposed to investigate an online adaptive intrusion detection system that can detect unknown attacks on the internet, adapt to changing traffic behavior, and operate with minimal memory and processing overhead. The framework is focused on the Adaptive Self-Adjusting Memory K-Nearest Neighbors algorithm. The streaming network traffic is processed by the system and the model is updated continuously without retraining. It has two memory structures: short-term memory, which holds recent observations, and long-term memory, which holds past behavior. To cope with changes in network patterns, the algorithm automatically adjusts the ratio of these memories based on prediction accuracy. With the help of a sliding performance window and a cooldown mechanism, memory updates are controlled and therefore kept stable. The framework uses a streaming ML platform to implement the framework and is tested on NetFlow-based industrial data. Zero-day detection capability is also tested using synthetic attacks generated by generative adversarial networks, and the model is compared with various traditional offline classifiers. There are high detection performance results in experiments. The system achieves detection accuracy greater than 92% for most attack types and up to 99.50% for specific attack categories. Each sample takes an average of 0.02 milliseconds to process, and the model itself requires only approximately 64 kilobytes of memory, compared to traditional methods that demand much more memory. These attributes show the applicability of this method to low-power IoT settings.

Hybrid, ML-based approaches to intrusion detection in IIoT networks have also been pursued, with the goal of producing a model that is at once efficient, accurate, and energy-conscious. One such design is SecureBlock, a framework that integrates ML-driven behavior analysis with blockchain-based trust management. The first component is a Hidden Markov Model that continuously analyzes device behavior through a three-stage process, rather than relying on a fixed set of historical rules. It begins by assessing operational behavior, including resource use and activity patterns; it then computes a device's trust level using the forward and backward algorithms of the Markov model; and finally, it distinguishes legitimate from malicious equipment based on probability indicators and intrusion classification. By estimating trust through probabilistic state transitions and binomial reputation updates, the model can tell cooperative from non-cooperative behavior over time. The second component is an intrusion detection module that sorts devices into four categories: legitimate, sensitive, under attack, and malicious, with devices judged malicious simply cut off from further communication. The third is a blockchain layer that records device interactions in an immutable registry, ensuring transparency and tamper resistance because any alteration becomes visible to all connected nodes. In this architecture, the Markov model detects abnormal behavior, while the blockchain ensures the trust and integrity of the records. The framework was evaluated in a simulated IoT environment of 250 devices with synthetic attack traffic, using true-positive rate, F-measure, miss rate, accuracy, and false-negative rate as performance measures. In detecting malicious devices, it achieved roughly 87% accuracy with an error margin below 2.5% as the number of devices varied, improving on older ML methods by about 2% and generating roughly 91% more credible reports. On the whole, blockchain augmented with intelligent behavior detection proved more accurate, produced fewer false negatives, and validated trust more effectively than traditional intrusion detection systems.

7.3.2 Application of DL techniques

One DL-based intrusion detection system, **AttackNet**, begins with data preparation, in which the network-traffic dataset is preprocessed through augmentation, shuffling, dummy encoding of categorical features, and standardization to improve generalization and reduce bias. The detection model itself adopts a hybrid architecture pairing CNN[21] with GRU[22]: the CNN component extracts structural patterns and feature relationships from the traffic, while the GRU component captures temporal dependencies in sequential communication behavior, and fully connected dense layers with a softmax activation perform the multiclass classification. This fusion of spatial and temporal learning lets the system recognize complex attack patterns more effectively than single-model approaches. Evaluated on the N-BaIoT dataset, where it distinguishes normal traffic from nine categories of botnet attack, AttackNet performs strongly, achieving 99.75% accuracy, 99.75% precision, 99.74% recall, and a loss of 0.0063, while improving accuracy by roughly 3.2% to 16.07% over existing methods. Overall, it classifies 10 traffic classes-benign traffic and several botnet attacks and performs well on real-world IIoT network data. A second framework takes a deep transfer learning approach, integrating data transformation, pretrained CNNs, optimization, ensemble learning, and model compression. The Edge-IIoTset dataset

[21] A Convolutional Neural Network is a type of deep neural network that uses convolutional layers to automatically learn spatial and hierarchical feature patterns from grid-like data such as images, making it highly effective for image recognition and feature extraction tasks.

[22] A Gated Recurrent Unit (GRU) is a type of recurrent neural network that uses update and reset gates to capture temporal dependencies in sequential data, offering performance comparable to LSTM but with fewer parameters and lower computational cost.

is first prepared by removing redundant attributes, encoding categorical features, and normalizing values, after which the tabular traffic records are converted into image-like representations to enable convolutional networks to capture the spatial patterns associated with attacks. Several pretrained CNN models: Xception, ResNet50, EfficientNet, MobileNet, and Inception are fine-tuned via transfer learning; their hyperparameters are adjusted via random search, and the most effective among them are combined into a bagging ensemble to improve generalization. Model quantization is then applied to compress the network and lower computational cost, enabling deployment on edge and IoT devices. The framework achieves very strong detection across fourteen attack categories: after optimization and ensemble integration, it reports perfect classification: 100% accuracy, precision, recall, F1-score, and Cohen's kappa, with no false alarms, while the individual optimized CNN models already reach roughly 99.7% to 99.9% accuracy, and the ensemble sustains comparable performance on a separate car-hacking dataset, evidence of good generalization. Rather than measuring energy consumption directly, resource efficiency is assessed through hardware metrics such as memory usage, inference time, CPU and GPU utilization, and computational complexity; the quantization step reduces memory requirements by roughly three to four times while preserving detection accuracy, indicating suitability for resource-constrained edge environments.

One end-to-end DL intrusion detection system, built on a one-dimensional CNN1D, addresses the difficulty of securing IIoT environments, where large numbers of interconnected industrial devices operate under strict reliability, latency, and resource constraints. The aim is a simple, lightweight, fully automated detection model that recognizes every attack category in a realistic IIoT dataset while generalizing well enough for real-world deployment. The approach performs automatic feature extraction and classification within a single learning framework, dispensing with separate feature-engineering steps. Its detection model is a CNN1D composed of four convolutional blocks, each combining Conv1D, batch normalization, average pooling, and dropout layers, followed by a flatten and dense layers with a softmax output for multiclass classification; the network uses LeakyReLU activation and cross-entropy loss, optimized with Adam to improve convergence and generalization. Folding feature extraction and classification into a single pipeline enables real-time operation in industrial settings. On the Edge-IIoTset dataset, which spans fourteen attack categories plus normal traffic, the model performs very strongly: 99.96% accuracy with a loss of 0.0011, correctly identifying all fifteen classes. Many attack types achieve perfect precision, recall, and F1-score, while the rest achieve 97-99%; cross-validation confirms consistent behavior at roughly 99.93-99.94% accuracy on unseen data, with stable convergence and no sign of overfitting. A second framework, GACO, is a hybrid combining GCNs, GRUs, and ACO[23]. Network traffic is

[23] Ant Colony Optimization is a nature-inspired metaheuristic optimization algorithm that mimics the foraging behavior of ants, using simulated pheromone trails to iteratively discover optimal or near-optimal paths and solutions to combinatorial problems.

first prepared through categorical encoding, normalization, and feature reduction via Principal Component Analysis. The GCN component captures the structural relationships among devices within the communication network, while the GRU analyzes temporal patterns in traffic to flag anomalous behavior, and the ACO algorithm automatically tunes hyperparameters such as learning rate, neuron count, dropout rate, and pooling size, removing the need for manual adjustment; its optimization function weighs detection accuracy, training time, false negatives, and computational complexity together to balance performance against efficiency. Evaluated on several realistic datasets: Edge-IIoTset, CICAPT-IIoT, and WUSTL-IIoT, the model detects a range of attack scenarios well, with detection rates of roughly 97% to 99% depending on the dataset and attack type and high recall and F1-scores for threats such as advanced persistent attacks, distributed denial-of-service, man-in-the-middle, and zero-day attacks. GACO delivers more stable and accurate detection than several existing approaches while requiring fewer training iterations. Resource efficiency is also addressed: rather than measuring energy consumption directly, the framework incorporates computational complexity as a proxy in its optimization objective, thereby minimizing processing time and resource use while preserving accuracy, making it suitable for resource-constrained industrial IoT environments. A third system is a CNN-based detector designed to learn spatial patterns in network-traffic flows. It is trained on the DNN-EdgeIIoT dataset[24], which contains more than 2.2 million traffic records with 63 features and 14 attack types grouped into five categories: DoS/DDoS, injection, malware, scanning, and man-in-the-middle attacks. Preprocessing removes corrupted records, encodes labels, normalizes values, and splits the data into 80% for training and 20% for testing. The CNN architecture is deliberately simple to keep computational cost low, comprising two Conv1D layers with 32 and 64 filters for feature extraction, max-pooling layers for dimensionality reduction, a fully connected layer of 128 neurons, and a softmax output for multi-class classification; it is trained with the Adam optimizer using dropout and early stopping to prevent overfitting, and no hybrid components are introduced, so as to support deployment on edge devices. Detection is strong throughout: binary classification reaches perfect performance: 100% accuracy, precision, recall, and F1-score while six-class classification exceeds 99% precision and recall, and fifteen-class classification attains an F1-score of about 0.946. Deployed on a Raspberry Pi, the system still maintains roughly 98.7% accuracy, demonstrating practical usability at the edge. It processes a sample in about 9 milliseconds, handles around 85 flows per second on Raspberry Pi hardware, reduces parameters by 30-40% through pruning, and lowers memory usage to about 120 MB through quantization-characteristics that suit

[24] The DNN-EdgeIIoT dataset is the deep-learning-oriented subset of the Edge-IIoTset benchmark, a realistic IoT/IIoT cybersecurity dataset generated from a seven-layer smart-factory testbed, containing 61 features and 14 attack types (grouped into DoS/DDoS, injection, MITM, malware, and scanning) for evaluating deep-learning-based intrusion detection systems

resource-constrained IoT and IIoT devices and point indirectly to reduced energy use.

A different approach is the DRL[25] based intrusion detection framework DC-IDS, which combines a Deep Q-Network with generative modeling. The detection problem is first formulated as a discrete-time Markov Decision Process, enabling the model to learn optimal classification policies via RL. The Deep Q-Network is strengthened with target networks, double Q-learning, and experience replay to improve training stability and accuracy. To detect both known and unknown attacks, a CAE[26] is embedded in the DQN's value network, separating the task into two functions: classifying known traffic and identifying unknown threats. The autoencoder reconstructs traffic features, and the resulting reconstruction error helps distinguish unknown attacks from legitimate behavior, with Extreme Value Theory then applied to set the decision thresholds for flagging unknown samples. Evaluated on the ToN-IoT dataset, which captures realistic industrial IoT network activity, the framework recognizes unknown attacks more effectively than earlier open-set methods. While those approaches achieved roughly 77% accuracy on unknown attacks, this model substantially improves on that figure while still reliably classifying known traffic. This technique also shows greater stability and stronger overall detection on the dataset than competing techniques.

ICS and IoT networks are becoming increasingly interconnected, widening their exposure to advanced cyberattacks that exploit communication behavior, routing patterns, and device interactions. Because such attacks can interrupt the operation of critical infrastructure, early detection is essential. One response is a hybrid DL intrusion detection framework that combines GCN[27] with LSTM[28] models. The IoT environment is modeled as a graph in which devices are nodes and communication links are edges: the GCN learns the spatial relationships among connected devices, while the LSTM captures temporal dependencies within traffic sequences. Using the IoT-23 dataset[29] of benign and malicious traffic, the GCN first

25 Deep reinforcement learning (DRL) is a machine learning approach that combines reinforcement learning with deep neural networks, enabling an agent to learn optimal decision-making policies through trial-and-error interaction with an environment guided by reward feedback.

26 A Conditional Variational Autoencoder (CVAE) is a generative model that extends the variational autoencoder by conditioning both encoding and decoding on additional input labels or attributes, enabling controlled generation of data samples belonging to specified classes or conditions

27 A Graph Convolutional Network is a type of neural network that operates directly on graph-structured data, learning node representations by aggregating and transforming feature information from each node's neighbors to capture relational and topological patterns

28 An LSTM (Long Short-Term Memory) is a type of recurrent neural network that uses gated memory cells to capture long-range temporal dependencies in sequential data while mitigating the vanishing-gradient problem that affects standard RNNs

29 The IoT-23 dataset is a labeled benchmark of real IoT network traffic, released by the Stratosphere Laboratory, comprising twenty-three captures (scenarios) of both malicious botnet traffic, such as Mirai and Toriiand benign device activity, widely used for training and evaluating IoT intrusion and malware detection systems.

extracts structural features from the network topology, and the resulting embeddings pass to LSTM layers that detect anomalies evolving over time, with training relying on cross-entropy loss, dropout, early stopping, and cross-validation to improve generalization and limit overfitting. The hybrid GCN-LSTM model achieves roughly 99.99% accuracy in identifying intrusion attempts in high-risk scenarios, with higher precision, recall, and F1-score than single-model approaches; notably, the combined architecture detects attacks that the GCN alone cannot, especially those characterized by abnormal timing behavior rather than purely structural anomalies. A related pair of methods, CVAE-ID and its federated extension FLCVAE-ID, is designed for ICS environments. CVAE-ID is built on a CAE trained only on normal network traffic; it learns the system's typical behavior by encoding selected network features and contextual information into a latent distribution and then reconstructing the expected traffic patterns, flagging anomalies whenever the reconstruction error exceeds a threshold set at the 95th percentile of validation errors. Its training objective combines reconstruction loss with KL divergence to ensure the model accurately captures the distribution of legitimate behavior. To preserve privacy, the approach adopts a federated architecture, FLCVAE-ID, in which each industrial node trains the model locally and shares only model parameters, not raw data; a central server aggregates these parameters via Federated Averaging and redistributes the updated global model across repeated communication rounds. Evaluated on the WUSTL-IIOT-2018 dataset[30]: millions of SCADA traffic records including reconnaissance and exploitation attacks, the model uses just six normalized traffic features and performs unsupervised anomaly detection, having been trained exclusively on normal data. The centralized CVAE-ID achieves 97.56% accuracy with an AUC-ROC of 0.9495, while the federated version performs comparably, with accuracy between 97.47% and 97.52% and F1-scores above 97% evidence that the federated method retains detection capability close to centralized learning while enabling privacy-preserving deployment across distributed industrial environments.

One attention-based DNN[31] model combines an attention mechanism with a multilayer NN to achieve high detection accuracy while reducing prediction time and computational overhead in IIoT systems. The attention layer assigns an importance weight to each input feature through a softmax-based weighting process and multiplies these weights by the original attributes, thereby emphasizing security-relevant features and dampening the influence of irrelevant ones. The refined feature vector then passes through a DNN with four fully connected layers, ReLU activation in the hidden layers, and softmax for classification. Evaluated on the X-IIoTID dataset, which spans multiple attack categories, the model is

[30] The WUSTL-IIOT-2018 dataset is an Industrial IoT intrusion detection benchmark developed at Washington University in St. Louis, generated from a SCADA-based industrial testbed and containing labeled normal and attack traffic for evaluating IDS in industrial control environments

[31] An attention-based Deep Neural Network is a neural architecture that incorporates attention mechanisms to dynamically assign different weights to input features or sequence elements, allowing the model to focus on the most relevant parts of the data for improved prediction and interpretability

supported by data preparation that includes label encoding, feature ranking with XGBoost, selection of sixty of the sixty-five features, min-max normalization, and stratified splitting into eighty percent training and twenty percent testing, with the Adam optimizer and sparse categorical cross-entropy loss used in training. This technique shows roughly 99.84% accuracy, 99.46% precision, 98.84% recall, and a 99.14% F1-score, with class-level analysis showing near-perfect detection of many attacks, including ransomware, reconnaissance, and command-and-control traffic. Inference is faster than with more complex DL methods while maintaining high accuracy, and pairing feature selection with reduced processing time points to lower computational cost and better suitability for energy-limited IIoT environments, though actual hardware power consumption was not measured experimentally. A second framework takes a deep transfer learning approach, integrating data transformation, optimization, and ensemble learning to build an adaptive system that can classify multiple attack categories while coping with heterogeneous data and limited labeled samples in modern IIoT settings. Network traffic from the NF-ToN-IoTv2, NF-BoT-IoTv2, and X-IIoTID datasets is first preprocessed and balanced via under-sampling and SMOTE, after which the NetFlow records are converted into RGB images to enable convolutional networks to learn spatial traffic patterns. Six pretrained CNN models: Xception, Inception, MobileNet, MobileNetV2, DenseNet121, and EfficientNetB0, are fine-tuned through transfer learning, a genetic algorithm optimizes hyperparameters such as the number of frozen layers, learning rate, activation functions, and dropout rate, and the three best-performing models are then combined in a soft-voting ensemble to improve robustness and generalization. After optimization and ensemble integration, the framework achieves 100% detection accuracy across all attack categories in all three datasets.

A further system pursues human-understandable decisions through an explainable ensemble of CNNs paired with interpretability techniques. The ToN-IoT dataset, telemetry data, operating-system logs, and network traffic from an industrial IoT environment are first normalized and scaled. Three distinct CNN architectures are trained independently, and their outputs are combined via a hard-voting ensemble to produce a reliable final prediction. For transparency, the framework incorporates two explainable AI methods, SHAP and LIME, which identify influential features and clearly explain why a given instance is labeled benign or malicious, helping analysts follow the decision process, while a baseline Extreme Learning Machine classifier serves as a point of comparison. The ensemble CNN outperforms the baseline across the dataset's nine attack categories while remaining consistently reliable; comparable explainable approaches have reported accuracies near 99.15% and F1-scores near 98.83%, indicating competitive performance for explainable industrial IoT security.

A final system offers a trustworthy, adaptive IDS that combines online ML with explainable AI, organized around three components: data acquisition and preprocessing, an adaptive detection engine, and an explainability layer. Rather than computationally heavy DL, it employs an ensemble of lightweight online algorithms such as Adaptive Hoeffding Tree, Online Bagging with Perceptrons, Incremental

Gaussian Naïve Bayes, and Passive-Aggressive classifiers, updated continuously through a streaming test-then-train strategy, allowing the system to learn from incoming traffic in real time. To handle changing network behavior, concept drift is detected via Page-Hinkley and ADWIN mechanisms, which automatically adjust model weights or reinitialize classifiers as needed, and SHAP-based explanations identify the influence of features such as packet size, protocol type, and device behavior, with a lightweight approximation generating explanations directly on edge devices without slowing detection. Evaluated on the ToN-IoT and BoT-IoT datasets and deployed on a Raspberry Pi 5 testbed, the framework achieves 96.4% accuracy, 96.1% precision, 95.7% recall, a 95.9% F1-score, and a 2.1% false-positive rate, processing each instance in about 34.8 milliseconds within real-time edge limits. In operation, the Raspberry Pi draws roughly 3-5 watts, detection latency remains under 50 milliseconds, and explanation generation takes about 55 milliseconds asynchronously. Because processing is local and free of heavy GPU-based models, the framework is well-suited for low-power edge deployment in Industrial IoT environments.

An Improved Binary Spider Wasp Optimization algorithm offers an optimized feature-selection mechanism for IDS in IIoT environments, designed to raise attack-detection accuracy while reducing computational complexity. It operates in two stages. In the first, the optimization algorithm performs feature selection by adapting the Spider Wasp Optimization technique to a binary search space, with additional strategies that enhance exploration and mitigate premature convergence, thereby enabling the identification of the most relevant network features and the discarding of redundant attributes. In the second, the selected feature subset is passed to ML classifiers, K-Nearest Neighbor among them, alongside other conventional models for comparison, so that reducing input dimensionality balances detection accuracy against computational efficiency. Evaluated on industrial IoT intrusion datasets containing both normal and malicious traffic, the optimization-based feature selection improves detection performance, achieving higher accuracy, precision, recall, and F1-score than traditional feature-selection methods and baseline optimization techniques, while the reduced feature set preserves strong detection capability and enhances both classification stability and convergence speed.

Applying DL-based intrusion detection in IIoT edge computing environments is challenging because network traffic data are highly dimensional, while edge devices have limited processing power, memory, and energy. Large feature sets raise computational complexity and impede real-time detection, yet industrial systems demand both high accuracy and low latency to safeguard safety and reliability. One response is a lightweight intrusion detection framework built on a compact DNN suited to resource-constrained edge devices. The Edge-IIoTset dataset is first preprocessed by removing duplicate entries, handling missing values, encoding categorical features, and normalizing the data, after which several dimensionality-reduction techniques: PCA, LDA, ICA, Factor Analysis, and UMAP, are examined to find the most informative feature subset, with class imbalance addressed through K-means-SMOTE oversampling. The processed data feed a fully CNN using

GELU activation, dropout regularization, the Adam optimizer, and early stopping, and performance is assessed both before and after dimensionality reduction to balance accuracy against computational cost. The reduction substantially improves efficiency while barely affecting detection: the UMAP-based configuration reaches roughly 99.96% accuracy, with a macro F1-score near 99% and a weighted F1-score near 100%, a negligible loss relative to the original 99.98% even as computational complexity falls sharply, and confusion-matrix analysis confirms reliable classification across fifteen attack categories. Rather than measuring energy directly, efficiency is gauged by resource usage: dimensionality reduction cuts the model's parameters from 15,439 to 3,087, lowering memory requirements, speeding inference, and reducing processing overhead, making the model well-suited to edge deployment.

A second framework, DTKD-IDS, is a lightweight DL system based on dual-teacher knowledge distillation, comprising two teacher networks and a compact student network. The student first learns feature representations from the first teacher through prototype distillation, in which the teacher's intermediate outputs guide the student to imitate its behavior; a second teacher then supplies complementary knowledge, and the two teachers' predictions are adaptively weighted to reduce the risk of transferring incorrect information from any single source. Training stability and class imbalance are managed through a hybrid loss that combines focal loss, mean squared error[32], and Kullback-Leibler divergence[33], while the student model employs one-dimensional depthwise separable convolution to markedly reduce its parameter count and computational complexity. Evaluated on the CICDDoS2019[34], NSL-KDD[35], and X-IIoTID datasets[36], the framework detects attacks effectively throughout: in binary classification it achieves roughly 99.97% precision and a 99.98% detection rate on CICDDoS2019, and about 99.88% accuracy on NSL-KDD, while in multiclass classification it attains around 99.76% on CICDDoS2019, 99.25% on NSL-KDD, and 99.61% on X-IIoTID. It consistently surpasses existing

[32] Mean Squared Error (MSE) is a loss/error metric that measures the average of the squared differences between predicted and actual values, penalizing larger errors more heavily and quantifying how closely a model's predictions match the true data.

[33] Kullback-Leibler (KL) divergence is a measure from information theory that quantifies how much one probability distribution differs from a reference distribution, indicating the information lost when the approximate distribution is used to represent the true one.

[34] CICDDoS2019 is a benchmark dataset developed by the Canadian Institute for Cybersecurity (CIC) that contains realistic, labeled network traffic featuring a wide range of modern reflection- and exploitation-based distributed denial-of-service (DDoS) attacks alongside benign traffic, designed for evaluating DDoS detection systems

[35] NSL-KDD is a refined benchmark intrusion detection dataset derived from the older KDD'99 dataset, which removes redundant and duplicate records to reduce bias and provide a more balanced and reliable basis for evaluating network intrusion detection systems

[36] X-IIoTID is a connectivity- and device-agnostic Industrial IoT intrusion detection dataset that captures multi-view features from realistic IIoT environments, labeled across normal activity and a broad range of attack behaviors mapped to the stages of the cyber kill chain.

ML and DL methods, improving the student network's performance by roughly 2-7% depending on the dataset and metric. Efficiency is again assessed indirectly, through model size rather than measured power: the distilled student reduces the parameter count by about 20 to 250 times relative to the teacher models while preserving high accuracy, enabling faster detection and real-time operation on resource-constrained IIoT devices and thereby lowering computational and energy demands.

7.3.3 Application of FL

Industrial Internet of Things (IIoT) environments comprise many distributed edge devices that continuously generate sensitive operational data. Deploying intrusion detection in such settings is difficult because detection models must run on limited computing power, storage, and energy while also protecting data privacy. Traditional centralized DL-based IDS require collecting raw traffic from many devices, which heightens privacy risk and communication overhead; federated learning enables distributed training but still contends with non-identically distributed data across devices, limited personalization, and the possibility of information leakage through shared parameters.

One way to address these difficulties is a federated learning approach called Federated Two-stage Knowledge Distillation (FTKD), which integrates several components. A lightweight neural model, MA-TBCLNN, is designed for resource-constrained edge devices while retaining strong feature-extraction ability. A two-stage knowledge-distillation process then follows: Adaptive Progressive Self-Knowledge Distillation allows each local model to learn from its own earlier states, while Personalized Knowledge Distillation uses aggregated global knowledge to tailor each model to its device. To cope with heterogeneous data distributions, the framework aggregates outputs through an entropy-maximum mean discrepancy weighting method. Crucially, devices exchange prediction logits rather than model parameters and apply differential privacy by adding uniform noise to forestall data leakage. Together these mechanisms support collaborative learning, personalization, and privacy protection across distributed IIoT systems. Evaluated on the ToN-IoT and Edge-IIoTset datasets, FTKD detects attacks effectively, achieving accuracy above 97% and outperforming conventional federated learning and traditional intrusion detection methods across multiple attack categories, with improved robustness under heterogeneous data conditions and better adaptability to diverse attack scenarios than standard federated approaches.

A further framework, **2DF-IDS**, is a decentralized, federated learning intrusion detection system that enables collaborative detection of diverse attacks across multiple industrial environments while preserving data privacy, eliminating dependence on a central server, and protecting communication against advanced cryptographic threats. It dispenses with a central aggregation server by having multiple factories form a peer-to-peer network and collaboratively train a shared detection model: each participant updates its local model and exchanges encrypted parameters with neighboring nodes until a consensus model emerges. To safeguard sensitive information, the framework applies Differentially Private Stochastic Gradient Descent, clipping gradients and adding Gaussian noise before sharing, while parameter transmission is secured through a post-quantum cryptographic scheme based on Ring-Learning-With-Errors combined with AES encryption, protecting communication against both present and future attacks. The detection component is a multilayer perceptron that performs multi-class classification on the Edge-IIoTset dataset, enabling collaborative learning without sharing raw data or relying on a central coordinator. Performance is comparable to centralized learning, achieving roughly 94.37% accuracy compared to 94.84% for a fully centralized approach, and surpassing traditional federated learning at 93.91%. Under strict privacy conditions, the framework improves F1-score by about 12%, recall by 13%, and precision by 9% relative to other federated IDS methods, achieves perfect classification of benign traffic in some settings, and remains stable across different numbers of participating clients.

A different framework, **EX-DFL**, combines federated DL intrusion detection with explainable artificial intelligence, aiming to achieve accurate detection that preserves data privacy while enabling administrators to interpret the resulting alerts. It follows a federated learning architecture in which multiple edge devices collaboratively train a global model without sharing raw data: each device trains a local DNN on its own private dataset and sends only model parameters to a central aggregation server, which averages them and redistributes the updated model over successive communication rounds. The model is trained on the CICIDS2017 dataset, which includes normal traffic and several attack types, and preprocessing includes normalization, handling missing values, and distributing the data across simulated edge nodes. For transparency, the framework integrates SHAP-based explainability, computing feature-contribution values that show how each network attribute shapes a classification decision and providing both instance-level explanations and overall feature-importance rankings. The federated model is also compared with centralized CNN, DNN, and RNN models to weigh privacy against detection performance. It detects attacks strongly while keeping data private, reaching up to roughly 99.97% accuracy, with precision near 99.96%, recall near 99.94%, and AUC near 99.96%; the centralized models likewise score highly, but the federated approach matches them without sharing sensitive data, and adding more participating edge devices further improves the global model through collaborative learning. A second framework is a foundation-model-assisted federated learning system that integrates generative modeling, knowledge distillation, and privacy protection, developed to support intrusion detection in drone-assisted Industrial IoT used for monitoring, inspection, delivery, and surveillance. Conditional generative adversarial networks first augment cyber-physical drone datasets to reduce imbalance, and a cloud-based foundation model then produces soft labels through knowledge distillation to guide local models. The architecture proceeds in three phases: the cloud model generates soft labels; each drone trains locally on its own data using the distilled knowledge; and a macro base station aggregates model parameters to update the global model. To improve stability and privacy, the framework combines FedALA and FedProx aggregation to reduce divergence between local and global models, applies differential privacy during parameter exchange, and uses secure aggregation to protect the global model's integrity. Evaluated on a drone cyber-physical dataset spanning both communication and flight-behavior attacks, it detects threats reliably, achieving about 91% accuracy on cyber-related attacks and about 99% on physical-attack scenarios, and improving on baseline approaches by roughly 0.47-3.24% for cyberattacks and 0.93-4.84% for physical attacks. A third framework examines intrusion detection in federated learning, enhanced with differential privacy mechanisms. Each edge device trains a local model on its own network traffic data and transmits only the updated parameters to a central server, which aggregates them into a global model and redistributes it across multiple communication rounds, enabling distributed learning without sharing raw traffic. To guard sensitive information against leakage through model updates, the framework applies several differential-privacy perturbation techniques: the Gaussian mechanism, the analytic Gaussian mechanism, various forms of Laplace noise (truncated, bounded, and bounded-noise), and uniform noise injection, evaluated across a range of privacy levels to expose the trade-off between privacy and detection accuracy. It also compares two aggregation strategies: traditional Federated Averaging (FedAvg) and Fed+, the latter designed to handle heterogeneous, non-IID data distributions more effectively. Tested on the CIC-ToN_IoT dataset of roughly 4.4 million traffic flows across multiple attack categories, the system uses a multiclass logistic regression model with a softmax classifier to evaluate privacy mechanisms rather than propose a new detection model. Introducing differential privacy does not meaningfully degrade performance, accuracy generally stays above 0.8 across mechanisms, and Fed+ edges out FedAvg, particularly in non-IID scenarios; in some cases the injected noise even improves results through regularization. Correlation analysis further shows that privacy protection strengthens as the privacy parameter decreases, while overall detection accuracy remains relatively stable.

7.3.4 Application of DL based hybrid techniques

DL techniques are frequently combined with additional security measures and network architectures to strengthen protection in Industrial IoT environments. One such design is a unified architecture that integrates blockchain technology with a DL-based intrusion detection system to provide secure communication, authentication, privacy preservation, and accurate attack detection together. Its blockchain communication layer secures the links among industrial devices, edge nodes, and cloud servers through session-based mutual authentication and key agreement; a Proof-of-Authority consensus mechanism validates transactions and forms blocks, while elliptic-curve cryptography handles secure identity verification, and the whole proceeds through registration, authentication, and consensus stages to prevent unauthorized access and data manipulation. The detection component combines a Contractive Sparse Autoencoder, an attention-based Bidirectional LSTM, and a softmax classifier: the autoencoder extracts representative features from network traffic, the Bidirectional LSTM analyzes temporal attack patterns, and the attention mechanism highlights salient information before classification. With data prepared through normalization, missing-value handling, and label encoding, the model attains roughly 98.88% accuracy on ToN-IoT and 95.80% on Edge-IIoTset in multi-class detection.

A second framework, DyGRA-Edge, is an attention-based DL system that blends three complementary mechanisms. Its Dynamic Gradient Controller recasts residual learning as an ordinary differential equation with an adaptive step size guided by Lyapunov stability, stabilizing gradients and curbing noise amplification in bursty traffic. The Anisotropic Diffusion Convolution module transforms conventional convolution into a diffusion process that sharpens salient edge features in low-contrast grayscale traffic images, making subtle anomalies more readily apparent. The Sparse Entropy Attention mechanism minimizes conditional entropy to trim redundant features and reduce false alarms. Network traffic is converted into small grayscale images and processed through this architecture, then evaluated on real industrial platforms, a benchmark dataset, and a Raspberry Pi edge device. It reaches roughly 98.83% accuracy, 98.05% precision, 97.90% recall, and a 97.97% F1-score on an oil-and-gas platform, and about 98.55% accuracy with comparable precision, recall, and F1 on a catalytic reforming system: overall accuracy above 98.5%, surpassing conventional convolutional and lightweight transformer models. Inference latency remains between 63 and 98 milliseconds, supporting real-time detection, and deployment on a Raspberry Pi shows average CPU usage near 5.3%, roughly 40% below comparable lightweight transformer methods, which suits resource-constrained edge environments and indirectly indicates low energy consumption.

A third design is a hybrid framework spanning ML and DL across several processing stages. The ToN-IoT dataset is first cleaned and normalized, SMOTE is applied to address class imbalance, and Singular Value Decomposition is then used to reduce feature dimensionality by removing redundant attributes while retaining essential data characteristics. Several classifiers are examined for detection: LSTM, Bi-LSTM, and GRU networks among the DL models, and Decision Tree, Ensemble Bagging Tree, and K-Nearest Neighbor among the traditional ones, across both binary classification (normal versus malicious) and multi-class classification over nine attack categories, with performance measured through accuracy, precision, recall, F1-score, and AUC-ROC. In binary classification, Bi-LSTM and GRU reach roughly 99.999% accuracy at an error rate of 0.001 and LSTM about 99.991%, while the traditional models trail slightly: Ensemble Bagging Tree near 99.94%, Decision Tree at 99.91%, and KNN at 99.826%. In multi-class classification, GRU achieves around 99.984% accuracy, followed by LSTM at 99.908% and Bi-LSTM at 99.9%, with Ensemble Bagging Tree at around 99.926% and Decision Tree and KNN at about 99.858% and 99.774%, respectively. The DL approaches thus offer superior detection for industrial IoT tasks.

A fourth analytical report compares three DL architectures: CNN, LSTM, and a hybrid CNN-LSTM. The UNSW-NB15 and X-IIoTID datasets are prepared by handling missing values, converting categorical attributes to numerical form, and applying min-max normalization. The CNN extracts spatial patterns from traffic automatically; the LSTM learns temporal relationships and sequence-based attack behavior; and the hybrid combines both forms of learning to improve detection performance, with all three assessed on accuracy, precision, recall, F1-score, and loss for binary and multi-class tasks. The hybrid performs best: on UNSW-NB15 the CNN reaches about 90.09% accuracy and the LSTM roughly 91.14% (binary) and 91.10% (multi-class), while the hybrid improves these to about 93.21% and 92.90%; on X-IIoTID the CNN attains around 99.15% (binary) and 99.26% (multi-class), the LSTM about 99.05% and 98.91%, and the hybrid the highest at roughly 99.84% and 99.80%. Combining spatial and temporal learning therefore enhances detection markedly across most attack categories relative to standalone models.

A fifth approach presents an integrated security architecture pairing a DL IDS with blockchain verification for layered protection. Its first component is a CNN-based IDS implemented as an application within a software-defined networking controller; this module inspects packet payloads to identify malicious commands and supports both binary and multi-class classification. It is evaluated on an industrial control-system natural-gas-pipeline dataset with 27 features, where attacks are grouped into normal, injection, reconnaissance, and denial-of-service traffic. The second component is a blockchain-based security layer on a private MultiChain network: the controller sends flow rules to network switches, while a detection node stores the same rules on the blockchain and then compares switch logs against the blockchain records, with any mismatch signaling a possible man-in-the-middle or rule-injection attack. The IDS thus protects data-plane traffic while the blockchain safeguards the control plane. The CNN-based IDS reaches about 94.75% accuracy for binary classification and 94.65% for multi-class, with binary metrics near 95.28% precision, 93.84% recall, and 94.48% F1-score, and multi-class metrics near 97.02% precision, 88.86% recall, and 92.31% F1-score, outperforming the decision-tree and RSL-KNN baselines; the combined framework successfully detects both malicious payloads and flow-rule manipulation.

A sixth design is a hybrid anomaly-based system, the **CNN2D-RNN-SVM framework**, which combines DL feature extraction with machine-learning classification. Traffic from the ToN-IoT dataset is preprocessed by removing missing values, standardizing features, and encoding labels into eight categories: normal, denial-of-service, distributed denial-of-service, injection, cross-site scripting, password attacks, scanning, and man-in-the-middle. One-dimensional traffic features are transformed into two-dimensional image-like representations to aid spatial learning; a two-dimensional CNN extracts spatial relationships within packets, a recurrent network captures temporal behavior across sequences, and a softmax layer provides an initial classification. In the final stage, the learned representation is fed into a support vector machine, which maps the features into a higher-dimensional space and learns nonlinear decision boundaries for accurate identification, marrying automatic feature learning with the SVM's classification strength. The framework achieves roughly 99.59% accuracy, an F1-score, and an AUC of 0.9977, and the linear-kernel SVM performs best because the deep feature representation becomes nearly linearly separable.

A seventh framework couples Long Short-Term Memory and Gated Recurrent Unit networks for accurate, adaptive, and scalable detection of sophisticated attacks in cloud-based IIoT environments. Evaluated on the Kitsune dataset of real industrial traffic, such as normal activity alongside botnet, man-in-the-middle, denial-of-service, and information-gain attacks, it draws on the strengths of both sequential models: the LSTM captures long-term dependencies and multi-stage attack behavior, while the GRU learns faster with fewer parameters and adapts quickly to new threats; their outputs are merged through dense layers for the final prediction. Adversarial training, dropout regularization, and dynamic thresholding improve robustness against evasion, and ten-fold cross-validation against standalone LSTM, GRU, and ConvLSTM2D approaches confirms its strength: roughly 98.68% accuracy, 98.44% precision, 98.62% recall, and a 98.62% F1-score, with a very low false-negative rate near 0.01% and detection time around 6 milliseconds per record. Real-time inference is supported, latency is reduced through pruning and quantization, and a hierarchical deployment performs detection at the edge with further analysis in the cloud while multi-core processing shortens training; characteristics well suited to resource-constrained industrial IoT settings.

Finally, a multi-level hybrid architecture combines edge and cloud intelligence to improve detection efficiency in Industrial IoT. At the edge, a Logistic Regression classifier performs rapid preliminary screening, forwarding only low-confidence flows, about 16% of total traffic, to the cloud, where a one-dimensional CNN analyzes complex attack patterns; this hierarchy reduces communication overhead, latency, and bandwidth use while preserving accuracy. To sharpen detection and lower computational cost, a Bowerbird Courtship-Inspired Feature Selection algorithm is applied, with the edge using a wrapper-based method optimized for recall-oriented F1 performance and the cloud using a filter-based method drawing on Fisher score and correlation penalties to strip redundant attributes, and a hybrid balancing pipeline combining SMOTE, ENN, and LOF improves the detection of minority attack classes. Evaluated on the WUSTL-IIoT dataset with normalized NetFlow features, the edge-level Logistic Regression reaches about 99.70% accuracy with high recall, while the cloud-level CNN approaches perfect performance at roughly 100% accuracy and an F1-score near 99.98%, and the combined architecture cuts false negatives sharply while remaining reliable. Efficiency is gauged by execution time, an indirect proxy for energy use: feature selection trims Logistic Regression inference from 52 ms to 38 ms and CNN processing from 27.86 seconds to 18.28 seconds, indicating lower overhead and better suitability for resource-constrained edge devices such as Raspberry Pi nodes.

Building on this line of work, a hybrid security framework called the **Quantum-Aware Secure Blockchain Intrusion Detection System (QASB-IDS)** integrates artificial intelligence, blockchain technology, federated learning, and post-quantum cryptography to secure Industrial IoT environments. Its detection component is a lightweight CNN-LSTM model in which the convolutional layers learn spatial patterns from network-traffic features while the LSTM analyzes temporal relationships and multi-stage attack behavior, a joint design that lets a single model perform both signature-based and anomaly-based detection. To support collaborative and tamper-resistant operation, a hierarchical consortium blockchain securely records alerts and model updates, and federated learning allows multiple devices to contribute to training without sharing raw data, preserving privacy while reducing communication overhead. The architecture further incorporates quantum-resilient mechanisms: lattice-based digital signatures authenticate blockchain transactions, and Quantum Key Distribution establishes secure communication keys, guarding the system against future quantum-computing attacks. Evaluated on several industrial intrusion datasets: Edge-IIoTset, SWaT, and X-IIoTID, it detects attacks strongly, reaching roughly 99.1% accuracy on Edge-IIoTset, 98.7% on SWaT, and 98.4% on X-IIoTID, with F1-scores above 0.985 and a false-positive rate near 1.3%. Efficiency analysis indicates low resource consumption, with edge inference drawing about 0.42-0.6 W per detection; the overhead from post-quantum cryptography remains below roughly 5%, blockchain latency is around 140 ms, and communication overhead is under 7%. The framework can therefore operate on resource-constrained industrial devices while delivering stronger, future-resistant protection.

A further framework takes an interdisciplinary DL approach, integrating data preprocessing, feature engineering, and multiple temporal neural models. The dataset is first prepared by removing missing values, normalizing attributes, and encoding labels, and SMOTE oversampling is then applied to provide minority attack categories with adequate representation. Feature engineering then proceeds in two stages: important attributes are selected using mutual information, information gain, and correlation filtering; dimensionality is further reduced with Sparse Principal Component Analysis (SPCA), thereby reducing redundancy and computational overhead while preserving essential attack characteristics. For detection, the framework uses an attention-driven architecture that combines Deep RNN, Deep LSTM, and Deep Bi-LSTM models, with the attention mechanism assigning greater weight to significant time steps in the network sequence, thereby capturing temporal attack behavior more effectively. Evaluated on three industrial control system datasets: SWaT, WADI, and GHL, representing water-treatment, water-distribution, and gas-heating processes and spanning both single-stage and multi-stage cyber-physical attacks, the attention-based Deep LSTM model performs best, reaching roughly 99.8% precision, recall, and F1-score across the datasets with similarly high ROC-AUC values. The framework steadily reduces both false positives and false negatives during training, and the LSTM converges faster than the RNN and Bi-LSTM alternatives. Feature reduction through SPCA reduces complexity and shortens training and testing times, while the computational cost scales with input size and network parameters. Table 7.2 presents a comparative analysis of the IDS techniques and models discussed above for the active control of Industrial IoT architectures and environments.

Table 7.2 Comparative analysis of sustainable IDS techniques in Industrial IoT (IIoT) environments.

Technique Category	Model/Framework	Core Methodology	Dataset/Evaluation	Detection Performance	Sustainability/Lightweight Contribution
ML	Z-classifier intrusion-prevention firewall	Iterative removal-and-refinement training to achieve zero false positives; CART used to derive firewall rules.	SmartGrid Attack, KDD Cup'99	Zero false positives; detects large volumes of malicious traffic	Suitable for IIoT edge devices; prioritizes operational reliability with lightweight rule generation.
ML	RF-PCCIF / RF-IFPCC	Pearson Correlation feature selection + Isolation Forest anomaly filtering + Random Forest classification.	Bot-IoT, NF-UNSW-NB15-v2	99.98% / 99.99% accuracy on Bot-IoT; 99.30% / 99.18% on NF-UNSW-NB15-v2	Reduces redundant features, prediction time, and computational overhead for constrained environments.
ML	Adaptive Self-Adjusting Memory KNN	Online adaptive KNN with short-term and long-term memory for zero-day attack detection in streaming traffic.	NetFlow-based industrial datasets, GAN-generated synthetic attacks	Above 92% accuracy for most attack types; up to 99.50%	Requires only about 64 KB memory and 0.02 ms per sample, supporting low-power deployment.
ML + Blockchain	SecureBlock	Hidden Markov Model-based trust estimation + blockchain-based immutable trust management.	Simulation with 250 IoT devices and synthetic attacks	About 87% accuracy; miss rate below 2.5%	Improves trust verification and reduces false negatives while maintaining efficient distributed operation.
DL	AttackNet	Hybrid CNN-GRU architecture for spatial and temporal attack pattern learning.	N-BaIoT	99.75% accuracy, 99.75% precision, 99.74% recall	High detection capability with automated feature learning for real-world IIoT traffic.
DL	Transfer learning + ensemble + quantization IDS	Pretrained CNNs (Xception, ResNet50, EfficientNet, MobileNet, Inception), bagging ensemble, model quantization.	Edge-IIoTset, car-hacking dataset	100% accuracy, precision, recall, F1-score, Cohen's kappa	Quantization reduces memory by about 3–4× while preserving accuracy for edge deployment.
DL	CNN1D-based IDS	End-to-end Conv1D architecture with automatic feature extraction and multiclass classification.	Edge-IIoTset	99.96% accuracy; 99.93–99.94% in cross-validation	Lightweight single-pipeline detection suitable for real-time industrial environments.
DL	GACO	Graph Convolutional Network + GRU + Ant Colony Optimization for hyperparameter tuning.	Edge-IIoTset, CICAPT-IIoT, WUSTL-IIoT	Detection rates generally between 97% and 99%	Optimization minimizes computational complexity and training time while maintaining strong accuracy.

continued on next page

Table 7.2 (*continued*)

Technique Category	Model/Framework	Core Methodology	Dataset/Evaluation	Detection Performance	Sustainability/Lightweight Contribution
DL	Lightweight CNN on DNN-EdgeIIoT	Simple CNN with pruning and quantization for edge deployment.	DNN-EdgeIIoT; Raspberry Pi deployment	100% binary accuracy; about 98.7% on Raspberry Pi	Processes about 85 flows/s, 9 ms/sample, memory about 120 MB; suitable for constrained devices.
DRL	DC-IDS	Deep Q-Network + Conditional VAE + Extreme Value Theory for known and unknown attack detection.	ToN-IoT	Stronger unknown-attack recognition than prior methods; improves beyond earlier 77% open-set accuracy	Supports adaptive detection of evolving threats without relying only on known signatures.
DL	GCN-LSTM hybrid IDS	Graph Convolutional Network for structural relations + LSTM for temporal dependencies.	IoT-23	About 99.99% accuracy	Captures both topological and temporal attack behavior with strong generalization.
DL / Federated	CVAE-ID / FLCVAE-ID	Conditional VAE trained on normal traffic; federated extension with FedAvg.	WUSTL-IIOT-2018	CVAE-ID: 97.56% accuracy; FLCVAE-ID: 97.47–97.52% accuracy	Privacy-preserving anomaly detection with only six normalized features; suitable for distributed ICS settings.
DL	Attention-based DNN IDS	Attention-weighted feature refinement + multilayer neural network.	X-IIoTID	99.84% accuracy, 99.46% precision, 98.84% recall, 99.14% F1-score	Reduced inference overhead through feature selection and focused attention on important features.
DL	Transfer learning + GA + soft voting ensemble	RGB NetFlow transformation + six pretrained CNNs + genetic algorithm optimization + ensemble voting.	NF-ToN-IoTv2, NF-BoT-IoTv2, X-IIoTID	100% accuracy across datasets	Strong generalization with optimized hyperparameters; suitable where high accuracy is needed.
Explainable / Online IDS	Trustworthy adaptive online IDS	Online ensemble learning + concept drift detection + SHAP-based explainability.	ToN-IoT, BoT-IoT; Raspberry Pi 5	96.4% accuracy, 95.9% F1-score	Runs at 3–5 W, under 50 ms detection latency; well suited for low-power edge IIoT use.
Feature Optimization	Improved Binary Spider Wasp Optimization	Binary optimization-based feature selection with conventional classifiers.	Industrial IoT intrusion datasets	Higher accuracy, precision, recall, and F1-score than baseline methods	Reduces dimensionality and computational complexity while preserving strong detection capability.

continued on next page

Table 7.2 *(continued)*

Technique Category	Model/Framework	Core Methodology	Dataset/Evaluation	Detection Performance	Sustainability/Lightweight Contribution
Lightweight DL	UMAP-based compact DNN	Dimensionality reduction (UMAP and others) + compact fully connected DNN.	Edge-IIoTset	About 99.96% accuracy; macro F1 about 99%	Parameters reduced from 15,439 to 3,087, lowering memory and processing overhead.
Lightweight DL	DTKD-IDS	Dual-teacher knowledge distillation + depthwise separable convolution student model.	CICDDoS2019, NSL-KDD, X-IIoTID	Up to 99.76% multiclass accuracy; 99.98% detection rate in binary setting	Reduces parameters by about 20–250× while maintaining high accuracy.
FL	FTKD	Federated two-stage knowledge distillation with personalized learning and differential privacy.	ToN-IoT, Edge-IIoTset	Above 97% accuracy	Supports privacy-preserving collaborative learning under heterogeneous edge data distributions.
FL	2DF-IDS	Decentralized peer-to-peer FL-based IDS with DPSGD and post-quantum secure communication.	Edge-IIoTset	About 94.37% accuracy	Removes central coordinator, preserves privacy, and secures parameter exchange against future threats.
FL + XAI	EX-DFL	Federated DL with SHAP explanations.	CICIDS2017	Up to 99.97% accuracy, 99.96% precision, 99.94% recall	Preserves privacy while enabling interpretable alerts and collaborative model improvement.
FL	FL with differential privacy and Fed+	Differential privacy mechanisms + FedAvg/Fed+ aggregation.	CIC-ToN_IoT	Accuracy generally above 0.8 across privacy settings	Strong privacy protection with limited performance degradation; useful for non-IID IIoT scenarios.
FL	Federated ResNet-based IDS	Modified ResNet + FedAvg for distributed industrial IDS.	X-IIoTID	99.16% federated accuracy; centralized accuracy 99.43%	Preserves data privacy while maintaining performance close to centralized learning.
Hybrid DL + Blockchain	Blockchain + CSAE + Attention BiLSTM	Proof-of-Authority blockchain + Contractive Sparse AE + attention-based BiLSTM.	ToN-IoT, Edge-IIoTset	98.88% on ToN-IoT; 95.80% on Edge-IIoTset	Provides secure communication, authentication, and accurate multiclass detection.
Hybrid DL	DyGRA-Edge	Dynamic Gradient Controller + Anisotropic Diffusion Convolution + Sparse Entropy Attention.	Real industrial platforms, benchmark dataset, Raspberry Pi	Overall accuracy above 98.5%	Raspberry Pi CPU usage about 5.3%; low-latency edge deployment with reduced overhead.

continued on next page

Table 7.2 (*continued*)

Technique Category	Model/Framework	Core Methodology	Dataset/Evaluation	Detection Performance	Sustainability/Lightweight Contribution
Hybrid ML/DL	SVD + LSTM/BiLSTM /GRU framework	SMOTE + SVD feature reduction + comparison of temporal DL and conventional ML classifiers.	ToN-IoT	Up to 99.999% binary accuracy; up to 99.984% multi-class accuracy	Feature reduction lowers complexity while deep sequence models maximize detection capability.
Hybrid DL	CNN-LSTM hybrid IDS	CNN for spatial features + LSTM for temporal behavior.	UNSW-NB15, X-IIoTID	Up to 99.84% binary and 99.80% multi-class accuracy on X-IIoTID	Hybrid design improves attack recognition over standalone CNN and LSTM models.
Hybrid DL + Blockchain	CNN IDS + MultiChain verification	CNN-based IDS within SDN controller + blockchain-based flow rule integrity verification.	Natural gas pipeline ICS dataset	About 94.75% binary accuracy; 94.65% multi-class accuracy	Multi-layer protection secures both data plane and control plane in industrial networks.
Hybrid DL	CNN2D–RNN–SVM	CNN2D feature extraction + RNN temporal learning + SVM final classification.	ToN-IoT	About 99.59% accuracy and F1-score; AUC 0.9977	Combines automatic feature learning with efficient decision boundaries.
Hybrid DL	LSTM-GRU hybrid IDS	Sequential fusion of LSTM and GRU with adversarial training, pruning, and quantization.	Kitsune	98.68% accuracy, 98.62% F1-score	About 6 ms per record; supports edge-cloud hierarchical deployment and low latency.
Hybrid Edge-Cloud IDS	Multi-level LR + CNN framework	Edge Logistic Regression for rapid screening + cloud CNN for difficult flows + feature selection.	WUSTL-IIoT	Edge: 99.70%; cloud CNN: nearly 100%	Reduces communication and processing cost by forwarding only about 16% low-confidence flows to the cloud.
Hybrid Secure Framework	QASB-IDS	CNN-LSTM + consortium blockchain + FL + post-quantum cryptography.	Edge-IIoTset, SWaT, X-IIoTID	99.1%, 98.7%, and 98.4% accuracy respectively	Edge inference about 0.42–0.6 W/detection; post-quantum overhead below 5%.
Hybrid Attention-based Temporal DL	Attention-driven Deep RNN / LSTM / Bi-LSTM framework	Feature engineering + SPCA + attention-weighted temporal neural models.	SWaT, WADI, GHL	About 99.8% precision, recall, and F1-score	SPCA reduces complexity and training/testing cost while preserving high detection quality.

7.4 Sustainable IDS in connected healthcare (IoMT)

Intrusion Detection Systems (IDS) play a critical role in smart healthcare environments, where interconnected medical devices, electronic health records, cloud platforms, and wireless sensor networks continuously exchange sensitive patient data. Modern healthcare systems rely heavily on IoT-enabled devices, such as wearable monitors, infusion pumps, smart imaging systems, and remote diagnostic platforms, to deliver real-time, personalized medical services. However, this high level of connectivity significantly increases the attack surface. Cyberattacks such as ransomware, denial-of-service, data manipulation, Mirai and Bashlite attacks, and unauthorized access can disrupt clinical operations, compromise patient privacy, and even endanger human life by altering medical device behavior. An effective IDS continuously monitors network traffic and device activity to detect abnormal patterns, malicious commands, and suspicious data flows, thereby helping to stop malicious network attacks. By identifying threats in real time, IDS solutions help prevent service interruption and protect sensitive medical information in smart healthcare infrastructures. In resource-constrained environments like smart healthcare systems, lightweight and adaptive IDS mechanisms are required for better. Not many attempts have been made in this direction, but the IDS designed to address the existing security challenges of smart healthcare systems is sufficient to ensure high security accuracy.

A statistical anomaly detection framework called **IoTBoT-IDS** offers a lightweight, anomaly-based intrusion detection system that models heterogeneous IoT traffic and detects unknown botnet behavior in smart, connected healthcare systems. It operates in three stages. First, raw PCAP traffic is processed to extract relevant network-flow features: timing information, byte counts, source and destination IP addresses, MAC addresses, and port numbers, after which a statistical feature-extraction mechanism computes summary statistics such as mean, standard deviation, and packet count within one-second sliding windows, capturing the subtle behavioral patterns associated with botnet activity. Second, a Beta Mixture Model models the probability distribution of normal network traffic; unlike Gaussian models, the beta distribution is better suited to semi-bounded traffic features, and the mixture's parameters are estimated through the Expectation-Maximization algorithm, allowing flexible modeling of legitimate behavior. Third, the posterior probabilities produced by the Beta Mixture Model are analyzed with a correntropy-based similarity measure, which captures nonlinear relationships and is robust to non-Gaussian noise; detection thresholds are set dynamically using the Interquartile Range method, and any observation falling outside the learned normal boundaries is classified as malicious. Because the system learns only normal behavior, it can identify previously unseen botnet variants. Evaluated on three benchmark datasets: the Kitsune dataset, the IoT Network Intrusion Dataset, and the ISCX 2012 dataset, IoTBoT-IDS achieved an average detection accuracy of roughly 99.2%, with precision and detection rates frequently above 99% and in some cases approaching 100%. It sustained strong performance across a range of attack categories, including SYN and SSDP flooding, man-in-the-middle attacks, Mirai-based botnet activity, scanning, spam, and UDP flooding. False-positive and false-negative rates were generally low, though performance dipped slightly where training data were limited. On the whole, the framework provides accurate and computationally efficient intrusion detection well suited to resource-constrained smart healthcare systems.

Another line of work addresses the practical obstacles facing existing Digital Twin (DT)-based Structural Health Monitoring (SHM) systems, namely their high implementation costs, technical complexity, and reliance on advanced computational resources. DT-enabled SHM systems provide continuous monitoring and predictive maintenance, yet many current solutions lean on expensive sensing technologies and sophisticated ML models. To make such monitoring more practical and affordable, a two-layer framework couples a hardware layer and a software layer through IoT infrastructure. The hardware layer integrates a low-cost potentiometer-based contact displacement sensor, a low-cost infrared non-contact sensor, and an Arduino Nano 33 IoT microcontroller with cloud connectivity. The sensors were calibrated against a digital height gauge to assess accuracy and noise. The potentiometer sensor proved highly linear, accurate to roughly ±80 micrometers, whereas the infrared sensor behaved nonlinearly and less precisely, at about ±363 micrometers. The software layer comprises a finite-element-based Digital Twin built in FEMAP, with nonlinear analysis carried out in ReConAn; concrete behavior was represented using a modified constitutive model, and reinforcement was modeled with bilinear steel properties; the twin was calibrated by iteratively adjusting material parameters against experimental load-test data. Over 72 nonlinear iterations, the optimal model achieved a mean relative error of 4.7%. A Python-based automation platform was then developed to update the model, predict structural response, estimate crack width, and diagnose damage against predefined deflection and crack thresholds. Static-cyclic and incremental loading tests confirmed the approach: the potentiometer sensor agreed closely with reference LVDT measurements, with a low mean absolute error and stable performance, whereas the infrared sensor exhibited greater variability. Taken together, the work shows that a cost-effective, accessible IoT-enabled Digital Twin framework can deliver reliable structural monitoring without recourse to expensive sensing or computational infrastructure. Table 7.3 presents a comparative analysis of IDS techniques and frameworks actively deployed in smart healthcare IoT environments to ensure smooth and effective performance.

7.5 Sustainable IDS in vehicle to everything (V2X) communication network

Vehicle-to-Everything (V2X) communication enables vehicles to exchange information with surrounding environmental entities, including other vehicles, roadside infrastructure, pedestrians, cloud platforms, communication tower networks and so on. Through technologies such as Dedicated Short-Range Communications (DSRC), Cellular-V2X, 5G/6G networking systems (based on IEEE 802.11p standard) and so

Table 7.3 Comparative analysis of IDS and monitoring frameworks in smart healthcare IoT networks.

Technique Category	Model/Frame-work	Core Methodology	Dataset/Evaluation	Detection/System Performance	Lightweight/Practical Contribution
Statistical Anomaly Detection	IoTBoT-IDS	Network traffic is first processed from PCAP files to extract flow-level features such as packet counts, byte source and destination addresses, communication ports, and statistics. Statistical characteristics of traffic behavior are computed using sliding time windows. A Beta Mixture Model is then trained.	Kitsune dataset, IoT Network Intrusion Dataset, ISCX 2012 dataset	Average detection accuracy approximately 99.2%; precision and detection rate frequently above 99%. Successfully detects SYN flooding, SSDP flooding, Mirai botnet activity, man-in-the-middle attacks, scanning attacks, spam, and UDP flooding.	Designed for resource-constrained IoT healthcare environments. Uses lightweight statistical modeling instead of complex DL models, enabling efficient deployment on healthcare IoT devices with limited computational resources while maintaining strong detection accuracy.
IoT-enabled Digital Twin Monitoring	IoT-integrated Digital Twin SHM framework	A two-layer architecture composed of a hardware sensing layer and a Digital Twin software layer. The hardware layer integrates low-cost sensors including a potentiometer-based displacement sensor and an infrared non-contact sensor connected to an Arduino Nano 33 IoT microcontroller for cloud communication. Sensor data is transmitted to a software-based Digital Twin built using finite element modeling in FEMAP and nonlinear analysis in ReConAn.	Experimental validation using static–cyclic and incremental load tests on structural components	Potentiometer sensor achieved approximately ± 80 μm accuracy with strong linearity. Digital Twin calibration achieved about 4.7% mean relative error after 72 nonlinear iterations. Results closely matched reference LVDT measurements.	Provides a cost-effective monitoring solution using inexpensive sensors and lightweight IoT devices. Reduces dependence on expensive sensing infrastructure and high-performance computing while still enabling reliable real-time monitoring and anomaly detection in healthcare-related infrastructure systems.

on, V2X supports real-time applications ranging from collision avoidance and emergency alerts to traffic optimization and autonomous driving coordination. By enabling continuous data exchange, V2X forms the foundation of intelligent transportation systems and modern smart mobility. However, this high level of connectivity also introduces significant cybersecurity challenges. Because V2X networks rely on open wireless communication and interact directly with vehicle control functions, cyberattacks such as spoofing, denial-of-service, replay attacks, message manipulation, brute-force attacks, probing, infiltration attacks and so on can threaten both data integrity and physical safety as well as unauthorized control of the vehicles. Compromised vehicular communications may lead to real-world consequences, including traffic disruption or endangerment of human life. In addition, the highly dynamic nature of vehicular environments renders conventional rule-based security mechanisms insufficient to detect evolving threats. To tackle these challenges, intelligent and energy-efficient intrusion detection systems are essential in V2X environments. Security mechanisms must provide accurate and real-time detection while operating within the limited computational and energy constraints of onboard vehicular devices. Achieving a balance between intrusion detection performance, processing overhead, and sustainable energy use is therefore a key requirement for secure and sustainable V2X-enabled transportation systems. Various IDS frameworks, security architectures and techniques are presented to achieve this goal. This chapter will briefly discuss each of the sustainable IDS available to date.

7.5.1 DL based Green IDS for V2X

A hybrid deep reinforcement learning framework that combines an Advantage Actor-Critic (A2C) algorithm with a Long Short-Term Memory (LSTM) network offers an intelligent, adaptive means of intrusion detection and mitigation, able to learn evolving attack patterns and respond dynamically in real time within **Software-Defined Vehicles (SDV)** environments. The LSTM component captures temporal dependencies in V2X communication data, drawing on sequential packet-level features: packet size, arrival rate, source and destination identifiers, signal strength, timestamps, sequence numbers, and error rates, that together represent the system state at each time step. The A2C architecture comprises two NN: an actor network that selects mitigation actions and a critic network that evaluates the expected reward of those actions. Four adaptive responses are defined: allow, flag, monitor, and block, and the reward function balances detection performance against resource efficiency, weighing true-positive rate, false-positive rate, and resource consumption while penalizing excessive defensive actions that would waste bandwidth or computing power; learning is guided by an advantage function based on temporal-difference updates. In testing, detection proves strong: model sensitivity, the proportion of actual attacks correctly identified, rises steadily during training and approaches nearly 100% after about 500 episodes, while overall accuracy also improves over time to roughly 95 to 100% near the end of training. The false-positive rate stays below 0.20 and the false-negative rate below 0.10, confirming reliable performance.

A further framework, CR-V2XR, offers a decentralized, trust-aware, and delay-sensitive cybersecurity design to maintain reliable coordination in V2X-enabled roundabouts under continuous adversarial conditions. Roundabouts are especially demanding, since traffic moves nonlinearly and changes constantly: vehicles merge, circulate, and interact with pedestrians without traffic lights or strict timing control, so safe coordination depends heavily on timely, trustworthy communication, and even small delays or manipulated messages can disrupt vehicle behavior and increase the risk of accidents. The CR-V2XR architecture is organized into three layers: the vehicle layer, the roadside-unit (RSU) edge layer, and a federated aggregation layer. Each RSU runs a lightweight anomaly detection model trained locally via supervised learning with binary cross-entropy loss, and rather than sharing raw traffic data, the RSUs periodically transmit model parameters to a central aggregator via asynchronous federated learning, thereby protecting privacy and reducing communication overhead.

The framework draws together several complementary techniques. Spatio-temporal trajectory modeling based on motion equations predicts vehicle paths and estimates potential collision risks, while latency-aware communication modeling analyzes propagation, queuing, medium access, and retransmission delays to ensure compliance with safety limits. A multi-modal trust mechanism fuses information from Basic Safety Messages, LiDAR validation, vehicle-to-vehicle corroboration, and behavioral consistency checks, and entropy-based anomaly detection flags irregular or uncertain communication patterns. A Stackelberg game-theoretic model lets the system adjust trust thresholds dynamically in response to strategic adversaries, and a multi-objective NSGA-III optimization process balances detection accuracy, collision probability, communication cost, and latency while respecting operational constraints such as minimum time-to-collision and trust thresholds. Evaluated through the OMNeT++, Veins, and SUMO simulation platforms across eleven adversarial scenarios, including Sybil attacks, wormhole attacks, and data injection and manipulation, CR-V2XR reaches roughly 95% detection accuracy even under challenging attacks. It markedly reduces collision probability, from 0.61 to 0.27 in high-density traffic with 300 vehicles, and keeps communication delay within acceptable safety limits, typically between 45 and 60 milliseconds under normal conditions and still controlled under heavy adversarial stress, where delays may reach around 180 milliseconds.

Another approach builds supervised DL models using Convolutional Long Short-Term Memory (ConvLSTM) architectures, integrating internal vehicle sensors and external IoT-assisted navigation data to improve detection accuracy and enhance the safety and reliability of connected vehicle systems. Modern autonomous vehicles depend on internal components such as Electronic Control Units, CAN bus communication, and an array of perception sensors including GNSS, IMU, and powertrain sensors. While these systems enable intelligent driving functions, they are also exposed to cyberattacks, hardware faults, and sensor malfunctions; corrupted or spoofed signals, particularly in the navigation and powertrain modules, can mislead control algorithms and create serious safety risks. To uncover these internal vulnerabilities and detect such attacks, two ConvLSTM models are developed. In the first, higher-rate IoT data are down-sampled through convolutional layers and then concatenated with On-Board Diagnostics II (OBDII) data before entering stacked ConvLSTM layers. In the second, lower-rate OBDII data are upsampled via transposed convolutional layers to match the IoT sampling rate prior to concatenation, thereby improving feature consistency across sensors. The input is arranged into three-dimensional time-series windows of 16 seconds using a structured stacking format, and both models are trained with the Adam optimizer, binary cross-entropy loss, 40 epochs, and a batch size of 32. The dataset was collected from a real vehicle trip via OBDII interfaces and smartphone sensors. After synchronization, synthetic anomalies were injected into two key variables: engine RPM and vehicle speed, with four anomaly types introduced to simulate realistic attack conditions. The results show strong anomaly-detection capability, and the second model consistently outperforms the first. When orientation-sensor data are included, the second model attains precision up to 98%, recall around 96% to 97%, and F1-scores of roughly 97% to 98%. The clear gain from including orientation sensors underscores the value of combining internal vehicle data with IoT-assisted sensing.

A stacking-based ensemble framework named **SFGL** integrates Gradient Boosting Decision Trees (GBDT), Random Forest, and Bidirectional LSTM models into a high-accuracy, computationally efficient, and imbalance-aware intrusion detection system for Internet of Vehicles (IoV) networks. It proceeds in three stages. The first is data preprocessing: categorical features are one-hot encoded, numerical features are normalized via Min-Max scaling, and class imbalance is addressed with a hybrid sampling strategy that combines ADASYN oversampling and Tomek-Links undersampling. The second is feature selection, in which Mutual Information ranks features by importance, and an adaptive threshold retains those with a cumulative importance of at most 0.9, thereby reducing dimensionality and improving efficiency. The third is the stacking ensemble itself, with Random Forest, GBDT, and Bi-LSTM serving as base learners, and a Bi-LSTM as the meta-learner: a two-layer design that enables the model to capture both nonlinear structural patterns and temporal dependencies in vehicular network traffic. On the CICIDS2017 dataset, the model achieves perfect precision, recall, and F1-scores of 100% for most attack classes, including benign traffic, DoS, port scanning, brute force, and web attacks; the Bot class reaches an F1-score of 99.6%, while the infiltration class falls to 86.3% owing to its limited original samples. On the NSL-KDD dataset, it likewise performs strongly, with F1-scores of 100% for normal and DoS traffic, 99.7% for probing, 95.1% for R2L, and 86.1% for U2R attacks, the minority classes again dipping slightly because of their sparse representation. Feature selection preserves nearly the same detection accuracy while cutting inference latency by roughly 37%, demonstrating improved computational efficiency alongside strong detection capability.

A lightweight DeepMLP-based intrusion detection framework balances accuracy and efficiency, offering a multiclass, adaptive, and computationally economical system that detects attacks in both in-vehicle and external networks without sacrificing performance. It follows a structured workflow of preprocessing, model training, and evaluation. SMOTE and random oversampling address class imbalance, and a central contribution is byte-level feature engineering: rather than treating the CAN data field as a single feature, each data byte is extracted individually, followed by feature normalization via Min-Max scaling and standardization. SHAP analysis confirms that timestamps and particular data bytes are the most influential features in classification. The NN is deliberately simple: an input layer, two dense layers of 128 and 64 neurons with ReLU activation, and a Softmax output layer for multiclass classification, and is trained with the Adam optimizer and categorical cross-entropy loss over 10 epochs at a batch size of 32; ablation analysis shows this configuration achieves high F1-scores while keeping computational complexity low. Validated on five datasets, three in-vehicle and two external communication, the model proves adaptable across environments. On in-vehicle datasets such as Car-Hacking and the Car-Hacking Attack and Defense Challenge, it achieves 99.99% accuracy with a 99.99% F1-score and extremely low false-positive rates; on the ROAD dataset, the false-positive rate remains very low at 0.03%. On the external communication datasets CICIDS2017 and CSE-CIC-IDS2018, it achieves 99.41% accuracy with strong precision and recall. Set against more complex GAN- and CNN-based methods, the DeepMLP approach matches or exceeds their accuracy while requiring substantially fewer computational resources.

A two-stage intrusion detection framework extracts rules from DNNs to build an accurate, explainable, and resource-efficient system that combines the strengths of DL and rule-based reasoning while maintaining high performance. A fully connected feed-forward NN is first trained using ReLU activation, a softmax output layer, and cross-entropy loss. Once trained, interpretable rules are extracted through two distinct approaches. The first, **DeepRed**, is a decompositional technique that analyzes hidden-neuron activations layer by layer and generates decision rules by merging the intermediate representations. The second, **HypInv**, treats the network as a black box and approximates its decision boundaries through hyperplane-based inversion. DeepRed thus examines internal structure, while HypInv approximates the model's behavior externally. The architecture operates in two stages: the first performs binary classification to determine whether traffic is normal or malicious; if it is deemed malicious, the second performs multiclass classification to identify the specific attack type. Three variants are implemented: a homogeneous DeepRed model, a homogeneous HypInv model, and a heterogeneous model combining both, alongside hybrid feature-selection methods such as mutual information, ANOVA, chi-square, linear SVM, and Extra Trees, and data-balancing strategies that pair undersampling with oversampling. Classification performance is strong: DeepRed achieves accuracy ranging from above 92% to nearly 99% across datasets, and the two-stage homogeneous DeepRed model reaches roughly 98% accuracy on CIC-IDS2017 and 97% on CSE-CIC-IDS2018. In terms of efficiency, DeepRed shows lower execution time, reduced CPU usage, and lower memory consumption, while HypInv also reduces resource use relative to the full DNN, though less efficiently than DeepRed.

7.5.2 ML based Green IDS for V2X

The Internet of Vehicular Things (IoV), in which connected vehicles communicate via V2V and V2X infrastructures, faces rising cybersecurity risks. One response is a hybrid ensemble IDS framework that integrates several strong ML algorithms through ensemble learning. As IoV ecosystems grow, their exposure to diverse cyber threats widens, and the aim here is a high-accuracy, resource-efficient, ensemble-based IDS that can detect multiple attack categories in IoV networks while addressing dataset imbalance and improving overall reliability. K-means clustering creates representative subsets to reduce computational overhead; Z-score normalization standardizes feature values; Information Gain-based feature selection removes irrelevant attributes and reduces noise; and the Synthetic Minority Over-sampling Technique (SMOTE) generates artificial samples for minority classes to counter class imbalance. After evaluating several algorithms, four high-performing classifiers are chosen as base learners: XGBoost, Random Forest, Decision Tree, and Gradient Boosting, and three ensemble strategies are compared: bagging, voting, and stacking. Stacking proves best: training a meta-classifier on the outputs of the base learners to correct individual model errors and lift overall predictive performance. Evaluation spans two well-known datasets, CIC-IDS2017 and UNSW-NB15, to cover diverse attack types. On CIC-IDS2017, the stacking ensemble achieves 99.75% accuracy and 99.74% F1-score, with consistently high precision and recall across attack categories; on UNSW-NB15, it reaches 100% accuracy and 100% F1-score in binary classification.

A closely related approach is a Multitiered Hybrid Intrusion Detection System that integrates supervised and unsupervised learning within a four-tier architecture, aiming for a unified, optimized system capable of detecting both known and zero-day attacks across intra-vehicle and external vehicular networks while preserving high accuracy and low latency. It begins with data preprocessing, in which K-means cluster sampling creates representative subsets, SMOTE addresses class imbalance, Z-score normalization scales features, and Bayesian optimization tunes hyperparameters to improve clustering and sampling efficiency. A three-stage feature-engineering process follows: Information Gain selects important features, the Fast Correlation-Based Filter removes redundant attributes, and Kernel Principal Component Analysis performs nonlinear dimensionality reduction, an IG-FCBF-KPCA pipeline that sharpens detection while lowering computational cost. The first two tiers handle known-attack detection through supervised learning, combining four tree-based classifiers, Decision Tree, Random Forest, Extra Trees, and XGBoost, into a stacking ensemble, with Bayesian optimization via a Tree Parzen Estimator to further refine the model parameters. The third and fourth tiers address zero-day attacks through anomaly detection: K-means clustering divides the data into groups and assigns labels by the majority class, and samples classified with low confidence are passed to biased classifiers trained specifically to handle false positives and false negatives. This hybrid design lets the system recognize both familiar and previously unseen attack patterns. Evaluated on the CAN-intrusion dataset for intra-vehicle attacks and the CICIDS2017 dataset for external network attacks, it achieves 99.99% accuracy on the CAN dataset and 99.88% on CICIDS2017 for known attacks, with very high detection rates and extremely low false-alarm rates; the stacking ensemble consistently outperforms individual classifiers. For zero-day detection, it attains an F1-score of 96.3% on the CAN dataset and 80% on CICIDS2017, showing strong capability in identifying unknown attacks.

A further framework, **S2VC (Secure Smart Vehicular Communications)**, is a comprehensive **hardware-software** design that brings together protocol design, cryptographic protection, threat modeling, and AI-based intrusion detection. The methodology starts by constructing robot-car testbeds from PiCarX vehicles equipped with Raspberry Pi 4 controllers, arranged on a structured road map that simulates real intersections to emulate realistic driving conditions. Normal driving scenarios are implemented first, after which internal and external cyberattacks are modeled, countermeasures are deployed, traffic datasets are collected, and ML models are trained for detection, an approach that ties practical vehicular experimentation to AI-driven cybersecurity evaluation. The testbed comprises multiple PiCarX autonomous vehicles, a GPU server acting as a roadside unit, Raspberry Pi 4 controllers, ultrasonic and grayscale sensors, and a structured road environment. Communication runs over TCP, with one port dedicated to normal traffic and another to secure traffic, and the roadside unit serves as a centralized authority that verifies and forwards messages between vehicles. A lightweight application-layer protocol is developed in which each message carries a vehicle identifier, a timestamp, and a message-type flag; these flags define operations such as route requests, hazard reporting, replay detection, edge verification, and debugging, and every message is first sent to the roadside unit, which validates its authenticity before redistribution. The framework also models several realistic attack scenarios. In a poisoning attack, a malicious vehicle transmits false obstacle information; in a replay attack, a man-in-the-middle adversary captures and retransmits earlier messages; and in a denial-of-service attack, the roadside unit is flooded with traffic via automated tools. All attacks are executed directly on the physical testbed to assess resilience. To counter them, S2VC integrates symmetric and asymmetric encryption, digital signatures, hash-based message authentication codes, and timestamp validation, with Unix timestamps embedded in authenticated messages to thwart replay attacks; the system additionally supports negotiation of cryptographic parameters and incorporates jammer-localization techniques. Beyond protocol-level protection, it employs AI-based predictive models for intrusion detection: traffic collected during normal operation and denial-of-service attacks is labeled and used to train several classifiers: J48, k-Nearest Neighbor, Regression, Random Tree, and Random Forest. Detection performance is high, with classification accuracy ranging from 99.23% to 100% across models. Live experiments with packet-capture analysis further validate the protocol's functionality, secure message negotiation, attack execution, dataset generation, and AI-based detection. Together, these results confirm that S2VC delivers both secure communication and intelligent attack detection within a smart vehicular environment.

A further design uses an Adaptive Tree-Based Ensemble Network as the core detection engine of an efficient, accurate, multiclass intrusion detection system for the IoV, one that mitigates class imbalance, reduces computational overhead, and sustains strong detection of both in-vehicle and external attacks. The methodology begins with data processing and balancing, drawing on the CICIDS2017 dataset for external attacks and the Car-Hacking dataset for CAN-bus intra-vehicle attacks. Correlation analysis and ML-based feature-importance techniques, including Random Forest and XGBoost estimators, reduce dimensionality while retaining the most informative attributes. Features are selected until the cumulative importance reaches 95%, and a quantile transformation is applied for normalization to improve robustness to outliers, while a hybrid strategy combining SMOTE oversampling with Random_Under_Sampler resolves class imbalance. The Adaptive Tree-Based Ensemble Network itself adopts a multi-layer cascading structure built from several tree-based models: XGBoost, LightGBM, Random Forest, and Extra Trees. Each layer functions as an ensemble, with its outputs concatenated and passed to the next layer in a cascade, using five-fold cross-validation and recall as the validation metric. The model depth is set adaptively, the cascading process stopping once performance ceases to improve, and softmax loss supports multiclass classification. This layered ensemble marries the efficiency of tree-based models with the representational advantages of deeper architectures, while avoiding the high computational cost of DNNs. Detection is strong throughout: on CICIDS2017 the model achieves an F1-score of 96.5%, reflecting effective multiclass classification and improved detection of minority attack categories, and on the Car-Hacking dataset it reaches an F1-score of 99.99%, indicating near-perfect detection of CAN-based intra-vehicle attacks.

7.5.3 BlockChain secured architecture based Green IDS

A framework named BDTwin integrates blockchain technology with DL-based intrusion detection, organized around two main components: a blockchain-and-smart-contract mechanism and a DL-driven IDS module. Its focus is the security and privacy of Cybertwin-driven V2X applications within the Automotive Industrial Internet of Things. Cybertwin technology creates digital representations of vehicles and infrastructure, anchors communication, and manages digital assets, but publishing and sharing user-generated digital assets can introduce privacy risks. V2X environments compound this difficulty by being decentralized, heterogeneous, and reliant on open wireless channels, leaving them exposed to replay attacks, impersonation, man-in-the-middle attacks, device capture, and data tampering; threats that blockchain-based authentication and secure communication, on their own, often fail to detect.

In BDTwin, the blockchain layer provides secure communication and decentralized trust among vehicles, roadside units, Cybertwin edge servers, and cloud servers. Elliptic Curve Cryptography handles secure registration and authentication; Zero-Knowledge Proof techniques enable identity verification without revealing sensitive credentials; smart contracts on the Ethereum blockchain automatically validate transactions; and an enhanced Proof-of-Work consensus reduces mining difficulty through prior Zero-Knowledge Proof verification. For scalability, raw sensor data are stored off-chain through IPFS and only cryptographic hashes are recorded on-chain, a structure that preserves integrity, authentication, privacy, and non-repudiation. The intrusion detection component runs at the Cybertwin edge servers to ease the computational load on vehicles and roadside units, and it combines three techniques: autoregressive modeling captures temporal patterns in V2X traffic, a DAE[37] performs unsupervised feature extraction and dimensionality reduction, and the resulting latent features are classified by an Attention-Based Bidirectional LSTM. The model is trained with cross-entropy loss and evaluated on the ToN-IoT and CICIDS-2017 datasets. Evaluation covers both blockchain performance and detection effectiveness. The blockchain experiments measure registration time, block creation time, mining delay, smart-contract deployment, gas consumption, and storage overhead, showing that processing time rises with the number of vehicles and the transaction volume while gas consumption grows in proportion to transaction size, and that IPFS improves scalability while keeping stored data securely linked to the blockchain records. The IDS component, for its part, classifies strongly: on ToN-IoT, precision ranges from 89% to 100% across classes, detection rates from 88.78% to 99.91%, and F1-scores from 88.92% to 100%, with a near-zero false-alarm rate; on CICIDS-2017, precision ranges from 83.52% to 99.11%, detection rates from 73.73% to 98.51%, and F1-scores from 71.46% to 98.33%.

A further design is a Collaborative Network Intrusion Detection System that integrates DL, blockchain technology, and reinforcement learning into a scalable, low-latency framework, pairing secure blockchain-based information sharing with reinforcement learning-based trust management to defend against advanced and zero-day attacks in 6G-enabled Vehicle-to-Everything (V2X) networks. It comprises two main components: a DL-based collaborative detection system and a trust-driven blockchain consensus mechanism. In the first component, each blockchain node hosts a local detection module. Incoming network traffic is transformed into two-dimensional binary images, enabling spatial feature extraction through CNNs, after which a dual-level ensemble classifier is applied: at the first level, multiple CNN models, such as ResNet50, DenseNet121, and EfficientNet-B1, extract deep features, and at the second, a Random Forest meta-classifier combines their outputs to improve accuracy. When malicious traffic is identified, a unique hash is generated and recorded as a blockchain transaction, then shared among nodes to enable decentralized threat-intelligence exchange and proactive defense. The second component centers on trust-based blockchain consensus enhanced by reinforcement learning. Each node carries a dynamic trust score derived from its detection accuracy, staking rate, and local blockchain behavior, and Bayesian inference updates these values based on the number of valid and invalid blocks and transactions associated

[37] A Deep Variational Autoencoder is a generative neural network that uses deep encoder and decoder networks to learn a probabilistic latent representation of input data, enabling it to both compress data and generate new samples by sampling from the learned latent distribution.

with the node. To optimize validator selection, a Q-learning agent is introduced, with the reinforcement learning model framed as a Markov Decision Process in which states represent node-behavior conditions and actions correspond to block validation or isolation decisions; the reward function rewards correct, secure choices and penalizes harmful behavior. In testing, the ensemble detection module reaches roughly 99% accuracy with a very low false-positive rate and effective zero-day detection; the reinforcement learning mechanism adapts trust scores and selects reliable validators while isolating malicious nodes, and the blockchain experiments show stable block-validation times, low transaction-propagation delays, and better scalability than traditional consensus mechanisms.

7.5.4 FL based Green IDS for V2X

A Distributed Intrusion Detection (DID) framework adopts a multi-layer C-V2X architecture integrated with federated DL, aiming to provide a distributed, low-latency, and resource-efficient IDS that preserves privacy, reduces communication overhead, and maintains strong detection performance. The system spans three layers: the Radio Access Network layer collects vehicular traffic data; the Multi-Access Edge Computing layer performs feature extraction using CICFlowMeter and trains local DL models; and the cloud layer aggregates the local model parameters into a global model and distributes it back to the edge nodes. This arrangement supports real-time detection at the edge while avoiding centralized data transmission. The framework is evaluated on the CIC-IDS2018 dataset, which provides realistic traffic and multiple attack categories, such as DoS, DDoS, botnet, brute-force, and infiltration. Preprocessing removes invalid records, eliminates irrelevant attributes, applies one-hot encoding, and splits the data into training and testing subsets. Feature selection reduces the original 80 features to 30 significant ones to lower computational complexity. The DL model comprises an input layer of 30 neurons, several hidden layers with ReLU activation, and a Softmax output layer with 12 classes, trained using the Adam optimizer and cross-entropy loss, with learning rate, batch size, and training epochs chosen experimentally. The federated mechanism follows the FedAvg algorithm: a global model is initialized in the cloud and distributed to the edge nodes, each of which trains on local data and returns only its model updates, after which the cloud aggregates them and redistributes the improved model; a collaborative process that strengthens privacy and substantially reduces communication load. The federated DID model detects attacks well, reporting 95.81% accuracy, 92.47% precision, 94.48% recall, a 96.44% F1-score, an AUC of 0.9985, and a false-alarm rate of roughly 0.0094.

7.5.5 Other Green IDS for V2X

A GAN-assisted Contextual Pattern-Aware Intrusion Detection System, called GPIDS, learns contextual cooperation patterns among electronic control units, rather than relying solely on the physical-layer characteristics of In-Vehicle Networks based on the Controller Area Network (CAN) protocol. CAN was designed for closed, isolated environments and offers no built-in encryption, authentication, or access control; once an attacker gains entry through a physical interface such as the OBD-II port or a wireless entry point such as the infotainment or telematics system, malicious messages can be injected onto the CAN bus with little to stop them. GPIDS follows a semi-supervised strategy and is evaluated against six representative attack types: bus-off, spoofing, masquerade, replay, fuzzy, and SOME attacks, with the SOME attack being the hardest to detect, as it preserves the source unit, frequency, voltage characteristics, and identifier sequence. CAN data were collected from four real vehicles under both running and stationary conditions; a 16-frame sliding window was applied, and payloads were standardized before the frames were converted into one-hot-encoded images suitable for GAN processing. The GPIDS architecture comprises a generator, an encoder-decoder structure, a discriminator, and a reconstruction network; rather than taking random noise as input, the model encodes real data into a latent representation, thereby improving convergence and contextual learning. During training, it learns the latent patterns of normal behavior, and during testing, it reconstructs abnormal data, computing the L2 distance between the original and reconstructed latent vectors as an anomaly score; when that score exceeds a predefined threshold, an intrusion is flagged. This mechanism enables detection even when the physical transmission features remain unchanged. Detection is strong across vehicles and attack types, generally above 93% accuracy and reaching 99.11% for spoofing attacks, while for the demanding SOME attack, accuracy ranges from roughly 93% to 98% across vehicles. Table 7.4 presents a comparative analysis of the IDS techniques and frameworks applied in Vehicle-to-Everything and in-vehicle systems for smooth and secure operation.

7.6 Sustainable IDS in indoor environment

Intrusion Detection Systems (IDS) play a critical role in securing indoor environments such as airports and smart homes, where interconnected devices, sensors, and control systems operate continuously over shared networks. In airports, indoor ICT infrastructure supports mission-critical subsystems, including passenger processing, air traffic coordination, surveillance, baggage handling, and energy management, where any cyber intrusion can disrupt operations, cause financial losses, compromise sensitive data, and even threaten human safety. Similarly, smart homes rely on heterogeneous IoT devices, such as cameras, smart locks, voice assistants, lighting systems, device-control systems, and thermostats that often lack robust built-in security controls, making them attractive targets for attackers. Indoor networks are exposed to a wide range of cyber and network-based attacks, including Denial of Service (DoS/DDoS) attacks that make the service-providing devices unavailable, Man-in-the-Middle (MITM) and ARP spoofing attacks that intercept or manipulate communications, reconnaissance and port scanning attacks that probe for vulnerabil-

Table 7.4 Comparative analysis of sustainable IDS techniques in V2X and in-vehicle enviroments.

Technique Category	Model/Framework	Core Methodology	Dataset/Evaluation	Detection Performance	Sustainability/Lightweight Contribution
DRL	A2C–LSTM IDS for SDV	Hybrid Advantage Actor–Critic and LSTM framework for adaptive IDS and mitigation in software-defined vehicle environments. LSTM captures temporal packet behavior, while the actor selects actions such as allow, flag, monitor, and block. The critic evaluates action quality through a reward function balancing true positives, false positives, and resource consumption.	SDV/V2X sequential communication scenarios	Sensitivity approaches nearly 100% after training; overall accuracy reaches about 95–100%; false-positive rate below 0.20 and false-negative rate below 0.10	Explicitly incorporates resource efficiency in the reward function, reducing unnecessary defensive actions and supporting sustainable onboard deployment.
Federated / Trust-aware V2X	CR-V2XR	Decentralized trust-aware framework for V2X roundabouts using local anomaly detection at roadside units, asynchronous FL, spatio-temporal trajectory prediction, latency-aware communication modeling, entropy-based anomaly detection, Stackelberg game-based threshold adjustment, and NSGA-III multi-objective optimization.	OMNeT++, Veins, SUMO; 11 adversarial scenarios	About 95% detection accuracy; collision probability reduced from 0.61 to 0.27; delay typically 45–60 ms under normal conditions	Preserves privacy by sharing parameters instead of raw data and controls communication delay and overhead under real-time safety constraints.
DL	ConvLSTM anomaly detection for connected vehicles	Two ConvLSTM models combine internal OBDII signals and external IoT-assisted smartphone sensing. One downsamples IoT data before fusion, while the other upsamples OBDII data using transposed convolutions. Time-series windows are classified using stacked ConvLSTM layers.	Real vehicle trip data with injected anomalies in engine RPM and speed	Precision up to 98%; recall about 96–97%; F1-score around 97–98%	Improves anomaly detection by fusing low-cost onboard and IoT-assisted sensing without relying on complex external infrastructure.
Hybrid Ensemble DL	SFGL	Stacking framework combining Gradient Boosting Decision Trees, Random Forest, and Bi-LSTM as base learners, with Bi-LSTM as meta-learner. Uses one-hot encoding, Min–Max normalization, ADASYN plus Tomek Links balancing, and Mutual Information feature selection.	CICIDS2017, NSL-KDD	Near-perfect precision, recall, and F1 for most classes; Bot class F1 = 99.6%; infiltration F1 = 86.3%	Feature selection reduces inference latency by about 37% while preserving very high classification performance.

continued on next page

Table 7.4 (*continued*)

Technique Category	Model/Framework	Core Methodology	Dataset/Evaluation	Detection Performance	Sustainability/Lightweight Contribution
Lightweight DL	DeepMLP-based IDS	Multiclass IDS using byte-level feature engineering on CAN data, SHAP-guided feature importance, and a simple multilayer perceptron with two dense layers. SMOTE and random oversampling are used for imbalance handling.	Car-Hacking, Car-Hacking Attack and Defense Challenge, ROAD, CICIDS2017, CSE-CIC-IDS2018	99.99% accuracy and F1-score on in-vehicle datasets; 99.41% accuracy on external communication datasets	Simpler than GAN- and CNN-based alternatives while achieving equal and higher performance with lower computational overhead.
Explainable DL	DeepRed / HypInv two-stage IDS	Two-stage framework where a DNN first performs binary and then multiclass classification. Interpretable rules are extracted using DeepRed and HypInv. Hybrid feature selection and balancing methods improve performance and efficiency.	CIC-IDS2017, CSE-CIC-IDS2018	DeepRed achieves about 98% accuracy on CIC-IDS2017 and 97% on CSE-CIC-IDS2018	Reduces CPU usage, execution time, and memory consumption while improving interpretability and maintaining strong performance.
ML Ensemble	Hybrid ensemble IDS for IoV	Uses K-means representative subset selection, Z-score normalization, Information Gain feature selection, and SMOTE balancing. Base learners include XGBoost, Random Forest, Decision Tree, and Gradient Boosting, combined using bagging, voting, and stacking.	CIC-IDS2017, UNSW-NB15	Stacking achieves 99.75% accuracy and 99.74% F1-score on CIC-IDS2017; 100% accuracy in binary classification on UNSW-NB15	Sampling and feature reduction lower computational burden while ensemble learning preserves high accuracy.
Hybrid ML / Anomaly Detection	Multitiered Hybrid IDS	Four-tier architecture combining supervised and unsupervised learning for known and zero-day attacks. Uses K-means sampling, SMOTE, Bayesian optimization, IG-FCBF-KPCA feature engineering, stacking ensembles, biased classifiers, and K-means-based anomaly filtering.	CAN intrusion dataset, CICIDS2017	99.99% accuracy on CAN; 99.88% on CICIDS2017; zero-day F1 = 96.3% on CAN and 80% on CICIDS2017	Multi-tier design reduces unnecessary complexity and supports both internal and external vehicular networks with low false alarm rates.
Hardware–Software Secure Framework	S2VC	Integrated robot-car testbed framework with protocol design, cryptography, replay protection, hash-based authentication, attack execution, and AI-based IDS using J48, kNN, Regression, Random Tree, and Random Forest.	PiCarX physical testbed with RSU and real attack scenarios	Classification accuracy ranges from 99.23% to 100%	Combines lightweight protocol protection with real-time ML-based attack detection on Raspberry Pi-class hardware.

continued on next page

Table 7.4 (*continued*)

Technique Category	Model/Framework	Core Methodology	Dataset/Evaluation	Detection Performance	Sustainability/Lightweight Contribution
ML Ensemble	Adaptive Tree-Based Ensemble Network	Cascaded multilayer tree-based architecture using XGBoost, LightGBM, Random Forest, and Extra Trees. Feature selection is based on correlation and cumulative importance, with quantile transformation and SMOTE plus undersampling.	CICIDS2017, Car-Hacking dataset	F1-score of 96.5% on CICIDS2017 and 99.99% on Car-Hacking	Avoids heavy DL overhead while retaining deep-representation-such as benefits through cascading tree ensembles.
Blockchain + DL	BDTwin	Blockchain and smart-contract based Cybertwin security framework with ECC authentication, Zero-Knowledge Proof validation, Ethereum smart contracts, IPFS off-chain storage, and an IDS combining autoregressive modeling, DVAE, and attention-based BiLSTM.	ToN-IoT, CICIDS-2017	ToN-IoT F1-score ranges from 88.92% to 100%; CICIDS-2017 F1-score ranges from 71.46% to 98.33%	Off-chain storage improves scalability; IDS is moved to Cybertwin edge servers to reduce burden on vehicles and roadside units.
Blockchain + DL + Reinforcement Learning	Collaborative NIDS for 6G-V2X	Local nodes convert traffic into binary images, classify it using CNN ensembles and a Random Forest meta-classifier, then share alerts through blockchain. Reinforcement learning and Bayesian trust update are used for consensus and validator selection.	6G-enabled V2X collaborative setting	About 99% detection accuracy with low false positive rate and effective zero-day detection	Distributes detection and trust decisions across nodes, improving scalability and reducing centralized latency bottlenecks.
Federated DL	DID framework	Multi-layer C-V2X architecture with CICFlowMeter feature extraction at edge nodes and federated DL using FedAvg. Cloud aggregates only model parameters rather than raw traffic data.	CIC-IDS2018	Accuracy 95.81%; precision 92.47%; recall 94.48%; F1-score 96.44%; AUC 0.9985	Reduces communication overhead and preserves privacy while enabling real-time detection at MEC nodes.

continued on next page

Table 7.4 *(continued)*

Technique Category	Model/Framework	Core Methodology	Dataset/Evaluation	Detection Performance	Sustainability/Lightweight Contribution
GAN-based Semi-supervised IDS	GPIDS	GAN-assisted contextual pattern-aware IDS for CAN networks. Uses sliding windows, one-hot encoding, latent-space reconstruction, and anomaly scoring based on L2 distance between latent representations.	CAN data from four real vehicles; six attack types	Detection accuracy generally above 93%; up to 99.11% for spoofing; 93–98% for SOME attack	Learns contextual ECU cooperation patterns without relying on expensive physical-layer features, supporting efficient in-vehicle deployment.
Airport IDS / DL	Deep-FFNN airport IDS	Deep feedforward neural network with feature selection through back-elimination regression, normalization, and binary attack classification.	DARPA/KDD 1999	Accuracy 99.86%; detection rate 99.83%; false alarm rate 0.16%	Achieves high detection accuracy with a relatively simple architecture and reduced feature set.
FL + Differential Privacy	DP-FL + KD + CNN-GRU	Federated learning architecture for airport IDS with Gaussian-noise differential privacy, teacher–student knowledge distillation, CNN-GRU teacher model, lightweight student model, and denoising adaptive optimization.	Airport subsystem client-server setting	Minority attack detection improves by up to 30%; converges under strong privacy budget $(0.1, 10^{-5})$	Maintains privacy, improves minority-class detection, and reduces model complexity through knowledge distillation.
Two-level AI IDS	Multi-level AI-based IDS for airport/indoor IoT	Two-stage system with binary detection followed by attack classification. Evaluates LDA, kNN, Bagging Ensemble, and Decision Tree after preprocessing, tokenization, one-hot encoding, and normalization.	Seven IoT subdatasets	Decision Tree achieves nearly perfect and perfect accuracy on most datasets; above 99.97% in many multiclass settings	Decision Tree offers the best balance between detection performance and execution time compared with more expensive ensemble models.

ities, ransomware targeting internal systems, botnet infections exploiting weak IoT credentials, replay attacks, firmware exploitation, and data leakage due to weak encryption. Because many of these attacks originate from the local network or through compromised IoT devices, IDS solutions, particularly those capable of anomaly detection, device profiling, and attack classification, are essential to continuously monitor indoor network traffic, identify malicious behavior in real time, and enable rapid response mechanisms to protect both operational continuity and occupant safety. In this section, the chapter discusses the current status of sustainable IDS in indoor environments, such as smart airports and homes.

7.6.1 Sustainable IDS in airport network

An anomaly-based intrusion detection system built on a Deep Feedforward NN (Deep-FFNN) achieves high accuracy while keeping a very low false-alarm rate in airport environments. Airports are highly interconnected environments where disruptions can cause significant economic losses, operational instability, and risks to passenger safety. The model is trained and evaluated on the DARPA/KDD 1999 dataset, which contains network-traffic records with 41 features across multiple attack categories. Feature selection is applied first, using a backward-elimination regression method based on statistical significance to discard irrelevant attributes and retain 36 meaningful features that support the detection of both known and unknown attacks. All features are then normalized to keep NN training balanced, and categorical attributes are appropriately encoded. The Deep-FFNN comprises two hidden layers of 18 neurons each and performs binary classification between normal and attack traffic. It performs strongly, achieving 99.86% accuracy, a 99.83% detection rate, and a false-alarm rate of just 0.16%.

A further framework combines differentially private federated learning with knowledge distillation and a hybrid CNN-GRU model to deliver an IDS that improves minority-attack detection while holding a balanced privacy-utility trade-off in time-sensitive airport environments. Its architecture spans three layers: the Security Operation Center serves as the server and coordinates model aggregation; IDS nodes within airport subsystems train local models using Gaussian noise injection to satisfy differential-privacy requirements; and aviation operation systems act as clients that generate local data and apply user-level privacy protection, with federated learning implemented under the (ϵ, δ)-differential privacy model. The detection engine adopts a teacher-student structure. The teacher model combines convolutional layers for spatial feature extraction with a two-phase GRU module for temporal pattern learning, followed by fully connected layers, while the student is a lightweight version guided by knowledge distillation through soft targets and a combination of cross-entropy and Kullback-Leibler divergence losses; Random Under-Sampling is applied to ease class imbalance. The framework also introduces a denoising adaptive parameter-update mechanism that modifies the Adam optimizer by incorporating a noise-regularization factor and correcting differential-privacy noise during aggregation, thereby improving convergence and mitigating the adverse effects of the injected noise. In testing, knowledge distillation speeds convergence and markedly improves minority-attack detection, the CNN-GRU with distillation achieving more balanced classification with minority-attack detection rising by up to 30%; and under strong privacy constraints with a target budget of $(0.1, 10^{-5})$, the denoising optimizer converges within a small number of communication rounds while sustaining higher accuracy.

A two-level artificial intelligence-based intrusion detection framework tailored to IoT environments is an intelligent, efficient, multi-level IDS that detects malicious activity and classifies attack types across heterogeneous IoT devices while maintaining acceptable processing time. It operates in two stages: the first performs binary classification to separate normal from malicious traffic, and the second, triggered when traffic is judged malicious, classifies the specific attack type. Several classifiers are evaluated including Linear Discriminant Analysis, k-Nearest Neighbors, a Bagging Ensemble, and Decision Tree with preprocessing that removes missing or irrelevant data, converts non-numeric attributes to numeric form, applies tokenization and one-hot encoding, and normalizes features. Across all of them, the Decision Tree offers the best balance of high detection accuracy and low computational cost. Performance is strong across all seven IoT subdatasets: in binary classification, the Decision Tree reaches near-perfect or perfect accuracy in most cases: 100% on the IoT-Fridge and IoT-Garage Door datasets and 99.99% on the IoT-GPS Tracker and IoT-Modbus datasets, and although the Bagging Ensemble often matches this accuracy, it requires considerably longer execution time. In multiclass classification, the Decision Tree again performs well, exceeding 99.97% accuracy on most datasets, with only a small number of attacks misclassified, such as occasional confusion between ransomware and XSS attacks or between scanning and password attacks.

7.6.2 Sustainable IDS in smart homes

Smart homes integrate heterogeneous IoT devices such as cameras, smart locks, voice assistants, lighting systems, and thermostats, which often lack robust built-in security controls, making them attractive targets for attackers. IDS solutions capable of anomaly detection, device profiling, and attack classification are essential for continuously monitoring indoor network traffic and identifying malicious behavior in real time.

7.6.2.1 ML based Green IDS for Smart Homes

A three-layer supervised intrusion detection architecture profiles heterogeneous IoT devices, detects malicious network activity, and classifies the type of attack targeting devices in a smart-home environment. Smart-home IoT devices have limited computational power, support diverse communication protocols, and lack robust built-in security. The first layer performs device profiling, identifying devices by their MAC addresses and learning their normal network behavior; the second classifies network packets as benign or malicious; and the third, invoked when malicious traffic is found, determines the specific attack category: denial-of-service, man-in-the-middle, scanning, IoT-toolkit attacks, and so on. A realistic smart-home testbed was built from eight commercial IoT devices, and network traffic was captured over several weeks, three of normal activity and two of malicious activity, with multiple attack scenarios implemented to mimic realistic adversarial behavior. Rather than relying on deep packet inspection, the system extracts 121 packet-level features from protocol headers, including Ethernet, IP, TCP, and ICMP fields, excluding payload data so as to remain compatible with encrypted traffic, and feature-selection techniques then isolate the most relevant attributes. Performance is strong across all three tasks: the weighted-average F-measure reaches 99.7% for device profiling, 97.0% for malicious-packet detection, and 99% for attack-type classification, dipping only slightly on unseen validation data while remaining high. The most influential features are TCP flags, IP flags, packet length, ICMP fields, and destination ports. With its lightweight, computationally efficient feature extraction and fast classification, the approach supports real-time operation and is well-suited for deployment in resource-constrained smart-home environments.

A modular IDS reference architecture is built from four main components. The first is a network-level anomaly module that performs network behavior analysis using flow-based statistics drawn from packet captures: IPFIX flows are generated from the network and converted into time-series features; ten indicators of compromise are defined to catch anomalies such as denial-of-service, scanning, spoofing, brute force, and command-and-control activity, and statistical methods including the Moving Average and Exponentially Weighted Moving Average flag deviations from normal traffic. The second is an application-level anomaly module that monitors smart-device telemetry to detect false-command and false-data injection attacks, combining a PCA-with-Q-residual detector that identifies inconsistent variable values with a K-Nearest Neighbor temporal detector that spots abnormal daily power-consumption behavior. The third integrates a signature-based system using Snort to detect known attacks via predefined rules, and the fourth is a correlation module that aggregates alerts from the others to produce meaningful alarms and reduce false positives. Validation drew on the AMPds dataset, which records electrical consumption for 21 devices over one year, and detection proved strong across the modules. The network-level module detected every network attack with at least one indicator of compromise, achieving detection rates near 100% for single attacks and between 86 and 100% for simultaneous attacks, depending on overlap conditions, and very low false-positive and true-negative rates, exceeding 99% in most cases. The PCA-based detector reached an average geometric mean of roughly 89%, rising to 99.4% when anomalous devices were excluded from training, while the KNN detector scored between 80 and 91% with true-negative rates consistently above 99%. The Snort signature module detected only four of twelve attacks, underscoring the complementary value of anomaly-based detection. In terms of efficiency, the network module processed more than 12 million packets in under 250 seconds, and the application module processed over 900,000 samples in less than a minute, with memory usage remaining below 165 MB.

An ensemble-based intrusion detection model, **LGB-IDS**, is built on the Light Gradient Boosting Machine classifier and achieves high accuracy, low false alarms, and strong time efficiency while effectively handling imbalanced datasets. It is evaluated on the DS2OS dataset, which collects network traffic from simulated IoT smart-home environments and comprises 13 features across 1 benign class and 7 attack classes; its pronounced imbalance makes classification challenging. Preprocessing covers data cleaning, removal of irrelevant attributes such as timestamps, conversion of categorical values to numeric form, label encoding, and one-hot encoding, while feature engineering and reduction eliminate redundant attributes and lower computational complexity. The model employs leaf-wise tree growth, gradient-based one-sided sampling, exclusive feature bundling, and histogram-based decision-tree learning, with hyperparameters such as tree depth, number of estimators, and learning rate tuned to optimize performance. Classification proves strong: the technique reaches 99.92% accuracy on both training and testing data, with very low mean absolute error and root mean squared error indicating minimal prediction error, and a threat-detection rate above 90% alongside low false alarms.

A two-layer ML-based IDS is lightweight, accurate, and decentralized enough to run directly on IoT devices while still enabling multiclass classification in the cloud. The first layer operates on the device, embedded in an ESP32-based smart thermostat via TinyML; it performs binary classification to distinguish normal from malicious traffic and shields the device against major attack types. The second layer is deployed in the cloud on AWS and performs multiclass classification to identify specific attack categories, including DoS, DDoS, brute force, injection, ransomware, port scanning, MITM, and backdoor attacks. The system is trained on the TON_IoT dataset, along with a custom dataset collected from a real ESP32 thermostat and a Raspberry Pi adversary. Several models are evaluated, including XGBoost, Random Forest, LSTM, MLP, and Conv1D for the cloud layer, and XGBoost, Decision Tree, Random Forest, and an ANN[38] for the device layer, alongside feature-selection methods such as Chi-square[39] and PCA[40], with TinyML[41] tools used to embed the trained models into the microcontroller. Both layers perform strongly. At the cloud level, XGBoost achieves the highest accuracy at 99.50%, with high precision and recall and very low inference

[38] An Artificial Neural Network is a computational model inspired by the structure of the biological brain, consisting of interconnected layers of nodes (neurons) that learn to recognize patterns and map inputs to outputs by adjusting weighted connections during training.

[39] Chi-square is a statistical test that measures the dependence between two categorical variables by comparing observed and expected frequencies, commonly used in feature selection to identify the input features most relevant to the target class.

[40] PCA is a dimensionality-reduction technique that transforms correlated features into a smaller set of uncorrelated variables (principal components) that capture the maximum variance in the data, simplifying datasets while preserving essential information.

[41] TinyML is a field focused on deploying lightweight, optimized machine-learning models on extremely resource-constrained, low-power devices such as microcontrollers, enabling on-device inference at the edge without reliance on cloud computing.

time; Random Forest closely matches it, while LSTM and Conv1D fare less well. At the device level, the embedded XGBoost model achieves 99.92% accuracy with very low false-positive and false-negative rates. Although the Decision Tree offers faster inference, XGBoost is chosen for its slightly better detection performance. Real-time testing on the custom dataset shows that the embedded IDS detects MITM and DoS attacks within a few milliseconds, achieving 97.59% accuracy. Together, these results confirm the feasibility of running a lightweight, accurate ML-based IDS directly on IoT devices while coordinating with a cloud-based multiclass detection system.

7.6.2.2 DL based Green IDS for Smart Homes

FDeep is a fog-based DL-IDS for smart-home IoT environments, organized across three layers: the IoT layer, the fog layer, and the cloud layer. Its central idea is to place the DL model in the fog layer, between the IoT devices and the cloud. Network traffic is first captured at IoT gateways using packet-sniffing tools and converted into feature sets, after which the fog-layer model performs attack detection and classification, with periodic retraining on newly collected traffic to keep detection accuracy from drifting over time. Three models are implemented and compared: LSTM, CNN, and a hybrid CNN-LSTM, using the TON/IIoT dataset, which contains real IoT device traffic and multiple attack types including DoS, DDoS, ransomware, scanning, password attacks, injection, backdoor, and cross-site scripting. The hybrid CNN-LSTM performs best overall: on the IoT weather-sensor dataset it reaches 98.02% accuracy, with comparable precision, recall, and F1-score, outperforming the standalone LSTM and CNN models. On the thermostat dataset, performance is lower: the CNN-LSTM achieves 76.19% accuracy, a drop attributable mainly to dataset imbalance.

FL-SUSP is a FL framework that integrates knowledge distillation, cognitive confidence scoring, personalized weighting, and server-side parameter optimization. In smart homes, devices such as cameras, thermostats, and smart locks generate traffic with distinct patterns and attack distributions; some clients may lack certain attack types entirely, while others hold only a narrow subset of classes. Under such heterogeneity, conventional FL algorithms like FedAvg suffer from client drift, in which local models become biased toward their dominant classes, weakening the global model and degrading detection performance. The architecture comprises a client module and a server module. On the client side, each participant keeps a local labeled dataset, an unlabeled distillation dataset, a local model, and a domain discriminator: the local model generates soft labels for the distillation data, while the domain discriminator gauges how familiar each sample is to the client, quantifying this as a Cognitive Confidence Score. Soft labels are then weighted by that score, so reliable predictions carry more importance and uncertain ones receive little or none; a personalized weighting strategy that curbs the harm of unreliable knowledge transfer. On the server side, weighted soft voting aggregates client predictions to produce higher-quality pseudo-labels for the distillation dataset; rather than simple parameter averaging, the server selects top-performing local models by cosine similarity, performs weighted aggregation, and further refines the global model using the newly labeled distillation data. This self-updating mechanism adapts better to heterogeneous data distributions and mitigates client drift. Evaluated on the N-BaIoT dataset, FL-SUSP achieves 83.94% accuracy and an 82.35% F1-score for benign traffic and botnet attacks such as Mirai and Gafgyt, a substantial improvement over weaker baselines.

HiFINS, a Hierarchical Federated Learning-based Interactive Network Security framework, offers a scalable, privacy-preserving, real-time intrusion detection system that joins hierarchical federated learning to human-centered interaction. It is organized into three coordinated tiers: at the first, edge devices or routers carry out local traffic monitoring and model training; at the second, edge servers aggregate and validate intermediate model updates; and at the third, a cloud-level global model coordinates and refines the overall learning process. The system is implemented using a modified hierarchical federated learning pipeline built on the Flower framework, with local models trained on real-world smart-home network traffic and the CICIoT2023 dataset. A discriminator component identifies adversarial inputs and reduces the risk of poisoning attacks during aggregation, while the optimization objective combines cross-entropy loss for classification accuracy, an adversarial loss for robustness, and a feedback-aware term derived from user interactions. HiFINS performs strongly across the standard metrics: accuracy, precision, recall, F1-score, and AUC. Although the initial training phase yields slightly lower precision due to traffic imbalance, a false-positive refinement mechanism, combined with user feedback, reduces redundant alerts by roughly 44% while maintaining recall above 99%. Computational performance is also assessed by training time, CPU utilization, and inference throughput, and the hierarchical refinement strategy further improves the global model's generalization without compromising privacy.

2FIDS is a Fog-Federated Learning-based Intrusion Detection System deployed at the fog layer, offering a privacy-preserving, scalable, low-latency design for fog-assisted smart homes that reduces communication overhead and energy consumption while maintaining strong detection performance. Its architecture spans three layers: an edge layer of IoT devices that collect network traffic; a fog layer of nodes, such as routers and hubs, that perform local model training; and a cloud layer that provides storage and management but takes no part in training, thereby limiting privacy exposure. The detection engine is an LSTM-based DL classifier trained through federated learning; each fog node trains a local LSTM on its private data and sends only model updates to the fog server, which aggregates them through a median-based method to blunt the effect of poisoning attacks, with secure communication ensured by gRPC over TLS encryption and 8-bit model quantization and compression applied to trim communication overhead. Detection proves stable and scalable. Across the BoT-IoT and TON-IoT datasets, overall accuracy holds around 96% even as the number of participating fog nodes grows, and on the more complex MQTTset dataset it stays above 86%. Per-attack evaluation shows high F1-scores for most categories, though some, including MitM, flood, and malformed MQTT messages, perform relatively less well. With quantization and compression, transmission delay falls from roughly 50 milliseconds to 5-10 milliseconds, and communication overhead drops from about 4 MB to 1 MB per training round, a reduction of around 75%. On the whole, the framework shows that federated DL at the fog layer can deliver accurate, efficient intrusion detection while preserving privacy in smart-home IoT systems.

A hybrid DL architecture combining CNNs with Long Short-Term Memory networks offers an accurate, low-latency, scalable, and energy-efficient IDS for smart homes. The framework moves through four stages: data collection, preprocessing, CNN-based feature extraction, and LSTM-based temporal classification. Data are collected from network traffic logs, IoT device logs, system logs, and application logs using monitoring tools such as Wireshark and Tcpdump. During preprocessing, corrupted and redundant entries are removed, numerical features are normalized, class imbalance is addressed, and relevant attributes such as packet inter-arrival time and payload entropy are extracted. The CNN component then learns spatial features from network-traffic matrices through convolution and max-pooling, reducing dimensionality and improving robustness to noise, after which the extracted features pass to the LSTM module to capture temporal dependencies in sequential traffic; through its forget, input, and output gates, the LSTM models long-term attack behavior and detects stealthy or slowly evolving threats. In testing, the CNN-LSTM model achieves 98.2% accuracy, higher than the CNN-RNN, Random Forest, SVM, and Decision Tree models, and achieves the highest precision and recall, indicating reliable classification of both normal and malicious traffic, with a false-positive rate of just 1.3%.

7.6.2.3 Blockchain based Green IDS for Smart Homes

A three-layer architecture combines ML, SHAP-based explainability, and blockchain integration to produce an intrusion detection framework that is accurate, explainable, and secure, drawing on Explainable Artificial Intelligence for interpretability and blockchain for tamper-resistant logging of activity on smart-home networks. It is trained and evaluated on the RT-IoT2022 dataset, which holds over 100,000 traffic records, 83 features, and 12 attack categories. Preprocessing removes non-informative attributes, converts categorical features to numerical form, handles missing values, and divides the data into training and testing subsets. In the first phase, six ML models: Naïve Bayes, K-Nearest Neighbors, Multi-Layer Perceptron, Support Vector Machine, Logistic Regression, and Random Forest, are trained on all available features. In the second phase, SHAP identifies the 30 most influential features by Shapley value, and the same models are retrained using only those features, thereby sharpening interpretability by making clear which attributes drive each prediction. Finally, a blockchain layer securely records detection outcomes: timestamps, attack types, affected devices, and detection results are stored in smart contracts, ensuring transparent auditing and tamper-proof storage of network logs. SHAP-based feature selection improves most classifiers, with Random Forest performing best: its accuracy rises from 98% to 99%, with near-perfect precision, recall, and F1-score after optimization, while K-Nearest Neighbors and Naïve Bayes show moderate gains, and the others remain stable or dip slightly. The framework holds up well even under class imbalance.

7.7 Sustainable IDS in smart agriculture

Smart Agriculture, also known as Agriculture 4.0, refers to the application of modern digital technologies to traditional farming practices. It combines information and communication technologies, the Internet of Things, artificial intelligence, cloud computing, and data analytics to improve productivity, sustainability, and profitability while reducing environmental impact. Sensors continuously collect environmental and operational data, which is processed locally or in the cloud to support real-time decision-making and automated control. The transition toward smart agriculture is motivated by global challenges such as food insecurity, climate change, water scarcity, and rapid population growth. By using digital tools, farmers can manage irrigation, fertilization, pest control, harvesting, and logistics with greater precision and reduced waste. A smart agriculture system consists of several interconnected technological components. IoT devices and sensors form the foundation of the system by collecting real-time data from soil, crops, and livestock. These include soil moisture sensors, temperature and humidity sensors, pH sensors, light intensity sensors, water level monitors, and animal health tracking devices. Actuators and automated control systems respond to sensor data by adjusting irrigation, dispensing fertilizers, regulating greenhouse ventilation, or supporting robotic harvesting. Communication infrastructure enables data exchange among devices and control platforms using technologies such as Wi-Fi, LoRaWAN, ZigBee, NB-IoT, cellular networks, and satellite links. This interconnected ecosystem is often described as the Internet of Agricultural Things. Data processing occurs either at the edge, through local gateways or embedded devices for low-latency decisions, or in the cloud for large-scale analytics, artificial intelligence modeling, and long-term storage. Artificial intelligence and data analytics support applications such as crop disease prediction, irrigation optimization, livestock anomaly detection, weather forecasting, and supply chain management. Farmers interact with these systems through management dashboards, mobile applications, and web-based platforms.

Despite its benefits, smart agriculture introduces significant cybersecurity risks due to its reliance on interconnected IoT devices, wireless communication, and cloud services. Device-level vulnerabilities include weak authentication, default credentials, outdated firmware, and limited processing power for security mechanisms. Network-level risks arise from unencrypted communication, insecure wireless protocols, and poor network segmentation, making systems vulnerable to interception and spoofing. At the cloud level, threats include data breaches, unauthorized access, insecure APIs, and insider misuse. Agricultural data may contain sensitive operational and financial information, which increases the consequences of security failures. Distributed Denial of Service attacks can disrupt irrigation or monitoring services by overwhelming network resources. Man-in-the-Middle attacks allow adversaries to intercept and manipulate communication between devices. Ransomware can lock access to farm management platforms or IoT controllers. Data injection attacks may falsify sensor readings, leading to incorrect automated decisions. Reconnaissance and scanning activities help attackers identify weaknesses before launching more serious intrusions. Compromised IoT devices may also form botnets to participate in large-scale attacks. In addition, insider threats can arise when authorized users misuse their privileges.

Given the dependence of smart agriculture on automated and real-time systems, security breaches can cause crop damage, financial loss, resource waste, supply chain disruption, environmental harm, and even risks to national food security. Intrusion Detection Systems play a critical role in protecting these environments. An IDS continuously monitors network traffic, detects abnormal behavior, and generates alerts when potential threats are identified. IDS solutions may be network-based, monitoring traffic across the agricultural network, or host-based, focusing on individual devices. Because traditional signature-based systems cannot identify unknown or evolving threats, ML and DL approaches are increasingly adopted. These intelligent systems analyze traffic patterns, detect anomalies, and classify multiple attack types, thereby improving the resilience and reliability of smart agriculture infrastructures. This section discusses the existing successful IDS techniques and frameworks applied in the Smart Agriculture area.

7.7.1 ML based Green IDS for smart agriculture

A hybrid framework named DKPLS-KELM provides a specialized intrusion detection approach for smart agriculture, aiming to improve detection accuracy while reducing computational complexity and redundant features. It works in two stages, dimensionality reduction and classification. The first applies a modified Downsized Kernel Partial Least Squares method for feature extraction: conventional Kernel Partial Least Squares handles nonlinear relationships well but generates large kernel matrices that inflate memory use and processing time, so the downsized version shrinks the kernel matrix by retaining only the most informative latent components and representative observations, preserving essential discriminative information at lower cost. The second stage uses a Kernel Extreme Learning Machine for classification; the Extreme Learning Machine is a single-hidden-layer NN prized for fast training, and the kernel-based extension sharpens its ability to model nonlinear data. By pairing efficient feature reduction with fast nonlinear classification, the framework supports both binary and multi-class detection in smart-agriculture environments. Evaluation drew on the X-IIoTID dataset, a modern industrial IoT intrusion dataset spanning multiple attack types and heterogeneous feature views such as network traffic, host logs, and alert data, and covered binary classification, nine-class attack detection, and eighteen-class attack detection. Performance is strong throughout: binary classification reaches 99.92% accuracy with perfect sensitivity and very high specificity; the nine-category setting attains nearly 100% overall accuracy, with particularly high detection rates for RDoS and Command and Control attacks; and in the eighteen-class scenario most categories hold accuracy above 99.75%.

7.7.2 DL based Green IDS for smart agriculture

A hybrid DL-based IDS deployed within a three-tier Agriculture 4.0 architecture offers a robust, scalable, and computationally efficient detection framework tailored to Agriculture 4.0 systems, with particular emphasis on reliable DDoS detection. The architecture comprises an Edge Agri-IoT Sensor layer, a Fog Intermediate Decentralized layer, and a Cloud Centralized layer, with the IDS implemented chiefly at the fog layer to enable near-real-time detection while reducing dependence on the cloud. It draws on the CIC-DDoS2019 dataset, which captures realistic DDoS traffic. Preprocessing includes data cleansing, encoding, Z-score normalization for robustness to outliers, and feature reduction, using a basic autoencoder to compress the original 85 features into an 18-feature latent representation, thereby reducing redundancy and computational overhead while preserving meaningful patterns. For binary detection, a deep autoencoder is trained on benign traffic only; this unsupervised approach allows the model to learn normal behavior and identify anomalies through reconstruction errors. The network combines multiple hidden layers, ReLU activation in the encoder, sigmoid activation in the decoder, mean squared error as the loss, and the Adam optimizer, with an anomaly threshold defined from the mean and standard deviation of the reconstruction errors; a strategy that naturally mitigates data imbalance by focusing on normal data and treating deviations as potential attacks. After binary detection, HDBSCAN clusters the multi-class attacks; it is chosen because it needs no predefined number of clusters, detects clusters of varying density, and handles noise well. Pairing deep-autoencoder anomaly detection with density-based clustering sharpens both granularity and robustness. On CIC-DDoS2019 the framework performs strongly, achieving binary classification accuracy above 98% with high precision, recall, and F1-score depending on configuration, and testing of different autoencoder architectures identifies the optimal depth and hidden-node structure. On the whole, the hybrid IDS delivers accurate, computationally efficient DDoS detection, well-suited to Agriculture 4.0 environments.

A hybrid DL-based IDS deployed within a three-tier Agriculture 4.0 architecture offers a robust, scalable, and computationally efficient detection framework tailored to Agriculture 4.0 systems, with particular emphasis on reliable DDoS detection. The architecture comprises an Edge Agri-IoT Sensor layer, a Fog Intermediate Decentralized layer, and a Cloud Centralized layer, with the IDS implemented chiefly at the fog layer to enable near-real-time detection while reducing dependence on the cloud. It draws on the CIC-DDoS2019 dataset, which captures realistic DDoS traffic. Preprocessing includes data cleansing, encoding, Z-score normalization for robustness to outliers, and feature reduction using a basic autoencoder to compress the original 85 features into an 18-feature latent representation, thereby reducing redundancy and computational overhead while preserving meaningful patterns. For binary detection, a deep autoencoder is trained only on benign traffic; this unsupervised approach allows the model to learn normal behavior and identify anomalies through reconstruction errors. The network combines multiple hidden layers, ReLU activation in the encoder, sigmoid activation in the decoder, mean squared error as the loss, and the Adam optimizer, with an anomaly threshold defined from the mean and standard deviation of the reconstruction errors; a strategy that naturally mitigates data imbalance by focusing on normal data and treating deviations as potential attacks. After binary detection, HDBSCAN clusters the multi-class attacks; it is chosen because it needs no predefined number of clusters, detects clusters of varying density, and handles noise well. Pairing deep-autoencoder anomaly detection with density-based clustering sharpens both granularity and robustness. On CIC-DDoS2019 the framework performs strongly, achieving binary classification accuracy above 98% with high precision, recall, and F1-score depending on configuration, and testing of different autoencoder architectures identifies the optimal depth and hidden-node structure. On the whole, the hybrid IDS delivers accurate, computationally efficient DDoS detection well suited to Agriculture 4.0 environments.

A similar kind of three-layer IDS for smart agriculture comprises a sensing layer, a fog computing layer, and a cloud layer. The sensing layer holds agricultural sensors and drones that gather real-time data; the fog computing layer hosts the intrusion detection system and performs local analysis to cut detection latency; and the cloud layer handles centralized storage and service management. Placing the IDS at the fog layer allows attacks to be identified and mitigated before traffic ever reaches the cloud. The evaluation draws on two benchmark datasets: APA-DDoS and ToN-IoT. The detection model, the **FOCB** framework, integrates several techniques: during preprocessing, label encoding converts categorical features to numerical values, and Min-Max normalization scales them to the range [0, 1]. At its core is a fusion model joining BiGRU[42] with CNN, structured as an input layer, a BiGRU layer that captures forward and backward temporal dependencies in network traffic, an attention layer that weights important features more heavily, a convolutional layer for deeper feature extraction, and a Softmax output layer; the BiGRU structure models sequential traffic patterns efficiently while keeping computational complexity lower than that of traditional recurrent networks. To further sharpen performance, the model employs Wild Horse Optimization, a nature-inspired metaheuristic that tunes parameters such as weights and biases by minimizing the classification error rate, thereby improving both accuracy and stability. On the APA-DDoS dataset the model achieves 99.35% accuracy, 99.90% precision, 98.99% recall, and a 99.08% F-measure, with the confusion matrix confirming accurate classification of DDoS-PSH-ACK, DDoS-ACK, and benign traffic. On the ToN-IoT dataset, it achieves 99.71% accuracy, 99.89% precision, 99.05% recall, and 99.85% F-measure, with reasonable training and prediction times and faster operation than ConvNeXt-based alternatives.

[42] A Bidirectional Gated Recurrent Unit (BiGRU) is a recurrent neural network architecture that processes sequential data in both forward and backward directions using two GRU layers, allowing it to capture context from both past and future states for richer temporal feature representation.

A multi-stage methodology integrates data preprocessing, feature engineering, image transformation, CNN-based classification, and hyperparameter optimization to yield an optimized CNN-based intrusion detection system that detects intrusions in agricultural IoT networks accurately while reducing computational complexity. It uses the NSL-KDD dataset, which contains 43 features and several attack categories: DoS, Probe, Privilege, and Access. Preprocessing removes null values, applies one-hot encoding to categorical features, and eliminates redundant or zero-variance attributes. Correlation and collinearity checks retain only the most relevant attributes. Because the dataset is initially imbalanced, SMOTE[43] generates synthetic minority samples to balance the class distribution. For further dimensionality reduction, Recursive Feature Elimination with a Random Forest wrapper identifies the most informative attributes, paring the feature set to 9 essential features, thereby lowering computational cost and improving stability. A distinctive element is the conversion of tabular traffic data into image form: after normalization to a 0-255 pixel range, groups of 27 consecutive records, each with nine features, are combined into $9 \times 9 \times 3$ RGB images, each labeled normal or attack by its composition; allowing convolutional networks, designed for image classification, to be brought to bear on intrusion detection. Three pre-trained CNN architectures are evaluated: VGG16, Inception, and Xception, each combining convolutional layers for feature extraction, pooling layers for dimensionality reduction, and fully connected layers for binary classification. To further improve performance, hyperparameter optimization combines Random Search with Particle Swarm Optimization, with the latter adjusting parameters such as the number of frozen layers, learning rate, dropout rate, number of epochs, and early-stopping patience to aid convergence and reduce the risk of local minima. The results show clear gains. With default hyperparameters, VGG16 reaches 97.89% accuracy and a 97.88% F1-score, outperforming Inception and Xception; after Random Search optimization, it rises to 98.26% accuracy; and when optimized with Particle Swarm Optimization, the VGG16 model attains 99.99% accuracy, precision, and recall, with a near-perfect F1-score. The optimized CNN-based IDS thus delivers highly accurate intrusion detection in smart agricultural IoT networks while remaining computationally efficient.

A three-part methodological framework combines standardized preprocessing, a lightweight NN design, and extensive multi-dataset benchmarking to produce a lightweight, reproducible, and dataset-independent DL-IDS; one that achieves high accuracy across heterogeneous IoT datasets while remaining suitable for resource-constrained agricultural edge devices. The first part is a unified preprocessing pipeline applying StandardScaler normalization, undersampling to curb majority-class dominance, SMOTE to balance minority classes, and Tomek Links to remove noisy or borderline samples; this standardized pipeline improves generalization and

[43] SMOTE is a data-balancing algorithm that addresses class imbalance by generating synthetic samples for the minority class through interpolation between existing minority instances and their nearest neighbors, rather than simply duplicating them.

reduces overfitting while addressing class imbalance. The second is a lightweight feedforward DNN with a 256-128-64-Softmax architecture, using ReLU activation, batch normalization, 30% dropout, the Adam optimizer at a learning rate of 0.0001, and categorical cross-entropy loss; with roughly 1.2 million parameters, this design shortens inference time, lowers memory use, and avoids extensive hyperparameter tuning, making it suitable for microcontroller-class hardware. The third is a comprehensive benchmark across 18 public IoT intrusion detection datasets, including CICIDS2017, BoT-IoT, UNSW-NB15, ToN-IoT, MQTT-IoT2020[44], CIC-IoT2022[45], Car-Hacking[46], WSN-DS[47], and the agriculture-specific Farm-Flow dataset collected from a hydroponic greenhouse.

Performance is strong and stable throughout. The model achieves an average accuracy of 99.14% and maintains at least 97% accuracy across all tested datasets, reaching a perfect 100% on Car-Hacking, N-BaIoT, and CIC-IoT2022; on CICIDS2017 it scores 99.2%, and on UNSW-NB15 and BoT-IoT it scores 99.7% and 99.8%, respectively. The agriculture-focused Farm-Flow dataset yields a multi-class accuracy of 93.32%, reflecting the complexity of real-world greenhouse traffic. Binary tasks produce near-perfect confusion matrices, while multi-class performance dips mainly in highly imbalanced or overlapping attack categories. In comparison, the lightweight network performs competitively with, and often better than, more complex CNN-LSTM, Transformer, federated learning, and blockchain-integrated models, confirming that a carefully designed lightweight architecture can achieve high detection accuracy while remaining practical for sustainable smart-agriculture deployment.

A hybrid DL architecture combines BiGRU, LSTM, and a Softmax classifier to produce an edge-deployable intrusion detection system that analyzes long time-series traffic efficiently and reduces computational overhead while preserving high accuracy. The model stacks two BiGRU layers of 200 and 100 neurons, followed by two LSTM layers of 100 and 50 neurons, with a dropout rate of 0.3 to mitigate overfitting; ReLU and Softmax activations are used, and training uses categorical cross-entropy loss with the Adam optimizer. The BiGRU layers capture both forward and backward temporal dependencies in network traffic; the LSTM layers model long-range dependencies and mitigate vanishing-gradient problems;

---

44 MQTT-IoT2020 (MQTT-IoT-IDS2020) is a benchmark intrusion detection dataset generated from a simulated MQTT-based IoT network, containing normal traffic and several MQTT-related attacks (such as brute-force, scanning, and flooding) for evaluating IDS in publish-subscribe IoT environments.

45 CIC-IoT2022 is a benchmark dataset developed by the Canadian Institute for Cybersecurity that captures realistic network traffic from a large testbed of diverse real IoT devices, profiling normal device behavior and various attacks to support IoT security analysis and intrusion detection.

46 Car-Hacking is an in-vehicle network intrusion detection dataset that contains Controller Area Network (CAN) bus traffic with normal messages and injected attacks (such as DoS, fuzzy, and spoofing of RPM/gear), used to evaluate IDS for automotive and in-vehicle security.

47 WSN-DS is a specialized wireless sensor network intrusion detection dataset that captures normal traffic and four types of denial-of-service attacks (Blackhole, Grayhole, Flooding, and Scheduling/TDMA) based on the LEACH routing protocol, designed for evaluating IDS in WSN environments.

and the Softmax layer performs multi-class attack classification. To further improve efficiency, the system applies TBPTT: rather than processing entire time sequences during training, it divides long sequences into smaller windows, reducing memory usage, lowering training complexity, and accelerating convergence; all of which are well-suited to edge deployment. Preprocessing removes missing and infinite values, normalizes the data, and configures the model for multi-class classification. Detection is strong across datasets, with the system reaching 99.82% accuracy on CIC-IDS2018, 99.55% on ToN-IoT, and 98.32% on Edge-IIoTset. Precision, recall, and F1-scores stay consistently high: F1-scores above 99% for CIC-IDS2018 and ToN-IoT and 97.82% for Edge-IIoTset, while false-positive and false-negative rates remain very low, confirming robust classification. The efficiency evaluation is notable: applying TBPTT cuts testing time on CIC-IDS2018 from 76 seconds to 14, with comparable reductions on ToN-IoT and Edge-IIoTset. The hybrid BiGRU-LSTM model with truncated training thus provides accurate, efficient, and edge-feasible intrusion detection for smart-agriculture systems operating in demanding environments.

A Privacy-Encoding-Based Enhanced Deep Learning (PEDL) framework integrates privacy protection with anomaly detection through two main components: a privacy enhancement unit and an intrusion detection unit. The privacy enhancement unit comprises feature mapping, feature selection, feature normalization, and a Sparse Capsule Auto-Encoder, while the detection unit employs an Attention-Based GRU. The defining idea is that detection operates on encoded representations of IoT data rather than on the raw data itself, thereby strengthening privacy. During preprocessing, categorical features are converted to numerical form, Mutual Information selects the most relevant features and discards redundant ones, and Min-Max normalization scales features to the range [0, 1] to stabilize training. The SCAE is central to privacy preservation, combining capsule-autoencoder principles with sparsity constraints enforced via Kullback-Leibler divergence; it minimizes reconstruction error using mean squared error loss and produces encoded vector representations that reduce the risk of inference or reconstruction attacks while retaining the patterns essential for detection. Using these encoded representations, the Attention-Based GRU then performs detection: alongside standard reset and update gates, it incorporates an attention mechanism that weights different time steps in the traffic sequence, allowing the model to concentrate on critical temporal features and improve detection of complex attack behavior. Evaluated on the ToN-IoT and IoT Botnet datasets, both spanning multiple attack categories, the framework performs strongly: roughly 99.9% accuracy, 99.7% recall, 99.9% precision, and a 99.8% F1-score, with confusion-matrix and ROC analyses confirming its detection strength. Crucially, the privacy encoding does not diminish accuracy, showing that strong security and robust privacy protection can be achieved together in smart-agriculture IoT systems.

7.8 Existing challenges in adapting IDS in different scenarios

Although many energy-efficient and fast-response IDSs have been proposed to protect IoT-enabled environments against cyberattacks and data theft, several persistent limitations persist across diverse smart application domains. In practice, many IDS solutions struggle with high false-positive rates, limited adaptability to new or zero-day attacks, performance degradation under class imbalance, and insufficient scalability for large-scale deployments. In addition, resource constraints at the edge, such as limited CPU, memory, bandwidth, and battery capacity, continue to hinder the practical deployment of advanced DL-based detection models. Privacy preservation, interoperability across heterogeneous devices, and real-time processing requirements further complicate IDS deployment in smart agriculture, healthcare, transportation, and smart home systems.

Therefore, despite notable progress, significant research gaps remain. This section outlines the major technical and operational limitations observed in existing IDS approaches and discusses potential directions for future work. These may include lightweight model design, federated and privacy-preserving learning frameworks, adaptive and self-learning detection mechanisms, improved strategies for handling class imbalance, explainable AI integration, and energy-aware optimization techniques. Addressing these challenges will be essential to developing robust, scalable, and sustainable IDS solutions for next-generation IoT ecosystems.

7.8.1 Limitations of existing IDS techniques in smart cities and potential solutions

Although intrusion detection systems have improved significantly in IoT-enabled smart cities, several important limitations still persist.

- First, centralized IDS architectures face scalability and latency challenges. Cloud-based detection frameworks require continuous transmission of large volumes of traffic data to central servers. This increases communication overhead and delays response time. Such delays are unacceptable for time-sensitive smart city services, including traffic management, smart grid control, emergency response systems, and healthcare monitoring.
- Second, IoT devices are inherently resource-constrained. Most sensors and edge nodes operate with limited battery capacity, processing power, and memory. As a result, deploying complex cryptographic algorithms or DL models directly on these devices is often impractical. Many IDS designs assume adequate computational resources, which does not reflect the reality of large-scale wireless sensor networks deployed across urban environments.
- Third, energy consumption remains a major concern. Security mechanisms increase both computation and communication costs, which can significantly reduce the operational lifetime of IoT networks. Many traditional secure

communication and routing frameworks focus primarily on detection accuracy while neglecting energy optimization. This threatens the long-term sustainability of smart city infrastructures.

- Fourth, centralized architectures introduce single points of failure and trust vulnerabilities. A compromised central controller or aggregation server can disrupt the entire detection process. Such bottlenecks reduce system resilience and increase exposure to targeted attacks.
- Fifth, IDS models often struggle to adapt to evolving threats. While artificial intelligence-based detection improves classification accuracy, these models are vulnerable to adversarial manipulation. Carefully crafted inputs can mislead detection systems, leading to false positives or false negatives and reducing operational reliability.
- Finally, lack of explainability and interoperability limits real-world deployment. Many ML and DL models operate as black boxes. Security administrators may find it difficult to interpret detection decisions. In addition, integrating IDS solutions across heterogeneous smart city infrastructures remains challenging due to differences in protocols, standards, and device capabilities.

To overcome these challenges, future IDS frameworks for smart cities should adopt distributed, energy-aware, and adaptive architectures.

- First, existing studies indicate that semi-distributed and fully distributed IDS models should move detection functions closer to the edge or fog layer. Edge-based analytics reduce latency, lower communication overhead, and prevent centralized bottlenecks. This approach supports faster response times for critical smart city services.
- Second, energy-aware security design must be integrated into IDS frameworks. Routing, clustering, and data aggregation strategies should consider residual energy and link stability. Combining security enforcement with energy-efficient communication mechanisms can extend network lifetime without compromising detection performance.
- Third, decentralized trust mechanisms, such as lightweight blockchain frameworks, can improve transparency, data integrity, and resilience to single points of failure. However, energy-efficient consensus mechanisms are necessary to avoid excessive computational overhead in IoT environments.
- Fourth, adaptive AI-driven detection models should be employed. Ensemble learning, metaheuristic optimization, and self-learning classifiers can improve accuracy while adapting to new attack patterns. Incorporating adversarial training and robust learning strategies can enhance resilience to adversarial attacks in ML.
- Fifth, federated learning offers a promising approach for privacy-preserving collaborative detection. It enables distributed nodes to share model updates instead of raw data. This improves global threat awareness while maintaining data confidentiality.
- Finally, integrating Software-Defined Networking (SDN) and Network Function Virtualization (NFV) can provide dynamic traffic monitoring and programmable

security policies. These technologies enhance flexibility, scalability, and rapid mitigation of detected threats.

In summary, addressing the limitations of existing IDS techniques requires a balanced combination of distributed intelligence, energy efficiency, privacy preservation, and adaptive security mechanisms. Such advancements are essential for building resilient and sustainable smart-city infrastructure.

7.8.2 Limitations of existing IDS techniques in IIoT and potential solutions

Despite rapid advances in ML, DL, federated learning, and blockchain-based security mechanisms, intrusion detection systems in Industrial Internet of Things (IIoT) environments still face several persistent challenges.

- One major limitation is the difficulty of maintaining extremely low false positive rates. IIoT systems often operate in safety-critical infrastructures such as power plants, manufacturing lines, and industrial control systems. In these environments, false alarms can interrupt production processes or trigger unnecessary shutdowns. Although many modern DL models report high accuracy, achieving near-zero false positives under real industrial traffic conditions remains challenging.
- Another critical issue is the resource constraint of edge devices. Many proposed IDS models rely on complex architectures such as CNN-LSTM hybrids, attention-based networks, or deep ensembles. These models demand substantial computational power, memory, and energy. However, IIoT edge nodes typically operate with limited hardware capacity. This mismatch makes direct deployment of heavy models impractical for real-time industrial monitoring.
- Data imbalance and scarcity also reduce detection reliability. Industrial datasets often contain a large proportion of normal traffic and very few samples of rare attacks. Even when techniques such as oversampling, generative models, or hybrid sampling are applied, minority-class misclassification remains a concern. Zero-day and open-set attacks further complicate detection, as models trained on predefined categories may fail to recognize previously unseen threats.
- Generalization and adaptability present additional limitations. Many IDS models are trained and evaluated on benchmark datasets. Their performance may degrade when exposed to heterogeneous industrial environments, evolving attack strategies, or adversarial manipulation. Offline training approaches struggle to maintain robustness in dynamic operational settings.
- Privacy and centralization issues further restrict deployment. Centralized learning architectures require transmitting sensitive industrial data to aggregation servers. This introduces privacy risks and creates single points of failure. While federated learning addresses some of these concerns, it introduces new challenges, including communication overhead, non-independent data distributions, model-poisoning risks, and trade-offs between differential privacy and accuracy.

- Interpretability and trust remain essential concerns. DL models often function as black boxes. Industrial operators and regulatory authorities require transparent explanations for security decisions. Without explainability, high-performing models may still face resistance in safety-critical deployments.
- In addition, optimization complexity and computational overhead complicate implementation. Metaheuristic-based tuning and hybrid architectures improve detection performance but increase training cost and system complexity. Blockchain-integrated frameworks enhance integrity and tamper resistance, yet they may introduce latency, scalability limitations, and additional resource consumption. Moreover, emerging threats such as adversarial ML and future quantum-capable attackers highlight vulnerabilities that current IDS designs rarely address.
- Finally, limited real-world validation remains a significant gap. Many studies demonstrate strong experimental accuracy but provide limited testing in large-scale, heterogeneous industrial deployments with strict timing constraints and protocol diversity.

To address these limitations, future IIoT IDS frameworks should focus for lightweight, privacy-preserving, explainable, and adaptive IDS architectures as discussed below:

- Future IIoT IDS frameworks adopt lightweight, adaptive, and privacy-preserving designs. Model compression techniques such as pruning, quantization, and knowledge distillation can reduce computational cost while maintaining accuracy. Two-tier architectures that combine edge-level pre-filtering with fog or cloud-level verification can balance real-time detection and analytical depth.
- Advanced data-balancing strategies and open-set recognition methods should be integrated to improve minority-attack detection and zero-day resilience. Continuous and online learning mechanisms, including reinforcement learning and incremental training, can help models adapt to evolving traffic patterns without catastrophic forgetting.
- Secure federated learning frameworks must incorporate robust aggregation, poisoning detection, and adaptive privacy controls to ensure collaborative yet secure training. Explainable AI techniques, such as feature attribution and attention visualization, should be embedded into IDS design to enhance operator trust and regulatory compliance.
- Lightweight blockchain mechanisms and consortium-based models may strengthen trust and secure logging without imposing excessive overhead. In parallel, research should explore post-quantum cryptographic approaches to future-proof industrial cybersecurity systems.

Ultimately, a cross-layer, multi-level IDS architecture that integrates network traffic analysis, device behavior profiling, and cyber-physical monitoring across the edge, fog, and cloud layers can provide greater resilience. By integrating anomaly detection, signature analysis, adaptive intelligence, and trust management, IIoT security frameworks can achieve a balanced combination of accuracy, efficiency, scalability, and robustness suitable for real-world industrial environments. In addition, federated learning, knowledge distillation, hybrid deep models, and blockchain-based trust management should be combined to build resilient and sustainable Industrial IoT security frameworks.

7.8.3 Limitations of existing IDS techniques in connected healthcare and potential solutions

Intrusion Detection Systems in healthcare environments, especially within Internet of Medical Things ecosystems, face several important limitations, which are listed below:

- One major concern is the reliance on centralized architectures. Many healthcare organizations store patient records and train detection models in centralized repositories. This design creates single points of failure and increases the risk of large-scale data breaches. It also raises regulatory concerns under frameworks such as GDPR and HIPAA. When IDS models are trained on centralized datasets, sensitive patient information may be exposed or misused.
- Another limitation arises from the heterogeneous and resource-constrained nature of IoMT devices. Healthcare networks include wearable monitors, implantable devices, bedside systems, and remote sensors. These devices operate with limited battery capacity, memory, and processing power. As a result, complex ML and DL models are often too heavy to run directly on them. This restricts the feasibility of real-time, device-level intrusion detection and shifts the burden to external infrastructure.
- High false-positive and false-negative rates also remain a serious operational challenge. Healthcare systems function in safety-critical environments where incorrect alerts can interrupt medical workflows and delay treatment. At the same time, undetected attacks may endanger patient safety and compromise sensitive medical data. Many data-driven IDS models are biased toward dominant traffic patterns and struggle to capture the diverse and dynamic behavior of medical networks.
- Limited adaptability to new and evolving threats further reduces system reliability. Healthcare infrastructure is a frequent target of ransomware, botnets, and data manipulation attacks. Signature-based detection methods cannot detect unknown attack patterns, whereas supervised models rely on labeled datasets that may not capture emerging threats. This makes long-term resilience difficult to achieve.
- Interoperability and trust management across distributed healthcare entities add another layer of complexity. Hospitals, clinics, laboratories, and remote monitoring services operate under different administrative and technical environments. Traditional IDS frameworks do not sufficiently support secure collaboration or coordinated model updates across these domains.

To address these limitations, future healthcare IDS solutions should focus on the following stated solutions:

- Future IDS targeting for connected healthcare systems should adopt decentralized, privacy-preserving, and adaptive designs. Federated learning offers an effective approach by enabling collaborative model training without sharing raw patient data. Each institution trains a local model and shares only the model parameters, thereby reducing privacy risks while maintaining detection performance.
- Blockchain technology can strengthen trust and accountability within distributed healthcare networks. Immutable ledgers and smart contracts can secure model update validation, identity management, and logging processes. This reduces reliance on centralized servers and enhances transparency across stakeholders.
- Lightweight anomaly-based detection techniques should also be prioritized. Instead of relying exclusively on labeled attack data, these approaches learn patterns of normal healthcare traffic and identify deviations as potential intrusions. Such methods are better suited to environments where labeled attack data is limited.
- Deploying IDS components at the edge layer can further improve responsiveness. By placing detection modules at IoT gateways or local servers, healthcare systems can reduce latency and mitigate threats more quickly before they propagate.
- Finally, explainable artificial intelligence should be integrated into healthcare IDS frameworks. In clinical settings, decision-makers must understand the reasoning behind security alerts. Interpretable models improve user trust and support regulatory compliance.

Overall, a multi-layer architecture that combines IoMT devices, edge computing, federated learning, blockchain, and explainable detection mechanisms can provide a balanced and resilient security framework. Such an approach enhances privacy, scalability, and reliability while meeting the strict safety and regulatory requirements of modern healthcare systems.

7.8.4 Limitations of existing IDS techniques in V2X and potential solutions

Intrusion Detection Systems in Vehicle-to-Everything and Internet of Vehicles environments face several persistent technical and operational challenges. They are:

- One major limitation is the computational complexity of many DL-based models. Although these models often achieve high detection accuracy, they require substantial memory and processing power. Vehicular onboard units and roadside edge nodes typically operate under strict hardware and energy constraints. As a result, many advanced IDS architectures are difficult to deploy directly in real-time vehicular systems.
- Another challenge arises from centralized training approaches. Centralized ML frameworks require large volumes of vehicular data to be transmitted to a central server. In highly dynamic V2X networks, where vehicles frequently change location and connectivity conditions fluctuate, centralized aggregation becomes inefficient and vulnerable. It increases bandwidth usage, introduces latency, and

creates single points of failure. Moreover, sharing raw vehicular data raises privacy concerns, especially when location and behavioral information are involved.

- Adversarial robustness and zero-day attack detection also remain significant concerns. V2X systems are exposed to sophisticated threats, including data poisoning, evasion attacks, and adversarial manipulation of ML models. Many IDS solutions are evaluated using benchmark datasets that do not fully capture the diversity and unpredictability of real vehicular traffic. Consequently, their performance may degrade in real-world deployments.
- Imbalanced datasets and complex multiclass attack scenarios further reduce detection reliability. Vehicular datasets often contain a large proportion of normal traffic and limited examples of certain attack types. While oversampling and ensemble methods help mitigate imbalance, many systems still rely on binary classification. This limits their ability to distinguish among multiple coordinated or multi-stage attacks, which are common in connected vehicle environments.
- Explainability and trust are equally important challenges. DNNs generally operate as black-box systems. In safety-critical automotive contexts, regulatory frameworks require transparent and interpretable decision-making. Without explainable outputs, security alerts may not be trusted by system operators or may fail to meet compliance requirements.
- Collaborative misbehavior detection mechanisms are not yet fully integrated with collective perception and cooperative communication standards. The absence of standardized coordination between intrusion detection, trust management, and cooperative awareness messages weakens overall system resilience in connected vehicle ecosystems.

To overcome these limitations for Green IDS in V2X, real practitioners need to adapt several precautions which are given below:

- Future V2X IDS frameworks should adopt lightweight, adaptive, and collaborative designs. Model compression, pruning, and knowledge distillation techniques can reduce computational overhead while maintaining acceptable accuracy. Resource-aware and slice-adaptive IDS models can further improve feasibility in real-time vehicular networks.
- Federated learning offers a privacy-preserving alternative to centralized training. Vehicles and edge nodes can collaboratively update global models without sharing raw data. This reduces bandwidth consumption and enhances privacy. However, secure aggregation and poisoning-resistant mechanisms must be incorporated to protect the federated process from adversarial manipulation.
- Blockchain integration can strengthen distributed trust and tamper resistance. Immutable logging, decentralized validation, and secure identity management can improve accountability in cooperative V2X communication. When combined with adaptive trust management strategies, blockchain-based frameworks can enhance resilience in large-scale vehicular systems.
- Hybrid and multitier IDS architectures also provide a balanced solution. Combining signature-based detection with anomaly-based analysis improves

zero-day detection while maintaining low latency. Two-stage and rule-extraction models can enhance interpretability and operational transparency.

- Advanced ensemble and multiclass classification strategies should be adopted to improve attack differentiation. Integrating data balancing methods, adaptive feature selection, and stacking approaches can enhance generalization and performance under diverse traffic conditions.
- A holistic security architecture that integrates intrusion detection, misbehavior detection, collaborative perception validation, and real-time risk assessment is essential for future autonomous and connected vehicle systems. Such a multi-layered framework will better align with the safety, scalability, and trust requirements of next-generation V2X environments.

7.8.5 Limitations of existing IDS techniques in smart airports and potential solutions

Smart airports represent highly complex cyber-physical ecosystems integrating IoT devices, industrial control systems, baggage handling systems, passenger flow management, surveillance, and airside operations. Existing intrusion detection techniques face several limitations in such environments. They are:

- One major limitation of existing IDS approaches is their reliance on centralized architectures. In many cases, security data from different airport subsystems are collected and processed at a central security operations center. While this approach simplifies monitoring, it introduces privacy risks, increases communication overhead, and creates single points of failure. Transmitting raw operational data, such as passenger flow statistics or baggage system logs, may also raise confidentiality and regulatory concerns.
- Another significant challenge is the highly imbalanced distribution of attack data. In real airport environments, malicious events occur far less frequently than normal operational traffic. Traditional supervised learning models depend on sufficient labeled attack samples to learn effective decision boundaries. When attack instances are rare, these models often fail to detect minority or emerging threats. As a result, detection performance for sophisticated or low-frequency attacks may degrade.
- Privacy-preserving solutions introduce additional complexity. Differential privacy techniques, often integrated with federated learning frameworks, protect sensitive data by adding controlled noise to model updates. Although this improves privacy protection, the injected noise can slow convergence and slightly reduce classification accuracy. Achieving an appropriate balance between privacy guarantees and detection effectiveness remains a key challenge for smart airport IDS deployment.
- Operational constraints further complicate IDS design. Many artificial intelligence-based detection systems focus primarily on maximizing accuracy. However, smart airports require real-time detection, high system availability, interoper-

ability across heterogeneous devices, and compliance with strict aviation safety standards. Edge devices may also have limited computational resources, which restricts the deployment of complex DL models. In addition, explainability is essential in aviation contexts, where security alerts must be transparent and justifiable.
- Traditional signature-based systems are also inadequate for detecting coordinated, multi-stage, or zero-day attacks that target interconnected airport subsystems. Static rule-based approaches cannot adapt quickly to evolving threat strategies in dynamic airport networks.

To address these limitations, various strategies and precautions need to be adopted to enable a Green IDS system for a smart airport. They are:

- A comprehensive and distributed IDS strategy is necessary. Federated learning-based architectures can reduce privacy risks by allowing local airport subsystems to train models independently and share only model parameters. This approach minimizes raw data transfer and reduces reliance on centralized aggregation. Advanced techniques such as adaptive clipping and denoising mechanisms can help maintain detection performance while preserving privacy.
- Imbalance-aware learning methods should also be incorporated. Techniques such as cost-sensitive learning, semi-supervised training, knowledge distillation, and synthetic minority oversampling can improve the detection of rare attack classes. These strategies enhance model sensitivity without excessively increasing false alarms.
- Deploying lightweight IDS modules at edge or fog nodes can significantly reduce detection latency. Localized analysis near operational systems allows faster response to anomalies, which is critical in time-sensitive airport operations. Explainable AI methods should be integrated to provide interpretable alerts and improve administrator trust.
- Hybrid detection approaches offer additional benefits. Combining anomaly detection with behavior profiling and contextual awareness enables better identification of complex or previously unseen threats. Finally, continuous learning mechanisms, including adaptive federated updates and transfer learning, can help IDS models evolve alongside emerging cyber threats. Such a multi-layered and adaptive framework can strengthen the long-term resilience of smart airport security infrastructures.

In summary, future IDS frameworks for smart airports should emphasize distributed privacy-preserving learning, lightweight edge deployment, imbalance-aware modeling, explainability, and adaptive threat-intelligence integration to achieve secure, resilient, and real-time cyber defense.

7.8.6 Limitations of existing IDS techniques in smart home and potential solutions

IDS in smart home environments have improved significantly through the use of ML, distributed architectures, and federated learning. However, several important limitations remain. They are:

- A major challenge is the presence of resource-constrained, heterogeneous devices. Smart homes include low-power IoT devices that operate over various communication protocols, including Wi-Fi, ZigBee, and proprietary stacks. Many advanced ML and DL models achieve high detection accuracy, including ensemble, gradient boosting, and CNN-LSTM approaches. Yet these models often require computational power and memory that exceed the capabilities of embedded home devices. Even lightweight or TinyML-based solutions introduce trade-offs between model simplicity, detection coverage, and scalability.
- Privacy and centralization issues also persist. Traditional IDS frameworks frequently rely on centralized data aggregation and model training, which increases communication overhead and raises concerns about user privacy. Although federated and hierarchical federated learning frameworks reduce the need to share raw data, they introduce coordination complexity, synchronization delays, and potential vulnerabilities, including model poisoning and unreliable edge nodes. Ensuring secure and efficient collaboration among distributed devices remains an ongoing challenge.
- Another limitation involves adaptability to zero-day and evolving attacks. Signature-based components cannot detect new or previously unseen threats. Supervised learning approaches depend heavily on labeled datasets, which may not accurately represent the diversity of real smart home environments. Furthermore, adversarial ML techniques can manipulate IDS models by introducing carefully crafted perturbations, thereby reducing detection reliability.
- False positives and usability concerns further restrict practical adoption. Smart home residents are usually non-technical users. Excessive false alarms, especially in anomaly-based systems, can lead to alert fatigue and reduced trust in the system. Many IDS solutions do not sufficiently consider economic constraints, ease of installation, and user experience in residential settings. As a result, technically sound systems may fail in real-world deployment.
- The absence of standardized architectures and benchmarking frameworks limits reproducibility and fair comparison. Many studies evaluate performance on public datasets that do not fully capture the heterogeneity and dynamics of real smart-home networks. This weakens generalizability and complicates large-scale adoption.

To overcome these limitations, a holistic and context-aware strategy is required. In addition to it, several precautions and updated techniques are required to adapt. They are discussed below:

- Hybrid hierarchical architectures can provide a balanced solution. Lightweight anomaly detection modules can operate on devices, while more complex analysis and collaborative learning can be performed at the fog or edge layer. Adaptive model partitioning can dynamically distribute computation according to device capability.
- Privacy-preserving federated learning frameworks should be strengthened with secure aggregation, differential privacy, and model validation mechanisms to reduce poisoning risks. Incorporating adversarial training techniques can further enhance robustness against manipulation.
- Semi-supervised and unsupervised anomaly detection methods can reduce reliance on labeled datasets and improve adaptability to evolving traffic patterns. Continual learning strategies can allow incremental updates without degrading previously learned knowledge.
- Human-centered design is equally important. IDS systems should provide clear, interpretable alerts and actionable recommendations through user-friendly dashboards. Integrating explainable AI techniques can increase transparency, reduce confusion, and improve trust among non-technical residents.
- Standardized and modular reference architectures should be developed to support reproducible evaluation and cross-comparison. Future benchmarking efforts should incorporate realistic multi-protocol traffic and real-world attack scenarios. Such comprehensive and practical approaches can enhance the reliability, scalability, and usability of IDS solutions in smart home environments.

To summarize, a future-ready solution for Green IDS in smart homes lies in lightweight hierarchical federated architectures, privacy-preserving and adversarially robust learning, adaptive anomaly detection, and human-centered system design. Such an integrated approach can significantly enhance the resilience and practical viability of IDS deployment in real-world smart-home ecosystems.

7.8.7 Limitations of existing IDS techniques in smart agriculture and potential solutions

Despite achieving very high reported accuracies (often above 99%), current IDS solutions for smart agriculture exhibit several recurring limitations. They are listed here:

- A primary concern is the presence of resource constraints at the edge. Many proposed models rely on DL architectures such as CNN-BiGRU, hybrid GRU/LSTM networks, or transfer learning ensembles. Although these approaches achieve strong detection performance, they require considerable memory, processing power, and energy. Smart agriculture environments depend on battery-powered sensors, low-power gateways, and unstable connectivity. Deploying heavy models in such conditions increases energy consumption and inference latency, which can limit real-time farm operations.

- Another limitation is the lack of adaptability to dynamic and extreme agricultural environments. Farming systems operate under changing weather conditions, seasonal variations, and fluctuating device availability. However, many IDS models are trained offline using static public datasets. These models are rarely designed to adjust continuously to seasonal traffic changes, new device deployments, or evolving attack strategies. As a result, runtime adaptability remains limited.
- Dataset dependency and weak generalization also pose challenges. Numerous IDS solutions are validated using benchmark datasets such as CIC-DDoS2019, ToN-IoT, or Edge-IIoTset. Although these datasets are useful for comparison, they may not fully represent real agricultural deployments such as greenhouse monitoring, irrigation systems, or livestock management networks. High performance on benchmark datasets does not guarantee robustness across heterogeneous farm environments or unseen attack types.
- Privacy protection is another area that requires stronger attention. Some studies propose privacy-preserving encoding mechanisms, yet many IDS frameworks still rely on centralized training or cloud-based aggregation. Agricultural data, including crop yield information, irrigation schedules, and operational configurations, can be sensitive. Centralized data collection may expose such information to unnecessary risks.
- The absence of coordinated multi-layer task placement reduces scalability. While certain designs adopt fog-cloud architectures, most systems do not specify how detection tasks should dynamically shift among the sensor, edge, fog, and cloud layers based on energy availability, latency requirements, or threat severity. Static deployment strategies limit flexibility and reduce long-term sustainability.
- Energy awareness is also often treated as a secondary objective rather than a core design principle. Although lightweight NNs have been proposed, few IDS solutions explicitly optimize detection decisions while accounting for computational cost, communication overhead, and battery usage. This contradicts the sustainability goals that smart agriculture aims to achieve.

To address these limitations, future IDS designs for smart agriculture should move toward adaptive, energy-aware, and context-driven architectures. In addition, some precautions and adaptable techniques are necessary for IoT-based Smart Agriculture. They are:

- Detection tasks should be distributed intelligently across multiple layers. Lightweight anomaly screening can be performed at the sensor or edge level, while complex deep analysis can be offloaded to fog or cloud layers only when necessary. Such utility-based allocation can balance energy consumption and latency requirements.
- Adaptive and online learning mechanisms should replace purely static training. Incremental learning, continual learning, and domain adaptation can allow IDS models to adjust to new device types, seasonal traffic patterns, and emerging

threats without complete retraining. Privacy-preserving federated learning can further support distributed model training while keeping sensitive farm data local.
- Energy-efficient model compression, pruning, and knowledge distillation techniques can reduce computational overhead while maintaining high accuracy.
- Cross-dataset validation and benchmarking with real agricultural traffic traces should be emphasized to improve domain-specific robustness.
- Integrating contextual information, such as irrigation cycles, weather conditions, and device roles, into detection logic can reduce false positives and help distinguish legitimate agricultural anomalies from malicious activity. Together, these improvements can enhance the reliability, scalability, and sustainability of IDS solutions in smart agriculture environments.

In summary, while existing IDS techniques for smart agriculture demonstrate impressive classification accuracy, they remain limited by computational overhead, dataset dependency, insufficient runtime adaptivity, and weak integration of energy and privacy considerations. The next generation of smart agriculture IDS must transition from accuracy-centric designs to sustainable, adaptive, and utility-driven detection ecosystems that align cybersecurity protection with the environmental and operational constraints of modern precision farming systems.

CHAPTER

Green intrusion detection for real-world IoT deployments

8

8.1 Introduction

The use and adoption of the Internet of Things (IoT) across transportation systems, smart cities, renewable energy networks, and industrial automation are increasing every day, transforming modern infrastructure into highly interconnected cyber-physical ecosystems. While this connectivity improves operational efficiency, automation, and data-driven decision-making, it simultaneously increases exposure to cyber threats. Intrusion Detection Systems (IDS) have therefore become a critical component in safeguarding IoT-enabled environments. However, unlike conventional IT networks, IoT systems operate under strict resource constraints, including limited computational capacity, restricted memory, intermittent connectivity, and constrained energy availability. In such environments, achieving high detection accuracy alone is insufficient. IDS frameworks must also be energy-efficient, scalable, adaptive, and suitable for deployment in real-world, low-power conditions.

This chapter introduces the concept of Green Intrusion Detection Systems (Green IDS) for real-world IoT deployments. Green IDS extends traditional intrusion detection by integrating cybersecurity objectives with sustainability considerations. It emphasizes lightweight model design, distributed intelligence across edge-fog-cloud layers, energy-aware ML, and lifecycle-oriented deployment strategies. The goal is to ensure that intrusion detection mechanisms not only identify malicious activities effectively but also operate within acceptable computational and energy budgets.

To ground the discussion in practical implementation, this chapter consolidates detailed case studies across three major domains: IoT-based transportation systems, renewable energy-enabled smart networks, and secured Industrial IoT automation. Each domain presents unique operational constraints and threat models. Transportation systems require millisecond-level response times and the feasibility of edge deployment. Renewable energy IoT networks must maintain availability under fluctuating power conditions. Industrial automation demands low false-alarm rates and protocol-aware detection within safety-critical control loops. By analyzing lightweight IDS models, distributed architectures, FL frameworks, blockchain-assisted designs, and energy-optimized DL techniques altogether, this chapter evaluates how green design principles can be translated into operational practice.

Green Intrusion Detection Systems for IoT. https://doi.org/10.1016/B978-0-44-344249-0.00015-6

Beyond performance metrics such as accuracy, precision, recall, and F1-score, this chapter incorporates computational overhead, inference latency, memory footprint, and energy consumption as primary evaluation dimensions. Through comparative analysis, best practices and deployment guidelines are derived to support future IDS development in sustainable IoT ecosystems. The central contribution of this chapter lies in bridging theoretical Green AI concepts with domain-specific implementation insights, providing a structured roadmap for designing intrusion detection systems that are secure, adaptive, and environmentally responsible.

8.2 Performance evaluation metrics

In ML, an Intrusion Detection System (IDS) is typically formulated as a binary classification problem, where the presence of an intrusion or security attack is treated as the positive class (1) and legitimate or normal network traffic is treated as the negative class (0). The objective of the IDS model is to accurately distinguish malicious activities from benign traffic using learned patterns derived from network features. This formulation enables the use of standard supervised learning algorithms and evaluation metrics derived from the confusion matrix. However, in IoT environments, detection accuracy alone is not sufficient. IoT devices are often highly resource-constrained, operating with limited computational capability, memory, and battery power. Therefore, IDS techniques designed for IoT systems must not only achieve high detection performance but also be energy-efficient. Excessive computational overhead can rapidly deplete device batteries and degrade overall system sustainability. To comprehensively evaluate IDS models in IoT-based systems, multiple performance metrics are considered. These include Accuracy, Precision, Recall, F1-score and so on for assessing detection effectiveness. At the same time, computational cost, inference time, memory usage, and energy consumption are evaluated to determine system efficiency. The collective assessment of these metrics helps determine whether a proposed IDS model achieves an optimal balance between high detection capability and low energy consumption, which is critical for practical deployment in IoT environments.

Let us consider in general,

- **TP (True Positive)** = Number of attack instances correctly detected as attacks
- **TN (True Negative)** = Number of normal instances correctly classified as normal
- **FP (False Positive)** = Number of normal instances incorrectly classified as attacks (False Alarm)
- **FN (False Negative)** = Number of attacks incorrectly classified as normal (Missed Attack)

8.2.1 Precision

Precision measures how many of the detected intrusions are actually real intrusions. It reflects the impact of the false-alarm rate. High precision means that the IDS does not frequently issue false alarms. Mathematically, it is calculated with the following equation:

$$Precision = \frac{TP}{TP + FP} \tag{8.1}$$

In practical IDS deployment, High precision means fewer false alarms, whereas low precision increases the operational burden because security analysts must investigate numerous false alarms.

8.2.2 Recall

Recall measures the number of actual intrusions successfully detected by the IDS. It reflects the system's ability to minimize missed attacks. Mathematically, it is calculated with the following equation:

$$Recall = \frac{TP}{TP + FN} \tag{8.2}$$

In cybersecurity, high recall means that most intrusions or attacks are detected, whereas low recall is considered dangerous for IoT networks because many attacks go undetected, potentially compromising the system.

8.2.3 F_1-score

The F_1-score is the harmonic mean of Precision and Recall, providing a single metric that balances between False alarms (FP) and missed attacks (FN). It is helpful to understand a technique's performance when it is applied to an imbalanced dataset (i.e., one that is not evenly distributed across classes). In mathematics, the F_1-Score is calculated using the following equation:

$$F_1 = 2 * \frac{Precision * Recall}{Precision + Recall} \tag{8.3}$$

In practice, a high F_1 Score indicates a good balance between attack detection and false-alarm mitigation, whereas a low F_1 Score indicates either poor accuracy in intrusion/attack detection or excessive false alarms. This metric is widely adopted in IDS studies because accuracy or precision alone can be misleading in highly imbalanced intrusion datasets.

8.2.4 Energy metric Joule

A joule (J) is the standard unit of energy in the International System of Units (SI). It represents the amount of work performed or energy transferred when a force produces motion or when a device consumes power over time. In computing and embedded environments, such as IoT devices and intrusion detection system (IDS) sensors, energy consumption is typically calculated as the product of power and time, expressed as $E = P \times t$, where E denotes energy in joules, P represents power in watts, and t indicates time in seconds. Because one watt corresponds to one joule per second, a value of one joule can be interpreted as the energy consumed by a device operating at one watt for one second.

In IoT-based security and transportation systems, energy, measured in joules, is commonly used to assess battery usage and operational efficiency. It quantifies the energy required to execute an IDS model, transmit data, perform computational processing on CPUs or GPUs, support network communication, and operate sensing components. Lower energy consumption, measured in fewer joules, indicates a more efficient system and directly contributes to a longer device lifetime and improved sustainability in resource-constrained deployments.

8.3 Green IDS for IoT-based transportation systems

The rapid expansion of the Internet of Vehicles (IoV) and Cooperative Intelligent Transportation Systems (CITS) has resulted in highly interconnected, data-intensive vehicular networks, in which smart devices, sensors, and cloud infrastructure enable automated and collaborative transportation management. In these environments, vehicles continuously exchange information through Vehicle-to-Vehicle (V2V) and Vehicle-to-Infrastructure (V2I) communications. Although existing cryptographic protocols and authentication mechanisms are effective at securing communication channels, they are insufficient to detect internal misbehavior. Such misbehavior may include falsified location information, replayed messages, malware attacks, unauthorized access, Sybil attacks, data manipulation threats, zero-day exploits, and denial-of-service (DoS) attacks. This limitation arises primarily from the dynamic, time-dependent characteristics of vehicular data, which make traditional rule-based approaches and classical ML-based intrusion detection systems less effective, particularly since they rely heavily on manually engineered features.

The primary objective of developing a Green Intrusion Detection System (IDS) for IoT-enabled active transportation systems is therefore to create an intelligent, scalable, and real-time solution capable of identifying multiple categories of vehicular misbehavior. The proposed system must be able to (1) process large-scale sequential vehicular data efficiently, (2) satisfy strict real-time operational requirements, and (3) support deployment at the network edge rather than relying solely on cloud infrastructure, thereby minimizing latency and operational costs. Numerous studies have been conducted to address these challenges. The following sections provide a detailed discussion and critical analysis of these existing approaches.

8.3.1 Application of ML

Various ML algorithms are applied to intrusion detection in IoT-based transportation systems. At the same time, ML algorithms are integrated with other techniques for better accuracy. One of them is GTBNN[1], a hybrid framework that integrates game theory with a BNN[2] and is optimized via Bayesian hyperparameter tuning. This framework aims to model the non-cooperative interaction between attackers and defenders within Intelligent Transportation System (ITS) cloud environments. In addition, this technique seeks to improve intrusion detection accuracy, reduce the false positive rate (FPR), and optimize decision-making time through a probabilistic neural framework. The interaction between attackers and defenders is formulated as a non-cooperative game, in which the defender's strategies include signature-based, anomaly-based, and honeypot-based detection, while the attacker's strategies include regular attacks, waiting, and sophisticated attacks. Payoff functions are defined for both parties to quantify strategic outcomes. In Nash Equilibrium analysis, the "wait" strategy is eliminated because attackers are assumed to always attempt an attack under equilibrium conditions. Consequently, the payoff matrix is reduced from a 3×2 structure to a 2×2 configuration using a graphical min-max method. The resulting equilibrium probabilities indicate that the signature-based module should be activated with probability 0.89 and the anomaly-based module with probability 0.11. From the attacker's perspective, regular attacks occur with probability 0.74, while sophisticated attacks occur with probability 0.26. This selective activation strategy prevents the simultaneous execution of all detection modules, thereby reducing unnecessary energy consumption. Following the selection of a strategic module, intrusion detection is performed using a BNN. In this framework, model weights are treated as probability distributions rather than fixed parameters, enabling uncertainty quantification and making the model particularly suitable for high-risk ITS environments. Hyperparameters are optimized using Bayesian Optimization, which is more efficient than Grid Search and Random Search. The identified optimal configuration comprises a learning rate of 0.01, 118 hidden units, and a batch size of 16. Feature selection is conducted using Recursive Feature Elimination (RFE), and the framework is evaluated on three benchmark datasets: UNSW-NB15, CICIDS 2017, and Bot-IoT. Experimental results demonstrate strong detection performance across all datasets. On UNSW-NB15, the model achieves 98.23% accuracy, 99.99% detection rate, and 98.12% F1-score. For CICIDS 2017, it achieves 99.98% accuracy, 99.99% detection rate, and a 99.92% F1-score. On the Bot-IoT dataset, the model attains 99.87% accuracy, 99.93% detection rate, and a 99.62% F1-score. False

[1] A Game-Theoretic Bayesian Neural Network is a model that combines Bayesian neural networks, which quantify uncertainty by treating weights as probability distributions, with game theory, framing learning or defense as a strategic interaction to produce robust, uncertainty-aware decisions under adversarial conditions.

[2] A Bayesian Neural Network is a neural network that treats its weights as probability distributions rather than fixed values, enabling it to quantify uncertainty in its predictions and offer more robust, well-calibrated outputs.

positive rates are also notably low, with 0.011% for the signature module, 0.015% for the anomaly module, and 0.102% for the honeypot module. Compared with prior approaches, the GTBNN framework achieves measurable improvements in detection rate across all datasets. Beyond detection accuracy, the framework demonstrates improved strategic and computational efficiency. It also exhibits significantly lower decision-making time, supporting real-time applicability. The algorithmic complexity is $O(mn)$, indicating scalability suitable for operational deployment. The framework accounts for the energy consumed by IDS components and honeypots, and module activation probabilities influence overall energy usage. By activating only the optimal detection module identified via Nash Equilibrium analysis and avoiding the simultaneous execution of all modules, the system reduces unnecessary energy expenditure.

8.3.2 Application of DL mechanisms

Several DL architectures have been developed for intrusion detection in network-assisted intelligent transportation systems, with particular attention to smart-city settings. One such approach adopts a hybrid design that couples two architectures: LSTM networks and CNNs, to model misbehavior detection in vehicular networks. LSTM networks are well-suited to capturing temporal dependencies in sequential time-series data, while CNNs extract localized temporal patterns and salient features. To further improve performance, the two are combined into hybrid configurations, such as two CNN layers followed by one LSTM layer (2-CNN + 1-LSTM) and two CNN layers followed by two LSTM layers (2-CNN + 2-LSTM). Such models are trained in a cloud environment to exploit ample computational resources and then deployed on edge servers for real-time inference. This line of work also introduces three distinct DL-based Classification Engines (DLCEs). DLCE-1 is a single-stage, fine-grained classifier that directly categorizes all eighteen behavior types within a unified framework. DLCE-2 adopts a two-stage approach: the first stage performs coarse-grained classification to separate normal from misbehaving activity, and the second conducts fine-grained classification to identify specific attack or fault categories. DLCE-3 also follows a two-stage design but introduces a hierarchical structure, first sorting data into three broad categories: normal behavior, faults, and attacks, and then applying separate fine-grained classifiers for faults and attacks. This hierarchical arrangement improves interpretability and offers greater flexibility, especially where real-time deployment constraints vary.

Performance is assessed using accuracy, precision, recall, and F1-score. DLCE-1, the single-stage fine-grained classifier, attains an accuracy of 99.63%, with precision of 96.86%, recall of 96.74%, and an F1-score of 96.75%; among the tested configurations, the 2-CNN + 1-LSTM architecture delivers the best overall results. DLCE-2, implementing two-stage normal-versus-misbehavior classification, reports an overall F1-score of 95.58%, while DLCE-3, with its hierarchical normal/fault/attack classification followed by fine-grained categorization, achieves an overall F1-score of 96.49%, combining strong performance with improved structural clarity. Deployment is evaluated on two representative edge platforms, the Nvidia Jetson Nano and the Raspberry Pi 3B. On the Jetson Nano, total execution time is 288.07 ms for the 4-LSTM model and 251.56 ms for the 2-CNN + 1-LSTM model; on the Raspberry Pi these rise to 570.48 ms and 337.16 ms, respectively. The hybrid 2-CNN + 1-LSTM model thus achieves both superior classification performance and lower inference latency on both devices. A closer look at the runtime is revealing: the prediction phase itself requires only about 0.3 ms, so inference is highly efficient, and the bulk of the execution time is consumed by data preprocessing and preparation rather than by the detection computation proper.

A related design, PIGNUS, is a hybrid DL intrusion detection model that integrates CNNs with GRUs. The CNN component extracts spatial characteristics from network traffic, while the GRU captures the temporal patterns associated with attack behavior. A feature-processing stage precedes classification, removing redundant attributes to improve detection and reduce computational complexity. Evaluated on the N-BaIoT dataset in a multi-class setting, the framework distinguishes normal traffic from nine IoT botnet attack types and is compared against several state-of-the-art detection models. The CNN-GRU approach identifies multiple botnet categories with high accuracy, separating benign from malicious traffic across attack classes, and outperforms conventional methods in multi-class identification, providing evidence of the advantage of combining spatial and temporal learning when analyzing Industrial IoT traffic.

A further framework, SDLMA-IITS (Secure Deep Learning-Enabled Malware Attack Detection for IoT-Enabled Intelligent Transportation Systems), integrates DL, explainable artificial intelligence (XAI), and cryptographic authentication. It aims not only to detect malicious activity but also to improve interpretability and the security of communication in IoT-enabled transportation environments. The detection core is an ensemble of CNN-GRU and CNN-LSTM architectures whose outputs are concatenated before final classification, a design that strengthens feature extraction, captures temporal dependencies in network traffic, and improves generalization. A preprocessing phase precedes the ensemble, handling missing values and outliers, encoding categorical attributes, normalizing features, and selecting features to remove redundant variables; correlation analysis, visualized as a heatmap, and protocol-distribution analysis further clarify feature relationships and traffic characteristics. These steps improve generalization, reduce dimensionality, and lower the risk of overfitting. For transparency, SHapley Additive exPlanations (SHAP) are incorporated, with the summary analysis identifying influential features such as RST_COUNT, INTER-ARRIVAL TIME (IAT), URG_COUNTER, and VARIANCE; by quantifying each feature's contribution to the outcome, this component helps analysts understand why traffic is flagged as malicious. Beyond detection, the framework integrates secure authentication and key establishment: session keys, nonces and timestamps, and pseudonymous identities to protect privacy, and is formally analyzed under both the Dolev-Yao (DY) and CK adversary models, ensuring resilience against replay, man-in-the-middle, impersonation, and session-key-disclosure attacks. The ensemble model achieves the highest performance, with an accuracy of 99.65%, precision of 0.99, recall of 0.989, and an F1-score of 0.991; the CNN-LSTM model reaches 99.28% accuracy and the CNN model 99.24%, with the full framework outperforming several recent state-of-the-art approaches.

Building on explainable AI and cryptographic authentication, the Explainable AI-Driven Intrusion Detection System (EAI-IDS) is designed for IoT-enabled transportation. It seeks to detect anomalies in high-dimensional, time-dependent sensor data in real time, explain its decisions transparently, and operate efficiently within resource-constrained systems by combining temporal DL, feature-based classification, explainability, and real-time mitigation in a single architecture. The anomaly detection engine is hybrid: LSTM networks capture temporal dependencies in sensor communication patterns, while a Random Forest classifier performs feature-level anomaly detection. An anomaly score is computed for each node using statistical deviation measures, and alerts are triggered when the score exceeds a predefined threshold. Hyperparameters are tuned via both grid search and Bayesian optimization to balance detection performance against computational cost. SHAP again provides interpretability, offering global and local explanations through feature-importance rankings, summary plots, and instance-level explanations. Latency, energy consumption, and node mobility speed emerge as dominant indicators of anomalous behavior, and exposing this rationale strengthens operator trust in safety-critical settings. The framework also implements real-time mitigation: when compromised nodes are identified, they are isolated, communication routes are dynamically reconfigured, and secure connections are re-established after validation, all supported by a dynamic network-graph model that monitors bandwidth, delay, packet loss, and energy consumption, with a multi-objective optimization function minimizing delay and energy expenditure while preserving packet delivery rate (PDR) requirements. In testing, the system attains 94.2% detection accuracy, roughly 92% validation accuracy, and an ROC AUC of about 0.85, with the confusion matrix confirming reliable separation of normal and anomalous traffic. Detection latency is about 15.2 ms, markedly faster than the 30.1 ms of SVM-based approaches, while inference takes 10.8 ms and training 45.3 s, all consistent with real-time autonomous deployment. Energy efficiency is central: the system consumes roughly 2.1 J per node, well below the approximately 4.0 J of an SVM-based IDS; secure communication requires about 7.5 J, compared to up to 11 J for compromised communication, and the IDS reduces communication delay by about 7.5 ms while maintaining a 98.5% packet delivery rate. A unified metric that combines delivery rate, delay, and energy consumption confirms its superior performance and resource optimization compared with existing frameworks.

Cybersecurity exposure is not confined to IoT-enabled vehicles and transportation infrastructure; Electric Vehicle (EV) charging infrastructure within smart urban transport introduces new risks as charging stations interconnect with IoT networks, smart grids, and cloud platforms. This connectivity invites denial-of-service attacks, malware injection, unauthorized access, and manipulation of charging parameters: incidents that can interrupt service, compromise user privacy, and undermine reliability. A hybrid DL framework addresses this by combining Extreme Gradient

Boosting (XGBoost) with CNNs: XGBoost processes structured, feature-rich charging data, while CNNs capture temporal and sequential patterns in communication traffic and charging activity, enabling the system to benefit from both feature-level decision learning and pattern-level representation learning. SHAP again provides transparency by quantifying each feature's contribution and clarifying why a charging session is classified as normal or anomalous. An adaptive learning mechanism continuously updates the model as charging behavior evolves. Through ongoing traffic monitoring, behavior analysis, and signature detection, the IDS stays resilient against emerging strategies. On the first benchmark dataset the hybrid XGBoost-CNN system attains 96% accuracy, 95.5% precision, 98.5% recall, a 97% F1-score, and an AUC of 0.975, with false-positive and false-negative rates of 2.5% and 1.5%; on the second, it records 94% accuracy, 92% precision, 94% recall, a 93% F1-score, and an AUC of 0.965. With SHAP-based explanations incorporated, accuracy rises to about 97.5% and the false-positive and false-negative rates fall to 1.8% and 1.2%. The framework is also practical, requiring roughly an hour of training and about 1 millisecond per sample at inference, supporting real-time detection in smart EV-charging environments.

A persistent challenge for DL-based IDS in any network is class imbalance: normal traffic dominates the data, while minority attack categories are underrepresented, biasing the learning and degrading the detection of rare but critical attacks. Reconstruction-based anomaly detectors compound the difficulty, since they often reconstruct anomalous and normal samples equally well, thereby losing discriminative power. ReMeNet (Reconstruction Memory Network) addresses these limitations by embedding a memory component within a Generative Adversarial Network (GAN), uniting reconstruction-based anomaly detection with adversarial learning to sharpen the distinction between normal and malicious traffic. Its memory-enhanced GAN comprises four components: a generator, a memory module, a filter, and a discriminator. The generator follows an encoder-memory-decoder design akin to an autoencoder but inserts an external memory module between the encoder and decoder; rather than reconstructing the latent representation directly, the encoded features query this module to retrieve the most relevant stored representation of normal traffic, yielding accurate reconstruction for benign samples and higher reconstruction errors for anomalies. Memory addressing uses an attention mechanism based on cosine similarity, and entropy regularization applied to the addressing weights encourages sparsity and prevents redundant storage, keeping the stored normal features diverse and representative. Robustness is further improved by a filter-enhanced adversarial mechanism: the filter removes anomalous samples before they reach the discriminator, so adversarial training focuses solely on normal traffic, while a modified reconstruction loss deliberately raises the reconstruction error for anomalies above a predefined threshold, keeping the generator from overfitting to malicious data. The final generator loss is a weighted sum of reconstruction, memory, and adversarial terms, a multi-objective strategy that stabilizes training and strengthens discrimination. To tackle severe imbalance, a VQ-WGAN mechanism couples VQ-VAE-2 (Vector Quantized Variational Autoencoder) with WGAN-GP (Wasserstein GAN with Gradient Penalty): VQ-VAE-2 discretizes the feature space and improves the quality of synthetic samples for minority classes, while WGAN-GP stabilizes training through gradient-penalty regularization, together producing high-quality synthetic data that improves dataset balance. Evaluated on the UNSW-NB15 dataset, about 2.54 million samples with substantial imbalance, the model reaches 91.70% accuracy, with weighted precision of 91.57%, weighted recall of 91.70%, and a weighted F1-score of 91.63%; macro-averaged metrics are lower, however, at 80.01% precision, 80.37% recall, and 80.19% F1-score, reflecting the continuing difficulty of minority classes. Category-wise, normal traffic achieves an F1-score of 98.92%, while Fuzzers and Reconnaissance attacks reach 92.72% and 90.28%, respectively, while extremely rare categories such as Worms (56.91%) and Backdoors (62.19%) remain hard to detect despite generative balancing.

A second persistent challenge is limited interpretability: many DL models behave as black boxes, offering little insight into their reasoning, which erodes the trust of security practitioners and obstructs deployment in safety-critical settings such as IoT-enabled transportation. The Cyber-Resilient Explainable DL-Based Intrusion Detection System (XDL-IDS) responds by pairing a hybrid CNN-GRU architecture with SHAP-based explainability. One-dimensional CNNs (1D CNNs) extract spatial and hierarchical features from network traffic, while GRUs capture temporal dependencies and mitigate problems such as vanishing gradients. The CNN layers learn structured feature representations, and the GRU layers process the sequential patterns of vehicular communication. The configuration comprises two 1D CNN layers with 32 filters and a kernel size of 2, followed by two GRU layers of 32 and 16 neurons, a dropout layer with a rate of 0.2 to limit overfitting, and a dense layer of 30 neurons before the output, with sigmoid activation for binary classification and softmax for multiclass classification. SHAP provides both global interpretability, through summary plots of overall feature importance, and local interpretability, through instance-level waterfall plots that show how individual features drive specific predictions, allowing operators to see which features shape each outcome. Performance is exceptionally strong: in the binary setting, the model achieves 100% accuracy, 100% precision, 99.99% recall, an F1-score of 100%, and an AUC of 1.0000, with only five false negatives and no false positives. In the multiclass setting, it reaches 99.64% accuracy, 97.23% precision, 98.48% recall, and a 97.69% F1-score, with AUC values of 1.00 for benign traffic, DoS, steering, and gas-spoofing attacks and near-perfect values for RPM and speed-spoofing attacks, giving a macro-average AUC of 0.9999; precision for the Spoofing-SPEED class is slightly lower than for the others. XDL-IDS thus combines high detection accuracy with enhanced interpretability, making it well suited to safety-critical IoT transportation environments.

8.3.3 Application of federated learning

FL is a decentralized ML approach that enables multiple clients (e.g., smartphones, IoT devices, or organizations) to collaboratively train a shared model while keeping their data on their respective devices. Instead of moving data to a central server, FL brings the model to the data, enhancing privacy and reducing data transfer costs. Although this approach is conceptually well-suited for IoT ecosystems, its practical deployment in Connected and Autonomous Vehicle (CAV) networks remains challenging. Edge platforms commonly used in vehicular environments, such as embedded onboard units and Raspberry Pi-class devices, have limited computational capacity, restricted memory, and constrained energy resources. These limitations make continuous or large-scale on-device training particularly challenging. Conventional centralized intrusion detection system (IDS) architectures require collecting and aggregating all data on a central server. While this approach simplifies model management, it raises serious concerns related to data privacy, bandwidth consumption, and communication overhead. In contrast, traditional FL-based IDS frameworks distribute the training process across devices, reducing data sharing but imposing substantial computational demands on individual nodes. In resource-constrained vehicular environments, where navigation systems, safety-critical modules, and infotainment services simultaneously compete for processing power, allocating sufficient resources for intensive local model training becomes impractical. Moreover, ensuring scalability across heterogeneous hardware platforms and maintaining reliable operation under dynamic network connectivity conditions introduces additional complexity to FL deployment in CAV networks.

To overcome existing limitations, a hybrid framework, termed Federated Fine-Tuning (FedFT), was introduced in the study. This approach integrates FL with Transfer Learning principles to reduce computational and memory demands on client devices while preserving collaborative model training. FedFT framework adopts a two-stage server-edge learning strategy. In the first stage, a central server pre-trains a global intrusion detection model on proxy data. This phase addresses the most computationally intensive portion of model development. In the second stage, client devices receive the pre-trained model and perform limited fine-tuning. Rather than retraining the entire architecture, the convolutional feature-extraction layers are frozen, and only the lightweight classification head is updated locally. By restricting training to a small subset of parameters, this strategy substantially lowers memory consumption and computational overhead on edge devices, while maintaining the benefits of collaborative learning. The underlying IDS architecture consists of three main components. The feature extraction stage is implemented using three one-dimensional convolutional blocks, each comprising a Conv1D layer and a max-pooling layer. These layers capture meaningful patterns in network traffic data. The extracted representations are then passed to a multi-layer perceptron (MLP) module composed of fully connected layers with ReLU activation functions. A final sigmoid output layer performs binary classification, distinguishing between normal traffic and intrusions. By freezing the convolutional layers and fine-tuning only the fully connected layers, the model retains strong representational capability while significantly reducing local computational requirements. The federated workflow is implemented using the Flower FL framework and employs the Federated Averaging (FedAvg) algorithm for parameter aggregation. The process begins with server-side pre-training using proxy data. The trained model parameters are then distributed to participating clients. Each client fine-tunes the designated layers and transmits updated parameters back to the server. The server aggregates these updates and redistributes the refined model across multiple communication rounds. For evaluation, the NSL-KDD dataset is partitioned among clients to simulate distributed IoT environments, and Principal Component Analysis (PCA) is applied for feature extraction. To evaluate performance, two FedFT configurations are evaluated: FedFT-3, which fine-tunes three fully connected layers, and FedFT-1, which fine-tunes only the final fully connected layer. FedFT-3 achieves an accuracy of 99.2%, with memory usage of 6.6 MB and an execution time of 1253 seconds. This performance closely approaches that of the centralized model, which achieves 99.8% accuracy, while reducing memory consumption by approximately 20%. In contrast, FedFT-1 achieves 94.3% accuracy, with memory usage reduced to 4.3 MB and execution time shortened to 564 seconds. This configuration reduces memory consumption by up to 42% and execution time by approximately 75%, albeit with a modest decrease in classification accuracy. In addition, the evaluation results demonstrate significant memory savings, faster training times, and stable scalability as the number of participating clients increases. Notably, accuracy degradation remains below 1% when scaling from four to eight clients. Because energy consumption in embedded systems is closely tied to CPU utilization, memory access, and runtime, the observed reductions strongly indicate improved energy efficiency. Furthermore, scalability analysis indicates that while communication overhead slightly increases training time as additional clients are added, memory usage remains stable and performance degradation is minimal, supporting energy-efficient deployment in IoT and CAV networks.

A privacy-preserving, decentralized, and computationally efficient FL-based Intrusion Detection System (FL-IDS) offers another approach, one designed for deployment on real embedded edge devices while maintaining high detection accuracy and low runtime overhead. Its emphasis is on operating effectively in practical edge environments, where hardware constraints and communication limitations must be weighed carefully. The system is built around the Flower FL platform: a global server model runs on an NVIDIA Jetson Xavier equipped with a GPU, while multiple client models execute on Raspberry Pi 4 devices. Communication between the server and clients occurs over a wireless LAN, and model aggregation is performed using the Federated Averaging (FedAvg) algorithm. This design enables collaborative model training without centralizing raw data. This FL-IDS framework supports two detection approaches. The first model is a Logistic Regression-based IDS (LR-IDS), which applies the Pearson Correlation Coefficient (PCC) for feature extraction and uses Logistic Regression for binary classification. The second approach is a DL-based IDS referred to as PCC-CNN. This model incorporates a modified one-dimensional CNN architecture comprising 1D convolutional layers, max-pooling layers, a 30% dropout rate to reduce overfitting, and fully connected dense layers with ReLU activation. The final classification layer uses a softmax activation function, and the model is trained with the Adam optimizer. The framework was evaluated under two real-world experimental testbeds. The first testbed consisted of two Raspberry Pi clients and one Jetson Xavier server, while the second testbed included four Raspberry Pi clients and one Jetson Xavier server. Two datasets were used for validation: the NSL-KDD dataset for network intrusion detection and the Car-Hacking dataset, which focuses on Controller Area Network (CAN) bus intrusions in autonomous vehicles. The federated training process follows the standard FL workflow, including model initialization, parameter distribution to clients, local training, weight uploading, server-side aggregation, and iterative updates until convergence. The performance evaluation demonstrates varying results across models and datasets. For the LR-IDS model, experiments on the NSL-KDD dataset achieved an accuracy of 96.82% with a loss of 0.127, a training time of 42.08 seconds, and a processing time of 10 seconds. On the Car-Hacking dataset, LR-IDS achieved 93.56% accuracy with a loss of 0.28, but required longer training (83.28 seconds) and significantly higher processing time (306 seconds). These findings indicate that while LR-IDS performs reasonably well on traditional network intrusion data, its effectiveness and efficiency decline in vehicular intrusion scenarios. In contrast, the DL-based PCC-CNN model demonstrated superior performance. On the NSL-KDD dataset, it achieved 97% accuracy, a loss of 0.12, and a training time of 75.98 seconds. On the Car-Hacking dataset, the model achieved 99.93% accuracy with a remarkably low loss of 0.005, although the training time increased to 557.65 seconds.

8.3.4 Application of graph networks

In the real-world Autonomous Transportation System, large volumes of vehicular data are generated and exchanged daily via wireless communication networks. Traditional intrusion detection approaches, particularly those based on conventional ML or Euclidean-structured data models, struggle to handle the non-Euclidean structure of vehicular communication networks. Moreover, standard graph models, such as GCNs, have limitations: equal weighting of neighbors, an inability to handle directed graphs effectively, and limited adaptability in dynamic environments. To address existing challenges, this study presents QnGSA (Hypercube-Driven Graph Self-Attention Intrusion Detection Model), an adaptive, scalable, and high-accuracy intrusion detection model that handles complex non-Euclidean vehicular graph data while remaining robust across both sparse and dense network conditions. The central point of this framework is the development of a hypercube-driven association graph constructed through a semi-supervised K-means++ clustering approach, referred to as QnSSKM. In this framework, each vehicle is modeled as a node in a graph. The feature representation incorporates static attributes, such as speed and position; dynamic characteristics, including acceleration; and time-series features, such as communication delay and transmission periodicity. Vehicles are first grouped into clusters based on feature similarity using semi-supervised clustering. Rather than forming fully connected subgraphs within each cluster, nodes are linked according to a hypercube connectivity rule, in which connections are established only when the Hamming distance equals 1. This design produces a sparse graph structure, mitigates the risk of edge explosion in high-dimensional spaces, enhances computational efficiency, and improves robustness in scenarios with uneven node distributions. After graph construction, the model applies a Graph Attention Network (GAT) to aggregate features and detect intrusions. The attention mechanism computes attention coefficients via a LeakyReLU activation, and softmax normalization assigns adaptive weights to neighboring nodes. Multi-head attention is incorporated to stabilize learning and enhance representational capacity, followed by a softmax layer for final classification. Compared to traditional Graph Convolutional Networks (GCNs), the GAT-based approach offers several advantages. It assigns distinct importance to neighboring nodes, accommodates directed and dynamically evolving graphs, and does not rely on Laplacian-matrix constraints. These characteristics enable the QnGSA model to adapt effectively to both dense urban vehicular networks and sparsely distributed rural environments. The experimental evaluation was conducted using a large-scale 223 GB Mountain View driving dataset in a multi-class intrusion detection setting. Training was performed over 500 epochs with a learning rate of 0.005. Performance was assessed using Accuracy, Macro Precision, Macro Recall, and Macro F1-score. The reported results demonstrate strong performance, achieving 99.01% accuracy, 98.90% macro precision, 98.66% macro recall, and 98.79% macro F1-score. It also evaluates the computational efficiency through architectural design choices. The use of sparse hypercube connectivity significantly reduces the number of edges in the graph. Specifically, each node maintains approximately $\lceil log_2(m) \rceil$ connections, thereby preventing exponential growth in adjacency relationships. The semi-supervised clustering method incurs minimal overhead, and the controlled multi-head GAT architecture reduces the complexity of adjacency-matrix operations. As a result, memory usage is lowered, and attention-based aggregation avoids unnecessary global computations. The model also demonstrates stable performance across both dense and sparse network conditions. Collectively, these characteristics indicate that the architecture is computationally efficient and scalable, thereby indirectly suggesting improved energy efficiency for active transportation system deployments, even in the absence of direct power-consumption measurements.

Fig. 8.1 shows an overall block diagram of various cybersecurity attacks and the techniques available so far to mitigate them in smart transportation systems.

8.4 Green IDS for IoT-based smart cities

Smart cities connect many components such as sensors, vehicles, infrastructure, cloud services, and user devices through large Internet of Things (IoT) networks. These connections support intelligent services including transportation control, energy management, healthcare monitoring, surveillance, and environmental monitoring. However, this high level of connectivity also increases security risks. Attackers may launch spoofing, denial-of-service, malware, data tampering, or unauthorized access attacks, which can disrupt critical city services, violate privacy, and threaten

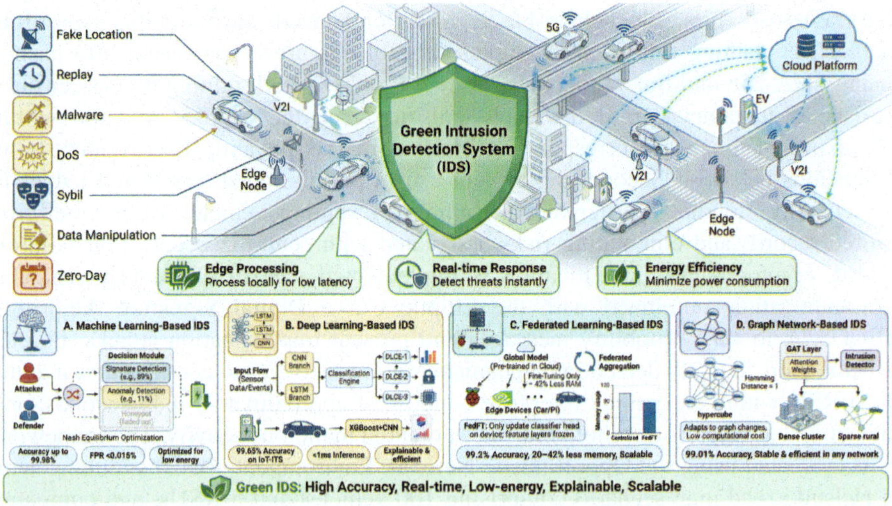

FIGURE 8.1

A block diagram of different Cybersecurity attacks and Green IDS approaches to prevent them in transportation systems.

public safety. Because many smart-city systems operate in real time and directly control physical processes such as traffic signals, autonomous vehicles, and power systems, traditional perimeter-based security approaches are not sufficient. Furthermore, centralized cloud-based intrusion detection systems often introduce significant delays, high communication overhead, and single points of failure, making them unsuitable for large, resource-constrained IoT environments. As a result, attacks may not be detected quickly or reliably. Therefore, intrusion detection systems (IDSs) are essential security components in smart cities, as they continuously monitor network activity, detect abnormal behavior, and enable rapid incident response. IoT networks play a dual role in this environment: they enable smart-city functionality but also represent a major target for attackers. Hence, developing IDS solutions that are accurate, adaptive, and energy-efficient is critical for maintaining reliability, trust, and resilience in smart-city systems.

A range of intrusion detection systems for IoT-based smart-city networks has been developed and implemented. One such framework, **BIDS (Blockchain-Enabled Intrusion Detection System)**, is a decentralized, tamper-resistant system designed to validate vehicular behavior in real time without relying on a central authority. It integrates vehicular networking with distributed ledger technology to strengthen trust and reliability in transportation environments. Within this framework, vehicles transmit their mobility information to nearby Roadside Units (RSUs), which relay the data to cloudlets; the cloudlets verify these mobility patterns and record them in blockchain blocks, after which the validated information becomes accessible to the traffic management system. Several complementary security mechanisms underpin the framework. First, blockchain-based validation converts each mobility report into a block containing time-location tuples. The blocks are cryptographically hashed using SHA-256 and linked together, while a Proof-of-Work mining process ensures resistance to tampering. If a vehicle fails to reach the claimed location within the expected time, the corresponding block is marked invalid, thereby identifying suspicious behavior. Second, the system uses a permissioned distributed ledger in which only cloudlets participate in mining, preventing vehicles from modifying stored records and eliminating risks associated with centralized detection failures. Third, cryptographic authentication is implemented via IEEE 802.11p vehicular communication, combined with the Elliptic Curve Digital Signature Algorithm (ECDSA), to verify mobility messages and prevent impersonation attacks. Fourth, a behavioral anomaly detection mechanism requires vehicles to confirm arrival at the next RSU within an optimal tolerance window of approximately ±49 seconds; any deviation beyond this threshold indicates potential malicious activity. The framework was evaluated using the Opportunistic Network Environment (ONE) simulator with a Helsinki road map scenario comprising 100 vehicles and 5 RSUs, and compared with ART, TMEC, and NOTRINO intrusion detection approaches. Performance was measured using precision, recall, and F-measure. The results demonstrate approximately 98% detection accuracy when only 5% of vehicles are malicious, and about 85% when the proportion of malicious vehicles increases to 40%. Under the highest attack rate, the system achieved a precision of 94%, recall of 89%, and an F-measure of 90%, indicating strong effectiveness in identifying anomalous vehicular behavior in distributed transportation networks.

Another existing framework aims to develop a scalable intrusion detection system architecture that operates efficiently across distributed IoT infrastructures while maintaining high detection accuracy, particularly against wireless impersonation attacks. To achieve this objective, the authors introduce two collaborative ML-based IDS architectures implemented within a fog-edge computing environment. The first design is a semi-distributed architecture in which edge devices perform feature selection in parallel, while a fog node executes the final classification using a Multi-Layer Perceptron (MLP) model. The second design is a fully distributed architecture in which each edge node independently performs both feature selection and classification, and a controller aggregates the final detection decision. By distributing processing tasks across multiple nodes, both approaches aim to reduce latency and computational overhead compared to traditional centralized detection systems. The detection pipeline follows a structured sequence of stages. The system is trained using the AWID wireless intrusion dataset, with balanced normal and attack traffic. Feature extraction is performed using a stacked autoencoder with a layered structure of 154, 100, and 50 neurons, combining original attributes with learned representations. Feature selection employs both wrapper and filter techniques, including Support Vector Machine and J48 decision tree methods, as well as Information Gain, OneR, and Correlation-based Feature Selection (CFS). The final classification step is carried out using an MLP neural network. Performance evaluation is conducted using multiple metrics, including accuracy, detection rate, false alarm rate, F1-score, Matthews Correlation Coefficient (MCC), and model construction time. The semi-distributed architecture achieves a detection rate of 99.96%, accuracy of 99.97%, F1-score of 99.97%, MCC of 99.95%, and a false alarm rate of 0.0001%, with a model build time of 186.26 seconds. The fully distributed architecture records a detection rate of 98.26%, accuracy of 97.80%, F1-score of 97.81%, MCC of 95.65%, and a build time of 73.52 seconds. For comparison, a centralized baseline model achieves similar accuracy (99.97%) but requires significantly longer processing time, approximately 12,073 seconds. These results indicate that the semi-distributed approach maintains nearly the same accuracy as centralized detection while dramatically reducing computation time, whereas the fully distributed model sacrifices a small amount of accuracy in exchange for substantially faster operation. This study assesses energy efficiency indirectly by analyzing computational cost and processing time, factors that are particularly important for resource-constrained IoT devices. The results show that the distributed IDS significantly decreases computation time from 12,073 seconds in the centralized approach to 73.52 seconds. The semi-distributed architecture likewise achieves a substantial reduction in processing overhead. Because shorter processing times generally correspond to reduced CPU utilization, these improvements imply lower energy consumption on resource-constrained edge nodes. Consequently, the proposed architectures enhance operational efficiency and are better suited for battery-powered smart-city deployments.

Smart Grid Control Systems (SGCS) in modern smart cities integrate IoT devices, communication networks, and cyber-physical infrastructure, making them particularly vulnerable to cyber threats such as false data injection and denial-of-service (DoS) attacks. Conventional intrusion detection systems, designed for traditional IT environments, depend on predefined attack patterns and balanced datasets, and so perform poorly in smart-grid contexts where attack data are scarce, and system behavior is highly complex and nonlinear. These shortcomings hinder adaptation to emerging threats and weaken the reliability of protection for critical energy infrastructure. Addressing them requires an intrusion detection approach that can learn from imbalanced cyber-physical data, recognize previously unseen attacks, and support proactive defense.

One such approach is a DL-based intrusion detection framework integrated with a Cyber-Physical Digital Twin. The framework first employs a specialized DL representation model that produces balanced feature representations from asymmetric SGCS datasets, mitigating the scarcity of attack samples. Detection is then performed by a hybrid classifier that combines Support Vector Machine (SVM) and K-Nearest Neighbor (K-NN) methods, a pairing that captures the nonlinear relationships within smart-grid data and detects both known and unknown attack patterns. At the heart of the framework lies the Cyber-Physical Digital Twin, which replicates both the physical and cyber elements of the grid: SCADA systems, sensors, substations, and communication networks. The twin is used to inject synthetic cyber threats, conduct scenario analysis, retrain the detection system, and simulate incident-response strategies, enabling the IDS to learn continuously from simulated attacks in real time and adapt to evolving threats. Evaluated on real smart-grid datasets with 10-fold cross-validation and compared against baseline methods such as DNN, SVM, Random Forests, and LSTM models, the framework achieves higher accuracy, precision, recall, and F1-score than all baselines, sustaining strong detection even under severe dataset imbalance. It consistently achieves the highest F1-score among all evaluated classifiers, confirming its effectiveness in securing cyber-physical smart-grid systems.

Smart-city sensing infrastructures are especially vulnerable to False Data Injection Attacks (FDIA), in which adversaries manipulate sensor readings to mislead automated decision-making. Such tampering can disrupt traffic, destabilize control systems, or create outright safety hazards. One way to counter this threat is a CycleGAN-based intrusion detection framework enhanced through hybrid metaheuristic optimization. Its core detection mechanism is a deep generative model that learns the distribution of normal sensor behavior without requiring paired training data. Using adversarial and cycle-consistency loss functions, the model treats abnormal behavior as a deviation from the learned normal patterns, allowing it to detect previously unseen attacks rather than only known signatures. To strengthen performance, hyperparameters are automatically optimized using two complementary metaheuristic algorithms: Biogeography-Based Optimization (BBO), which mimics migration processes to search for optimal parameter configurations, and the Whale Optimization Algorithm (WOA), which dynamically refines parameters through cooperative search behavior: a combination that accelerates convergence and improves anomaly-recognition accuracy. FDIA itself can be expressed mathematically, with normal sensor measurements perturbed by malicious variations to yield corrupted estimates. Evaluated in a simulated smart-city environment of 100 IoT devices and traffic-monitoring sensors, with real-time anomaly spikes injected to emulate attack conditions, the framework achieves a detection rate of roughly 95% at a 5% false-positive rate, and responds to an FDIA in about two minutes; fast and effective enough for real-world smart-city infrastructure. Taken together, these results indicate robust and timely detection of anomalous data within large-scale smart-city IoT networks.

To ensure communication between cloud computing-supported IoT devices and other interconnected cyber-physical infrastructures, a hybrid intrusion detection framework called REPOStack was introduced, combining optimized feature selection with ensemble learning to improve classification reliability. Initially, the NSL-KDD dataset is preprocessed with one-hot encoding, so categorical attributes can be represented numerically and processed effectively by learning algorithms. The framework then applies a hybrid feature-selection strategy. Recursive Feature Elimination (RFE) is used to identify informative attributes, while a Self-Adaptive Equilibrium Optimizer combined with Particle Swarm Optimization (SAEO-PSO) searches for an optimal subset of features through evolutionary optimization. The intersection of the feature sets produced by these two methods is selected as the final input representation, ensuring that only the most relevant characteristics are retained for intrusion classification. After feature selection, the system constructs

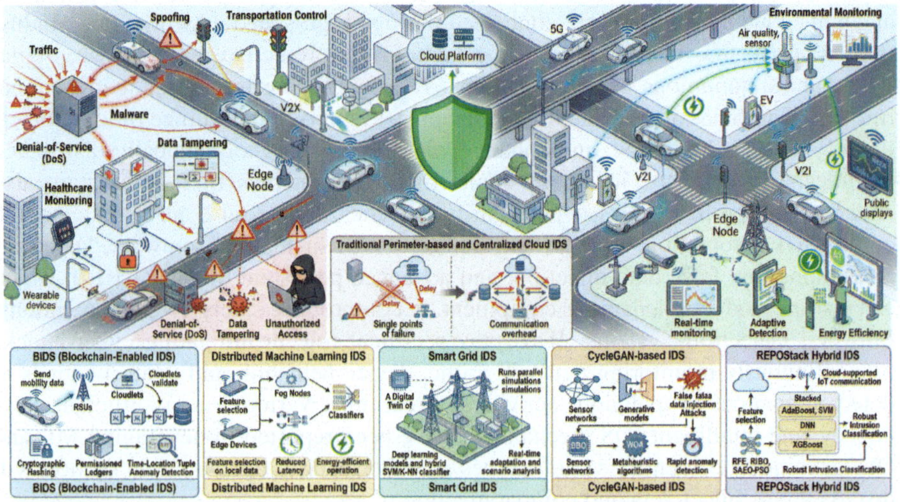

FIGURE 8.2

A block diagram of probable attacks present in Smart Cities and available Green IDS to mitigate them.

a probabilistic stacked ensemble model. The base learners consist of AdaBoost, SVM, and a DNN, while XGBoost acts as the meta-learner. Rather than relying on individual predictions, the stacked model learns from the base classifiers' probability outputs, thereby enhancing robustness and reducing misclassification in complex network traffic scenarios. The framework's performance is evaluated using accuracy, sensitivity, specificity, precision, and F1-score across multiple benchmark datasets. Experimental results demonstrate strong detection capability. On the NSL-KDD dataset, the model achieves 98.95% accuracy, 99.61% sensitivity, 99.23% specificity, 99.98% precision, and an F1-score of 97.80%. For the UNSW-NB15 dataset, the accuracy is 99.90%, and for the CICIDS dataset, it is 98.27%. Overall, the REPOStack framework improves performance by approximately 2 7% compared with existing intrusion detection approaches across multiple evaluation metrics.

Fig. 8.2 shows potential cybersecurity attacks in a smart city environment and the available green IDS to mitigate them.

8.5 Green IDS for secured industrial IoT automation

Industrial Internet of Things (IIoT) automation represents the convergence of traditional industrial automation systems, such as PLCs, SCADA, DCS, robotics, and sensor-actuator networks, to modern connected systems. This is possible because of advances in connectivity, edge computing, cloud platforms, and data-driven intelligence. In modern smart factories and industrial environments, machines, controllers, and embedded devices are interconnected through high-speed networks (e.g., Industrial Ethernet, 5G) to enable real-time monitoring, predictive maintenance, digital twins, and autonomous decision-making. This integration transforms conventional rule-based automation into intelligent, adaptive systems that optimize production efficiency, reduce downtime, and enhance visibility across geographically distributed facilities. However, the increased connectivity that enables IIoT automation also enhances the probability of cybersecurity breaches. Industrial control systems, the core of IoT automation, are now exposed to threats such as ransomware, DDoS attacks, spoofing, false data injection, and advanced persistent threats (APTs), which can disrupt production, damage equipment, or compromise safety-critical operations. Intrusion Detection Systems (IDS) play a critical role in mitigating cyber-attacks by continuously monitoring network traffic, device behavior, and control signals to detect anomalous or malicious activities in real time. Various energy-efficient, low-latency, and intelligent IDS mechanisms have been reported by leveraging ML and DL techniques to identify various types of cybersecurity attacks. This section will discuss them collectively and comparatively.

8.5.1 Green IDS for ZigBee supported IoT systems

The ZigBee network is widely adopted as a networking technology in Industrial IoT systems for its low power consumption, low cost, and overall suitability. Built for wireless sensor networks, it is deployed extensively in smart grids, healthcare facilities, and industrial monitoring environments. Conventional ZigBee security, however, rests primarily on bit-level identifiers such as MAC addresses and encryption keys, credentials that can be spoofed with publicly available tools, allowing unauthorized devices to join the network. Industrial systems may consequently face rogue device insertion, unauthorized access, and the potential manipulation of physical processes. To counter these weaknesses, physical-layer device authentication via radio-frequency (RF) fingerprinting can reliably verify legitimate ZigBee devices and reject spoofed ones.

This RF fingerprinting framework follows a structured pipeline for device identification and verification. The first stage is **signal acquisition and preprocessing**: wireless signals transmitted by ZigBee devices are captured under different operating conditions, then down-converted to baseband, digitized, and prepared for further processing, ensuring that the captured emissions take a consistent digital form suitable for analysis. The second stage is **feature extraction**, in which three instantaneous physical-layer characteristics, amplitude, phase, and frequency responses, are derived from each synchronization-header transmission. These parameters reflect inherent hardware-level imperfections unique to each device, and the combined statistical measurements yield a high-dimensional RF fingerprint of 729 features. The third stage is **dimensionality reduction and feature projection**: because high-dimensional feature spaces raise computational cost and may introduce redundancy, **Multiple Discriminant Analysis** projects the fingerprints into a lower-dimensional space, sharpening inter-device separability and improving classification efficiency.

The fourth stage is **device classification**, in which the projected feature vectors are processed by a **Maximum Likelihood classifier** that assigns each fingerprint to the most probable device class based on statistical models of feature distributions. The fifth stage is **device identity verification**: the claimed device identity is compared against its RF fingerprint using a statistical verification test based on **multivariate Gaussian posterior probabilities**, with the decision mechanism determining whether the observed fingerprint matches the legitimate device profile, and **Receiver Operating Characteristic** analysis used to assess performance through true and false verification rates. The final stage is computational optimization through feature ranking: to reduce complexity and enable deployment on resource-constrained platforms, feature selection is applied, with pre-classification ranking performed using the **Kolmogorov-Smirnov** test and post-classification relevance ranking conducted using GRLVQI. The experimental results demonstrate strong device identification and verification capabilities. Using all 729 features, approximately 90% classification accuracy was achieved at a signal-to-noise ratio of around 10 dB, with each device achieving at least 80% classification accuracy. When dimensionality reduction was applied, the 90% accuracy benchmark was achieved at about 18 dB signal-to-noise ratio. In rogue device rejection experiments involving six unauthorized devices across multiple spoofing scenarios, the framework achieved more than 90% rejection in all but one case. These findings confirm that RF fingerprinting can effectively detect spoofed devices even when they replicate legitimate bit-level credentials.

8.5.2 Blockchain-based Green IDS

A Blockchain-Based Collaborative Intrusion Detection System (BC-IDS) offers another approach by combining AI-driven intrusion detection with Ethereum blockchain technology within a multilayer architecture. The design comprises three layers: an IoT device layer, a controller layer housing distributed IDS servers, and a blockchain layer for decentralized storage. Within this framework, each IDS server detects attacks and extracts the associated malicious IP addresses, which are then submitted to a smart contract deployed on the Ethereum blockchain. A notable feature is a duplication-check mechanism, implemented in Solidity using the Keccak256 hashing function, that prevents repeated storage of identical IP addresses and thereby curbs unnecessary blockchain usage. The overall workflow spans alarm generation, blockchain validation, block creation, and the distribution of updated blacklists across collaborating domains. Evaluation centers on five criteria: decentralization, collaboration, trust, adaptability, and privacy preservation, and the framework improves scalability by more than 50% relative to earlier blockchain-based defense systems, successfully storing and advertising over 100 malicious IP addresses per transaction while supporting multiple IDS models in parallel without overloading any single node. It is also lightweight at the device level, since IoT devices need not run blockchain nodes; blockchain operations are handled by IDS servers, thereby easing the computational burden on resource-constrained devices. The duplication-check mechanism further reduces redundant storage and lowers transaction costs, indirectly improving operational efficiency. That said, detailed experimental energy benchmarking is not reported, and the framework remains at a proof-of-concept stage, without a comprehensive evaluation of detection accuracy, latency, or real-time throughput.

8.5.3 Deep learning based Green IDS

The Distributed Network Protocol 3 (DNP3), widely used in Industrial Control Systems and SCADA-based smart grid environments, has notable security weaknesses that warrant close examination. Although DNP3 is deployed extensively across critical infrastructure, it was not originally designed with robust built-in security mechanisms and therefore remains vulnerable to cyberattacks that can disrupt services, manipulate operational data, or trigger denial-of-service conditions. Incidents such as the attack on the Ukrainian power grid and the Stuxnet worm illustrate the severe consequences that can follow when such weaknesses are exploited. Two objectives follow from these limitations. The first is to systematically identify and then experimentally implement DNP3-specific attack vectors to demonstrate the protocol's vulnerabilities in realistic ICS environments. The second is to design a machine-learning-based intrusion detection system that accurately detects and classifies DNP3-targeted attacks. This pairing of offensive analysis with defensive system design forms a single, unified framework.

Eight DNP3-focused attacks were implemented, including disabling unsolicited messages, cold and warm restarts, slave discovery, data initialization through man-in-the-middle manipulation, stopping application processes, and replay attacks using ARP poisoning, each exploiting application-layer function codes or weaknesses in the protocol's design. Network traffic was generated in two ways: the first employed CICFlowMeter to extract roughly 80 TCP/IP-based features, while the second used a custom DNP3-specific flow generator to extract over 100 protocol-level attributes. All flows were labeled by attack type to enable supervised learning. Detection itself relied on a DNN: two separate DNN models were trained, one on the TCP/IP flow features and the other on the DNP3-specific features. The network architecture comprises ten fully connected layers with ReLU activations and a softmax output layer, trained with the Adam optimizer at a learning rate of 0.0001 and categorical cross-entropy loss over 1000 epochs. The system performs multi-class classification across the eight DNP3 attacks and normal traffic, and the TCP/IP-based model additionally detects ARP poisoning. Evaluated on accuracy, precision, recall, and F1-score, the DNP3 flow-based DNN achieved an accuracy of 99.0%, with precision of 95.8%, recall of 95.49%, and an F1-score of 95.65%.

The integration of Software-Defined Networking (SDN) with Industrial Internet of Things (IIoT) environments presents a distinct set of security challenges. While SDN improves scalability, flexibility, and centralized control, it also introduces new attack surfaces, including flow-rule injection, man-in-the-middle attacks, and command injection targeting packet payloads. Conventional protections such as firewalls, encryption, and access control prove insufficient for securing multilayer

SDN-based IIoT architectures, particularly against coordinated or advanced attacks. A two-component security framework addresses this by combining a CNN-based IDS for application-layer protection with a blockchain-based verification mechanism for network-layer protection. The architecture brings together sensors and actuators, PLC and RTU devices, SDN switches, a Ryu SDN controller, an IDS implemented as a controller application, a private MultiChain blockchain, and a Detection Node. The IDS runs inside the SDN controller and inspects packet payloads before new flow rules are installed in the switches, while the attack model accounts for command-injection attacks that alter packet content, flow-rule injection attacks that manipulate packet headers, and man-in-the-middle attacks occurring at the southbound interface.

The CNN-based IDS is trained on the ICS natural-gas-pipeline dataset, from which 18 relevant features are selected from the original 27 after preprocessing, with attack classes spanning normal traffic, injection attacks, denial-of-service attacks, and reconnaissance. Its architecture consists of two one-dimensional convolution layers followed by max-pooling and average-pooling layers, and two fully connected layers, using ReLU activation and a softmax output layer for classification. For network-layer security, a private multi-chain blockchain verifies the integrity of flow rules: when the controller installs a rule, a copy is stored on the blockchain, and the Detection Node later retrieves both the blockchain record and the switch flow-table logs, comparing the number of entries, the rule content, and the Hard age field that indicates modification time. Any inconsistency between the stored rule and the active rule signals a possible flow-rule injection or man-in-the-middle attack. The results show strong detection performance: in binary classification, the IDS reaches 94.75% accuracy, with precision of 95.28%, recall of 93.84%, and an F1-score of 94.48%, while in multi-class classification it attains 94.65% accuracy, 97.02% precision, 88.86% recall, and a 92.31% F1-score. Integration testing further confirms that the IDS detects and blocks malicious payloads, while flow-rule manipulation and man-in-the-middle attacks are caught through blockchain-based verification, thereby delivering coordinated protection for both data-plane traffic and control-plane flow rules in SDN-enabled IIoT systems.

The closed-set assumption in Industrial IoT systems deserves scrutiny, and the DC-IDS framework offers one way to move beyond it. IIoT systems frequently operate in open, dynamic environments where new and previously unseen attacks emerge regularly, yet closed-set classifiers tend to misclassify such unknown attacks as benign traffic or as known attack types. DC-IDS addresses this shortcoming through an RL[3]-based approach tailored to IIoT scenarios, integrating a Deep Q-Network (DQN)-based RL module, a CVAE[4], and Extreme Value Theory. The

[3] Reinforcement learning is a machine learning paradigm in which an agent learns to make optimal decisions by interacting with an environment through trial and error, taking actions and adjusting its behavior based on rewards or penalties received to maximize cumulative long-term reward.

[4] A Conditional Variational Autoencoder is a generative model that extends the variational autoencoder by conditioning both the encoding and decoding processes on additional information such as class labels, enabling controlled generation of data samples belonging to specified categories or conditions.

intrusion detection task is first cast as a discrete-time Markov Decision Process, in which network-traffic features represent system states, traffic labels correspond to actions, and a reward mechanism assigns positive rewards for correct classifications and negative ones for errors. Training stability is reinforced by a target network, double Q-learning, an epsilon-greedy exploration strategy, and an experience replay buffer. The CVAE is embedded within the DQN framework to enable open-set recognition and comprises a prior network, a recognition network, and a decoder network. The detection task is thereby divided into two components: known-traffic classification, which the DQN handles by learning latent representations and producing classification outputs, and unknown-attack recognition, which proceeds by analyzing reconstruction error. Because unknown samples tend to yield higher reconstruction errors than known traffic, those errors are modeled using Extreme Value Theory and a Generalized Pareto Distribution, after which a probability threshold determines whether a given instance belongs to an unknown class. In practice, DC-IDS improves recognition of unknown attacks compared with earlier open-set approaches while maintaining strong classification performance on known traffic.

Intrusion detection in SCADA[5] networks carries an important practical limitation. Most DL models, CNN-, LSTM-, and RNN-based approaches among them, require large volumes of labeled attack data to train effectively, yet real industrial environments rarely supply such data, particularly for newly emerging or rare attack types. This is especially true of SCADA systems supporting critical infrastructure such as gas pipelines and power grids, which seldom provide abundant labeled attack samples for model development. The Few-Shot Learning-Based Intrusion Detection System, known as FS-IDS, addresses this constraint, achieving high detection accuracy even with only a handful of attack samples. The framework unfolds in three phases: data preprocessing, model training, and detection. During preprocessing, continuous features are standardized via Z-score normalization and reduced via Principal Component Analysis to preserve important variance while lowering dimensionality, and discrete features are one-hot encoded, with an additional bit reserved for unknown categories. The processed features are then reshaped into two-dimensional matrices for use with a CNN. The core detection model pairs Prototypical Networks with a two-dimensional CNN: the CNN learns an embedding function that maps input features into a latent space, a prototype vector is computed for each class as the mean embedding of its support examples, and classification proceeds by measuring the Euclidean distance between query samples and class prototypes, with the model optimized through a negative log-likelihood loss. Evaluated on the Gas Pipeline SCADA dataset, which contains both frequent and rare attack categories, FS-IDS attains roughly 83.78% accuracy and an 82.78%

[5] SCADA systems are industrial control systems that monitor, control, and collect real-time data from distributed industrial processes and infrastructure, such as power grids, water treatment, and manufacturing, through sensors, controllers (e.g., PLCs/RTUs), and centralized supervisory software

macro-F1 score across few-shot tasks. Performance improves as more attack samples become available, rising from about 74.96% accuracy in one-shot settings to 89.06% in ten-shot scenarios, with marked gains across several rare attack types, evidence that the model remains robust even when training data are scarce.

Wireless Sensor Networks (WSNs) pose growing cybersecurity concerns of their own, as they are widely deployed across critical sectors such as industrial automation, environmental monitoring, healthcare, and defense. Because sensor nodes have limited energy, memory, and processing capacity and are often installed in unattended or hostile environments, they are highly exposed to attacks such as eavesdropping, spoofing, and denial-of-service. Traditional ML and DL models tend either to impose heavy computational overhead or to adapt poorly to continuously evolving threats. MultiNet-IDS addresses this difficulty as an ensemble detection framework that combines Exhaustive Feature Selection, DRL, and LSTM networks to produce an intrusion detection system that is adaptive, accurate, and computationally efficient for heterogeneous, time-varying WSN environments. Feature selection proceeds in two stages: first, Pearson correlation and mutual information filters out redundant or weakly relevant features; second, an exhaustive combinatorial search evaluates all remaining feature subsets with five-fold cross-validation, selecting the subset that maximizes the F1-score while minimizing computational cost; thereby reducing dimensionality without sacrificing predictive power. The Deep RL module casts intrusion detection as a learning task in which the agent interacts with the traffic environment, earning rewards for correct classifications and penalties for errors, and applying Q-learning updates to refine its policy over time, an adaptive mechanism that lets the model respond to shifting attack patterns. In parallel, the LSTM network analyzes sequential traffic to capture long-term temporal dependencies; through gated memory units, it overcomes vanishing-gradient problems and detects slow or distributed attacks that unfold gradually. The outputs of the DRL and LSTM components are then merged through a late-stage ensemble strategy to improve robustness and precision. Across three benchmark datasets: UNSW-NB15, CIC-DDoS2019, and Kitsune, standalone LSTM models reached moderate accuracy of 80 to 85%, while the DRL component performed more strongly, attaining about 96.2% accuracy on UNSW-NB15 and 94.7% on CIC-DDoS2019, though convergence was less stable on Kitsune. When integrated into the full **MultiNet-IDS** ensemble, the approach achieved up to 99.1% accuracy with substantially lower false-positive rates, demonstrating that combining feature optimization, RL, and temporal modeling can yield a robust and adaptive intrusion detection framework well suited to Wireless Sensor Network environments.

In addition to the growing cybersecurity risks in Wireless Sensor Networks (WSNs), cybersecurity challenges are increasing in Industry 4.0 and Industrial Internet of Things environments, where manufacturing systems integrate WSNs with IoT devices, cloud platforms, artificial intelligence, data-driven monitoring, and so on. Although these technologies improve automation and machine-to-machine communication, they also increase exposure to cyber threats such as denial-of-service, distributed denial-of-service, ransomware, man-in-the-middle, backdoor insertion, injection, and scanning. To detect these attacks, a Hybrid Intrusion Detection Model (HIDMN) was introduced, integrating an optimized CNN, a Long Short-Term Memory network, transfer learning techniques, and the Grey Wolf Optimizer for hyperparameter tuning, to effectively identify multi-class attacks in Industry 4.0 networks. The CNN component is enhanced using the Grey Wolf Optimizer, which adjusts important parameters such as batch size, number of epochs, pooling size, kernel size, and number of filters. This optimization improves feature extraction, reduces overfitting, and stabilizes model convergence. The hybrid CNN-LSTM architecture enables the CNN layers to extract spatial features from traffic data, while the LSTM layers capture temporal dependencies and sequential attack behaviors. Transfer learning is incorporated by freezing early CNN layers and retraining the final layers for classification. This approach allows the model to reuse previously learned representations and improve learning efficiency for complex multi-class detection tasks. Experimental analysis on the ToN-IoT dataset suggests that the optimized CNN-LSTM model with transfer learning achieved an accuracy of 94.4%, precision of 92.7%, recall of 52.39%, and an F1-score of 56.6%. On the UNSW-NB15 dataset, the model achieved a precision of 94.25%. Overall, the study shows that combining hyperparameter optimization, hybrid DL, and transfer learning can enhance multi-class intrusion detection performance in Industry 4.0 environments.

8.5.4 Other techniques to support Green IDS

Network-history analysis offers another effective basis for detecting intrusions in Industrial Control Systems. One such approach examines security in ICS by analyzing historical Siemens TIA Portal project archives, rather than relying solely on network traffic or real-time process data. The focus falls on historical PLC configuration files, program code, metadata, and timestamps preserved in long-term backups. From roughly three years of archived TIA Portal projects collected at an automotive manufacturing plant, a heuristic-based anomaly detection framework is constructed. The dataset comprises structured JSON representations of PLC blocks: OB, FB, FC, and DB, together with their associated metadata. Seven timing-related variables are considered: creation time, modification time, code modification time, interface modification time, load-relevant modification time, compile time, and download time. Two storage-related variables are also analyzed: required load memory and required work memory.

To represent realistic threats, three attacker scenarios are evaluated. The first is a stealthy PLC programmer who inserts malicious code during normal working hours; the second is a backup coordinator who modifies data outside legitimate working hours, before backups are saved; and the third is a non-stealthy attacker who makes random, distributed modifications. Together, these scenarios permit a systematic assessment of detection effectiveness. The time-based detection approach performs very unevenly across them. It achieves an AUC of 0.999 for the backup-coordinator scenario; near-perfect discrimination when attacks fall outside normal working hours, but the AUC drops to 0.297 for the stealthy PLC programmer and 0.506 for the various-attacker scenario. Time-based rules thus prove highly effective against night-time activity yet inadequate for insiders operating within legitimate time windows, leaving precision and recall unbalanced in stealthy cases and limiting the overall F-measure.

The size-based method, which examines relative changes in load and work memory, performs better for some attacker types, reaching an AUC of 0.812 for the various-attacker scenario and 0.683 for the PLC programmer, and so detects distributed or memory-intensive modifications more reliably. Its performance is worse in the backup-coordinator scenario, with an AUC of 0.493; although storage analysis improves recall in stealthier cases, it remains vulnerable to carefully controlled modifications that keep memory changes minimal. Combining timing and storage features yields more balanced performance across all three scenarios, with the combined method achieving AUCs of 0.624 for the PLC programmer, 0.899 for the backup coordinator, and 0.834 for the various attacker. Relative to the single-feature approaches, this combination raises AUC by roughly 32.7% for the PLC programmer, 40.6% for the backup coordinator (against size-only detection), and 32.8% for the various attacker, reflecting better trade-offs between precision and recall and higher overall F-measure values. Even so, false positives on legitimate project updates can reach as high as 19.87%, meaning that while detection sensitivity improves, some normal modifications are still flagged as anomalies: a limitation that affects precision in real-world deployment.

Modbus/TCP is widely used in Industrial Automation and Control Systems for its simplicity and reliability, yet it provides no built-in mechanisms for authentication, encryption, or data-integrity protection. Attackers can therefore manipulate values within the Modbus Protocol Data Unit and mount false data injection, spoofing, denial-of-service, and reconnaissance attacks. One way to strengthen ICS security against these threats is to implement a plant-specific, misuse-based intrusion detection system designed to identify malicious manipulation of process values carried over Modbus/TCP. To support such work, a cyber-physical testbed simulating a water-treatment plant was built, comprising two Siemens S7 programmable logic controllers, a PcVue SCADA system, a managed switch with mirrored traffic, and a Security Onion platform running the Suricata intrusion detection engine. Guided by the ISA/IEC 62443 security-level framework, three principal attack types were designed: denial-of-service through TCP SYN flooding, spoofing via man-in-the-middle false data injection, and intelligence gathering through network scanning. Without an intrusion detection system in place, these attacks went either undetected or were misread as ordinary communication failures.

The detection system itself is misuse-based and built on Suricata, chosen for its advanced Modbus/TCP parsing and acceptable detection latency. Crucially, it introduces process-aware rules that inspect the Modbus data field rather than network headers alone. Custom rules were written to flag abnormal register values, unauthorized write operations, suspicious function codes, and excessive traffic patterns; 82 tailored rules in total that monitor process-specific behavior and are deliberately structured so that operational engineers can modify them easily, keeping the system practical for industrial deployment. Detection performance proved strong: the system identified 100% of denial-of-service and reconnaissance attacks and roughly 96% of spoofing attacks, with the slightly lower figure arising when attackers injected values that fell within acceptable operational ranges. The system generates detection alerts but provides no automatic mitigation. On the whole, process-level, misuse-based intrusion detection markedly improves the visibility of Modbus/TCP attacks in industrial control environments.

8.6 Renewable energy-based Green IDS for IoT networks

Renewable energy in the context of the Internet of Things (IoT) refers to the use of naturally replenishable ambient sources, such as solar radiation, thermal gradients, mechanical vibrations, radio-frequency signals, and biochemical reactions, to power sensing and communication devices via energy-harvesting mechanisms, rather than relying solely on batteries. These techniques enable long-term autonomous operation and reduce carbon footprint, but they also fundamentally change the security dynamics of IoT networks because device availability now depends on fluctuating environmental power rather than stable electrical supply. When energy becomes intermittent or scarce, IoT devices may reduce processing, skip authentication, or downgrade encryption, thereby exposing them to attacks such as man-in-the-middle interception, side-channel inference, and replay attacks. In real-world environments like smart homes, industrial monitoring, agriculture, healthcare wearables, and smart cities, attackers can also launch denial-of-service and energy-depletion attacks by repeatedly triggering communication or sensing operations, draining harvested energy and forcing nodes offline; routing-based attacks (blackhole/selective forwarding) disrupt packet delivery; malicious trigger requests and control-plane flooding increase overhead and congestion; fake aggregated data corrupts decision making; and physical tampering or blocking of solar/RF sources disables entire sensing regions. The impact on network communication is severe: increased latency, packet loss, unreliable routing paths, compromised data integrity, and intermittent connectivity, ultimately leading to service failure in safety-critical applications such as traffic control, health monitoring, and environmental surveillance. Therefore, renewable-powered IoT improves sustainability while simultaneously broadening the attack surface, making energy availability itself a cybersecurity factor rather than merely a performance metric.

DEPRONN-ES (Dual Energy Profile for IoT with Enhanced Security) is a framework that jointly addresses energy efficiency and privacy protection in IoT networks. It models the network as a multi-objective optimization problem in which conventional battery-powered nodes seek to minimize energy consumption, while renewable-powered nodes aim for energy-neutral operation. Rather than solving the computationally expensive optimal formulation directly, the framework adopts a heuristic routing strategy: during parent selection, paths powered by renewable nodes are preferred, and where none is available, the path with the highest minimum residual energy is chosen. Data aggregation is likewise adaptive, increasing when battery-powered nodes are low on energy to reduce transmissions and decreasing when renewable energy is plentiful. This cooperative arrangement lets heterogeneous devices work together while each preserves its own energy objective. To safeguard sensitive battery information, the framework applies differential privacy, adding Laplace noise to shared energy values so that attackers cannot single out weak nodes; the degree of privacy is governed by a configurable privacy budget, with smaller values yielding stronger privacy at the cost of precision, which allows useful network statistics to be retained while individual device conditions remain concealed. The system is implemented with realistic IoT technologies: Contiki OS and the Cooja emulator, RPL routing, CoAP communication, IEEE 802.15.4 with 6LoWPAN, the KiBaM battery model, and solar energy-harvesting traces enabling evaluation under practical smart-city conditions, where it delivers significant gains in both security and efficiency. In attack scenarios, the attacker success rate decreased from 100% to approximately 13.33%, representing an 87% reduction due to obfuscated battery information. Under normal operation, the framework balanced routing paths, reduced unnecessary transmissions, and maintained connectivity across nodes with different energy capabilities. Energy analysis showed that protected nodes saved roughly 286 μAh on average during attacks, and traditional nodes consumed less power when energy was limited. Networks with more renewable nodes harvested more energy than they consumed, and the best privacy-energy trade-off occurred around a privacy budget of approximately 0.36. Overall, the framework simultaneously enhances resilience and improves energy efficiency in heterogeneous IoT environments.

An integrated cyber-physical resilience framework brings together optimization, ML, and secure communication to address these challenges in concert. Its aim is a unified design that simultaneously ensures secure operation, adaptive recovery, and resilient energy management in renewable-energy-driven IoT power grids. A vulnerability assessment module begins by analyzing system risk in light of renewable-energy variability, communication dependencies, and network-topology relationships. Resilient operation is achieved through a hybrid control strategy that pairs distributionally robust optimization (DRO) with multi-agent RL (MARL): the DRO component ensures reliable energy allocation under uncertainty, while MARL enables decentralized agents to learn adaptive control policies and recover from cyberattacks. Several security layers reinforce the framework, including blockchain-based authentication for trustworthy data exchange, lightweight cryptographic techniques suited to constrained IoT devices, and a deep-learning intrusion detection mechanism that recognizes abnormal behavior. The model captures the supply-demand balance, the corrupted measurements produced by attacks, and the degradation of resilience, and is validated on IEEE benchmark distribution networks under simulated false data injection, denial-of-service, and spoofing attacks. In evaluation, the approach performs markedly better than conventional optimization methods, rule-based control, and single-agent learning strategies. The framework reduces resilience loss by approximately 63.9% and achieves intrusion detection accuracy of about 92.8%

while lowering operational costs. The resilience index reaches around 0.847, compared with less than 0.754 for baseline approaches, and the system shows faster recovery and stable energy allocation across different attack intensities. Renewable-rich configurations also benefit from improved operational stability through adaptive, learning-based control. Energy performance is assessed using operational efficiency, renewable utilization, and system stability rather than direct power measurement. The proposed method reduces the operational cost to approximately $44.1/MWh$ and maintains supply-demand balance during disturbances. Renewable energy curtailment decreases by about 12 18%, and carbon emissions decline by approximately 5 8% due to better coordination of distributed energy resources. A combined resilience metric that incorporates energy continuity, communication reliability, and detection capability indicates that improved security directly contributes to sustainable and reliable energy operations.

Secure and efficient energy management in smart cities poses a distinctive challenge, since renewable energy sources, electric transportation, and IoT-enabled infrastructure now operate in a tightly interconnected environment. Modern urban systems weave together smart grids, microgrids, electric vehicles, charging stations, and energy hubs to improve sustainability and operational performance, but this dense connectivity also widens their exposure to cyber threats. Variability in renewable generation, bidirectional vehicle-to-grid interactions, and the continuous, large-scale exchange of data introduce uncertainty and instability that, if exploited, could disrupt essential urban services. The aim, therefore, is a unified framework that can optimize energy transactions, manage uncertainty in renewable energy, and protect communication processes all at once. The solution takes the form of a cyber-physical, digital-twin-based architecture that integrates simulation, optimization, and intrusion detection. A digital twin reproduces the real-time operation of the smart grid, transportation system, microgrid, and energy hub from sensor data, allowing control decisions to be evaluated safely. Energy management is optimized with the Honey Bee Mating Optimization algorithm, which determines charging-station placement and coordinates energy exchange among electric vehicles, the subway system, and the grid, while uncertainty in renewable generation is handled through the Point Estimate Method 2m-scheme, which converts stochastic variables into deterministic equivalents. Cybersecurity is provided by a GAN-based intrusion detection system trained via an evolutionary optimization process to detect false data injection and related attacks. In simulation, the framework improves both operational efficiency and security performance. The optimization approach produces higher-quality solutions and requires less computation time than genetic and particle-swarm algorithms, taking about 54 seconds instead of 82 seconds for genetic optimization. The intrusion detection component achieves approximately 85.29% precision, 96.61% recall, 90.69% F1-score, and about 91.43% overall accuracy, indicating reliable detection with low missed attacks. These outcomes enhance the safety of data exchange across the smart-city network. Energy evaluation demonstrates better utilization and cost efficiency across transportation and grid components. The framework supports bidirectional energy transfer between vehicles, the grid, and the subway system, improving resource balance. Modeling renewable uncertainty further reduces operational costs, while optimal charging-station placement improves energy-flow coordination. Electric vehicles effectively use stored energy, and the integrated management maintains supply-demand balance. The digital twin also enables adaptive optimization by testing different operating scenarios without affecting the real infrastructure.

8.7 Energy-focused comparative evaluation of available IDS models

8.7.1 Energy-focused comparative analysis of available Green IDS in transportation systems

In Internet of Vehicles (IoV), Cooperative Intelligent Transportation Systems (CITS), and connected or autonomous vehicle environments, an intrusion detection system can be deployed only if it satisfies strict real-time constraints while operating on resource-limited edge hardware and under intermittent connectivity. Decision windows are often measured in milliseconds, and delays can directly affect the system's safety measures. For this reason, Green IDS evaluation in transportation must treat energy efficiency as a primary objective rather than a secondary consideration. In practice, energy performance is reflected in several measurable indicators: inference latency and throughput, model size and memory footprint, communication overhead, and the frequency of computationally expensive operations such as retraining, graph reconstruction, or explainability analysis; especially in FL settings. When direct power measurements are available, they provide the strongest validation. In many cases, however, runtime and memory usage serve as justified and transparent proxies for energy consumption.

An energy-aware comparative evaluation of IDS families reveals meaningful differences. Explainable and real-time mitigation frameworks provide the strongest direct evidence when they explicitly report energy per node, as well as latency and packet delivery metrics. For example, systems that measure joules per node and maintain millisecond-level latency demonstrate that detection, explanation, and mitigation can be integrated within bounded energy budgets. However, explainability and mitigation modules must be carefully engineered to avoid unnecessary overhead. Rate-limiting explanation processes and activating them only for uncertain or high-impact alerts helps maintain low average energy usage.

FL-based IDS deployed on real edge devices highlights a different energy challenge. In such systems, local training time and communication rounds often dominate energy consumption. Training and processing times can vary significantly with dataset complexity, directly affecting computational load and battery usage. Therefore, energy-aware federated IDS designs should minimize on-device training complexity and reduce participation frequency without compromising the benefits of collaborative learning. Federated fine-tuning strategies offer a practical compromise between accuracy and efficiency. By freezing heavy feature-extraction layers and updating only lightweight classification components, these approaches reduce the memory footprint and execution time while preserving acceptable detection performance. This balance makes partial fine-tuning highly aligned with Green IDS principles in transportation systems.

Graph-based IDS approaches introduce additional considerations. Vehicular environments naturally generate dense interaction graphs, which may lead to high computational overhead. Energy-aware graph designs that constrain connectivity and enforce sparsity reduce memory requirements and message-passing cost. Event-triggered graph updates, rather than continuous reconstruction, further improve efficiency in dynamic mobility conditions. Model compression techniques provide a broadly applicable energy-saving mechanism. Parameter reduction, pruning, quantization, and dimensionality reduction decrease memory usage and accelerate inference while maintaining near-baseline accuracy. Reporting feasibility on embedded platforms, such as millisecond-level inference times and manageable memory consumption, strengthens the case for deployability in transportation edge environments.

From a deployment perspective, several practical guidelines emerge. Energy should be measured explicitly whenever possible; otherwise, latency, throughput, memory usage, and CPU utilization should be reported transparently as proxies. Always-on edge inference must remain lightweight, while computationally heavy modules, such as explainability, retraining, or advanced correlation, should be triggered only when necessary. In FL settings, reducing local training cost and limiting communication rounds are critical for energy control. Sparse graph construction and compression-by-design should be incorporated early in system design to ensure scalability.

Overall, energy-centric evaluation is essential for validating Green IDS in transportation IoT systems. Detection accuracy alone is insufficient. Sustainable deployment requires balancing security effectiveness with latency, computational overhead, communication cost, and hardware feasibility. Only by integrating these dimensions can Green IDS frameworks support safe, efficient, and environmentally responsible intelligent transportation ecosystems.

Table 8.1 compares the IDS models evaluated in Smart Transportation systems.

8.7.2 Energy-focused comparative analysis of available Green IDS in smart cities

Energy efficiency is a central requirement for intrusion detection systems deployed in smart city environments. Unlike traditional IT networks, smart cities integrate battery-powered sensors, vehicular units, fog nodes, renewable microgrids, and cloud services into a single interconnected ecosystem. These components operate under limited power budgets and dynamic workloads. For this reason, IDS evaluation should extend beyond detection accuracy. It should also consider computational cost, communication overhead, latency, scalability, and system resilience under constrained energy conditions.

Table 8.1 Energy-Focused Comparative Analysis of Green IDS Frameworks in Transportation IoT.

IDS/Framework	Target Environment	Core Technique	Learning Setting	Edge Suitability	Green/Energy Mechanism	Energy Evidence	Reported Performance	Main Limitations
GTBNN	ITS / Transportation IoT	Game-theoretic module selection + Bayesian NN + Bayesian optimization + RFE	Supervised	Medium	Selective module activation avoids running all classifiers and reduces redundant computation	Indirect (architectural efficiency)	Acc 98.23% (UNSW-NB15), 99.98% (CICIDS2017), 99.87% (Bot-IoT)	Energy not directly measured; depends on accurate threat modeling assumptions
CNN+LSTM DLCE-1	Vehicular misbehavior detection	Hybrid CNN–LSTM classifier	Supervised	High	Optimized edge inference with low latency	Indirect (latency proxy; inference ~0.3 ms)	Acc 99.63%; F1 96.75%	Preprocessing overhead dominates; training heavy
DLCE-2	Vehicular networks	Two-stage hierarchical classification	Supervised	High	Early filtering reduces invocation of deeper models	Indirect (structural efficiency)	F1 95.58%	Error propagation between stages
DLCE-3	Vehicular networks	Hierarchical multi-branch classifier	Supervised	High	Selective deeper classification reduces unnecessary computation	Indirect	F1 96.49%	Pipeline complexity increases
PIGNUS	IoT botnet / vehicular traffic	CNN + GRU hybrid model	Supervised	Medium–High	Feature redundancy removal lowers dimensionality and compute cost	Indirect	Strong multi-class performance	Model size and latency not fully detailed
SDLMA-IITS	IoT-enabled ITS	Ensemble CNN-GRU + CNN-LSTM + SHAP + authentication	Supervised	Medium	Feature selection + ensemble robustness reduce retraining cost	Indirect	Acc 99.65%; F1 0.991	Explainability and ensemble add overhead
EAI-IDS	IoT-enabled transportation	LSTM + Random Forest + SHAP + mitigation optimization	Hybrid	High	Multi-objective optimization minimizes delay and energy per node	Direct (approx. 2.1 J/node)	Acc 94.2%; latency 15.2 ms; PDR 98.5%	Higher architectural complexity
Hybrid XGBoost–CNN	EV charging infrastructure	XGBoost + CNN + SHAP	Supervised	Medium	Efficient inference (approx. 1 ms/sample) and adaptive updating	Indirect (time-based proxy)	Acc 94–96%; AUC 0.965–0.975	Continuous updates may increase long-term energy cost

continued on next page

Table 8.1 (*continued*)

IDS/Framework	Target Environment	Core Technique	Learning Setting	Edge Suitability	Green/Energy Mechanism	Energy Evidence	Reported Performance	Main Limitations
ReMeNet	Transportation CPS intrusion	Memory-enhanced GAN	Hybrid / Generative	Medium	Synthetic minority generation reduces imbalance retraining	Indirect (training heavy)	Acc 91.70%; macro F1 80.19%	GAN training intensive; limited edge suitability
XDL-IDS	Safety-critical vehicular systems	1D CNN + GRU + SHAP	Supervised	Medium–High	Stable GRU architecture improves inference stability	Indirect	Binary acc near 100%; multi-class 99.64%	SHAP adds computational overhead
FedFT-3 / FedFT-1	Federated Transportation IoT	Server pretrain + client fine-tune head only	Federated + Transfer	High	Freezing feature extractor reduces memory and runtime on clients	Indirect (memory/time proxy)	FedFT-3: 99.2%; FedFT-1: 94.3%	Communication rounds consume energy
FL-IDS (LR-IDS)	Transportation IoT FL	PCC + Logistic Regression	Federated	High	Lightweight classifier reduces compute demand	Indirect (processing time reported)	NSL-KDD 96.82%; Car-Hacking 93.56%	Lower modeling capacity
FL-IDS (PCC-CNN)	Transportation IoT FL	1D CNN with dropout	Federated	Medium–High	Balanced accuracy–compute trade-off	Indirect (training time proxy)	Car-Hacking 99.93%	Training and communication overhead
QnGSA	Autonomous transport systems	Sparse hypercube graph + GAT	Supervised / Graph	Medium–High	Sparse design limits edges to $\lceil \log_2(m) \rceil$ reducing compute	Indirect	Acc 99.01%; macro F1 98.79%	Graph updates costly in high mobility
PRADA	Navigation route security	Proactive risk assessment	Hybrid	Medium	Preventative mitigation reduces repeated detection cost	Not specified	Not specified	Not a conventional IDS classifier

Blockchain-enabled intrusion detection systems provide strong integrity and decentralization, but they introduce notable energy costs. In Internet of Vehicles environments, permissioned blockchain systems that depend on cryptographic hashing and Proof-of-Work consensus mechanisms significantly increase computational demand, particularly at infrastructure components such as cloudlets and roadside units. Although mining is not performed on vehicles themselves, repeated hashing and block verification consume processing resources and add communication overhead for block propagation. This architecture improves system robustness and reduces the risk of centralized failure, potentially saving energy by preventing large-scale disruptions. However, compared to lightweight ML approaches, blockchain-based IDS generally require higher processing energy and are better suited for infrastructure-powered nodes rather than battery-driven edge devices.

Distributed and semi-distributed ML IDS architectures offer a more energy-efficient alternative. By shifting computation from centralized servers to fog and edge nodes, these systems reduce latency and processing bottlenecks. Empirical comparisons show significant reductions in model-building time when moving from centralized to distributed settings. Lower computation time directly implies reduced CPU usage and energy consumption. Edge-level processing also decreases the need to transmit large volumes of data to the cloud, thereby lowering communication energy. Although semi-distributed models may slightly improve accuracy, fully distributed architectures often provide a better balance between detection performance and energy efficiency. For smart cities partially powered by renewable sources, such architectures demonstrate strong scalability under energy constraints.

Digital twin-based DL IDS models for smart grid control systems introduce another dimension to energy evaluation. These systems combine synthetic attack simulation, representation balancing, and hybrid classifiers. The training phase of deep models and digital twin simulations requires substantial computational resources. Once deployed, inference costs become moderate. In energy-critical infrastructures such as power grids, the higher training energy cost is often justified because preventing grid disruptions preserves macro-level energy stability. In this context, operational reliability outweighs computational efficiency.

Generative adversarial approaches, such as CycleGAN-based detection for false data injection attacks, also demand careful energy consideration. Adversarial training and metaheuristic optimization loops increase training complexity and energy consumption. After training, inference remains moderately expensive, and detection can be achieved within acceptable time windows. Although such methods consume more energy than simpler classifiers, their ability to detect previously unseen anomalies may prevent cascading failures in traffic or sensing systems. This preventive capability can indirectly protect broader energy infrastructure.

Hybrid ensemble frameworks that incorporate feature selection techniques offer a more balanced energy profile. By applying recursive feature elimination and optimization strategies, redundant attributes are removed before classification. Reduced dimensionality lowers model complexity and shortens processing time. While ensemble inference may require additional computation per instance, the optimized feature space compensates for this overhead. Compared with deep generative models, such hybrid approaches often achieve high accuracy at moderate computational cost, making them practical for fog- or cloud-assisted smart-city deployments.

From a broader architectural perspective, zero-trust and end-to-end security frameworks also influence energy consumption. Continuous authentication, encryption, and integrity verification increase processing load, particularly for constrained IoT devices. Overly aggressive security provisioning may unintentionally drain node resources. Therefore, energy-aware IDS design should employ lightweight cryptographic mechanisms at the edge, adaptively activate detection modules based on context, and offload heavy analytics to the fog or cloud layers.

Overall, from an energy-focused perspective, distributed ML-based IDS architectures provide the most practical balance between detection accuracy and computational efficiency for smart-city IoT deployments. Blockchain-based IDS offers strong integrity guarantees but introduces significant hashing and mining overhead. DL and generative adversarial approaches improve anomaly generalization but require careful placement at fog or cloud layers to avoid draining edge resources. Hybrid feature-selection frameworks (e.g., REPOStack) demonstrate a promising direction for reducing computational complexity without sacrificing detection performance. However, across all evaluated systems, explicit energy metrics, such as Joules per detection or CPU-cycle profiling, are largely absent, highlighting a major research gap in green IDS evaluation for smart cities.

Table 8.2 compares the Green IDS models evaluated in Smart Cities.

Looking ahead, truly sustainable IDS frameworks for smart cities must integrate renewable-powered fog nodes, model compression techniques, federated or hierarchical learning, and standardized energy metrics. Evaluation should include not only precision, recall, and F1-score, but also measurable indicators such as inference latency, CPU utilization, communication overhead, and energy per detection event. By making energy-aware evaluation a primary benchmarking dimension, smart-city security solutions can achieve long-term resilience, scalability, and environmental sustainability.

8.7.3 Energy-focused comparative analysis of available Green IDS in industrial automation

Industrial automation systems operate under stricter energy and computational constraints than traditional IT networks. Programmable logic controllers (PLCs), remote terminal units (RTUs), wireless sensor nodes, and edge gateways often have limited processing capability, memory, and power availability. Therefore, evaluating intrusion detection systems (IDS) for Industrial IoT (IIoT) must extend beyond detection accuracy. A proper energy-oriented evaluation should consider computational complexity, memory usage, communication overhead, feasibility at the edge, training versus inference cost, federated or blockchain aggregation overhead, and real-time latency requirements.

Table 8.2 Energy-Focused Comparative Analysis of IDS Frameworks for Smart City Environments.

IDS/Framework	Target Environment	Core Technique	Learning Setting	Edge Suitability	Green/Energy Mechanism	Energy Evidence	Reported Performance	Main Limitations
BIDS (Blockchain-Enabled IDS)	Internet of Vehicles (IoV), Smart Transportation	Permissioned Blockchain + SHA-256 + Proof-of-Work + Mobility Validation	Rule-based + Behavioral validation	Low for IoT nodes; Moderate for RSUs/Cloudlets	Decentralized validation reduces single-point failure; prevents large-scale disruption	No direct energy metric; PoW implies high computational overhead at cloudlets	98% detection (5% malicious); 85% detection (40% malicious); F1 ≈ 90%	High computational cost due to mining; scalability concerns; not lightweight for edge devices
Semi-Distributed / Distributed ML IDS	IoT-enabled Smart Cities (Fog–Edge Architecture)	Stacked Autoencoder + Feature Selection + MLP	Supervised ML (Anomaly-based)	High (especially distributed version)	Parallel processing; reduced cloud transmission; latency reduction	Build time reduced from 12,073 s (centralized) to 73.52 s (distributed)	Accuracy ≈ 99.97% (semi-distributed); 97.8% (distributed); FAR ≈ 0.0001%	Slight accuracy trade-off in fully distributed model; requires coordination overhead
Digital Twin-Based DL IDS (SGCS)	Smart Grid Control Systems (Cyber-Physical Infrastructure)	Deep Representation Learning + SVM + KNN + Digital Twin Simulation	Supervised + Synthetic Data Augmentation	Moderate (Primarily Fog/Control Center)	Balanced representation reduces retraining cycles; proactive simulation prevents grid-level energy disruption	No explicit Joule metric; high training computation; real-time inference moderate	Outperforms DNN, RF, LSTM in accuracy, precision, recall, F1-score	High training complexity; digital twin simulation overhead; resource intensive
CycleGAN-Based FDIA IDS	Smart City IoT Sensing Infrastructure	CycleGAN + BBO + Whale Optimization	Unsupervised (Generative Anomaly Detection)	Low–Moderate (Better for Fog/Cloud)	Learns normal data distribution; optimized hyperparameters reduce re-training waste	No direct energy metric; 2-minute detection response time	Detection rate ≈ 95%; FPR ≈ 5%	High adversarial training cost; optimization overhead; not lightweight for constrained devices
REPOStack Hybrid IDS	Cloud-supported IoT Smart Cities	RFE + SAEO-PSO + AdaBoost + SVM + DNN + XGBoost (Stacked Ensemble)	Supervised ML	Moderate (Best suited for Fog/Cloud)	Hybrid feature selection reduces dimensionality and processing load	No explicit energy metric; reduced feature set lowers inference complexity	Accuracy: 98.95% (NSL-KDD); 99.90% (UNSW-NB15); strong precision and F1-score	Ensemble complexity; optimization overhead; not explicitly evaluated for energy metrics
ANT-Centric Security Architecture (Conceptual)	Multi-Domain Smart Cities (Utility, Transport, Healthcare, Homes)	Zero-Trust End-to-End Data Lifecycle Security	Architectural / Policy-driven	Adaptive (Depends on implementation layer)	Context-aware security placement; avoids over-provisioned security at edge	No quantitative metric; conceptual energy-awareness via lifecycle-based protection	Not performance-focused; framework-level guidance	Conceptual; requires integration with concrete IDS mechanisms

Lightweight and process-aware IDS models demonstrate the strongest energy efficiency. Rule-based systems, such as misuse-oriented Modbus detection implemented through engines like Suricata, operate with deterministic rule matching and do not require ML training. These systems consume minimal CPU resources, require no GPU acceleration, and impose almost no communication overhead. As a result, they are highly suitable for PLC-level deployment. However, they are limited in their ability to detect unknown or zero-day attacks. Similarly, historical configuration analysis approaches that audit PLC project archives operate offline and incur energy cost only during scheduled audits. While highly energy-efficient, they cannot provide real-time protection.

DL-based IDS models introduce significantly higher energy demands. DNP3-based DNNs with multiple fully connected layers and extensive training epochs consume substantial computational resources. Although inference energy is lower once the model is deployed, these architectures are better suited to gateways or cloud servers than to embedded devices. Hybrid models such as optimized CNN-LSTM frameworks improve performance through transfer learning and parameter tuning. Freezing the early layers reduces retraining costs, yet convolutional and sequential components still incur moderate-to-high energy consumption. These models are optimized compared to naive DL designs but remain heavy for low-power PLCs.

RL and open-set detection frameworks further increase computational overhead. Architectures combining Deep Q-Networks, conditional variational autoencoders, and experience replay require iterative updates and continuous policy refinement. While these methods enhance adaptability and reduce false alarms, they demand considerable computational cycles. Consequently, they are more appropriate for fog or cloud layers than for field-level devices. Their indirect energy benefit lies in improved detection of unknown attacks, which may prevent repeated mitigation cycles and broader system disruption.

Ensemble and hybrid IDS models attempt to balance energy and performance. MultiNet-style systems use staged feature selection to reduce input dimensionality before applying DL components. Although training remains expensive, optimized inference can lower operational energy cost. Blockchain-integrated IDS architectures introduce another dimension of energy consumption. When blockchain validation and hashing mechanisms are deployed at controllers or SDN layers, computational and storage overhead increases. However, shifting these tasks away from constrained IoT devices preserves device-level energy budgets. Collaborative blockchain frameworks may reduce redundant storage, yet consensus mechanisms still add network-layer overhead.

Federated and fog-based IDS architectures offer a more balanced solution. FL reduces raw data transmission by sharing model parameters instead of traffic logs. This lowers communication energy while preserving data privacy. However, aggregation rounds and synchronization introduce additional overhead. Few-shot learning approaches provide another energy-efficient alternative. By training on smaller datasets and using lightweight prototype-based networks, these methods reduce retraining frequency and data collection cost. Although detection accuracy may be lower than large-scale DL models, few-shot strategies are practical for SCADA and edge deployments where energy conservation is critical.

From a cross-model perspective, **rule-based and historical audit IDS** models exhibit the lowest energy consumption and are suitable for field devices. Few-shot and federated fog-based systems offer balanced energy-performance solutions well-suited to smart factory environments. In contrast, DRL, blockchain-integrated systems, and multi-layer DNNs provide high detection capability but incur higher computational and communication energy costs, making them more appropriate for fog or cloud layers.

Several key insights emerge from this analysis. **Feature selection and dimensionality reduction** are among the most effective strategies for lowering computational load. Transfer learning reduces retraining energy by freezing early layers. FL minimizes communication overhead compared to centralized training. Blockchain mechanisms should be deployed only at infrastructure-powered layers, not on constrained IIoT devices. RL improves adaptability but should be reserved for scenarios where open-set detection is essential.

Table 8.3 presents a comparative analysis of available IDS frameworks and models for the effective implementation of Smart Industrial Automation.

In summary, an energy-centric classification of IIoT IDS models can be defined in three tiers. Energy-optimal models, such as rule-based and few-shot approaches, are suitable for field-level deployment. Balanced energy-performance models, including federated fog-based IDS and optimized CNN-LSTM systems, are recommended for smart factory environments. High-accuracy but high-energy approaches, such as RL and blockchain-based IDS, should be confined to fog or cloud layers. In practical industrial automation, edge-level IDS should emphasize lightweight inference and feature reduction; fog-level IDS should leverage FL for scalability and privacy; blockchain should never operate on constrained devices; and RL should be deployed only when adaptive detection is operationally necessary.

8.7.4 Energy-focused comparative analysis of available renewable energy-based IDS

Renewable-powered IoT networks change the traditional relationship between energy and cybersecurity. In conventional battery-based systems, energy is mainly a resource constraint. In renewable IoT environments, however, energy becomes both a constraint and a security variable. Because nodes rely on intermittent harvesting sources such as solar, thermal, mechanical, or radio-frequency energy, fluctuations in power availability directly influence system behavior. At the same time, adversaries can exploit energy characteristics through energy-depletion attacks, harvesting-blocking attacks, or by forcing devices into low-power states where cryptographic protections may be downgraded. As a result, renewable energy-aware intrusion detection systems must balance detection accuracy with energy neutrality and long-term sustainability.

Table 8.3 Energy-focused comparative analysis of IDS frameworks for Industrial IoT automation.

IDS/Framework	Target Environment	Core Technique	Learning Setting	Edge Suitability	Green/Energy Mechanism	Energy Evidence	Reported Performance	Main Limitations
ZigBee RF Fingerprinting (PHY ID verification)	ZigBee / IEEE 802.15.4 in industrial control and building automation	RF fingerprint features (amplitude/phase/frequency) + MDA projection + ML classifier + statistical verification; KS / GRLVQI feature ranking	Supervised (device ID verification / classification)	High (feature reduction + lightweight classifiers)	Uses dimensionality reduction and feature ranking to reduce compute; avoids cryptographic-heavy device-side operations for ID verification	Indirect (reduced feature sets and simple classifiers imply lower CPU/energy; no joules reported)	True verification rate > 90% and false verification rate < 10% (reported); rogue reject rate > 90% in most spoofing scenarios	Needs RF capture/receiver support; channel/SNR sensitivity; device aging and environment changes may affect fingerprints
BC-IDSs (Blockchain-Based Collaborative IDS Framework)	IoT/IIoT cross-domain security (blacklist sharing)	Multiple IDS servers extract malicious IPs + Ethereum smart contract storage + duplication-check (Keccak256) + blacklist distribution	Hybrid (depends on local IDS models; blockchain coordination)	Medium (IoT devices not mining; servers handle blockchain)	Offloads blockchain to controller/IDS servers; duplication-check reduces redundant writes and transaction cost	Indirect (no direct power results; efficiency argued via reduced redundancy and improved scalability)	Scalability improved by about 50%; supports advertising/storing >100 malicious IPs per transaction (reported)	Proof-of-concept; limited detection metrics/latency reporting; blockchain overhead and deployment cost not energy-benchmarked
DNP3 DNN IDS (multi-model)	ICS/SCADA smart grid networks using DNP3	Implemented 8 DNP3 attacks + flow feature extraction (TCP/IP and DNP3-specific) + DNN classifiers (multi-class)	Supervised	Medium (inference possible at gateway; training heavy)	No explicit green module; operational savings only via automated detection vs manual inspection	Not reported (no energy/power/CPU profiling; only performance metrics)	Accuracy 99.0% (reported); precision 95.8%, recall 95.49%, F1 95.65% (DNP3-flow DNN, reported)	Training cost and dataset dependence; potential generalization issues across plants; energy and real-time constraints not quantified
SDN-CNN IDS + MultiChain Verification	SDN-enabled IIoT (ICS pipeline-like traffic; control/data plane protection)	CNN IDS as SDN controller application (payload inspection) + private MultiChain to verify flow-rule integrity + detection node log comparison	Supervised	Medium (controller-side; not sensor-level)	Centralizes heavy compute at SDN controller; avoids running IDS/blockchain on constrained end devices; private chain reduces openness	Indirect (no joules; energy shifted to controller nodes; extra blockchain verification overhead implied)	Binary: Acc 94.75%, Prec 95.28%, Rec 93.84%, F1 94.48%; Multi-class: Acc 94.65%, Prec 97.02%, Rec 88.86%, F1 92.31% (reported)	Blockchain adds processing/storage overhead; relies on SDN infrastructure; may not capture all physical/process anomalies

continued on next page

Table 8.3 (*continued*)

IDS/Framework	Target Environment	Core Technique	Learning Setting	Edge Suitability	Green/Energy Mechanism	Energy Evidence	Reported Performance	Main Limitations
DC-IDS (DQN + CVAE + EVT)	IIoT intrusion detection under open-set (unknown attacks), e.g., ToN-IoT	Open-set modeled as MDP + DQN for known-class classification + CVAE reconstruction error + EVT thresholding for unknown recognition	Deep reinforcement learning + generative (hybrid)	Medium (better on fog/edge server than tiny nodes)	Focuses on reducing misclassification of unknown attacks (reduces repeated mitigation/forensics cycles indirectly)	Not reported (no direct energy; compute overhead expected from DRL/CVAE)	Reported improved unknown-attack recognition rate and stability vs prior open-set methods (paper reports comparative gains)	Higher compute/training complexity; hyperparameter sensitivity; energy and latency not explicitly profiled
FS-IDS (Few-Shot Learning for SCADA)	SCADA networks (e.g., gas pipeline) with rare/limited attack samples	PCA + one-hot preprocessing + prototypical network with CNN embedding; few-shot adaptation	Few-shot / supervised (episodic)	Medium–High (few-shot reduces data needs; inference moderate)	Fewer labeled samples reduce retraining/data-collection cost; compact prototypes support efficient adaptation	Indirect (no joules; reduced training data and limited fine-tuning imply lower energy)	About 83.78% accuracy and 82.78% macro-F1 (few-shot tasks, reported); improves with more shots (up to about 89.06% at 10-shot)	Lower accuracy than large-data DL; depends on representative support set; deployment tuning needed per site
MultiNet-IDS (EFS + DRL + LSTM)	WSN/industrial monitoring networks (resource-constrained sensing)	Two-stage exhaustive feature selection + DRL adaptive decision + LSTM temporal modeling; ensemble fusion	Hybrid (DRL + supervised temporal modeling)	Medium (feature reduction helps; DRL training heavy)	EFS reduces dimensionality and compute; aims to cut false positives (saves downstream resource usage)	Indirect (efficiency argued via dimensionality reduction; no device energy metrics)	Up to 99.1% accuracy across datasets (reported) with reduced false positives	Exhaustive selection can be costly offline; DRL convergence cost; energy/latency on real sensor nodes not fully quantified

continued on next page

Table 8.3 (*continued*)

IDS/Framework	Target Environment	Core Technique	Learning Setting	Edge Suitability	Green/Energy Mechanism	Energy Evidence	Reported Performance	Main Limitations
HIDM (Optimized CNN–LSTM + TL)	Industry 4.0 / IIoT enterprise networks (ToN-IoT, UNSW-NB15)	CNN–LSTM hybrid + Grey Wolf Optimizer tuning + transfer learning (freeze/reuse representations)	Supervised (multi-class)	Medium (edge gateway feasible; training best on server)	TL reduces retraining cost; GWO tuning aims for efficient convergence (indirect energy efficiency)	Indirect (no joules; efficiency implied via TL reuse and tuning)	Reported precision 92.7% (ToN-IoT) and 94.25% (UNSW-NB15) for OCNN-LSTM with TL (reported)	Recall/F1 may be lower under class imbalance; hyperparameter optimization overhead; energy not measured
FFL-IDS (Fog-enabled Federated CNN IDS)	IIoT (jamming/spoofing) with fog-assisted FL (Edge-IIoTset, CIC-IDS2017)	CNN-based IDS trained via federated learning + fog layer for low-latency aggregation	Federated (privacy-preserving)	High (designed for distributed/edge + fog)	Avoids raw data transfer (lower comms + privacy); fog reduces cloud latency and repeated long-haul transmissions	Indirect (performance/architecture; no joules, but comms reduction is a strong energy proxy)	Edge-IIoTset: Acc 93.4%, Rec 91.6%, Prec 88%, F1 87%; CIC-IDS2017: Acc 95.8%, Prec 94.9%, Rec 94%, F1 93% (reported)	Communication rounds still cost energy; non-IID data and client drift; no direct power profiling
TIA Project History Anomaly Detection (Hartmann & Wendzel)	ICS engineering artifacts (Siemens TIA Portal project history/backups)	Heuristic anomaly detection on timestamps and memory/storage variables across long-term backups; attacker-scenario analysis	Unsupervised / heuristic	High for offline audit (not real-time inline IDS)	Offline analysis reduces always-on monitoring cost; uses compact metadata features (timestamps/memory)	Indirect (no energy metrics; low operational overhead since not continuous packet inspection)	Reported AUC varies strongly by scenario (e.g., very high AUC for some scenarios; weaker for stealthy insiders) (reported in paper)	Not real-time network IDS; vulnerable to stealthy in-window edits; false positives for legitimate updates
Misuse-Based Modbus/TCP IDS (Suricata rules)	Industrial automation networks using Modbus/TCP (water treatment testbed)	Process-aware signature/rule IDS: out-of-bound register/value rules + function-code/traffic-pattern rules (plant-specific)	Rule-based (misuse/signature)	High (IDS runs on monitoring host; minimal ML compute)	Very low compute vs DL; rule evaluation and protocol parsing; avoids training cycles	Indirect (no joules; lightweight rule matching implies low energy)	Detected 100% of DoS and reconnaissance; about 96% spoofing (reported)	Cannot detect truly novel attacks beyond rules; needs expert rule engineering and per-plant tuning; no automatic mitigation

To evaluate renewable-based IDS frameworks from an energy perspective, several dimensions are important. These include how the framework integrates renewable sources, the type of energy optimization strategy used, the interaction between energy management and security mechanisms, the type of energy evidence reported, and the overall level of operational sustainability. Unlike traditional IDS evaluation, renewable environments require explicit consideration of how security decisions affect energy harvesting, consumption, and resilience.

One representative node-level approach is DEPRONN-ES, which models partially sustainable IoT systems with both renewable-powered and battery-powered devices. In this framework, renewable nodes aim to achieve energy-neutral operation, while traditional nodes prioritize energy conservation. The system applies renewable-aware routing, adaptive data aggregation, and differential privacy to protect shared energy information. Direct energy evidence is reported, including microampere-hour savings and a significant reduction in attack success rates. By preventing attackers from identifying weak nodes through exposed energy information, the framework strengthens both privacy and energy stability. This approach demonstrates strong micro-level energy-security coupling and provides measurable energy savings under realistic solar harvesting traces.

At a broader scale, cyber-physical resilience frameworks that combine multi-agent RL, distributionally robust optimization, blockchain authentication, and DL-based detection address energy security at the grid level. These models explicitly consider renewable variability, supply-demand balancing, and attack-aware control strategies. Reported results include reductions in resilience loss, operational cost savings, lower renewable curtailment rates, and decreased emissions. In this context, security mechanisms contribute directly to energy continuity. By maintaining stable operation under false data injection, denial-of-service, or spoofing attacks, these systems protect both grid integrity and renewable utilization. Their strength lies in macro-level optimization and comprehensive energy-resilience integration.

Digital twin-enabled frameworks provide another perspective by co-optimizing energy management and intrusion detection within a unified cyber-physical simulation environment. These systems incorporate renewable-energy uncertainty modeling, charging-infrastructure optimization, and generative-adversarial-network-based detection. Reported evidence includes improved operational runtime efficiency, high detection performance, and better energy balance between electric vehicles and the grid. Although they may not provide detailed micro-level energy measurements, they demonstrate strong system-level integration between energy optimization and cybersecurity. In contrast, broader Green IoT exiting techniques and ecosystems offer a conceptual foundation by classifying renewable harvesting mechanisms and identifying associated vulnerabilities. These works emphasize the security risks posed by energy-source blocking, energy-based denial-of-service, and low-power cryptographic weaknesses. While they often lack direct joule-level measurement, they provide an essential taxonomy that informs the design of renewable-aware IDS frameworks. Across these models, three architectural philosophies emerge. Node-centric energy-aware IDS approaches focus on battery-state awareness and privacy-preserving energy information sharing. System-level resilience frameworks integrate renewable variability modeling, optimization, and adaptive learning to protect grid stability. Digital twin-based systems emphasize coordinated energy-security optimization at the urban scale.

A key distinction also arises between energy neutrality and energy robustness. Energy neutrality aims to ensure that harvested energy meets or exceeds consumption at the node level. Energy robustness ensures that the system remains stable and resilient under energy-targeted attacks. Node-level frameworks primarily pursue neutrality, while grid-scale models emphasize robustness. Table 8.4 presents a comparative analysis of renewable-energy-based IDS models for Smart IoT-enabled environments.

Overall, renewable energy in IoT systems is no longer simply a performance parameter. It becomes a determinant of security posture. The most mature renewable-based IDS frameworks explicitly model energy variability, integrate learning and optimization techniques, provide quantifiable energy metrics, and avoid unnecessary computational or cryptographic overhead. Such approaches align security objectives with sustainability goals and support long-term, resilient operation in renewable-powered smart environments.

8.8 Best practices for IDS implementation in diverse IoT networks

Smart infrastructures are becoming pervasive across cities' services, transportation systems, industrial automation, and renewable-energy infrastructure. For these applications, cybersecurity must be designed in concert with operational considerations and sustainability. IDS needs to optimize for accuracy and detection capabilities, detection latency, false-alarm reduction, privacy preservation, interoperability, deployment scale, and energy constraints. Off-the-shelf IDS pipelines that only optimize for classification performance are therefore inadequate.

Adapting IDS solutions for green environments requires us to think beyond simply compressing a state-of-the-art IDS. A Green IDS is one in which detection intelligence is pushed down to the appropriate layers of the stack, computational intensity is minimized, energy costs are considered, and context-aware adaptability is built in by design. In a smart-city context, IDS solutions must be composable and interoperable, with carbon-aware security guarantees. Transportation systems require intrusion detection to operate at ultra-low latency under high-mobility conditions. Intrusion detection in industrial automation needs to ensure safety, respect process semantics, and tolerate zero false positives. Renewable-powered infrastructure needs IDS that are tolerant of intermittency and maximize availability. Because of these issues, there is no single-rule, deploy-all model that is present or applicable. Green IDS is an intrusion detection paradigm that emphasizes domain-aware deployment practices. It integrates distributed intelligence, zero-trust security principles, adaptive

Table 8.4 Energy-focused comparative analysis of renewable-energy-based IDS/security frameworks for smart environments.

IDS/Framework	Target Environment	Core Technique	Learning Setting	Edge Suitability	Green/Energy Mechanism	Energy Evidence	Reported Performance	Main Limitations
DEPRONN-ES	Partial sustainable IoT in smart-city settings (mix of traditional and energy-harvesting nodes)	Heuristic routing (renewable-preferred parent selection + max–min path energy) + adaptive data aggregation + differential privacy (Laplace noise) for energy information sharing	Heuristic / privacy-preserving	High	Dual energy profiles (energy-neutral for sustainable nodes; energy-saving for traditional nodes); adaptive aggregation reduces transmissions; differential privacy reduces energy-oriented attack success	Direct/proxy: attack success reduced by about 87%; indoor light harvesting traces used; reduced resource consumption under attack reported	Attack success reduced from 100% to about 13.33%; best privacy–energy trade-off around $\epsilon \sim 0.36$	Tuning needed for privacy budget and aggregation; privacy noise reduces fidelity of shared energy stats; focuses on routing/energy-leak attacks rather than full-spectrum IDS
MARL–DRO + blockchain + DL-IDS cyber–physical resilience framework	Renewable energy-driven IoT power grids (DERs, smart meters/controllers, communication networks)	Vulnerability assessment + distributionally robust optimization (DRO) + multi-agent reinforcement learning (MARL) + blockchain authentication + lightweight cryptography + deep-learning IDS	Hybrid (optimization + RL + DL)	Medium	Resilient energy allocation and recovery under renewable variability and cyber-attacks; security layers protect integrity of energy transactions and control signals	Indirect but strong sustainability proxies: curtailment reduced about 12–18%; operational cost reduced about 7–10%; emissions reduced about 5–8%	IDS/detection accuracy about 92.8%; resilience loss reduced about 63.9%; resilience index about 0.847 (reported)	No device-level joule/Wh profiling; computational/communication overhead of RL and blockchain not fully quantified; scaling and interpretability challenges
Digital Twin smart-city energy management + GAN-based IDS (HBMO-trained)	Smart city energy and transportation ecosystem (smart grid, microgrid, energy hub, EVs & charging)	Digital twin + Honey Bee Mating Optimization (HBMO) for planning/optimization + GAN-based IDS; renewable uncertainty via point-estimate method (2m-scheme)	Deep learning + optimization	Medium	Co-optimizes energy transactions and security; IDS supports trusted data exchange without degrading energy-management coordination	Indirect: reduced optimization runtime (reported faster than GA); energy gains expressed through improved coordination/transactions rather than device power	Precision about 85.29%, recall about 96.61%, F1 about 90.69%, accuracy about 91.43% (reported)	No joule/Wh evaluation; GAN training and optimization can be expensive; depends on simulator fidelity; real-time constraints not fully established
Green IoT renewable integration and security implications	Cross-domain renewable-powered IoT (smart homes & healthcare, industry, smart cities, WSNs)	Survey/taxonomy of energy harvesting and energy-saving strategies; security implications (energy depletion, intermittency-driven vulnerability, overhead of security tasks, benchmarking gaps)	Not applicable	Not applicable	Identifies harvesting-aware operation and data reduction (aggregation/compression/prediction); calls for unified energy-security benchmarks and low-power security support	Conceptual/analytical evidence; highlights lack of standardized energy measurement and comparable benchmarks	Not applicable	No single deployable IDS; broad scope; provides research gaps and guidance

learning and inference mechanisms, and energy-efficient ML models. In addition, it considers lifecycle sustainability, ensuring that security solutions remain effective, resource-conscious, and environmentally responsible throughout system design, deployment, and operation.

The following subsections present structured guidelines for implementing Green IDS across these major smart environments. Together, they provide a practical and forward-looking framework for designing intrusion detection mechanisms that are secure, efficient, resilient, and environmentally responsible.

8.8.1 Implementing guidelines for Green IDS deployment in smart city

The development of smart cities requires security solutions that are not only accurate and intelligent but also sustainable, adaptive, and context-aware. As urban infrastructures increasingly depend on interconnected IoT devices, communication networks, and cloud services, intrusion detection systems must evolve to meet both cybersecurity and environmental goals. Green Intrusion Detection Systems (Green IDS) represent this shift by integrating strong threat detection with energy efficiency and long-term sustainability. In this section, the best practices and guidelines to implement Green IDS in Smart Cities are discussed below:

- A fundamental best practice for Green IDS deployment in smart cities is the adoption of a data-centric, zero-trust architecture. Instead of relying on traditional perimeter defenses, security mechanisms should protect the entire data lifecycle, from collection and transmission to processing and storage. Every device, gateway, and service should be continuously authenticated and verified. This approach reduces insider threats and eliminates reliance on centralized trust models, which may become single points of failure.
- Another essential practice is to distribute intelligence across the edge, fog, and cloud layers. Purely centralized IDS architectures often create latency, high communication overhead, and unnecessary energy consumption. By deploying lightweight anomaly detection models at the edge, systems can respond quickly to local threats while minimizing data transmission. More complex analytics can be handled at fog or cloud layers when necessary. This layered design reduces processing delay and lowers the overall computational load, thereby directly supporting energy-efficient operation.
- Energy optimization must be treated as a primary design objective. Feature reduction techniques and hybrid feature selection methods help decrease redundant computation. Model compression strategies, such as pruning and knowledge distillation, can significantly reduce memory and processing requirements without severely affecting accuracy. Furthermore, IDS complexity should adapt to contextual risk levels. During low-risk periods, lightweight detection can operate, while higher-complexity models may activate only when abnormal activity is detected. Such adaptive strategies support greener deployments.

- Smart-city environments generate diverse and high-speed data streams across transportation, utilities, healthcare, and public services. Therefore, IDS frameworks must integrate artificial intelligence with context-aware monitoring. DL models can detect complex anomalies, but they must be carefully optimized to avoid excessive energy consumption. The goal is to maintain a balance between detection performance and computational sustainability.
- Interoperability is also critical. Smart cities rely on heterogeneous communication technologies, including 5G, WiFi, low-power wide-area networks, and vehicular networks. Green IDS architectures should be modular and flexible to operate across different subsystems without duplicating computational tasks. This reduces redundant processing and improves scalability.
- Distributed trust technologies, such as blockchain, may enhance transparency and tamper resistance in selected domains. However, traditional blockchain mechanisms can consume significant energy. For Green IDS deployment, permissioned ledgers and lightweight consensus protocols should be preferred. Blockchain integration should be selective and applied only where strong integrity guarantees are required.
- Looking ahead, Green IDS frameworks should incorporate carbon-aware security strategies. Detection complexity can be dynamically adjusted based on energy availability, particularly in cities powered by renewable sources. Self-adaptive and autonomous defense mechanisms, including federated and reinforcement learning, can further enhance resilience by enabling continuous learning in response to evolving threats. Security must also be embedded at the system design stage rather than added later. Early integration ensures alignment between protection mechanisms and infrastructure constraints.
- Evaluation criteria for smart-city IDS should expand beyond detection accuracy. Metrics such as false alarm rate, response latency, scalability, energy consumption, and environmental impact must be jointly assessed. Energy-aware benchmarking will be essential to validate sustainable IDS deployments.

In summary, Green IDS in smart cities integrates cybersecurity, artificial intelligence, distributed computing, and sustainability engineering. The objective is not only to detect intrusions but to do so efficiently, responsibly, and in harmony with environmental constraints. By combining distributed intelligence, zero-trust principles, adaptive modeling, and energy-aware optimization, future IDS frameworks can support resilient and sustainable smart-city ecosystems.

8.8.2 Implementing guidelines for Green IDS deployment in smart transportation

Green Intrusion Detection Systems (IDS) for IoT-enabled transportation environments, such as the Internet of Vehicles (IoV), Cooperative Intelligent Transportation Systems (CITS), and Connected and Autonomous Vehicles (CAV), must go beyond achieving high detection accuracy. These systems operate under strict latency requirements and are deployed on resource-constrained edge hardware. They must also remain reliable in highly dynamic traffic and mobility conditions. Recent trends in Green IDS show a shift from fully centralized IDS architectures toward edge-fog-cloud and federated designs. These distributed approaches aim to reduce bandwidth consumption, preserve data privacy, and maintain low response times. Therefore, Green IDS in smart transportation must balance security effectiveness with operational feasibility and sustainability. This section discusses best practices and guidelines for implementing Green IDS to enable an effective smart transportation system.

- A key best practice is adopting a tiered edge-cloud detection pipeline. Lightweight detection models should operate at the edge to enable immediate response to threats. More complex and computationally intensive models can run in fog or cloud layers to analyze ambiguous or advanced attack patterns. This layered design minimizes latency while avoiding unnecessary computational load on constrained devices.
- Another important practice is to design for resource realism rather than focus solely on accuracy. Edge devices in transportation systems often have strict limits on memory, energy, and bandwidth. IDS frameworks should treat these constraints as core design requirements. Resource-aware FL offers a practical solution. Instead of full on-device training, models can be pre-trained on the server and then lightly fine-tuned at client nodes. Expensive layers can be frozen, and only small classification components can be updated locally. This reduces memory and computational overhead while preserving the benefits of collaborative learning.
- Model configuration should also reflect the accuracy-efficiency trade-off required by the deployment scenario. Fine-tuning more layers may increase detection accuracy but consume additional resources. In contrast, updating fewer layers improves efficiency but may slightly reduce accuracy. Selecting the appropriate configuration depends on the node's hardware capability and the safety-critical nature of the application.
- Validation on representative embedded platforms and domain-specific datasets is equally essential. Experiments on realistic hardware, such as edge servers and lightweight clients, highlight performance differences across datasets. Models that perform well on general intrusion datasets may show weaker results in vehicular-specific environments. Therefore, transportation-focused datasets and testbeds must be used to ensure deployment readiness.
- Future deployment strategies should prioritize an edge-first architecture for time-critical decisions. Immediate anomaly detection should occur at the edge, while fog or cloud layers can handle deeper classification and historical analysis. FL workflows should be structured carefully, including model initialization, local updates, aggregation, and repetition. Connectivity interruptions must be anticipated in highly mobile vehicular networks.
- From a training perspective, hybrid server-edge federated strategies are recommended. Centralized pre-training, followed by lightweight client fine-tuning, re-

duces the device burden while maintaining collaborative intelligence. The choice of fine-tuning depth should be aligned with node capability and energy budget.

- Scalability challenges must be addressed explicitly. Bandwidth limitations, synchronization delays, dynamic client participation, and communication overhead can interfere with real-time vehicular functions. During deployment, memory usage and execution time should be monitored alongside detection accuracy. Green IDS success depends not only on classification performance but also on operational cost and efficiency.
- Disciplined data handling and evaluation procedures are necessary. Class imbalance must be addressed using appropriate balancing strategies. Stable and transparent training and testing methods should be applied before system hardening. Deployment-ready evaluations should report latency, memory footprint, runtime, and resource usage in addition to accuracy metrics. Only by combining security performance with measurable efficiency can Green IDS solutions truly support sustainable and resilient smart transportation systems.

8.8.3 Implementing Guidelines for Green IDS deployment in Industrial Automation

In secured Industrial IoT (IIoT) automation, a Green Intrusion Detection System must achieve more than high detection accuracy. Industrial communication is time-sensitive and tightly coupled with safety-critical control processes. Therefore, an effective IDS must maintain low latency and minimal false alarms while operating within strict CPU, memory, and energy constraints of PLCs, SCADA components, and edge gateways. This requirement naturally leads to layered architectures. Lightweight, process-aware checks should run close to the industrial plant, while computationally intensive analytics and model training can be placed on more capable controllers or servers. At the same time, the IDS itself must not introduce operational bottlenecks or become an additional attack surface.

- A key best practice is to adopt a layered, process-first detection pipeline that combines plant-specific rules with learning-based mechanisms. Misuse-based and protocol-aware rules can quickly detect clear violations at low computational cost. For example, protocol parsers can enforce function codes, register addresses, and value thresholds that reflect real plant constraints.
- In safety-critical systems, it is also essential to prioritize near-zero false positives, since unnecessary blocking of legitimate traffic may disrupt industrial processes.
- Lightweight detection should be deployed at the edge, while heavier verification and correlation can occur at controllers or servers. IDS models should be trained using realistic, protocol-specific attack scenarios rather than only generic datasets.
- Designers must also consider operational response windows and ensure that detection latency remains within acceptable limits for human or automated intervention.

- Rule-based systems should be complemented with temporal or cross-sensor validation to detect stealthy attacks that remain within normal value ranges. Because IIoT environments evolve, IDS frameworks should include mechanisms to detect previously unseen attacks and support incremental learning with limited new samples.
- For future deployment, IDS components should be placed according to available computational and energy budgets. Fast inference and plant-specific checks belong at PLC or gateway level, while model retraining, correlation, and integrity verification can be handled at higher layers.
- Evaluation should extend beyond accuracy to include false-positive rate, detection latency, CPU and memory usage, and energy-related indicators.
- Rule governance and maintainability are also critical, as industrial systems may require numerous plant-specific rules that must be auditable and version-controlled.
- Deployment should include explicit testing for stealth, replay, and control-plane manipulation scenarios to ensure resilience against bypass attempts. IDS alerts must provide interpretable, process-aware information so that operators can respond quickly and correctly.
- If collaborative or blockchain-based threat sharing is implemented, it must be designed carefully to avoid excessive computational overhead, thereby preserving the sustainability goals of Green IDS in Industrial IoT environments.

8.8.4 Implementing guidelines for renewable energy-based Green IDS deployment in smart environments

In renewable-powered smart environments, such as smart cities, intelligent grids, electric-vehicle charging systems, and large-scale sensing networks, energy availability becomes integral to the security model. Many nodes rely on intermittent energy harvesting and may periodically share residual energy information to support routing and aggregation decisions. However, this practice introduces new vulnerabilities. Adversaries can analyze energy-related information and deliberately target weaker nodes, generating legitimate-looking traffic that gradually drains their power and disrupts connectivity. In such contexts, a renewable energy-aware Green IDS must focus not only on detection accuracy but also on sustaining availability, protecting privacy, and ensuring real-time protection under fluctuating power conditions. The best practices for implementing Renewable Energy-based Green IDS and guidelines for deploying Green IDS in Smart environments are listed below:

- A fundamental best practice is to treat energy as a critical security indicator and to prevent its exposure. Energy information can support adaptive routing and IDS decisions, yet it should be protected through obfuscation or privacy-preserving mechanisms to prevent leakage.
- Networks that combine renewable and battery-powered devices should adopt dual operational profiles. Renewable nodes may aim for energy-neutral operation, while battery-based nodes require stricter conservation policies.

- Routing, aggregation, and IDS task allocation should reflect these differences to prevent premature battery depletion. Lightweight privacy mechanisms, such as differential privacy applied to shared energy metrics, offer a practical alternative to heavy cryptographic solutions. These methods reduce the attacker's ability to identify vulnerable nodes while maintaining acceptable routing performance.
- IDS logic must account for intermittent power conditions. Instead of failing when energy drops, detection pipelines should gracefully degrade by reducing feature sets, switching to simpler models, or triggering event-based analysis.
- Standardized evaluation of security-energy trade-offs is essential. Renewable-powered IDS performance should be assessed not only by detection metrics but also by energy overhead, harvesting conditions, and long-term network sustainability.
- For effective deployment, renewable-energy-based Green IDS should be implemented as a coordinated policy framework rather than a single detection model. Energy-aware routing, privacy-preserving energy information sharing, and intrusion detection should operate together to maintain availability during power fluctuations.
- Differential privacy parameters must be carefully tuned to balance routing accuracy and exposure risk, and validation should include energy-depletion adversaries, not only traditional attack scenarios. Evaluation should also consider service continuity, route stability, and the impact on connectivity.
- Hardware-aware design further enhances sustainability by incorporating low-power cryptographic modules, wake-up mechanisms, and lightweight accelerators that reduce computational burden.
- Benchmarking should document harvesting conditions, energy-neutrality targets, and security overhead to ensure reproducibility and facilitate knowledge transfer across renewable-powered smart deployments.

This chapter has examined the design and deployment of Green Intrusion Detection Systems across transportation networks, smart-city infrastructures, renewable energy-based IoT environments, and industrial automation systems. Through detailed case studies and comparative evaluations, it demonstrates that energy efficiency is not a secondary optimization factor but a fundamental design requirement for modern IoT security. The analysis reveals that lightweight and process-aware IDS mechanisms are highly suitable for field-level deployment where computational resources are limited. Federated and fog-based architectures offer a balanced trade-off between privacy, scalability, and energy efficiency. DL and RL techniques provide strong detection capability but require careful placement at gateway or cloud layers to prevent excessive energy consumption at edge nodes. Blockchain-assisted IDS architectures enhance trust and decentralization but must be offloaded from resource-constrained devices to remain sustainable. Renewable-aware IDS frameworks further illustrate that energy availability itself becomes part of the security model in harvesting-based IoT systems.

Across all domains, several common principles emerge. First, feature optimization and model compression significantly reduce computational overhead without compromising accuracy at high scale. Second, distributed intelligence reduces communication energy and latency compared to centralized architectures. Third, adaptive activation mechanisms, where high-complexity models operate only when necessary, help maintain operational sustainability. Fourth, energy-aware evaluation metrics must accompany traditional detection metrics to ensure deployment feasibility.

Ultimately, Green IDS represents the convergence of cybersecurity engineering, artificial intelligence, distributed systems, and sustainability science. The future of IoT security depends on systems that are not only accurate and resilient but also energy-conscious and context-aware. By consolidating practical lessons from multiple real-world application domains, this chapter provides implementation-oriented guidance for researchers and practitioners seeking to develop intrusion detection systems that align with long-term sustainability goals while maintaining robust protection against evolving cyber threats.

CHAPTER

Future directions in sustainable IoT security

9

9.1 Introduction

The IoT is expanding exponentially and is transforming modern digital infrastructure, enabling intelligent services across smart cities, industrial automation, transportation, healthcare, and critical cyber-physical systems. However, this large-scale interconnectivity has significantly expanded the attack surface of digital ecosystems. IoT devices often operate under strict resource constraints, heterogeneous communication protocols, and dynamic network conditions. As a result, traditional intrusion detection systems (IDS) designed for conventional IT environments are no longer sufficient. The future of IoT security requires intelligent, scalable, energy-efficient, and regulation-aware protection mechanisms that can operate sustainably across distributed infrastructures.

Recent trends in the adoption of ML, DL, FL, RL, and generative AI (GenAI) consistently point to one conclusion: artificial intelligence has become central to next-generation intrusion detection. AI-driven IDS models make possible adaptive anomaly detection, behavioral analysis, and automated response across complex and evolving IoT environments. At the same time, they bring critical challenges to the fore: computational overhead, the realism of training datasets, adversarial vulnerability, gaps in interpretability, and the practical feasibility of deployment on resource-constrained devices. The future of sustainable IoT security must therefore move beyond accuracy-centric evaluation toward architectures that are deployment-aware, energy-conscious, and secure across the entire system lifecycle.

In parallel, blockchain technologies are increasingly integrated into IDS frameworks to provide decentralized trust, immutable logging, secure aggregation, and automated policy enforcement. Rather than functioning as standalone detection engines, blockchain mechanisms act as coordination and integrity layers that support ML, FL, and distributed intrusion detection. However, scalability, communication overhead, storage growth, and energy consumption remain open challenges in blockchain-enabled IoT security architectures. Sustainable deployment, therefore, requires lightweight consensus mechanisms, off-chain computation, and hybrid edge-cloud coordination models.

Another transformative development is the emergence of post-quantum cryptographic approaches in IoT security. As advances in quantum computing threaten classical public-key infrastructures, next-generation IDS must incorporate quantum-

Green Intrusion Detection Systems for IoT. https://doi.org/10.1016/B978-0-44-344249-0.00016-8

resistant cryptographic primitives, secure key management, and blockchain frameworks hardened with lattice-based digital signatures. In this evolving paradigm, intrusion detection is no longer limited to identifying malicious traffic; it must also guarantee long-term integrity, secure model lifecycle management, and verifiable operational provenance. Post-quantum IDS architectures combine intelligent detection models with cryptographically resilient trust infrastructures.

Energy efficiency and sustainability represent foundational design requirements for future IoT security systems. Smart cities, industrial automation platforms, vehicular networks, and distributed sensor systems generate continuous high-volume telemetry under strict latency and power constraints. DL-based IDS and RL-based network defense mechanisms emphasize the importance of hierarchical edge-fog-cloud architectures, model compression techniques, federated collaboration, adaptive detection pipelines, and resource-aware learning frameworks to balance detection performance and energy consumption. Sustainable IDS must therefore incorporate measurable energy budgets, communication efficiency, and lifecycle-aware model management. Beyond technical innovation, policy and standardization play a critical role in shaping the deployment of next-generation energy-efficient IDS. International standards and regulatory frameworks provide governance structures for risk management, data protection, industrial control security, and incident response. However, current standards rarely define explicit energy-efficiency metrics or sustainability criteria for intrusion detection. Governments, regulatory bodies, and industry leaders must therefore collaborate to establish measurable guidelines, interoperability frameworks, certification mechanisms, and compliance benchmarks to support the widespread adoption of green IoT security solutions.

This chapter explores emerging technologies and architectural trends shaping the future of sustainable IoT security. It discusses AI-driven IDS advancements, blockchain-based security integration, post-quantum cryptographic resilience, and energy-efficient deployment strategies across smart cities, industrial systems, and transportation infrastructures. It further examines scalability challenges, interoperability barriers, adversarial robustness concerns, and policy implications. By integrating intelligent detection, decentralized trust, quantum-resilient cryptography, and energy-aware engineering principles, next-generation IDS can evolve into resilient, scalable, and sustainable cybersecurity ecosystems for the IoT era.

9.2 Future of AI-driven IDS in sustainable IoT security

Artificial intelligence has moved to the center of intrusion detection, reshaping it from static signature matching into adaptive, data-driven defense capable of recognizing patterns that conventional rules would miss. In sustainable IoT settings, however, this capability cannot be pursued solely for accuracy. The devices that populate smart cities, homes, vehicles, and industrial plants operate under tight constraints on energy, memory, and computation, and are deployed at a scale and level of heterogeneity that strain any centralized defense. The promise of AI-driven intrusion detection therefore lies in reconciling two demands that once seemed opposed: strong, evolving threat detection on the one hand, and resource-conscious, lifecycle-aware operation on the other. Realizing that promise calls for advances across several fronts, from lightweight model design and edge-first deployment to federated coordination, adversarial robustness, and standardized, energy-inclusive evaluation. This section discusses these focuses in three different directions. The first considers the future of ML-based IDS for sustainable IoT security, where traditional, computationally modest models remain valuable for lightweight and embedded deployment. The second turns to the future of DL-based IDS, whose richer representational power must be tempered through compression, distillation, and hierarchical edge-cloud architectures to fit constrained environments. The third focuses on the particular demands of machine and DL-based IDS for Industrial Control Systems, where deterministic timing, legacy protocols, and safety-critical processes impose constraints unlike those of any other domain. Together, these perspectives chart how intelligent intrusion detection can mature into a discipline that protects IoT ecosystems without compromising their sustainability.

9.2.1 Future of ML based IDS for sustainable IoT security

The evolution of intrusion detection systems (IDS) mirrors the broader transformation of cybersecurity in the age of artificial intelligence (AI) . Early IDS implementations were primarily signature-based, relying on predefined rules to identify known threats. Effective as they were against previously documented attacks, such systems lacked adaptability and could not respond to zero-day exploits or evolving adversarial behavior. As networks expanded and IoT ecosystems grew more complex, these traditional approaches proved insufficient, and ML emerged as a critical enabler of intelligent, adaptive, and scalable intrusion detection.

The field has since progressed clearly from conventional statistical learning techniques toward DL and hybrid, AI-driven architectures. Several factors drove this shift. First, modern network traffic generates high-dimensional, heterogeneous data streams that manual feature engineering alone cannot handle effectively. Second, contemporary attacks often unfold as multi-stage, stealthy campaigns that demand temporal and behavioral modeling. Third, IoT and cyber-physical systems introduce distributed, resource-constrained environments in which adaptive, automated detection becomes essential. ML-based IDS frameworks now predominate in both research and experimental deployment across smart cities, industrial automation, healthcare IoT, and vehicular networks.

One important advancement is the introduction of Automated ML (AutoML) for network intrusion detection. Unlike traditional pipelines that rely heavily on manual feature engineering and expert-driven model tuning, AutoML frameworks automate feature selection, hyperparameter optimization, neural architecture search (NAS) , and combined algorithm selection and hyperparameter (CASH) optimization. These techniques enable systematic exploration of model configurations and reduce human dependency during model development. In IoT contexts, AutoML offers adaptive tuning and scalable model discovery. However, from a practitioner's perspective, AutoML and NAS require substantial computational resources and large search spaces, which limit their direct applicability to constrained edge devices. Therefore, while AutoML strengthens model robustness and adaptability, it is better suited to cloud or high-performance fog infrastructures than to sensor-level deployment. Neural Architecture Search further enhances this automated paradigm by dynamically identifying optimal DL structures for complex and evolving IoT traffic patterns. NAS is particularly valuable in heterogeneous multi-layer IoT networks where manually designed architectures may not generalize across domains. Nevertheless, NAS incurs significant computational overhead, making edge deployment challenging without resource-aware constraints.

Another emerging direction is Multi-Task Learning (MTL). Instead of training independent models for each attack category, MTL simultaneously learns multiple related detection tasks while sharing internal representations. This approach improves knowledge transfer, reduces redundant model training, and enhances detection consistency across correlated attack types. MTL-based IDS architectures are therefore more scalable and efficient in environments where diverse but interrelated threats coexist. Last but not least, another critical development is the recognition of lifecycle-aware ML security models. Recent IoT security frameworks and firmware highlight vulnerabilities across the entire ML lifecycle, including data collection, training, testing, deployment, and maintenance. Threats such as data poisoning, model poisoning, adversarial examples, and model extraction attacks demonstrate that IDS models themselves can be targeted. Therefore, modern IDS design must incorporate robustness mechanisms throughout the complete lifecycle, rather than focusing solely on inference-time adversarial defense.

Traditional ML algorithms represent the foundational stage of intelligent intrusion detection. These methods operate on structured features extracted from packet headers, network flows, or statistical summaries of communication sessions. Common algorithms include Decision Trees, Random Forests, Support Vector Machines, K-Nearest Neighbors, Naïve Bayes, Logistic Regression, Gaussian Mixture Models, K-Means Clustering, and Linear Discriminant Analysis. Early IDS work relied heavily on these models because network traffic datasets such as KDD99 and NSL-KDD were primarily tabular and structured. Tree-based and kernel-based classifiers performed particularly well in such settings: Decision Trees and Random Forests offered interpretability and robustness, while Support Vector Machines generalized strongly in high-dimensional feature spaces, and Gaussian Mixture Models and clustering methods served anomaly detection in unsupervised contexts. SVM, RF, DT, and KNN were among the most frequently used algorithms in this early period, often exceeding 99% accuracy on benchmark datasets such as UNSW-NB15 and CICIDS2017. Their popularity owed much to moderate computational requirements, ease of implementation, and the relative transparency of their decision-making.

Nevertheless, traditional ML approaches exhibit inherent limitations. They depend heavily on handcrafted features and domain expertise. They struggle to model temporal dependencies in sequential traffic data. Moreover, their performance often declines when applied to heterogeneous IoT environments characterized by evolving device behavior and dynamic traffic patterns. Despite strong experimental results, ML-based IDS faces substantial challenges in real-world IoT deployment. They are:

- Resource constraints remain a primary concern. IoT devices typically operate with limited CPU power, memory capacity, and battery life. DL models may introduce unacceptable latency or energy overhead.
- Dataset limitations also undermine generalization. Many benchmark datasets are outdated, imbalanced, or synthetically generated. As a result, models may overfit and perform poorly in diverse real-world conditions.
- Scalability presents another difficulty. Smart cities and industrial IoT systems involve billions of heterogeneous devices using multiple communication protocols. Deploying and coordinating IDS across such ecosystems remains complex.
- Zero-day detection remains a topic that warrants further discussion. Supervised models depend on known attack patterns and may fail against novel threats. Moreover, adversarial ML techniques can manipulate model predictions.
- High false-positive rates create alert fatigue and reduce trust in IDS systems. Privacy regulations further complicate centralized data aggregation. Although FL mitigates some risks, it introduces additional operational complexity.
- Model interpretability remains a barrier to regulatory compliance. Black-box DL decisions are difficult to justify in critical infrastructures.
- Integration with legacy systems, edge-cloud coordination, and continuous model updates increases deployment complexity.

ML has fundamentally reshaped intrusion detection, turning it from static signature matching into adaptive behavioral analysis. Despite their limitations, traditional ML methods remain highly relevant for lightweight deployments, particularly on embedded or edge devices where DL inference may be infeasible under energy or memory constraints. Accuracy alone, however, is not enough. Sustainable IDS deployment requires balancing detection capability against computational efficiency, scalability, privacy preservation, adaptability, and interpretability. ML techniques have undeniably improved detection performance in controlled experimental settings, frequently achieving exceptionally high accuracy, precision, recall, and F1-scores on benchmark datasets. Yet the next generation of intrusion detection systems for IoT environments must move beyond accuracy-centric evaluation. Real-world IoT ecosystems present distinctive challenges: large-scale deployment, device heterogeneity, limited computational capacity, energy constraints, privacy requirements, and a continuously evolving threat landscape. The future of ML-based IDS therefore lies in architectural redesign rather than in merely incremental gains in predictive accuracy.

A deployment-oriented perspective is essential. Traditional IDS research has largely focused on maximizing classification performance using publicly available datasets. While these results are valuable, they often overlook the practical realities of IoT systems. Large-scale IoT infrastructures involve millions or even billions of devices operating across distributed networks. These devices differ in hardware capabilities, communication protocols, and operational roles. Future ML-based IDS frameworks must therefore prioritize scalability, efficient resource utilization, and compatibility with heterogeneous technology stacks. Lightweight models, including pruned deep networks, quantized neural architectures, and TinyML-based implementations, represent promising directions for edge deployment. Furthermore, hybrid edge-cloud architectures should be adopted to distribute detection tasks appropriately. Incremental and continual learning mechanisms are also necessary to avoid frequent full retraining cycles, which are computationally expensive and operationally disruptive.

Energy awareness will play a central role in the design of future IDS. IoT devices typically operate under strict power budgets, especially in smart grids, wireless sensor networks, and industrial automation environments, where deep ensembles and large neural networks that excel in the laboratory may prove impractical in the field. Attention is increasingly turning to energy-efficient anomaly detection, adaptive sampling strategies, and event-driven processing. A hierarchical IDS architecture is likely to become the dominant model: lightweight anomaly detectors operate at the edge for rapid screening, while deeper analysis and model updates are performed in the fog or cloud layers. Techniques such as model compression, knowledge distillation, and optimized feature-selection pipelines are essential for reducing computational overhead. Just as importantly, future work must report energy consumption, runtime latency, memory footprint, and throughput alongside the conventional detection metrics.

Another major direction concerns dataset realism and standardized benchmarking. Several widely used datasets, such as KDD99 and NSL-KDD, carry well-recognized limitations: they are outdated and do not faithfully reflect modern IoT traffic patterns, often containing synthetic flows, duplicated samples, and unrealistic attack distributions. Severe class imbalance further biases many experimental results. Future work must therefore prioritize IoT-native datasets that capture modern communication protocols such as ZigBee, LoRaWAN, BLE, and NB-IoT, and that incorporate cross-layer threats, zero-day attacks, and traces of real device behavior. Cross-dataset validation should become standard practice to guard against overfitting to any single benchmark, and standardized evaluation frameworks will be needed to enable fair comparison and reproducibility from one study to the next.

Explainability and trustworthiness represent another critical frontier. DL models often function as black boxes, making it difficult for operators to interpret detection outcomes. In safety-critical domains such as healthcare, transportation, and industrial control systems, explainability is not optional but mandatory. Regulatory compliance and operational accountability require transparent reasoning behind alerts. Techniques such as SHAP, LIME, and rule-based explainers are increasingly integrated into IDS pipelines. However, interpretability introduces additional computational cost and complexity. Future systems must carefully balance detection precision and transparency. Human-in-the-loop validation mechanisms may further enhance operational trust and reduce false positives.

Privacy preservation is equally important in IoT ecosystems. Centralized ML approaches require aggregation of raw traffic data, which raises privacy and regulatory concerns. FL has emerged as a promising solution by enabling decentralized model training without sharing raw data. At the same time, blockchain integration has been proposed to enhance decentralized trust, secure alert propagation, and enable immutable forensic logging. Nevertheless, blockchain mechanisms can introduce latency and energy overhead due to consensus protocols. Therefore, lightweight consensus mechanisms and modular blockchainIDS interoperability frameworks are required. Future works and strategies must rigorously evaluate communication latency, synchronization cost, and energy overhead in distributed security architectures.

Robustness against adversarial and evolving attacks remains a pressing concern. IoT networks are increasingly targeted by sophisticated zero-day exploits, adversarial machine-learning attacks, and cross-layer coordinated attacks. Static supervised models trained on historical datasets are insufficient in such dynamic environments. Continuous learning, self-supervised representation learning, and semi-supervised detection frameworks will likely become more prominent. Generative models can be used to simulate rare attack scenarios and improve resilience. Adversarial training strategies should be incorporated to strengthen model robustness against evasion attempts. Moreover, the integration of post-quantum cryptographic mechanisms may become increasingly relevant as advances in quantum computing threaten existing cryptographic infrastructures.

Automation through AutoML and NAS is another important trend. Automated model selection and hyperparameter optimization reduce human intervention and allow IDS architectures to adapt to changing IoT conditions. However, given the high computational cost of large search spaces, future work must focus on constrained NAS strategies that account for IoT resource limitations. Lightweight search methods and edge-aware model optimization will be critical to ensure feasibility.

Scalability and heterogeneity-aware architectures are fundamental for sustainable IoT security. IoT systems involve multiple communication protocols, diverse device capabilities, and cross-platform behaviors. Future IDS frameworks should adopt multi-layer detection strategies spanning perception, transport, and application layers. Modular architectures will facilitate interoperability and policy consistency across platforms. Collaborative threat intelligence sharing across domains may further enhance detection coverage and resilience.

Ethical considerations are drawing increasing attention in the design of intrusion detection systems. ML models may inadvertently introduce bias or disproportionately affect certain network segments, and their privacy implications must be managed carefully to avoid intrusive monitoring practices. Transparent auditing mechanisms and fairness analysis should be built into IDS evaluation procedures, and responsible-AI principles must guide the deployment of security technologies within societal infrastructures.

In summary, the emerging paradigm in ML-based IoT intrusion detection emphasizes holistic system design. The field is transitioning from isolated, accuracy-driven experimental models toward scalable, lightweight, explainable, privacy-preserving, and adversarially robust security ecosystems. The future of IDS in IoT security depends on interdisciplinary collaboration among artificial intelligence researchers, networking engineers, embedded system designers, and cryptography experts. Sustainable, resilient, and trustworthy cybersecurity in IoT ecosystems can be achieved only through integrated, well-coordinated architectural innovation across system layers.

9.2.2 Future of DL based IDS in sustainable IoT security

Recent advances in IDS show that the evolution of ML-based intrusion detection systems in IoT environments extends far beyond conventional supervised and DL models. Contemporary research highlights the emergence of automated, adaptive, distributed, and lifecycle-aware AI paradigms that are significantly reshaping IDS design in modern IoT and IIoT ecosystems. As network complexity increased and traffic data became more intricate, DL techniques gained prominence in developing strong IDS. Deep models provide automatic feature extraction and hierarchical representation learning, which are particularly beneficial for high-dimensional and unstructured data.

DL architectures and models have already been developed and experimented with in the IoT security domain, and their advances have been reported. They are discussed below:

- Artificial Neural Networks (ANN) and Deep Neural Networks (DNN) use multiple fully connected layers to learn nonlinear relationships between input features and attack classes. These models are widely applied in binary and multi-class classification tasks. Deep architectures enable abstract feature learning without extensive manual preprocessing. However, increasing depth also increases training time, memory requirements, and energy consumption. Consequently, DNN-based IDS models are generally deployed at fog or cloud layers rather than directly on resource-constrained IoT devices.
- Convolutional Neural Networks (CNN) are effective in capturing spatial correlations within data. In IDS applications, CNNs are used for packet-level pattern recognition, flow-based feature extraction, and even transforming tabular traffic data into image-like representations. CNNs are relatively efficient during inference compared to fully connected networks, especially when optimized using pruning or quantization. For this reason, CNN-based IDS models have been successfully deployed on edge platforms such as Raspberry Pi and Jetson Nano devices in several experimental studies.
- Because network traffic exhibits sequential and temporal characteristics, recurrent architectures are particularly valuable. Recurrent Neural Networks (RNN) , Long Short-Term Memory (LSTM), and Gated Recurrent Unit (GRU) models capture temporal dependencies in communication flows. These architectures are well suited for detecting distributed denial-of-service attacks, botnet propagation, insider threats, and multi-stage intrusions. LSTM mitigates vanishing gradient issues and captures long-term dependencies, while GRU offers comparable

performance with fewer parameters. However, sequential computation introduces latency and increases computational cost, which may limit their applicability in real-time industrial control systems.

- Autoencoders (AE) are widely used for anomaly detection in unsupervised settings. They learn compressed representations of normal traffic and identify anomalies by reconstructing them. This approach is particularly useful in dynamic IoT environments where labeled attack data are scarce. However, selecting appropriate thresholds remains challenging, and legitimate but rare traffic patterns may be incorrectly classified as anomalies.
- Generative Adversarial Networks (GAN) are increasingly used in IDS research for data augmentation, class imbalance mitigation, and adversarial robustness enhancement. GANs generate synthetic attack samples to improve minority-class detection. However, adversarial training is computationally intensive and increases energy consumption, making GAN-based approaches more suitable for offline model enhancement rather than continuous real-time deployment.
- Graph Neural Networks (GNN) represent an emerging direction in IDS ecosystems. They model communication relationships between devices, capturing structural dependencies in IoT and vehicular networks. By leveraging network topology, GNN-based IDS can detect coordinated or distributed attacks more effectively. Nevertheless, graph construction and message passing operations can become computationally expensive if graph density is not controlled.
- Closely related to generalization challenges is the adoption of Domain-Adversarial Neural Networks (DANN) and transfer learning frameworks. IoT deployments are inherently heterogeneous, involving diverse protocols, traffic characteristics, and hardware capabilities. Models trained on one dataset often fail when deployed in different domains. DANN mitigates this issue by learning domain-invariant representations, thereby improving cross-dataset robustness and reducing overfitting to benchmark environments. This capability is essential for practical IoT security deployments.
- Beyond classical ML and DL models, research increasingly explores optimization-enhanced learning frameworks. Metaheuristic algorithms such as Grey Wolf Optimization (GWO), Particle Swarm Optimization (PSO), and evolutionary search methods are integrated with classifiers to optimize feature selection and hyperparameters. These optimization layers reduce dimensionality, minimize redundant computation, and improve detection performance while maintaining manageable computational overhead. Such approaches represent a hybrid class of optimization-driven IDS architectures.
- Federated Learning (FL) has become a central paradigm in IoT security. Instead of transmitting raw traffic data to centralized servers, FL enables distributed training across edge or fog nodes while sharing only model parameters. This architecture preserves privacy, reduces bandwidth consumption, and supports decentralized intelligence. However, communication rounds, aggregation overhead, and potential model leakage remain important concerns. Recent work emphasizes

privacy-preserving aggregation, secure off-chain storage, and lightweight consensus mechanisms to address these challenges.

- Deep Reinforcement Learning (DRL) introduces adaptive decision-making capabilities into IDS systems. Unlike static supervised models, DRL-based IDS can dynamically adjust defense strategies in response to environmental feedback. These systems are particularly useful in response to network resource management and intrusion response scenarios. Nevertheless, DRL requires iterative policy learning and continuous interaction with the environment, which increases computational complexity and energy consumption.
- A major conceptual advancement is the emergence of (NeSy AI). Neurosymbolic models integrate symbolic rule-based reasoning with neural DL pattern recognition. This hybrid framework enhances interpretability, structured reasoning, and logical consistency while retaining high detection capability. Although NeSy improves transparency and trustworthiness, it may incur additional inference overhead due to symbolic reasoning. Careful architectural optimization is therefore required for deployment in resource-constrained IoT systems.

As noted above, DL models have been widely adopted in intrusion detection systems for their ability to capture complex, nonlinear relationships in network traffic. Deep Neural Networks (DNNs), in particular, are frequently used to learn high-level feature representations from raw or preprocessed traffic flows. Several limitations exist, however. Although DNNs often achieve very high accuracy, frequently exceeding 99% on benchmark datasets, these results are often dataset-specific and generalize poorly to real IoT traffic, especially because public datasets are commonly outdated, imbalanced, or synthetic, which heightens the risk of overfitting and weakens the realism of deployment. Effective training also demands large labeled datasets that are difficult to obtain in dynamic IoT settings, and the high parameter count of these models carries substantial computational overhead, making real-time inference challenging on resource-constrained devices. Because DNNs operate largely as black boxes, they offer limited interpretability and hinder forensic analysis. They are likewise vulnerable to adversarial attacks, from small input perturbations to manipulation of the model during training or inference.

CNNs are often used to transform network traffic into grid-like or image-based representations to extract spatial features. While this approach can improve classification accuracy, it introduces certain drawbacks. Converting sequential network data into two-dimensional matrices may distort temporal relationships that are essential for intrusion detection. Convolution operations are computationally expensive and increase inference time, especially on embedded devices. Moreover, CNNs do not inherently model temporal dependencies, which limits their ability to capture evolving attack patterns. Like other deep models, CNN-based IDS solutions are susceptible to adversarial perturbations and may suffer from robustness issues in real-world deployments.

RNNs, including LSTM and GRU architectures, are specifically designed to model sequential data and time-series traffic behavior. They are suitable for detecting anomalies that evolve over time. However, RNN-based models face training instability issues such as vanishing and exploding gradients. They often require long convergence times and careful hyperparameter tuning. Their sequential nature increases inference latency, which can be problematic in real-time IoT and industrial control systems. LSTM architectures introduce additional gates and memory states, which increase computational complexity and memory usage. In industrial control and operational technology environments, where deterministic timing and strict latency constraints are required, delays introduced by RNN processing may disrupt physical processes and compromise safety.

AE are commonly applied in unsupervised anomaly detection. They learn compressed representations of normal traffic and identify anomalies based on reconstruction error. Although effective in many scenarios, autoencoders face several challenges. A high reconstruction error does not always correspond to malicious behavior, leading to ambiguity in detection decisions. Selecting an appropriate anomaly threshold is difficult and often environment-specific. Unsupervised training also makes these models vulnerable to data poisoning, since they may learn malicious patterns as normal if the training data is contaminated. Over time, latent representations may drift as network behavior changes, which degrades detection performance unless continuous retraining is performed.

GANs are used for synthetic attack generation and class imbalance mitigation. They consist of a generator and a discriminator that compete during training. While GANs can enhance dataset diversity and improve detection performance, they are computationally expensive due to dual-network training. They also suffer from instability issues such as mode collapse and non-convergence. The balance between generator and discriminator can be exploited by adversaries, and synthetic samples may not accurately reflect the diversity of real-world IoT traffic. Therefore, GAN-based IDS solutions require careful validation before deployment.

GNNs have emerged as a promising approach for modeling relational structures in IoT networks. They represent devices and communication flows as nodes and edges in a graph. Although GNNs capture topological information effectively, they face scalability challenges. Large IoT graphs increase memory consumption and computational complexity. Dynamic network topologies require frequent graph updates, which adds processing overhead. Node embeddings generated by GNNs are often difficult to interpret, and storing large adjacency matrices can be costly in massive IoT environments.

DANNs are introduced to address cross-domain generalization problems. They aim to reduce dataset bias by learning domain-invariant features. However, DANN assumes that domain discrepancies can be clearly identified and aligned. Training with gradient reversal layers can complicate convergence and increase instability. Moreover, adapting models across heterogeneous IoT protocols, such as ZigBee, LoRaWAN, and NB-IoT, remains challenging due to structural differences in traffic characteristics.

FL has been proposed as a privacy-preserving distributed training strategy for IoT-based IDS. Instead of sharing raw data, devices exchange model parameters. While this approach enhances privacy and reduces the risks of centralized data collection, it introduces communication overhead due to frequent parameter aggregation. Non-independent and non-identically distributed data across IoT devices can slow convergence and degrade global model performance. FL systems are also vulnerable to model poisoning and gradient inversion attacks, which can compromise the aggregated model. Therefore, secure aggregation and robust validation mechanisms are required.

DRL has been explored for adaptive intrusion response and dynamic defense strategies. DRL enables systems to learn optimal policies through interaction with the environment. However, exploration in live IoT systems can be risky, as trial-and-error learning may disrupt operations. DRL models require extensive training episodes and careful reward engineering. Poorly designed reward functions can lead to unstable or suboptimal defense policies. Additionally, policy learning is computationally intensive and may not be suitable for low-power edge devices.

Across all DL approaches, several cross-cutting limitations persist. IoT devices operate under strict CPU, memory, and energy constraints, thereby limiting the feasibility of deploying large models. Many IDS solutions are evaluated primarily on synthetic or benchmark datasets, with limited real-world validation. Deep models are vulnerable to adversarial attacks, including fast gradient sign method attacks, projected gradient descent, model inversion, and poisoning attacks. Their black-box nature creates an interpretability gap, reducing trust and regulatory compliance. Furthermore, vulnerabilities may arise throughout the ML lifecycle, including data collection, training, deployment, and maintenance. Finally, the massive scale and heterogeneity of IoT ecosystems pose significant scalability challenges, requiring models that are efficient, adaptable, and robust under diverse operational conditions.

Future DL-based IDS models must be adaptive, scalable, interpretable, energy-efficient, and suitable for deployment in heterogeneous, resource-constrained environments. Taken together, developments in DL, RL, FL, and neurosymbolic AI suggest that the architectural future of IoT IDS can be understood through several major trends. These directions for DL and related models in IoT security IDS are discussed in detail below.

- One important direction is the adoption of multi-task and transfer-aware DL models. MTL enables a single model to learn multiple related intrusion detection objectives simultaneously, such as binary attack detection and fine-grained attack classification. By sharing internal representations across related tasks, MTL improves generalization and reduces retraining costs when IoT environments evolve. Transfer learning further supports cross-domain adaptation, allowing models trained in one IoT setting to be fine-tuned in another with limited additional data. In heterogeneous IoT infrastructures, where devices and protocols differ significantly, these approaches reduce computational burden and enhance adaptability.
- Transformer-based architectures represent another emerging direction. Compared to traditional recurrent neural networks, transformers can model long-range

temporal dependencies using attention mechanisms. This makes them particularly well-suited to detecting slow, stealthy attack patterns in IoT traffic. Transformer models can overcome the training instability problems found in RNNs while improving sequence modeling performance. Future work in IDS is expected to focus on lightweight transformer variants suited to edge devices, as well as hybrid CNN-transformer models that combine spatial and temporal feature extraction. Attention mechanisms may also enhance interpretability by highlighting the traffic features that most influence a decision.

- DRL is reshaping IDS from passive detection tools into adaptive defense agents. Recent progress in DRL-based intrusion detection techniques has led to the increasing application of DRL methods such as DQN, DDQN, actor-critic models, and policy-gradient methods in communication networks and industrial systems. In future IoT IDS architectures, DRL agents may dynamically adjust detection thresholds, allocate resources, and initiate automated mitigation actions. Such systems will learn optimal defense strategies through interaction with network environments. However, future research must address convergence stability, safe exploration in live systems, and computational efficiency for edge deployment.
- Federated and distributed DL will become central in large-scale IoT deployments. IoT ecosystems often involve privacy-sensitive data collected from distributed sensors, vehicles, and industrial devices. FL enables collaborative model training without sharing raw traffic data. Future IDS frameworks will incorporate communication-efficient aggregation, robustness against model poisoning, and mechanisms to handle non-independent and non-identically distributed (non-IID) data. Federated-RL may also emerge, combining adaptive defense with privacy-preserving distributed training. These approaches are especially relevant for smart cities and industrial IoT networks.
- Hybrid DL architectures are expected to dominate future IoT IDS designs. Combinations such as CNN-LSTM, autoencoder-GAN, and multi-modal deep networks are seeing growing use in intrusion detection, drawing on the complementary strengths of their components: convolutional layers extract spatial patterns, recurrent or transformer layers capture temporal dependencies, and generative models detect anomalies through reconstruction. In the heterogeneous traffic environments characteristic of IoT, such hybrid architectures offer both flexibility and improved detection robustness.
- Generative and self-supervised learning models will play a crucial role in addressing data scarcity. IoT intrusion datasets are often imbalanced and lack labeled examples of emerging attacks. Autoencoders, variational autoencoders, GANs, and contrastive learning methods enable representation learning without extensive manual labeling. Synthetic attack generation through GANs may improve robustness against zero-day threats. Self-supervised learning can extract meaningful representations from large volumes of unlabeled traffic data, which is common in IoT networks.
- NeSy DL introduces a promising paradigm that combines neural representation learning with symbolic reasoning. Neurosymbolic architectures integrate rule-

based logic, protocol knowledge, and graph reasoning into deep models. This fusion improves interpretability and supports structured reasoning over IoT communication rules. For critical infrastructure such as smart grids and industrial control systems, where explainability and regulatory compliance are essential, neurosymbolic IDS may provide a balanced approach that strikes a balance between accuracy and transparency.
- GNNs are also gaining attention due to the inherently relational nature of IoT networks. IoT devices interact through dynamic communication graphs. GNN-based IDS models can capture device relationships, traffic propagation patterns, and coordinated attack behavior. These architectures are particularly relevant for smart grids, vehicular networks, and distributed industrial systems. Future work must address scalability, dynamic graph updates, and memory-efficient graph representations.
- Edge-optimized and lightweight DL models will define the practical future of IoT IDS. Resource constraints in IoT devices require model compression, pruning, quantization, and efficient inference strategies. Emerging techniques such as hyperdimensional computing and TinyML architectures aim to enable on-device intelligence. Future DL-based IDS must prioritize energy efficiency, low latency, and real-time operation while maintaining acceptable detection accuracy.
- Across all architectural trends, several research drivers remain consistent. Adversarial robustness must be strengthened to defend against data poisoning, model inversion, and gradient-based attacks. Dataset realism and cross-domain validation are necessary to avoid overfitting to outdated benchmarks. Explainability must be integrated into model design rather than added as an afterthought. Privacy-preserving mechanisms must protect both data and model parameters in distributed settings.

In summary, the future of DL architectures for IoT intrusion detection systems will move toward adaptive, distributed, automated, interpretable, and resource-aware security frameworks. Rather than relying solely on deeper or more complex models, next-generation IDS solutions will integrate RL, federated collaboration, neurosymbolic reasoning, graph modeling, and lightweight edge optimization. This architectural evolution reflects a broader shift from accuracy-driven experimentation to deployment-ready, resilient, and sustainable IoT security ecosystems.

9.2.3 Future of machine and DL based IDS for industrial control systems

Industrial Control Systems (ICS) constitute a distinct class of cyber-physical environments in which security mechanisms must adhere to strict operational constraints. Unlike conventional IT networks, ICS environments operate under real-time communication requirements, deterministic traffic patterns, dedicated operational technology OT protocols such as Modbus, DNP3, and PROFINET, and safety-critical production processes. ICS architectures typically follow the Purdue model and exhibit predictable communication flows, fixed connection lifetimes, and tightly regulated timing behavior. These characteristics strongly influence how ML- and DL-based IDSs must be designed and deployed in industrial environments.

Traditional ML models remain widely adopted in ICS intrusion detection due to their interpretability, modest computational requirements, and stable behavior. Tree-based techniques, such as Decision Trees and Random Forests, are widely used because they provide transparent decision paths and handle structured industrial data effectively. Random Forest, in particular, offers improved robustness against overfitting while maintaining a manageable computational cost. Probabilistic models, including Naïve Bayes, Bayesian Networks, and Hidden Markov Models, are well-suited for ICS networks because industrial traffic often exhibits repetitive, structured patterns. Given the regular packet timing and predefined communication flows described in the ICS-related works, probabilistic modeling can capture normal process behavior with reasonable efficiency. Boundary-based methods, such as Support Vector Machines, are also common in ICS IDS, especially for binary classification between normal and malicious traffic. Instance-based approaches, such as K-Nearest Neighbors, have been applied in water treatment and manufacturing systems, where deterministic traffic patterns enable similarity-based detection; however, these models require regular updates to remain effective.

DL architectures have increasingly been explored for ICS anomaly detection as industrial networks generate larger volumes of data and more complex behavioral patterns. ANN and DNN enable nonlinear feature learning and hierarchical representation extraction, thereby improving detection accuracy compared to shallow models. Recurrent neural networks, including LSTM and GRU variants, are particularly relevant because ICS traffic is inherently sequential and time-dependent. These models can capture temporal dependencies and detect slow, stealthy attacks that evolve over time. AEs are also widely adopted in ICS due to the scarcity of labeled attack data. By learning the reconstruction profile of normal traffic, they can identify anomalies through reconstruction error without relying on extensive labeled datasets. Hybrid architectures that combine lightweight edge-level detection with cloud-based deep analytics are emerging as practical solutions for secure and sustainable ICS monitoring.

Despite these advances, both ML and DL architectures face significant limitations in industrial environments. Real-time constraints stand among the most critical. ICS networks prioritize availability and deterministic timing over confidentiality, so any additional latency introduced by complex inference pipelines risks disrupting physical processes. Because packet timing and sampling intervals are tightly controlled, IDS-induced delays can interfere with control-loop stability. Resource constraints complicate deployment further: many ICS components are legacy PLCs and embedded controllers with limited processing capability and memory, whereas DL models often demand substantial computational resources for both training and inference; a tension that runs counter to the sustainability and energy-efficiency goals of industrial facilities.

Legacy integration is another major barrier. Historically, ICS environments were air-gapped and relied on proprietary or weakly secured OT protocols. The convergence of IT and OT networks has increased exposure to cyber threats while introducing heterogeneous communication standards. ML and DL models must generalize across diverse protocols, thereby complicating feature engineering and model portability. In addition, publicly available ICS datasets are limited and often synthetic. Validation challenges nonetheless remain unresolved, since many experimental evaluations fail to capture the full complexity of real industrial operations. This raises the risk of overfitting and weakens confidence in real-world deployment.

Explainability and trust are particularly important in safety-critical systems. Industrial operators require clear justification for IDS alerts because false positives may halt production lines or trigger costly shutdowns. Black-box DL models, therefore, face resistance unless accompanied by interpretable reasoning mechanisms. Furthermore, ML-based IDS themselves introduce new attack surfaces. Data poisoning, model manipulation, and evasion attacks can compromise the reliability of detection. Given that ICS infrastructure is a high-value target, AI-based defenses must also be protected throughout their lifecycles.

Looking forward, the future of ML and DL architectures for ICS IDS will likely focus on distributed, explainable, and resource-aware solutions. FL presents a promising direction for collaborative model training across geographically distributed industrial plants while preserving data privacy. XAI techniques are expected to enhance operator trust and regulatory compliance. Lightweight, edge-optimized DL models, supported by pruning and quantization techniques, will become essential for meeting strict latency and energy constraints. Hybrid edge-cloud architectures can provide scalable analytics while maintaining local real-time responsiveness. Recent ongoing exploration also suggests that large language models may support threat intelligence analysis and incident response automation, complementing core detection engines.

In summary, the application of ML and DL in ICS intrusion detection requires careful adaptation to operational technology constraints. Future research must balance detection accuracy with deterministic timing, computational efficiency, interpretability, and sustainability. Only through context-aware architectural design can AI-driven IDS achieve reliable and safe deployment in industrial control environments.

9.3 Future of BlockChain-based IDS in sustainable IoT security

Blockchain-based intrusion detection systems (IDS) in IoT environments are rarely implemented as standalone solutions. Instead, they are integrated with complementary techniques to strengthen trust, decentralization, and resilience across distributed networks. In most designs, blockchain serves as a security-enhancing layer that supports ML, FL, smart contracts, and edge-based detection mechanisms.

One of the most common integrations is the combination of blockchain and ML- or DL-based anomaly detection. In this approach, the IDS model performs traffic analysis using classifiers such as CNN, LSTM, GRU, or optimized variants like Quantum BiGRU with metaheuristic tuning, while blockchain provides immutable storage of detection results and model updates. This integration ensures tamper-proof logging of anomaly scores and prevents unauthorized modification of IDS decisions. In several implementations, blockchains securely store model parameters and validate updates before they are applied, thereby protecting collaborative detection frameworks against manipulation. This design strengthens integrity and decentralized trust in IoT security monitoring.

Another significant integration is the combination of blockchain with FL, particularly in IIoT systems. As explained in various technical reports and case studies on blockchain and FL for IIoT, FL enables distributed model training without sharing raw data, while blockchain can replace or supplement the central aggregation server. Smart contracts are used to manage model aggregation and validate client updates. This approach improves transparency and reduces reliance on a single trusted entity. It also helps mitigate model poisoning and backdoor attacks by verifying contributions before updating the global model. However, technical reports on this technique also highlight challenges, including communication overhead, client heterogeneity, and aggregation complexity, which remain open research issues.

Blockchain is also integrated with smart contracts to automate IDS response and rule enforcement. In Internet of Vehicles (IoV) and smart city systems, smart contracts validate IDS alerts before storing them on-chain. They automatically execute predefined security policies, enforce access control decisions, and trigger mitigation procedures. This reduces manual intervention and enables decentralized policy management. Similarly, in blockchain-SDN architectures, SDN monitors traffic flows in real time, while blockchain stores verified alerts and ensures that security logs cannot be altered. This combination mitigates the single point of failure problem in centralized controllers.

In green IoT frameworks, blockchain has been combined with energy-aware clustering mechanisms. Cluster head selection algorithms reduce energy consumption, while blockchain secures inter-cluster communication and manages certificate revocation for malicious nodes. In fog and edge computing architectures, lightweight anomaly detection is deployed at the edge to enable low latency, while blockchain-based decentralized validation is performed at higher layers. This multi-layer design supports real-time intrusion detection while maintaining distributed trust.

Despite these advantages, blockchain-integrated IDS solutions face significant practical limitations. They are listed below:

- Scalability remains a primary concern. IoT systems generate large volumes of alerts, and storing every IDS event on-chain leads to throughput bottlenecks and high latency. Consensus mechanisms introduce additional delay and computational overhead, which may be unsuitable for resource-constrained IoT devices. Even when permissioned blockchains are used, validation and replication processes increase processing cost.

- Energy consumption is another critical issue. Mining, block validation, and ledger synchronization require additional computational resources. In green IoT or battery-powered environments, this overhead may contradict sustainability goals. Communication overhead also increases when blockchain is combined with FL, as model updates and verification messages must be transmitted across distributed nodes. The IIoT report highlights that aggregation and communication costs are the key bottlenecks in such systems.
- The growth in storage of the blockchain ledger poses further challenges. IoT devices typically cannot store the entire ledger and must rely on lightweight nodes or off-chain storage mechanisms. Smart contracts may contain vulnerabilities, and once deployed, coding errors are difficult to correct due to blockchain immutability. In safety-critical applications such as IoV or industrial control, blockchain validation delays may conflict with millisecond-level decision requirements. Additionally, although blockchain enhances transparency, transaction metadata may expose behavioral patterns, creating a privacy paradox.
- **Operational cost** is another limitation. Smart contract execution fees, on-chain storage costs, and infrastructure maintenance can increase deployment costs, making large-scale IoT implementations financially challenging.

The future of blockchain-integrated models for intrusion detection systems in IoT security is evolving toward more decentralized, adaptive, and efficiency-oriented architectures. From a practitioner's perspective, Blockchain is no longer viewed merely as a logging mechanism but as a coordination and trust layer that complements ML-based detection. The next generation of systems will integrate blockchain with FL, DL, smart contracts, and software-defined networking to form robust and scalable IDS ecosystems suitable for smart cities and industrial IoT.

In the context of blockchain-based FL, the trajectory clearly points toward decentralized aggregation without relying on a single trusted server. Replacing the centralized FL coordinator with a blockchain-based consensus mechanism reduces reliance on trust assumptions and prevents single points of failure. This enables collaborative intrusion detection across multiple organizations, such as factories, utility providers, or municipal infrastructures, while maintaining data locality and privacy. However, poisoning and backdoor attacks against federated updates remain critical threats. Future systems are therefore expected to embed secure aggregation, anomaly scoring of client updates, and robust model validation as default components. At the same time, practitioners and potential researchers acknowledge the overhead introduced by blockchain coordination and emphasize the need for lightweight consensus mechanisms and optimized communication protocols. Consequently, permissioned blockchains, cluster-based federation, personalization strategies, and drift detection mechanisms will likely become standard practices to address heterogeneity and model drift in industrial IoT deployments.

When blockchain is combined with DL-based detection models, the trajectory points toward adaptive, online IDS capable of handling non-stationary IoT traffic. In vehicular settings especially, dynamic data and continually evolving attack strategies demand real-time anomaly detection and ongoing model adaptation. Future DL pipelines will increasingly run at the edge or fog layer for low-latency inference, while blockchain serves chiefly for secure logging, auditability, and the validation of model updates. Optimization-driven approaches, including metaheuristic feature selection and temporal architectures such as bidirectional GRU variants, are likely to remain valuable for managing noisy and imbalanced telemetry. Adversarial robustness, too, will become mandatory, since AI-based IDS are themselves vulnerable to evasion and manipulation. Adversarial training, robust model validation, and secure on-chain parameter storage will thus form integral components of future blockchain-DL IDS frameworks.

The integration of blockchain with smart contracts is also expected to mature significantly. Smart contracts will increasingly function as the automation layer for IDS, encoding response policies, quarantine actions, trust scoring, and incident workflows. Hybrid fog-blockchain architectures are proposed to meet latency constraints in smart city environments. In such models, computationally intensive ML computations run off-chain on fog or edge nodes, while smart contracts enforce security policies and validate intrusion alerts before immutably recording them. However, scalability and computational overhead remain key blockers. Real-world case studies and technical reports identify throughput limitations, processing delays, and energy costs as major deployment challenges. Therefore, future focus should prioritize sharding, sidechains, layer-2 solutions, pruned ledgers, and permissioned blockchain configurations to reduce delay and resource consumption.

Blockchain, combined with SDN (software-defined networking) and NFV (network function virtualization), is also moving toward a unified security fabric for smart cities. SDN provides fine-grained traffic visibility and programmable control, while blockchain ensures integrity and decentralized trust. NFV enables elastic deployment of security services across the infrastructure. Future systems will likely perform intrusion detection analytics within programmable SDN controllers or distributed edge nodes, store security attestations and trust proofs on-chain, and orchestrate mitigation using NFV-based service chaining. This layered architecture enhances resilience while avoiding overloading constrained IoT devices.

Across all these integrations, several cross-cutting best practices are emerging. Scalability and low overhead must serve as primary design goals, a point that recurs across work on the IoV (Internet of Vehicles) and blockchain-based security alike. Heavy computation should be shifted off-chain, with only essential hashes, alerts, and integrity proofs committed to the ledger. Edge- and fog-first execution is crucial to meet real-time latency requirements. Secure aggregation and poisoning defense are essential in federated contexts. Device heterogeneity and data drift must be addressed through personalization, cluster-based federation, and continual learning. Strong identity management, certification, and revocation mechanisms, such as those proposed in energy-aware blockchain frameworks like BENIGREEN, must be tightly integrated with IDS pipelines to ensure trusted telemetry and authenticated communication. Finally, energy-aware security design is becoming indispensable in green IoT environments. Future blockchain-enabled IDS must consider energy-efficient clustering, duty cycling, and sustainable consensus protocols without sacrificing visibility or detection capability. In summary, the future of blockchain-integrated IDS in IoT security lies in hybrid, layered, and efficiency-driven architectures. Blockchain will increasingly serve as a substrate for trust, auditing, and coordination rather than a computational engine. ML and DL will operate closer to the edge for real-time analysis. FL and distributed learning will support cross-organizational collaboration. Smart contracts will automate enforcement and policy validation. Lightweight consensus, off-chain computation, and energy-aware design will determine practical feasibility. Only by balancing security strength, computational efficiency, scalability, and sustainability can blockchain-enhanced IDS achieve robust protection in next-generation IoT ecosystems.

Overall, blockchain-integrated IDS architectures enhance integrity, decentralization, and collaborative trust in IoT security systems. They support anomaly-based, signature-based, hybrid, and federated IDS models through immutable logging, secure aggregation, and automated policy enforcement. However, scalability, latency, energy consumption, communication overhead, storage growth, and smart contract vulnerabilities remain unresolved challenges. Future attention should be paid to lightweight consensus mechanisms, off-chain storage integration, scalable aggregation protocols, and energy-aware blockchain designs to ensure practical deployment in real-world IoT environments.

9.4 Future of post-quantum cryptographic approaches in sustainable IoT security

Post-quantum intrusion detection systems (IDS) for IoT security represent an emerging architectural shift in which advanced detection models are combined with quantum-resistant trust mechanisms. In this paradigm, ML and DL models continue to serve as the primary detection engines, while post-quantum cryptography (PQC), quantum-resilient blockchain, and secure key management frameworks protect the integrity, authenticity, and confidentiality of the entire IDS lifecycle. The objective is not only to detect malicious activity but also to ensure that communications, model updates, alerts, and forensic logs remain secure even in the presence of future quantum-capable adversaries.

One important direction is the integration of post-quantum cryptography (PQC) directly into IDS ecosystems. Lattice-based cryptography stands out as a leading candidate for post-quantum digital signatures and secure key exchange in IoT environments. Lattice-based identity-based signature schemes are especially well-suited to IoT networks, since they provide authentication, non-repudiation, and traceability without relying on a classical public-key infrastructure that may become vulnerable to quantum attacks. Alongside lattice-based methods, hash-based and code-based cryptographic schemes offer viable alternatives for lightweight IoT deployments, particularly when paired with DL-based IDS pipelines. Within such architectures, PQC protects the communication channel, the identities of participating nodes, and the integrity of IDS model parameters throughout the training, aggregation, and update phases.

Another major trend is the development of quantum-resilient blockchain frameworks that act as the trust backbone of IDS infrastructures. Traditional blockchain systems often rely on classical cryptographic primitives such as RSA or ECC, which are susceptible to quantum algorithms. Quantum-aware blockchain IDS designs therefore incorporate lattice-based post-quantum signatures to ensure that stored alerts, audit trails, and model updates remain tamper-proof over the long term. The LQB-IDS architecture explicitly demonstrates this approach by integrating a post-quantum-secure blockchain database (LLM-QBc-DB) to preserve IDS knowledge and alert provenance while combining lightweight ML and LLM modules for adaptive detection. This architecture highlights that post-quantum blockchain is not a replacement for detection models but rather a mechanism to ensure secure lifecycle management of IDS intelligence.

In highly critical infrastructures, quantum key distribution (QKD) is also proposed as a complementary mechanism for securing key exchange between gateways and cloud or control layers. QKD enables information-theoretically secure key establishment and incorporates error-correction and privacy-amplification mechanisms to mitigate real-world channel imperfections. Although QKD deployment at the IoT scale remains operationally complex, hierarchical key management strategies at the gateway level are proposed to enable integration into industrial and smart grid environments.

DL remains central to post-quantum IDS (PQ-IDS), but it is increasingly deployed in hybrid architectures. For example, lightweight CNN-LSTM models can perform initial detection at the edge, while unknown or complex attack patterns are analyzed using more advanced modules such as LLM-based analyzers. In the LQB-IDS framework, a dual-switch learning mechanism allows a lightweight ML model to handle known attacks with minimal latency, while the LLM module dynamically analyzes unknown traffic patterns and updates the knowledge base stored on a post-quantum-secure blockchain. This design addresses both adaptability and security by combining intelligent detection with quantum-resilient storage and validation.

A useful taxonomy for PQ-IDS in IoT security can therefore be organized into several categories. First, crypto-hardened IDS pipelines integrate PQC primitives to secure communication and authentication throughout the detection workflow. Second, blockchain-integrated post-quantum IDS architectures ensure immutable and auditable storage of alerts and model histories. Third, QKD-enhanced infrastructures protect high-value communication links. Fourth, hybrid intelligence systems that combine ML, DL, or LLM-based detection with post-quantum-secure trust frameworks. Fifth, recent works explore post-quantum-secure FL, in which model aggregation and update verification are protected against both privacy leakage and quantum-enabled attacks.

Despite their advantages, PQ-IDS frameworks introduce several practical limitations. First, PQC schemes often require larger key sizes and greater computational overhead than classical cryptography. When combined with DL inference or FL synchronization, this can increase CPU usage, memory consumption, and energy demand, which is problematic for resource-constrained IoT devices. Second, latency becomes a critical concern. Blockchain confirmation delays, cryptographic verification, and LLM-based reasoning can introduce additional processing time. The real-world case studies related to LQB-IDS acknowledge this trade-off and mitigate it by using a lightweight ML module as the default fast path, while reserving LLM analysis for unknown traffic. Third, the complexity of system integration is significant. Combining IDS lifecycle management, PQC key management, blockchain governance, and possibly QKD networking requires careful architectural coordination.

Furthermore, QKD deployment faces practical constraints, including limited key generation rates and sensitivity to channel noise, necessitating hierarchical gateway-based designs. There is also an inherent tension between security strength and detection performance. Stronger cryptographic protections and comprehensive logging may reduce agility or increase operational cost. Finally, although blockchain improves auditability, not all proposed systems fully log both detection outputs and model evolution histories in a verifiable manner, leaving gaps in end-to-end provenance.

The future of blockchain-integrated PQ-IDS in IoT environments is moving toward a fully integrated, end-to-end trustworthy security lifecycle. Recent frameworks, such as quantum-aware secure blockchain IDS architectures and adaptive LLM-assisted PQ-IDS designs, treat intrusion detection not as a standalone classifier, but as a continuous operational process. This process includes detection outputs, model updates, provenance tracking, secure information sharing across distributed nodes, and quantum-resilient integrity protection of the entire pipeline. In the V2X domain, next-generation IDS must simultaneously address deployment realism, adversarial robustness, federated coordination, and PQC integration. In this emerging paradigm, an IDS will no longer be evaluated solely by accuracy or F1-score. It will also be judged by its ability to provide forensic-grade traceability of alerts, verifiable model lineage, secure update attribution, and resistance against quantum-capable adversaries.

Another clear trajectory is the adoption of edge-cloud split PQ-IDS architectures. Adaptive systems, such as LLM-assisted blockchain-secured IDS, demonstrate that lightweight ML or DL models can operate at the edge to enable low-latency detection of known attacks, while more computationally intensive reasoning modules, including large language models, handle unknown-attack analysis, concept drift, and knowledge refinement in the cloud. In these architectures, a permissioned post-quantum-secure blockchain serves as the trusted knowledge plane. It stores validated alerts, unknown-attack intelligence, and model updates in an immutable, quantum-resilient manner. This approach enables controlled dissemination of verified intelligence across IoT or IIoT devices while preventing silent tampering or poisoning. Technical reports on V2X-related case studies further emphasize that scalable deployment requires careful management of communication overhead, latency, and energy consumption, reinforcing the need for lightweight, hierarchical designs.

Across post-quantum blockchain IDS (PQ-BIIDS) technical reports and evaluations, lattice-based cryptography has emerged as the dominant cryptographic foundation. Lattice-based digital signatures, such as Dilithium-class schemes, are repeatedly proposed to secure ledger transactions, model updates, and alert verification under quantum threat models. Hash-based and code-based schemes are also considered, but lattice-based primitives are often preferred due to their performance and the momentum of standardization. In parallel, most practical architectures favor consortium or permissioned blockchains rather than public proof-of-work systems. Lightweight consensus mechanisms, including proof-of-authority or hierarchical consortium models, are chosen to reduce computational and energy overhead in IoT and IIoT deployments. In high-criticality environments such as smart grids and V2X gateways, selective integration of post-quantum key exchange or even quantum key distribution is proposed for securing critical communication links. However, these mechanisms are applied selectively due to cost and deployment complexity.

Secure collaborative learning is becoming a central element of future PQ-IDS models. Quantum-aware secure blockchain IDS frameworks highlight the need to unify federated or distributed model training with blockchain-based provenance and post-quantum cryptographic guarantees. Model aggregation processes must be verifiable, privacy-preserving, and resistant to poisoning or backdoor attacks. By anchoring model versions and update histories on a post-quantum-secure ledger, it becomes possible to audit which participant contributed each update and to detect anomalous or malicious contributions. The V2X study underscores that FL, adversarial robustness, and blockchain-based security enhancements are essential components for the scalable deployment of vehicular and IoT IDS. In the post-quantum era, these mechanisms must also withstand cryptanalytic advances that threaten classical public-key cryptography.

From a deployment perspective, several practical adaptations are consistently implied. First, **blockchain should function** as the provenance backbone of the IDS, recording alerts, model versions, and update histories to support traceability and forensic readiness. Second, **post-quantum digital signatures** should protect both detection outputs and model updates to ensure long-term integrity. Third, **permissioned consensus mechanisms** should be preferred to maintain scalability and energy efficiency in resource-constrained IoT systems. Fourth, **adaptive detection pipelines** should combine fast edge-level machine learning with selective cloud-level reasoning, rather than relying exclusively on large models. Fifth, governance of permissioned blockchains must be partially automated, potentially through AI-assisted trust evaluation, to support large and dynamic IoT ecosystems without excessive manual intervention. In conclusion, the future of post-quantum IDS for IoT security is converging toward a hybrid architecture that combines intelligent detection, cryptographic survivability, and verifiable operational provenance. Real-time edge-based DL models will handle immediate detection. Selective use of advanced reasoning models will support the analysis of unknown attacks and adaptation. Permissioned blockchains upgraded with lattice-based signatures will provide tamper-resistant governance and auditability. In critical links, post-quantum key exchange or quantum-secure mechanisms will strengthen communication security. At the same time, system designers must balance detection accuracy against computational efficiency, energy consumption, latency, and scalability. It is increasingly clear that next-generation IDS will need to reconcile theoretical AI models with the constraints of real-world deployment, adversarial robustness, federated coordination, and post-quantum cryptography. Only by uniting intelligent detection with quantum-resilient trust infrastructures can IoT ecosystems attain cybersecurity protection that is durable, auditable, and genuinely future-proof.

In summary, post-quantum IDS for IoT security represents a convergence of quantum-resistant cryptography, secure distributed ledgers, and intelligent detection mechanisms. The future of this field lies in designing lightweight, latency-aware, and energy-efficient architectures that integrate PQC, blockchain, FL, and adaptive AI models in a cohesive and scalable manner. Such systems must ensure not only accurate intrusion detection but also long-term cryptographic resilience, secure model lifecycle management, and trustworthy auditability in the emerging quantum era.

9.5 Future of next-generation energy-efficient IDS deployment

The deployment of IDSs in modern IoT ecosystems has reached a critical stage where detection accuracy alone is no longer sufficient to define an effective security solution. Emerging environments such as smart cities, connected vehicles, medical devices, and industrial automation systems (IAS) generate continuous streams of high-volume data while operating under strict constraints related to energy consumption, latency, and computational resources. The scale, diversity, and dynamic nature of these environments have exposed the limitations of traditional centralized, cloud-based detection approaches. As a result, the development of next-generation IDSs is increasingly guided by a common set of design principles. These include moving detection capabilities closer to data sources through edge and fog computing, reducing computational overhead by employing model compression techniques such as pruning, quantization, knowledge distillation, and enabling collaborative learning through federated and privacy-preserving frameworks. In addition, modern IDS architectures are beginning to allocate computational resources adaptively, adjusting processing intensity based on the operational context rather than executing all detection models at maximum capacity.

Despite these shared trends, each application domain presents unique challenges. Healthcare environments must meet stringent privacy, security, and patient safety requirements. Vehicular and V2X networks demand ultra-low latency, rapid decision-making, and resilience in highly dynamic and mobile conditions. Industrial automation systems, meanwhile, must operate within deterministic timing constraints while integrating with legacy protocols and infrastructure.

This section explores the future of energy-efficient IDS deployment through four interconnected domains: smart cities, transportation and V2X systems, the Internet of Medical Things (IoMT), and industrial automation. Collectively, these perspectives demonstrate the ongoing evolution of the field from an emphasis on detection accuracy alone toward a broader focus on sustainable, deployment-ready cybersecurity engineering. In this emerging paradigm, energy efficiency, scalability, operational reliability, and security effectiveness are treated as equally important design objectives rather than secondary considerations.

9.5.1 Future of energy-efficient IDS in smart cities

The rapid digitalization of smart cities has created a densely interconnected environment of surveillance cameras, intelligent transportation systems, smart grids, environmental sensors, and building-automation platforms, all of which continuously generate large volumes of heterogeneous data. Next-generation IDS must therefore achieve not only high detection accuracy but also operate within strict energy, latency, and scalability constraints. In both DL-based and RL-based IDS architectures, deployment realism, computational efficiency, and adaptive intelligence are becoming as important as raw detection performance. In smart-city settings, energy efficiency is no longer optional but a fundamental design requirement.

One dominant direction in energy-efficient smart-city IDS is the adoption of edge and fog computing architectures. Instead of transmitting raw data streams to centralized cloud servers, detection mechanisms are increasingly deployed closer to the data source. Lightweight models operate on gateways, roadside units, access points, or building controllers, thereby reducing communication overhead and enabling faster response times. This hierarchical architecture typically follows a layered model: sensors perform basic filtering, gateways execute lightweight anomaly detection, fog nodes conduct deeper analytics, and cloud platforms handle large-scale correlation and model training. Such distributed placement significantly reduces bandwidth usage and lowers communication energy consumption while maintaining situational awareness.

Lightweight DL models are central to this transformation. Modern IDS techniques and frameworks highlight CNNs, RNNs, transformer-based models, and hybrid architectures as powerful detection engines. However, these models must be optimized for the constraints of smart-city infrastructure. Techniques such as pruning, quantization, knowledge distillation, and model compression reduce parameter size and computational demand. Instead of deploying large transformer models, compact variants and efficient attention mechanisms are increasingly preferred. In many cases, model training occurs in high-performance environments, while inference is deployed in compressed form on edge devices. This separation ensures both high model capability and operational efficiency.

FL represents another important development for smart-city IDS. Smart cities handle sensitive data, including mobility traces, video streams, and residential telemetry. FL allows distributed nodes to collaboratively train detection models without sharing raw data. This approach enhances privacy and reduces the need for large-scale data transmission. FL pipeline nevertheless brings challenges of its own, arising from heterogeneous data distributions and non-independent and non-identically distributed (non-IID) traffic patterns. To address this, personalized FL and adaptive aggregation strategies are emerging as practical solutions. From an energy perspective, efficient FL mechanisms, such as compressed model updates and selective client participation, are necessary to prevent excessive device-side energy consumption.

Adaptive IDS using RL and DRL is also gaining attention in smart-city contexts. RL-based IDS can dynamically adjust inspection policies, allocate resources, and decide when to offload computation to fog or cloud nodes. The review of DRL-based IDS in communication networks identifies energy efficiency and edge deployment as open research challenges. In smart cities, DRL models can optimize trade-offs between detection accuracy and power consumption. However, DRL training can be computationally intensive and must be carefully engineered to ensure stability and safe deployment in critical infrastructure.

Emerging neural paradigms further support energy-efficient detection. GNNs are well-suited for modeling transportation systems, smart grids, and communication topologies where relational structure is central. Spiking neural networks (SNNs) are being explored for ultra-low-power inference in always-on sensor environments. These architectures offer promising directions for scalable and structured anomaly detection in graph-like smart-city systems.

Despite these advancements, several practical limitations remain. First, trade-offs among accuracy, latency, and energy are unavoidable. Centralized deep models may achieve higher detection accuracy, but they increase latency and communication energy consumption. Edge-based models reduce delay and bandwidth usage but may sacrifice some predictive performance. Second, smart-city environments experience frequent concept drift due to seasonal patterns, events, infrastructure upgrades, and evolving attack strategies. Personalized learning and continual adaptation mechanisms are therefore essential. Third, FL and RL frameworks introduce additional energy overhead and security risks, including poisoning attacks and unstable training dynamics. Finally, a persistent deployment gap remains between experimental results and real-world operation. Many IDS models perform well on benchmark datasets but struggle under continuous, large-scale, and heterogeneous smart-city conditions. For sustainable and practical deployment, several best practices can be adopted. Energy and latency budgets should guide model selection from the outset. Compression and pruning must be treated as mandatory design stages rather than optional optimizations. Hybrid detection pipelines, combining lightweight local anomaly filters with more sophisticated regional classifiers, can balance efficiency and robustness. Concept drift should be addressed through periodic recalibration and online learning strategies. FL and RL loops must incorporate integrity verification and robust aggregation mechanisms. Most importantly, energy consumption should be explicitly measured and reported in terms of inference cost, communication overhead, and device-level impact. Without quantifiable metrics, claims of "green IDS" remain incomplete.

The evolution of smart cities is generating unprecedented volumes of continuous data from traffic systems, surveillance cameras, environmental sensors, smart grids, and intelligent buildings; all operating under strict latency and energy constraints. As a result, the future of IDS in smart cities is moving toward architectures that prioritize energy efficiency, scalability, and real-time responsiveness alongside detection accuracy. DL plays a central role in extracting patterns from distributed urban sensors, yet edge computing is becoming equally essential, since centralized processing cannot scale sustainably as telemetry volumes grow. This shift establishes energy-efficient, deployment-aware IDS as a core requirement for the cybersecurity of future smart cities.

One dominant trajectory is the transition to edge-first and fog-assisted IDS architectures. Rather than routing raw data streams to centralized cloud servers, detection is increasingly placed near the data sources themselves. Lightweight models run on gateways, roadside units, or building controllers; fog nodes perform intermediate analytics; and cloud servers are reserved for large-scale training and cross-domain correlation. This hierarchical structure, device to gateway to fog to cloud, reduces both communication energy consumption and backhaul congestion. Edge inference is a practical means of enabling localized anomaly detection while minimizing cloud overhead, particularly in intelligent IoT applications and advanced V2X intrusion detection. In future deployments, only compressed features, anomaly scores, alerts, or cryptographic hashes will travel upstream, while the bulk of real-time inspection takes place at the edge.

A second major development is the replacement of accuracy-centric DL with efficiency-by-design DL. While convolutional, recurrent, and transformer-based models achieve strong detection performance, they often require significant computational resources. Reports on Smart-city applications repeatedly warn that increasing model complexity is incompatible with the limited memory and processing power of edge devices. Therefore, next-generation IDS will rely on model compression techniques such as pruning, quantization, and knowledge distillation. These techniques reduce model size and computational load without severely degrading accuracy. Future smart-city IDS will standardize on deployable DL models carefully tuned to device-level power budgets.

FL is also expected to become a foundational mechanism in smart-city IDS. Urban environments involve privacy-sensitive data, including mobility traces, surveillance feeds, and household telemetry. FL enables collaborative training across distributed nodes without transferring raw data to centralized repositories. Existing state-of-the-art works on intelligent IoT security emphasize FL as critical for both privacy preservation and network efficiency. However, FL introduces challenges, including non-IID data across city zones, communication overhead, and local training energy consumption. Personalized FL is increasingly recognized as necessary to handle data heterogeneity across districts and infrastructure types. Future smart-city IDS will adopt hierarchical FL structures, district-level aggregation feeding into city-level coordination, combined with compressed updates, sparse gradient sharing, and selective client participation to reduce energy expenditure.

Another emerging direction is the adaptive, energy-aware IDS that dynamically adjusts its computational complexity. Rather than operating at a constant intensity, next-generation systems will modulate detection depth according to context: network load, energy availability, levels of suspicious activity, or emergency conditions. V2X and smart-city security increasingly call for mechanisms that scale model complexity to real-time constraints. The result is a multi-stage gating pipeline: an ultra-light anomaly filter monitors traffic continuously at the edge, more powerful deep models activate only when anomalies are suspected, and cloud-based analytics perform cross-domain correlation for large-scale incidents. Such adaptive architectures conserve energy under normal conditions while preserving strong detection capability during high-risk periods.

RL and DRL are also gaining importance in energy-efficient IDS design. Beyond anomaly detection, RL can optimize operational decisions such as when to inspect specific data flows, when to offload computation to fog nodes, and how to allocate resources among subsystems. Energy efficiency remains an open research challenge for RL-based intrusion detection, particularly in resource-constrained IoT environments. Future smart-city IDS may use DRL agents to manage inspection frequency, prioritize alerts among transportation and utility systems, and dynamically schedule computational tasks. This energy-aware decision-making layer supports both operational resilience and sustainable energy consumption.

Structured neural paradigms are likely to become more prominent in city-scale IDS. Smart-city infrastructures are inherently graph-structured, including road networks, communication topologies, and power grids. GNNs are well suited for modeling multi-hop attack propagation and coordinated anomalies across interconnected systems. At the same time, SNNs are recognized for their energy efficiency in always-on scenarios. These paradigms hold clear potential for low-power inference in autonomous and large-scale environments. Future work may integrate GNN-based relational reasoning with lightweight inference engines to improve both detection quality and energy efficiency.

Several other limitations will still continue to shape the advancement of IoT-IDSs. The trade-off between energy consumption, latency, and detection accuracy remains fundamental. Centralized models may achieve slightly higher accuracy, but they introduce latency and communication energy overhead. Edge-based models reduce delay and energy consumption but may experience modest degradation in accuracy. Consequently, future IDS evaluations must report comprehensive metrics, including energy per inference, communication overhead, and end-to-end latency, rather than accuracy alone. Another limitation is the lack of realistic datasets and operational testbeds. Many DL and RL IDSs rely on simulated or outdated datasets, which limits confidence in real-world deployment. Next-generation smart-city IDS must be validated through cross-dataset testing, realistic traffic traces, and privacy-preserving benchmarking frameworks.

Collaborative learning (CL) approaches also introduce governance and security challenges. While FL improves privacy, it can increase communication overhead and expose systems to poisoning attacks. In AIoT surveillance systems in particular, collaborative training across multiple locations demands efficient compression and careful bandwidth management. Future work must therefore combine robust aggregation mechanisms, anomaly detection applied to client updates, and adaptive training schedules to ensure both energy efficiency and resilience.

In conclusion, the future of energy-efficient IDS in smart cities is moving toward hierarchical edge-first architectures, compressed and deployable DL models, efficient federated collaboration, adaptive multi-stage pipelines, RL-based resource optimization, and graph-aware intelligence. The field is transitioning from accuracy-driven experimentation to sustainable, deployment-ready cybersecurity engineering. Next-generation smart-city IDS must balance detection performance with energy efficiency, privacy preservation, scalability, and operational reliability to protect complex urban ecosystems over the long term.

9.5.2 Future of energy-efficient IDS in transportation and vehicle-to-everything

The evolution of transportation and Vehicle-to-Everything (V2X) systems is reshaping the design principles of intrusion detection systems (IDS). Modern vehicular ecosystems generate continuous, high-volume, latency-sensitive data streams from in-vehicle networks, roadside infrastructure, and cloud services. As highlighted in reports on V2X and in-vehicle IDSs, next-generation IDS architectures are increasingly designed around energy efficiency, low latency, distributed intelligence, and operational realism. The future direction is therefore not merely about improving detection accuracy, but about building sustainable, edge-aware, and scalable security frameworks for mobility infrastructures.

A central trend is the adoption of edge-native IDS at Roadside Units (RSUs), On-Board Units (OBUs), and vehicle Electronic Control Units (ECUs). Instead of transmitting raw telemetry to centralized cloud servers, anomaly detection is performed near the data source. This reduces backhaul communication energy, minimizes latency, and enables faster response to safety-critical events. Localized detection at RSUs and vehicle nodes improves responsiveness and eases the energy burden of continuous uplink transmission. In practice, this leads to hierarchical architectures in which lightweight inference models operate at the vehicle level, intermediate analytics are performed at RSUs or fog nodes, and only aggregated alerts or compressed features are forwarded to the cloud for large-scale correlation.

FL is emerging as a foundational mechanism for collaborative IDS in transportation systems. Because vehicular data often contains sensitive mobility and behavioral information, centralizing raw traffic logs is impractical. FL enables distributed training across vehicles and infrastructure nodes without sharing raw data. Works and technical reports on V2X systems highlight hierarchical federated architectures, vehicle-to-RSU-to-cloud, as a scalable approach for large fleets. However, energy-efficient FL is becoming a core focus of future study. Techniques such as federated pruning, sparse gradient exchange, adaptive client participation, and reduced communication rounds are proposed to mitigate communication overhead and battery consumption. The future of vehicular FL-IDS will therefore combine privacy preservation with communication-aware and energy-aware optimization.

Another defining direction is the shift toward lightweight and deployable DL models. While CNN-LSTM pipelines and other deep architectures demonstrate strong performance for spatio-temporal traffic analysis, their computational demands are often incompatible with strict real-time vehicular constraints. Consequently, next-generation V2X IDS increasingly relies on model compression techniques such as pruning, quantization, and knowledge distillation. These methods reduce memory footprint and inference cost while preserving acceptable detection performance. Emerging references to TinyML-inspired approaches further suggest that compact, task-specific models will become standard for on-vehicle IDS deployment. Generative and self-supervised techniques are likewise gaining importance, particularly for handling rare or zero-day attacks. Transportation environments often lack sufficient labeled real-world data, and generative models, GAN- and VAE-based approaches among them, help fill this gap by augmenting datasets and improving generalization under evolving attack patterns. By reducing how often models must be retrained, these methods also lower the computational and communication energy costs of long-term deployment.

Hybrid security stacks are also shaping the future of energy-efficient vehicular IDS. Blockchain-integrated FL frameworks are proposed to ensure tamper-resistant aggregation of model updates, while differential privacy and secure aggregation protect against gradient leakage. Forward-looking discussions also consider integrating post-quantum cryptography with hardware security modules to secure federated coordination. However, blockchain and advanced cryptographic mechanisms must be carefully engineered to avoid undermining energy-efficiency goals, as consensus overhead and ledger maintenance can significantly increase computational cost.

Despite these advancements, several persistent limitations continue to influence next-generation design. They are listed here:

- First, the trade-off between accuracy, latency, and energy remains unavoidable. Centralized models may achieve higher detection performance due to global visibility but introduce latency and increased communication energy. Conversely, decentralized edge-based IDS reduces latency and energy consumption but may sacrifice some detection robustness.
- Second, communication overhead in FL acts as an energy tax, particularly in highly mobile vehicular networks with unstable connectivity. Adaptive aggregation strategies and participation control are therefore essential to maintain sustainability.

- **Mobility and intermittent connectivity** further complicate distributed learning. Non-independent and non-identically distributed (non-IID) data across vehicles leads to model drift and inconsistent updates.
- **Adaptive federated learning** schemes that dynamically adjust aggregation frequency and client selection are increasingly necessary. Additionally, federated IDS introduces new attack surfaces, including poisoning and Byzantine update manipulation, requiring robust aggregation and anomaly detection on model updates.
- **Real-time feasibility** is another major constraint. Vehicular systems operate under strict timing guarantees. Heavy DL models, and even some traditional ML approaches such as large-scale k-NN or SVM, may struggle to meet hard deadlines without hardware acceleration. Model compression alleviates some of this burden but does not eliminate the fundamental computational tension.
- **Vehicular data** is inherently noisy due to sensor inaccuracies, environmental changes, and wireless interference. This increases false alarms and adds computational overhead for filtering and verification.
- A further limitation lies in **dataset realism and evaluation** practices. Many IDS models are validated on synthetic or limited datasets that do not capture the complexity of real-world vehicular communication. Poor generalization leads to frequent retraining and recalibration, thereby increasing operational energy costs. Therefore, future research must emphasize realistic testbeds, cross-dataset validation, and energy-aware benchmarking.

The future of next-generation energy-efficient intrusion detection systems (IDS) in transportation and Vehicle-to-Everything (V2X) environments is increasingly shaped by strict real-time requirements, high mobility, and limited on-board resources. Traditional cloud-centric detection models are gradually being replaced by edge-native architectures. In upcoming V2X deployments, intrusion detection inference will primarily run on Roadside Units (RSUs), On-Board Units (OBUs), and even Electronic Control Units (ECUs). This shift is motivated by the need to reduce detection latency, maintain operation under intermittent connectivity, and limit the energy consumed by continuous uplink communication to remote servers. Existing works, models and technical reports on V2X security consistently emphasize that edge inference enables faster reaction to malicious events while reducing backhaul bandwidth and communication-related energy expenditure. As vehicular networks move toward 5G and 6G integration, such localized intelligence becomes essential for maintaining both responsiveness and energy efficiency. Some of the near future advancements of next-generation energy-efficient intrusion detection systems in transportation and Vehicle-to-Everything (V2X) environments are given below:

- **FL** is expected to remain central in V2X IDS, but its primary role is evolving beyond privacy preservation. In large vehicular fleets, transmitting raw data to centralized servers is both bandwidth-intensive and energy-expensive. FL avoids this by allowing vehicles to train models locally and share only model updates. A hierarchical structure is especially well suited to V2X settings: vehicles communicate with nearby roadside units (RSUs), which in turn coordinate with regional or cloud-level aggregators. This multi-tier architecture reduces long-distance communication and improves scalability. However, FL introduces its own computational and communication overhead. Therefore, future research focuses on energy-aware FL mechanisms, including compressed updates, adaptive participation strategies, and efficient aggregation protocols. Robust aggregation is also necessary to defend against poisoning and Byzantine attacks, which are significant concerns in open vehicular ecosystems.

- Model efficiency will become a foundational requirement rather than an optional optimization. DL architectures such as CNNs and LSTMs have shown strong detection capabilities in vehicular intrusion detection, particularly for time-dependent and sequence-based attacks, yet they often impose computational demands that conflict with the strict energy budgets and real-time constraints of vehicular systems. Pruning, quantization, and knowledge distillation are essential techniques for reducing model size and computational load while preserving detection accuracy, and federated pruning further reduces both training computation and communication overhead during collaborative learning. In practice, next-generation vehicular IDS will follow compression-by-design principles, so that efficiency is built into the architecture from the start.
- Another important direction is adaptive-complexity IDS. V2X environments are highly dynamic. Traffic density, channel quality, and threat levels fluctuate continuously. A single static model configuration cannot remain optimal under all conditions. Future IDS frameworks are expected to dynamically adjust their computational footprint in response to contextual factors. Lightweight models may operate during low-risk periods, while more complex analysis is activated during suspected attacks or abnormal traffic bursts. This adaptive scaling lets systems conserve energy where possible and commit resources where necessary. Adaptive learning and dynamic aggregation stand out as key priorities for sustainable large-scale V2X intrusion detection.
- Vehicular IDS will also evolve toward multi-layer and multi-signal defense strategies. While Controller Area Network (CAN)-based intrusion detection remains critical in in-vehicle systems, next-generation approaches will integrate multiple perspectives. These include statistical traffic features, timing characteristics, physical-layer indicators, information-theoretic measures, and learning-based detectors. In in-vehicle settings, combining physical-layer fingerprints with behavioral and learning-based analysis strengthens resilience against spoofing and masquerade attacks. Hardware-assisted security mechanisms and trusted execution environments are emerging as complementary defenses. Such system-level strategies support both robustness and energy-aware design, filtering anomalies at multiple layers before escalating to more intensive analysis.
- Energy efficiency has become a first-class design metric in V2X-IDS because computational load, latency, and energy consumption are tightly coupled. DL models improve detection rates but increase processing overhead and power consumption. Centralized models can offer a global perspective and potentially

higher accuracy, yet they introduce latency and communication costs. Distributed and edge-based approaches reduce latency but may suffer from inconsistent training or reduced model capacity. The dominant challenge, therefore, is to explicitly balance accuracy, latency, and energy rather than optimizing a single dimension. Future IDS evaluations are expected to include metrics such as energy per inference, communication cost, and end-to-end detection delay alongside traditional accuracy measures.

- Communication overhead represents a hidden but significant energy drain in vehicular IDS. Even when inference is computationally efficient, collaborative detection, sensor fusion, and federated training generate continuous network traffic. Although FL reduces raw data transmission, it can increase communication overhead for model updates. In high-mobility scenarios with intermittent connectivity, repeated synchronization attempts may further inflate energy use. Efficient aggregation schedules, sparse model updates, and event-triggered synchronization are therefore expected to become standard design practices.
- To support realistic deployment, next-generation V2X-IDS must also attend to robustness and operational practicality. Vehicular environments are marked by noise, sensor inaccuracies, wireless interference, and rapidly shifting network conditions, all of which can trigger false alarms, leading to unnecessary processing and wasted energy. Noise-aware preprocessing, robust training techniques, and anomaly-filtering mechanisms are therefore critical. XAI (Explainable Artificial Intelligence) is an important direction in its own right, since interpretability is essential to both operational trust and regulatory compliance. Clear explanations reduce needless human intervention and speed up triage, thereby indirectly improving energy efficiency by reducing repeated diagnostic cycles.
- A persistent limitation is the reliance on synthetic or limited datasets. There is a recurring need for realistic vehicular testbeds and cross-dataset validation to ensure that reported gains in efficiency and accuracy translate into real-world performance; without representative datasets, claims of energy efficiency remain difficult to verify. Future work must therefore prioritize standardized benchmarks, real traffic traces, and evaluation frameworks that incorporate energy and latency metrics alongside detection quality.
- Emerging security integrations likewise call for energy-conscious redesign. Blockchain-based IDS aim to provide tamper-resistant logging and decentralized trust in vehicular networks, yet combining blockchain with DL can sharply increase energy consumption if it is not carefully engineered; permissioned or lightweight blockchain mechanisms are accordingly better suited to vehicular contexts. In a similar vein, future V2X systems are expected to adopt post-quantum cryptography in preparation for quantum-capable adversaries, particularly within 6G-enabled ecosystems, but these quantum-safe mechanisms must be optimized for computational efficiency, lest they undermine the very energy constraints that govern vehicular deployment.

In summary, the future of next-generation energy-efficient IDS in transportation and V2X systems is converging toward a multi-layered and adaptive architecture. Detection will increasingly occur at the edge, supported by hierarchical FL, compressed DL models, and adaptive decision mechanisms. Energy-aware optimization, communication-efficient collaboration, and structured intelligence models will become central design principles. At the same time, researchers and practitioners must explicitly address trade-offs among detection performance, latency, energy consumption, and security robustness. Sustainable vehicular cybersecurity will depend not only on intelligent algorithms but also on careful architectural engineering that aligns security objectives with real-world operational constraints.

9.5.3 Future of energy-efficient IDS in the Internet of medical

Next-generation energy-efficient IDS for Connected Medical systems are increasingly designed with the realities of the Internet of Medical Things (IoMT) in mind, where devices operate under strict resource, privacy, and safety constraints. In IoMT security, wearable sensors, infusion pumps, implantable devices, and bedside monitoring systems consistently operate with limited processing power, memory, and battery capacity. As a result, future IDS architectures prioritize lightweight detection at the device or gateway level, while reserving computationally intensive analytics for higher layers. In practice, this means deploying simplified ML or compressed DL models on medical gateways or local hubs, and combining local monitoring with centralized analysis to reduce latency, conserve energy, and maintain global visibility across hospital networks. This layered approach improves responsiveness without overwhelming fragile endpoint devices.

A defining architectural direction in connected medical environments is edge-fog-cloud partitioning. At the edge, fast anomaly triage identifies suspicious behavior in real time; at the fog layer, short-term correlation and aggregation enable near-real-time response across wards or departments; and at the cloud layer, long-term analytics, heavy model training, and cross-institutional intelligence sharing take place. In IoMT and Healthcare 5.0 contexts, such multi-tier placement is not optional but necessary, because medical systems demand both low latency and continuous availability. Centralized-only IDS strategies are often impractical in clinical settings, where delayed decisions can compromise patient safety. Next-generation IoMT IDS are therefore increasingly defined by hierarchical orchestration rather than monolithic deployment.

FL and distributed learning further shape the future of energy-efficient medical IDS. Healthcare systems face strict regulatory requirements and strong privacy obligations. Centralizing raw patient data is frequently infeasible. FL allows collaborative model training across hospitals and medical devices while keeping data local. This reduces the direct exposure of sensitive information and can lower the overhead of continuous raw data transmission. However, the technical reports and case studies also note that FL must address device heterogeneity and uneven data distributions across sites. Personalized FL is emerging as a solution that enables models to adapt to the characteristics of specific hospitals or departments while still benefiting from global collaboration. In extremely constrained settings, Split Learning is also discussed as a complementary mechanism that partitions computation between the device and the server to balance privacy, energy, and latency constraints.

Another important development is the use of semi-supervised and self-supervised learning. Medical intrusion datasets are scarce and difficult to label, particularly when real attack traces are limited or confidential. Semi-supervised learning reduces dependence on large labeled datasets by combining small annotated samples with abundant unlabeled data. Self-supervised representation learning further enables feature extraction without manual labeling. These approaches reduce operational costs and make large-scale deployment more realistic in healthcare settings, where annotation is costly and clinical workflows cannot be disrupted for data collection.

Temporal modeling remains central to IoMT-IDS, since many attacks unfold as time-dependent deviations in telemetry or network flows. RNNs such as LSTM and GRU have been widely used for this purpose, but they are often computationally expensive for edge medical devices. Temporal Convolutional Networks (TCNs) offer an efficient alternative, modeling long-range temporal dependencies with better parallelization and lower training cost. This makes them attractive for energy-aware medical IDS, where sequential analysis is necessary yet heavy recurrent architectures are impractical.

XAI is likewise becoming essential in connected medical systems. Healthcare professionals must be able to trust automated alerts, especially when those alerts shape clinical decisions, and clear IDS explanations improve both operator confidence and regulatory compliance. Yet XAI mechanisms carry their own costs: they add computational overhead and may expose the model's reasoning pathways in ways that attackers could exploit. Future IoMT-IDS must therefore balance interpretability, efficiency, and resilience, integrating lightweight explanation mechanisms that strengthen trust without compromising system performance.

Despite these advances, significant limitations remain. Some of them are listed here:

- Resource constraints continue to create an unavoidable trade-off between detection accuracy, latency, and energy consumption. DeepCNN models often require substantial computational and memory resources, making direct deployment on wearable or implantable devices infeasible. Heterogeneous protocols, device malfunctions, and measurement noise further degrade reliability.
- In medical contexts, sensor errors and wireless interference can resemble malicious anomalies, increasing false positives and unnecessary computational load. Real-time constraints are particularly strict; IDS must not interfere with life-critical operations or delay clinical workflows.
- Privacy and regulatory requirements also raise the deployment threshold. Healthcare environments operate under strict compliance frameworks. IDS must protect confidentiality while remaining auditable and secure.

- Adversarial ML threats add further complexity. AI-driven IDS can be targeted through evasion attacks, data poisoning, or the exploitation of explanation interfaces, and adversarial perturbations and model manipulation pose serious reliability risks in IoMT contexts. FL, though privacy-preserving, presents challenges of its own: it incurs communication overhead and relies on robust aggregation to defend against malicious participants, while heterogeneity across devices and institutions can destabilize the collaborative learning process.
- Scalability presents another open challenge. Healthcare systems may rapidly expand due to new equipment, emergency surges, or pandemic conditions. Maintaining secure, energy-efficient IDS performance under sudden growth remains unresolved. The evaluation of many existing techniques relies on limited datasets or simulated environments, leaving a gap between research prototypes and continuous deployment at hospital scale.

The future of next-generation energy-efficient IDS in connected medical systems is increasingly shaped by the operational realities of the Internet of Medical Things (IoMT). In these environments, devices such as wearable sensors, infusion pumps, implantable monitors, and bedside systems operate under tight limits on processing power, memory, and battery life. Future IDS solutions must therefore be lightweight by design rather than optimized only after development. High detection accuracy alone no longer suffices; models must be deliberately engineered to minimize computational complexity, memory footprint, and energy consumption while still supporting real-time detection in safety-critical healthcare settings. This points toward ultra-compact edge models or lightweight feature filters running on devices and gateways, paired with escalation-based detection in which heavier analysis is triggered only as risk levels rise. Energy budgeting, captured through metrics such as joules per inference, duty cycling, and adaptive scheduling, is expected to become a formal evaluation criterion in clinical IDS design. Several near-term advances in energy-efficient IDS for connected medical systems are outlined below.

- Architecturally, connected medical IDS are converging toward mature Cloud-Fog-Edge pipelines. Hybrid deployment is consistently seen as the only scalable way to balance the low-latency demands of clinical care, the need for continuous monitoring, and the energy constraints of individual devices. In this model, the edge performs continuous, inexpensive anomaly triage; the fog layer, often situated at hospital gateways or departmental servers, aggregates alerts across wards and devices to enable rapid correlation and localized response; and the cloud layer handles computationally intensive tasks such as large-scale training, cross-hospital benchmarking, and long-term threat-intelligence analysis. This layered design strengthens resilience and availability while reducing unnecessary data transmission from constrained endpoints. As Healthcare 5.0 systems expand, such hybrid architectures are likely to become the standard for clinical-grade IDS frameworks.
- FL is also positioned as a default strategy for future IoMT-IDS, provided that it evolves to meet efficiency and robustness requirements. Healthcare

regulations and patient privacy constraints make centralized data collection difficult. FL enables hospitals and medical devices to train models locally and share only parameters, thereby preserving confidentiality. Existing analytical reports further highlight split learning as an alternative when devices are extremely resource-constrained or when model confidentiality is essential. However, FL introduces new challenges, including communication overhead, heterogeneous data distributions, and vulnerability to poisoning attacks. Future work, therefore, focuses on efficient FL mechanisms that reduce communication rounds, compress updates, and selectively involve participants based on energy or risk conditions. Robust aggregation methods and governance policies aligned with hospital compliance standards will also be necessary to ensure secure collaborative learning across institutions. In some proposals, blockchain is integrated with FL to provide decentralized trust, model provenance, and auditability, especially in multi-hospital deployments.

- Another important direction for future work is the adoption of semi-supervised and self-supervised learning. IoMT intrusion detection suffers from limited labeled attack data and high annotation costs. Semi-supervised approaches leverage small labeled datasets combined with large volumes of unlabeled telemetry. Self-supervised learning enables representation learning from raw medical and network data without extensive manual labeling. These approaches improve scalability and reduce operational burden. They also support energy efficiency by enabling smaller models to achieve comparable performance. Heavy pretraining tasks are expected to be performed at fog or cloud layers, while edge devices primarily rely on efficient inference.
- Temporal modeling remains critical in connected medical systems, as many cyberattacks and anomalies manifest through time-dependent patterns such as burst activity, repeated protocol misuse, or gradual manipulation of physiological readings. While recurrent architectures such as LSTM and GRU have been widely applied, existing technical reports emphasize that they can be computationally demanding. TCNs are increasingly recognized as efficient alternatives, offering parallelizable training and strong long-range dependency modeling with reduced computational overhead. In future IoMT-IDS deployments, TCN-based architectures, possibly combined with lightweight attention mechanisms, are likely to replace heavier recurrent pipelines in many edge and fog scenarios due to their hardware-friendly characteristics.
- Explainability will likewise become a mandatory requirement in Healthcare 5.0 environments. Clinical staff, security teams, and regulatory authorities must be able to understand and justify IDS decisions, which makes XAI increasingly central to trust, transparency, and patient-centered reasoning. Yet XAI techniques can carry additional computational costs and may expose the model's reasoning pathways in ways that attackers could exploit. Future IoMT-IDS must therefore adopt lightweight explanation mechanisms, efficient feature-attribution methods among them, and tailor explanations to the roles of different users. Datasets and evaluation frameworks must also integrate biomedical context alongside network

features, so that the resulting explanations are both meaningful and clinically relevant.

- Data realism and benchmarking represent a decisive bottleneck in the evolution of IoMT-IDS, not least because of the scarcity of publicly available, representative Healthcare 5.0 datasets. Many existing datasets lack authentic biomedical streams or do not accurately reflect real hospital traffic patterns. This limitation reduces confidence in deployment readiness and hinders cross-study comparison. Future progress will require standardized datasets that combine network and biomedical features, realistic clinical testbeds, cross-hospital validation, and evaluation metrics that include energy consumption and latency alongside detection accuracy. Without such comprehensive benchmarking, claims of energy-efficient security remain difficult to verify.
- Blockchain technology is expected to play a selective but important role in connected medical IDS. Rather than serving as a universal solution, it will most likely function as an audit and compliance layer, providing immutability, decentralized trust, and tamper-resistant logging for alerts and model updates. In clinical environments where forensic traceability and regulatory compliance are essential, permissioned or authority-based consensus mechanisms are preferred because they reduce energy and latency overhead compared to public blockchains. Future systems will store alerts, model provenance, and compliance logs on-chain, while avoiding the storage of raw medical data to preserve privacy and efficiency.

In summary, next-generation energy-efficient IDS in connected medical systems will be defined by lightweight-by-design models, hierarchical Cloud-Fog-Edge architectures, privacy-preserving collaborative learning, efficient temporal modeling, and clinically meaningful explainability. Energy, latency, robustness, and regulatory compliance will become primary design constraints rather than secondary considerations. By integrating architectural efficiency, adaptive learning, secure governance, and realistic evaluation, IoMT-IDS can move closer to sustainable, trustworthy protection in modern healthcare environments.

9.5.4 Future of energy-efficient IDS in the industrial automation

Next-generation energy-efficient IDS in IIoT and automation environments are increasingly shaped by strict real-time requirements, legacy-system constraints, and sustainability goals. ICSs operate under deterministic traffic patterns, tight latency bounds, and safety-critical processes, so energy efficiency is not merely a matter of cost but a factor that directly affects system stability and availability. Future IDS must accordingly balance detection accuracy, computational overhead, and operational continuity while advancing long-term sustainability objectives.

A dominant direction in IIoT security is the deployment of lightweight ML and DL models at the edge or fog layer. Bringing detection closer to sensors, programmable logic controllers (PLCs), and gateways reduces the need for continuous backhaul to centralized cloud servers. This lowers communication energy consumption and improves response time. However, edge deployment requires compact and resource-aware models. As a result, future IDS architectures in industrial automation are expected to adopt hierarchical detection strategies. A lightweight anomaly filter may operate continuously at the edge, while more computationally intensive analysis is triggered at fog or cloud levels only when suspicious behavior is detected. Event-triggered inference and early-stage filtering reduce unnecessary computation. Feature slimming, through careful feature selection or dimensionality reduction, further decreases model complexity without significantly compromising accuracy.

FL has emerged as a promising approach for distributed industrial environments where sharing raw operational data is restricted. Industrial telemetry, production metrics, and control logs often contain sensitive or proprietary information. FL allows collaborative model training across plants or sites without transferring raw data. Existing technical reports on FL-based IDS in IIoT emphasize its potential to reduce data movement and improve privacy. However, energy efficiency remains a critical concern because frequent model updates and aggregation rounds can increase communication overhead. Future FL-based industrial IDS will likely adopt communication-efficient strategies such as compressed model updates, adaptive client participation, and hierarchical aggregation through fog nodes. Differential privacy and secure aggregation mechanisms are expected to become standard for protecting against gradient leakage and update manipulation while maintaining manageable computational costs.

DRL is also being explored in industrial networks as a mechanism for adaptive defense and resource control. Unlike static classifiers, DRL treats intrusion detection and response as a sequential decision process, adjusting detection thresholds, sampling rates, and mitigation actions in response to changing network conditions. In IIoT settings, this adaptability is especially valuable for dynamic process monitoring and the orchestration of responsive countermeasures. DRL models can be computationally intensive and difficult to deploy under strict real-time constraints. Attention is therefore shifting toward lightweight DRL implementations suited to edge or fog deployment, and energy-aware policy learning, in which the agent folds computational cost and communication overhead into its reward structure, is likely to become an important direction.

Feature selection and dimensionality reduction are central to energy-efficient industrial IDS. Metaheuristic optimization techniques are increasingly used to identify compact and discriminative feature subsets from high-dimensional industrial traffic and telemetry data. By reducing the number of input features, inference time and memory consumption decrease significantly. Many industrial IDS pipelines now follow a structured approach: raw network or process data are first preprocessed and filtered, then metaheuristic-based feature selection is applied, and finally, a lightweight classifier operates at the edge. Hybrid IDS approaches that combine signature-based detection with anomaly-based learning further help balance computational cost and detection coverage.

Despite these advances, several limitations shape the future development of energy-efficient IDS in industrial automation. Some of them are listed here:

- Real-time constraints remain one of the most critical challenges. Industrial processes depend on predictable timing, and excessive computational delay can disrupt physical operations. Temporal complexity and processing overhead frequently conflict with strict latency budgets, so future solutions must explicitly measure and report detection delay and energy consumption alongside accuracy.
- Another significant limitation is the scarcity of realistic industrial datasets. Much of the available work relies on outdated or synthetic data that fail to capture the full reality of modern IIoT traffic, protocol diversity, and process-specific behavior, thereby weakening confidence in real-world deployment. Site-specific traffic patterns, legacy protocols such as Modbus and DNP3, and varying operational modes collectively produce non-independent and non-identically distributed (non-IID) data.
- FL-related case studies and reports emphasize that client heterogeneity and inconsistent benchmarking complicate cross-site model generalization. Addressing these challenges requires more representative datasets, standardized evaluation frameworks, and testbeds that reflect real industrial constraints.
- Collaborative learning approaches also introduce new security risks. Even when raw data remain local, model updates in FL systems may be vulnerable to poisoning or backdoor attacks.
- Industrial adversaries can be strategic and persistent, targeting the model's integrity rather than network traffic alone. Guarding against them calls for robust aggregation, anomaly detection applied to model updates, and defensive mechanisms against evasion attacks. These protective measures must, in turn, be carefully designed to avoid excessive computational overhead.
- A persistent structural tension exists between energy efficiency and security strength. Increasing monitoring frequency, adding more features, or deploying complex deep models enhances detection capability but raises energy consumption. Conversely, overly simplified monitoring may miss sophisticated attacks. Industrial IoT protocols themselves often balance security features against energy and latency requirements, and IDS design inherits this trade-off. Future works will increasingly treat energy consumption as a measurable design constraint, integrating metrics such as energy per inference, communication cost, and memory footprint into evaluation protocols.

The future of next-generation energy-efficient IDS in IIoT and industrial automation is moving toward tightly integrated, resource-aware, system-level security architectures. Industrial environments differ from traditional IT systems in that they operate under strict latency requirements, deterministic traffic patterns, and safety-critical constraints. Future IDS solutions must accordingly achieve high detection accuracy while also respecting energy budgets, computational limits, and operational continuity. Energy efficiency is no longer a secondary optimization goal but a fundamental design requirement for sustainable and secure industrial automation. Several promising directions for achieving energy-efficient IDS in IIoT and industrial automation are outlined below.

- A dominant direction is the adoption of cooperative Edge-Fog-Cloud IDS architectures. Instead of relying on centralized, cloud-only detection, future IIoT deployments will distribute intelligence across multiple tiers. At the edge level, lightweight anomaly detection models will operate close to programmable logic controllers (PLCs), sensors, and gateways. These models will provide rapid screening and immediate mitigation actions such as traffic filtering or node isolation. The fog layer will perform contextual analysis, correlating events across devices, production lines, or plant zones. The cloud layer will handle computationally intensive tasks such as model retraining, cross-site intelligence sharing, and long-term threat analysis. This tiered architecture balances low latency, reduced communication overhead, and scalable analytics. Such hybrid deployment models represent the most realistic path toward energy-efficient IDS in operational industrial environments.
- Another major evolution concerns the integration of energy-aware learning principles into IDS design. RL-based IDS research has identified energy optimization in resource-constrained environments as a significant open challenge. Future IIoT IDS will likely incorporate multi-objective optimization strategies that explicitly couple security performance with power consumption. For example, models may adjust their complexity depending on device battery state, workload intensity, or process criticality. Budgeted inference strategies can dynamically scale up computation under high-risk conditions and scale down during stable operational phases. Workload-aware scheduling will also become important, ensuring that heavy inspection processes are activated only when the industrial process enters vulnerable states, such as configuration changes or abnormal control-loop behavior.
- Event-driven and adaptive sampling strategies are also expected to play a central role in "Green IDS" data pipelines. Rather than continuously processing all traffic and telemetry, next-generation systems will work to reduce the volume of data that is sensed and transmitted. Adaptive sampling, event-triggered processing, and lightweight anomaly detection stand out as practical strategies for balancing energy consumption against detection quality. In industrial automation, this translates into process-aware triggers, where monitoring intensity increases during state transitions or alarm conditions. Feature-on-demand approaches will compute expensive features only when lightweight detectors signal potential anomalies. Local aggregation at gateways will replace continuous streaming of raw data to higher layers, further reducing communication energy.
- Model-level efficiency will also shape future architectures. Technical evaluation reports in related constrained domains emphasize the importance of lightweight and resource-efficient IDS models. Heavy recurrent architectures such as traditional LSTM stacks may gradually be replaced by more efficient temporal modeling techniques. TCNs, e.g., provide strong long-range dependency modeling with better parallelization and lower computational cost. In IIoT time-series traffic and process monitoring, TCN-like models, compressed neural networks, and quantized architectures are likely to dominate edge deployments. Early-exit inference mechanisms, in which computation stops once sufficient confidence is

achieved, can further reduce energy consumption. Compact models designed for hardware-friendly execution will increasingly replace accuracy-only optimized deep models.

- Distributed and privacy-preserving learning mechanisms will also be central to future IIoT IDS. Industrial organizations often hesitate to centralize sensitive operational data. FL enables collaborative training across multiple sites while keeping raw data local. Both FL and split learning are promising approaches for distributed industrial ecosystems, particularly where device capabilities vary significantly. However, communication rounds and aggregation steps introduce additional energy costs. Therefore, future FL-based IIoT-IDS will prioritize communication-efficient updates, hierarchical aggregation across edge and gateway layers, and selective participation strategies. Secure aggregation and privacy-preserving mechanisms must be integrated carefully to avoid excessive computational overhead.
- DRL is expected to grow in importance within industrial networks, particularly for adaptive defense and resource management. DRL can model intrusion detection and response as sequential decision-making processes. It can dynamically adjust thresholds, select mitigation actions, and allocate monitoring resources in response to changing network conditions. Before large-scale deployment in IIoT environments, however, DRL must become both energy-aware and adversarially robust. Lightweight DRL implementations, edge-compatible policy models, and robust training under adversarial scenarios will all be necessary to ensure reliable operation in safety-critical settings.
- Robustness against adversarial manipulation is becoming a mandatory design principle, given risks such as evasion attacks, data poisoning, and feature manipulation in ML-based IDS. In industrial automation, attackers may exploit characteristics of structured traffic or predictable control patterns. Future IDS evaluation will therefore include adversarial testing, structured robustness assessments, and secure feature extraction pipelines. Robustness must be engineered specifically for industrial protocols and deterministic traffic, rather than borrowing defenses developed for unrelated domains.
- Explainability is also emerging as an operational requirement rather than a purely academic objective. In industrial environments, false alarms can lead to production interruptions and financial losses. Operators need clear explanations to justify mitigation actions, and XAI enhances trust, auditability, and compliance in critical infrastructures. In IIoT, explainability will support faster incident triage and more transparent safety audits. Lightweight explanation techniques that do not impose heavy computational overhead will be preferred for edge and fog deployments.
- Improved benchmarking and realistic validation will further define what counts as a "next-generation" energy-efficient IDS. Many existing frameworks and techniques rely on limited or outdated datasets that fail to reflect modern industrial traffic or site-specific variability. What is needed instead are new benchmarking protocols, digital-twin environments, and industrial testbeds that capture realistic workloads and operational constraints. Future evaluations will increasingly report

energy consumption, detection latency, communication overhead, and operational impact alongside accuracy and F1-score, and both cross-dataset generalization and system-level validation will become essential to ensuring practical relevance.

In summary, the future of energy-efficient IDS in IIoT and automation converges toward system-integrated, tiered architectures that combine edge responsiveness with cloud intelligence. Energy-aware learning, adaptive sampling, and lightweight temporal models will reduce computational and communication costs. Distributed privacy-preserving learning will support multi-site collaboration, while adversarial robustness and explainability will strengthen operational trust. Most importantly, energy, latency, and resilience will be treated as primary evaluation metrics alongside detection performance. By aligning intelligent detection mechanisms with industrial sustainability and safety requirements, next-generation IIoT IDS can provide secure, scalable, and energy-conscious protection for modern automated systems.

9.6 Role of policy-making organizations in deploying IDS

The deployment of IDS in IoT environments must move beyond accuracy-driven design toward energy-aware, resource-constrained, and lifecycle-sustainable operation. Green IDS is not achieved through model compression alone, but through coordinated policies spanning sensing, deployment architecture, FL operations, governance, evaluation, and adaptive control. The structured policy framework that follows summarizes the key practices required for sustainable IoT IDS deployment.

- **Energy-Aware Sensing and Data Collection Policies** Energy efficiency begins before model inference. In many IoT systems, sensing, transmission, and logging consume more power than classification itself. Therefore, Green IDS must regulate data collection and processing.
  - **Adaptive Sampling Policy** IoT devices should dynamically adjust sampling frequency based on contextual risk. During normal behavior, low-frequency sampling conserves energy. When anomalies or suspicious signals appear, sampling rates increase temporarily. This adaptive strategy reduces sensing and communication overhead while maintaining detection reliability.
  - **Event-Driven Processing Policy** Continuous streaming and feature extraction are inefficient in constrained IoT networks. Event-triggered data capture ensures that logging, feature extraction, and deeper inspection are triggered only when predefined thresholds are met or abnormal state transitions occur. Adaptive, event-driven anomaly detection stands out as an effective strategy for conserving energy in IoT IDS.
  - **Lightweight Pre-Filter Policy** Low-cost statistical or rule-based anomaly checks should act as a first-stage filter. Only when suspicion exceeds a threshold should heavier ML/DL models be executed. This multi-stage defense architecture significantly reduces unnecessary computation.

- **Edge-Fog-Cloud Placement Policies** Deployment location strongly influences energy, latency, and communication overhead.
  - **Edge-First Inference Policy** Inference should be executed as close as possible to data sources (sensors, gateways, edge nodes). AI integration at the edge improves responsiveness and reduces uplink transmission requirements. Localized detection lowers bandwidth use and, in turn, cumulative network energy.
  - **Workload Splitting Policy** Feature extraction and lightweight detection should occur at the edge, while heavy retraining, deep analytics, and global correlation should be performed at fog or cloud layers. This hierarchical deployment balances energy use and detection strength.
  - **Offloading Governance Policy** Edge devices should offload tasks only when energy, latency, or security thresholds justify it. Offloading must be managed to prevent unnecessary reliance on the cloud.
- **Model Efficiency and Deployment Engineering Policies** Energy-efficient IDS requires disciplined model engineering practices.
  - **Deployment-Aware Model Design Policy** Models must satisfy explicit constraints on latency, memory, compute, and hardware compatibility. Pruning, quantization, and compression are deployment necessities here, not optional optimizations.
  - **Quantization and Compression Policy** Weight quantization (e.g., 4bit/8-bit), pruning, and knowledge distillation reduce model size and communication payload. This lowers both inference energy and update transmission costs in distributed environments.
  - **Feature Economy Policy** Metaheuristic-based feature selection, dimensionality reduction, and compact embeddings reduce computational burden. Feature slimming directly lowers inference power consumption.
  - **Hybrid Detection Policy** Combining signature-based, anomaly-based, and learning-based components allows balancing energy cost and detection coverage. Lightweight modules handle common attacks, whereas advanced modules are activated selectively.
- **FL Operational Policies for Sustainable IDS** FL is widely proposed for distributed IoT IDS, but its sustainability depends on strict operational controls.
  - **Participation-Aware Scheduling Policy** Client participation should depend on device energy state, connectivity stability, and data relevance. Client heterogeneity and resource constraints are core challenges in FL-based IDS, and intelligent scheduling helps avoid wasted communication rounds.
  - **Communication Reduction Policy** Reduce aggregation frequency, compress updates, and prune models before transmission. Federated pruning and sparse updates directly lower bandwidth and energy consumption.
  - **Heterogeneity-Resilient Aggregation Policy** Classic FedAvg is vulnerable to non-IID data and device variability. Robust aggregation mechanisms reduce failed rounds and retraining cycles, improving long-term sustainability.

  - **Secure Aggregation and Differential Privacy Policy** To prevent gradient leakage and poisoning, secure aggregation and differential privacy mechanisms must be applied. While these mechanisms introduce overhead, optimized implementations can preserve privacy without excessive energy cost.
- **Lifecycle Monitoring and Secure Update Policies** Energy waste often results from unstable or poorly governed model updates.
  - **Continuous Lifecycle Monitoring Policy** Concept drift detection and performance monitoring prevent silent degradation, which would otherwise trigger frequent retraining. Controlled adaptation reduces redundant computation.
  - **Secure Update and Logging Policy** Encrypted logging and authenticated update channels prevent adversarial poisoning that could force costly redeployment cycles.
  - **Safe Rollback Policy** Rollback mechanisms enable rapid recovery from degraded or compromised updates, preserving operational stability and reducing the need for repeated energy-intensive rollouts.
- **Governance and CI/CD Policies for IoT IDS** Institutional-level governance ensures repeatable, compliant, and sustainable IDS operation.
  - **CI/CD-for-IDS Policy** Continuous integration pipelines adapted for federated and edge environments ensure controlled, secure, and efficient updates.
  - **Model Governance and Regulatory Compliance Policy** IoT deployments often span jurisdictions. Governance must coordinate auditability, logging, and compliance without introducing excessive overhead.
  - **Auditability and Transparency Policy** Blockchain-based or secure logging mechanisms may be used selectively to ensure provenance, but must be optimized for lightweight operation to avoid undermining energy goals.
- **Real-World Evaluation and Benchmarking Policies** Green IDS claims must be validated with transparent metrics.
  - **Longitudinal Evaluation Policy** Models must be tested under real drift, mobility, and evolving attack conditions. Short lab evaluations are insufficient.
  - **Standardized Telemetry and Energy Reporting Policy** IDS technical and evaluation reports should report: i) Joules per inference, ii) Bytes per federated round, iii) Communication energy, iv) Latency impact. Without energy telemetry, "efficient IDS" claims remain unverified.
- **DRL-Specific Green Operation Policies** RL-based IDS introduces additional energy concerns.
  - **Energy-Constrained Reward Policy** RL agents should incorporate energy cost directly into reward functions, balancing detection accuracy and resource consumption.
  - **Edge-Compatible RL Architecture Policy** Lightweight RL architectures suitable for edge/fog execution must replace heavy centralized training loops.
  - **Safe Exploration Policy** Exploration strategies must be bounded to prevent costly false alarms or unsafe defensive actions in real deployments.

- **Integrated Green IDS Vision** Taken together, these insights indicate that Green IDS is a system-level discipline rather than a single optimization technique. It requires:
  - Selective sensing and event-driven data collection.
  - Hierarchical edge-fog-cloud deployment.
  - Deployment-aware model compression and feature economy.
  - Communication-efficient and secure FL.
  - Continuous lifecycle governance and rollback stability.
  - Explicit measurement of energy and latency metrics.
  - Adversarial robustness integrated with efficiency constraints.

  Only through coordinated enforcement of these policies can IoT intrusion detection achieve sustainable, secure, and scalable operation across diverse application domains.

The transition toward energy-efficient, AI-enabled IDS in IoT ecosystems is not solely a technical evolution. It is an organizational and governance transformation. Sustainable IDS deployment consistently requires coordinated action among regulators, standards bodies, industry alliances, and operational teams. Green IDS must therefore be treated as a system-level objective supported by policy, engineering discipline, lifecycle governance, and measurable accountability. The role of policy-making organizations in governing the proper deployment of Green IDS are given in the following sections

9.6.1 Roles of policy-making and standards organizations

- **Establish Minimum Energy-Aware Security Requirements** Policy-making bodies-national regulators, cybersecurity agencies, critical-infrastructure authorities, and sectoral standardization groups-play a central role in formalizing energy-aware IDS engineering as a baseline requirement rather than an optional feature. Because IoT devices operate under strict resource constraints, their security mechanisms must be designed with computational and energy awareness from the outset. On this basis, regulators can:
  - Define minimum acceptable energy budgets for IDS operation in constrained IoT/IIoT devices.
  - Require that security analytics do not compromise system stability, latency, or availability.
  - Mandate that detection mechanisms be evaluated under realistic energy and performance constraints.

  This transforms "green security" from a research concept into enforceable operational compliance.
- **Standardize Metrics and Benchmarking for Green IDS** A recurring issue in IDS work is the lack of standardized reporting for energy and communication overhead. Without standard metrics, vendors may claim "energy-efficient IDS"

without providing verifiable evidence. Standards organizations and industry alliances should therefore define a Green IDS Metrics Framework, including:
  - Energy per inference (e.g., Joules/inference or power/time window).
  - Communication overhead (bytes per round in federated settings).
  - Memory footprint and hardware class.
  - Latency and processing overhead.
  - Model update frequency and retraining cost.

  FL brings a particular need for communication-aware reporting and reproducibility across distributed IDS deployments. Standardized benchmarking guards against misleading claims and supports fair comparison across systems.
- **Define Governance Frameworks for Lifecycle and Secure Updates** IoT IDS deployments are long-lived and subject to continual updating. Lifecycle management, model-drift detection, and secure update mechanisms are therefore central concerns, and policy-making bodies can formalize governance rules such as:
  - Mandatory model versioning and update traceability.
  - Secure distribution channels for model updates.
  - Audit logging requirements for IDS decisions and retraining events.
  - Rollback mechanisms in case of degraded performance or adversarial compromise.

  These governance policies reduce unnecessary retraining cycles and unstable deployments, which in turn improves both security and energy sustainability.
- **Align Privacy Baselines with Energy Constraints** Green IDS often relies on collaborative mechanisms, such as FL, to reduce the transmission of raw data. However, FL introduces privacy and aggregation risks. Secure aggregation, differential privacy, and protection against gradient leakage are critical concerns for FL-based IDS. Policy-makers must accordingly define:
  - Minimum privacy guarantees for distributed IDS.
  - Acceptable cryptographic protections that do not create excessive energy overhead.
  - Secure aggregation standards that balance confidentiality with efficiency.

  The objective is to prevent privacy enforcement from becoming so computationally heavy that it undermines energy goals.
- **Support Infrastructure for Evaluation and Certification** A persistent gap separates laboratory experiments from real-world IoT deployment. Policy ecosystems can help close it by:
  - Funding shared IoT security testbeds.
  - Promoting standardized datasets and digital twins.
  - Publishing reference architectures (e.g., edge-fog-cloud IDS placement).
  - Establishing certification programs for energy-efficient IDS solutions.

  Such institutional support enables reproducibility and responsible adoption at scale.

9.6.2 Roles of practitioners and operational stakeholders

While policy defines requirements, practitioners implement them. Engineers, security operators, and DevSecOps teams operationalize Green IDS through concrete technical and organizational practices.

- **Implement Adaptive and Event-Driven Detection** Practitioners must translate energy-aware policies into system behavior. This includes:
  - Adaptive sampling to reduce sensing and communication overhead.
  - Event-driven processing instead of continuous heavy inspection.
  - Lightweight anomaly-first pipelines before escalating to deeper models.

  Intelligent IoT architectures should optimize operations across the entire data lifecycle. Practitioners therefore ensure that data collection itself is efficient before applying ML/DL detection.
- **Enforce Telemetry-Driven Operations** Energy-efficient IDS requires continuous measurement. Operational teams must:
  - Monitor power consumption and device-level resource utilization.
  - Track bytes exchanged during federated rounds.
  - Record latency, memory usage, and inference cost.
  - Report metrics regularly, not only during deployment.

  This measurement-driven culture ensures that sustainability goals remain visible and enforceable.
- **Manage Model Lifecycle and Drift** IoT environments are dynamic. Devices are added, firmware changes, and traffic patterns evolve. Practitioners must:
  - Detect concept drift in real time.
  - Retrain models only when necessary.
  - Secure update pipelines against poisoning or tampering.
  - Roll back degraded models promptly.

  Effective lifecycle control prevents repeated costly retraining and operational instability.
- **Coordinate Resource-Aware Federated Learning** When FL-based IDS is deployed, practitioners determine:
  - Which devices participate in training.
  - How often updates are sent.
  - How to handle stragglers and heterogeneous hardware.
  - How to reduce unnecessary communication rounds.

  Heterogeneity and communication overhead stand out as major operational barriers in federated IDS. Participation-aware scheduling and aggregation policies reduce wasted energy and improve convergence stability.
- **Engineer Deployable and Compact Models** Operational teams are responsible for translating research models into production-ready artifacts. This includes:
  - Model pruning and quantization.
  - Update compression for federated rounds.
  - Hardware-accelerated deployment formats (e.g., edge-friendly runtimes).
  - Validation under device-level resource budgets.

Many IDS failures arise because research models do not meet deployment constraints. Practitioners bridge this gap.

- **Balance Energy Reduction with Security Coverage** Practitioners must avoid excessive optimization that weakens detection capability. For example:
  - Aggressive sampling reduction may miss slow or stealthy attacks.
  - Heavy compression may degrade anomaly sensitivity.
  - Over-offloading may introduce latency risks.

  Thus, Green IDS must remain **risk-aware**, not merely energy-minimizing.

9.6.3 Coordinated organizational model for Green IDS

A clear division of responsibilities emerges, as set out below:

- **Policy-Making Organizations Define What Must Be True**
  - Minimum energy-aware design standards.
  - Standardized benchmarking and reporting.
  - Governance and lifecycle requirements.
  - Privacy-preserving but feasible security baselines.
  - Certification and compliance frameworks.
- **Practitioners Implement How It Becomes True**
  - Adaptive sampling and multi-stage detection.
  - Telemetry-first monitoring.
  - Resource-aware federated scheduling.
  - Secure lifecycle management.
  - Model compression and deployment engineering.

In summary, the deployment of Green IDS in IoT ecosystems is not solely a technical optimization problem; it is equally a challenge of governance, engineering, and lifecycle coordination. Energy efficiency must be woven into system design, evaluation, and operations across the entire data lifecycle. Future IoT security architectures will succeed only when policy-makers establish measurable sustainability baselines and practitioners implement adaptive, resource-aware, and secure operational pipelines. Sustainable IDS, in the end, demands institutional alignment as much as algorithmic innovation.

9.7 Standards of sustainable IDS

Sustainable, or Green IDS for IoT security, is best understood as mechanisms that not only detect attacks effectively but also operate in a resource-aware, privacy-preserving, and standards-aligned manner. IDS is widely recognized as a critical component for protecting modern networks, particularly in IoT and Industrial IoT environments, where connectivity, automation, and data exchange are pervasive. Traditional IDS approaches, however, often rely on centralized processing and incur heavy computational overhead, making them difficult to deploy in resource-constrained, distributed settings. A sustainable IDS must therefore align with established security-governance standards while treating energy efficiency, scalability, and robustness as core design principles.

At the governance level, Sustainable IDS should be mapped to internationally recognized information security management frameworks, including ISO/IEC 27001, ISO 27002, NIST SP 800-53, and the NIST Cybersecurity Framework. These standards do not prescribe specific IDS algorithms, but they define requirements for control selection, risk management, incident handling, monitoring, and auditing. In practice, IDS deployment must therefore support measurable controls, continuous monitoring, and documented response procedures. In industrial environments, alignment with IEC 62443 is essential, as this standard defines security requirements for Industrial Automation and Control Systems (IACS). In such contexts, IDS must respect strict operational constraints, including deterministic communication, low latency, and system availability. Sustainable IDS in IIoT must therefore guarantee bounded resource consumption, predictable performance, and safe integration within zone-and-conduit architectures.

From a technical standardization perspective, Sustainable IDS must also reflect best practices in detection-strategy design. IDS approaches fall broadly into signature-based, anomaly-based, specification-based, and hybrid categories. Green IDS should favor adaptive and hybrid mechanisms that balance detection accuracy with computational efficiency. ML and DL techniques have significantly enhanced detection performance in recent years, but they also introduce higher computational costs. Consequently, sustainability requires careful model selection, lightweight architectures, feature reduction strategies, and edge-oriented deployment models. Meta-heuristic feature selection and dimensionality reduction approaches help reduce model complexity and improve efficiency in distributed networks.

Privacy and data protection standards also shape Sustainable IDS requirements. FL has emerged as a standards-aligned approach that preserves data sovereignty while enabling collaborative intrusion detection. FL-based IDS frameworks address privacy leakage and communication overhead issues common in centralized systems. In regulated environments, this supports compliance with data protection laws and privacy-by-design principles. Sustainability in this sense encompasses minimizing raw data transmission, reducing bandwidth consumption, and limiting storage requirements, thereby lowering energy usage.

Another essential standard dimension concerns robustness and adversarial resilience. ML-based IDS are vulnerable to adversarial manipulation. A Sustainable IDS must therefore integrate adversarial testing, robust aggregation mechanisms in federated settings, and evaluation against evasion and poisoning attacks. RL and adaptive IDS models further contribute to dynamic threat response in complex communication networks. Such adaptability ensures long-term operational sustainability by reducing the need for frequent retraining and manual intervention.

Finally, a sustainable IDS calls for standardized evaluation and reporting practices. Dataset imbalance, outdated benchmarks, and inconsistent evaluation metrics remain persistent challenges in the field. Green IDS standards should therefore mandate the reporting of both security metrics: accuracy, precision, recall, F1-score, detection rate, and false-alarm rate, and resource metrics such as CPU usage, memory footprint, communication overhead, latency, and energy consumption. In IoT environments, where communication technologies such as ZigBee, 6LoWPAN, LoRaWAN, and NB-IoT operate under strict energy budgets, such reporting is essential to gauge realistic deployment feasibility.

9.7.1 Future adaptation in standards of sustainable IDS

The current landscape of standards for Sustainable IDS, with a focus mainly on Green IDS, remains incomplete. Most existing standards focus on security governance, privacy, or industrial safety, but they rarely define explicit requirements for energy efficiency, carbon impact, or lifecycle sustainability. In light of the evolution of IoT and AI-based IDS, several important standards remain either missing or underdeveloped and may need to be incorporated into future energy-efficient IDS frameworks. Some of the potential adaptations required are listed below:

- First, there is no formal Energy Efficiency Standard for IDS. Existing frameworks, such as ISO/IEC 27001 or NIST CSF, define what to protect and how to manage risk, but they do not define measurable energy constraints for security controls. A future Green IDS standard should include defined energy budgets (e.g., Joules per detection cycle), CPU duty cycle limits for edge nodes, communication energy caps, and reporting templates for power consumption. This would allow organizations to compare IDS solutions not only by detection accuracy but also by energy performance.
- Second, there is no standardized Energy-Aware Evaluation Benchmark for IDS models. Technical reports and real-world case studies repeatedly emphasize dataset limitations and inconsistent evaluation metrics. However, most benchmarks report accuracy, precision, recall, and F1-score without reporting computational cost. A missing standard is a unified evaluation protocol that mandates reporting of:
  - inference latency,
  - memory footprint,
  - bandwidth usage,
  - retraining cost,
  - energy per inference.

  Without this, "high-performing" IDS models may be unsuitable for IoT environments.
- Third, there is no formal Green AI Compliance Framework for IDS. DL-based IDS significantly increases computational demand. Future standards could require:
  - model compression (quantization, pruning),
  - lightweight architectures for edge devices,
  - carbon-aware training policies,

    - lifecycle energy accounting for all the phases of a model (training + deployment + update cost).

  This would align IDS development with broader Green AI initiatives.
- Fourth, a Standard for Sustainable Federated IDS Deployment is missing. FL improves privacy and reduces centralized data transfer, but there is no formal guideline defining:
    - optimal aggregation frequency,
    - communication budget limits,
    - client selection policies for energy balancing,
    - secure aggregation efficiency thresholds.

  Future sustainable IDS standards may integrate privacy-preserving learning with energy-aware communication protocols.
- Fifth, there is no Adversarial Robustness and Energy Trade-off Standard. IDS must defend against adversarial attacks, but robustness mechanisms often increase computational cost. A future standard could define acceptable trade-offs between:
    - adversarial defense overhead,
    - model complexity,
    - energy cost.

  This would prevent over-engineered defense models that are secure but unsustainable in IoT environments.
- Sixth, there is a lack of Edge-Cloud Sustainability Coordination Standards. IoT architectures operate across the device, gateway, fog, and cloud layers. Sustainable IDS standards should define:
    - hierarchical detection responsibilities,
    - optimal placement of detection tasks,
    - load balancing rules to minimize redundant processing and communication energy.
- Seventh, lifecycle and circular sustainability standards are largely absent. Future Green IDS standards may include:
    - secure hardware recycling policies,
    - firmware update efficiency standards,
    - sustainable procurement requirements,
    - long-term model maintenance guidelines to reduce retraining frequency.
- Eighth, there is no internationally recognized Sustainable IDS Certification Program. Similar to ISO certification for management systems, a future certification could validate that an IDS:
    - meets minimum detection performance,
    - complies with privacy regulations,
    - operates within defined energy thresholds,
    - reports environmental impact transparently.

In summary, the Standards of Sustainable (Green) IDS for IoT security can be defined as a multi-layered alignment framework. It combines (1) governance and risk management standards such as ISO 27001 and NIST frameworks, (2) domain-specific standards such as IEC 62443 for industrial systems, (3) operational IDS guidance such as NIST SP 800-94, and (4) sustainability-oriented technical criteria including energy-aware design, privacy preservation, adversarial robustness, distributed learning, and standardized evaluation metrics. Future Sustainable IDS frameworks will likely integrate cybersecurity compliance, AI governance, energy-efficiency metrics, and environmental accountability into a unified standard. This integration is essential for IoT and Industrial IoT systems, where security, scalability, and sustainability must coexist without compromising operational reliability.

Overall, the evolution of sustainable IoT security reflects a fundamental transformation in the design, evaluation, and deployment of intrusion detection systems. As discussed throughout this chapter, the future of IDS in IoT environments is no longer defined solely by detection accuracy. Instead, it is shaped by the need to balance intelligence with efficiency, adaptability with stability, and innovation with regulatory responsibility. The increasing scale of IoT ecosystems spanning smart cities, industrial control systems, transportation networks, and critical infrastructures demands security architectures that are resilient, energy-aware, and capable of long-term operational sustainability.

Artificial intelligence has become the core enabler of next-generation IDS. ML, DL, RL, federated learning, and hybrid neurosymbolic models collectively reframe intrusion detection as an adaptive, data-driven process. These technologies allow systems to move beyond static signature matching toward behavioral modeling and autonomous response. However, the chapter also highlights that AI-driven IDS must address practical deployment realities. Resource constraints, dataset bias, adversarial robustness, interpretability, and lifecycle vulnerabilities remain pressing challenges. Sustainable IoT security therefore requires not only advanced models, but also careful architectural redesign that supports scalability, explainability, and real-world feasibility.

Blockchain integration introduces a complementary dimension of trust and decentralization. Rather than serving as a computational engine, blockchain increasingly functions as a coordination and provenance layer that secures model updates, immutably logs alerts, and automates policy enforcement through smart contracts. When combined with FL and edge intelligence, blockchain strengthens collaborative security across distributed infrastructures. Yet its scalability limitations, consensus overhead, storage growth, and energy demands remind us that trust mechanisms must also be engineered sustainably. Lightweight consensus, off-chain processing, and permissioned architectures represent necessary adaptations for practical IoT deployment.

The emergence of post-quantum cryptographic approaches further extends the security horizon. As quantum computing threatens classical cryptographic schemes, IDS frameworks must integrate quantum-resistant digital signatures, secure aggregation protocols, and tamper-proof lifecycle management. In this emerging paradigm, intrusion detection is not merely a classification task; it becomes part of a verifiable, end-to-end trustworthy ecosystem. The convergence of AI-based detection with post-quantum cryptography and secure distributed ledgers ensures that both operational intelligence and cryptographic survivability are addressed simultaneously.

Energy efficiency is central to sustainable IDS design. IoT devices operate under strict power budgets, limited processing capabilities, and latency-sensitive environments. The chapter emphasizes hierarchical edge-fog-cloud architectures, model compression, adaptive inspection pipelines, federated collaboration, and RL-based resource optimization as essential strategies for reducing computational and communication overhead. Future IDS systems must explicitly measure and report energy consumption, latency, memory footprint, and communication costs, in addition to traditional detection metrics. Without quantifiable sustainability indicators, claims of "green IDS" remain incomplete.

Equally important are governance, interoperability, and policy considerations. The deployment of next-generation energy-efficient IDS requires alignment with international standards, regulatory frameworks, and industry-driven best practices. Governments and regulatory bodies play a critical role in defining compliance requirements, certification models, and cross-domain collaboration mechanisms. Industry leaders must translate research advances into deployable, interoperable, and scalable security products. Standardization efforts should increasingly incorporate energy-efficiency benchmarks, lifecycle security requirements, and quantum-resilient design principles to ensure coherent global adoption.

In conclusion, the future of sustainable IoT security lies in integrated and multidisciplinary innovation. Intelligent detection models, decentralized trust infrastructures, quantum-resilient cryptographic safeguards, and energy-aware engineering principles must operate together rather than in isolation. The field is moving from experimental, accuracy-driven research toward holistic, deployment-ready cybersecurity ecosystems. Achieving durable and scalable protection for IoT environments will require collaboration among artificial intelligence researchers, cryptographers, network engineers, policymakers, and industry practitioners. Only through such coordinated efforts can next-generation intrusion detection systems provide resilient, efficient, and future-proof security for the increasingly interconnected world.

CHAPTER

Conclusion

10

10.1 Introduction

This book examines the evolution of IDS in IoT systems, from foundational principles to advanced sustainable architectures. This book systematically examines the foundations, constraints, vulnerabilities, architectural principles, and future directions of sustainable IDS in these interconnected ecosystems. Across Chapters 2 through 9, a central argument has been consistently developed: cybersecurity in IoT cannot be separated from energy efficiency, lifecycle sustainability, and environmental responsibility. Sustainable IoT security is not an optional enhancement; it is a structural necessity dictated by scale, heterogeneity, and global sustainability imperatives. These structural characteristics reshape how security must be engineered. Intrusion detection in IoT cannot simply replicate enterprise network models; it must be lightweight, adaptive, distributed, and energy-aware.

Chapter 3 further demonstrated that lightweight security is not merely an optimization strategy but a system-engineering discipline governed by strict computational, memory, timing, and energy constraints. Security mechanisms must operate within tightly bounded duty cycles and microjoule-level energy budgets. This constraint-driven perspective laid the groundwork for redefining IDS as an embedded cyber-physical control component rather than a standalone classification engine.

Chapter 4 introduced formal energy models for IoT systems and established energy as a measurable state variable in security design. By decomposing total device energy into computational, communication, memory, and security components, the chapter demonstrated that radio transmission typically accounts for the majority of energy consumption. Consequently, sustainable IDS must reduce redundant communication, support local inference, and dynamically adjust detection thresholds based on residual energy. The energy-aware framework transforms IDS optimization into a multi-objective control problem that balances detection strength and long-term device viability.

Chapter 5 extended this foundation by proposing Green IDS as a structural redesign paradigm. Rather than treating energy efficiency as an afterthought, Green IDS embeds carbon awareness, cross-layer optimization, federated coordination, and adaptive scheduling into the architecture. The hierarchical integration of IoT devices, edge gateways, fog intelligence, and cloud orchestration illustrates how sustainable detection can be achieved through distributed collaboration. The closed-loop control

Green Intrusion Detection Systems for IoT. https://doi.org/10.1016/B978-0-44-344249-0.00017-X

models presented in this chapter show that intrusion detection must continuously adapt to both threat intensity and energy dynamics.

Chapter 6 examined IoT vulnerabilities through a formalized risk perspective. By modeling vulnerability as a function of exploit probability and impact across confidentiality, integrity, availability, and privacy dimensions, the chapter highlighted the cascading effects of compromised nodes in interconnected ecosystems. This analysis reinforced the need for a proactive and energy-efficient IDS capable of mitigating both direct attacks and lateral propagation risks.

Chapter 7 demonstrated how sustainable IDS principles can be applied in real-world smart environments, including smart cities, renewable energy systems, transportation networks, and industrial automation. Case studies illustrated that energy-efficient anomaly detection, lightweight statistical learning, edge-based inference, and blockchain-assisted trust mechanisms can enhance both system resilience and environmental responsibility. These implementations confirm that sustainability and cybersecurity are not competing objectives but complementary design goals.

Chapter 8 focused on Green IDS deployment in practical IoT domains, emphasizing performance metrics that extend beyond accuracy to include energy consumption (measured in joules), inference latency, and memory footprint. This evaluation perspective reflects a paradigm shift: detection performance must be assessed alongside environmental cost and operational feasibility.

Chapter 9 explored future directions, including AI-driven IDS, federated and multi-task learning, blockchain-based trust layers, lifecycle-aware security, adversarial robustness, and post-quantum cryptographic resilience. The convergence of these technologies defines the trajectory of next-generation sustainable IoT security.

10.2 Key insights from the chapters

Across the chapters, several cross-cutting insights emerge:

- **Energy is a first-class security variable** Sustainable IDS must treat energy not as a secondary constraint but as a dynamic system state influencing detection thresholds, communication frequency, and model complexity.
- **Distributed intelligence is essential** Edge-fog-cloud hierarchies reduce communication overhead and align computational intensity with available resources. Lightweight anomaly screening at the edge, combined with deeper analysis at higher layers, provides balanced protection.
- **Lifecycle security is critical** IDS models are vulnerable to poisoning, adversarial manipulation, model extraction, and drift. Sustainable systems must protect the entire ML lifecycle, including data collection, training, deployment, updates, and retirement.
- **Evaluation must incorporate sustainability metrics** Reporting detection accuracy without energy metrics creates incomplete conclusions. Future benchmarking

standards must mandate reporting on energy per inference, communication costs, and environmental footprint.

- **Security and sustainability reinforce global development objectives** Sustainable IDS supports resilient digital infrastructure (SDG 9), safe and secure smart cities (SDG 11), and reduced carbon emissions through energy-aware cybersecurity (SDG 13).

10.3 Strategic roadmap and actionable recommendations

The collective findings of the surveyed literature indicate that the evolution of IDS in IoT, Industrial IoT, Smart Cities, Transportation, 5G, and AIoT ecosystems is steadily progressing toward intelligent, distributed, privacy-aware, and energy-conscious architectures. At the same time, recurring challenges continue to limit large-scale deployment. These challenges include unrealistic benchmarking datasets, limited adversarial robustness, inconsistent evaluation metrics, privacy risks in centralized learning, energy constraints at the device layer, and insufficient interoperability across vendors and infrastructure. Addressing these gaps requires a coordinated strategic roadmap that spans academia, industry, policymakers, and standards organizations.

10.3.1 Strategic directions for academia

From an academic standpoint, the most urgent priority is the development of realistic, standardized evaluation frameworks. Much current work still relies on outdated or imbalanced datasets, and many efforts report detection accuracy without regard to deployment feasibility. Future research must move toward IoT-native benchmark environments that reflect multi-layer architectures, heterogeneous traffic behavior, concept drift, and emerging zero-day attacks. Evaluation protocols, too, should reach beyond accuracy to include resource-aware metrics. In particular, sustainable IDS research should emphasize:

- Energy consumption per inference
- Communication overhead in FL
- Memory footprint and model complexity
- Latency and throughput constraints in edge environments

Shifting the research focus from accuracy-only metrics to resource-aware benchmarking will produce models that are truly deployable in real-world IoT ecosystems.

Adversarial robustness represents another fundamental research direction. ML-based IDS models remain vulnerable to evasion, poisoning, and model extraction attacks. Academic research must treat robustness as a primary design objective rather than an afterthought. This requires systematic investigation of adversarial training methods, GAN-assisted defense mechanisms, Byzantine-resilient aggregation in federated environments, and explainable AI techniques to reduce black-box vulnerabilities. IDS research should integrate robustness testing as a standard experimental requirement.

Privacy-preserving collaborative learning also demands deeper academic exploration. FL has strong potential to protect data sovereignty while enabling distributed model training. However, unresolved issues such as client heterogeneity, non-IID data distribution, communication efficiency, and secure aggregation overhead remain open research problems. Advancing differential privacy mechanisms, homomorphic encryption, and federated-RL will be critical for secure large-scale IDS collaboration across smart cities and industrial infrastructures.

Lightweight and edge-centric intelligence must also become a central research focus. DL techniques significantly improve detection performance, yet IoT devices operate under strict computational and energy constraints. Academic work should prioritize TinyML frameworks, model compression techniques, meta-heuristic feature selection, and hierarchical detection pipelines that distribute tasks across device, edge, and cloud layers. Sustainable IDS research must align intelligence with hardware feasibility.

10.3.2 Strategic directions for industry

For the industry, the transition from centralized IDS models to distributed and hierarchical architectures is essential. Large-scale IoT environments cannot rely solely on cloud-based detection. Instead, detection responsibilities should be distributed across edge gateways and device-level screening mechanisms to reduce bandwidth usage and latency. Industry should emphasize:

- Edge-based anomaly detection for latency-sensitive environments
- Federated IDS frameworks to reduce raw data sharing
- Selective blockchain integration for auditability and trust coordination

Embedding adversarial testing into development lifecycles is equally important. IDS products must undergo systematic red-teaming, adversarial validation, and drift monitoring. AI models deployed in IoT networks should be continuously evaluated against evolving attack patterns. Security validation must extend throughout the AI lifecycle, from training and deployment to retraining and updates. The integration of generative AI and synthetic data offers additional opportunities but must be handled carefully. GAN-based and generative approaches can address class imbalance and simulate emerging threats, yet they introduce ethical and dual-use risks. Industry deployment should therefore incorporate statistical similarity validation, misuse-prevention safeguards, and ethical risk-assessment frameworks. Generative tools should enhance robustness without increasing systemic vulnerability.

Energy-aware cybersecurity engineering must also become standard practice. IoT communication protocols often prioritize energy efficiency over strong security controls. Industry stakeholders should implement explicit energy budgets for IDS modules, monitor communication overhead during federated updates, and optimize model update cycles to reduce carbon impact. Cybersecurity must be integrated into environmental, social, and governance (ESG) strategies.

10.3.3 Strategic directions for policymakers

Policymakers play a crucial role in shaping sustainable IoT security ecosystems. Current regulatory frameworks focus heavily on privacy and compliance but rarely address energy-aware cybersecurity or lifecycle AI governance. Governments should consider establishing certification programs for sustainable IDS solutions that incorporate both security and resource-efficiency metrics. Policy initiatives should encourage:

- Mandatory reporting of detection performance and resource consumption
- Lifecycle security management standards
- Energy-efficiency benchmarks for large-scale IoT deployments

Cross-sector collaboration must also be promoted. IoT ecosystems span public infrastructure, private enterprises, and critical services. Policymakers should facilitate secure federated data-sharing frameworks, incentivize public-private partnerships in cybersecurity research, and support funding for privacy-preserving AI innovation. Collaborative defense strategies enhance systemic resilience without compromising regulatory compliance. Importantly, sustainable IDS deployment aligns directly with global development priorities. Energy-efficient cybersecurity strengthens resilient infrastructure (SDG 9), supports secure smart cities (SDG 11), and contributes to climate-conscious digital transformation (SDG 13). Cybersecurity policy should therefore be framed as a pillar of sustainable development.

10.3.4 Strategic directions for standardization bodies

Standardization bodies must address persistent inconsistencies in benchmarking and reporting practices. A unified evaluation framework is necessary to ensure reproducibility and comparability across IDS solutions. Standards organizations should define common evaluation criteria that combine security performance and sustainability metrics. These should include:

- Detection accuracy and per-attack performance
- Energy and latency measurements
- Communication overhead in distributed learning
- Adversarial robustness validation

Federated and edge-based IDS architectures also require standardized design principles. Clear guidelines should define secure aggregation requirements, communication budget thresholds, and interoperability protocols across vendors. Without standardization, cross-domain deployment remains fragmented and inefficient. In addition, AI governance standards must evolve to accommodate emerging technologies, including DRL, GAN-based detection, and generative AI integration. Standardization efforts should emphasize model explainability, lifecycle governance, secure update mechanisms, and ethical risk assessment. AI governance must become inseparable from cybersecurity standardization.

In summary, the collective research landscape indicates that sustainable IoT security depends on coordinated convergence across multiple dimensions. The future of IDS is not defined by a single centralized detection engine, but by a distributed, adaptive, privacy-preserving, and energy-conscious cyber-physical intelligence framework. Achieving this transformation requires alignment among academic research innovation, industrial deployment practices, regulatory policy frameworks, and international standardization efforts. A secure and sustainable IoT ecosystem is attainable only through structured collaboration and long-term commitment to intelligent, privacy-aware, robust, and environmentally responsible cybersecurity design.

10.4 Current state of IDS in IoT and SDG alignment

The reviewed body of work clearly demonstrates that the Internet of Things has evolved into a central technological driver of sustainable development. Across smart cities, digital agriculture, intelligent infrastructure, transportation, city traffic management, and environmental monitoring, IoT systems are increasingly deployed as operational tools that support the objectives of SDG 9 (Industry, Innovation, and Infrastructure), SDG 11 (Sustainable Cities and Communities), and SDG 13 (Climate Action). IoT ecosystems are no longer limited to conceptual pilot studies; they are now embedded in real-world infrastructures, shaping transportation networks, energy grids, healthcare systems, and agricultural production.

Despite this rapid expansion, the security dimension, particularly IDS, has not kept pace with sustainability planning. While IoT technologies are explicitly positioned as enablers of resilience and environmental efficiency, IDS architectures are often designed primarily around detection performance rather than the integration of sustainability. Current IDS deployments in IoT environments tend to exhibit several recurring characteristics:

- Heavy reliance on centralized architectures
- High computational and energy overhead
- Limited interoperability across heterogeneous devices
- Minimal integration of sustainability metrics

This imbalance creates structural tension. For example, in smart city deployments, IoT systems optimize traffic flows, dynamically control lighting, and monitor environmental conditions. However, these interconnected infrastructures significantly expand the cyber-attack surface. If IDS mechanisms are inefficient, fragmented, or overly centralized, disruptions may compromise essential public services, directly undermining SDG 11's goal of building safe and resilient cities.

A similar challenge is visible in smart farming systems, where IoT supports precision irrigation, disease monitoring, and climate-adaptive decision-making. These technologies align closely with SDG 2 and SDG 13, promoting food security and environmental sustainability. Yet agricultural IoT deployments often operate under low-power conditions, intermittent connectivity, and limited technical support. Conventional IDS models rarely consider:

- Energy-constrained rural deployments
- Limited communication bandwidth
- Socio-behavioral adoption factors

As a consequence, IDS research has largely prioritized detection accuracy at the expense of long-term sustainability integration.

10.4.1 Sustainability gaps in current IoT-IDS deployments

Several structural limitations hinder the alignment of IDS architectures with sustainable development objectives. One major concern is energy inefficiency. Sustainable IoT systems require careful resource allocation and minimal waste. However, many IDS approaches, particularly those based on DL, depend on continuous high-volume data processing and intensive communication between devices and cloud servers. These models often require frequent retraining and model updates. Such practices increase energy consumption and contradict the climate-conscious digital transformation envisioned under SDG 13.

Another persistent issue is centralization. Many IoT security architectures still depend heavily on cloud-based processing. While centralized systems simplify monitoring, they also increase latency, create single points of failure, and raise overall energy demand. In developing regions, where infrastructure and connectivity are limited, centralized IDS models are often impractical. This structural dependency restricts scalability and reduces resilience.

Interoperability challenges further complicate sustainability alignment. Smart city and industrial IoT deployments typically involve systems from multiple vendors using incompatible APIs. Without standardized IDS interoperability frameworks:

- Security monitoring remains fragmented
- Cross-subsystem anomaly detection is weakened
- Urban resilience is reduced

Finally, governance and ethical concerns cannot be ignored. AI-driven predictive models enhance urban efficiency and sustainability planning, yet they introduce issues related to Algorithmic bias, Lack of transparency, Accountability gaps, and Data privacy risks. Current IDS systems rarely integrate explainability or governance-aware mechanisms. As AI becomes embedded in critical infrastructure, the absence of ethical safeguards risks amplifying inequalities or generating unintended social harm.

10.4.2 Vision for a secure and sustainable IoT ecosystem

Addressing these limitations requires a fundamental shift in how IDS systems are conceptualized. Future IDS architectures must move beyond detection-centric optimization toward sustainability-integrated cybersecurity design.

- **SDG 9: Resilient Infrastructure and Innovation** To support resilient and innovative infrastructure, IDS must evolve into adaptive, decentralized, and resource-aware systems. Instead of relying exclusively on cloud processing, next-generation models should incorporate:
  - Edge-native anomaly detection
  - Federated and distributed learning architectures
  - Low-power detection mechanisms
  - Interoperable security standards

  Goal-oriented engineering approaches demonstrate that sustainability constraints, such as energy efficiency, latency bounds, and scalability, can be embedded at the requirements stage. IDS frameworks should therefore integrate sustainability metrics directly into system design, enabling dynamic resource optimization and long-term maintainability. Resilience in digital infrastructure requires security systems that are efficient, interoperable, and adaptive across heterogeneous IoT environments.
- **SDG 11: Safe, Inclusive, and Sustainable Cities** Smart cities depend on predictive AI, real-time monitoring, and integrated operations centers. Security mechanisms must therefore evolve into cyber-physical resilience systems rather than passive alert generators. A sustainable urban security ecosystem should incorporate:
  - AI-enhanced integrated security operations
  - Real-time cross-subsystem anomaly correlation
  - Transparent decision-support interfaces
  - Citizen-centered data governance policies

  IDS in urban environments must detect infrastructure stress early, prevent cascading failures, and support emergency response coordination. Moreover, ethical AI principles must guide deployment. Sustainable IDS should integrate Explainable AI mechanisms, Bias detection and mitigation strategies and Governance-aware auditing capabilities. Security in smart cities must reinforce social responsibility alongside technical robustness.
- **SDG 13: Climate-Conscious Digital Security** Climate action requires reducing the environmental footprint of digital infrastructures. Cybersecurity itself must become energy-aware. A sustainable IDS ecosystem should therefore:
  - Monitor its own energy consumption
  - Adjust detection intensity based on dynamic risk levels
  - Minimize redundant data transmission
  - Operate efficiently on renewable-powered edge devices

  In rural and agricultural IoT systems, this implies compatibility with LPWAN communication technologies and low-energy sensor networks. IDS mechanisms should shift from **always-on** heavy processing toward Risk-adaptive monitoring, Event-driven activation, and Lightweight edge filtering. By embedding cybersecurity into climate-resilient digital transformation, IoT infrastructures can support sustainability without increasing environmental burden.

10.4.3 Integrated vision: toward sustainable cyber–physical intelligence

A secure and sustainable IoT ecosystem demands convergence across multiple technological and governance domains. Future architectures must integrate:

- AI-enhanced predictive modeling
- Intelligent operations management
- Sustainability-driven requirements engineering
- Context-aware decentralized design

Based on these discussions, the next generation of IDS systems should focus on energy-aware, federated, and edge-centric interoperability across vendors; explainability; governance compliance; and design informed by sustainability-oriented engineering frameworks. Under this paradigm, IDS evolves from a reactive security mechanism into a core component of resilient, climate-aligned cyber-physical intelligence.

In summary, Intrusion Detection Systems in IoT environments have advanced considerably in both technical capabilities and analytical sophistication. However, their integration with broader sustainability goals remains limited. As IoT infrastructures increasingly contribute to global development priorities, it is essential that cybersecurity frameworks evolve in parallel with these long-term objectives. A meaningful transition is therefore required, from centralized, energy-intensive, and isolated detection models toward adaptive, distributed, explainable, and sustainability-oriented cyber-physical intelligence architectures. By aligning IDS innovation with SDG 9 (Industry, Innovation, and Infrastructure), SDG 11 (Sustainable Cities and Communities), and SDG 13 (Climate Action), digital security can reinforce, rather than compromise, the resilience and environmental sustainability of emerging smart infrastructures.

Index

D

E

F

G

H

I

J

L

M

N

O

P

Q

R

S

Printed and bound by CPI Group (UK) Ltd, Croydon, CR0 4YY
14/09/2026
02216409-0017